THE
GOOD
DEATH

THE
GOOD
DEATH

The New American
Search to Reshape
the End of Life

Marilyn Webb

BANTAM BOOKS
NEW YORK   TORONTO   LONDON
SYDNEY   AUCKLAND

THE GOOD DEATH
A Bantam Book / November 1997

Parts of this book have appeared in
different form in *New York* magazine, *Glamour*,
and *Ladies' Home Journal*.

Book design by Caroline Cunningham

Library of Congress Cataloging-in-Publication Data

Webb, Marilyn, 1942–
    The good death : the new American search to reshape the end of
life / Marilyn Webb.
        p.   cm.
    Includes bibliographical references and index.
    ISBN 0-553-09555-2
    1. Death—Social aspects—United States.   2. Death—United States—
Psychological aspects.   3. Death—Moral and ethical aspects—United
States.   4. Pain—Treatment—United States.   5. Hospice care—United
States.   6. Bereavement—United States.   I. Title.
HQ1073.5.U6W43   1997
306.9'0973—dc21   97-24486
                                                                          CIP

Published simultaneously in the United States and Canada

Bantam Books are published by Bantam Books, a division of Bantam
Doubleday Dell Publishing Group, Inc. Its trademark, consisting of the words
"Bantam Books" and the portrayal of a rooster, is Registered in U.S. Patent and
Trademark Office and in other countries. Marca Registrada. Bantam Books,
1540 Broadway, New York, New York 10036.

PRINTED IN THE UNITED STATES OF AMERICA

BVG   0   9   8   7   6   5   4   3   2   1

To my sister, Netta Marjorie Salzman,
and my father, William Salzman, who first
showed me the problem.
To my stepfather, Macy Halpert,
who showed me the way.
To my father-in-law, Jack Sheedy,
who confirmed it.

And to my husband, John Sheedy,
my mother, Esther Halpert, and
my daughter, Jennifer Webb,
whose love has always been there for me.

Contents

Acknowledgments

No book is the endeavor only of its author. In this case, there is a near army of people—some now gone and some still alive—without whom this book would not have been written. The depth of emotion began with relatives who have now died: Netta Salzman, William Salzman, Jacob and Anna Salzman, Frank and Anna Wein, Macy Halpert, and Jack Sheedy.

The idea for a book took root with the help of Deborah Harkins, my editor at *New York* magazine; James Levine, my literary agent; and Toni Burbank, my editor at Bantam. The confidence to do it, though, was inspired by my family: my husband, John Sheedy; my mother, Esther Halpert; my children, Jennifer Webb and Ally, Meghan, and Patrick Sheedy; my mother-in-law, Marie Sheedy; my cousins, who have been like siblings to me, Natalie and Howard Shawn and Barbara and Sam Bobrow; and Joe Weintraub, David Lansbury, Jason Kiefer, Jacob Hoye, Rachel Sheedy, Jay Antonangelli, Honey Bear, Tobi, and Blue. Of special importance was my writers' group: Ann Banks, Gwenda Blair, Cate Breslin, Carol Brightman, Jane Ciabattari, Kathryn Kilgore, Grace Lichtenstein, Robin Reisig, and Anne Sommers; and my close friends and advisers: Barbara Stewart, John Sennhauser, Holly Brown, Carole Feld, David Levy, Susan Linfield, Joe Michenfelder, and Laurene Glynn.

My first and most profound guide to dying was the Buddhist teacher, the late Venerable Chögyam Trungpa, Rinpoche. The very gifted Sister Loretta Palamara helped me to understand at the bedside and to see. She died the day I finished writing this introduction.

I am forever grateful to those who let me into their lives at the most private and vulnerable of times: Peter Ciccone, Ron Burris, Fran Mack, Dominick and Marsha Ciccone; Glenn Leung, Sharon and Emelia Siens, and Dave Turner; Father Tom Sheedy, Dr. Larry

Killebrew, Sister Martina Fox, Father Vincent Keenan and Father Tommy Conway; Audrey and Jonathan Hill and Margaret Hill Andrews; Ed Sennhauser; Heidi Fernandez and Carmen Fernandez-Hyde; Moh, Justin, and Cecily Hardin, Adele Obodov; Gramps, John, Jackie, Micki, and the two Maries; and others whom I cannot name.

I am also grateful to the large numbers of medical professionals, end-of-life care specialists, and families who helped me in my research: Mary Cooke and Cabrini Hospice; John Finn, M.D., Carolyn Fitzpatrick-Cassin, Joan Hull, Ph.D., and the Hospice of Southeastern Michigan; Jay Mahoney and the National Hospice Organization; Kathleen Foley, M.D., Russell Portenoy, M.D., William Breitbart, M.D., Nessa Coyle, R.N., and others at Memorial Sloan-Kettering Cancer Center, who taught me to understand the management of pain.

Arthur Kennish, M.D., and the specialists, residents, and interns at Mount Sinai Hospital in New York, who took me along on rounds on the cardiac intensive care unit; Joanne Lynn, M.D., who guided me through years of research on dying; Joan Teno, M.D., and staff of SUPPORT and at the Center to Improve Care of the Dying at George Washington University Medical Center; the Hastings Center, especially Daniel Callahan, Ph.D., Joseph Fins, M.D., Strachan Donnelley, Ph.D., Hilde Lindemann Nelson, M.A., and James Lindemann Nelson, Ph.D., Eric Parens, Ph.D., Marna Howarth, Bette Crigger, and Mary Jane Wild.

Elisabeth Kübler-Ross, M.D., and her staff at the Elisabeth Kübler-Ross Center; Samuel Bobrow, M.D., of the oncology staff at Yale University Medical School; Mathy Mezey, R.N., Ph.D., Ganga Stone, Kay Mitchell, and Cynthia Burke, who first showed me where to look. Janet Good, the Survivors, and the friends of Jack Kevorkian, M.D.; Kenneth Ring, Ph.D., Jack Lardis, and others at the International Association of Near-Death Studies; and families who spoke up about loss, personally helped me to understand, and have since changed the way we all die: Joe and Julia Quinlan, Chris Cruzan, Julie Delio, Ron Adkins, Carol Poenisch and Connie Frederick, Carol Loving, Dave Ball, Judy Brown, Janet and Ray Good, and Minna and Lou Barrett.

I'd like to thank the following centers for allowing me working space and solitude: the Virginia Center for the Creative Arts, the

Allen Room at the New York Public Library, the Writers Room in New York; and Steve Isaacs and others at the Graduate School of Journalism at Columbia University for collegial friendship and support.

The world of research has been made enormously easier by Court TV and the Internet. Especially helpful were America Online, CompuServe, Dialog, Knowledge Index, Medline, PsychInfo, the on-line editions of newspapers nationwide, John Hofsess for DeathNet and "Nothing but the News," and Derek Humphrey for ERGO.

And finally, while I take full responsibility for any omissions or errors in this book, I am tremendously indebted to my expert readers, who so carefully pored over sections or whole chapters, tirelessly correcting medical or legal facts, and details of stories: Moh Hardin; Adele Obodov; Connie Berman; Victor Sierpina, M.D.; Arthur Kennish, M.D.; Joanne Lynn, M.D.; Daniel Callahan, Ph.D.; Ron Burris; Dominick and Marsha Ciccone; Fran Mack; Kathleen Foley, M.D.; Russell Portenoy, M.D.; William Breitbart, M.D.; Richard Patt, M.D.; Paul Armstrong, Esq.; Alan Meisel, Esq.; William Colby, Esq.; Jim Lindemann Nelson; Barbara Karnes, R.N.; Jay Mahoney; Jon Harris; Barbara Stewart; Derek Humphrey; John Sennhauser; Heidi Fernandez; Joe and Julia Quinlan; Timothy Quill, M.D.; Elisabeth Kübler-Ross, M.D.; Rachel Remen, M.D.; Stephen and Ondrea Levine; and Therese Schroeder-Sheker.

Thank you to the many, many other physicians, philosophers, patients, and families who so generously shared their time, their feelings, their thoughts, and their vast expertise. And finally, thank you to those who helped tirelessly with the endless details: Melissa Rowland, Daniel Greenberg, and Arielle Eckstut, in the office of James Levine Communications, Inc.; Bantam associate editor Robin Michaelson, copy editor Anne Cherry, and attorney Elizabeth McNamara.

Foreword

As medical treatments became more effective at extending life in the latter part of this century, the physician's age-old duty to treat suffering and provide support for dying patients and their families was largely forgotten. Death became viewed as a medical failure rather than a natural and inevitable part of the life cycle. Beginning with Elisabeth Kübler-Ross, and later with the hospice movement, American medicine began to refind a vision about caring for dying patients. Careful attention to pain and other physical symptoms is the foundation. When patients are relatively free from physical suffering, they are better able to attend to the psychological, social, spiritual, and existential aspects of the final phase of their lives. The dying process is in no way simple or uniform, but when approached with skill and caring by medical professionals, death can usually be made meaningful, or at least tolerable, for most patients.

There is ample evidence that we in medicine do not always do an adequate job providing palliative care for our dying patients. Yet, it is hard to find a more contentious issue than whether a physician should help a suffering patient to die. Too many patients still die in acute care hospitals where their final days are dominated by futile technological interventions that aggravate rather than alleviate suffering. Because of reluctance by both medical professionals and families to face the possibility of death, hospice care is frequently offered very late if at all. Many patients are thereby deprived of the opportunity to achieve a meaningful closure to their lives, to say nothing of losing access to adequate pain relief and a multidisciplinary team of support services. Many doctors, patients, families, and regulators still have unrealistic fears about addiction, and insufficient knowledge about the potential effectiveness of modern pain relief. Although there are signs of improvement, physicians are still not adequately trained to communicate openly with dying patients and families, nor to provide pain management. Furthermore, the multidisciplinary team support at home for patients on hospice programs is available only to those with proper insurance and a relatively certain prognosis of six months or less. Hospice programs work for patients with cancer, but for those dying more slowly and uncertainly from cardiac, respiratory, or neurological diseases, access to similar systems of care is unavailable. With all these inadequacies, how can we possibly talk about doctors' more actively helping some of their patients to die?

I have never met a terminally ill patient who actually wanted to die, but I have met many who want to stop living the way they are forced to as a result of their disease. Such patients definitely exist, and not all of their dilemmas can be solved by improving access and delivery of palliative care. In fact, we negotiate openly with these patients if they happen to be on a life-sustaining treatment such as a mechanical ventilator, kidney dialysis machine, or feeding tube. There is a societal consensus that these patients should be "allowed to die," and physicians are implored to listen more carefully to their requests. However, for patients whose suffering is similarly severe and unrelievable, but who aren't receiving life-sustaining therapy, many in our culture are willing to question and devalue their requests, and suggest that doctors should be prohibited from responding. Many physicians do provide potentially lethal medication in response to these requests, but they do so in secret, without the benefit of consultation by those with expertise in palliative care. Unlike the cessation of life supports, where we utilize our most experienced clinicians in the decision-making process to ensure that all possible alternatives have been considered, the practice of physician-assisted death is almost completely underground, and kept that way by laws that are completely unenforced as long as one does not publicly talk about it.

Is this secret, arbitrary, unpredictable process better for patients and families than a more open process subject to safeguards and mandatory consultations? Many patients fear dying in the midst of severe, unrelieved suffering that their health-care providers will be afraid to address because of the legal and ethical uncertainties. Yet those who know that their physicians will be responsive can spend their last days, weeks, and months free of the worry that if their suffering becomes extreme, they would not have access to an escape. In reality, few persons will need such assistance if they receive adequate palliative care, but the freedom from fear is very important to many who have witnessed severe suffering by a family member or a loved one.

Of course, there are many frames of reference that must be considered in addressing this complex topic. Suffering patients and their families have the most compelling interests, but the interests of potentially responding physicians must also be considered, as should the potential effects on the larger communities of patients and physicians. Physician-assisted death intersects with clinical medicine, ethics, law, religion, and public policy. It touches on individual liberty as well as on the kind of commitment and responsibility we want doctors to have to their dying patients. There is an inevitable tension between the narratives and experiences of real individuals and the interests of the larger community. The challenge is to create a public policy that ensures access to palliative care as the standard of care for the dying, that is responsive to individual persons whose suffering becomes extreme in spite of unrestrained efforts to care, and that at the same time protects other potentially vulnerable populations. With 40 million Americans currently uninsured, and medicine in the midst of radical reform driven much more by cost containment than quality improvement, the stakes of this debate could not be higher or more complex. Are these forces more dangerous in a secret or an open system? Is not the cessation of life supports subject to similar pressures? How does keeping some dying patients alive against their will protect the larger community?

Many pundits addressing these issues overemphasize one side or the other in this debate in support of their ideological positions. Thoughtful, accessible reviews with a balanced, unbiased presentation are rare. Marilyn Webb's remarkable book provides such a synthesis. Her approach integrates landmark legal cases, personal interviews with nationally known experts from a variety of disciplines and points of view, literature reviews from pain management, hospice, law, and medical ethics, and personal narratives by patients and families with firsthand experience. The result is a highly readable integration of ethical, legal, religious, and clinical perspectives, in a historically accurate account of the evolution of the American way of death over the last thirty years that emphasizes the persons involved and their families.

Those who find themselves struggling in the middle ground of today's "right to die" movement—feeling we should be able to respond to troubling cases, but worried about the social consequences in today's complex world—should read this book. You will find no shortage of complexity, nor any overly facile conclusions. *The Good Death* should improve your depth of understanding and your ability to look at the issues in the context of recent history and clinical reality. Since we all have to die at some point, we should learn to explore the middle ground in all of its complexity and ambiguity before our own time comes.

—Timothy E. Quill, M.D.
Professor of Medicine and Psychiatry
University of Rochester School of Medicine

Introduction

Americans commonly claim that we are a death-denying society. Mostly, though, we are simply unfamiliar with death—at least with the kind of dying that most of us actually face. At the turn of this century, most people died quickly and at any age. The average age at death was just forty-six years old, and most people died of infections and accidents. Now, however, most of us will live into old age. Three-quarters of Americans die after age sixty-five, and the average age at death for adults is nearly eighty.

Until the last half century, young people would become familiar with death when siblings and parents died. Now, most of adulthood passes without personal contact with dying. Often we become caregivers for a loved one who will be "sick unto death" without any sense of how that person or the family could live well under the shadow of death—and we have so little guidance. Our popular culture almost completely ignores the life experience of people with serious chronic illness that will end in death. No evening television shows tell the story of old people slowly dying. Even newspaper obituaries tell the deceased's life story only until retirement—and say nothing of the life that was led in the ensuing twenty years, including telling nothing about the dying except its putative "cause."

We are a nation that desperately needs stories—perhaps even myths—about dying to provide some guides to appropriate roles and worthy behavior. For a long time, my elderly patients claimed that they would not want to survive "like Karen Quinlan." The fate of being persistently unconscious yet still breathing is exceedingly rare. Nevertheless, the shared mythic figure gave us all some language by which to communicate the claim that some fates are too awful to condone. Recently, the decent, even graceful, dyings of Jacqueline Kennedy Onassis, Richard Nixon, and Cardinal Joseph

Bernardin have told stories which celebrate a style and pattern of dying.

Marilyn Webb here tells some much less public stories, mostly of people whose lives will soon end, and who are finding ways to have worthy lives. The stories are richly spun, enough so that one can tell whether one's own experience might follow that path or might find it unwelcome.

Any retelling of such a story must fail to tell it all. The storyteller has a perspective and has to craft a coherent tale. There is always more to be said, and not all of it can be said coherently. However, this is the strength of stories, not their shortcoming. The stories are not the stuff of myth. The people are real enough to be flawed and the stories complicated enough to avoid simplistic summary. Readers can engage this book as interesting tales of our age, or as a cafeteria of experiences from which to pick and choose as one contemplates what to admire in good dying, or as a reminder of the array of often-ignored possibilities in shaping one's life at its end.

At the close of the twentieth century, America is at a crossroads. One of the fondest hopes of the start of the century surely was that most people could live long and mostly healthy lives. As we learned in childhood fairy tales, having the genie grant the wish does not ensure that the wish maker will be happy with the outcome! Within the first quarter century of the next millennium, we will nearly double the aggregate challenge of disability in old age. Death will once again come back home, as we will not use hospitals for most who are old and dying. Families and nursing homes will have to learn how to make good on the promise of old age, even with illness and disability. The shortcomings that these stories illuminate are real—people really don't know how to talk about or plan for dying, services to relieve pain are unreliable, costs of care are often crippling, and many people have little help in finding meaning and cherishing their own lives.

We could do better. We could set about reshaping our social institutions so that the end of life is worthy and valid, comfortable and comforted. Some of what needs to be done lies in the realms of public policy and professional education—to change Medicare reimbursement formulas, to demand measurement of the quality of care, and to learn the new sets of skills for professional caregivers, for example. However, much improvement requires that we once again become familiar with what is possible, and that we reinvent a meaningful language. For that, we need stories, and those you will find here.

—Joanne Lynn, M.D.
Center to Improve Care of the Dying
George Washington University

A Personal Introduction

During the six years it has taken to research and write this book, people have asked me whether it wasn't depressing, even morbid, to report about death in America. They are surprised when I say that not only has this been the most inspiring work of my life, but the most magnificent times were spent with people who were dying.

I came to this book haltingly, no doubt out of personal need, but in the end I realized I have been preparing to do this book all my life. I was a child of the fifties, when death was not spoken of, most particularly not to children. So when death came, it came as a shock.

I was sixteen when my sister died, and she was thirteen and a half. Her name was Netta, after my mother's sister, Nettie, who'd also died at thirteen and a half, when my own mother was sixteen.

Nettie was run over by a hit-and-run taxicab driver one afternoon on her way to buy bread for dinner. She lingered in a Brooklyn hospital in a coma for nearly a month before she died, but the family had known it was just a matter of time.

It was different with my sister. Netta died in 1959 at North Shore Hospital on Long Island, after she'd been sick for three years. We thought all along that modern medicine would cure her.

Netta contracted nephrosis, a kidney infection, as a complication of a strep throat when she was ten. Those were the days just before kidney dialysis or transplants. What she had was fatal, but I never knew, not for any part of those three long years it took her to die. I later learned that her doctor had told my father, but he'd tried to "protect" my mother by not telling her. The doctors went along with the lie. My mother still says she never knew. She functioned on dreams, fantasies of medical miracles, and denial.

I lived in dreams of my own. I remember nights of dreams pockmarked by noise outside my bedroom door. My room was at the end of a long hall; my sister's was closer to my parents' room, the bathroom between her room and theirs. Many nights they were all up, dashing back and forth from their bedrooms to the bathroom. Sometimes I'd wake up and get ready for school with just a neighbor in the house, telling me that my parents had to take Netta to the hospital once again.

The last time I saw Netta alive was a Friday afternoon, the day before I went off to a boarding school weekend dance. By then, I'd already gotten used to what I saw. Her body had swelled, she'd grown weak, she'd long been vomiting blood, her skin had yellowed. She never complained, but—also by then—she'd become nearly tyrannical toward me. Maybe I should have known the end was near when she gave me her vanilla ice cream.

When I returned on Sunday evening, my house was filled with people, many of them strangers. My mother was in the living room, crying. Crowds enveloped her. That wall of people soon symbolized for me the muzzle our family put on talk of death.

Years later, I discovered that Netta had had a final heart attack while my mother rushed to change the sheets on her hospital bed. She'd soiled herself—as frequently happens in death—but my mother didn't know, or couldn't admit, that Netta was in the process of dying.

When I came home, someone at the front door merely told me that Netta had died, and also that my mother needed me to be strong. It was better if I would try not to ask too much. Our family shut down. I imagined that Netta had died in great pain, and the not-knowing made me scared. I didn't know what death was; I wasn't prepared, nor was I helped afterward to understand or to grieve. I adopted a pose of black humor, with a literary twist. I called Netta's story "Death by Vanilla Ice Cream."

In 1963, while I was away at college, my father died. He went to dinner and never made it home. The police found him slumped over the steering wheel, his car parked around the corner on the side of the road. My mother later identified him in a drawer at the morgue. They said he'd had a heart attack. I thought he'd died of a broken heart.

We never talked about this death either, but this time there was something more: My dad and I had been in the midst of a feud about someone I was dating. No surprise, we broke up, but my relationship with my father remained unresolved. Now I was filled with guilt, unfinished business, and anger. I called this story "Death by Bad Boyfriend."

Over the next few years, all four of my grandparents died. By then, my family—or what was left of it—began using black humor, too. On a scale of deaths, my paternal grandfather's was the best: He died at home at the age of ninety-five, sitting in his dark leather chair, feet up, reading the *Wall Street Journal*. It was still open to the page with the stock market quotes when they found him. On that day, Grandpa's stocks had gone way up.

I've since learned that the way death occurs in families has tremendous weight and can leave a legacy that is lasting. Those deaths that are good pull families together and leave a legacy of peace. Those that are bad leave a legacy of grief, anger, and pain that can continue across many generations. Our family used silence, which compounded the pain. And I've since learned that our way was no different from that of most families in America.

When my sister became ill, antibiotics were still so new that her doctor didn't even know the correct one to prescribe for her infection, and later, as her kidneys failed, there were no dialysis machines or transplants. My father died swiftly because that was what heart conditions meant at the time. But America was on the cusp of enormous change.

Today, thanks to modern antibiotics, heart bypasses, cancer treatments, organ transplants, life-support equipment, dialysis, and intravenous fluids, medicine has changed the way this nation dies, giving us a life expectancy at birth of an extra twenty-seven years since the turn of the century. But, as I discovered in researching this book, it has also made the dying process harder.

In defeating many previously lethal diseases, new ailments have taken their place that instead keep people in long-term decline and even less sure than my family was about when an illness is likely to lead to death. Medical success may have even allowed death to become *more* hidden, lulling Americans into losing knowledge not just of the physical process of dying, but of the psychological and spiritual dimensions of death.

This was brought home to me by a later family death. My stepfather, Macy, was a funny, street-smart attorney, but during the mid-1980s, this ruddy and raucous man began dying inch by terrible inch of Alzheimer's disease.

Like D. Hale Cobb III, whom you will meet in Chapter 7, as his dementia grew worse, his doctors continued to treat his physical ailments aggressively—heart attacks, diverticulitis, infections, pneumonia—as if there were something they might do by treating his body that would end up curing his mind. All of this in the face of our explicitly stated family wishes against such treatment. In a way, it was lucky his mind was gone, though, since Macy's death was so slow and so debased that had he known what was going on he would have been humiliated beyond all enduring.

About the time my stepfather had already lost track of our names and faces, he was hospitalized for pneumonia. One day I found him sitting alone in a regular chair. He wasn't braying, or hanging off his walker or wheelchair, or cursing, as he usually did. In fact, he looked almost normal. He turned to me when I walked into the room, and with full recognition, he said, "Your father was here to see me this morning."

By then, my father had been dead for twenty-five years. My stepfather had never met him, nor did he know a lot about our relationship, yet when I asked what my father had to say, he answered, "He told me to tell you that he loves you very much, even though you don't think so." He also said some personal things my father would likely have said, things my stepfather could never have known. Then he went back to his braying.

Over the next few months, this incident ended up unraveling and ultimately healing my unresolved anger with my father. It also made me realize that far more is going on as we prepare to die than medicine might have us think.

Journalists cope with their personal lives by writing stories about other people. After Macy died in 1989, I wrote an article for *New York* magazine about how Americans are coping with the vastly altered landscape of modern medicine and with illnesses like Alzheimer's, cancer, and AIDS.

I learned that such cataclysmic changes are occurring in how we die that these issues may well be among the most crucial challenges we face as we enter the twenty-first century.

In fact, a confluence of crucial events occurred in June 1990:

· Dr. Jack Kevorkian, a retired Michigan pathologist, helped Janet Adkins, an Alzheimer's patient from Oregon, die in the back of his rusty Volkswagen van, using a makeshift suicide machine.

· Dr. Timothy Quill, a former hospice physician from Rochester, New York, helped Patricia Diane Trumbull, a leukemia patient of his, die by giving her a prescription for "barbiturates for sleep," knowing that she would take them when she felt it was time. But to protect him and her family from prosecution, she would have to take them and die alone.

· The U.S. Supreme Court decided in the case of Nancy Beth Cruzan—a thirty-three-year-old woman who lay comatose in a Missouri hospital, subsisting on a feeding tube and in a persistent vegetative state—that patients legally could refuse feeding tubes, just as they could any other medical treatment, even if that refusal meant death. The Cruzan decision spurred Congress to pass the Patient Self-Determination Act, requiring hospitals and nursing homes to let patients know they had the right to sign an advance directive about the kind of treatment they preferred at the end of life.

· The family of eighty-five-year-old Helga Wanglie appealed to a Minnesota court to prevent doctors from disconnecting Mrs. Wanglie's respirator and feeding tube against her family's wishes. Her doctors called her condition hopeless, but the Wanglies argued that Helga, a religious woman who'd suffered irreparable brain damage after a heart attack, would not have wanted life supports removed.

Changes in medicine and the law have now penetrated into the most intimate areas of life, confounding all our prior ways of handling illness and death. As this book was being finished, the Supreme Court ruled on the issue of legalizing assisted suicide. The nation as a whole was struggling with what improvements might need to be made in health-care finance and in the care of the dying. More significant, it was also struggling with the question: When it comes to each of our own deaths, who decides? and how?

I realized at the start of my reporting that individual deaths—like those in my family—are played out against a vast scope of medical, legal, social, cultural, political, and financial issues. I began to search this larger background, trying to examine death not just as the private ordeal it always is, but as part of an enormous and shifting social fabric.

In undertaking this book, I wanted to take death out of the shadows of secrecy. I wanted to talk to those who are dying about what their dying is like, to learn more about what happens to our fading bodies and minds. I wanted to look at how the seriously ill and dying are treated, and what we might do to bring about an eventual *good* death for ourselves and for those whom we love.

That search set me on a lengthy investigative path. For six years I immersed myself as a reporter in America's medical and health-care system, probing the medical environments and styles in which most people die.

At the very beginning of my work, I practically moved onto the inpatient unit of Cabrini Hospice in Manhattan for a month. There I spent days and nights with patients and staff members and was lucky enough to learn at the start about the psychological dimensions of dying. My guide was Sister Loretta Palamara, one of the most gifted people in the care of the dying that I have ever met, who died of a cerebral hemorrhage just as I was finishing this book.

At Cabrini Hospice I also met two extraordinary patients. Audrey Hill, who died of ovarian cancer, helped me understand the spiritual dimensions of dying, and that those moments like the one I had with my stepfather are available to many, if we know how to listen. Peter Ciccone, who died of AIDS, was the first to show me that pain management in America is not always what it could be.

They were the first of some fifteen patients and their families who allowed me into their lives, who let me follow them, talk with them—in person, on the phone, at their deathbeds—week after week, month after month, telling me in detail what they were feeling and thinking, nearly until the moment they died. I am particularly honored that except in those few places noted in the text, everyone I interviewed or wrote about allowed me to use his or her real name. They helped me to know the dying process itself, and in sharing that process with me, they allowed me to reshape the private puzzle of my life. It was an immense gift, and for that I will always remain grateful.

Needing to understand more, I began attending intensive medical training seminars at major teaching hospitals and their nursing home affiliates. I also went to conferences held by professional organizations—for example, the American Society of Clinical Oncology, the National Hospice Organization, and the Academy of Hospice Physicians—and to workshops and training intensives on more highly focused medical issues held by a variety of medical groups.

I crisscrossed the nation, going to small communities like Pass Christian, Mississippi, or Sebastian, Florida, places where there are modest hospitals and quieter ways of death, and visiting or interviewing those at large teaching hospitals and medical centers in New York, Detroit, San Francisco, New Haven, Washington, Boston, Los Angeles, San Antonio, Chicago, Minneapolis, Montreal, Philadelphia, and Houston.

I went on cardiology rounds at Mount Sinai Medical Center and to pain management sessions at Memorial Sloan-Kettering Cancer Center and Beth Israel Hospital, all in New York City. I visited palliative care centers and hospices like the Royal Victoria Hospital in Montreal, the Hospice of Michigan and its inpatient affiliates at the Detroit hospitals, and the Coming Home Hospice in San Francisco's Castro district.

To learn what doctors are taught about dying I studied textbooks—often under the guidance of medical school faculty members—used in the best medical schools today. I focused particularly on texts on internal medicine, pain management, and palliative care. And I pored over the history of medicine in the reading rooms and rare book rooms of the New York Academy of Medicine's vast library. I also interviewed nearly three hundred physicians, nurses, and health-care workers about their work, their training, their relationships with patients, and about their general understanding and views of modern medical care.

Among those interviewed were people who now play a significant part in our modern saga of dying—familiar names like Dr. Elisabeth Kübler-Ross, Dr. Joanne Lynn, Dr. Jack Kevorkian, and Dr. Timothy Quill, as well as countless other people actively involved on the front lines in shaping, and changing, our American culture of dying: doctors, nurses, psychologists, social workers, hospice volunteers, hospital administrators, ethicists, lawyers, spiritual advisers, and philosophers on death.

While I talked extensively with Jewish, Catholic, and other Christian clerics and theologians, I also explored how influences from the East, particularly Tibetan Buddhism, are changing the terrain of dying in America. And I reported on the new kind of spirituality emerging from hospice care and from popular accounts of near-death experiences.

I was also interested in differing political points of view and what impact they have on our care of the dying. To that end, I interviewed people with diverse opinions—from pro-choice liberals involved with the Hemlock Society, Choice in Dying, and AIDS organizations to pro-life conservatives involved with the National Committee for the Right to Life, or disability activists with a group called Not Dead Yet.

I tried to understand the new ethical and legal issues involved in dying, spending a month as a journalist-in-residence at the Hastings Center in Briarcliff Manor, New York, and interviewing noted end-of-life attorneys and ethicists. I listened to the families who were key to the growing body of ethics and case law that we are learning to live by—the Quinlans, the Cruzans—and I talked with their lawyers, their doctors, their priests.

When I began reporting, I could not understand why someone might want to die in the back of Dr. Jack Kevorkian's rusty van. Now I do. But I also learned that if we are to have good deaths, the culture of dying needs to change.

These needed changes involve the way we make our own personal decisions, and they involve altering the sociomedical context in which we die. We need to change the way ill patients are treated, the way health-care financing is handled, the way we care for those who are at the edges of life. I also learned that there is hope, since many of the changes that I found were needed in medicine, end-of-life care, and the law may now be on the way.

Surely, none of us wants to die, but there are decisions to be made that can make our dying easier. Each person, of course, will make his or her own choices and they will not be the same for everyone. I have learned in writing this book which choices can help make death less painful.

All decisions require open conversations rather than secrecy about death. Against the backdrop of confusion and sorrow that is always there when someone we love dies, I have also learned something more: It *is* possible to have a good death in America, but as a nation that has grown used to medical miracles, we now have to develop the will to learn how to bring closure to life when a cure is no longer likely.

THE
GOOD
DEATH

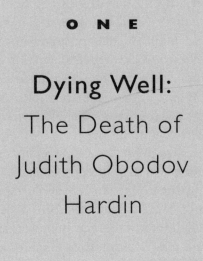

ONE

Dying Well: The Death of Judith Obodov Hardin

Except for the fact that his mother died, the summer he was ten was the best summer of Justin Hardin's life. At least, that's how he tells it now that he's fourteen.

That year, he moved with his mother, Judith, his father, Moh, and his five-year-old sister, Cecily, from Nova Scotia to a house high on a hill in the Sangre de Cristo Mountains of southern Colorado. Standing on their front deck or looking out through the picture window in the living room, Justin could see over the San Luis Valley for two hundred miles. Inside, standing in front of the picture window, he could look up through two huge skylights and watch traffic jams of clouds traveling above. At night, when Justin loved it best, if he tilted his head back and squinted hard, he could see clear through the black sky and beyond, into a kaleidoscope of galaxies and stars, and imagine universes filled with the most awesome fantasies.

During the days, Judith would swing in her hammock, strung outside the deck between two tall pine trees. When it was hot, a window fan would blow on her, propped up on the grass and plugged into an extension cord that wormed its way to a socket back in the bathroom. She was like a squid feeding on the house. Near the extension cord lay another tentacle, this one fatter and clearer, a tube that brought her oxygen wherever she went, seeping through two little prongs in her nose.

At night, Judith slept in her La-Z-Boy recliner in the living room in front of the picture window, directly beneath the skylights—an egg being cooked by the moon. And every third night Justin would have a "spendover," those nights when he'd sleep on the couch beside her, under the stars and that moon. Before they went to sleep, he and Judith would play Monopoly or Gameboy, or read aloud to each other from novels.

One novel they read over and over. It wasn't something out of great literature, something Judith picked to be sure Justin thought great thoughts. It was a book called *Borgel*—his all-time favorite. "It's about this kid whose uncle—whom he didn't even know he had—comes and takes him in a car that turns into a spaceship and they fly out into space," Justin says. "Halfway through the book, you realize the uncle is trying to find this big monument in space to show him. In the end, they find it, but it turns out it's a giant Popsicle. It's a really cool story."

But mostly, they'd just stare at the stars and talk, especially when they both woke up in the middle of the night, which they often did. By that summer of 1990, Judith had been fighting breast cancer for three years. Yet now, even four years later, Justin still thinks of that time as totally magical.

Judith was dying, and everyone knew it. Weird as it sounds, that's probably what made the summer so special. "It was so quiet and peaceful," Justin says. "There weren't any screams and tears. Nobody got in any big fights. Everything was just focused on her dying. I felt closer to her than I ever had, because we spent more time together, just talking. We had that house on the hill and I built a fort outside and she slept under those big skylights. It was so beautiful."

The thing Justin remembers most about Judith's dying is the

love that filled the house. It was euphoric and absolute. When he talks one hears one of those few people who have been completely and unconditionally loved by their mothers, even if for a brief period of time. There is a calmness, a certain wisdom, a feeling of confidence, a tinge of humility mixed with good-natured humor. Never had Justin felt so utterly surrounded by such intense, immensely accepting love. Nor had his father or sister.

"To us, it became just ordinary," Moh says. "It's what we did day after day. But when people came to visit, they were always blown away. Judith had gotten so thin, and she had this oxygen tube attached to her wherever she went, but she was so bright and had such a great sense of humor. Friends would say they never felt so much love and real caring."

Watching Judith, holding her, being with her, saying good-bye, transformed everything her family and friends had thought before about death and dying. "She was so inspiring to be around," Moh says. "It was like seeing her off on a great journey, very uplifted and humane." The way she died taught them something profound: Awful, wrenching, painful as it is to lose someone you love, the process of dying isn't necessarily terrifying. That feeling has changed the lives of Judith's family.

Judith Hardin was just thirty-six when she died. Moh was ten years older. They were, though they didn't know it, part of an American movement that is beginning to explore the notion of *natural dying,* much as the Lamaze movement explored natural childbirth several decades ago.

This movement affects not only those who are the Hardins' age—baby boomers at midlife—but almost every American. People of the Hardins' generation are now the nation's caretakers: They are rearing children, succoring their ill and dying peers, and taking on responsibility for their often frail, elderly parents. At the same time, some are facing painful, early deaths of their own.

Just as members of this generation have altered everything else they have passed through in their life cycle—from sex to childbirth to marriage—they are now in the process of altering how Americans handle the experience of dying. What they are doing may well be the most important social change we will see as we enter the twenty-first century. This move toward natural dying is predicated on a revolution in medicine—on sea changes in medical technology and cultural thinking, on a revamping of end-of-life law, and on changes in the basic definitions of life and death.

Rather than being organized, this movement is a spontaneous, grass-roots response to how difficult dying seems to have become. To die "naturally" is to find a way to have a graceful death when the prognosis is terminal and further treatments are of questionable value. It is not a rejection of medical science, but rather an attempt to use the sophistication of modern medicine to treat—in a different, better way—those who are seriously ill or near death.

Just as medical advances—such as pain medications and fetal monitors—have been incorporated into natural childbirth, modern medications can be incorporated into natural dying, helping us manage pain or other uncomfortable symptoms at death. New laws have given us the unprecedented ability to say no to unwanted treatments.

This movement is an attempt to return dying to the intimacy of American families—whether it occurs at home, in a hospital, or in a nursing home. Like natural childbirth, natural dying is a way to cope with one of the great milestones in life, a movement searching for ways to bring closure to lives well lived, and to help us appreciate that all of life is about connections, relationships, and unconditional love. It is helping us feel comfortable again holding, kissing, caressing loved ones as they die, and reinvesting death with a new kind of sacredness.

Some of those involved are eminent physicians—many of them working in the most prestigious medical centers—who are worried about what they see as overly aggressive treatments that prolong life excessively and grant a paucity of attention to care that could give comfort to the dying.

Some are psychologists or philosophers in the process of developing new fields—for instance, medical bioethics or psycho-oncology (treating the psychological and emotional issues of cancer patients).

Some are hospice doctors, nurses, social workers, aides, or volunteers who believe that home care with social and nursing support and pain and symptom management is the best way to care for those who are terminally ill. But most are ordinary Americans—like the Hardins.

Judith first found the lump about two years after Cecily was born. She was taking a rare lazy bath that day, soaping up her right breast, and there it was, a hard little acorn hiding in the soft tissue. It had been about three years since they'd moved to Nova Scotia from Vermont, and life was good. She and Moh had bought a greenhouse in rural Maitland (about an hour and a half from Halifax), they had a lot of friends, Moh had a job he loved, writing government publications, the babies were thriving, and Judith adored running the greenhouse. She thought the lump must be nothing. Her mother and her cousin both had fibrocystic breasts.

But six months later, the lump was still there, so she consulted her doctor, who sent her to another doctor in Halifax for a needle biopsy. As Moh tells it now, Judith and that Halifax doctor didn't get along. "Judith was one of those independent women, a Leo," Moh says, "with long, flaming red hair and a fiery spirit. It sounds like this was an old-time male doctor who didn't have much patience with women who asked a lot of questions and had their own strong opinions. And she certainly did."

Not only did Judith come home from his office in tears—with her breast slowly turning black and blue where he'd poked her—but the doctor didn't get the tissue he needed for the biopsy. Judith was so upset that she didn't return to any physician for another six months—a wait, Moh says, "that probably had implications for her future."

She stopped thinking about the lump. Judith had a knack for making friends, and one of the traits her friends most loved about her was how involved she got in listening to what was happening in their lives. She'd walk around hanging on to the phone, saying things like, "No, he didn't!" and "How did it make you feel?" and "Then what?" She'd sit on the porch, making it fun for people to be around, organizing little outings like cross-country ski trips or telling lively, raucous jokes to cheer up friends. She'd agree, disagree, give advice, have intense, emotional fights, but she was always there when she was needed.

Judith wasn't really beautiful, but with her long orange-red hair, her face full of freckles, her lean, tanned body, her sharp humor, her witty, foxy ways, she seemed more beautiful the longer you knew her. She was at home in Nova Scotia, rather like an Anne of Green Gables grown up and come back.

But in another six months, the lump was not only still there, it felt larger—maybe as large as a walnut now, but definitely bigger than an acorn. This time she went to a woman doctor. "That day Judith drove to Halifax with a girlfriend for a mammogram," Moh says. "I remember no one was particularly concerned. But then she called me at work and told me it was positive. I was scared out of my mind.

"When she got home, Judith said the doctor wanted to do a full mastectomy as soon as possible, which was in three days. This was in December of 1987, right after Christmas. Cecily was only three and Justin was about to turn seven. They were going to do it on New Year's Eve, that's how serious they thought it was. All she wanted to do then was lie in bed and go to sleep. I was in shock. I remember going outside and thinking, 'Who can I talk to, who will understand if I cry?' "

At that time Judith was thirty-three, Moh forty-three. They'd met in San Francisco when she was just twenty-two, wild, fresh out of acting school and Boston's Emerson College. Moh was more sophisticated—a musician and a landscape designer who'd gone to Duke University, the best in North Carolina, where he'd grown up—and he thought he could tame her. He fell in love. Moh, the son of a Methodist minister, was a man who could be relied on—devoted, steady, loving, brilliant. He often thought that since he was Judith's senior, he was the one in charge. But sometimes, especially times like this, he caught a glimpse of Judith's vast emotional strength.

For the operation, her mother, Adele Obodov, flew in from Colorado Springs, where Judith had grown up. Adele, Moh, Justin, and Cecily all stayed at a bed-and-breakfast in Halifax to be near Judith. Fourteen of Judith's women friends also took turns being with her at the hospital around the clock.

"Before the surgery Judith and I were alone in her hospital

room," Moh says, "and she took her breast out and said, 'Goodbye, it's been nice.' I felt so embarrassed; I didn't know what to do. Afterward, the doctor said he'd taken out fourteen lymph nodes and the cancer had spread to nine of them. It wasn't twelve or fourteen, so it wasn't the worst, but she had to start on chemotherapy the next morning." That's how Moh and Judith spent New Year's Eve.

On the first day of 1988, Judith woke up with bandages where her right breast had been and a needleful of chemicals slowly seeping into her arm. She wasn't given Adriamycin, one of the strongest chemotherapy drugs, which would have made her striking red hair fall out and menopause begin. Doctors were trying to avoid that, since she was so young. But over the next six months, she had to come back to Halifax every three or four weeks for four more chemo treatments targeted to her particular type of cancer.

Each time, she'd sit in a room in the hospital while the poison dripped into her veins. She could feel it going in, a sense of cold marauding through her body, like little frozen threads continually spreading. If it wasn't done right, if even a drop got out of a vein and under her skin, it could cause a serious burn. She wondered why it didn't burn the veins. But within a few hours, she began to feel it burn something deeper; her consciousness began to dim as the poison within her slowly started to work.

That was when the fear would come, when she and her oncology nurse would talk. Judith shared secrets with her that she didn't talk about at home—fear of dying, fear of leaving her children, fear that they were too young to grow up without their mother. The nurse told her she'd seen chemotherapy work wonders, but that she understood why Judith would be scared. She had kids of her own.

Usually a girlfriend would drive Judith in for chemo. On the long drive back to Maitland, Judith would sit in the car, hoping to get home before the exhaustion set in. Then she'd lie in bed, rolled up in a ball under the covers, for three days, not eating. "The strange part of having cancer," Moh says, "is that the illness doesn't make you feel at all sick at first. It's the chemotherapy that's so rough. It sapped her energy, took away her spirit. In a way, it took away her very being, her sense of who she was, her confidence. And as soon as you begin to feel better, they zap you again. It made her sick for months."

After the treatments ended, Judith was fine for almost a year. They decided to sell the greenhouse and move to Halifax to be nearer Judith's friends. She wanted to be around women, have them there for advice and support. Moh got a job doing economic consulting for mining companies. Judith took charge of selling their greenhouse. She began looking herself again, tanned and lean and healthy, so much so that Moh felt he'd better start jogging lest *he* be the one who looked sickly and soft-bodied. Their lives slowly came back together. Judith was glad to be alive.

She found herself falling in love with Moh all over again. He'd been so loving, so supportive. She was glad to feel his body next to hers at night, to watch his eyes at dinner, to hear his voice when he talked with the children. And he fell in love again with her. She also realized how desperately she loved her kids. Only then did she begin to have nightmares about what it would be like to leave them. She'd wake in the night and find her pillow wet with tears. She'd roll over and cling to Moh like one half of a twin Popsicle, grateful to be there.

But within the year the cancer returned, this time in the skin around Judith's mastectomy and in her armpit. The day they told her, Moh found her lying on the couch, just staring. For weeks after that, she hardly moved. Secretly, when her husband and children weren't around, she would talk on the phone long-distance to her mother about her terror of dying.

Doctors cut out the lumps and she had another round of chemotherapy, which was stronger this time and made her sicker than ever. Her hair fell out in bunches, and though she wasn't entirely bald, she mourned how much it had thinned. Then she had radiation, which she found wasn't as bad. But with this recurrence, her prognosis grew more bleak. Her friends deluged her with books on breast cancer, books on treatments of one kind or another, but she found she didn't want to read them. Judith was overwhelmed, and Moh and her friends began looking for other doctors to consult.

During this time, Judith's mother flew from Colorado Springs to be with her, to help her, to talk with her. She must have gone back and forth six times. Judith's father was ill, having attacks of nausea. Adele was trying to take care of him and run their family business, but Judith kept wanting her to come again and again. Finally they had a fight. Judith was asking for more than Adele could give.

Adele is a Holocaust survivor, one of a trainload of children smuggled into England from Germany during the war. Many of her relatives perished in Auschwitz. She didn't want to lose Judith, but she had learned something about pain and survival. "Judith would say, 'Mother, you are my strength,' " Adele says. "I knew I couldn't be her strength. I wanted her to build her own strength, because I felt if she didn't, she wouldn't get through this. Most of the really important things in life you do alone. Your husband may be there with you when you have your baby, but you're going it alone. You lose your mother or your father and you're alone. You're born alone and you have to die alone. But out of that fight—as terribly guilty as I felt at the time—I think Judith found her strength."

Like many Americans, once traditional methods seemed to be failing them Moh and Judith began to look to alternative therapies for help. Reliable researchers estimate that 40 percent of all cancer patients, most of them highly educated like Judith, ultimately turn to alternative treatments when their hope for a cure is running out. A dying Steve McQueen went to Mexico to try laetrile when he had cancer. Michael Landon went on an all-juice diet before he, too, died of cancer.

When traditional medicine can't cure by attacking the invading microbe or the marauding cancer cell through chemotherapy or radiation or surgery, other patients will do what McQueen and Landon did. They might also sign up for cancer camp, seek out self-help and meditation groups, try acupuncture, dose themselves with vitamins, take Tibetan or Chinese herbs, go on macrobiotic diets, or buy books on visualization—like those of Bernie Siegel, M.D., author of the best-seller *Love, Medicine and Miracles*. Most of these alternative treatments are based on Eastern views of medicine, which seeks to revitalize the body's immune system so that the system itself, rather than drugs or chemotherapy, can fight off illness.

These therapies made sense to the Hardins. By the time Judith discovered her cancer, they had been studying Buddhism for more than ten years. (Buddhism often uses visualizations in meditation— imaginary images, like the mental pictures of a perfect high jump or spectacular dive that athletes create to help them achieve peak performance.) She and Moh liked the idea of using visualizations to try to battle cancer, of trying to stimulate the immune system by imagining healthy cells galloping through the body, sweeping away cells that had become sick. This new, self-help culture of illness also seemed a lot like the familiar self-help culture of natural childbirth.

In 1979, when Judith had had Justin, and again in 1984, when Cecily was born, they had prepared with the help of natural child-birth classes. Just as Moh had coached Judith then, he began coaching her now to fight cancer. "We found a book that was one of the early self-help programs for cancer patients, with visualization and relaxation exercises," Moh says, "and we started doing them every night before we went to sleep. I'd say the visualization instructions out loud to her: 'Relax, starting from your toes, going to your feet, to wherever.' It's hazy now, but you imagine yourself in a meadow, you create your own space so you can relax and find comfort. Then you visualize the cancer, with white knights coming in to kill the cancer cells. For months, we lay next to each other in bed and did this for twenty minutes almost every night before she fell asleep."

But as the weeks went by, although the visualizations may have helped Judith sleep, they ended up having another, unexpected effect. "They set up the notion that you can heal yourself if you really want to," Moh says, "and if you don't [heal], you don't *want* to get well. Judith began to feel guilty, thinking that if she couldn't do it all right—if she couldn't visualize well enough so that the cancer went away—then death was some kind of failure; it was all her fault. Finally, the whole thing made her mad." She stopped wanting her friends to come over or call to tell her to try harder. Then, in the fall of 1989, she noticed new lumps in profusion.

The lumps were removed. Judith began relying more and more on the meditation practices she'd learned in her study of Buddhism. When a Tibetan Buddhist doctor came to town, she went to see him. He gave her a different kind of visualization: She had to picture cutting herself into little pieces and offering all her parts to the deities. The image was powerful—comforting, in a weird way, because it created a visceral feeling that even if the body is diseased, some other, healthy consciousness exists separate from the body and might conceivably live on.

She also plunged into ever more experimental treatments— shots of 714x, a black-market cure offered by a Montreal doctor;

gulps of an underground drug, said to have been used by the Indians to cure cancer and produced by an old farmer in Arkansas who sent it in reused milk cartons; a seventy-year-old European treatment called anthroposophy, based on Rudolf Steiner's teachings and practiced by a physician near New York City that Judith's sister, Janet, told her about. None of these had any noticeable effect.

"While we were in New York," Moh says, "the beginning of a 'what-the-hell' attitude started growing. We were away from the kids for four or five days, we had a little money, and we just decided to have some fun. Well, on the way back we were sitting in traffic at the George Washington Bridge saying what a great time we'd had, and a cement block came through the windshield, hit the gearshift, and jumped onto Judith's knee. We could have been killed right there. It made us remember something the Tibetan Buddhist doctor had said: 'Remember, life doesn't work very well, things *don't* work out. *That's* the nature of life.' " The near-death experience with the cement block brought back Judith's sense of humor.

The Hardins were part of a generation that grew up on medical miracles—including the Pill—a generation that explored Eastern religions, psychedelics, New Age ideas, and the literature of near-death experiences. Theirs is the first generation in history that didn't see its women die in childbirth, that counted on its children living to old age, that saw disease after disease eradicated, radiated, eliminated, that got polio shots and vaccinations and antibiotics and organ transplants.

It is also a generation with many members who do not have profound religious beliefs or who (when they do) frequently choose not to follow the beliefs they learned in childhood. In addition, many of their families—the traditional sources of comfort—have been radically altered, shaken by divorce, new sexual choices, and multiple generations needing simultaneous care. This generation didn't *expect* to die; its members are, perhaps, more emotionally unprepared for their mortality than any generation before it. Yet here they are, moved and outraged by early, shocking deaths from AIDS and cancer, and by the hard, protracted deaths of aging parents.

Still, this generation has unique strengths. It is not prepared to accept the dictates of any authority, doctors included. Demanding personal autonomy and control, it has taken charge of every stage in its life cycle and altered everything it has passed through. It strengthened the civil rights movement. It revived feminism. It divided over the Vietnam War. As its members have reached middle age, they have altered the way Americans view menopause, health, physical fitness, even aging. And now they are in the vanguard of those changing the American way of death. As members of this generation, Judith and Moh were savvy about questioning what medicine could and could not do.

By the fall of 1989, almost two years after Judith was first diagnosed, the cancer had spread to her bones—the beginning of the end. Though her chances of survival were lessening, doctors offered still more chemo, this time in a sack surgically placed inside her chest wall. No one mentioned it right then, but down the line there were still more high-tech treatments, including experimental bone marrow transplants.

Judith thought hard. She had begun to lose faith in Western medicine. She wanted to live, to be with Moh and the children. She thought maybe she could bargain for a few more years. She'd stare at Cecily, who was so little. She'd watch Justin shedding his baby-ness, sprouting into a boy.

But she also didn't want to be disfigured any more than she already was, nor did she want to lose her hair again or to be ill or isolated in a hospital, where she would miss spending her final days with her family. Her doctors would give her chances for survival in terms of statistical odds, and her odds kept getting longer. It was also impossible to know whether or not she, Judith Hardin, would be among the small percentage who would "make it" and, if she were, what the long-term prognosis might be, or what costs— emotional, physical, and financial—were involved.

She and Moh did research of their own. And soon Judith realized she had no confidence that more chemo would work if it hadn't worked already. She also realized she'd rather do anything than go through chemotherapy again, that the pain and chaos of more aggressive treatments were not worth the slim odds they might give her. Judith made a critical decision: She said no to further standard medical treatments.

■   ■   ■

That Christmas, the Hardins visited Judith's parents in Colorado Springs. Judith wanted to show Justin and Cecily where she'd grown up, how she'd walked to school, where she had played as a child. She took them to her old house, showed them her room, those secret places where she'd scribble or hide things, places she'd go when she cried.

While they were in Colorado, Judith felt better. It was sunny and bright there. She also went to see a psychic healer who had been recommended by a friend. He told her she needed to be where it was warm and sunny if she was going to get well.

Back in Nova Scotia, it was cold and dark. The snow seemed never to stop; the night ate up more and more of the days. Judith said her bones felt as if they were filling with deep arthritis. She never complained about the pain, but she began to limp and to walk more slowly. She thought of the greenhouse and the plants. By spring, they'd been without enough sun for so long that their energy was nearly depleted. She felt as drained as a late March plant. She suggested they move to Colorado for a while.

Judith was thinking of the psychic healer, of the warmth, of going back home to her own roots for new growth, of getting some distance from well-meaning friends who wouldn't stop giving her advice and suggestions about various treatments. She was overwhelmed. She thought she and Moh and the children would go on a family adventure. She talked about taking the kids out of school and traveling around the world. Though she hadn't said it out loud yet, Judith was becoming more sure that she was probably going to die, and that Moh and the children weren't ready. She wanted them all to have one final, wonderful family retreat, a last intoxicating good-time fling. But she wasn't able to stop all treatments yet. There were still some spiritual healing therapies she said she would try; she wasn't willing to dash everyone's hope—most of all her own.

"We were exhausted with the roller coaster of treatments—one day feeling, 'Oh, she's getting better'; the next day thinking, 'No, it's not working,'" Moh says. "And the cycles began getting shorter. I never gave up hope, but for Judith, there was a mix. She was still dealing with the psychology of the healing movement, thinking that death was some kind of failure, an enemy to be fought rather than a natural process. In the end, I think that was probably the biggest obstacle to our accepting her dying, but at the time, going to Colorado sounded like a good idea." At least Judith felt better there.

There was also something else: Since the Hardins had been living in Canada, which has a national health-care system, they had no health coverage in the United States. "We knew when we left," Moh says, "that that was *it* for more aggressive Western medicine. Unless we went back to Canada, we would only be able to afford alternative treatments."

They took Judith's parents up on their offer of financial help, Moh took a leave from work, they rented out their Halifax home, and were on the road within seven days after they'd decided to move.

"We set off for Colorado to have an adventure," Moh says. "I felt extremely young again, back to the hippie days of 'Well, let's see what will happen.' We had no objective, just to have Judith heal. I was forty-five, she was thirty-five, Justin ten, and Cecily five. And it was a great trip. We'd drive, stop in motels, play Ping-Pong, get in bed, order room service and a movie. We were lucky. We had some money. We'd always been paranoid about spending money, but we started to say, 'Yeah, sure, room service costs a little more, but who cares?' "

By February, they'd settled in the mountains near the town of Crestone. For three hours a day, while the children were at school, Moh and Judith would do healing exercises and cook macrobiotic food. To Moh, "healing" meant that Judith would be cured. He was so intent on this that the psychic healer showed him a technique to use, and Moh gave her "treatments" himself every day.

He swore that when he put his hands over her body he could feel the "holes" in the energy above her where the cancer was, just as the healer told him he would. Then he would concentrate hard: He'd hold his left hand on Judith's heart and move his right hand in the air several inches above her body, back and forth. When he felt a hole, he'd touch her there and try to balance out the energy between her heart and that hand where the hole was. He wanted so much to close up those holes. The healer told him that it would help her body make the cancer disappear. He nearly *willed* it to go away, doing what the healer had taught him. Pretty soon, Judith realized it wasn't working. But she loved Moh. So she let him try.

She also made new friends, among them Joe Vest, a filmmaker and composer who was dying of AIDS. Together he and Judith formed a black-humor club, The Terminals. Moh argued that anyone could join—since everyone is terminal—but Judith and Joe said no, because other people weren't as imminently terminal as they were. Both knew they didn't have much time, and they clung to each other for support.

By April, Judith's lymph system began to fail, and her lungs started filling uncomfortably with fluids. The cancer was eating away, marching on, chomping ever deeper into her lungs and bones. Judith felt herself growing weaker. She began having trouble breathing, and growths appeared around her chest wall and in her arms.

Then she met Sam MovesCamp, a Native American medicine man whom she grew to love and trust. Sam was a Lakota from the Pine Ridge Reservation of South Dakota. He told Judith that the Lakota people were given particular healing ceremonies by the "grandfathers," among them the pipe, the sweat, the vision quest, and the sun dance. This tradition of healing rituals was almost wiped out by attempts at assimilation and by laws, since rescinded, that had made the ceremonies illegal for many years. Younger Native Americans, like Sam, were trying to relearn this tradition from their own grandparents and share it with those in need.

Unusual as these healing rituals may have seemed, Judith felt she had nothing more to lose. While Moh still thought "healing" meant she might be cured, Judith began to think that "healing" could also mean she would find some spiritual strength in facing her own death. And that is exactly what happened, although not in the way anyone expected.

In May, Sam set up special sweat lodges for her. Then he brought Rudy RunsAbove, an elder medicine man from Pine Ridge, to perform two high-powered Yuwipi ceremonies. Rudy was aging and ill, and has since died, and he didn't leave Pine Ridge very often. But he came to Colorado for Judith.

When Rudy thought the time was right, he instructed Moh to line the windows of a room in the Hardins' house so that not a flicker of light could get in. In the middle of that room, Sam and Rudy made an altar of sand, placing flags and small pouches of tobacco—tied in cloths of black, red, yellow, and white—on each of the altar's four corners and put gourd rattles next to the altar.

Then they asked Judith, her friends, and her family to file in, and they turned out the lights. Standing on a bed of sage, Rudy recited words calling on the vision that he said gave him his power, and he sang songs to invite in the healing spirits.

Moh was credulous. "The spirits made their presence known by flashing lights and shaking the rattles all over the room," he maintains. "I mean on the ceiling and the floor and here and there. It was pretty wild, and there was a very strong feeling of presence."

"After the ceremony, there was a feast in which food was offered to the spirits and then to everyone at the ceremony. Judith told Rudy and Sam that she was disappointed: She thought it was all a trick, that the flashing lights were done with a Bic lighter, and Rudy had been doing the rattles," Moh says. "When they heard this, Rudy and Sam were hysterical, they thought it was so funny. Rudy was in his late sixties and one of his sides is paralyzed from a stroke; Sam would have had to race around the room in the pitch black and would have fallen over everyone in the process."

Judith was skeptical, but she was willing to try again. The next night, when Rudy called in the spirits and the rattles moved, she felt relaxed enough to let the rattles touch her. She was amazed; Judith said they found the exact spots where the cancer had made her bones so sore. But in the weeks afterward, Judith's soreness didn't recede; it got worse.

The cancer had begun to spread more deeply into her arm and through her chest wall. Judith began having terrible dreams, with chaotic, disconnected images. "There was a lot of fighting going on," Moh says, "an aggressive person fighting with a nice person, and it turned out they both were her." She'd wake up, terrified, many times a night. By June, she found it hard to walk or breathe. Judith knew for sure she was going to die. And something about her began to change.

"I think what happened," Moh says, "was that she stepped through her fear of the unknown. These ceremonies became a turning point in Judith's approach to death." It was as if she'd frantically searched here and there for a cure, and now, as she began to realize the end was near, she decided just to settle in with her life as it was. For Judith, that meant she would use the Buddhist meditation practices she'd already learned to help her in dying, and spend the rest of her days focused on her husband, her family, and her close friends.

From then on, she stopped *all* treatments. No psychic healing. No macrobiotic diet. The spreading cancer was making her uncomfortable, though, so Adele consulted with her own doctor. He sent Moh and Judith to a radiologist in Colorado Springs, who suggested that Judith come for radiation therapy to try to reduce the size of the new tumors. It was a long drive from Crestone to Colorado Springs, and the radiation was for "comfort only," not for any cure.

Judith and Moh decided to call Paul McIntyre, M.D., in Halifax, for advice. He had been their family doctor and had also delivered Cecily. They trusted him. Coincidentally, by then he had gotten special advanced training in palliative (comfort) care in treating the terminally ill and was in the process of refocusing his practice solely on caring for the dying.

"Normally, Paul McIntyre is a low-key kind of guy," Moh says, "not really one to give strong opinions, but this time he was stronger than we'd ever heard him. 'Look, Judith is too weak and it's too hot to make that drive,' " Moh says he said. " 'She'll probably die in the car. Judith wants to die at home, right where she is, so it's better if she doesn't go.' We were really grateful he told us that."

After that, Judith became very joyful. "A kind of groundlessness developed. It's so negative in our culture to 'give up,' because it implies that you've lost, so she went through various phases of feeling guilty, defeated," Moh says. "And then she came out the other side. She stopped seeing death as giving up and began to see it as the last of many life passages."

To help her, however, they decided to call their local Colorado doctor, Victor Sierpina, M.D. As the only doctor in their area, he treated everyone for everything from the flu, to sore throats, to broken bones. Judith wanted to know that he would be there if things got rough. Dr. Sierpina recommended hospice. They knew what that meant: Judith had, at most, six months to live.

Since Hospice Del Valle had no doctors of its own, Dr. Sierpina began to see her weekly, or to check in by phone. He ordered the oxygen machine and the hospice sent a visiting nurse, who also came weekly. She brought medical advice, pads and ointments for Judith's growing bedsores; Dr. Sierpina prescribed steroids and had the hospice bring her morphine to help her sleep through the night.

Dr. Sierpina was a physician as thoroughly trained in alternative medicine—especially in acupuncture and in home deliveries—as he had been in traditional medicine. "I think that's why she felt so comfortable with me," he says. "I told her I thought the patient was in the pilot's seat, and in a way, her death brought me back to home births, where young children are around, just walking in and out, participating, watching the whole birth process. It was a very sacred time—for me, for her, for her family."

Connie Berman, Judith's best friend from Halifax, came to visit, and she decided to return in a few weeks to help. Judith began spending more time just lying outside in the hammock strung between the two tall pines—four, five, six hours a day, sometimes with Connie or another friend, often with one of the children, sometimes by herself, often just with Moh.

"Sometimes we would talk," Moh says. "A lot of the time we were just together. She wrote letters to both Justin and Cecily for me to read to them after she died. And we cried a lot." One day, she turned to Moh and said: "It's so beautiful here, and I love you all so much. I don't want to leave. It's strange. All my life I've always wanted something else, but now that I'm about to die, I'm completely happy where I am."

In June, Judith was so ill that her family gathered at her house for last good-byes. Her parents drove down from Colorado Springs. Her brother and his wife and children came from Israel, her sister and her family from Sacramento, California. Judith told them all good-bye, one by one, and she told them she loved them. And she also made out a will.

But Judith didn't die. Shortly afterward, she realized that she might have been having a bad reaction to the morphine. So, rather than just accept the regular hospice prescription they decided to talk to Drs. Sierpina and McIntyre, and to do some research of their own. From their psychedelic days, they knew that pharmacology can always be fine-tuned.

Judith wanted to be as pain free as possible so she could sleep, but she didn't want to feel ill and dazed; she wanted to spend her final days alert. They learned that the original morphine prescription was probably too strong for her, and that there were other medications—and other dosages and combinations—she could try.

Dr. McIntyre suggested a highly diluted mixture of liquid morphine. Dr. Sierpina wrote the prescription, but the Hardins had trouble getting it filled. This particular dosage wasn't available at all pharmacies; it needed to be specially mixed, and not all pharmacies would do that. Moreover, not all pharmacies even carried the morphine.

"This wasn't an underground drug," Judith's mother says, "but a prescription written by a licensed Colorado doctor. Moh tried where they lived, and then I called pharmacies in Colorado Springs. I must have called seven or eight. Maybe more. I just kept calling—I even called the pharmacy in our local hospital—until I finally found a pharmacy [that would mix it]. It's so frustrating. They make you feel like you are doing something illegitimate." From then on, Adele drove regularly to southern Colorado to take Judith her pain medication.

"That was all she needed," Moh says. "After that she would take it only at night, as a nightcap before bed, and she'd joke, 'It's just for kicks.' "

By then, everyone had new routines. In the morning, Moh would help Cecily and Justin get ready for their day, while Connie helped Judith move from her chair in the living room up the stairs, step by step, on her backside, to take a bath and get dressed. Then she and Connie and Moh would begin meditating—for an hour or so.

Moh and Connie would sit on cushions on the floor at the foot of the bed in the Hardins' bedroom, facing the lavish shrine they'd built on top of the dresser. Judith sat on the bed, propped up against a mound of pillows, calming, focusing her mind, chanting in the traditional way. All the while, she would hold her mala—Buddhist prayer beads, like a rosary—clicking the beads and saying the prayers to herself.

Sometimes at night, Moh would wake up and hear Judith's

mala clicking away, knowing she had also begun meditating alone. If he asked, she'd say she was thinking about her Buddhist teacher and what he had taught her about living and dying. Moh says she kept growing calmer, that the house became so joyous it was nearly luminous. Family life went on, but it was accommodating more and more to Judith's diminished abilities and her coming death.

Justin went to day camp or played with friends, building his fort, running in the woods. He was part of a flock of neighborhood ten-year-olds who came and went on their bikes, one house to the next. Cecily also went to day camp, but she mostly wanted to stay close to Judith. At five, she was too young to understand what was going on, but often, not knowing frightened her.

"I was scared she just had one breast," Cecily says later, at eleven, "and I started not to want her to put me to sleep because I was afraid she'd die then." Judith would nuzzle and laugh with her, kiss her soft hair, whisper to her, tell her stories, calm her.

Slowly, among the things she whispered to Cecily, or talked to Justin about—as they looked at the stars at night—was what might happen if she didn't get well: They would stay here with Moh, go to school, be with friends. She would leave them each a precious possession of hers, something that might especially comfort each child. She wanted Cecily to have her mala, an unusual one, with blue-green stone beads the color of Judith's eyes. Justin would have her special backpack.

The most important thing Connie noticed was that Judith started to "kind of move at a different speed. My natural tendency was to organize the household. Judith was dying, and there I was, cleaning. I had to learn to be still, to slow down, and then to see what was needed," she says. "What I saw was that over the summer, Judith didn't get better, but she figured out how to live with her parameters, with the slowing down."

"There was a feeling of 'nowness' about her," Moh says, "which I think had a lot to do with understanding what it meant to give up the future. She had no sense of being dead or alive, but was just living in the present, a far more intensified present. It was also vivid. She wasn't transformed, or anything. She still yelled at me and the kids, but there was a nakedness about it, a vividness about it. Something like living in a time continuum with no plans for the future or memories of the past. The kids and I experienced it as an enormous sense of love, but it became very ordinary to us because we were in it. That's the interesting thing about death: When it happens, it's just ordinary."

Day after day, Moh and Connie and Judith fixed dinners so wonderful that they were nearly feasts. "There were no holds barred. Steak, salmon, trout, buffalo burgers, chicken, stews—we ate really well," he says. "After dinner, we might play Pictionary or talk." Judith couldn't eat much, but she loved the whole climate of preparing. Justin remembers they spent a lot of time sitting outside at night around a campfire, telling stories.

Judith began calling her women friends again. She was especially interested in hearing stories of others' experiences with breast cancer, stories she hadn't wanted to hear for a long while. Friends came to visit. Connie helped take care of the house. Judith slowly began teaching Moh to take over the cooking, the cleaning, the caring for the kids. "Lucky for me," he says, wryly, "I had this chance to run a household under her experienced, sharp, and critical eye."

Through the summer they watched movies on TV, sat around the fire, or read novels to each other aloud. And at night, after the children went to sleep, Connie and Judith and Moh also read aloud Buddhist stories and books, among them *The Way of the Warrior*. They began to think about how to get ready to die, about how to prepare to face death well.

And they would talk—about relationships, about whether Moh might find someone new after Judith died, about Justin and Cecily, about illness, and about dying itself. "Judith would hate me for saying this," Moh says, "but she was inspiring to be around. She was really happy, and also very sharp, with a wry sense of humor and without much hesitation to say what she thought."

They also began to talk about whether some consciousness lives on after death. "We had this question about the reports of people who have had near-death experiences," Moh says, "and said they could see and experience what was happening around them in the room." They made a pact. Judith joked that if she could—after she left her body—she'd make the pictures hang crooked on the walls of her bedroom. Connie, the most meticulous of housekeepers, was sure to notice! She also agreed to let

them know as much as she could what it was like to die as she was
in the process of actually dying.

J udith turned thirty-six on Friday, August 3. That weekend she had
a birthday party. Several friends dropped by, among them a young
Native American named Alex. Moh remembers the moment well:
Judith was in her recliner, in front of the big picture window and
under the skylights. Friends were gathered on the couches around
her; others were sitting or standing nearby.

At the other end of the large room, Connie and Moh were
cooking great heaps of lasagna—Connie's specialty—in the
kitchen area. Moh heard Alex tell Judith that the ceremonies and
the spirits had helped him after he'd almost died in a car accident,
and he started lecturing her about how she must not want to live—
otherwise Sam and Rudy's healing ceremonies would have worked.
That was when Moh heard Judith announce her acceptance of her
own death. Her voice was loud and clear—not shrill, but powerful.
She didn't have much strength by then. She needed help getting in
and out of her chair. But she sat up straight and looked incredibly
strong. Somehow, the intensity in her voice made everyone stop
speaking so they could hear her. She looked Alex directly in the
eyes.

"Alex, I'm at a place in my life where I am facing my death,"
Judith said. "I didn't choose to be here. I am not here because I gave
up. This is not bad. I do not feel bad about myself; it just is what is.
When I die, it is not a defeat. Believe me. I have tried everything,
and right now, I am facing my death.

"Someday, you'll be here. I don't care how many spirits you
have out there, and how many ceremonies you do, and how much
you pray, you are going to die. Sam is going to die; all of your
medicine men have died or are going to die. The Indian way has
helped me very much, but a real warrior sees that death is not giving
up. A real warrior knows that someday we are all going to die." At
that moment, Judith became a warrior herself.

On Monday, August 20, they heard that Mira, Judith's friend
and acupuncturist in Halifax, with whom she'd shared her fears at
the very beginning, had died of breast cancer. The oncology nurse
in Halifax—the one who'd so carefully put those chemotherapy

needles into her arm so not a drop would burn her—had also died, of a sudden aneurysm while she was driving. Another friend was about to die of AIDS. Judith thought how lucky she was to have had this time to get ready.

The next day, Tuesday, Connie and Moh came down with the flu. By Wednesday, Judith had gotten sick, too. Still, she had more energy than she'd had in months; she even got up out of her chair to make oatmeal and clean the kitchen. Throughout the day, though, her temperature kept going up and down. Sometimes her heart beat very fast. They called Dr. Sierpina, who came over on the way home from his office.

"Judith was alert, alive, vibrant, like a flower that had bloomed," he says. "It was astonishing. She'd gotten so frail and there she was with this life energy in full force. In retrospect, it seemed as if the spirit was making its last effort. It was like seeing a birth in reverse." He told Moh and Connie that Judith was doing fine. They felt relieved. But Judith just smiled a sly smile.

Late Thursday afternoon, Justin said he wanted to sleep at a friend's house, something he usually did about twice a week. For the first time he could remember, Judith told him no. He pleaded, so she said okay. That night, Moh had a "spendover." Judith wasn't feeling well, so even though Moh was supposed to be sleeping on the couch beside her, he was up every fifteen or thirty minutes trying to help her get comfortable. She had trouble breathing. He kept watching her, touching her, trying to help her adjust her position, looking at her to be sure there wasn't anything more he could do.

"Very little was said. She apologized for waking me up. I said, 'Don't worry, whatever you want, I'm here.' She said, 'I love you, Moh.' I said, 'I love you, too.' We had that conversation several times," Moh says. "Thinking back, I've wondered why she didn't say more, or I didn't see what was happening and say more—but actually, what is there to say—'Well, this is it, folks, good-bye forever'?"

Not until nearly five in the morning did it cross Moh's mind that this might be the day that Judith would die. "Her fingernails and lips started turning purple," he says, "and it became very difficult for her to talk; it was like the words wouldn't form." He didn't go back to sleep, but just sat with her, making feeble attempts to do something—take her temperature, something. At seven, he got scared enough to call Dr. Sierpina; he asked him to prescribe antibiotics. Connie went to get them.

"Twice during this time," Moh says, "Judith sat straight up, with her eyes wide open, and looked around, just for a few seconds. It was like she was looking right through everything, taking one last look. It was very powerful to watch. Connie came back and got very concerned." She and Moh both sat with Judith, who was lying in her recliner, totally relaxed.

All of a sudden, Judith pointed to her mouth, so Moh handed her the cup of tea by her side. She shook her head no and pointed to her mouth again. He asked if she wanted a glass of water, and again she shook her head no. "That's when either Connie or I said, 'Oh, you can't talk!' " Moh says, "and she shook her head yes. She was lying in her La-Z-Boy with her eyes closed, relaxed; there was no agitation or tension. A few minutes later, she got my attention and pointed to her eyes. I said, somewhat incredulously, 'Do you want your glasses?' and reached for them. Boy, was I missing the point, or what? She shook her head no. Again, one of us said, 'Oh, you can't see!' and she shook her head yes."

Moh called Dr. Sierpina again, who was at the door in five minutes. "He came in and said very loudly, 'Judith, can you hear me?' She shook her head yes. There was a definite sense of her being far away, but still in touch," Moh says. "He took her pulse, blood pressure, those kinds of things that doctors do. I remember him saying, 'This is really bad.'

"He asked me to get an oxygen mask, rather than the nasal cannula she was wearing, and he told Judith in a very loud voice that he was going to try a couple of acupuncture points to stimulate her, and that it might hurt a little. She responded to him that she understood. It was like she understood, but she really didn't care. She was kind of slumped back in her chair. He did one on her foot, and was doing one on her lips when he felt her pulse again and said, 'She's going.' Just like that, a very simple statement. Then he said: 'She's gone.' He said she might take a couple more sporadic breaths, but that was natural. And I remember thinking that maybe on one of those breaths she'd 'catch' again and come back to life.

"Then I saw Connie standing over her and saying, 'Good-bye, Judith.' So I stood up and said, 'I love you.' We stood there for a minute. The doctor's wife was crying near the door, the doctor was putting his things in his bag. I was in shock. I thought we should carry her upstairs and put her in our bed, so the doctor helped me lift her."

The death certificate would say it was 8:05 on Friday morning, August 24, 1990. Cecily woke up. Every morning, she went into Moh and Judith's bedroom to watch television, but when she went in that day, she found Moh sitting in the rocking chair, crying. He told her her mom had died and they both cried. Then Justin came back from his friend's, so Moh picked Cecily up and they went downstairs.

"I told Justin the words I had been dreading for a couple of years: 'Your mom died,' " Moh says. "At first he was in shock, just sat at the edge of the couch and stared out the window for three or four minutes." Then Moh hugged him and they all held each other. And just sobbed.

Justin and Cecily wanted to see Judith, but neither child wanted to be alone in the room with her body. Justin began to feel guilty that he'd begged to go to his friend's, but they all realized that somehow Judith had known this was the night she would die. And by telling him he could go, she had let Justin know it was okay that he wasn't right there.

One of the things Judith had told Moh and her family in the months before she died was that she wanted to have a Buddhist funeral and be cremated. So later that day, Moh and Connie and Joe Vest, her fellow "Terminal" who had come over, washed her body. When people die, they'd been told, bodily fluids usually escape as their sphincters and other muscles relax. So they were ready. But not much happened. Connie picked out one of Judith's favorite dresses and dressed her. Then they said Buddhist prayers and began the funeral preparations they had all made.

Connie called friends and family. In the Buddhist tradition, the body is left undisturbed for three days while people meditate in the room with it. "My strongest experience," Moh says, "is that when Judith died there was no more 'Judithness,' but there was a strong feeling of release, a strong presence in the room." Those who came said that when they sat in that room, they felt Judith's presence, too. Slowly, that feeling and their meditation seemed to transform the environment, making them feel as if the house had become sacred, even uplifted.

In the middle of all that, Judith's family arrived from Colorado Springs, and then Moh's family arrived from North Carolina. They were devastated. Judith's family is Jewish; Moh's family is Methodist. They weren't used to wakes or funerals like this. But Judith's mother and her sister, Janet, each wanted to spend some time alone in the room with her body. (By then, dry ice had been packed around it under the bedcovers.)

When Janet came out, she told Moh that something strange had happened. She'd been sitting there, depressed, when all of a sudden she looked at Judith's face. She could have sworn it moved into a kind of smile that Janet interpreted as Judith saying, "Oh, come on!" *Just like Judith,* she'd thought; *trying to unnerve me.* She shook her head and looked again, but Judith's mouth was back to normal. It actually scared her, she told Moh, just as Judith used to when they were kids. But after that phantom smile, she felt far less sad.

When Adele came out, she, too, told Moh that something strange had happened. She had stayed in the room for just a short time, and she'd cried most of the time. When she got up to leave, she looked one last time at Judith and saw a tear on her cheek—a tear that Adele swears wasn't there when she had arrived. "It touched me greatly," Adele says. "Now I realize that maybe, since she was not embalmed, it was bodily fluids escaping. But there I was, sitting there and crying very, very hard, and talking to her—crying—and then this tear appeared. The most painful thing I can imagine is for a mother to lose a child. I was thankful that we had those last months. Judith said her good-byes and died gracefully."

On the day before the funeral the strangest thing of all occurred. Moh, Connie, Joe Vest, and some other friends had been meditating with Judith's body, as they had every morning. When they got up, Connie walked over to Moh and said, "Did you notice the pictures?"

"I had no idea what she was talking about," Moh says. "But she said, 'The pictures on the wall over Judith's bed. They are crooked.' I remember thinking, 'Okay, Connie, I'll go straighten them, but you are getting really particular.' Then she said: 'Don't you remember the conversation?' Which I didn't until she reminded me."

Connie, Moh—and even Cecily and Justin—all say that the three pictures around Judith's bed were now hanging crooked. Moh says they were tilted by as much as 45 degrees. "The time around Judith's death felt very magical," he says. "It didn't take away the loss, the grieving. When she died I felt like a wide open slit had been cut through my heart. But these things, these funny coincidences, were there."

It hardly matters when or how the pictures actually moved. What matters is how comforting it was to all of them to have a sign that Judith might still be near in spirit form.

Even now, four years later, Moh says that the peace, the calm, even the mystery, surrounding Judith's death were the greatest gift anyone has ever given him.

"Judith's death changed me a lot," he says. "Obviously, my wife died, but the way she died was so powerful, so extraordinary an experience for all of us. It made me realize that death is a journey, that Judith had taken that journey so well, and that she left us feeling so loved and so inspired. All I can say is that for me, for Justin, for Cecily—for all of us, but especially speaking for me—in Judith's death I felt extremely lucky and unlucky at the same time."

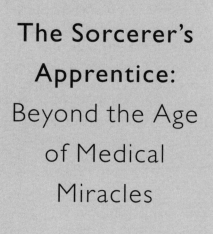

T W O

The Sorcerer's Apprentice:
Beyond the Age of Medical Miracles

The way Judith Hardin died was consistent with the life she had lived and with what she valued most—the health and well-being of her family. In the process of dying she managed both to enhance that well-being and to give her own life its uniquely appropriate closure. Very few people have a death better than Judith's.

A good death was once a matter of sheer luck, simply because some terminal illnesses are far more painful and debasing than others. Today, a good death has more to do with the decisions we—and our health-care providers—make about our medical treatment and terminal care, and with our psychological preparation for dying, than it does with good or bad fortune.

Those deaths that seem good often have these things in common: Excessive treatment—treatment that extends the process of dying longer than a patient wants it extended—is not given; pain and other disquieting or humiliating symptoms are managed aggressively and well; the dying person is granted as much decision-making power as he or she wants; emotional issues are addressed; and the patient, his family, and his friends get all the psychological, spiritual, and physical help they need. Unfortunately, few patients today are lucky enough to die this way.

Judith was fortunate in that her cancer spread so that a relatively gentle death was possible. "She went into respiratory failure and shock," Dr. Sierpina says. "It's usually a complex thing at the end, involving nutritional failure, toxins circulating. In her case, it was a matter of the cancer in her lungs overwhelming her system metabolically. It just reached a certain natural stopping point."

Had the cancer metastasized to her brain, or had it eaten more deeply into her bones, her death might have been more torturous and more psychologically devastating—involving delirium, more severe pain, or serious disabilities.

However, the decisions Judith made about her medical care and the way she managed her final days also made her dying process easier. She refused heroic, last-ditch treatments that might have caused her cancer to spread in different, more painful ways, and she did what she felt she needed to do to bring closure for her family. She also had the good fortune to look for—and find—physicians skilled in palliative medicine (end-of-life symptom management and care).

Dr. Sierpina was able to control her pain and difficulty in breathing, and that relief of suffering let her continue to be her vital and witty self until the day of her death. Medical skill, combined with Judith's fierce sense of how to finish life whole, allowed her to leave her husband and children with a mix of feelings that Moh describes as "brokenhearted and uplifted." Indeed, Judith handled her death so poignantly and so well that the way she died not only moved her family and friends but also inspired her doctors.

Medicine has become sophisticated in its power to cure *and* in its ability to engineer a better death than most of us would have if we depended solely on fate. Unhappily, though, advanced, comfort-oriented medical care is available to too small a percentage of the six thousand people who die in this country every day.

Judith's doctors—Dr. Sierpina and Dr. McIntyre—are rarities among modern physicians: They have both now given their practices over to caring for families and the terminally ill within a palliative-care context. Dr. Sierpina is on the medical faculty in family medicine at the University of Texas Medical Branch in Galveston. His students learn that death is a natural transition, not a medical failure, and that there are things they can do to make that transition better.

"We've institutionalized death and birth—both ends of the life spectrum—and because we have we are not in touch with either of them and go to such great lengths to intervene," says Sierpina. "But the more important thing about Judith's death was the spiritual process—and I've seen this now with many patients as they die. We have a will to live—maybe until a certain life event we may be waiting for, like a birthday or an anniversary—and then we go. That's how it was with her. I think it's the ability of the spirit. The will to resist death is strong. But I don't think death is a sad thing anymore. It's a holy thing."

Palliative techniques are the focus of Dr. McIntyre's practice at the Queen Elizabeth II Health Sciences Center in Halifax, and as a faculty member at the medical school of Dalhousie University. In Canada, palliative medicine is an integral part of the continuum of treatment in serious illness; indeed, in Great Britain and Australia it is a medical specialty. In the United States, though, few doctors are trained to be experts in palliative care—to weigh, as Dr. McIntyre did with Judith, when radiation might or might not be helpful in meeting a particular patient's goals, and to know which pain medications are more effective than others for the way the patient wants to spend his or her final days.

Still, when Dr. McIntyre hears people talking about "peaceful death" he warns them that "dying well" must be defined solely by how the particular patient who is dying interprets it. "Beware of those who say there is a 'correct way to die.' Because then people who don't die that way are seen as failures," he says. "They can't even die right! True 'patient-centered' care isn't about 'peaceful' death. It's about dying, and dying can take many forms, depending on the person who is doing it."

One of the most remarkable things about Judith Hardin's death, he says, was her personal honesty and courage in being aware of what was happening to her. "The fearful thing is to *keep having* treatments to the day you die and not address your dying. She did her best *not* to die, doing more than most—things most people had not even dreamed of, like the Native American rituals— but then when she realized she was dying, she had the courage to live, and share, her death with her family." In America today, that is a rare combination of blessings.

At the turn of the twentieth century, most Americans died at home, surrounded by their family and friends. But by the 1930s, more and more people were going to hospitals to try to get well, or to spend their final days. By the 1970s, a hospital room was where nearly all Americans died, their last glances taking in ventilating machines, the next bed in the intensive-care unit, a surgeon, a dangling IV bag, or a cardiopulmonary resuscitation team.

Since then, a variety of studies suggest that the trend has begun to reverse (astonishingly, there are no good, definitive data). Different studies show that of the 2.2 million deaths that occur in America each year, between 50 and 80 percent of them take place in medical institutions, 5 to 14 percent in nursing homes, and 10 to 14 percent at home with the help of a hospice. The rest of us either die at home without hospice care, or away from home, for example, as the result of an accident or an act of violence.

Most of us have learned, at the hospital bedside of a friend or loved one, that while medicine can miraculously save lives, it often makes dying more drawn out, more painful, and more debasing than it has ever been before. Many of us have seen loved ones with fatal underlying illnesses brought back—against their will—from heart attacks or severe bouts of pneumonia, only to go on to die days, weeks, or painful, humiliating months later. We have seen friends or elderly parents who would have welcomed death put on respirators or feeding tubes against their will and left there indefinitely.

Now, as we approach the twenty-first century, the dying and those who care for them face extraordinary dilemmas: Medical science has become so successful that what people fear most is not death itself but a slow death—locked behind hospital doors—that prolongs life but makes it a living hell. It is largely *because* our success is so new that death has became so troublesome: We have few traditions to guide us through this unprecedented, and greatly protracted, dying process.

Only a hundred years ago, so crude were the indicators of death that alarm bells were sometimes attached to coffins in case someone awoke underground to find he or she had been buried alive. Some funeral homes hired guards to watch the recently deceased for any signs of life.

Today, electrocardiograms, brain-scanning equipment, and other high-tech medical machines are capable not only of giving doctors the ability to postpone death but of providing delicate measures that have led to far more esoteric definitions of death itself. The cessation of heart or lung functions has been supplemented by the cessation of whole-brain functions as the legal definitions of death. It is our ever-changing technology that has allowed us to continue to redefine the margins not only of death—but of life.

In 1900, the average life expectancy at birth for most Americans was only fifty years—today's marker of middle age. People died young—and usually quickly—of accidents or of diseases whose progression from sickness to death was relatively swift. Except in cases of tuberculosis, death generally took no longer than a month, maybe two at most. And once someone became ill, doctors couldn't do much except provide comfort and give something to numb the pain.

By then, improvements in anesthesia had already started making more sophisticated surgery possible, and public-health programs were put into place to curb the spread of epidemics like cholera. Bacteria and viruses began to be isolated as disease-causing agents. But only in 1908 did the age of chemical therapy truly begin—when scientist Paul Ehrlich won the Nobel Prize for discovering that certain chemicals that the body could tolerate could also kill bacteria.

Life expectancy slowly began to increase, with the discovery, in the first half of this century, of medications to fight yellow fever, typhoid, and cholera; with the creation of vaccines against epidemic killers such as smallpox and diphtheria; and with the routine use of insulin and blood transfusions. Then came the introduction of antibiotics in the 1940s, notably penicillin, a history-altering medical triumph. Antibiotics could treat previously common, lethal conditions. This was followed only a few years later by medications to cure that longtime scourge, tuberculosis.

Medicine entered the modern age (an age when illness could truly be prevented or cured) only at the time the front-runners of the baby boom generation were born. People the ages of Judith and Moh Hardin became the first generation in history to grow up without regularly seeing their parents, aunts, uncles, schoolmates, or siblings succumb to illnesses such as strep throat, scarlet fever, and pneumonia, or to what we now consider minor respiratory, stomach, and intestinal bacterial infections.

Just as the older members of this generation were entering Little League and Girl Scouts came a second miracle: The Salk vaccine could successfully ward off polio. So astonishing was the success of this one vaccine that in this country cases of paralytic poliomyelitis dropped from 55,000 in 1954 to fewer than 200 cases a year later. The Salk vaccine and vaccines against measles, German measles, and later, mumps, practically eliminated all these illnesses as childhood maimers and killers.

By the late 1960s, when modern medicine began to emerge full blown, parasitic and infectious diseases were no longer the major causes of American deaths. Those diseases that once killed most of us young—and killed us swiftly—were all but replaced as major killers in the industrialized world. Instead, the Big Four—heart disease, cancer, cardiovascular disease, and lung disease—took their place. Americans began dying of degenerative illnesses involving long-term, chronic decline.

Demographers and public-health specialists refer to this change from quick death by infection to drawn-out death by chronic illness as an "epidemiologic transition," a term first used in 1971 by Abdel R. Omran, Ph.D., a sociologist from the University of North Carolina. Dr. Omran showed how improved sanitation and health-care advances in developing nations cause a change in mortality from swift-killing infections to degenerative disease.

Recent studies and reports—including best-sellers such as *The Hot Zone* and *The Coming Plague*—have focused our attention on the rise of new infectious diseases. Yet, even with the spread of AIDS (which accounts for the largest number of cases of new infectious diseases today), degenerative illnesses are still our major American killers. Indeed, medical advances over the past decade have transformed even AIDS from a swift killer into a degenerative condition.

And now, the degenerative illnesses themselves have changed. As late as the 1960s, cancer was such a sure label of death that doctors feared even using the C word. But by the 1990s, cancer was a "managed condition." According to the National Cancer Institute, the five-year survival rate for testicular cancer in 1973 was 74 percent; by 1985 it had risen to 92 percent. In that time span, the five-year prostate cancer survival rate rose from 61 to 77 percent, and the survival rate for Hodgkin's disease went from 61 to 81 percent. We were living with fatal diseases far longer than we ever had before.

The late 1960s and early 1970s also saw the introduction of a dazzling array of medical techniques. Respirators and feeding tubes went high-tech. Bringing people back from massive heart attacks by means of methods and machinery for cardiopulmonary resuscitation became a regular occurrence. Every hospital in the nation put into place the technology for giving artificial food and intravenous fluids. Advanced methods of diagnosis, with CAT scans, MRIs, mammograms, sonograms, and angiograms, came into use.

Today, heroic operations that once made international news—like the first heart transplant, in 1967 by South Africa's Christiaan Barnard—have become nearly commonplace. Heart bypasses, open-heart and valve-replacement operations, and procedures like angioplasty have become surgical routine. With newer anti-rejection medications, other organ transplants—lungs, liver, kidneys, pancreas, bone marrow—are now regularly performed in hospitals across the nation.

Medications such as beta-blockers, anticoagulants (often called "blood thinners"), and vasopressors are in everyday use. And so, between 1965 and 1985, death from heart disease was dramatically postponed. During the 1960s, deaths in the hospital following heart attacks fell from 22 to 17 percent; by 1993, they had plummeted to some 4 to 6 percent. New methods of cerebrovascular diagnoses, venous surgery, and new medications have transformed vascular disease and the potential for stroke; other medications, portable oxygen machines, respirators, even lung transplants, have given years to those with previously fatal lung problems.

By 1995, Americans' life expectancy at birth had reached seventy-seven years; the average life span had increased by some twenty-seven years since the twentieth century began. S. Jay Olshansky, Ph.D., and A. Brian Ault, Ph.D., medical demographers from the University of Chicago's medical school and its Center on Aging, Health and Society, offer this perspective on the magnitude of this change: "It took the previous two thousand years to achieve a comparable increase for the entire human species."

But though we are living longer with what were once lethal illnesses, we aren't always living better. When heart patients seen in the 1950s are compared with those seen today, says Daniel Levy, M.D., director of the famous Framingham Heart Study, today's patients are far sicker. "The early mortality is lower, so sicker patients are surviving," he says. They may survive heart attacks and bypass surgeries and live with the help of newer medications, but they are now living in a condition that is far more seriously ill and more impaired.

Success has led physicians to view death as a malady that can (and should) be outwitted. The medical breakthroughs of just the past few decades have given patients the same view, raising our expectations of cures that were once only dreamed of by human beings, and lulling us into the sweet notion that death may always be successfully fought.

The result is that we aren't reconciled to death. Those diseases that are lethal to the young—such as AIDS or cancers without a good prognosis—catch us off guard. Neither are we ready for the unpleasantness of some of the treatments that hold death at bay or for the condition those treatments might put us in. We have wished for something and, like the sorcerer's apprentice, we may now be overwhelmed with what we got.

It's 8:30 A.M. on Monday, August 23, 1993. Daily teaching rounds are about to begin for medical residents on the cardiac intensive care unit (ICU) on the fifth floor of the new wing at Mount Sinai Hospital. The building is in a sliver of blocks between the posh Upper East Side and poor Spanish Harlem in Manhattan. Patients here come from both of those areas, from across the country, and from around the world.

Mount Sinai is a teaching hospital affiliated with the City University of New York's Mount Sinai Medical School and has earned an international reputation for expertise in treating heart disease. It specializes in bypass surgery, angioplasty, valve replacements, transplants, highly sophisticated diagnostics, and management of heart disease with up-to-the-minute medications. Inside a hospital, especially a world-class hospital like this one, medical miracles are wrought daily.

Doctors here grew up in medicine's golden era, and this hospital fostered many breakthroughs. While this floor is new, the luster of discoveries past burnishes the corridors. The photos on the walls, the legends, the medical textbooks—doctors walking the halls today can't help but pick up the message: A good physician can fix whatever is wrong, if he or she only figures out the solution.

These doctors aim to cure at all costs. Death is a sign of their own failure—rather like getting an *F* in a course. Their training is like a game of Strategy, the object being to learn how to choose the right treatment option, to hedge the bets, to push the window of survival. That's what these residents are here to learn today.

We're standing, waiting, around the nurses' station in the center of the shiny, fourteen-bed intensive care unit, waiting for all ten of the residents to arrive, plus the two attending physicians who will lead them—Arthur Kennish, M.D., and Salmin Sharma, M.D., members of the teaching faculty. The residents are in their late twenties and thirties, in their first and third postgraduate years, graduates of the best medical schools in the nation. The doctors leading them, both in their forties, rank as senior attending physicians.

Dr. Kennish is also an internist and cardiologist with a thriving Park Avenue private practice. As usual, he has been up since 4:30 A.M., and he has already seen his own hospitalized patients and is ready to begin rounds. Dr. Kennish may be doing well, but he lives life on the run, with very little sleep.

Dr. Sharma, an invasive cardiologist (one who performs sophisticated, high-tech cardiology procedures) is known for his pioneering work in angioplasty. This is an advanced method of clearing blocked arteries in the heart by inserting a tiny wire into a vein in the leg and winding it up through the body to open an artery with a tiny, expanding balloon. His office is this hospital; his patients are those that other doctors call him in to see. He is the expert brought in when other doctors need his more specialized skills.

Soon the residents are all here—eight men and two women, stethoscopes strung over their necks, each of them wearing a white coat and clutching a clipboard, ready to take notes. Most of them are training for a specialty field like cardiology or surgery, rather than for general practice.

The past two decades have seen a dramatic increase in specialization in medicine—a movement away from the more personalized general or family practices like Dr. Kennish's and toward specialties like Dr. Sharma's. Only very recently have managed-care plans and a shortage of primary-care doctors exerted pressure on the medical system to train more family doctors. Indeed, generalists, with their larger view of medicine, are seen as relics of the past. They have been mostly replaced by specialists whose training gives them a fine-tuned ability to keep on searching for a cure, organ by organ by organ.

Whatever its cause, distance—rather than closeness—marks the doctor-patient relationship today. Residency programs may help foster that distance by scheduling such frequent rotations through various specialty areas that young physicians cannot stay with a patient long enough to develop a deep relationship.

They are also famously tiring and grueling, despite the impact of recent court cases—such as the one brought by the parents of Libby Zion—that have served to limit the number of consecutive hours interns and residents can work. Exhaustion can create a risk of error and also may prevent doctors from getting too emotionally involved, especially with patients who are dying. Many of the residents following Drs. Kennish and Sharma around today seem tired. The shifts in this group overlap—half will finish and go home to bed when their rounds are over, and half have just begun their next shift.

One woman resident, whom I'll call Linda, is hugely pregnant; she is scheduled to give birth to her first child right at the end of this ten-week rotation and before her next one begins. She's been up for her all-night shift, something each of these physicians does every third or fourth night, and is one of those who is about to go home. Occasionally she puts her hands to her back or tries lifting her swollen belly under her white doctor's coat.

Linda confides that on her first day, a patient of hers died, a woman just about her own age. "I fell apart," she says. "I thought it was my fault, though it really wasn't. I kept thinking, 'If she could die, so could I.' That's how much I identified with her. I cried and cried. So they sent me home. I thought maybe I'd get to stay home for a few days, but they said to be back on the floor the next day. I just slept and slept. When I got back, I got the message: Pay attention to the heart [as just a bodily organ]. Keep your emotional distance [from the patient]. And that's it. You learn that's what you have to do to stay professional and to be most effective."

With the young doctors on rounds today, as on many days, is Abe Schaffer, M.D., a retired cardiologist who likes to keep his hand in, mostly with ethical issues. "Sometimes students think he's loony and ignore him," Dr. Kennish whispers to me later, "but often he reminds them to look for the obvious, things they would have missed by focusing too much on the technology, the options, the technicalities."

Although patients' own physicians determine their treatment, residents are responsible for daily care. Several are on duty at a time, under the supervision of the teaching faculty. Together, they also monitor quality: If they disagree with the private physician's treatment plan, someone from this team will speak to that doctor.

We're ready. The head resident takes the charts from behind the nurses' station. Like a flock of geese, we start rounds by following the cart with the charts, stopping outside each room as a senior doctor and head resident take turns leading a discussion about the patient inside.

We are standing, some fifteen of us now, outside the first room on the unit. The door is open and we start with a summary of who has been brought onto the unit and who has left since yesterday. No one ever mentions what happened to those who left—whether they got well and went home; whether they will play golf again or go back to work; whether they have died.

Visible through the open door is a jovial-looking man, dressed in a hospital gown with its back slightly open. He smiles and listens. He is actually standing up, trying to walk around. (I've identified him, and all other Mount Sinai patients, by a pseudonym.)

"Mr. Novack, in bed one," the chief resident says, ignoring Mr. Novack, "is a sixty-two-year-old white male who's been waiting several weeks for a heart to arrive for a transplant. He's Status One." (That means he's a priority patient.) The team whooshes in to see Mr. Novack.

"How do you feel?" Dr. Kennish asks. "Great," Mr. Novack smiles wryly, "for someone who's seven-eighths dead." Gallows humor is the way doctors—and Mr. Novack—get through the day.

Mr. Novack has been kept relatively stable on medications, so he really could go home until a heart arrives, the chief resident tells me. But to maintain his priority status, according to regulations from the national organ transplant bank, he must be in an ICU, maintained on dopamine, even though he doesn't really need it. To meet the rules, the team members prescribe a minor amount of the drug, look at his chart, tell a few more jokes, and leave.

Bed two is empty. Someone's gone. No one says where. So is bed three. In bed four is forty-eight-year-old Mr. Levine, described as a "white male." The team thinks Mr. Levine has had a heart attack. A layperson might assume doctors know whether or not someone has had a heart attack. But diagnosis is often ambiguous.

Mr. Levine has had a complete workup. His doctor found that he has several blocked arteries in his heart and has scheduled him for "coronary artery bypass graft" surgery. That, in medical lingo, makes Mr. Levine "a CABG" (pronounced "cabbage"). But the team disagrees with his doctor. There are a number of reasons why an artery or a vein may be blocked, as well as differences in the manner or intensity of the blockage, each of them requiring a different best-treatment option.

The team members argue outside his door. They give percentages and cite various studies. They end up thinking that Mr. Levine should be catheterized before surgery so the doctors can know for sure whether a bypass is his best option. Catheterization is a way to do an interior exam of the arteries of the heart. Since bypass surgery will help only a specific condition, and since it's also the most invasive procedure, it's arguably also the most dangerous. Other conditions may be helped by an angioplasty, or by a second new technique called an atherectomy, in which the inside of the vein can be gored out with a microscopic knife, or by one of an arsenal of new medications like thrombolytics. (An even newer method is now used at Mount Sinai—stents, or tiny, thin tubes, put into blocked arteries to expand them.)

The studies differ on the efficacy of the various treatments. The doctors cite them outside Mr. Levine's open door. Study one, in the *Lancet,* shows that recovery after CABG takes longer than angioplasty but leads to less risk of angina. Study two, from Duke University Medical Center, and scheduled to appear in the *Annals of Internal Medicine,* shows that there is no difference between the two in return-to-work rates one year after treatment, but the study doesn't say what the long-term effects of either might be. Study three, in *JAMA,* says the risk-versus-benefit ratio depends on which hospital and which doctor does the angioplasty or the CABG. Study four discusses the newer method, and though it has promising results, Drs. Sharma and Kennish say it may be too soon to tell whether it's really effective or safe.

Had Mr. Levine listened, he would have discovered that his doctor's choice of the bypass surgery (or CABG) was essentially a crapshoot. They don't know how many arteries in his heart are *severely* involved—they say only a catheterization can tell—and the level of severity determines the best treatment. If two vessels are severely involved, or if all three are, CABG would improve his chance of surviving for five years by 36 to 63 percent, angioplasty by only 10 percent. But if he has less severe heart disease, angioplasty would reduce the likelihood of death by almost 50 percent over CABG. Mr. Levine may have found comfort in the fact that the team decided to talk with his doctor and to suggest a catheterization first to see exactly how many vessels are involved, and how severely.

Everyone agrees that if, after the catheterization, angioplasty is indicated, and if Dr. Sharma does it at Mount Sinai, Mr. Levine's odds might improve. The data measure only survival rates, and since these procedures are all so new, the survival time being measured is still relatively short.

While these doctors argue odds, Dr. Schaffer sits nearby on a rolling typewriter chair, staring at Mr. Levine's chart and watching his heart-monitor screen through the open door. When they finish arguing, Dr. Schaffer says the medication they are using to try to stabilize Mr. Levine isn't working. His heart is still doing flips. So the team orders changes in his drugs, deciding to talk to his physician at length.

Dr. Schaffer also notices that Mr. Levine's most recent electro-cardiogram (EKG) printout somehow doesn't match his past ones. After the discussion is finished, Dr. Sharma says he noticed it, too. He asks the nurses to do another EKG. It turns out that the EKG had been mistakenly switched with that of another patient—every patient's worst nightmare. After looking at the new one, the team still has the same recommendations to make to Mr. Levine's physician about the surgery. And we move on.

In bed five, Ms. Loman, fifty-four years old, described as a "black female," has just come in, transferred from a feeder hospital in an outlying borough. This is her fourth heart attack, and when Dr. Sharma looks at her chart, he sighs. He says he's seen her during all her past three hospitalizations, and mutters that this is horrible. She definitely needs a CABG, he says, but has no insurance or Medicaid, so the doctors at the feeder hospital simply stabilized her medically and sent her on. She's applied for Medicaid and is apparently eligible, Dr. Sharma says, but it takes the system six weeks to process an application, and in the meantime she's had this fourth heart attack. "That's a lot for the body to handle," he says.

Ms. Loman is on a respirator, a clear plastic tube stuffed into her mouth, pumping air from a small box nearby. Heart failure has caused her body to swell with fluids, particularly her lungs. She's conscious, though, and they tell her that as soon as the medications reduce the fluid they can begin to wean her from the respirator so she can breathe on her own. She looks scared, but with the respirator tube going in through her mouth, she can't talk. Her eyes give her away and she starts to cry. Dr. Kennish nods and tells her he knows it's tough. The other doctors, seemingly uncomfortable, try to ignore her tears and start drifting out of her room, one by one.

Back outside, Dr. Kennish tells the reassembled group that the lungs get stiff when they fill with fluids and when a respirator is used, causing a lot of strain on the heart merely to breathe. So it's a deepening spiral down. Respirators were originally intended to get a person through an acute episode like this, he says. As soon as patients were stabilized, they were supposed to be weaned off, but once a technology exists, it can be misused. Families may want to keep an ill relative alive even though he or she is terminal, or doctors may fear lawsuits if they don't use it. Dr. Kennish informs these fledgling physicians that they will need to think about these issues in their practices. Meanwhile, it doesn't seem as if any of these doctors have high hopes for Ms. Loman, even if she were a Rockefeller, but no one comes out and says it.

Bed six is empty. Bed seven is a special case: Going into the room requires special precautions. The patient has an illness for which the hospital has put him into isolation—possibly tuberculosis, which has recently reemerged in New York, particularly among people with AIDS. Nobody mentions what the problem is. We rush in, talk to him for a minute—far, far less than the other patients, and without really saying much—and rush out. It seems as if this patient is essentially being ignored.

The problem just might be, although no one says it, that he is highly likely to die. Diane Meier, M.D., a gerontologist at Mount Sinai, tells me later that it's most instructive, when looking at how doctors are trained during their internships and residencies, to pay attention to the omissions in addition to what's overtly being taught. "At teaching hospitals like this one, it's a social process," she says. "Doctors see that their mission is to cure, not to care for a dying patient. When they see dying patients ignored in rounds, that's worth at least thirty lectures." One study, she says, found that young doctors like these thought that the time they had to spend caring for dying patients took away from the more important knowledge they had to learn as physicians.

We move on. In bed eight is Mr. Levy, an eighty-five-year-old "white male" up from Florida, who had a heart attack on the golf course when he got a hole in one. He starts to tell the team about how he got his heart attack, but he gets so excited that his heart monitor goes kaflooie when he gets to the part about the hole in one, so the doctors tell him to stop. His own doctor had put him on medications, but obviously they aren't keeping him stable.

Outside, in the hall, the head resident says Mr. Levy needs a pacemaker, but begins quoting journal articles about the risk-benefit ratios of surgery for someone his age. Dr. Schaffer balks. He says he detects ageism. Data from other studies, he says, shows the percentages of survival to be much higher if everything else about the patient's condition is fine, which—from looking at Mr. Levy and his chart—it seems to be.

Another set of rules requires that Mr. Levy have a diagnostic catheterization before he gets the pacemaker, but Linda objects.

Why put him through an invasive, and possibly dangerous, procedure, given his age, she asks, when it's clear he needs a pacemaker? The team decides to skip the catheterization here and recommends the pacemaker. Almost immediately, Mr. Levy is on a gurney, waving good-bye as he goes off to surgery. Afterward, he'll be relocated on the surgical floor, so the residents will never learn what happened to him unless they make a special effort to ask.

Six more patients still to see in the next fifteen minutes. In bed eleven, Ms. Norris, a "black female," sixty-four, surprises the team. Though no one has discharged her, when they come in she is getting dressed to go home. Last year she had bypass surgery, but she's just had another heart attack. Her doctor told her she needed a second bypass, but she says she wants to go home to take care of her four-year-old grandson. Drs. Sharma and Kennish try to persuade her otherwise.

"You know, doctors," she finally says, "I appreciate all you are trying to do. I appreciate all this machinery, but we're all gonna die someday, and I've had enough surgery. I just want to take my chances now being at home. Some things, only God can decide." But she does get back into bed after agreeing to stay just a few more days so they can try to readjust her medications.

After bed fourteen, rounds are over for the day. The shift changes; half of these young doctors go home to sleep and the other half take over the care of these patients. Watching these doctors in action, I find it disquieting to realize how inexact a science medicine is, how much impact survival percentages, conflicting research studies, and social, political, financial, and bureaucratic issues have on the care their patients are given.

"The more complicated medicine becomes, the more pressure on you to feel you should have chosen another treatment option," Dr. Kennish tells me as we leave the unit. "Death becomes your fault, your failure to properly strategize. Mount Sinai is very different from other hospitals. Here there is more discussion of possibilities and more willingness on the part of the doctors to say, 'We don't know,' if they don't know. But in other hospitals, they just communicate that *they know,* which makes it all the more difficult to deal with when they fail, and it opens them up to patient criticism, or worse."

In a way, he says, things were actually much better before medicine became so sophisticated, and those unsophisticated days were only two or so decades ago, when he was a resident himself.

"The locus of decision making has shifted to the patient," he says. (Many would disagree.) "But what do you do if they aren't capable of understanding everything that goes into a decision, or understanding that there are always risks—that nothing, not even walking across Park Avenue, is risk-free? And medicine has gotten so complicated that even doctors aren't sure which way to go. These ethical issues didn't exist twenty years ago. Then a doctor made the decisions; patients didn't want to know. They got better. Or they died. But there was a much greater understanding that life ends in death."

Most of us grew up thinking, "Doctor knows best," so it's sobering to learn how many interpretations there are for various symptoms, how many treatment options there are, and how terribly experimental modern medicine is. The layperson isn't used to thinking about treatment decisions in terms of survival statistics. We just want to know that chemotherapy will cure our mother's cancer, or that bypass surgery is exactly what we ourselves, or our husband or wife, need.

And it's especially surprising to discover that doctors actually *make* their choices by means of probability theory. They think in terms of "chances are," or "one-in-ten," or "40 percent," not in the absolute terms ("*this* will make him better") that laypeople expect when a treatment is suggested. Even more surprising to learn is that in some hospitals—in emergency rooms and intensive care units—across the nation, highly sophisticated computer models are used to project a person's likelihood of survival based on calculations using the results of various tests and the status of various fluids and organs.

Still, physicians' decisions are really just informed trial and error, based on their own and others' research, whether these doctors use computer projections or not. And medical trials today are so narrowly focused, and provide such a short track record, that in many cases there is little good research on the long-term outcomes of particular treatments. Most physicians just keep trying treatment after treatment in hopes that one will work—or at least that the patient will not get worse.

In rounds at Mount Sinai that day, no one ever mentioned what would happen if none of the treatment options worked, or what impact the various treatments might have on a patient's ability to function well afterward—and for how long and at what level. Nor did the doctors discuss what level of functioning a patient might find acceptable, or how to assess or discuss that with a patient, or how the treatment itself might affect a patient's daily life.

Nearly three years later, for example, Dr. Sharma told me that Mr. Novack did end up getting his heart transplant about six weeks after I first saw him. "For almost two years he did fine, but then he got cancer," Dr. Sharma said. "The antirejection drugs cause cancer. It's a big, big problem with these antirejection medications." He died shortly afterward of lymphoma.

Death, once understood as the final result of life, has been transformed into a "doctor's fault." So teaching hospitals train young physicians to try every possible play, whatever the odds. They focus on one organ at a time; the specialist's tunnel vision keeps him (or her) from questioning whether a repaired heart could actually work well with damaged lungs, or whether repairing a heart is beneficial for someone who is bedridden, in great pain, or who has kidneys or lungs that are also failing.

The fierce focus on technical innovation and the decision to "keep on treating" have given us our increased longevity, but physicians like Dr. Kennish lament whether the future of medicine will continue to be an art or become a mere craft guided by strict sets of rules and devoid of a sense of patient as person.

If we examine how American doctors are trained we begin to understand why dying has become so difficult in this country. The deficiencies of the modern medical curriculum have prompted a growing number of highly influential doctors to propose radical changes in the way terminally ill patients are treated as well as the way future generations of physicians will be educated.

Doctors today know less about how people die, and less about how to make their dying easier, than they knew at the turn of the century. In 1906, William Osler, M.D., founder of the Johns Hopkins School of Medicine in Baltimore (the first medical school in America), documented the last days or hours of a consecutive 486 of his dying patients, describing the symptoms and signs he saw in patients as they approached death. Astonishingly, Osler's work is still the largest and most comprehensive sequential study (a study that tracks the course of the illness of each patient that comes in) of exactly how hospital patients grow progressively sicker and finally die.

Osler used these and his earlier findings to train generations of physicians with his textbook *Principles and Practice of Medicine* (which has been reprinted and updated over and over). He enumerated the various illnesses that people died of at the turn of the century, their recommended treatments, and the course—and precise length of time—each illness generally took from its inception until the patient's death. An obvious method, a layperson would assume. And yet—significantly—today's doctors do not get this kind of information about their dying patients.

Modern medical textbooks provide up-to-date material on illnesses and treatments—but the emphasis is on the *treatment,* not on the patient or the normal course of the disease. Conspicuously lacking are sections on the paths each of these illnesses might take to death. Therefore, doctors have little idea what to expect, little knowledge of how to treat symptoms of decline—pain included— little understanding of how to differentiate each disease's constellation of symptoms so that they can be addressed in order to make a dying patient more comfortable, little training on how to judge when and how treatment should stop, and not enough knowledge about how to provide palliative care.

Cecil Textbook of Medicine—one of the textbooks of general medicine most often used—devotes fewer than 25 of the 2,300 pages in its nineteenth edition, published in 1992 (the most recent as of this writing), to the treatment of dying patients. None of these pages are in the same section of the book where illnesses and treatments are described. Only 5 of the 2,300 pages discuss pain, and only 3, set off by themselves, directly treat the terminal stage of death. "It's as if death were generic, as if each individual disease, if treated correctly, would not lead to death," comments Christine K. Cassel, M.D., chief of the geriatrics department at Mount Sinai School of Medicine and one of the major voices in efforts to change end-of-life care.

Another major text, *Harrison's Principles of Internal Medicine,* in its thirteenth edition, published in 1994, also neglects to discuss what happens as specific diseases cause the body to shut down and on ways the symptoms of decline can be eased. It offers, instead, extensive data on treatment options.

In 1996, researchers at the Center to Improve Care of the Dying, at George Washington University Medical School, did a comparison study of *Harrison's, The Washington Manual,* and the *Merck Manual,* all texts that guide physicians today. They found "that all three books have substantial opportunities for improvement in addressing how to care for a dying patient, and often did not even discuss the prospect of death as an outcome."

Indeed, the texts did not mention death or dying even in the sections they devoted to nine of the leading causes of death today: AIDS; renal, heart, or lung failure; cancer; liver disease; dementia; diabetes; and stroke. They did not describe the kinds of deaths these patients would undergo, nor did they talk about how to ease the deaths these diseases led to. And they rarely mentioned symptoms that might need to be addressed to keep a patient comfortable, the burdens the family would assume in caring for a patient, or how treatment and care decisions might be made. All this led the researchers to conclude that "general medical textbooks provide almost no guidance on the care of the dying patient."

This study's essential findings were reiterated by the AMA's Council on Scientific Affairs in a well-documented 1996 report in *JAMA,* "The Good Care of the Dying Patient," and has subsequently led the AMA to develop its own education program to try to retrain American doctors in better care of the dying. The reason "suffering patients are now requesting physician-assisted suicide," the *JAMA* report lamented, may be because American physicians know so little about how to care for and help the dying.

Even specialty texts like pain and anesthesiology textbooks often focus far more on acute, postsurgical, wound, or injury pain syndromes than on the chronic pain of those who are terminally ill and dying. "In Osler's day, little could be done to alter the rapid course of fatal illness or injury," the *JAMA* report read. "Now successful medical treatment regularly causes a slow course to death. Yet, modern medicine has largely failed to note how a patient lives during the now prolonged course toward dying."

It wasn't until the spring of 1993 that the first modern palliative-care textbook, *The Oxford Textbook of Palliative Medicine*, was published. And not the World Health Organization nor the American Pain Society nor the American Society of Clinical Oncology nor the U.S. Department of Health and Human Services' Division for Clinical-Practice Guidelines published pain-management guidelines or curricula until the end of the 1980s and the beginning of the 1990s. As of 1996, experts concerned with end-of-life care were *still* campaigning to introduce these guidelines into medical school and residency training programs, to have questions about these issues added to medical-licensing exams, and to add pain-management and palliative-care standards to the criteria for hospital accreditation.

As the AMA reported in its study "The Good Care of the Dying Patient," as of 1993, only 5 of the nation's 126 medical schools had a separate course required on death and dying, although 117 of them did include such information in other required courses. And only 26 percent of all medical residency programs offered instruction on end-of-life issues.

"In the current system of care, many dying persons suffer needlessly, burden their families, and die isolated from family and community," the AMA report concluded. It called for improvements in disease-specific research on illnesses and death, on palliative care, on insurance coverage for this care, and for an end to "overly aggressive, unwarranted [treatment in order] to help improve the care of the dying patient."

The technology, training methods, and go-for-the-Rose-Bowl ethic of today's medical culture have all worked against the development of this kind of knowledge. Through its spectacular accomplishments, this "we-can-lick-disease" culture has unwittingly expanded—perhaps even contorted—the modern dying process without addressing the consequences.

Many physicians and policymakers were advocating a decrease in overly burdensome end-of-life treatments as early as the 1970s. But in 1996, the AMA's serious concern over this issue was grounded largely on the recently released—and shocking—findings of a study that had been finalized in 1995. The Study to

Understand Prognoses and Preferences for Outcomes and Risks of Treatment (SUPPORT) was arguably the most massive piece of research into the end stage of dying in America since Dr. Osler's at the turn of the century.

The $28 million SUPPORT project was codirected by Joanne Lynn, M.D., now head of the Center to Improve Care of the Dying, and William A. Knaus, M.D., now chief of the department of health evaluative sciences at the University of Virginia School of Medicine and a faculty member in a program to teach doctors better care of dying patients.

SUPPORT had a dramatic impact because it included a large slice of the medical establishment, involving interviews with some sixteen hundred doctors, five hundred nurses, and many other health-care professionals at prestigious medical institutions nationwide. More than two hundred researchers—physicians, nurses, and social scientists—were involved, all of them affiliated with major research institutions. Some of these researchers were caring for patients. Others were interviewing patients, their families, and doctors and nurses at the five participating hospitals. Still others were coordinating these efforts or collecting and analyzing data. The study sent a clear warning from deep within America's heartland about how difficult dying in American hospitals has become.

Osler could document nearly the entirety of his patients' disease processes from diagnosis to death because in 1900 that process took only a short period of time. Because dying today is more drawn out, SUPPORT could observe patients only during the critical end stage of life. From 1989 to 1994, the researchers followed some nine thousand patients, roughly five thousand of whom had died by the time the study was over.

All of these were seriously ill people who had come into five medical centers, all teaching hospitals—in Boston; Los Angeles; Durham, North Carolina; Cleveland, Ohio; and Marshfield, Wisconsin. Those patients enrolled in the study were in the final stages of one of nine specific illnesses; they were well enough to survive the first forty-eight hours after hospital admission but sick enough to only have an average of a 50-50 chance of surviving another six months. Researchers intended to find out what happened to patients and their families in the weeks and months following this acute episode.

The study took place in two phases. In Phase I, which lasted from 1989 to 1991, researchers examined how patients were treated when they entered a hospital, how medical decisions were made, and what happened to them and their families during the acute treatment period and for six months afterward. The researchers looked at patients' medical records, and interviewed doctors, nurses, patients, and families. Among their discoveries:

· Half of the patients who were still conscious had moderate to severe pain at least half of the time before they died.
· Thirty-one percent of the patients preferred not to have cardiopulmonary resuscitation (CPR) attempts to bring them back if their hearts stopped; therefore, their doctors should have written "do not resuscitate" (DNR) orders and entered them into their hospital medical charts.
· More than half of their doctors did not know about these patients' DNR preferences.
· Just under half of the patient DNR orders that were placed in charts were written only within two days before the patient died.
· Nearly 40 percent of the patients spent at least ten days in an intensive care unit.

Researchers believed that these findings meant that the patients had often undergone overly aggressive treatment that had been pushed until the very end without sufficient discussion ahead of time about what it would mean for someone who had a terribly poor prognosis to receive aggressive treatment and be resuscitated. (Bluntly put, that means undergoing a resuscitation that doesn't work, or being brought back in the same condition—or a worse condition—than the patient had suffered before his heart stopped.)

In Phase II, from 1992 to 1994, SUPPORT researchers tried to remedy what they considered the medical system's failures. They divided the patients into two groups. One group continued to have the usual treatment, as in the first phase of the study. For the other group, interventions were put in place that researchers believed would make the patients' decision making better, and therefore their experiences of dying easier.

These interventions were grounded in both medical knowledge acquired over the past thirty years and in doctors' cultural and legal experience with new laws about advance directives (living wills and health-care proxies, which we will discuss in Chapter 6). But the researchers even went beyond that: They hired nurses whose job was to talk with patients and families to find out if the patients had living wills, to discuss in depth how they wanted care to proceed, to be sure that patients and families understood their situation and prospects, to ensure that the patients' wishes were inserted in their medical charts, and to communicate these wishes to the patients' doctors.

The doctors were also given medical information that doctors do not ordinarily get—graphic reports on the experimental group of patients that described their statistical probability of surviving up to six months, the likelihood of their having severe functional impairment in two months if they did survive, and the probability of their surviving cardiopulmonary resuscitation. Doctors were also given reports that included the severity of their patients' pain and their patients' understanding of their own prognoses. They had regular conversations about all of this with the specially hired nurses who had talked to patients and their families about their wishes.

Astonishingly, the researchers found that these interventions— all of them quite extraordinary efforts to learn about patients' wishes about their end-of-life care and to empower them to determine their own treatment—seemed to have no effect. Those patients who received the interventions (efforts that every expert on end-of-life medicine or law thought would change patients' treatment patterns) ended up being treated exactly the same as those patients for whom no such efforts were made. Half of all patients still reported uncontrolled moderate to severe pain, and doctors paid little attention to finding out whether patients wished to end life-extending treatment earlier. "We are left with a troubling situation," the study concluded. "The picture we describe of the care of seriously ill or dying persons is not attractive."

Physicians, nurses, policymakers, and social scientists have struggled to make sense of these devastating findings. "It used to be that death was the worst thing that could happen to you," Dr. Knaus, SUPPORT's codirector, told one reporter, "but medical technology now has allowed doctors to create a situation that's even worse."

Dr. Lynn, the other codirector, believes that it is partly because dying has so greatly changed—in such a short period of time—that neither patients nor doctors know quite what to do. Since then, she, Dr. Knaus, and a near tidal wave of others have become outspoken advocates of the need to improve the care that modern medicine gives to the seriously ill and dying.

In 1995, she established the Center to Improve Care of the Dying and, with other esteemed doctors, lawyers, and policy-makers, helped organize the Project on Death in America—an effort by the Soros Foundation to pour upward of $15 million into medical care and education "to transform the culture and experi-ence of dying." She also worked with the AMA and the National Academy of Sciences' Institute of Medicine to develop programs to improve the medical care of the dying.

"Twenty years from now, we are going to look at the way people approach dying today and shake our heads over it, the way we now shake our heads about the way the Victorians viewed sex," Dr. Lynn says. "People really die now by inches rather than by miles. We die in a very slow, chronic way, but our views of dying are based on old views of death—when you were run over by a carriage at the turn of the century and died the next day. We've now con-verted the causes of death into chronic diseases, so the decisions made about dying these days are more about living day to day. It isn't only the problem of removing a patient from a respirator. It's 'Will you give antibiotics or not for this pneumonia?' A person who's had multiple complications with his main underlying illness comes to understand what is involved each time he gets sick, and comes to see how difficult [such choices] can be."

These days, patients and families must ask new kinds of ques-tions as they navigate through the last stage of life: "Should I have that last round of chemotherapy? That delicate, high-tech surgery or radiation? Should I take blood thinners or not? Should I have kidney dialysis, antibiotics, even a glucose intravenous drip?" These are not mere treatment decisions. They depend on the disease one has and on our individual prognosis, our personal hopes, and our private goals. These are private, emotionally complex, highly consequential choices. And they can make all the difference between a decent extended life, a thicket of nightmares, and a gentler death.

"With chronic dying," Dr. Lynn says, "people die in small steps, so it's important to have conversations ahead of time to make these small decisions in a better way. I'd ask, 'What is really important to you?' For some, it may be avoiding being a burden; for others, it may be avoiding family bankruptcy, or how they look, or living to see their eight-months-pregnant daughter's baby. First you have to deal with unrealistic goals, shaping them to be realistic. Then you have to work with people to make a plan of care that makes sense with their plan of life."

Her conclusions echo words written by S. Jay Olshansky, Ph.D., the influential researcher from the University of Chicago's Center on Aging, Health and Society, and two of his colleagues. "The dilemma we face as a society is that medical ethics oblige physicians and researchers to pursue new technologies and therapeutic interventions in efforts to postpone death, [but] without a parallel effort to improve the quality of life," they argued, "it may also extend the frequency and duration of frailty and disability. . . ."

They warned that "society will soon be forced to realize that death is no longer its major adversary." That dubious honor goes to torturously prolonged dying, with poor management of the conditions longer life has now bequeathed us.

THREE

Dying Hard: The Death of Peter Ciccone

On September 11, 1993, a week before he died, Peter Ciccone made a tape recording as part of his personal journal. "Please, God, let me die," he said. "I can't stand this pain anymore." That's what he said to his lover, Ron Burris, every day. That's what he'd told his friends constantly since he had made dying his 1993 New Year's resolution. He was recording his journal because he could no longer move his hands to write. "The pain is unreal," he said. "Just when you think it can't get any worse, it does."

That August 10, Peter had turned thirty-four. By then, he'd already been sick for six years. For two and a half years he had not been able to walk without someone's help. For the past seventeen months he'd been bedridden, and Cabrini Hospice, in Manhattan, had been giving Ron help in caring for him at home. When he was accepted for hospice care, Peter was thought to have no more than six months to live. But he hung on, and no one could understand why.

The day of his birthday it was hot and sticky—outdoors *and* indoors—in Brooklyn Heights, where Peter lived. For thirty-five days that summer the temperature reached at least 90 degrees; on three of those days, it went over 100. Peter had an air conditioner in his one-bedroom apartment, but it never made the rooms quite cool enough.

Every day, all day, he lay in the bedroom in the back, in a hospital bed cushioned by an air mattress to prevent bedsores. His bed had been pushed up against the queen-size bed in which he used to sleep beside Ron. For the past two years, though, Ron had slept in the big bed alone.

But the air mattress hadn't prevented bedsores, those places where the skin had rotted away from the pressure his body exerted when he lay in one spot. That day, his largest sore—the one on his back—was an inch wide and an inch deep. In the morning, Ron washed the sore thoroughly and put on antibiotic ointment, proud that he never let the bedsores get infected. On this day, Peter wanted to be sure that giant sore didn't weep or smell, because he was having a party.

Around four o'clock, his older brother, Donny, his older sister, Fran, and both their families climbed the three flights to apartment 3L, first building on the left inside the ornate gate of a wrought-iron-enclosed garden courtyard. Peter's apartment house complex looked as if it belonged in New Orleans, not Brooklyn Heights. To reach his apartment, his guests had to climb a narrow, circular ironwork staircase encased in a tube of stone, then crisscross a filigree-trimmed outside passageway. As they twirled from floor to floor, they carried cakes and flowers, ready to celebrate who knows what.

Ron remembers that at Peter's birthday party seven years before—the year they'd first met—Peter had been a vibrant host, running from room to room to make sure everyone had a good time—his friends at the television set, drinking beer and watching the game; his Twelve-Step group in the kitchen sipping ginger ale; and his family talking in the back room.

Peter was a different kind of host today. He lay emaciated in his bed, slurring his words as he spoke. He worried that the place stank. He hoped he wouldn't have diarrhea while the guests were there. He smiled and told them all he was sorry if he'd made anyone mad, if he'd done anything to hurt them. He said he loved them, and he thanked them for taking care of him. Then he said good-bye. Some said he was waiting until his birthday to die. But that didn't turn out to be the reason he was hanging on.

That night, Peter had a dream. He was walking in a field filled with deep, blue-green grass and wildflowers—pinks, whites, golds, reds, blues, yellows, kinds he'd never seen before, absolutely beautiful, a galaxy of flowers that looked like the fields Dorothy passed as she walked to the Emerald City to meet the Wizard of Oz. The scene was sunny, clear, blindingly bright, the meadow vivid with color, but none of the brightness hurt his eyes. It felt utterly wonderful to be in this lush field. Soon he saw a wooden post-and-rail fence, like the kind that surrounds old farms or pastures out West. A wide gate crossed the fence. And that's where he noticed *them*. Both his parents were standing on the other side of the gate, watching him closely, smiling, waving, and blowing kisses. They had died years before.

Running to them, gesturing, calling, Peter yelled, "Mom, Mom!" hollering for them to take him with them, wanting to get closer. He tried opening the gate to go through, but his mother quickly stopped him. Peter felt his throat and chest tighten; he begged and began to cry, heaving huge sobs. Then his mother gently touched his cheek and kissed him. "You can't come yet," she told him softly, "but I promise to let you know when it's time." When he awoke, Peter was wet with tears. Across their beds he whispered to Ron. "It's too much here," he said, "and that field was so beautiful there." But it would take him another month and eight days to go, most of it filled with unnecessary pain.

Peter had not died swiftly of pneumonia, as did most of the other six members of his 1980s AIDS support group. Instead, he died after suffering a lengthy, painful condition called peripheral neuropathy—the kind of degenerative condition that has transformed AIDS into the model of a modern fatal disease—slow, debilitating, painful.

Laboratories all over the world have produced remedies that

boost the immune system and slow down the HIV virus that causes AIDS, as well as medications that protect against a range of lethal AIDS-related illnesses such as PCP pneumonia. These medications do not cure the underlying HIV virus, but they can extend by years the time that those infected are able to live before their weakened immune system allows a particular end-stage AIDS condition to kill them.

It is difficult to measure accurately when someone initially became infected with HIV and to determine exactly how long a patient has carried the disease before the onset of full-blown AIDS. Today, anecdotal reports and long-range studies indicate that more and more people are living with the HIV virus for upward of ten and twelve years, especially with the advent of protease inhibitors and "cocktail" combinations of antiviral drugs. From 1983, when the AIDS epidemic crashed into public awareness in the United States, until 1993, when Peter died, studies show that survival time with full-blown AIDS had increased from twenty-eight months to thirty-eight months.

However, researchers lament a lack of attention paid to the need for skilled palliative care to handle the horrific problems associated with AIDS—pain, confusion, dementia, severe nausea, vomiting, diarrhea, depression, anxiety, fatigue, fever, shortness of breath, wasting syndrome, and dehydration. Studies also show that the presence of these multiple problems can compound the psychological despair of those afflicted with AIDS (or any chronic illness), further disabling the body's immune system and crippling the person's will to go on.

Peter endured severe, long-term, intractable pain. He also suffered psychologically—from humiliation, debilitation, an inability to lead a normal, functional life—suffering that added significantly to his growing despair. As he moved closer to death, none of these afflictions was entirely controlled, though the means to relieve some of them did exist.

Peter took care of both his parents before they died. By all accounts, their deaths—terrible as they were—were a lot prettier than his. When Peter was fifteen, his father died of lung cancer in a Brooklyn hospital. As the baby in the family, he was the last child at home, the one closest to his mother during his father's painful last year. Just before his father died, his mother told Peter she'd found some lumps in her breasts, but she waited until after the funeral to get them checked.

"Two weeks after my father was in the ground, my mother had a radical mastectomy," Peter said in an interview about a year before he died. "Then a month after that she had another." Peter nursed her while she had radiation and chemotherapy, heard her swear she'd never go through it again. A year later, she fell in love with, and married, the father of a girlfriend of Peter's sister, Fran. But in 1985, not quite ten years after her mastectomy, Peter's mother got sick again. This time she said, "No more chemo. Just take me home and give me morphine."

Although Peter had gone to art school, he became a hairdresser—one of the most popular in stylish Brooklyn Heights. But he quit his job to take care of his mother. In those last weeks, she loved the way they'd talk, laugh, tell jokes, watch TV. She loved teaching him to crochet and do needlepoint. While she slept, he finished an afghan and two needlepoint portraits.

Near the end, she slept most of the time. When she awoke, he washed her, fed her, held her, and gave her Dilaudid or morphine. "It was bad. She went blind toward the end and said things like 'Please get a gun and shoot me.' She finally passed on. I saw her spirit go right up. The minute she died the phone rang. It was the priest, who was coming to visit her every day. We were very religious—holy water and everything. After she died I went home and threw up blood, I was such a wreck. I thought, 'Oh shit. I have cancer like my mother and father.' " It turned out that Peter merely had an ulcer. But things were about to get much worse.

In April 1986, just four months after his mother died, Peter had taken to sitting on benches day after day, staring at the water from the Brooklyn Heights Promenade, thinking about being only twenty-seven and orphaned, trying to recover. One Saturday toward the end of the month, Ron walked by. He was thirty-one at the time, and shy. He happened to look at Peter. And Peter happened to smile.

Peter was handsome then, with rich, black hair, a trimmed, racy beard, dark eyes. His face came alive when he smiled. He loved dancing, getting dressed up. When he was younger, people said he looked like John Travolta in *Saturday Night Fever*. When he got older, he developed muscles, so they began saying he looked more like Sly Stallone—a cross between Rambo and Rocky.

Ron Burris had been a high-school weakling back in Ohio. "When I met Peter," he said, "I had been working out for about four years, lifting weights for an hour or two each day, going to the gym so much they used to tell me to leave. But I had always been a skinny, blond nerd, and I was tired of it." After college he'd worked at two bookstores, Scribner's and Rizzoli's, and became a model on the side, perhaps as a kind of triumph over his wimpy past. "It felt weird to me," he said, "but Peter was so proud of me and my new muscles."

By June they had fallen in love. By August, they'd moved into that Brooklyn Heights apartment, decorating it in marble and tones of pink and red. Peter taught Ron to do needlepoint, and in the evenings they'd sit together sewing in front of the TV, framing their needlepoints and putting them up on the walls as soon as they were finished. Peter had never been happier.

Almost immediately after they moved in together, Peter began getting strange bruises. "At first I didn't think anything of it, but it happened again and again," he said. "It was like hickeys all over me. I called the Gay Men's Health Crisis [in New York City] for a referral to a doctor, and that doctor sent me to an oncologist. He took a blood test, and two days later he said my platelet count was low. He asked me if I was promiscuous and I said, 'No. I mean, I'm not an angel, but I don't run in front of trucks.' Well, he said, in a small number of HIV cases the virus affects the blood platelets, and it's either AIDS or leukemia."

In October 1986, six months after they met, Ron went with him for the final test results. "By the time we hit the lobby of the New York University [NYU] Medical Center, Ron was hysterical," Peter said. "He said, 'I just met you, and now I'm going to lose you.' We took a cab to my sister's house in Brooklyn. Well, Fran got hysterical, too, saying, 'We just lost Mom, and now you!' "

Peter had AIDS. He read everything he could about it, but in 1986, AIDS was still barely known. Indeed, it had just recently been recognized not as a "gay men's cancer" but as a series of end-stage illnesses with names like cryptococcal meningitis, toxoplasmosis, and Kaposi's sarcoma (KS), and was still being referred to in its early stages by diagnostic terms like GRID and ARC. Not much was understood about it other than that it was fatal, most often because the failing immune system couldn't fight off infections, parasitic diseases, and fast-killing cancers. Few physicians or lay-people realized the devastating moment-by-moment damage it could do.

Often after that, Peter was back in the hospital at NYU with thrombocytopenia (a low-blood-platelet condition that interferes with clotting), then with pneumonia, then with tuberculosis, and having test after painful test: a lung biopsy, bone biopsies, nerve tests.

Afterward, he would break down and cry, clinging to Ron. Peter was terrified, guilt-ridden, mortified. "Ron could have said, 'Get out. I don't want to live with you anymore,' but he was an angel," Peter said. "He said, 'I'm going to take care of you.' We went to NYU for treatment and Ron stayed with me the whole time." (NYU Medical Center has a co-op care program in which patients' families or significant others can live with the patient during treatment.) While they were there, Ron got tested; he, too, turned out to have the virus that causes AIDS. But Ron wasn't sick yet.

In March 1987, the Food and Drug Administration (FDA) approved for use the antiviral drug AZT, which was designed to bolster the failing immune system, and Peter was among the first group of AIDS patients to be given it. He was also taking newer medications to ward off the possibility of getting pneumonia again and to treat tuberculosis.

For a time, doctors thought his loss of muscle tone was a side effect of AZT, but it turned out to be part of the disease. The AZT kept Peter from dying of the swifter killers, but he got peripheral neuropathy instead, which doctors now say can be caused either by AIDS or by AZT-related spinal cord injury. A syndrome affecting the peripheral nerves, it can cause paralysis and burning, unremitting, intolerable pain.

S tarting in 1987, Peter cut back on his hours at work. "At first, my hands started falling asleep, just out of nowhere. But after a year, my legs started going numb. Soon I had pain in my legs and I had trouble standing. I noticed I was leaning on my customers more while I was doing their hair and that my hands hurt in cold water. I worked less and less, only a few days a week. Finally I needed a cane. Then I couldn't stand, so I had to leave work and go on disability. Within a year I went from a cane to a walker to a wheelchair, and then I couldn't even move the wheelchair with my hands, I was in so much pain. Nothing they gave me would help. I had written in my journal all the time, but soon I couldn't write, so Ron gave me a computer. Then I couldn't even use my hands, so Franny and Donny bought me a tape recorder and a speaker phone."

One day, Peter panicked; he had tried to get up to go to the bathroom, and he couldn't. "I realized I couldn't move my legs at all. I told Ron, 'I can't get up,'" Peter said. "Well, he tried to pull me up. He said, 'Maybe your legs are asleep.' But when he stood me up, my feet went every which way. My legs were like noodles. I had no power." That was in 1990; Franny and Donny got him a reclining chair so he wasn't confined to his bed.

"For ten months I sat in that chair all day," Peter said. "I ate and slept in it, and when I went to the bathroom I'd roll over onto the commode and Ron would help me back on. Though they are paralyzed, my legs are not numb. They don't move, but I'm in constant pain. Touch me and it kills. My feet go their own way. I have no power from the waist down. It really gets me scared."

Then Peter's bowels stopped functioning and he became unable to urinate on his own. So in 1991, he asked Ron to take him to the hospital. There they inserted a catheter, which Peter never again could do without. They gave him laxatives and taught Ron how to handle the catheter and how to rid Peter of his fecal impactions. By the time I met Peter in April 1992, a year and a half before he died, he was totally bedridden.

"I'm in mourning for the Peter I met and the relationship we had for the first three years," Ron said at the time. "Now even the dog can do more than he can. At least the dog can go to the bathroom by himself. You're supposed to have this happen after years of marriage—when you're ninety-four years old, not when you're thirty-two. But you don't just tell someone you'll leave if they get sick. In all of New York I chose Peter, so why would I leave him now that he's so sick? With Peter it's like we're married.

You wouldn't leave your husband if he were sick. Still, you know, it's for better or worse." For Peter, it went only from worse to worst.

In those early days of AIDS, KS lesions (tumors that discolor the skin) or bruises like Peter's (which indicated AIDS-related thrombocytopenia) were often the first symptoms noticed in those who were stricken. Because of this, dermatologists became early AIDS medical specialists. They were generally the first to see these symptoms, the first to try to figure out what was wrong, the first to begin research on the expanding epidemic.

The doctor that Peter first saw, the one that the Gay Men's Health Crisis referred him to, was a dermatologist who—somewhat out of default—was in the process of building a large AIDS practice. But this doctor was not a pain specialist, nor was AIDS pain as yet a major concern. At this time, all AIDS medical treatments were just being invented by a medical community taken by surprise. And even these fledgling specialists, like Peter's, had no idea what the disease was that they were dealing with, nor what the full range of its terrible symptoms was, nor what could be done to treat any of it. And, in those early days, the few doctors focusing their attention on AIDS were considered heroic even to try, since most of the medical community had simply ignored it.

But as Peter grew sicker, as he became less able to get to his physician, the dermatologist/AIDS specialist understandably became reluctant to take care of him over the phone, to prescribe the pain medications that Peter told him he needed. Nor was the doctor able to make house calls. Peter's psychiatrist, however, was able to come. He prescribed Valium for Peter's anxiety and milder painkillers like Percocet and codeine for his pain. As Peter's pain got worse, the psychiatrist wrote prescriptions for Dilaudid and then for a Duragesic skin patch (both narcotics).

Peter began to take these medications tentatively at first, taking them over the vehement objections of his Twelve-Step group. So opposed was the group to his taking drugs to treat pain that the group divided over the efforts of some to kick Peter out. But as the disease progressed further, Peter needed even more help.

Studies of patients today show that between 40 and 80 percent of all AIDS patients, depending on the study, have significant levels of pain—including severe headaches, agonizing abdominal cramping, and, worst of all, neuropathies (the kind of nerve pain that Peter had)—and that their pain increases as the illness progresses.

Nerve pain is the hardest kind to control even for pain specialists, but little was known about it in AIDS patients at the time. In any case, according to Ron, Peter's psychiatrist did not recommend evaluation by a pain specialist; rather, he suggested that Peter get care from a hospice.

Peter was ready. "One day I said to Ron, 'Look, the disease is progressing now. It's in my spine, it's working its way up. When it hits my diaphragm, I die.' I said, 'Ron, we have to talk. I don't want to go to the hospital again. I made my will a year ago.' I said, 'With this disease, things happen fast.'

"On Easter morning [of 1992] I woke up in my regular pain, but by evening I was hysterical, I was in such pain. I said, 'Ron, if something happens to me, what are you going to do? How will you get me down the stairs? I want to be in a place where I'll be treated how I want to be treated.' In the hospital, you'll be in pain from tests. At home, you'll be in pain with pain. I had heard about Cabrini Hospice. I wanted to be in a place where I could get all the pain relief I need and be taken care of."

Ron was frightened to hear Peter talking like this, but he wasn't surprised, either. "We held each other and we cried and cried," Peter said. "Then I called Cabrini Hospice. When they talked to me, there was so much love coming through on the phone. I wanted to go to their inpatient unit. But it was so hard to admit how sick I was."

Hospices hark back to the Middle Ages, when they were havens—often run by religious orders—where weary travelers, the sick, the hungry, or the orphaned could rest, find hospitality (that's the origin of *hospice*), and be well cared for. Today, hospices focus only on the terminally ill.

The modern hospice movement began in England in 1967, when Dame Cecily Saunders, M.D., opened St. Christopher's Hospice in the Sydenham section of London. The first American hospice was established in Connecticut in 1974. As of 1997, there were nearly 3,000 hospice programs in the United States. They cared for

14 percent of all Americans as they died, some 400,000 people a year (about 35 percent of all cancer and AIDS deaths, and a smaller percentage of deaths from other illnesses). Hospice's mission is to treat dying patients with compassion and personal attention, giving special emphasis to the relief of pain.

According to hospice philosophy, death is easier when pain and other symptoms are well controlled, and when the patient's family and friends can surround him—care for him, love him—throughout the dying process. Most hospice patients in America are cared for in their homes; the hospice program supplies home visits by doctors and visiting nurses; drugs and other medical supplies; aides to bathe, feed, and toilet the patient; psychological and spiritual counseling for patients and family members; and volunteers to help with everything from shopping and dog walking to driving a terminally ill patient to take a last, wistful look at the sea.

But in America, dying people are forced to make a hard bargain: To join a hospice they must be given a doctor's prognosis that they have no more than six months to live, stop aggressive treatments that are aimed at a cure, and focus only on comfort care as they are dying. In 1983, when Congress voted to cover hospice care through Medicare and Medicaid, it imposed these requirements in an attempt to cut end-of-life medical costs. (This was in part at the suggestion of hospice advocates, who feared the program might not otherwise receive any coverage.) Private insurers soon followed suit. Peter and Ron had to admit up front that Peter was dying and to make a major turnabout in his care.

Hospices themselves decide which patients are "appropriate" for them to take on, and by appropriateness they mean patients who have at most six months to live—and are willing to keep to the decision to forgo treatment. And, while they don't *force* patients into this bargain at Cabrini, its director, Mary Cooke, says that in initial interviews, her staff will examine patients' goals. "If someone wants to have aggressive treatment, then they are not a candidate for our program," she says. "We don't say it quite that bluntly, but *comfort* is our goal."

(In fact, by 1996 the federal government—through its Operation Restore Trust—was so forcefully attempting to make hospices stick to this six-month prognosis that it was asking for a return in funds for patients in hospices who survived longer.)

It is hard for doctors to make accurate predictions about how long their patients will live—and particularly difficult when the patients have diseases other than certain kinds of cancer (the illness on which the hospice model was first constructed). An AIDS patient's survival depends on the ability of his or her body to fight off opportunistic infections. Any illness an AIDS patient gets could be curable, or could be lethal. And though there are markers to test for the immune system's degree of impairment, it's impossible to know which illness is the one that will kill.

In addition, studies show AIDS patients who make peace with their dying—by stopping treatment, for example, or just by psychologically resolving that they will not get well—tend to survive a shorter length of time. Those who keep on hoping have increased psychoimmunological strength (no one yet knows why).

Since Peter died, protease inhibitors and new antiviral combinations seemed so promising that by 1997, AIDS deaths had begun to drop and a few AIDS hospices had closed. But experts also said it was too soon to assess the long-term prognosis of patients treated with these new drugs, or to know whether they would ultimately alter the symptomatic course of the disease. Their high cost ($10,000 to 15,000 a year) and the rigid schedule required for taking the pills also restricted their availability for many AIDS patients.

But Peter agreed to the bargain: Just to receive the kind of home care and pain control hospice offers, he stopped life-prolonging treatment. Stopping AZT, or any antiviral medications that might have kept up his immune system, meant that Peter was limiting his ability to ward off lethal illnesses. He also stopped the treatments designed to prevent TB and pneumonia, though he did take antibiotics until near the end.

Hospice care can be incredibly healing in a psychological way—transformative, loving, enormously helpful. But because of the funding limits imposed today, the hospice way of death isn't for everyone. In addition to stopping treatment and acknowledging that they have just a short time to live, most hospice patients are cared for in their own homes, and must have a full-time caretaker available. Ron could devote his time to nursing Peter—and had the enthusiasm to try to learn how to do it—partly because he, too, had AIDS. He wasn't as sick as Peter yet, but he was too weak to work any longer. By then, both of them were on disability, with their medical care partially covered by a complex mix of health insurers.

To get his pain under control, Peter quite literally sat down and wrote his funeral plans. "My doctor couldn't say how long I had. All he could say is that it wouldn't be years. But I decided I wanted to go to a hospice anyway. I couldn't stand it anymore. This pain kills. I know there's no cure, but at least in a hospice I can get all the pain relief I need and I won't be treated like a leper."

Cabrini Hospice offers, in addition to home care, a floor of fifteen beds within a separate wing of Cabrini Hospital, near Gramercy Park in Manhattan. Peter was admitted to this inpatient unit to get his pain under control as quickly as possible. And there, in April 1992, I first met him and Ron. That month, I had practically moved into Cabrini. I was following Sister Loretta Palamara on her rounds, to see what she did in helping the dying. Sister Loretta, Cabrini's spiritual counselor, is known in hospice circles to be particularly gifted.

For Peter, hospice seemed to work just fine at first. Daniel Kao, M.D., an internist in private practice and Cabrini Hospice's part-time medical director, put him on round-the-clock oral morphine, and Peter began to relax.

"You just hit the buzzer and the nurses come in," he said. "The first night I was here I had hot flashes, pain, sweat, nausea; I wanted to scream and yell from the pain of this disease. Well, a nurse came running in here and stripped off my sheets. I was drenched. She put cold compresses on my head and sat with me and talked all night. I was amazed. She said, 'You know, Peter, I love you. You're special.' You're treated with love and compassion here. And Ron can relax and get some rest. I can't repay them enough for what they gave me."

Slowly, Peter even began to smile. He was grateful for the smallest things. "I don't have to wait an hour for pain medications like in the hospital, when I was across from the nurses' station and no one came. And when my medication isn't working, I beep and they give me more. Or if my hands don't move, they will open my sandwich for me," he said.

"At hospice, I [was able to have] a bath the first night I was here. Before, I could only wash off in a commode. Here, I felt clean for the first time in a year. They washed me all over, and dried and powdered me. I felt so clean. It's phenomenal. The word should be put out to gay men, women, children, or anyone with AIDS, that hospice won't shut the door and leave you screaming in pain until you die."

When his pain medications were stabilized, Ron took Peter home in an ambulance. A hospice home-care aide visited each day, helping Ron with the chores of bathing and intimate care he'd been doing for so long. Drugs were delivered to them in Brooklyn. A nurse and a doctor came regularly. Sister Loretta would call, visit, and send notes. Peter felt more secure. He also felt secure in knowing that he could go back to the inpatient unit if he needed to, or if Ron needed a break. (He ended up going back three times, all during pain crises.)

But then, his pain got worse. He began suffering from abdominal pain, pain from severe herpes infections and yeast infections that spread inside and out, and, always, nerve pain that seemed to be everywhere. In the weeks and months after Peter got home, the numbness and pain began marching up his legs into his torso, setting his spine on fire. It traveled up his hands, through his arms, and stayed there, waiting for that final ambush. And Peter knew it. If he moved or turned on his side, if his dog Mikey wriggled over him, if a sheet happened to flutter from a breeze, his body would be racked with stabbing pain.

Then came months of uncontrolled diarrhea. Since his bladder was paralyzed so that he needed a catheter, that brought infection after infection—on top of the infections he already had from bedsores, herpes run wild, and a host of other maladies. Peter began to suffer psychologically—from hopelessness and despair on top of the pain. And the honeymoon with hospice began to wear off.

Peter began begging, pleading, for more pain medication. From home, he'd call the hospice nursing station every evening. When he was in Cabrini's inpatient unit, he'd ask repeatedly. Some nurses began getting annoyed, angry, labeling his calls "drug-seeking" behavior. So did Dr. Kao.

Over the past twenty years, there has been a revolution in the medical understanding of pain and how to control it. Different kinds of pain—such as bone pain or nerve pain—must be treated in different ways, often with different medications and techniques. Tough as it sometimes is to manage pain arising from tumors, it is often even more difficult to ease the pain of peripheral neuropathy—the kind of nerve pain that Peter had. This can be among the most severe pain syndromes, and the hardest to assuage, even for pain experts. Neuropathic pain—found in some cancer patients—now shows up in about 30 to 40 percent of all AIDS patients, and is the most common pain syndrome of those AIDS patients who do have pain. Yet, its severity has been almost ignored. In addition, long-term, chronic pain like Peter's does not produce the same responses in sufferers as acute pain. The health-care worker who is looking for wincing and grimacing and screaming as signals of severe pain may not see those responses, but, instead, expressions of apathy or depression.

"Knowledge currently available about how the damaged nervous system responds to pain is not generally known by the average physician, and, more tragically, is not being taught to the majority of current medical-school students," notes C. Stratton Hill Jr., M.D., an internationally known pain specialist from M. D. Anderson Cancer Center in Houston. "Tension between the doctor and the patient almost invariably arises in this scenario. . . . Usually the patient is ultimately suspected, and often accused, of being a street addict—a consequence of the illegal image of drugs."

That is exactly what happened to Peter. Dr. Kao considered him an addictive patient. He didn't look as if he was in pain, Dr. Kao told me many times before Peter died. And four months *after* his patient died, Dr. Kao explained further: "With Peter, you'd go in, he'd be smoking, watching TV, and you'd say, 'Are you in pain?' And he'd say, 'Yes, my arm, my legs,' but he didn't seem it. He had a drug history. He was an IV drug user before. [According to Ron, Peter was not an IV drug user, although he *had* used Valium and cocaine. But for the six years before he got sick, Peter had been "clean and sober."] Morphine can have a psychological effect. I think that's what he wanted. Thank God we don't have a lot of patients like that."

Pain, of course, *is* subjective. While there are assessment scales that pain experts use to determine the levels of a patient's pain, these scales, too, depend on patients' reports. But Dr. Kao said he didn't believe in these scales. The bottom line was that Dr. Kao didn't believe Peter *or* the level of his pain.

Various members of Cabrini's staff told Peter—on many different occasions—that they couldn't give him more morphine than they were giving him. Their explanations repeated myths about narcotic use that are all too common in this country: (1) If you take high doses of narcotics at the beginning, they won't work when you need them at the end. (2) Nerve pain isn't responsive to narcotics anyway. (3) If you get too much, it might cause respiratory depression and kill you.

Pain experts believe these statements are falsehoods long taught in American medical schools, falsehoods that keep patients like Peter chronically undertreated for pain. "I fought over and over again with Dr. Kao," Peter's brother, Donny, told me, "I didn't fight with the hospice, just with the doctor. 'He's dying!' I'd say. 'Put him out of pain.' He'd say that Peter was an addict. I'd say, 'So what? Knock him out.' And he'd say he couldn't do that. The bottom line is, when it came to pain, my brother suffered unduly, unnecessarily."

Dr. Kao is, in fact, a good and caring physician—indeed, he was one of the first doctors in this country to sign on with a hospice. "In 1978, when I came to New York to do my residency at Cabrini Hospital, the patients I saw were basically abandoned," he told me. "They were elderly people; their families couldn't take them to the doctor, and their doctors wouldn't prescribe over the phone because of fears of malpractice. Families aren't that close here, so I saw that this was an area I could help with." Dr. Kao even made house calls to those who were too sick to go out.

In 1982, he agreed to be the medical director of Cabrini's fledgling program, becoming one of a very few hospice doctors in the nation. By 1994, there were still only 2,000 hospice doctors nationwide. And nearly all of them—97 percent—worked at their hospice only part-time.

When Dr. Kao began his internship, it wasn't chic to be a hospice doctor—it still isn't—but he relished the freedom and the opportunity to help families.

"Hospice medicine is nothing new," he said. "It's just using common sense. It doesn't take a specialist to give pain medications. Part of the relief is that patients and families sign a consent [form] that they won't get aggressive care, so the threat of a lawsuit is low. That's the beauty of this—doctors are free to do what they'd like to do.

"Once you have that paper in hand, and since the idea of hospice is known," he said, "you can practice how you want, how it should be practiced with pain medications. Ninety to ninety-five percent of the patients respond very well. But some patients are very difficult, either because they have a bad disease or have psychological problems—a patient who has a known drug history, who doesn't look as if he is in pain, and has a high tolerance. There are a lot of AIDS patients with neuropathies. They are difficult to treat because we don't have a lot of good medications. They are not very morphine responsive."

When Peter first came onto Cabrini Hospice's inpatient unit, Dr. Kao slowly decreased the dosages of the Duragesic patch and the Percocet he had been on and gave him liquid morphine, eventually increasing an every-three-hour dose from 10 mg to 40 mg, until the patch was completely removed the third day. He also gave him anticonvulsants like Tegretol and Dilantin, and antidepressants like Elavil—all of them medications pain specialists recommend for neuropathic pain. But when the pain came back, Dr. Kao began to blame Peter and get mad.

"Peter had my phone number, and he'd call a lot," Dr. Kao told me, in an interview after Peter died. "Well, after a while you lose patience if you see nothing's working, and especially if you think he's not really in all that much pain. The people with neuropathies, usually you see them moaning in their sleep, uncomfortable most of the time. Peter never looked that way. Patients can manipulate you, especially HIV patients, but also cancer patients. They think they should have whatever they want because they're dying. You have to give appropriate care. We feel we have to set limits. Families can be manipulative, too."

Peter was one of the first of Dr. Kao's patients with AIDS neuropathy; the treatment protocols he had learned through hospice had been primarily for cancer. "When AIDS started coming along, I talked with doctors who treat AIDS patients at Cabrini and at Saint Vincent's [hospitals]," Dr. Kao said. "When you double the doses of medications and the patient doesn't respond, you usually understand [that the medication] doesn't work. Peter was difficult."

But the fact is, he may have needed even more than double the doses he was getting. And Dr. Kao may not have known that.

To Dr. Kao's credit, when he realized that he was having difficulty handling Peter's pain, he suggested that Peter go to a pain specialist at Memorial Sloan-Kettering for a consultation.

But Peter never did. He loved his Cabrini nurses, and to get treatment at Memorial, hospice rules meant that Peter might have had to go off the hospice program. He could have gone back on it, but Peter and Ron seemed too overwhelmed to get an ambulance to take him to Sloan-Kettering, and too exhausted to try to juggle their health insurance benefits—or sort through how Cabrini might otherwise cover the costs—so that Peter's consultation and transportation would have been paid.

Had he gone to Sloan-Kettering, however, Peter might have learned firsthand that the high doses of narcotics he actually may have required were *far* higher than the medical staff at Cabrini was giving him, and that these high doses were also legal, ethical, and considered good medical care, and that additional medication-delivery systems (such as an intraspinal catheter, which probably would have required expensive surgery to insert) were also available.

In addition, they might have given him additional medications to those he was already on, and also in high doses—drugs targeted specifically to neuropathic pain, including additional tricyclic antidepressants, antiarrhythmics, local anesthetics in internal preparation—and higher doses (even seizure-level doses) of anti-convulsants such as Tegretol and Dilantin.

Because I couldn't get Peter's pain out of my mind, after he died I asked many other physicians and nurses—especially pain specialists—about his case. In all, I asked more than a dozen world-renowned experts whether his pain could have been controlled, going over with them the treatment that he had been given.

These were specialists in AIDS pain, neuropathies, chronic pain, and in the psychiatric components of all of these. They worked at the forefront of pain research, in a range of state-of-the-art treatment centers, including Memorial Sloan-Kettering, where Peter might have gone, Saint Vincent's Hospital and the Long Island College of Medicine, both in New York, M. D. Anderson Cancer

Center in Houston, and San Francisco General Hospital. These specialists all told me essentially the same thing.

"They were *very cautious*," Russell K. Portenoy, M.D., an internationally known expert on pain and palliative care at Memorial Sloan-Kettering, said of Peter's pain management at Cabrini. "We titrate [raise the doses of medications] up fast, even on a daily basis."

Dr. Portenoy also wondered whether the equianalgesic dosages had been figured correctly when Peter's pain medications were changed. (These are the calculations made to assure equivalency when narcotic medications are switched or the mode of administration is changed.) The numbers I'd been given didn't seem to add up properly.

Based on reports provided both by Ron and by Cabrini Hospice Director Mary Cooke, Peter's medical record shows that after three days at Cabrini's inpatient unit, he was taking 40 mg of liquid morphine orally every three or four hours (Mary's and Ron's reports differed here). Then the dosage was raised to 60 mg, then 100 mg, then 120 mg, having gone up in increments of 20 mg over a year. The pain kept intensifying, but Peter took the 120 mg every three or four hours until September of the year before he died. "They said anything over 120 would be ineffective," Ron says. "The side effects would be worse than the benefits, so they had to find another solution."

From the beginning, Dr. Kao also gave Peter what Dr. Portenoy termed *safe but low* doses of Dilantin, Sinequan—an antiseizure medication and an antidepressant, both to address the nerve pain—and Valium, an antianxiety medication. At times, he also got Ativan. These were intended to treat the neuropathy, but Dr. Portenoy said the doses used may not have been high enough.

When Peter's pain got worse, Cabrini requested special AIDS funds—allocated as Ryan White funds by the U.S. Congress—to get Peter a morphine pump. This is a patient-controlled analgesic (PCA) pump, rather like a morphine-filled cassettelike skin patch that is capable of supplying a steady stream of morphine through the skin of his abdomen. He could also give himself a set amount of extra doses if he needed it. This was a stronger, more intensive way of giving him morphine.

Near the end, after he came back into the inpatient unit, Mary

Cooke says, Peter was put on an IV, getting 40 mg of morphine an hour. Ron says that at times it went up to 50 mg. Either 40 or 50 mg an hour of morphine would quickly kill most of us. But for people in pain, people whose tolerance has been raised by slowly increased doses, that amount may not be enough. And though the Cabrini staff felt otherwise, it didn't seem to be enough for Peter.

In his final week at Cabrini, Peter got between 960 mg and 1,200 mg a day intravenously for his pain. In a much-quoted 1990 study of cancer patients at Memorial Sloan-Kettering, staff at the neurology pain service followed ninety people in the last four weeks of their lives. This study, of which Dr. Portenoy was a co-author, found that most of these dying people needed—and got—between 7 and 699 mg a day (either of IV morphine or an equianalgesic dose of a similar narcotic, depending on their individual needs), with slightly higher doses given as they grew closer to dying.

Some patients had tough pain syndromes—as Peter had—and Dr. Portenoy said they required more. Two people got between 900 and 1,999 mg a day four weeks before they died, one got between 2,000 and 5,000 mg, another 8,000 to 11,000 mg, and a third got 15,984 mg.

In the twenty-four hours before death, these doses increased significantly. One patient got in the 900 to 1,999 mg range, five got 2,000 to 5,000 mg, one got 19,200 mg, and one got 35,164 mg over those last twenty-four hours. Patients at Cabrini got *significantly* less. Members of the hospice staff there said that Peter's was among the highest doses they *ever* gave—so high that various health professionals said that they were afraid it might kill him.

"What is appropriate care?" Dr. Kao asked me rhetorically, after Peter died. "Does it mean whatever the patient wants? Is getting patients high appropriate care? That's a misuse of hospice philosophy. So why waste good medicine? It's expensive, but that's not really a factor. Mary Cooke has never called and said to cut down on costs, but I know hospice loses money. It's an ethical issue. I want to give appropriate care, not something that's inappropriate, when a patient is dying. We get patients who want high doses because they want to die. Well, we don't help with euthanasia."

The world-renowned pain experts I interviewed work under different assumptions. "The pain in AIDS starts quite early in the disease," said Richard B. Patt, M.D., deputy director of the pain service at M. D. Anderson and codirector of the International Association for the Study of Pain's task force on AIDS pain, "so it makes doctors reluctant to treat. The piece that physicians often don't look at is function. My observation is that when people feel their pain is controlled they become more functional, not less functional. So I think it's important to help them with their quality of life so they can go on living. Neuropathic pain is hard, but not impossible. It's important to bring it down to tolerable levels."

The confusion that Dr. Kao faced, he said, might stem from controversies within the medical community about how best to treat neuropathies. "We've got two sets of treatment for it," Dr. Patt said. "The pain community has clearly, with one voice, been advocating for opioids, but neuropathic pain has been called opioid-resistant. What we're discovering now is that it isn't opioid-resistant. It just takes higher doses and requires a little better management. It means more aggressive treatment of the side effects."

While doctors treating pain once thought solely in terms of amounts that were needed, "the dose concept is now out the window," Dr. Patt said. "Treating pain with an opioid is more like treating diabetes with insulin than treating a person who's sick with antibiotics," he said. "You give as much painkiller as is required to relieve the pain, or until a side effect occurs. Then you treat the side effect. [Psychostimulants, for example, can counterbalance a feeling of sedation.] And go up still higher if you have to. There isn't a set amount. It's whatever works for the particular patient and the particular pain."

Robert V. Brody, M.D., director of the pain service and chairman of the ethics committee at San Francisco General Hospital, and the medical director of the Visiting Nurses and Hospice of San Francisco, the largest AIDS hospice in the Bay Area, put it bluntly.

"Fifty milligrams an hour of intravenous morphine is usually not enough for a dying AIDS patient," he said. "Enough is whatever works to relieve the pain for the particular patient. 'Believe the patient' is the first principle of good medicine. If [Peter's pain] were regular pain, it would have been relieved with that much morphine. Since it wasn't, it was probably neuropathic pain. And if the other medications didn't work, they probably should have gone up on the morphine. Did he endure pain that he didn't have to endure? The answer is probably yes."

Dr. Portenoy, trying to explain in a more dispassionate way why Peter's pain wasn't relieved, told me, "Neuropathic pain can be very challenging and can become unresponsive to most or all of the commonly used techniques, and the physician will require more sophisticated ways to respond." Among the solutions might have been more aggressive use of narcotics and additional medications, better management of their side effects, more high-tech or surgical techniques to give those medications, and sometimes, when the end was near, even sedation—using narcotics, barbiturates, or anesthesia alone or in combination—until death.

"He was in need of highly sophisticated pain management that was beyond the skills of hospice," Dr. Portenoy concluded. "Could we have handled it here? Who knows? He may have been in that group of patients—I think it's less than ten percent—whose pain cannot be adequately controlled. And then you would have been writing about our failure instead of theirs."

Studies by Dr. Portenoy and other researchers show that psychological distress is associated with physical pain, and that for some people a syndrome of pain and distress can spiral out of control. Neither Peter's physical nor his psychological pain seemed to be adequately resolved.

Peter didn't want people to see him in the condition he was in— the constant diarrhea, the catheter, the infections the catheter caused, the herpes, the fungus, the pain, the confinement to bed, having to go to the bathroom in bed, the total dependence on others. He was a human being so ill that he was beginning to lose his personhood.

Yet, when I asked Mary Cooke how hospice could have helped Peter address his pain, she told me the same thing over and over: Peter's pain was *spiritual,* not physical. "If you are giving someone maximum amounts of drugs and it's not working, something else is going on. Especially someone like him with a history of drugs— alcohol—any addiction. It's pretty self-evident that there is spiritual pain involved," she said. "That's why people like that go to AA and Twelve-Step and why those programs are so effective. Sister Loretta is the expert on this."

"Peter had the trouble of being Catholic and gay," Sister Loretta told me, "and they have many issues with the Church. Instead of [seeing] the loving-kindness of Jesus, they equate him with the strict rules of the Church, so it's hard to go toward him. I break the rules. Some priests say, 'I'll love you *if* you change.' But you're loved [by God] *unconditionally*. So I won't do that. But sometimes patients' anger toward this makes them unlovable. Their anger about it keeps them from going."

Those who are not religious are more inclined to talk solely about the relief of psychological pain, but even this can be subjective. "We tried to pull in other people to help him deal with the emotional pain," Peter's hospice home-care nurse said, "but he wouldn't let anyone else in [except herself and Sister Loretta]. He was very vain. He had a big photo of him[self] dressed as a female and he looked great." Maybe, she seemed to think, he didn't want other people to see it. When asked about it later, Ron said that picture she referred to actually wasn't even of Peter.

Such comments suggest that homophobia might have played a role in Peter's treatment. A 1994 study of members of the Gay and Lesbian Medical Association—all doctors and other health-care providers—found that 52 percent of them "had observed colleagues providing reduced care or denying care to patients because of their sexual orientation; 59 percent felt they had suffered discrimination, harassment, or ostracism from the medical profession because of their sexual orientation."

Another factor in his treatment was cost. "There is a lot of controversy among hospices right now over treatment for AIDS patients," Cooke told me, three years after Peter died. "Many hospices will not accept AIDS patients at all because of the costs." (Hospices are reimbursed a set fee per day for every patient enrolled, and the fee was based on the needs of cancer patients.) "Now my philosophy is that we have other patients who can balance the expense of the AIDS medications. We grappled with the whole issue pretty early on—in 1985—about how to deal with AIDS. Some on our board wanted to take them before the six months' prognosis, but we decided it is our mission to treat only those with six months to live."

But if Peter had chosen to go to a hospital, he might have been embroiled in yet another catch-22 for patients in pain. There were no provisions under Medicare, Medicaid, or third-party reimbursement systems *solely* for palliative care in hospitals. And yet, it is not in hospices but in hospitals—most particularly, hospital pain clinics like Memorial Sloan-Kettering's—that most sophisticated pain-control experts are employed. Perversely, reimbursement through insurance may also be lacking for the cost of outpatient palliative care, treatments, or drugs.

In 1996, the U.S. Health Care Financing Administration (HCFA) approved a reimbursement code on a trial basis that would allow hospitals to bill Medicare for palliative-care admissions for dying patients. The HCFA plans to study this before it will create a regular, diagnosis-related group (DRG) code for palliative care, but as of the start of 1997, no dollar amount had been attached to the trial code, nor was it being used. "It's not known yet," one pain expert said, "whether it will help improve access to palliative care."

To hospitalize a patient for pain control, doctors say, they have to use subterfuge. They have to say, for the record, that they are treating AIDS or colon cancer and provide some additional treatment, even if it isn't needed, or give medicines intravenously so that the hospitalization is justified. "What we usually do is put them in and do a workup," says one physician, who is now trying to craft revisions in these funding limitations, "even though we don't need it. It doesn't really harm the patient, but it's costing Medicare money and it's outrageous."

P eter kept begging, sobbing, pleading, asking for more medication, yet all the while he was dying, I never once thought he was using those drugs to get high or to kill himself. In fact, Peter was so determined not to take drugs that in the beginning, when his pain began growing more and more severe, he didn't even want to take medication to relieve it because his Twelve-Step group was so opposed to it.

If he'd wanted to, Peter could actually have killed himself all along. He had a secret stash of drugs at home, Ron said, "enough to kill the whole block." Like many people with AIDS, Peter kept them for final security. But the fact is, he didn't want to die.

"I believe in God," Peter said a few months before he died. "I always thought that if I ever get that bad, I'll kill myself first. But when I hit that plateau, well, you never know what you'll do until you get there. I thought, 'I'll never get catheterized.' But once I did, I'd never go without it. And then there was having to [have my bowels] disimpacted. Well, if you aren't disimpacted, you can die."

It turned out that Peter wasn't hanging around waiting until after his birthday to die. He was clinging to life just to be around Ron. He'd tell anyone who would listen: Ron was the best family he'd ever had, and he never, ever wanted to leave him. Peter wanted to be out of pain, not to die.

Three weeks after his birthday, the pain got so bad he could hardly breathe. He asked Ron if it would be okay to go, and Ron knew exactly what he meant. Cabrini admitted him as an inpatient for the third and last time. Peter said good-bye to Mikey, the dog who could pee better than he could, and an ambulance came to get him.

Because the circular stairs were so narrow, because they twirled within a wall of fine-cut stone, the ambulance crew couldn't take Peter down on a stretcher. It just wouldn't fit. Instead, they had to sit him up on a chair. By then, Peter's legs had long stopped being able to bend. They just dangled if left alone in space, but the pain of his dangling legs was great. Peter could feel every move, each time his legs jiggled or shook.

As the ambulance crew lifted him from the air mattress onto the chair, Peter let out a groan, though he was trying not to. Tears leaked from the corners of his eyes. As they took him down those three flights of circular stairs, his legs swung against each stone in the wall, hitting every turn in the ironwork railing. Screams, guttural howls, bloodcurdling shrieks came up from deep inside him. Every step downward. Every turn in the stair and the wall. And as he rode in the ambulance from Brooklyn, across the bridge to Manhattan, every bump in the road or short stop in traffic made Peter heave with sobs.

For most of the next eighteen days, Ron shuttled between being constantly near Peter—standing, sitting, or sleeping in a chair next to his bed—and running back home for brief moments to walk their dog, Mikey. Peter's temperature soared to 103°, 104°, higher. They said he had a blood infection. This time Peter said he'd had enough. He refused antibiotics that had cured infections before, letting this particular opportunistic infection become the one that would finally kill him.

When Peter's fever spiked, he would quiver, sweat, become delirious, moan. The nurses would pack him in ice. When the temperature came down, he would open his eyes and speak quietly, his eyes looking out intently at those who were near him from their ever-hollowing sockets. Always, there was constant pain. He had become a skeleton curled into a deformed fetal position. His wrist turned back on itself, his feet drooped, his legs had withered, his bones practically showed through his skin. His mouth and tongue were covered with thrush. All he talked about was the constant, burning pain.

Franny, his older sister, stayed close by, fluffing his pillows, kissing him, praying for God to have mercy. And she prayed for her mother to come and take him, to tell him it was finally time.

Peter's brother, Donny, rarely left, watching nights as Peter quietly moaned, trying to run his Long Island painting business by day from Peter's hospice room. He had promised Peter he wouldn't die alone. Sitting up in a chair by the bed, he watched as Peter finally could no longer swallow. Donny became an expert on breathing. He heard the breaths change from deep groans to breaths with big spaces in between to breaths so shallow you only knew they were there at all if you put your head on Peter's chest and listened.

Then, on that Saturday morning, September 18, just when most people in New York were sitting down to brunch, and Ron had gone to walk Mikey, Donny woke up in his chair beside Peter's bed, listened closely, and found Peter lying there with no breath at all. "I called the nurse," he said, "and she said he was gone. It freaked me out. His eyes were open when I listened to his chest, so I didn't know. Then I closed them."

For weeks, Peter had yelled, gotten angry, harangued people around him about the pain. But in the days right before he died he also worried—the constant diarrhea might smell, he might look so terrible that visitors might be offended. He thanked everyone for the slightest little things—for sips of juice, for ice, for arranging his pillow, for just being there and holding his hand.

Sitting with him much of that week in September as he lay dying, I heard him ask, beg, plead for more morphine, even with that 40- or 50-mg-an-hour intravenous morphine solution in his arm, until he could no longer speak. And even then, I heard them say no. Peter finally gave up hope and stopped asking. Stroking his forehead as he groaned, holding his hand as he sighed, I never once thought he was out of pain. Except when he finally died.

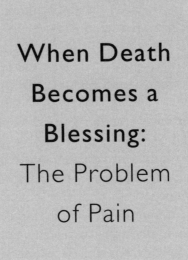

F O U R

When Death Becomes a Blessing: The Problem of Pain

On Saturday, September 18, 1993, at the exact time that Peter died—Kathleen M. Foley, M.D., was standing at a lectern in a downstairs meeting room at a Pittsburgh hotel, pointing to the slides projected behind her and speaking about pain.

The night before, I'd made a tough decision. I left Peter's side at Cabrini's inpatient hospice in Manhattan to see Dr. Foley, knowing that Peter probably wouldn't survive until I returned after the weekend. Pain management has gone through a revolution over the past twenty years, and Dr. Foley has emerged as one of the most eminent pain specialists in the world. This was the first time I would be able to hear her lecture about state-of-the-art treatment. More than anything, I wanted to know if there was something that might have been done to curb Peter's pain.

That weekend, the American Society of Clinical Oncology

(ASCO)—a professional organization of cancer and AIDS doctors—was holding its first national training conference on its newly adopted pain-management curriculum. The doctors and pain researchers speaking that weekend—twelve others in addition to Dr. Foley—were all pioneers in modern pain control, and the lectures and slides they presented over the two days were the content of a course that would be taken to medical lecture halls nationwide.

At the time, Dr. Foley was the director of the neurology pain service at Memorial Sloan-Kettering Cancer Center, and world renowned for her voluminous research and pathbreaking books. That day she would be sharing some twenty-five years of pain management experience.

There are two different kinds of pain, Dr. Foley explains, each the result of a different physiological mechanism. *Nociceptive* pain is the first type. It comes from tumors eating into tissue, but it is described as either *somatic* or *visceral* pain, depending on what kind of tissue it happens to eat.

Somatic pain is most common among cancer patients. It is well localized, characterized as "intermittent or constant, aching, gnaw-ing, throbbing, or cramping." It comes from bone tumors or inju-ries pushing into the surrounding tissue, or other kinds of tumors moving into soft tissue, muscle, lymph nodes, or skin.

Visceral pain, on the other hand, generally comes from cancer of the cardiovascular, respiratory, gastrointestinal, and genitourin-ary tracts. Patients describe it as "deep, squeezing, or colicky." The site at which the pain is felt, however, might not be where the problem lies. Visceral pain is often "referred" pain; that is, nerve pathway interference makes it seem as if the pain is coming from a place that it is not—shoulder pain, for instance, when a tumor might really be located in the diaphragm, liver, or lungs. The cancer is actually pressing on nerves that happen to pass through these diseased spots. The body mistakenly interprets skewed nerve mes-sages as originating elsewhere.

The second type of pain, Dr. Foley says, is *neuropathic* pain, which comes from an illness-related injury to portions of the ner-vous system itself, rather than from nerves being pressed. This kind of pain can also be further subdivided—into three categories, de-pending on where and how the nervous system has been invaded.

Peripherally generated pain comes from some type of injury to a nerve or nerves. *Centrally generated* pain comes from damage to the central nervous system, say, in the spinal cord, brain stem, or thalamus. *Sympathetically mediated* pain can come from either peripheral or central nervous system problems, but it is more pervasive—characterized, Dr. Foley says, by regional problems, say, vasomotor changes, swelling and sweating abnormalities, and/ or atrophy.

In addition to the need to know where pain comes from in order to treat it properly, pain experts need to assess the way it operates. Pain that comes only at certain times, and in specific blasts, is described as *acute*. Pain that comes episodically is called *intermittent*. Pain that persists on and on is *chronic*.

An injection, IV drip, or oral medication may help patients over an episode of acute pain, but chronic pain requires a longer-term treatment plan. "Adaption of the autonomic nervous system occurs and chronic pain patients lack the objective signs common to acute pain," Dr. Foley says, meaning those patients may not grimace or scream. "Chronic pain leads to significant changes in personality, lifestyle, and functional ability." How great these changes are is often dependent on how intense the pain actually is.

Pain intensity can range from *mild* to *moderate* to *severe* to *excruciating*. Without using a pain scale that allows a patient to describe this intensity it's hard for the person who is ill, or for his or her family or physicians, to know the levels of pain being experienced, how much of an emergency it is to treat it, and when medication has brought the pain down to a more tolerable level.

Making treatment even more complicated, all these different types of pain, their intensity, and their duration may occur in the same patient, at the same time, coming from many different pain sources and sites. "One-third of cancer patients in active therapy and sixty to ninety percent of patients with advanced cancer have significant pain," Dr. Foley says. "Patients with cancer will frequently have multiple causes of pain. In one survey, 81 percent of patients reported two or more distinct pain complaints; 34 percent reported three different kinds of pain [and] the whole issue is worse with AIDS pain."

Each of these pain periods and kinds of pain can require exacting assessment, and different treatment approaches, often given at the same time. Although most pain can be controlled by measures that are now routine to pain specialists, difficult pain syndromes such as neuropathic pain can require complicated, high-tech procedures, such as epidural catheters (catheters that spill narcotics directly into the spine) or nerve blocks. Sometimes they may require total and complete sedation until death, a controversial treatment option rarely acknowledged in most American hospitals.

The weight that Kathleen Foley conveys when she speaks is great. She has been among the driving forces putting proper pain treatment onto the international medical agenda, yet she is younger by far than many of her mentors and world-famous peers. Most important, she understands baby-boom culture, commanding respect among patients and other physicians alike.

If a patient is suspected of wanting pain medication to get high, or if he or she has a history of drug abuse, or even if he or she is a current drug abuser, Dr. Foley's view is "So what? Pain is pain and it should be relieved." After years of research her medical message is: Just say yes to drugs.

"This whole issue is worst for AIDS patients, many of whom *are* drug users, melodramatic, and/or gay," she says, "but *suffering pain,* particularly with neuropathy. They split staffs because of prejudice about all this. Comfort care requires giving them whatever is needed, [but] it's hard for doctors like us because we're often seen as complicit in addicts' need for drugs. And AIDS patients *are* often drug abusers, so it [ends up being] hardest for them."

Dr. Foley first became concerned about drugs and pain during the late 1970s, when she was fresh out of Cornell University Medical School and newly on the job at Memorial Sloan-Kettering. As a cancer specialist, she worried about the levels of suffering, and the longer periods of time during which this suffering was beginning to occur, that resulted from more successful cancer cures. As a neurologist, her job was to manage the pain of treatment as well as the pain of disease. The numbers of patients for whom this was a major problem kept on growing, along with the increasing numbers of cancer and, later, AIDS survivors.

Nearly from the start, Dr. Foley began research about how pain works in the human body—what nerve channels it travels along, how it can best be curbed depending on the specific pain site or pain channel. The more she learned, the more concerned she became to redress the tarnished reputation of good pain medications like narcotics as well as the fact that they weren't readily available and were sadly underused.

Dr. Foley was in excellent company. At Memorial Sloan-Kettering she worked with Raymond Houde, M.D., and Ada Rogers, R.N., both more experienced researchers and clinicians, who for twenty years had already been studying the physiology of pain and how to assuage it using narcotics and other drugs. Together, Houde and Rogers had done the classic research that underlies the equianalgesic dose table now in use worldwide. The table established equivalent doses of drugs for doctors to use when they switched patients between different narcotic drugs or ways of administering these drugs. Houde and Rogers also studied narcotics—often in high doses, and in new, sometimes synthetic forms and combinations—to treat difficult pain syndromes.

Across the continent, they were linked in their interest in treating pain with John Bonica, M.D., perhaps the father of modern pain treatment, at that time the chairman of the University of Washington's (Seattle) Multidisciplinary Pain Center, director of the medical school's department of anesthesiology, and founder of the International Association for the Study of Pain. For almost forty years he had been researching pain physiology, anesthesia, new surgical methods, and a team approach to pain treatment.

Kathy Foley joined this small, elite group of like-minded researchers, which was in turn joined by colleagues from around the world, to address this issue. Under the auspices of the World Health Organization (WHO), the group eventually helped draft a series of crucial pain treatment guidelines.

In 1982, when the WHO group came together, eleven of these experts—led by Dr. Bonica—gathered in Pomerio, Italy. Joining Dr. Foley and Dr. Bonica were physicians from India, Sweden, England, Japan, and Israel, experts in the fields of anesthesiology, neurology, neurosurgery, oncology, pharmacology, nursing, psychology, and surgery.

The group wanted to share with one another what they had learned about how pain operates in the human body, and how to manage the kind of moderate and severe pain that patients were experiencing as they lived longer because of successful cancer treatments.

In 1983, the first draft of its WHO guidelines was disseminated internationally; the American College of Physicians published similar principles of pain management in the *Annals of Internal Medicine*. In 1984, in *JAMA*, the American Medical Association (AMA) did likewise.

In December 1984, again under WHO auspices, the international pain management group met in Geneva. Dr. Foley was selected as the chairman of a gathering that was now expanded to include physicians from France, Nigeria, the USSR, Germany, Finland, Sri Lanka, Brazil, and the Netherlands. This time they wanted to use the 1983 working draft to set up cancer pain guidelines that could establish the principles of modern pain control worldwide.

By 1986, the organization had been named the WHO Comprehensive Management of Pain group; had set up eight WHO Collaborating Centers for Cancer Pain Relief worldwide, and had published a book under the WHO imprint. *Cancer Pain Relief* has since become the "gold standard" for state-of-the-art pain treatment. It uses a staged theory of pain, requiring physicians to think in terms of an *analgesic ladder* with different levels of treatment for mild to severe pain. The bedrock of treatment success is sufficient use of narcotics, given in steady doses around the clock. This book is accessible and readable and since publication has been sent to physicians, professional organizations, public agencies, and medical publishers the world over.

That same year, 1986, using the work of the WHO group, the American Pain Society created guidelines of its own and began to pressure health-care agencies within the U.S. government to issue federal guidelines on pain control.

In 1992, the U.S. Department of Health and Human Services' Agency for Health Care Policy and Research (AHCPR) issued what they called *Clinical Practice Guidelines* for acute, postsurgical pain management. Finally, in March 1994, with many of those early pain researchers on its advisory board, the agency published a second clinical practice guideline, *Management of Cancer Pain*, a guide on the treatment of long-term, chronic pain, and this included pain from cancer and from AIDS. A technical version went out to the nation's physicians, policymakers, medical centers and schools, and professional organizations. A layperson's version was also distributed to cancer and AIDS organizations, to patients and families, and to the media.

During these years, Dr. Foley published seminal papers and texts of her own. She was a whirlwind of energy, vociferously spreading the word on proper pain treatment. In fact, it became her life's mission. And that's what she was doing at that first ASCO pain training conference in Pittsburgh on that September morning in 1993 when Peter died.

B y then, Dr. Foley had been speaking about pain for more than a decade. But it had become apparent that getting state-of-the-art pain guidelines followed in everyday medical practice was not just a matter of education but a highly political, uphill battle.

In the late 1980s, the World Health Organization had enlisted Charles Cleeland, Ph.D., a professor of neurology at the University of Wisconsin's medical school, and others in his Pain Research Group, to assess the prevalence of patients' pain in the United States. The Wisconsin group became the WHO Collaborating Center for Symptom Evaluation of Cancer Care; WHO wanted them to discover what barriers might be standing in the way of good pain control.

Cleeland's team of researchers reported their findings in a series of disturbing articles published over the first half of the 1990s in the *New England Journal of Medicine,* the *Annals of Internal Medicine,* and other prestigious medical journals. They revealed not only how uninformed American doctors were about how to treat serious pain—despite the raft of new guidelines—but that they were under considerable pressure *not* to treat pain.

In 1991, Dr. Cleeland's Wisconsin Pain Research Group surveyed patients with recurrent or metastatic cancer from fifteen cancer centers in the eastern United States, all of them part of the Eastern Cooperative Oncology Group (ECOG), a National Cancer Institute–supported cooperative treatment group for the development and conduct of cancer-related clinical trials.

The researchers found that 61 percent of the patients treated by doctors in this group experienced pain, and 40 percent of them rated their pain as "significant" (more than 5 on a scale from 0 to 10). Yet *no* patient in this survey was receiving morphine or a morphinelike opioid, as the WHO and American Pain Society guidelines recommended. Researchers wondered why.

In 1992, the Wisconsin researchers conducted a nationwide survey of 322 members of state medical boards—the organizations that oversee physician licensing and medical practice in each state. The physicians on these boards have the power to censure other physicians—even take away their licenses to practice—for what they consider to be inappropriate treatment decisions. Researchers wanted to know whether these boards were a factor in the under-treatment of pain.

Their findings revealed an astounding information gap:

· To treat prolonged moderate to severe cancer pain, most board members recommended medications that pain experts consider grossly inadequate. Only 25 percent of them said they would give morphine as either their first, second, or third choice of medication; another 15 percent said they would use Dilaudid (hydromorphone, chosen by 13 percent) or levorphanol (2 percent), which are the other two opioids recommended by pain specialists.

A full 47 percent of these board members said they would give only aspirin or acetaminophen with codeine as their first, second, or third choice for prolonged moderate to severe cancer pain, and 21 percent said they would give just aspirin or acetaminophen alone. Pain experts say that these medications are useful for mild pain only. These numbers add up to more than 100 percent because respondents could give more than one answer.

"Codeine-combination products were recommended by many respondents," the Wisconsin research group noted, "but are generally considered too weak for prolonged moderate to severe pain. Meperidine [Demerol], which is inappropriate because of its toxicity, was recommended [for] about as often as it was recommended against [18 percent for; 17 percent against]. Opioid analgesics that are useful were recommended against by many respondents, including levorphanol, methadone, and hydromorphone [Dilaudid]."

·   These board members also had imprecise knowledge of the law. When asked about the legality and medical acceptability of prescribing opioids for more than several months in four patient scenarios involving cancer and nonmalignant pain, with and without a history of narcotic drug abuse, their answers were not only wrong, but often shocking.

Some 25 percent of them didn't realize that using opioid drugs for extended periods of time is lawful and considered acceptable medical practice for cancer pain; 14 percent thought that even though it is lawful, it is not generally acceptable medical practice and should be discouraged. Another 5 percent thought it violated medical practice laws and regulations, and 5 percent thought it a probable violation of federal or state controlled substance abuse laws and should be investigated. Seven percent said they didn't know.

Even more alarming, only 12 percent realized that using narcotics is lawful and good medical practice for chronic, serious noncancer pain—for example, pain that comes with AIDS or other illnesses. A full 47 percent said it violated acceptable medical practice, and 27 percent thought that it was probably a violation of federal or state controlled substance abuse laws and should be investigated. Again, 7 percent said they didn't know.

"It should be noted," the Wisconsin researchers said, "that in general, proceedings for violations of medical practice laws usually involve disciplinary action, including revocation of license, while state or federal controlled-substances law proceedings often involve criminal prosecutions, forfeitures, revocation of controlled substances registration, or a combination, and may include substantial fines or civil penalties. . . . The fact that 80 percent of the medical board members [also] said that their medical board was the agency most likely to investigate improper prescribing of controlled substances in their state underscores the significance of these data."

When the inquiry went back to cancer specialists after the WHO, American Pain Society, and other professional guidelines had had a chance to circulate among these physicians for an additional two years after the Wisconsin group's first study, the results were scarcely more encouraging.

In 1993, Dr. Cleeland reported his follow-up study of ECOG

physicians. Of the 897 doctors surveyed, 86 percent felt the majority of American patients in pain were undertreated; 49 percent of them also rated pain control for patients *in their own medical practice* as either *fair, poor,* or *very poor;* 31 percent of them said they would wait until their patients had only six months to live before using maximum pain medication. That, pain specialists say, is a tragic error.

A year later, when all these pain guidelines had had an *even longer* time to be well circulated among physicians in professional circles and in prestigious medical journals—and after the cancer specialists' curriculum guide was prepared by the American Society of Clinical Oncology, their own organization, and the group to whom Dr. Kathleen Foley was speaking that September day—these researchers went back again to these doctors' patients. Astoundingly, they found that nothing much had changed since they first reported talking with ECOG patients three years earlier.

In March 1994, the Wisconsin researchers reported speaking with 1,308 cancer patients of oncologists at fifty-four different ECOG treatment centers throughout the eastern United States. Dr. Cleeland and his colleagues found that 67 percent of those patients reported they had been in pain the week before, 36 percent with pain severe enough to impair their ability to function. In the researchers' estimation, 42 percent of those with pain were not given adequate medication.

"Despite published guidelines for pain management," the researchers concluded, basing their view on the standards for treatment first established by the WHO guidelines, "many patients with cancer have considerable pain and receive inadequate analgesia."

The ECOG group of physicians are hardly the only cancer doctors in America undertreating patients in pain. At the core of this tragic failure is a virtual phobia about narcotics. "The guidelines very clearly state that pharmacotherapy is the mainstay of cancer treatment," Dr. Foley says. "In a patient with severe chronic pain, you would choose a strong opioid from the beginning. But you can see from the numbers that that's not how it's done."

Dr. Foley and other researchers estimate that about half of all Americans spend the last days, months, or years of their lives in pain, more than half of which could be controlled but isn't. Federal AHCPR cancer pain guidelines estimate that 90 percent of all pain can be effectively managed. The numbers vary, depending on the study. Yet the sad fact is, in America today, undertreated pain is endemic.

The problem isn't limited only to cancer or AIDS patients. Indeed, those with cancer pain have the best chance of having their pain addressed, because cancer pain (and more recently AIDS pain) has been most intensively studied. The SUPPORT study of nearly 10,000 hospitalized American patients reported in 1995, and discussed in Chapter 2, found that half of all patients with a variety of other illnesses—including heart, liver, lung, or respiratory diseases, or organ system failures—spent the end of their lives in moderate or severe pain at least half of the time.

Yet doctors fear using narcotic drugs like morphine, the most effective medications for treating severe, long-term pain, and when they do prescribe opioids, they do not do so in high enough doses, which is often the only way these medications will work.

They believe, wrongly, that massive doses of narcotics will turn patients into addicts. They fear, wrongly, that narcotics will so build up their patients' tolerance for the drugs that they will no longer release them from pain. They fear, wrongly, that the drugs will accidentally cause patients to die of respiratory depression (which slows breathing down to nothing), or—plain and simple— from an overdose.

So great is our cultural fear of addiction that we have been blind to the virtues of these miracle medications: their ability to relieve severe pain and, when used wisely over long periods of time, to let seriously ill patients who would otherwise be bedridden lead relatively normal lives. In other cultures, narcotics have been the treatment of choice for centuries to ease the terrible pain of the mortally ill and dying. Indeed, until the beginning of this century, they were here as well.

Adding to American physicians' apprehension about using narcotics is stringent and increasing pressure from law-enforcement agencies. Indeed, by now the legal scrutiny provoked by narcotics use makes even suffering patients and their families fearful of using opioid drugs—and it has left doctors terrified.

Consider what happened to Ronald Blum, M.D., a physician

and research colleague of Dr. Foley. Dr. Blum is now the director of the Salick Cancer Center at Saint Vincent's Hospital in New York. In 1987, however, he was the deputy director of the Kaplan Cancer Center at New York University Hospital (he later became its director), a professor of oncology at NYU's medical school, and a highly regarded cancer specialist at Bellevue Hospital.

That year, 1987, Dr. Blum was participating, with his patients at Bellevue and NYU Medical Center—and with Dr. Foley's patients at Memorial Sloan-Kettering—in one of the first national drug trials of MS Contin, a sustained-release morphine tablet that has since become a favored drug for severe cancer pain.

"I was in the middle of office hours on a Friday morning at my NYU office," he says, "when my nurse came in and said there were two people in the waiting room from the state Department of Health. I put my patient in the examining room and went out. They flashed their badges, showed their sidearms, and told me that I had the right to remain silent and to seek counsel." When they read him his Miranda rights, he knew they meant business.

The Department of Health officials asked to see Dr. Blum's patient records. "I said I wanted to call my office manager to get them," he says. "They said, 'Oh, your accomplice!' and they proceeded to get more abusive."

According to officials at the New York State Department of Health's Bureau of Controlled Substances, which polices doctors, Dr. Blum was suspected of writing phony prescriptions and dealing drugs. The state's computers had flagged him because he was prescribing large quantities of high-dose narcotics.

Dr. Blum had to hire a criminal defense lawyer, and though he was able to prove his legitimate prescribing of narcotics for cancer pain, he still faced administrative charges on three counts: He'd failed to fill out the state's required triplicate prescription form properly; he hadn't kept every single one of his prescription books for the previous five years—as was required by the state—and he'd failed to report his cancer patients as *habitual users* or *addicts,* as was also required.

Dr. Blum's case was eventually dismissed, but it took eighteen months, cost him $10,000 in legal fees, and intimidated doctors from coast to coast. It turned out that Dr. Blum had made some reporting mistakes, errors that any doctor could have made, but he was no drug dealer. If the charges had stuck, though, he could have been required to pay a large fine and/or go to jail, and also lose his medical license. "There is a big problem of drug abuse," says Dr. Blum. "And there have been doctors legitimately convicted for prescribing narcotics, but then there are the rest of us."

Federal drug control laws first went into effect at the beginning of this century, for political reasons having to do with the opium trade from Asia. These laws were an attempt to prevent the sale of opioids in every corner-store bromide and through mail-order catalogs. They were also an attempt—on the part of missionaries—to lobby to protect the Philippine Islands (acquired after the Spanish Civil War) from the dangers of opium from China, and to curb doctors who, ostensibly, were dealing drugs.

Under political pressure from the United States, momentum was gathering internationally. In 1913, treaties under the auspices of the Hague Convention mandated an International Narcotics Control Board to restrict the amount of raw materials each nation might have and manufacture designated amounts of narcotics.

The federal Harrison Narcotic Act was passed in 1913, but it was vaguely worded and little enforced until the 1930s. After that, new laws were added and enforcement tightened—especially regarding doctors' prescribing practices—resulting in the almost universal perception that narcotics were bad.

That was the state of affairs until 1953, when Dr. Bonica—one of Dr. Foley's mentors and the original convener of the WHO pain relief group—lifted this veil slightly with the publication of his first crucial book. *The Management of Pain*, a 1,500-page text that has since been translated into many languages, has become the bible of pain diagnosis and therapy. It was the first time that cancer pain was brought into clear focus, yet laws regulating opioid use after that didn't get looser but rather tighter.

Today our laws are governed by a quirky set of federal and state legislation passed in the war-against-drugs fervor of the early 1970s, which put even more stringent restrictions in place for their legitimate use by patients.

The federal Controlled Substances Act (CSA) of 1970 established, among other regulatory mechanisms, a ranking system by which drugs were weighed—and monitored—according to their alleged relative dangers. Drugs were set into specific categories, called *schedules,* that are now in use worldwide.

CSA explicitly states that there are valid medical reasons for using narcotics. But when the CSA bill was first introduced into Congress, the Department of Justice was to have been the sole regulatory agency for both illegal and medical uses of narcotics. Under attack from the medical community, this section of the law was changed. Federal regulation for medical purposes was put under the aegis of what is now the Department of Health and Human Services, while the Justice Department's Drug Enforcement Administration remained responsible for monitoring illegal—and nonmedical—drug use.

Also created during this time were several other sets of laws—including the federal Food, Drug and Cosmetic Act—that set drugs into categories for medical use and for surveillance purposes. This part of the law is administered by the Food and Drug Administration, under which many drugs were accepted as safe and effective for human use, including narcotics, when prescribed by a physician for specific medical purposes. The regulatory categories were established on the safety and potential for abuse of certain drugs; in those categories drugs were ranked in terms of five schedules, each with different regulations and different mechanisms for their monitoring.

Psychedelic drugs, including marijuana, heroin, and LSD, were deemed Schedule I drugs; enforcement agencies consider them to have the highest potential for dependency and for abuse, so they have the most stringent monitoring requirements.

All Schedule I drugs are considered by the FDA to have no medical use, a determinant that has caused intense recent controversy, particularly among some AIDS and cancer patients and physicians who disagree. In 1996 ballot initiatives, Arizona voters approved a measure that would allow physicians to prescribe any Schedule I drug for medical use; California voters approved the medical use of marijuana only. But the federal government vowed to penalize doctors who prescribed these drugs, and to fight these state bills with federal legal clout.

Schedule II drugs are the narcotics that doctors may prescribe for moderate to severe pain, including opium derivatives such as morphine, Demerol, amphetamines, short-acting barbiturates such as Seconal, and codeine. A written prescription is required (some states require that it be written on a special form), no refills are allowed, and telephone prescribing is prohibited. Schedule I and Schedule II drugs are both tracked by enforcement agencies.

Schedule III drugs are considered to have some potential for abuse, but they are deemed less likely to cause dependence and/or harm, and they, too, have medicinal use. Included here are medications such as codeine combinations and some appetite suppressants. Though telephone prescribing is allowed, a pharmacist must convert it to written form; prescriptions must be written every six months and refills are limited to five.

Schedule IV drugs are those deemed even less likely to cause dependence or abuse. They include Darvon, benzodiazepines such as Valium (although New York State also has stricter laws against these medications, which are the mainstays for treating anxiety in terminally ill patients), and certain hypnotics. Prescription requirements are the same as for Schedule III drugs.

Schedule V drugs are those with the lowest potential for abuse, including diarrhea medications like Lomotil and Imodium, and certain preparations—such as cough medications—that contain some codeine. Some require a doctor's prescription; others just require signing a pharmacy log.

While federal regulations established standards for what constitutes a legal prescription for drugs in Schedules II to V and set limits on numbers of refills—recognizing the medical value of these drugs and the flexibility doctors might need in treating patients—they did not limit the amount that a doctor could prescribe at one time. However, states—as we shall see—would not be as lenient, nor would international regulation.

Federal law seemed to allow doctors to give patients as much as they might need, but international law—strengthened by the 1961 Single Convention on Narcotic Drugs and the 1971 Convention on Psychotropic Substances—tightened production limitations for these drugs. If doctors prescribed too many narcotics, the country-by-country production limits would end up reducing their use once each nation's quota had been met.

There have been recent efforts—particularly in 1990 by the WHO and by the U.N.'s International Narcotics Control Board— to allow more opioids to be produced so there would be enough available for medical use, but even the amount that can be produced has been tightly determined worldwide. Each country sets what it believes to be its quota of legitimate need and can then manufacture (or import) only that amount. The use of this limited supply is then carefully monitored and tightly controlled.

But in 1970, as federal lawmakers and agencies began to juggle how these laws would finally read and who would enforce them, the states jumped the gun and began passing drug laws of their own, creating a crazy quilt of laws that have become troublesome for doctors and patients.

Many state laws were patterned after the initial federal bill that failed to adequately distinguish—and create different enforcement mechanisms—for drug abuse and legitimate medical use. Nearly all presented problems for patients who needed opioid drugs.

In 1990, attempting to rectify problems, the National Conference of Commissioners on Uniform State Laws—which prepares model laws consistent with state policies—devised the Uniform Controlled Substances Act. It wanted to create one drug law that states could pass to make state-to-state regulation the same. The proposed model law recognizes that using opioid medications for pain is part of normal medical treatment; it also suggests that terms such as *addict* or *habitual user* should not be applied—as many states still do—to ill patients. But it is up to each state legislature to adopt this model law and make appropriate statewide legal and regulatory changes.

The New York State law under which Dr. Blum was charged was among the most restrictive in the nation. Like most other state laws at the time, it made no distinction between narcotics obtained for illicit or proper medical use, and it restricted prescriptions to a thirty-day supply, which is not good news for patients who for various reasons may need more.

But in that state, as in just a handful of others at the time, doctors were required to use triplicate forms to prescribe all Schedule II drugs. And, as in *no* other state, even some other drugs—benzodiazepines, such as Valium, used to calm anxiety for seriously ill patients—required triplicates just as narcotics did.

One copy went to the state, a second to the pharmacy, and the third had to be kept on file by the doctor for five years. The result of these regulations, many physicians said, was chilling, causing fear of regulatory agencies, and therefore reducing a physician's incentive to use the proper pain medications and additional necessary drugs.

"To keep their licenses, many doctors just don't give any narcotics," says Dr. Arthur Kennish, the Mount Sinai Hospital cardiologist we followed on rounds in Chapter 2. "That's your livelihood, and anyone can complain about you. It's common knowledge that doctors don't give enough pain medications. And that's true because they live in fear. It's easier to just say, 'I don't have a triplicate pad.' So it's a really, really tough problem."

Triplicate forms or not, however, almost all states have some surveillance mechanism in place—now computers are frequently used—to monitor doctors. Let one doctor in a community begin using higher doses of narcotics than other doctors in his town, and that doctor is bound to come to the attention of a law-enforcement official. David Joranson, Ph.D., of the University of Wisconsin's Pain Research Group, and June L. Dahl, Ph.D., director of the Wisconsin State Cancer Pain Initiative, have led a massive effort against the prescription drug reporting laws. They are joined by such patient-advocacy groups as Cancer Care. Opposing them are enforcement authorities who say that scrutiny is needed to keep doctors from writing phony prescriptions.

After officials in Texas cited doctors for diverting drugs to illegal users, that state passed a triplicate-prescription-form law. How prevalent was this alleged diversion of drugs? When Dr. C. Stratton Hill, Jr. (of M. D. Anderson and one of the world-renowned pain specialists who helped create the AHCPR cancer pain guidelines) and other experts examined state records, they discovered that a mere 0.08 percent of all drugs had been diverted.

"But we found," says Dr. Hill, "that the prescribing of opioids went down after the triplicate law went into effect—54 percent in one teaching hospital alone—and patients were getting something not as effective." Texas and California have since adopted more enlightened legislation that protects physicians who prescribe controlled substances for pain, and critics like Dr. Hill hope that other states will do the same.

State (and federal) tracking systems also monitor pharmacies, and this, too, can prevent patients from getting adequate pain relief. (Recall that Judith Hardin's mother, Adele, had to go to another city and call at least seven drugstores before she could find one that would fill a legitimate prescription for a cancer patient.) Some pharmacists are wary even of *stocking* opioids. A 1988 study of ninety-four New York City pharmacies found that 29 percent carried no morphinelike narcotics, 25 percent carried nothing stronger than Percodan, and though 37 percent of them did have some narcotic substitute, only three pharmacies carried the first-choice drug—oral morphine. National studies show similar numbers.

"Stocking opioid drugs is very troublesome," says Ivan Jourdain, owner of a New York City pharmacy. "God forbid you have a dishonest clerk or lose something, you're in big trouble. So we don't like to stock it, though we can order it for the following day. If we know the patient and the doctor, we will try to stock it, especially if we know the patient has cancer. But I don't think it's really hurting people, because there are so many other medications a doctor can use. Often a doctor will ask the pharmacist, 'What do you have in stock?' And we'll give the patient what's there." But that may not be the medication most able to blunt severe pain. Again, the patient is the one who loses.

These days, Dr. Kathleen Foley spends much of her time flying around the country to give lectures on the benefits of narcotics, but she's also broadened her concern to the improved care of the dying. In 1995 she became the director of the Soros Foundation's $15 million education effort, the Project on Death in America, and Dr. Russell Portenoy joined her as cochief of Memorial Sloan-Kettering's newly created pain and palliative-care service. Pain and symptom control have become Dr. Foley's political mission, particularly as they relate to physician-assisted suicide.

Whether it's her Catholicism—as some of her detractors say— or her medical conviction, Foley has come to disagree vehemently with those attempting to legalize assisted suicide. But she is very concerned about how to respond to the frequent requests from her own patients for help in dying.

While dying patients might have multiple kinds of pain, they also have a host of other symptoms. Memorial Sloan-Kettering studies show that terminal cancer patients have an average of thirteen different intolerable symptoms—ranging from shortness of breath to fatigue to constipation to general weariness with life. AIDS patients average eighteen. The plight of those with illnesses whose pain and other symptoms have not been as well addressed— diabetes, for example, or kidney, heart, or lung disease—is likely to be much worse.

Pain can greatly compound these other symptoms, causing a cycle of psychological distress, intense anxiety, and hopelessness. It is precisely the mounting psychological stress of these multiple problems, Dr. Foley says, that can put these patients at high risk for suicide.

Yet, in an age when most hospitals are still used to giving patients the antiquated shot of Demerol after surgery, Dr. Foley and other pain experts warn of its potential toxicity—particularly Demerol's risk for causing psychosis at modest doses and seizures in long-term use. In heading off direct pleas for help in dying, Dr. Foley always responds with the swift treatment of pain.

Here are her pain principles:

· Morphine, Dr. Foley says, is the "gold standard" of effective treatment, primarily because it works but also because it is readily available. Also effective, depending on the reactions of the particular patient, are several other narcotics, including Dilaudid and methadone.

While pain medications were once given only when the patient was writhing in pain—and in one big shot, as with Demerol— narcotics should instead be given at regular intervals around the clock in order to prevent pain from recurring in the first place. Extra doses should be provided for patients to use themselves if they feel the need.

· Morphine and other narcotics, she says, might also be given with methods invented in the last twenty years—oral suspensions, sustained-release capsules, intravenous drips, patient-controlled pumps, skin patches, and catheters implanted in specific areas— say, the spine, the brain, or specific nerves or nerve pathways.

· There are other new medications that mimic or improve on

standard morphine in their ability to quell pain. Still others head off
a variety of possible side effects of both illness and treatment, such
as nausea, diarrhea, constipation, itching.

· There are medications that can be used in combination with
narcotics for nerve pain. These include antidepressants, anticonvulsants, antiarrhythmics, and local anesthetics in injectable preparations.

· New surgical techniques have been devised, including the
use of a kind of microsurgery, with minute needles capable of
stilling or killing very tiny, site-specific nerves.

· Proper pain treatment begins with mild analgesics—say,
Tylenol—for mild pain. But for moderate to severe pain, doctors
must quickly give narcotics, sometimes in doses that may seem
terrifically high. Properly prescribed, these doses are as much as a
person feels he or she requires to relieve pain, or until an intolerable
side effect occurs. Then doctors must treat the side effect, and go up
even higher on the doses of narcotics, if they are still required.

The constant monitoring and changing of dosages takes particular
skill. Yet, if doctors follow these six rules outlined by Dr. Foley, most
patients whose pain is currently undertreated might find some relief.

1. *Don't limit drugs for fear of an overdose.* If junkies so
commonly overdose, why don't patients die when they are given
high amounts of narcotics? In a way, the answer is simple: The
patients are in pain; junkies aren't. Junkies are looking for a high,
an immediate rush that comes from one high-dose injection.

Proper treatment for pain is a steady dose of opioids, given
around the clock, either orally, in a high-tech, continued-supply
patch or pump, or in an IV drip. Tolerance to the drugs builds up,
and the body safely adjusts. (Junkies also use street drugs—not
pure narcotics in regulated concentrations—so they have no way of
knowing the drug's actual strength, what it's been mixed with, or
how much they are getting.)

Doses of narcotic medications can be safely and quickly raised
as they are needed to treat patients' pain. Pain acts as a brake. It
stimulates the nervous system, greatly reducing the chance of serious side effects like depressed respiration. The risks of narcotics
most Americans have heard about can happen, but they are rare

when these drugs are prescribed and monitored by skilled medical professionals. Those who are still fearful of an accidental overdose should know that doctors normally get ample warning preceding respiratory depression (which shows up as a marked slowing down of breathing). If health-care professionals are available, specific medications can be given that immediately reverse it. Problems generally arise only when doses are aggressively raised under poor or unskilled supervision.

2. *When narcotics are used for pain control, there is little risk of addiction.* While many drugs—steroids, say, or heart medications—can cause physical dependence, similar physical dependence can also occur with narcotics. That's why doctors need to taper off slowly with both of them. But psychological addiction—which is what junkies have—is a completely different story. That, Dr. Foley says, is unlikely unless the patient has psychologically addictive tendencies to begin with. And remember, she points out, even addicts get terrible diseases, and they, too, are entitled to relief of pain. Those with a drug history may need far higher doses of narcotics, not less, than other patients, she's learned. If they ask for more than they're getting, attention should be paid: They might actually need more.

3. *Believe the patient.* A person in pain doesn't always scream, writhe, cry, moan. Chronic (long-term) pain can show up as depression; it has gone on so long that life seems hardly worth living. Only those in acute pain (short-term, intense, recently acquired pain—say, the result of surgery) act the way most of us believe tormented people act. To find out how great someone's pain really is, a complete pain assessment is necessary.

To help physicians, patients must learn how to be more articulate about describing pain. (Is it dull? Burning? Stabbing?) Those differences indicate different sources of pain, which need to be differently treated. (Even if the source remains unknown, however, the pain should be treated.)

Assessment scales indicate intensity. There are several kinds of tests, but one popular one asks patients: "On a scale of one to ten, with ten being the most terrible pain you can imagine, where would you say your pain is?" If a patient says his pain is at the level of five or more, that's an indication to health-care providers that he needs immediate help.

4. *Severe pain can occur for months or years before someone dies.* It is acceptable to use narcotics for all of those months or years. Pain relief contributes to a human being's ability to lead a normal life. Aside from the agony it causes, undertreated pain can interfere both with quality of life and with a patient's ability even to try to fight off illness and heal.

Pain can occur at any stage of an illness. As people live longer with chronic disease, they find themselves in severe pain for longer and longer periods. Pain control during these times can make all the difference between carrying on a normal life and being bedridden and in agony. Yet many doctors hesitate to treat pain, if they treat it at all, until the final stages.

5. *A patient need not forgo morphine or another narcotic now in the hope that it will still be effective when the pain gets worse.* It will. Since there is no medical or legal ceiling on how much one can take, doses can keep being increased.

If someone regularly requires more and more pain medication, he might be gradually growing used to the amount of drugs his body is able to handle, but—more likely—his disease might be getting worse. He'll need another assessment to find out what additional medications should be offered. Patients often need to have their narcotics given in several different ways, to treat several different pain syndromes at the same time.

6. *Pain relief is always the objective when someone is dying, even if the high doses might have the unintended consequence of contributing to death.* Sometimes, doctors increase the dose of narcotic to control the pain and the patient gets sleepy. Sometimes, a sedating medicine is used specifically to induce unconsciousness because there is no other way to get symptom relief. As long as this is done openly (patients, if they are mentally aware, or caregivers, are informed), experts say this can be appropriate therapy at the end of life.

This treatment is not only legal and ethical but a well-established principle of good medicine, so long as a patient has let his doctors and his family know that he wants all the pain medication he can get at the end, even on the slim chance that it could cause death. (In fact, that risk is slim; someone who has been on narcotics over time has built up such a tolerance that the chance of an accidental death is practically nil.

Most patients whose pain is managed in this way will find some relief. However, Dr. Foley says, one can't say *all* pain can be treated, because it can't. "I'm very sensitive about this issue, because if you make big promises about treating pain and you don't deliver, it doesn't look good. So I won't say, 'All pain can be treated.' People choose a certain level of pain or symptoms they are willing to live with or not. But we do know that when pain is intense, it's hard for them to focus on anything else. So first we focus on pain relief at bedrest, then sitting in a chair, then walking around."

Because there is often a power imbalance—the doctor holding more cards (and access to the medication!) than the patient in pain—Dr. Foley says that patients and families may need to become more assertive about their need for care.

Among the options she suggests are getting another doctor, requesting a consultation with a pain specialist or a hospital or nursing home ethics committee, being sure the patients' preferences for pain management are included in an advance directive, and getting a copy of the federal AHCPR's *Cancer Pain Guidelines* to study and to show the physician.

Happily for patients, *failure* to treat pain may eventually be considered malpractice. In 1990, a North Carolina jury awarded $15 million to the family of a man who died in uncontrolled pain in a nursing home, where the head nurse refused to give this aged man with cancer the amount of narcotics he needed.

"Patients have to understand that pain should be treated," Dr. Foley says. "They have a right. So they should say to their doctors: 'My pain should be treated.' The public needs to know you're not an addict if you need pain medications, and the family needs to back it. Actually, I'm impressed that the public knows it better than doctors do."

C learly, one of the biggest problems for patients is the believability of their complaints about pain, for the experience of pain is highly subjective. It is no accident that Dr. John Bonica, the father of the international pain-management movement, suffered greatly himself.

In December 1993, about a year before he died at the age of

seventy-seven, Dr. Bonica came to New York to lecture at Memorial Sloan-Kettering. As usual, he was energetic and cheerful, but also as usual, he had to walk with the help of two silver canes, lumbering at each step. In his lifetime, Dr. Bonica had had thirty-six operations for broken bones—many of which had never properly healed—yet he was proud of these injuries and proud as well of his cauliflower ears.

To make money when he was still in his teens—and chesty, bulky, and sturdy—young John became a wrestler, coming up from poor neighborhoods, much as Sly Stallone had done in *Rocky*. In high school, Bonica trained by running along deserted Brooklyn streets at five in the morning carrying sandbags on his shoulders. To put himself through medical school, and later, to support his beloved wife, Emma Louise, and their family, John wrestled professionally, using the name Johnny "Bull" Walker to hide his identity as a fledgling doctor.

In 1937, he became the Canadian light-heavyweight wrestling champ; in 1941, he was the world light-heavyweight champion. Those were the years before professional wrestling associations had strict rules on potentially damaging maneuvers. John Bonica's years of wrestling left him with what would become a professional legacy in a different way. With years of broken bones, maimed tissue, and destroyed cartilage, Dr. John Bonica always fought pain of his own.

During World War II, he also learned to fight the pain of others. Dr. Bonica was assigned to run the anesthesiology department at Madigan General Hospital at Fort Lewis, in the state of Washington, which cared for wounded soldiers coming from the Pacific front. They were coming not only for surgery, but with injuries that were causing long-term pain. There, Dr. Bonica popularized a pioneering method for doing nerve blocks in specific regions of the body. After Emma Louise had trouble with anesthesia while giving birth to their first child, he invented the modern epidural.

From his work grew the basic principles of modern pain treatment. Since he suffered pain himself, he also understood pain's emotional and psychological ramifications. At the University of Washington he began the Multidisciplinary Pain Center, and in his classic teaching text, he advocated a team treatment approach. Essential to this team were the requisite neurologists and anesthesiologists, but also crucial were orthopedists (to deal with limb loss, limb pain, phantom limb pain, or bone injuries), rehabilitation specialists, and, of course, psychologists and psychiatrists to help patients cope with the emotional impact that injury, illness, and the very fact of pain itself might create.

While a revolution has occurred in the understanding and treatment of physical pain over the past two decades, a similar revolution has occurred in the understanding and treatment of psychological pain. Dr. Bonica has been at the forefront in this revolution as well.

Good palliative care these days means good management, not only of physical pain but of psychological syndromes, emotional pain, and other disturbing—often disease-specific—symptoms. This is the approach that physicians who are highly skilled in palliative treatment, like Dr. Foley, use in caring for their terminally ill and dying patients.

It is 9:30 in the morning, on Thursday, January 6, 1994. On the first floor of a wing at Memorial Sloan-Kettering, in a room large enough to fit nearly a hundred folding chairs, doctors, nurses, and social workers file in for pain rounds.

Up in front of the room sits Kathy Foley, together with her other mentor Dr. Ray Houde, and Dr. Russell Portenoy, Nessa Coyle (the nurse who directs patient care for the Supportive Care Program, the pain- and symptom-management team for particularly difficult cases), Terry Altillio, A.C.S.W. (the team's social worker), and several oncologists and other cancer specialists. One of them, Dr. Beth Popp, is the physician whose leukemia patient is about to be wheeled in.

When the room is nearly full—not only with nurses, social workers, and doctors, but also with the hospital's team of cancer-specific psychologists and psychiatrists—Dr. Popp goes out a door at the front and wheels in a small bundle of a patient in a wheelchair, from which dangles an IV bag actively dripping into this frail patient's arm.

The patient is Laura (not her real name), a twenty-nine-year-old woman wrapped in a colorful American country quilt, with a turban encircling her head, since chemotherapy has made her bald.

When she is settled, Dr. Popp stands by her side and tells the assembled group her story. Laura looks occasionally from Dr. Popp to the audience, seeming very relaxed in front of this large group.

Laura has leukemia and has recently had a bone marrow transplant. Her prognosis isn't good. She is the mother of three children—a ten-year-old boy and two little girls, aged two and three, and a single parent. Laura has support—her mother, friends, family, and her church—but she is experiencing a lot of anxiety about her illness and her likely death, and a large amount of bone pain.

Right now, however, says Dr. Popp, Laura's biggest problem is this: She knows she has a limited amount of time in which to live, and she wants to be able to spend that time with as little pain as possible, yet she also wants to be alert enough to try to lead a normal life at home with her kids.

Then Laura takes over. Speaking in a strong voice from beneath her turban and quilt, Laura tells the group that what's happening for her is that she is able to strike a livable balance taking Demerol—she isn't totally out of pain, but it gives her enough of an energized feeling so that she can get up out of bed and even give her children their baths or put them to bed. Yet the doctors want to take her Demerol away. Laura strongly objects. She says: "It makes me feel like a normal person. It lets me go through one day not thinking I have leukemia. When they told me they wanted to take me off, we had a battle."

Laura knows she's dying, but Demerol allows her to function— she can get up out of bed, she can sleep at night without taking sleeping pills, so why won't they let her keep it? Dr. Foley begins asking questions. She wonders why Laura can't take morphine, along with "uppers," which will stimulate her and allow her not to feel so sedated. She says it will be the same as Demerol, but Laura doesn't want to do it. She says she knows her body and this is the best she'll feel.

It seems that Laura has a past drug history, so Dr. Foley asks her to describe it. Laura says she took cocaine on weekends, but it made her feel paranoid and depressed. She drank beer with it and that made her throw up. Her church got her to go into rehab, and she stopped. Then she got leukemia.

At first, her doctors gave her Percocet, which also made her throw up. Morphine made her joints hurt and made her feel heavy. Demerol by IV was too strong, but acupuncture really worked. Still, after all this, she's adamant that oral Demerol is the best.

Laura's doctor speaks. She doesn't want her on Demerol. Period. Laura's home-care nurse gets up to speak. She says Laura isn't alert, as she claims, but she sleeps most of the time. The home-care nurse blames Demerol, yet she admits Laura doesn't have a good chance to survive, and having the Demerol regularly reduces her anxiety.

Dr. Foley turns to Laura. "They are concerned," she tells her, before the assembled crowd, "that you might develop seizures on Demerol. They are concerned that you aren't energized but sleeping, and then when you wake up, you're hyperactive.

"An addiction expert here would tell us we're all enablers and to stop your drugs and tell you to get out of bed and that's that. Well, we're not addiction experts, we don't have a[n addiction] center here, and we have a person with a terrible illness. So what do we do?"

Dr. Houde stands up and turns to Dr. Foley, his prize student. "I don't think all addiction experts would agree," he says. "Look, she was using a spree drug. That's what cocaine is. And she responded well to treatment, to counseling, and to acupuncture. This woman—without having to say we'll take your drug away—can be helped to deal with this problem. . . . I'm sure that if she were on a drug rehab program and got methadone and was able to function at home, we'd have no problem. So why do we now?"

The concern—Nessa Coyle and a staff therapist reiterate for everyone to hear—is whether to believe Laura that she's awake, not asleep. Is it the physician's responsibility, even right, to make this choice, they ask, or is it Laura's?

The concerns are whether by giving her *her* drug of choice they are enabling her addiction; whether *they* or *she* should be in control of her final days; and whether she remains awake or asleep, on their drug of choice or hers. The pain service staff hears that Laura *wants* to be awake, *wants* to have energy to be with her kids, and that she *feels better* with the risks of Demerol than taking morphine along with its potential requisite of uppers (for alertness) and downers (for sleep).

Laura responds: She is as concerned about addiction as they are. As soon as she realized she needed pain medication, she called her church, the one that sent her to rehab in the first place years ago, and they wanted her to go off drugs. She tried. But the pain was horrendous and she couldn't take care of her kids. Still, she wants to be baptized before she dies, and if she's on drugs the church says she can't. Morphine is considered a street drug in her neighborhood, so is Percocet, and uppers and downers, whereas everyone knows that Demerol is *medicine* and that it's given in hospitals specifically for pain. And for her, the pain management and the reasoning seem to work just fine.

For now, the staff decides, Laura can keep her Demerol. In balance, it's the drug that will allow her—until she dies—to have a life. And that's what this team is all about.

Sloan-Kettering is known worldwide for its aggressive, advanced cancer research and treatment, as well as for its vanguard attempts to care in a sophisticated way for life as a whole for dying patients. These patients need to handle—as Laura did—the emotional issues of their lengthy declines and decreased abilities.

They also need to cope with organic components of their illnesses, and with treatments and treatment decisions that can have a direct impact on their psychological states. This might include toxicity from drugs or failing organs, tumors pressing on certain areas of the brain, metabolic imbalances, or nutritional failures.

In focusing on these issues, those therapists, working here today with physicians like Dr. Popp, Dr. Foley, and Dr. Houde, have created an entirely new field called psycho-oncology, launched by Memorial Sloan-Kettering psychiatrist Jimmie Holland, M.D. This is the treatment of the psychiatric and psychological aspects of cancer, from the moment of first diagnosis to the time when treatment options need to be decided upon, through the course of treatment itself until death. Cancer was the first disease to spawn an illness-specific field of psychological treatment, but this model has since been expanded for use with other afflictions such as AIDS.

Dr. Foley's patients are followed during their hospital stays, and some, after they go home, remain under the pain service's care through its specialized at-home Supportive Care Team. Under this program, patients with multiple, hard-to-control pain and/or symptoms can have the medical assistance of visiting home-care nurses and social workers, cancer specialists, and pain specialists.

They may also see psycho-oncologists like Dr. Holland, coeditor of the seminal *Handbook of Psycho-Oncology*, and her colleague, William Breitbart, M.D. Together with a handful of other doctors, psychologists, and social workers, this Sloan-Kettering group has garnered international recognition for creating this new psychiatric field.

In addition to behavioral and talking therapies, psycho-oncologists have at their disposal a bevy of new medications to manage the emotional issues of dying patients. They also have the medical expertise to match the treatment aimed at curing cancer patients with the psychological and symptomatic impact of their treatment and decline. Just as Laura's pain was managed by this team in a way that was uniquely right for her, the team has learned to manage other symptoms in their patients' dying processes.

On Tuesday morning, December 14, 1993, the Supportive Care Team, led by Dr. Kathleen Foley, is meeting in private—as it does every Tuesday—in a small library-conference room on the third floor of Sloan-Kettering. Books and journals on pain and psychiatry line these walls. Sitting around a large table in the room's center are Dr. Foley, Dr. Portenoy, Nessa Coyle, and Terry Altillio. Joining them today are psycho-oncologists Dr. Holland and Dr. Breitbart, and several cancer specialists, nurses, and medical residents and interns. There are probably fifteen people in the room.

Many of this team's patients have left the hospital to spend their final days at home, while remaining under the aegis of Memorial Sloan-Kettering. Patients can return to the hospital whenever they feel they need to, but the team will also see that they get high-intensity care right in their apartments or homes.

As the team members discuss their current cases one by one, it becomes clear how much expertise, empathy, and ingenuity palliative-medicine specialists must employ in their quest to give their patients good end-of-life care. They must deal with problems such as prior overtreatment, massive physical assaults on the body, and insufficient prior discussion of when enough is enough. There are always insurance costs and reimbursement issues, and treatment choices often depend largely on what is covered. And there is a crucial point when pain might not be manageable without seemingly unacceptable side effects such as dementia or profound sedation.

This is the point when patients sometimes bring up the request doctors dread—assistance in dying. "Patients often say, 'Well, if you can't cure me, kill me,' " Dr. Foley says. "Palliative care isn't in their repertoire." A visitor here today, Frits Van Dam, Ph.D., of the Netherlands Cancer Institute, is an expert on quality-of-life studies and was part of the WHO pain-management group. Assisted suicide isn't legal in the Netherlands but is condoned so long as doctors meet certain guidelines (See Chapters 11 and 12). Doctors there have been criticized by physicians in this country, however, as not providing good enough palliative care, which some critics say leads patients to opt for assisted suicide. Dr. Van Dam scoffs at this, but he is here to watch what this team does, and likewise, they are questioning him about assisted suicide, since the patients this team sees are similarly tough cases.

Because of the overwhelming number of symptoms many dying patients experience, *all* of their symptoms might not be able to be addressed: The team physicians try to pick the three that are most distressing to the patient and manage those, because even partial relief gives patients hope.

Today they are talking about a woman with breast cancer that has aggressively metastasized into her brain. "Almost all her body parts have been assaulted," her physician tells the team. "She now has missing limbs and two mastectomies." Dr. Foley and Nessa Coyle think she was extensively overtreated, but that seems to be what the woman wanted.

"She was a securities analyst," Dr. Foley says, "and not able to say or hear when enough is enough, just: 'What's next.' Now she has, at most, two months. The radiation department wants to do palliative treatment to her head and back. I think it will destroy her to hear that nothing more can be done. She's in a lot of pain, but she won't admit it. She just keeps saying, 'When's the next chemo?' But she has beautiful blond hair and to lose it now would be the assault she couldn't take."

Radiation to shrink her tumor temporarily might be a solution.

But the woman highly values her beautiful hair; losing it would demolish her remaining self-esteem. She'd been bald through two prior chemotherapy treatments, and she doesn't want to go through that again. She wants to spend her final days with her newly grown locks of hair.

Dr. Breitbart, the psycho-oncologist, tells the team that he has seen this patient, that her pain and psychiatric symptoms are well controlled with appropriate medications—Dr. Holland concurs—but the woman is also trying to prolong her life until her nineteen-year-old daughter can get through some important—and very difficult—final college exams.

"How long will it take for her hair to fall out if we start the radiation now?" Dr. Foley asks her cancer physician. "And how long does she need to survive?"

The decision to recommend radiation was made, but only after the team concluded that the woman would likely die *after* the daughter's final exams—but *before* she lost her beautiful hair.

Such careful monitoring of patients' disease processes and concerns is crucial to help people handle the despair that today's illnesses can bring on. These are the kinds of questions this team asks, addressing how medical advances can help patients meet their last goals, and giving a new kind of hope by helping to orchestrate—in the patient's own terms—a psychologically dignified closure.

Even when a patient is truly incurable, these supportive-care specialists try to suggest treatment that will allow the patient to function at his or her highest possible level, rather than continuing to search for the perfect cure. These doctors well understand not only excruciating pain but the humiliation and distress that other symptoms cause and the despondency that comes with the near disintegration of the self. But this team understands the situation so well because at least one of them, Dr. Breitbart, has experienced firsthand how troublesome the *psychological* components of serious illness are.

William Breitbart is a physician whose own battle with illness—like Dr. Bonica's—helped him forge a new way to treat people who are desperately ill. Today, he is a world-renowned psycho-oncologist and an expert on the psychology of sickness and dying. He wrote the sections on psychological pain and suffering for the *Oxford Textbook of Palliative Medicine* and for the guidelines on the management of cancer pain issued by the AHCPR. He is the cochairman of the International Association for the Study of Pain's task force on AIDS pain and a research specialist on the reasons patients contemplate suicide.

It was his own life-threatening bout with cancer that propelled him into this new field. "My next-door neighbor, who was in medical school," he says, "was studying for her anatomy exam on the head and neck. She wanted to feel my face and neck to prepare for her exam, but when she got to my thyroid, she stopped. 'Bill,' she said, 'do you realize you have a lump?' It turned out I had cancer of the thyroid gland."

Dr. Breitbart, a tall, jovial, bearded teddy bear of a guy, was treated successfully, but in the process he went through hell. "When I went back to the doctor for my six-week checkup after surgery, he asked how I was," Dr. Breitbart says. "I told him, 'This was very difficult.' I had to repeat myself three times, because all the doctor would say was, 'What's difficult? The scar has healed really well.' So I realized he had no idea that I was talking about psychological difficulties. And that's when I decided to go into consultation-liaison psychiatry, which was a new field in the 1960s and 1970s, and to specialize in oncology."

The specialty of consultation-liaison psychiatry was created expressly to deal with the difficulties that modern treatment and chronic decline have created. Psycho-oncology is the subspecialty dealing with cancer. There are also a few consultation-liaison psychiatrists who specialize in the medical difficulties that afflict patients facing organ transplants, heart disease, multiple sclerosis, and other complex conditions.

In the late seventies, Dr. Breitbart came to Memorial Sloan-Kettering specifically to work with Dr. Jimmie Holland, coeditor of the authoritative *Handbook of Psycho-Oncology*. Together with a few others, they pretty much defined the field.

Recent research in mind/body medicine shows that those who reduce stress and anxiety improve their disease-fighting abilities, increase their immunity, and, in fact, live longer than those who don't reduce stress. But though physical pain is to be dreaded, it is psychological pain—the humiliation of lost control over bodily functions, the loss of independence and fear of being a burden, the despair when no improvement can be expected—that patients describe as their number one stressor, indeed, their reason for asking for assistance in suicide.

Dr. Breitbart has studied such requests among both AIDS and cancer patients at Memorial Sloan-Kettering. Terribly ill patients can suffer *fatigue,* "in the form of exhaustion of physical, emotional, spiritual, financial, familial, communal, and other resources," he says. "To focus on pain only is a simplistic notion. Those who focused on physician-assisted suicide in our studies were distressed, depressed, anxious. Palliative care involves more than pain control. We have to deal with these psychological issues when we talk about physician-assisted suicide."

In fact, Dr. Breitbart—since he has looked specifically at the mounting despair that seriously ill patients face as they decline—understands more than most physicians the reasons for these requests. And he thinks—as many other physicians do—that these are not all irrational requests or the result of a kind of depression that might be curable. Still, he is also passionate about heading off patients' possible desire to ask for help in dying by providing adequate psychological and psychiatric care. Part of his passion to curb requests for assisted suicide comes directly from two elements of his personal family history.

"My grandpa, Zishe Breitbart, was a famous strongman, known all over Europe for punching nails through boards with his bare fists," Dr. Breitbart told me. "One day in 1929, a nail scratched his hand and he got a severe infection that spread all over his body and killed him. That was before antibiotics. He was dead within six months." From this, Bill Breitbart learned that physical prowess mattered little; there was nothing that could be done to save Zishe.

The second contributing element of his family history was that his parents were Holocaust survivors from Poland. "My parents came here in 1949," he says. "I was the firstborn son, so there was a lot of pressure to succeed and to be a doctor. My father became the general manager of Ratner's [the famed Jewish restaurant in New York]. I went to a yeshiva, then to Brooklyn College, and then to Albert Einstein Medical School." He came away not so much religious, but with a strong survivor's sense that a weight of traditional wisdom rested with him.

The story of Grandpa Zishe and his parents' stories of who lived and who died in concentration camps taught Bill Breitbart two important things: Life requires a good sense of humor. And, in both living and dying, well-being has more to do with emotional than with physical strength. Today, emotional strength is what Dr. Breitbart tries to impart to his patients.

From the moment someone learns he or she has cancer, a crisis looms. A woman, he says, who has found out she has, say, breast cancer, has difficult choices to make. Is it better to have a mastectomy? A lumpectomy? Radiation? Chemotherapy with Adriamycin? Chemotherapy before surgery? After surgery? And what about the special treatments and diets?

Patients need help in reducing the intense feelings of isolation that a terminal illness brings, help sorting through medical information applicable to their particular case, help understanding the impact of various treatments. Psycho-oncologists might help them ask: What does it mean to you to lose a testicle? A breast? A voice box (larynx)? What does it mean in terms of self-image? Assurance of a cure? Adjustments during and after treatment? How people cope with difficult issues like this can greatly affect their treatment results, their state of mind, and their strength merely to endure.

In working with patients, a psycho-oncologist like Dr. Breitbart might employ the talking psychotherapy most Americans are familiar with. But also available today are new antidepressants and antipsychotic and antianxiety medications. As patients' disease processes progress, these physicians are trained to help sort out the psychological difficulties that may arise from the treatment or the disease, or both, and find new ways to treat them.

Most important, Dr. Breitbart draws on those new medications to treat the physical and emotional pain and depression that surround dying. The most prevalent cause of depression in dying patients, he says, is untreated pain, with organic causes and drug or toxic interactions coming next, but in the background is always the sadness that comes from the overwhelming loss of one's ability to function and the knowledge—whether conscious or not—of the imminent approach of death.

Dr. Breitbart estimates that 25 percent of cancer patients have severe depression, and by the disease's end stage, as many as 77 percent. But should the goal of treatment be to eradicate all depression, or is it at least in part a rational response to a terrible situation? Dr. Breitbart often refers to studies of physicians' attitudes on assisted suicide, one of which has found that 60 percent of physicians in a 1988 study in California said they "had been asked by patients to hasten death, and nearly all agreed that such requests could be considered 'rational.' "

"Those of us who provide clinical care for cancer patients with pain and advanced illness are sympathetic to the goals of symptom control and relief of suffering," Dr. Breitbart has written (with his colleague Dr. Steven Passik), "but are also obviously influenced by those who view suicide or active voluntary euthanasia as rational alternatives for those already dying and in distress. The danger lies in the premature assumption that suicidal ideation or a request to hasten death in the cancer patient represents a 'rational act' that is unencumbered by psychiatric disturbance."

Dr. Breitbart refers in his work to the following criteria for evaluating the request for "rational suicide"—which others who embrace this concept suggest: that the person have clear and unimpaired mental processes (unimpaired by depression or psychological illness or emotional distress); that he have a realistic assessment of his situation; and that the motives for suicide are understandable to most uninvolved observers.

Still, to some who disagree—like Dr. Foley—there is no rational reason for suicide. Others—like Dr. Van Dam—who disagree for different reasons feel that it is patronizing for physicians to assume they are able to make such determinations for someone else. (We will discuss this at length in Chapter 12.)

To still others—including psycho-oncologist Rachel Naomi Remen, M.D., medical director of Commonweal Cancer Help Retreat in Bolinas, California—to medicate against the existential angst of life or to use medications in ways that prevent patients from addressing—and wrestling with—the deeper issues of life and death is not only clearly wrong but can prevent them from completing the psychological and spiritual work they need to do in the process of dying.

As the field of psycho-oncology has grown, the fine lines between organic illness, justified despair, maladaptive psychological response—and, indeed, even spiritual ecstasy—have created other controversies. Among them is debate over the meaning of what some, like Dr. Breitbart, call *hallucinations* at the end of life, and what others, like Dr. Remen, might call *deathbed visions*. According to Breitbart, some 25 to 40 percent of all cancer patients have delirium, which is marked by confusion and hallucinations; in the terminal stage, some 85 percent have these symptoms. An even higher percentage of AIDS patients have depression and delirium, too.

"There are different kinds of hallucinations that occur in delirium," Dr. Breitbart says. "The function of the brain is screwed up in some major way, like when you're watching cable TV and it goes whacko, scrambled. So something causes the brain to go off in a gross, major way. And just as you have problems getting a clear picture when the cable goes off, [these patients] have problems with attention, focusing, memory, language, remembering to do things—problems even with the sleep-wake cycle."

Most of the time delirium is treatable, but when the patient is actively dying, delirium is hard to reverse, he says, mainly because dying can't be reversed. But while some delirium might be inspiring—many patients feel uplifted when they see, for example, angels or the coming of now-deceased relatives—hallucinations can also be terribly frightening, filled with disconnected or terrifying images, or even sounds and smells.

"What's the difference between a hallucination and a near-death experience, or dead relatives taking you to the afterworld? Well, I guess it's perspective," Dr. Breitbart says. "If you know there's an afterworld, well, I guess you'd be reassured. But since I don't know that there is, I'd treat for hallucination. . . . There are mysterious things in life, and I have a nonmysterious explanation," he says. "So I'm going to choose the known."

Dr. Breitbart and other psycho-oncologists with views like his may interpret pre-death restlessness (groaning, tossing) as severe anxiety needing treatment, and pre-death visions as hallucinations requiring psychiatric drugs, rather than psychological or spiritual phenomena that naturally occur as someone dies. It's all a matter of perspective. Some other psycho-oncologists—Dr. Remen, for example—look to these hallucinations for psychological or spiritual content.

Sedatives and psychotropic drugs can quiet delirium or take visions or restlessness away, but the debate centers on whether these drugs should be used and when. Some people claim that they are calming to the patient and the family. Others say that they take away the patient's chance to resolve issues and to finish life psychologically and spiritually whole.

"We know from one study at Sloan-Kettering that 85 percent of all cancer patients had terminal delirium. Not all had visual hallucinations," says Jon Levenson, M.D., a psychiatrist at Columbia Presbyterian Medical Center in New York, who specializes in the care of AIDS and cancer patients. (He has shared research projects and written articles with Dr. Breitbart.) "There are times when the family can't tolerate what's happening. And the family members live on, so we try to look at the terminally ill patient as a system that includes the family."

The psychiatric view is that these hallucinations are caused by the breakdown of body organs or the side effects of drugs. Since many doctors believe that everything is over once the body shuts down, they feel that the psychological comfort of the family is more important than the journey the dying person is trying to make.

"The patient may develop delirium—which is common in the weeks before death," says Dr. Levenson. "He or she may not recognize family members; the patient may be hallucinating, restless, agitated. It may be that these visual hallucinations are driven by the medical process. But they can still have meaning for an individual as he attempts to cope with these perceptual disturbances."

To some in the natural-dying movement, like Dr. Remen, the dying person's personal journey is primary—more important than whatever fear hallucinations may induce in the family. So anything that can help both the patient and the family calm down—anything that will allow family members to sit quietly and be with the dying person, hold his hand, stroke his brow, and anything that can help, rather than hinder, him in making that journey better—will also aid the whole family. To others, like Dr. Levenson and Dr. Breitbart, however, the kind of real horror that a few patients might experience at the very end of life, and the need to give them aggressive and immediate relief, might come first.

The disturbing truth—the stark truth that Sloan-Kettering and other palliative-care doctors know all too well—is that even if they provide state-of-the-art narcotics treatment and treatment of all disturbing symptoms, and even if they prescribe extremely high doses of opiates, the torment of some of their patients will not be relieved unless these patients are anesthetized into unconsciousness.

Vittorio Ventafridda, M.D., is an internationally known cancer specialist who served on the WHO pain committee and practices at the National Cancer Institute in Milan, Italy, a state-of-the-art pain-management center and the site of the WHO Collaborating Centre for Cancer Pain Relief. In 1990, he shocked pain specialists around the world by reporting in a prestigious medical journal, the *Journal of Palliative Care,* that more than 50 percent of his patients with advanced cancer experienced such unbearable suffering as death approached that they had to be sedated into unconsciousness. Half of the "unbearable suffering" Dr. Ventafridda saw was caused by pain, the other half by shortness of breath.

Dr. Ventafridda reported that he had followed 120 of his terminal-cancer patients in their last weeks and days of life. Only 43 of them got adequate relief from narcotics alone; 63—more than half—needed total sedation to get relief. He said that patients in this last category died within a few days after being put into this state.

Some American hospitals—most of them national comprehensive cancer centers or particularly sophisticated hospices—also use this practice: A drug coma is induced to achieve complete control of unbearable suffering. Patients are given either narcotics, usually in combination with barbiturates, or an anesthetic (of the type used for patients undergoing surgery).

The doctors expect these patients to die. With the patients' and families' consent, food and water may also be withheld. (Such patients may not be able to tolerate food and water anyway. Dr. Ventafridda noted in his article that many of his patients also suffered from severe vomiting and nausea.) Death is caused either by the progression of the disease process or, for weak patients, by the withholding of artificial nutrition and hydration, or from pneumonia that sets in because of lack of physical movement and sedated breathing.

Physicians at state-of-the-art medical centers where this kind of sedation is offered—like Memorial Sloan-Kettering and Fox Chase Cancer Center in Philadelphia—say that death usually occurs within, at most, ten days of the patient's sedation.

Though doctors at these medical centers acknowledged using what is also referred to as "terminal sedation" or "sedation of the imminently dying," or "unconscious sedation," they disagreed about the number of patients who required it. Most thought that Dr. Ventafridda's 50 percent figure was too high.

At Memorial Sloan-Kettering, Dr. Foley and Dr. Portenoy estimate that roughly 70 percent of the patients referred to their palliative-care team are helped with narcotics alone. Another 20 percent *might* get relief with a combination of treatments. Whether or not they do depends on what each patient considers to be an acceptable quality of life. That leaves some 5 to 10 percent who do not get adequate relief. "At the end of life," Dr. Portenoy says, "these patients might be candidates for sedation to achieve control of suffering.

"Under informed consent and medical self-determination," Dr. Portenoy explains, "it is a patient's legal right to reject sedation for symptom control if it is offered but it is not something patients can demand from a doctor. The possibility of sedation to treat intractable suffering at the end of life should be discussed with patients and families. Most patients and families do not reject it, if suffering is unrelieved and they are given the choice."

But this method has only recently become known and it is not yet extensively used in most American hospitals or hospices. And waiting days to die in an unconscious and sedated state—sometimes without receiving any nutrition or water—may not be a death everyone would choose.

While sedation to unconsciousness at the end of life may well sound like physician-assisted suicide, doctors, ethicists, and the courts have not considered it so. It is legal because our laws permit physicians to end suffering, if the intention is to do this, even if the treatment aimed at pain relief might hasten death. This ethical reasoning rests on medicine's timeless potential for creating what is called the "double effect," which in lay terms is akin to saying "the operation was a success but the patient died."

Some doctors consider terminal sedation appropriate—and legal—only for those who have physical pain or shortness of breath as they are actively dying. Others add severe nausea to the list, and still others add delirium, even psychospiritual concerns, or any other uncontrollable or terrible symptom.

Still other health-care professionals may feel uncomfortable about offering this approach if the suffering experienced by the dying patient is emotional or spiritual, rather than physical. It is usually not considered at all for patients who are not at the terminal stage, even though they might find their symptoms unbearable. Nor has it been widely available—except, perhaps, on an underground basis—to patients with illnesses other than cancer.

In less sophisticated medical centers, in places where old myths or outdated laws on the use of narcotics prevail, in the offices of physicians across the nation whose knowledge of pain and symptom management isn't up-to-date, the debilitating symptoms of chronic decline can, and do, remain ineffectively treated. In addition, cancer is a special context, because of the acceptance of pain control, Dr. Portenoy says. "Other patients with chronic pain due to other progressive medical illnesses probably fare much worse, for instance, patients with AIDS or hemophiliacs. It's very difficult. I think this is a problem that goes way beyond cancer."

Just how difficult the end of life can be, is evidenced by an important 1990 study of the final days of ninety cancer patients who had been referred to Memorial Sloan-Kettering's Supportive Care Program. The study was conducted by Dr. Foley, Dr. Portenoy, Nessa Coyle, and another nurse, Jean Adlehart, R.N. Though not named in the study, Dr. Breitbart and other psychiatrists participated in treatment.

All these patients had been referred to this team because they were experiencing very difficult-to-control symptoms. All of them suffered from pain; two-thirds of them had more than one kind of pain. In addition, they had a range of other disturbing symptoms that included fatigue, shortness of breath, anxiety, confusion, and general weakness. Many medications were used, including psychiatric medications and drugs for the range of their symptoms. A variety of narcotics were used for pain, depending on their effectiveness in a particular patient—including morphine, Dilaudid, methadone, and levorphanol—often given in several different ways at once. For purposes of the study, the researchers converted all drugs and dosages to morphine equivalents.

These highly sophisticated researchers and pain-control experts still found that eighteen of their ninety patients—20 percent— could get relief from their pain *only* if they lay completely still in bed. In fact, they found: "Our experience suggests that it is extremely important to set realistic goals for pain relief, lest unrealistic goals increase the level of frustration experienced by the patient, family, and staff. *For most patients, freedom from pain with activity is unrealistic* [italics are mine] and, indeed, it may be appropriate for some advanced cancer patients to remain in bed continuously if control of pain is not otherwise possible."

All eighteen of these immobilized, bedridden patients expressed thoughts of suicide to their doctors as a vague option "somewhere in the future."

An additional four of the original ninety patients actually had made plans for suicide. And another four specifically requested euthanasia, or help in dying.

Severe pain was an issue for some; for others, it was depression, hopelessness, and profound fatigue with their present condition of life. A man with lung cancer had terrifying episodes of acute shortness of breath—a feeling of imminent suffocation. One woman wanted help in dying when new metastases were found; another when additional paraplegia set in, after her brain cancer had already "led to an inability to talk, hear, swallow, and walk."

"All patients who expressed the possibility of suicide had progressive disease, with accumulating debility," the researchers noted. "They had neither the hope of prolonged survival nor of return to normal function."

When their feelings were more fully explored, most likely by the staff psycho-oncologists, these patients also talked about fears of excruciating pain, becoming a burden on their family, losing the ability to think, being demeaned by the loss of bowel and bladder function, and becoming paraplegic.

Researchers deemed all four of the patients who had made real plans for suicide as clinically depressed. They said that two also had episodes of delirium. These *two actually went ahead and killed themselves;* it isn't clear whether they were at home or in the hospital at the time.

While it also isn't stated directly in this study, *promises* of sedation at the end—which is what my own interviews show happens in Memorial's pain service—likely helped three of the suicidal patients to go on.

But the fourth—the man with lung cancer—was so terrified by an episode of acute shortness of breath that he'd already had, so afraid that it would recur again at the end, that—though he agreed to postpone his suicide plans—he didn't find complete comfort in their promises. He said he just wanted to die, but his doctors encouraged him to go on.

In the end, he had an acute, terrifying episode of shortness of breath, a feeling of drowning in his own fluids as he died. His family believes that for him, suicide would have been a far better solution.

What does this mean? All of the patients in this Sloan-Kettering study were receiving the best palliative care there is, from arguably the best physicians in the world. They got medications addressing pain, shortness of breath, constipation, depression, and delirium. They had promises of unconscious sedation if they couldn't bear their agony any longer.

Yet, even with all of that sophisticated help, eighteen patients (20 percent)—reduced to a life of pain that could be controlled only if they lay perfectly still in bed—talked of suicide, and an additional four patients had real plans.

Of these, two actually went through with their plans. And—judging from the high levels of narcotics given in the twenty-four hours before they died to two additional patients—it seems likely that they were helped to easier deaths with sedation. As opposed to assistance in suicide, these researchers take comfort that such deaths are deemed legal and medically ethical, since their intent was the relief of suffering, but it is clear from the numbers that 5 percent of their patients were either helped to their deaths or wished that they had been.

It is sobering to contemplate what the situation for tormented patients must be like in hospitals less skilled in palliative care than Memorial Sloan-Kettering. Dr. Foley's own conservative estimate that 5 percent of the patients she sees are in unassuageable pain may sound like relatively few. However, there are some 6,000 deaths in America every day. That means that 300 people a day, or 109,500 a year, die with unrelieved suffering.

The actual numbers are probably far higher: Dr. Foley's 5 percent refers only to the 5 percent of cancer patients she sees in her specialty practice, which is about 5 percent of the dying patients in her own hospital. Granted, her patients have difficult pain syndromes, but they are lucky enough to be in a sophisticated cancer pain center and to have treatment by physicians who are among the best pain experts in the world.

Most dying cancer patients are not as lucky. Nor, as we have seen, are those who are dying of other illnesses. Dr. Foley's study shows that the patients most in need of help in dying were those patients with progressive, deteriorating illnesses for whom there was no hope of a cure. When such an illness becomes terminal is largely arbitrary because it's the progressive deterioration in the patient's quality of life that is at stake. The issue is, who decides when enough is enough?

Most of the sophisticated research and treatment in palliative-care work addresses only what is considered the *terminal* phase of disease. Because cancer is the disease best studied, the terminal phase for it has been best demarcated. Still, even cancer specialists say the end is difficult to predict, and other illnesses are even harder.

"Doctors had the hardest time predicting the life spans of dying patients with congestive heart failure, the most common cause of death in the United States," read a 1997 report in *The New York Times* on the famed SUPPORT study, codirected by Dr. Joanne Lynn. In one part of the study, "28 percent of [these patients] who were expected to die in six months were still alive a year later. [And] among lung cancer patients . . . 13 percent who were expected to die in six months were still alive a year later and a very few even lived for two years."

But for patients who were actually ready to die, Dr. Lynn discovered, doctors were overly optimistic. "She and her colleagues looked at doctors' prognoses the day before patients' deaths," *The New York Times* reported. "Almost never, she said, did the doctors believe there was no hope. Doctors gave patients with congestive heart failure a 50 percent chance, on average, of living another two months. As a group, on the day they died, the patients in the study were expected to have a 17 percent chance of living for two months and a 7 percent chance of living six months. A week earlier, they were thought to have a 35 percent chance of living six months and a 51 percent chance of living two months."

"It is not clear that society desires to categorize individuals who still have a '50-50' chance to live as 'terminally ill' and certainly not as imminently dying," Dr. Lynn reportedly wrote, "[but] what we forget in our myths and our stories is just how ambiguous these situations are."

During these prolonged periods before they are considered terminal, patients may experience anything from impaired sexual and physical functioning to foul odors to adhesions to fluid buildup to loss of a tongue to the prospect of drowning in their own fluids. They may have to deal with fear of recurrence, fear of the disease, fear of treatment itself, and the despair brought on by the recasting of their very selves from functioning and healthy to fragile, un-steady, and sick. It is not hard to recognize how desperate their situation is.

In the latter half of the 1990s, most Americans die after their doctors withhold or withdraw one or another kind of treatment—whether it is chemotherapy, a blood transfusion, a respirator, or something as simple as antibiotics. Nontreatment, or "letting nature take its course," has become the modus operandi of end-of-life American medicine, but generally after highly aggressive treatment has already taken place. So long as a patient, or his or her proxy agrees, that is considered ethical, legal, even good medical practice, but assistance in suicide or straightforward euthanasia is not.

There is, certainly, a whiff of legal and verbal sophistry here, and that is the issue the U.S. Supreme Court considered in its landmark cases on legalizing assisted suicide. Whether or not one can get legal help in dying in America today depends on what disease one has. And then, "letting nature take its course"—depending on the disease—may be a more or less harsh way to die. Those who have a feeding tube or a respirator can, if they so choose, have both of these legally turned off, with morphine to ease discomfort and fear at the end.

Those with cancer can hope for a doctor knowledgeable and sophisticated enough to provide whatever high doses of narcotics are necessary to ease suffering, even if the treatment hastens death. None of this is considered assisted suicide or euthanasia. But patients with other illnesses or symptoms may not find such legal or straightforward solutions.

Proponents of legalized assisted suicide argued that because there are different rules for different illnesses, terminally ill people do not have equal protection under the law. Opponents charged that while the law should allow relief of suffering, it should not condone taking life. (See Chapter 12 for a fuller discussion.)

Even more important, physicians—and lawmakers—have not seemed willing to let patients decide for themselves when their suffering is so great that they might prefer death. Instead, that right has been left to doctors to decide. And this, proponents also argue, is a violation of our right to die in the way that we wish.

Those who are religious argue that the choice of life or death is God's, yet, given the sophistication of medicine today, this is a choice that is often manmade. The issue of more aggressive help— of legalizing assisted suicide—is the next battleground in what is already a twenty-year struggle through courts, legislatures, and state ballot measures for Americans to take back from medicine control over their own bodies and their own deaths.

X

Tough Love: The Legacy of Karen Ann Quinlan

About a week before she lost consciousness forever, Karen Ann Quinlan was sitting around with some friends, reading palms. When they got to hers, they were shocked: Karen had a lifeline so long that it went way across her hand and down her wrist. She was ecstatic—so happy that she drove straight over to show her mother. " 'Look, Ma,' " Julia Quinlan says Karen told her, waving her hand in the air, " 'look how long my lifeline is. It's the longest of all my friends'. You know what that means? I'm going to live forever.' "

Karen's excitement delighted her mother. Karen was normally a bubbly, outgoing person, but sometimes of late she'd seemed sad. Her aunt and a friend's father had recently died of cancer and another relative had died of a brain tumor. Julia remembers how upset Karen had been after she came home from sitting with her friend's family in the hospital waiting room, day after day. She'd watched them *all* suffer as her friend's father went through treatment after treatment. "Karen told me she would never want to suffer like that if she were so ill," Julia says. "She said, over and over, 'I'd never want to put my family through that.' "

At twenty-one, Karen was young to be thinking like this. But for some time she had been dwelling on a morbid fear: If she were ever in a hopeless condition, she'd said, she didn't want to be kept alive if that would just prolong her suffering. Luckily, as it turned out, she'd said this to many of the one hundred friends who'd come to her surprise birthday party the year before. They remembered and would later repeat at her trial what she had said.

In rural Landing, New Jersey, just off Lake Hopatcong, where Karen grew up, she was a born leader, a great athlete, usually optimistic. Not the kind to be overwhelmed by dark thoughts. But the summer before, she had begun reading books on reincarnation, clairvoyance, and ESP. "Karen had ESP herself," Julia says. She told her ex-boyfriend and her best friend that she was having premonitions. "I'm going to die young," she'd said. "But I'm going to go down in history."

That day, as Karen stared at her long lifeline, she must have wondered why, since she was to live forever, she had this foreboding that it wouldn't be long before she'd die—and why, if she hadn't done anything unusual, she would go down in history. Unfortunately, *both* of her predictions were accurate.

Karen Ann Quinlan did die young, and her name became a household word. In 1975, she fell into a coma; in 1976, a legal precedent was set when her family became the first in the country to win the right to refuse unwanted—and extraordinary—medical treatment. The Quinlans' travail was the nation's first public recognition that modern medicine's new power to prolong life had gone too far, and that Americans needed some legal shelter from that power.

In fact, as few people remember, Karen Ann Quinlan didn't die after the Quinlans won their court battle, but on June 11, 1985, over ten years after she first went into her coma. Yet the subsequent national focus on what kind of treatment a patient wants as he or she lies near death—and who has the right to decide that treatment—began with this one young woman and her family's New Jersey trial.

Roused by the life-in-death that Karen endured, state legislatures began passing laws that enable patients to say no to the kind of protracted treatment Karen had—treatment that merely extends the physical process of dying but makes what is left of life torturous.

Indeed, her case became the springboard for the growing body of end-of-life law that developed in this country over the past two decades—for the wave of court cases after hers, and for the subsequent legislation that made advance directives—such as living wills and health-care proxies—into state and federal law.

In 1991, five years after Karen finally died, the federal government enacted the Patient Self-Determination Act (PSDA), which requires that any medical center receiving federal funds must inform patients and their families about the legality of these advance directives, that they have the right by signing one of them (these documents differ state by state) to make the crucial decisions about their terminal care.

It is not widely understood that patients who are conscious and mentally competent have long had the right to decide on their own medical treatment, that court cases and common law have all supported a patient's right to make his or her own medical decisions, even if others disagree with those decisions, and even if those decisions might ultimately result in death.

Until Karen's case, however, this right did not clearly extend to those who were no longer conscious or mentally competent, even if medical decisions that needed to be made were the kinds of decisions those who knew and loved the patient were sure she might have made if she were still able to speak and decide for herself. Instead, as medicine has grown more complex, life, death, and treatment decisions have been generally left to doctors to decide.

Karen's case was a national watershed. It underscored the right patients have to make treatment decisions themselves. It clarified what happens when people are no longer competent and able to decide by extending that right even after consciousness has been lost.

This was a gigantic milestone. It gave us a framework to deal with issues that had long been in doctors' hands, dependent on the individual relationship between patient and physician.

Recently created state laws—reinforced in 1991 by the

PSDA—further extended that right by designing legal documents as vehicles by which we could make our wishes known in advance (thus called advance directives) with living wills, or to designate a decision maker in advance who would either act as a substitute—or proxy—for the patient, making such decisions on his or her behalf, or in that patient's best interests.

Karen's story has since gone down in medical and legal history, the laws her misery spurred into passage saving many patients and their families from the unwanted imposition of medical treatment. These new laws also allow us to have a legal vehicle stipulating treatment we might *want*—as well as not want—if that is what patients and their families might prefer instead.

And yet, as many patients and families have sadly learned—and as we will see in Chapter 6—even these new legal precedents and new laws might not be good enough. They still might not ensure that patients and families have any real say over our chronic declines, or any real clout in deciding how we spend our final days or, finally, how we die.

On Monday evening, April 14, 1975, Karen, her two roommates, and a girlfriend, Terry, went out to Falconer's, a local restaurant, to celebrate Terry's birthday. Karen was on a diet, since she was planning a trip to Florida and wanted to look good in her bathing suit. She hadn't eaten much in the previous few days, and she ate hardly anything for dinner. But her roommates later told her mother, Julia, that Karen did have a few drinks. After dinner she began to seem strange, they said, and told them she wasn't feeling well. Around midnight, they drove her back home to their small rented house in Cranberry Lake—near Lake Hopatcong, where her family still lived—and put her to bed.

About an hour later, one of the roommates checked on her, found she wasn't breathing, tried to give her mouth-to-mouth resuscitation, and called an ambulance. When paramedics arrived, Karen was given cardiopulmonary resuscitation. Then in the early hours of the morning of April 15, 1975, she was taken—already in a coma—to nearby Newton Memorial Hospital, in suburban Morris County, New Jersey.

At two in the morning, Karen's parents, Joe and Julia Quinlan, were awakened by a phone call from an emergency room nurse. When they arrived at the hospital's intensive care unit, it seemed to them as if Karen were merely asleep—albeit with a series of tubes, including one from a respirator already placed down her throat, hooking her up to life supports. She was in a coma from which she would never emerge.

Doctors in the emergency room worked on Karen and did test after test to determine what had caused her coma. The kind of treatment they gave her and her prognosis both depended on how it was caused, but physicians at Newton Memorial came up with nothing. After a few days, Paul McGee, M.D., an ICU doctor there, called in a consultant, Robert Morse, M.D., D.O., a young neurologist and osteopath who had been in practice just six years but was well respected in that suburban New Jersey area.

"Every means was used to save her life," Julia says. "Nine days later, Karen was transferred to the ICU at Saint Clare's Hospital, in Denville [a larger hospital, where Dr. Morse practiced]. Every available test was taken to determine the cause of her coma, but they were inconclusive or negative."

When Karen was transferred to Saint Clare's Hospital she was surrounded night and day by a bevy of health-care workers. At first Dr. Morse had hopes that Karen would come out of the coma spontaneously. Arshad Javed, M.D., a pulmonary internist and Dr. Morse's assistant, monitored her breathing on the respirator that was keeping her alive; she had IV bottles and a nasogastric feeding tube that wound through her nose to her stomach, and she was attached to a heart monitor. Nurses and doctors continually checked her vital signs.

When her body began slowly to curl inward, they sent physical therapists to work with her—stretching, massaging, even tying her limbs to boards and to the bed—to try to keep her limbs supple and straight for the day when she might revive. By the end of May 1975, Karen showed signs of severe brain damage and Dr. Morse finally told Joe and Julia that he'd classified her condition as a "persistent vegetative state" (PVS).

There are different kinds of comas—some are lighter, with a more positive prognosis than others. But the signs that Karen began showing were those of a coma so deep that the likelihood of recovery was bleak. "Karen's hands and feet were flexed; her knees and elbows were bending inward, becoming rigid and harder to move," Julia recalls. The doctors' prognosis was disheartening. Her coma was irreversible; there was no reasonable possibility of her emerging from a comatose condition to a cognitive, sapient state.

A high-protein liquid diet was pumped through the tube in her nose, a Foley catheter emptied her bladder, and intravenous fluids and antibiotics seeped into veins in her arms. A respirator helped her breathe through a tube inserted into a tracheostomy, a hole cut into her throat. Karen Ann would never again be the bubbly daughter that Julia and Joe Quinlan once knew.

M ost of us probably know that much of the story. At the time, newspaper reports attributed Karen's coma to drugs and alcohol at a wild party, rather than to a restaurant dinner with some friends. Her reputation was attacked because her two housemates, both high school friends, were male. It was a rabidly antidrug time, a time of changing cultures, and Karen became an object lesson, a warning about the damage that alleged loose living or drug use could inflict. What most of us *don't* know is that the facts don't support this theory. There are two more likely explanations.

At the restaurant, Karen reportedly drank only three gin and tonics. Though Valium was found in her purse, there were no illegal drugs in her blood or in her urine. "One lab found quinine, which used to be used to cut heroin, but it was from the tonic," says Julius Korein, M.D., a coma specialist from New York University Medical Center, who examined her at the time. He says an empty bottle of Darvon was also in her purse, but blood tests were done too late to determine how much Darvon she'd taken.

The tests did show aspirin and a barbiturate—both ingredients of Fiorinal, a common migraine medication that Karen might have been taking because of premenstrual syndrome. Although Dr. Korein testified at Karen's trial, he says he had only seen Karen's urine tests, not her blood tests at that time. He later learned these additional test results, which caused him to revise his opinion from what he'd already testified, and from what had been widely reported.

"There was no evidence of heroin, cocaine, or any of that. There was no evidence of alcohol, but we do know she was drinking," Dr. Korein says. "In the *Physicians' Desk Reference* there are big warnings not to drink with Darvon. So it was probably PMS, with her taking Darvon, Fiorinal, and Valium. That first night in the hospital, while she was in a coma, her period started. Darvon was used then for menstrual cramps, so you can assume that's what it was [for]. All that can cause a cardiac arrest and that led to a respiratory arrest."

Karen probably didn't realize the danger of mixing alcohol with these medications, most especially with Darvon. "This is not a rare occurrence," Dr. Korein says. "People have died from these Darvon-alcohol-Valium-barbiturate mixes. Darvon is not used commonly anymore, but at the time, Darvon was used commonly for pain, and these levels can be fatal."

Before Karen reached Newton Hospital, she'd had two episodes in which she'd stopped breathing for a total of fifteen minutes each before she was resuscitated with modern equipment that during the 1970s came into regular use in hospitals all over the nation. We now know that brain damage can occur after the brain has been deprived of oxygen for six minutes, but this wasn't clearly known back then. Dr. Korein surmises that lack of oxygen—the result of Karen's having no heartbeat and no breathing—caused brain damage.

But other reports indicate—even though Dr. Korein doubts them, based on the medical evidence he had—that her coma might also have been the result of an undetected injury to her brain. While Julia was stroking Karen's hair one day as she lay in her coma, she felt an egg-shaped bump on the back of her head. The New Jersey state attorney general would convene a grand jury to investigate whether she had been the victim of an assault the night she went into her coma, but the investigation was later dropped, since no evidence for this was found.

Julia says that almost two weeks before she went into the coma, Karen had hit her head, hard, when she fell down some outdoor cement steps at her house. A clot could have formed in her head that ultimately put enough pressure on her brain to cause a coma—something that is now showing up as a culprit, as diagnosis improves, in traumatic brain injury (TBI) syndromes. And, in fact, this pressure could have been progressive and mimicked the pain of migraine.

Karen was unfortunate enough to lapse into a coma during a window of time when technology could keep comatose patients alive, but when doctors did not yet have as sophisticated an understanding of TBI as they do now. CAT scans—which could have determined more reliably than the older electroencephalograms (a brain wave scan, called an EEG) what was wrong in Karen's brain—weren't in regular use until 1980. Only over the past decade have MRIs, PET, and SPECT scans appeared, all of which are commonly used today in diagnosing the causes of comas.

Doctors never figured out with absolute certainty what triggered Karen's coma, even though Dr. Korein conducted a brain autopsy, using high-tech methods, thirteen hours after she died—ten years after she went into her coma. All he could say with certainty, even after reviewing autopsy data as late as 1994—nine years after the autopsy—was that oxygen deprivation "was clearly the culprit, but what triggered it is still unknown."

During the first month of her coma, as April turned into May, Karen began having cycles of waking and sleeping within her coma. If nurses and doctors checked her for pain stimuli when she was "awake," Karen would jump as if from great pain. When the respirator pushed air down her throat, she'd grimace and sweat. When it stopped for a moment, she'd moan, even scream. Tears would stream down her face. Her eyes would be open wide, staring, darting around the room, as if there were some agony only she could see. And she began pulling her tubes out—the Foley catheter collecting her urine, the feeding tube that had also been placed down her throat. But still she seemed to see nothing and recognize no one.

Her doctors said these signs did not really mean she could feel pain or know what she was doing. They said these were primitive reflex reactions; the fact that Karen remained what physicians termed "unresponsive," even during those times when she was clearly awake, made them realize how deep Karen's coma was—and how unlikely it was that she would ever revive. These were signs that Karen's brain damage was severe.

Meanwhile, she also continued a slow physical demise. By the end of May, her limbs were becoming rigid, crimping, contorting farther into her chest. Her head started to flail sideways, back and forth, her neck craning backward as if her spine had broken. Soon, her body shrank smaller and smaller. Over the next few months, not even a year into her coma, her body wound itself into a grotesquely distorted, three-foot-long fetal ball.

Since then, medicine has improved its accuracy in prognoses for many conditions, head injury and coma among them. Medical practice has also begun to replace the technological imperative to do everything possible—just because there were things possible to do—with more sober assessment. In looking at a patient's total picture, doctors—and patients and families—have learned to assess the consequences of treatment and acknowledge that sometimes, some things are better left undone.

As a result, cardiopulmonary resuscitation is no longer used as aggressively as it was with Karen, not when it is clear that someone has been without oxygen for the length of time that she was. And faced now with the dilemma of whether someone has any chance of coming out of a coma, families would know the grim prospects for recovery with greater certainty when someone has entered a persistent vegetative state.

There is also more information about what a comatose person is experiencing. As more sophisticated neurological research has flourished, those who have recovered from coma have sometimes reported that they could hear what was going on around them, even though they could not respond. This has led nurses to be trained to speak as if the person in the bed could hear.

Some health-care professionals now suspect that those in comas can actually feel pain as well. This supposition is based on neonatal research, which discovered that infants (whose brains are as yet undeveloped) can experience pain. (For example, surgery is no longer performed on babies without using anesthesia, but it was, as late as the late 1970s and early 1980s.) This new information on pain might necessitate a reassessment of how much pain a coma patient can feel, and the efficacy of allowing someone to endure such a long-term and possibly hopeless condition.

Yet, other physicians say that none of this is true for patients in persistent vegetative states. "The very definition of PVS precludes the diagnosis in any situation in which the patient might yet have any higher cortical function," says Dr. Joanne Lynn, who had looked closely at the Quinlan case when, in the early 1980s, she served as staff medical director of a federal commission. "They are 'vegetative' only—able to breathe, maintain blood pressure, and other functions needed for mere existence, but have no thought or experience. Thus no pain. You could do an amputation or a surgery with only paralytic agents [to prevent reflexes], though few have noted that fact.

"We know in a variety of indirect ways," she says. "No responses, no electrical responses on [an] EEG, no change in blood pressure or pulse with things that ordinarily would cause pain, and autopsy or imaging findings of extensive destruction of key parts of the higher brain with preservation of the brain stem."

In 1992, Raj Narayan, M.D., a neurologist at Baylor College of Medicine in Houston, explained in an article in *The New York Times* that when a person has been in any kind of coma for a month or so following a head injury, "you can say with a high degree of certainty that this is likely to be permanent. After three months in a persistent vegetative state, the chance of regaining any function is vanishingly small." (Other neurologists say that to be safe, they might wait six months to a year before declaring such a person permanently unconscious.)

Those whose coma was caused by lack of oxygen or blood to the brain have a slightly more positive prognosis. Still, Dr. Narayan said, "three months of a persistent vegetative state gives a good indication that the coma is permanent."

Ronald Cranford, M.D., a neurologist at Hennepin County Medical Center in Minneapolis and chairman of the ethics committee of the American Academy of Neurology, told *The Times:* "If a person is in a vegetative state for two to three years, it is absolutely unthinkable that they would start recovery at that point." He knew of *no* cases where that had happened.

"Karen Quinlan would have been handled very differently today," he told me in 1996. "It still makes all the difference in the world whether the coma is caused by oxygen deprivation or trauma, but we know now that with oxygen deprivation, recovery after three months is practically zero. With trauma, the brain starts to recover later. It can get better after three to six months. But after a year, recovery is nonexistent. If there is any, the person is severely paralyzed."

Sometimes hopeful families point to miracle recoveries, such as that of Gary Dockery, a Tennessee policeman who awoke in 1996 and began speaking after spending seven and a half years in what some understood as a coma. Dockery was never in a *real* coma, medical experts say, but in what they call a "locked-in state." (Dockery has since died.) While it is admittedly rare even for someone in that state to regain consciousness, the likelihood of someone recovering from as deep a coma as Karen Quinlan was in is probably nil.

Twenty years after he first examined her, neurologist Dr. Julius Korein said that with a patient who is truly in a PVS, as Karen was, "after four or five months there may be a 1 percent chance, but there is essentially no recovery after that, assuming there was no error in the diagnosis. And [this] could go on for ten years. I think *all* treatment is extraordinary in a state like this. They should not even be turned or given antibiotics. Just left alone, and in a week they will expire. Giving *everything* is an abuse of medical technology."

For the Quinlans, seeing Karen lying there, her body twisting up, permanently unreachable yet ostensibly still alive, was unspeakable. Dr. Morse assured them that Karen couldn't feel pain "as we know it," but others who came to consult with him mused that if she could, her body was now becoming so gnarled that she would be in the most terrifying pain imaginable to a human being. Her physicians suggested she be permanently moved to a nursing home.

Slowly, wrenchingly, from mid-May through June, into July, after endless consultations with Dr. Morse and Dr. Javed, Julia—and then Joe—began talking with Father Thomas Trapasso, their parish priest, and with Father Paschal Caccavalle, the chaplain at Saint Clare's Hospital. The Quinlans were devout Roman Catholics. A statue of the Virgin Mother sat on their front lawn, and Julia worked as the secretary at Father Trapasso's church office. The Quinlans needed help with their emotional and spiritual pain and with prayer, and they also asked these priests for moral and spiritual guidance about Karen.

Both Father Trapasso and Father Caccavalle told the Quinlans the same thing: The Catholic Church has a long history of believing that while life should always be prolonged by ordinary means, one is under no moral obligation to use *extraordinary means*. This theological position harks back to the sixteenth century—practically to the beginning of medicine as a science, when questions of ethics arose over amputations—and has been reaffirmed ever since.

One such reaffirmation came in 1957 during a speech by Pope Pius XII to a conference of anesthesiologists. In cases where there is no hope for recovery, the pope said, any extraordinary medical means to preserve life might be refused if these means might cause unbearable suffering, even if that refusal was sure to result in the patient's death.

In hopeless situations like Karen's, the priests told the Quinlans, a mechanical respirator was an extraordinary kind of care. They said that the Church would consider it morally acceptable for them to ask that it be disconnected.

As Joe and Julia recalled in their 1977 book, *Karen Ann*, Father Trapasso told them: "Often a terminally ill patient, in pain or blessedly unconscious, has a disease that is being held back by a technology-designed dam. Nature is demanding death, and the dam is preventing it from happening. If you make the decision that there is no need to keep the dam in place and it is taken away, then the process of nature just takes place.

"Now, this decision is not without its moral implications," they remembered Father Trapasso as saying. "You have to ask if, by keeping the dam in place, you are allowing this person to continue to live a human life. Or is the dam retained simply because of some kind of obligation to keep the purely biological organism functioning? If that is the case, then there is no longer respect for life, for the dignity of human life."

The Quinlans reached their decision separately—tense, trying weeks apart. Julia came to it first. Then their other children—Mary Ellen, who was twenty at the time, then John, who was seventeen—and then Joe. But they all finally agreed: Karen's condition was hopeless, and though they weren't willing to ask that the doctors stop her feeding tube or her antibiotics, they would ask that Karen's respirator be turned off.

It was a box, Julia says, a machine sitting next to her by the bed, loud, noisy, so unnatural and harsh. "As a family, we were under tremendous stress," she says. "There were days when I couldn't mention Karen's name at the dinner table because our son, John, would leave the room." They wanted to let Karen find some peace, to do what was right for their daughter. But their stress was about to get worse.

O n Wednesday, July 30, 1975, Father Caccavalle, the chaplain at Saint Clare's, called a meeting, with Father Trapasso's approval. According to Paul Armstrong, who would later become the Quinlans' attorney, Dr. Morse and Dr. Javed both suggested removing Karen's respirator. The Quinlans, with the support of Father Caccavalle, officially told them they agreed. Joe said he wanted Karen to be returned to her "natural state" and then let the Lord do with her as He would. He thought it was up to God. Dr. Morse, too, was Catholic. Julia remembers that when they told him their feelings, he said only, "I think you made the right decision."

"There was nothing in the world he could do for her," Julia and Joe remembered Dr. Morse had said, "except to sustain her physically. Her brain damage, he said, was extensive and irreversible." But the next morning, Dr. Morse phoned Joe Quinlan at his Warner-Lambert Pharmaceuticals office. He said he had been thinking about it, and wanted to consult with a neurologist at Mount Sinai Medical Center in New York, who had been his professor.

On Friday, Dr. Morse called Joe again. He said he wasn't going to do it. He told Joe that he had a moral problem, that he didn't think there was sufficient moral or medical justification for such a step.

Saint Clare's was a Catholic institution; its board of directors was headed by a nun, Sister Mary Urban. It turned out that there were divisions at the hospital over theology. These divisions centered now on Karen and her respirator, but they foreshadowed the divisions that would become even more apparent all across the nation as modern medicine has altered the definitions of life and death.

Father Trapasso arranged a meeting with the hospital's administrators for Saturday. When he and the Quinlans arrived, Dr. Morse was there, and so was Theodore Einhorn, the hospital's attorney. He told the Quinlans straight out: He'd advised the hospital not to honor their wishes. He said further that because Karen was twenty-one, Joe Quinlan would have to go to court to be appointed her guardian. And, Einhorn said, he couldn't say for sure whether the hospital would honor their wishes even then.

The Quinlans were stunned. All along, Karen's doctors had consulted with them about Karen's care, asking them to sign whatever releases for treatment were needed. Now the Quinlans were told that what they had just asked for was very different; the treatments they'd approved before were aimed at *preserving* life.

Other doctors at major teaching hospitals would later testify at the Quinlans' trial that removing a respirator was a common, if covert, practice when a patient's condition was as hopeless as Karen's was, but doctors and administrators at Saint Clare's Hospital had never confronted such a situation. The only other times a respirator had been removed at Saint Clare's were when the patient was clearly brain dead, meaning that the EEG showed that the patient had no brain waves.

To save Karen, paramedics and doctors had used new, high-tech cardiopulmonary resuscitation equipment; to keep her alive they used feeding tubes and respirators. This machinery was so successful that it spared Karen physically, but the condition she was in was entirely new for this small hospital. Karen wasn't dead, nor was she really alive.

Karen still had some brain-wave activity and what physicians call "primitive brain functions." She could grimace, turn, move; her heart, kidneys, and vital organs worked. Doctors said that meant that her brain stem was working, but not her higher brain, which is responsible for consciousness, speech, reasoning. Had extraordinary means not been used to resuscitate her, had the respirator and feeding tube not been in place, Karen would clearly be dead. But now, because of this miracle-working equipment, she was in a physical state totally different from any condition the physicians at Saint Clare's were used to dealing with.

In addition to their theological qualms, the doctors and hospital administrators had fears that disconnecting the respirator of a person who was *technically* alive might constitute homicide. Nor were they sure—even though her parents had approved all of Karen's medical treatment—that parents *could* decide that it was time to remove medical treatments and thereby deliberately risk letting her die. The Quinlans felt they had no other choice but to go to court.

Since Karen was twenty-one, and since she was between jobs and not in college, she was deemed an unemployed, emancipated adult. Medicaid covered her bills and, fortunately for her family, Karen's Medicaid status also made her eligible for legal aid.

After work the next Wednesday, August 6, Joe Quinlan drove to his local Legal Aid office in Dover, New Jersey, and that's where he met thirty-year-old Paul Armstrong, now a professor at Rutgers law school. By the end of their first meeting, Armstrong had realized the significance of the case that Joe Quinlan brought him.

Over the next few weeks, he spent hour after hour in law libraries. He found that while there was case law that established a patient's right to refuse medical treatment, these cases had been argued—and won—on religious grounds, generally by those who were Christian Scientists or Jehovah's Witnesses. And while these were doctors who had been found guilty of mistreating patients, those decisions were made solely on grounds of malpractice. Only the recent U.S. Supreme Court's decision—the *Roe v. Wade* case that in 1973 legalized abortion, based on a woman's right to privacy over her own body—seemed relevant.

Then Armstrong visited Karen, and his heart was forever seared. He talked with Julia and the Quinlans' other two children, Mary Ellen and John, and he talked with his own wife, Maria. By the end of the month, he'd decided. Paul Armstrong quit his job to devote himself to the Quinlan case. He would take no fee, but it was a chance in a million—not only to help Karen, but to change U.S. constitutional law regarding the end of life.

On Friday, September 12, 1975, Armstrong filed papers at the Morris County Courthouse, the local court in suburban Morristown, New Jersey, asking that Joe Quinlan be named Karen's official guardian, with the intent of asking that all extraordinary means of medical treatment for her be stopped.

The next morning, when Julia Quinlan opened their front door to pick up the morning paper, the headline on the *Newark Star-Ledger* read: "Father Seeks the Legal Right to Let His Gravely Ill Daughter Die." And their now public tragedy began. "We were unobtrusive people, known only in our community and in our parish," Julia says, "but suddenly we had reporters from every country but Russia parked in our driveway and on our front lawn."

Pretrial hearings started on September 22, 1975, and on October 20—before Judge Robert Muir Jr.—their trial officially started. By now, Paul Armstrong had been joined by a Notre Dame college friend, thirty-three-year-old James Crowley, an attorney with the Wall Street law firm of Shearman & Sterling, which had agreed to back the case for free.

Opposing them were powerful attorneys including: Daniel Coburn, a Morristown lawyer representing Thomas Curtin, whom Judge Muir had named Karen's guardian ad litem; William Hyland, the New Jersey state attorney general, and two deputy attorneys general, David Baime and John DeCicco; Donald Collester, the Morris County prosecutor; Ralph Porzio for Drs. Morse and Javed; and Theodore Einhorn for Saint Clare's Hospital.

While the hospital's attorney said he was seeking guidelines that would protect Saint Clare's and its physicians—giving them immunity from homicide charges should they have to remove life-sustaining equipment—attorneys for the doctors (who were concerned about upholding the traditions of medical practice) and the state argued straight out that disconnecting Karen's respirator indeed was homicide. But Karen's lawyers argued that she wasn't alive as most people would define life. Physicians called to testify on Karen's condition described it like this: "If you took a child like this in the dark," one said, "and you put a flashlight in [the] back of the head, the light comes out the pupils. They have no brain." On some days Julia barely got out of the courtroom before she began sobbing.

Karen was the eldest of the Quinlan children, and the only one who had been adopted. She was also the one closest to her father, but lawyers impugned both her parents' motives, asking Joe Quinlan why he wanted to "terminate" his daughter, and implying that Joe and Julia's decision making might be poor.

That Karen had told so many people of her desire "not to suffer like that" turned out to be the crucial factor in their case. One by one, her family and her friends took the stand to testify that she had said to many people that she'd never want to be kept alive in the kind of condition she was now in.

The fact that patients have long had the right to decide their own medical treatment—based on the notion of informed patient consent—became the pivotal issue: Karen's wishes at the time when she was competent to have expressed them should now—through the words of her family and friends—substitute for her own words, her attorneys argued. The right to affirm one's own treatment choices when competent should, they said, extend equally when we are no longer consciously able to do so.

Meanwhile, the theological controversy over Karen's case had reached the Vatican. "On October 31 [1975], an official Vatican spokesman, Frederico Alessandrini, announced that the Vatican would take no official stand on the morality of disconnecting a respirator from Karen Ann Quinlan," Joe and Julia wrote in *Karen Ann*. " 'The Vatican cannot make pronouncements on individual cases of this nature,' he said.

"However, the morality of the case . . . could be decided by the local ecclesiastical jurisdiction—which, in this case, would be . . . The Most Reverend Lawrence B. Casey, Bishop of the Diocese of Paterson, New Jersey." Bishop Casey was terminally ill with cancer himself; he'd just suffered through two cancer surgeries that seemed unlikely to cure him.

"Despite his condition," *Karen Ann* read, "the seventy-year-old bishop drafted, on November 1, a lengthy and eloquent statement affirming the moral correctness of the Quinlans' request to discontinue use of the respirator 'as an extraordinary means of sustaining the life of Karen Ann Quinlan.' " He said he did not consider this euthanasia.

Bishop Casey was weak, but so strongly did he feel about this issue that he got up from his hospital bed and donned his robes to read the opinion he had written: "The decision to request discontinuance of this treatment is, according to the teachings of the Catholic Church, a morally correct decision," he proclaimed.

Judge Muir didn't agree that this theological position should have the force of law, however, and on November 10, 1975, he issued an opinion of his own: He did not believe there was a right to die. The respirator (the only piece of machinery the Quinlans really wanted to disconnect) would stay, and Joe Quinlan would no longer be Karen's official guardian. For one thing, the judge felt, this father was too emotionally involved. For another, even though Joe Quinlan was a religious person, what he wanted to do constituted homicide. Medical treatment was something only a doctor could decide.

Armstrong immediately appealed to the New Jersey Supreme

Court. Seven justices, headed by Chief Justice Richard J. Hughes, a former governor of New Jersey, weighed the testimony that had been given in Judge Muir's court. The New Jersey Catholic Conference filed an amicus brief consisting of Bishop Casey's statement that it was theologically correct for the Quinlans to request that Karen's life support equipment be rejected. "The rights and duties of the family depend on the presumed will of the unconscious patient if he or she is of legal age," Bishop Casey had said, "and the family, too, is bound to use only ordinary [not extraordinary, as in this case] means."

Judge Hughes, too, was Catholic, and in his opinion he drew extensively from the theological evidence presented, in order to understand the Quinlans' motivations. In his decision, he recognized the long legal right granted under U.S. law to act in a way that is consistent with—and guided by—one's own faith. This, in fact, is a protection guaranteed to Americans under First Amendment law, but Judge Hughes's court based its decision largely on an affirmation of our right to privacy and self-determination, even when incompetent.

On March 31, 1976, two days after Karen had turned twenty-two, the New Jersey Supreme Court unanimously reversed Judge Muir's opinion. Joe Quinlan would be Karen's guardian. Whatever he decided for his daughter would be acceptable—not unlawful, and not homicide. If the doctors thought her condition was truly hopeless, the hospital should convene an ethics committee. If the committee agreed that the prognosis was correct, Karen's medical equipment could be removed. If her own doctors did not want to do it, the Quinlans could find doctors who would.

This was an historic decision. A year after Karen went into her coma, the New Jersey State Supreme Court became the first in the nation to rule that doctors could remove all life-sustaining medical treatments.

The language of the court decision said that the Quinlans had the right to remove all the extraordinary treatments that were merely postponing Karen's death. Respirators were considered extraordinary treatments, but there was confusion about whether artificial nutrition and hydration belonged in that category.

"Karen never had what's called a feeding tube, which is inserted surgically into the stomach," Joe Quinlan told me. "She was fed through a nasogastric tube [which goes down through her nose]. Since [we thought that] Karen was not uncomfortable and it wasn't hurting her, we did not ask to have it removed."

No one thought that this mere "food deliverer" really mattered, anyway, since everyone expected Karen to die shortly after she was taken off the respirator. And she might have. But over her family's protests, Dr. Morse refused to shut it off. He procrastinated. He went to Puerto Rico for two weeks. Then, when pushed, the doctor told the Quinlans he wanted to try to *wean* Karen from the respirator, to take her off slowly. Joe says Morse patted him on the shoulder and told him to have patience and to trust him.

On Mother's Day, in May 1976, Julia took her mother out for dinner. On the way home, they stopped at Saint Clare's to visit Karen. Julia found that not only had doctors *not* been seriously trying to wean Karen from the respirator, but she had begun running a fever, and they had now put her on a body temperature control machine. No one had consulted the Quinlans; in fact, the hospital's staff members had stopped letting them look at Karen's chart or telling them what medications they were giving her.

By then, Karen had become a living skeleton, wasted from 120 to 68 pounds. "That night I thought my mother was going into shock," Julia later wrote, "not because of the machine—because it was the first time she had seen Karen without the bedclothes covering her body. . . . Mama could see what I never thought she would have to see—Karen's little figure, shrunken and twisted in a position that seems inhuman, with a blanket stuck between the legs so the bones don't cut into the flesh, and the gauze pads between her toes to keep them from bruising each other, and the bedsores that go so deep you can see the hipbone exposed. And my mother was just standing there, with her mouth open but not saying a word. That night I knew we couldn't wait any longer." Julia set a time and confronted Dr. Morse.

A federal commission that was later established to investigate end-of-life medical policies gave this astonishing report on what happened: "When, some six weeks after the New Jersey Supreme Court opinion authorizing the discontinuance of the respirator for Karen Ann Quinlan, the family asked her attending physician, Dr.

Robert J. Morse, why the respirator care was still being continued. Dr. Morse explained, 'I have tried to explain to you, I am following medical protocol.' When asked how long he would keep her on the respirator if she could not successfully be weaned, Dr. Morse replied, 'For as long as it takes. Forever.' "

The Quinlans discovered that it wasn't only Dr. Morse but the hospital administrators as well who refused to abide by the court's ruling. On May 18, 1976, Joe, Julia, and Paul Armstrong asked for a meeting. This time, Sister Mary Urban, the president of Saint Clare's board of trustees, came. " 'Speaking on behalf of the Board of Trustees of Saint Clare's—twenty-one people, and I know how each of them feels about this,' " Joe Quinlan later wrote that she told them, " 'I would like to say that we are a small community hospital, and we feel that it is morally incorrect.' "

Joe asked whether she'd seen the bishop's pronouncement. " 'I read Bishop Casey's statement,' " he says that she had said. " 'But there are other bishops in the Church who disagree with him. . . . You have to understand our position, Mr. Quinlan. In this hospital we don't kill people.' "

The fight had exhausted the family, Paul Armstrong says. They could have simply taken Karen to another hospital or fired Dr. Morse. In fact, at that point they threatened to. Armstrong had already gathered a team of doctors, led by a neurologist who would have supervised the respirator's removal. But instead, Julia and Joe wanted to reach a compromise. They agreed to let Dr. Morse try *seriously*—as he said he now would—to remove the respirator slowly.

From March 31, 1976, when the court's decision came down, until then, he had slowly, inch by inch, let Karen spend some time off her respirator. But he was weaning her in the way doctors would wean someone put on a respirator only temporarily—for instance, to get over a severe bout of pneumonia. Now he told them the truth: Whenever he had found that Karen wasn't able to breathe on her own without the respirator, he would neither take out the breathing tube nor turn the respirator off. Since they had started protesting, he had taken her off for some hours at a time. Now he upped those hours.

On May 22 the respirator was finally turned off, but Karen "miraculously"—still comatose—continued to breathe on her own. Doctors later surmised that she could breathe because swelling to the brain stem—which controls breathing—had only temporarily disabled her respiratory system until the swelling went down. But, they said, the injury to her higher-brain functions was permanent. She would never come out of her coma.

"The doctor didn't want to remove [the respirator at all but] if he had done what the court said," Armstrong says, "Karen would have had a more peaceful death." Meaning, if Dr. Morse had removed the respirator abruptly, as the family expected him to, Karen would have died. Instead, after the careful, slow weaning process, she was merely at the beginning of her ordeal.

K aren had stayed at Saint Clare's Hospital for thirteen months. She was now transferred—comatose, feeding tube still in place—to the Morris View Nursing Home in rural Morris Plains, to a room painted sunny yellow. The Quinlans had a steel security door installed in front of her door to keep out streams of faith healers and gawkers. One tabloid allegedly had a standing offer of more than $100,000 for a photo of Karen in her bed.

Sometimes she'd gag and have seizures. Sometimes she'd sweat, racked with fevers. They came from infections: from the catheter, the tube going into her stomach, from lying in bed, from pneumonias. She had wake and sleep cycles. Her eyes would stare; she'd often moan or grimace. Sometimes it seemed as if she could follow voices, looking right or left as people spoke. But Karen recognized no one, said nothing. Her body was now so horribly, torturously twisted that if, by some chance, she could feel anything, doctors continued to say that the pain would be intolerable.

"Karen was in limbo, and we were in limbo," Julia says. Each day, for all of the nine years, Julia visited her daughter after her work at the church. Joe would visit twice a day, morning and night. Mornings, he'd awaken at 5:30 A.M., drive forty minutes to see her, play her the radio, kiss her, talk to her. Then he'd go to his job at Warner-Lambert Pharmaceuticals. If Karen had a good day, Joe had a good day. But if she seemed miserable, it would ruin his day, too. She definitely had good days and bad days.

Sometimes she gagged on her liquid diet. She'd grimace and show discomfort at each sign of fever. She was no longer on antibiotics, though; doctors put only aspirin into her feeding tube when she got infections. At her bedside, the Quinlans would pray, asking God to perform a miracle or help Karen finally let go.

However, even if the law had allowed their daughter's feeding tube to be removed (and the New Jersey Supreme Court did not make this right explicit until 1985), the Quinlans wouldn't have done it. And in fact, the matter was controversial: Whether it is moral to remove a feeding tube would trigger heated discussion within the Church throughout the eighties.

In 1992, the Committee for Pro-Life Activities of the National Conference of Catholic Bishops finally issued its definitive paper, "Nutrition and Hydration: Moral and Pastoral Reflections," that stated that artificial nutrition and hydration can—like any other medical treatment—constitute extraordinary treatment if a person is in a condition that is either hopeless or causing intolerable suffering. By then, the Church had also begun to change its language; instead of talking in terms of *extraordinary treatments,* it now talked about deciding when the *burdens* of a treatment might outweigh its *benefits.*

When I interviewed him on this subject in the spring of 1996, Richard Doerflinger, assistant director for policy development of the National Conference of Catholic Bishops' Secretariat for Pro-Life Activities, in Washington, D.C., defined the Church's position in this way:

"We all have an obligation to make reasonable efforts to preserve life and health, but no one is obliged to accept a treatment that would have more burdens than benefits. This includes pain, suffering, and expense, for patients as well as for families. You never take life, but we are not called on to preserve life by every means possible. There are limits beyond which people are not asked to go in preserving life over death."

Decisions like this, he said, cannot be made by edict; individual situations must be mulled over one by one by one. Doerflinger suggested these decisions must be shared by patients, their families, their doctors, and their God.

But the question of whose burden should be given the greatest weight—the patient's or the family's—remains complex. That is a matter for prayer, a matter for each person and family member to search out in his or her own heart, to find a moral solution, to make his or her own peace with God. Still, Doerflinger pointed out that the Church has become worried about terms like *quality of life,* which sound as if they might lead to judgments about when particular patients' lives are not worth preserving. Fear of such judgments has led some in the Church toward efforts to protect people who are physically or intellectually disabled or impaired, or who become so after some illness or accident.

"It's a matter of intent," Doerflinger said, distancing the official pro-life arm of the Church from more conservative groups like the National Right to Life Committee. "Withdrawal of treatment should not be to *cause* death, but to relieve excessive burden."

According to Church teachings, it is permissible to fail to treat, even though a patient may die as a result, so long as the intent is to help ease severe pain or suffering and not specifically to end life. In religious terms, that's a moral point at which prayer is needed. And defining that point has also been the intent of the past twenty years of medical ethics and end-of-life law.

During their legal struggle, public sympathy for the Quinlans was tremendous. Responding to concern over Karen's case, Congress passed legislation, signed by President Jimmy Carter, for the landmark President's Commission for the Study of Ethical Problems in Medicine and Biomedical and Behavioral Research. Civil rights attorney Morris B. Abram, M.A., J.D., L.L.D., was appointed the commission's chairman. Dr. Joanne Lynn became the staff medical director.

The commission began its work in 1979. In a little more than three years, it made crucial recommendations—in a series of ten reports—on how law, medicine, and ethics should deal with what science had wrought, not only at the end of life but in medical research, in health care, and in genetic counseling. It began with the issues that Karen's case had raised.

As late as 1968, the definition of death was considered to be the cessation of heart, lung, and respiratory functions. That year, however, in light of medical and technological advances—including the emerging possibilities for organ transplants—an ad hoc committee at Harvard University suggested redefining death as the cessation of all brain functions. But this definition did not yet have any legal weight.

In 1977, individual states began adopting statutes that supplemented cessation of heart, respiration, and lung functions—as defined by the Harvard ad hoc committee—with whole-brain death as the legal definition of death.

In 1981, the President's Commission proposed a uniform state law that would officially expand the medical and legal definition of death from only *the cessation of heartbeat and breathing*—which could now be maintained unnaturally with life-sustaining equipment—to *the cessation of whole-brain function* as an alternative (meaning a flat line on an EEG and the body's inability to carry on basic brain-stem functions, such as digestion). Even under this new standard, Karen, lying helpless and unresponsive in her bed, was officially alive, since her brain stem still worked. But at least this new alternate definition acknowledged that medical technology had made the old definition of death outmoded.

Slowly, state by state, the commission's recommendations were adopted into law, until both the cessation of heart and lung functions or the cessation of whole-brain function became the two alternative national definitions of death. Aside from the plight that Karen and other long-term coma victims found themselves in, the change in definition was prompted also by the ethical and moral dilemmas that had suddenly arisen from medicine's ability to use the organs of dying people for transplants. (These organs had to somehow be kept "alive" long enough to be safely reused, even though their donors—in whose bodies they might still reside— were officially "dead.") The invention of ever more sophisticated equipment that could measure brain function made such a change in definition possible.

Today there is vehement debate about whether even this most recent definition is good enough. Some experts believe that "death" should be narrowed from "brain death" to "death of higher brain functions." That is controversial, particularly for those groups concerned with the disabled, but the effort is largely because more is now known about the poor prognoses of those in long-term comas.

Between 1975, when Karen went into her coma, and 1981, when the President's Commission first reported, CAT scans, MRIs, and other sophisticated diagnostic tools let doctors determine which portion of the brain was damaged, make better distinctions between brain injuries caused by accidents or traumas and those caused solely by lack of oxygen, and develop more accurate predictions of patients' likelihood for recovery.

In 1983, the commission released its most important report, *Deciding to Forego Life-Sustaining Treatment,* based on its own extensive hearings. The report broke new policymaking ground by recommending that artificial nutrition and hydration, respirators, antibiotics, kidney dialysis, and blood transfusions *all* be considered medical treatments that could be removed (or refused) as long as the patient's condition was hopeless and the patient—or someone speaking for him if he could not speak for himself—had requested it. (Doctors had pointed out that when a feeding tube or an IV is removed, or when kidney dialysis is stopped, death is not, in fact, horrible or painful. Indeed, if it is well managed, it can be far more peaceful than if those tubes were left in. The body slowly shuts down, putting itself into a natural, self-anesthetizing sleep.)

"The commission decided," Dr. Lynn says, "that artificial nutrition and hydration were the same as any other medical treatment." Rather than view certain treatments as "extraordinary," it decided to weigh any medical treatment in terms of whether its continued benefit to the patient outweighed its burdens—the same position that the Roman Catholic Church was to take in 1992. When the burdens begin outweighing the benefits, Dr. Lynn says, the commission recommended that treatment should stop. It also recommended that only a patient—or someone close who is speaking for him or her—can really know when that point has been reached.

These recommendations helped doctors, patients, and families clarify the appropriateness of procedures like turning off a respirator—procedures that could have helped Dr. Morse help Karen die sooner. "Weaning a permanently unconscious patient from a respirator when death is an acceptable outcome [as in Karen's case]," the report read, "might well be done rather differently for patients for whom survival is of paramount importance."

For instance, the commission report noted, patients who might be on a respirator only to get through a medical crisis—such as severe pneumonia—would be weaned from it slowly and carefully until they were able to breathe normally on their own. But for patients in irreversible comas like Karen's—patients who would never be able to return to a normal, conscious state—a respirator might be quickly removed. (Morphine can be used to calm any distress as death comes.) And when the patient died, her doctors need not fear legal reprisals. Dr. Morse withdrew Karen's respirator the way a doctor would wean a patient who would get well, who could be expected to return to a healthy state, instead of doing it in the manner that was appropriate for someone whose condition was as hopeless as hers was.

Courts considered the recommendations made in *Deciding to Forego Life-Sustaining Treatment* so significant that those ideas have been cited in court cases and used as the basis of legislation on advance directives ever since. Indeed, those recommendations are now part of the legal, medical, and ethical consensus under which doctors all around the country practice today.

But they weren't set anywhere into law until 1985, two years after the final President's Commission report appeared. That year, Paul Armstrong again went before the New Jersey Supreme Court to argue yet another landmark case. The family of a permanently comatose nursing-home patient, eighty-four-year-old Claire Conroy, wanted to remove her feeding tube. By then, attitudes had so changed that the President's Commission entered a brief recommending that the court approve removing the tube, as did the Catholic Conference. In January 1985, the New Jersey court agreed. It decided there was no difference between ordinary and extraordinary medical treatments, *including* artificial nutrition and hydration. These, like any other medical treatment, could legally be removed.

Just after the New Jersey Supreme Court ruling in the Conroy case, Karen's condition changed dramatically for the worse. During the ten years she was in a coma, she'd successfully battled infection after infection. And she did this without antibiotics, which the Quinlans had eventually decided should also be removed. But in the months after the court decision, her infections became more frequent, and things began to look bleak.

Karen got pneumonia. Then on June 9, 1985, she went into

shock. Her family, Father Trapasso, and Paul Armstrong gathered at Morris View Nursing Home, inside her locked gate in her sunny yellow room, and prayed. On June 11, 1985, as Julia wept and held her, as Joe, Mary Ellen, and John all cried, thirty-one-year-old Karen Ann Quinlan gasped for air. And she finally died.

Karen had held on for a decade, until New Jersey's law on all end-of-life medical treatments had been completely changed. "After Karen died, I realized her life had meaning far beyond what she or I could have imagined," Julia says. "She helped to break the lock of technology on the medical world. Before her case, people didn't know they had the right to refuse treatment. Now we all have the right to die in peace and dignity."

In 1980, using $50,000 they had received from their book, *Karen Ann*, and from a made-for-TV movie based on that book, Julia and Joe established a hospice in Karen's name to provide the kind of humane care at the end of life that the Quinlans—and Karen—would have wanted.

About a decade later, Joe Quinlan became ill with bone cancer. In the fall of 1996, he was hospitalized for treatment for the last time, then discharged in October, and returned home to Wantage, New Jersey, where the Quinlans had since moved. Staff from the Karen Ann Quinlan Hospice of Hope helped care for Joe until December 7, 1996, when he died.

Joe was then seventy-one, and the hospice he and Julia had founded served about four hundred families in Sussex and Warren counties in northwestern New Jersey and Pike County in eastern Pennsylvania. He and Julia had remained cochairmen of the hospice, actively guiding its growth for more than fifteen years.

"They believed in the right of people to die with dignity in their homes, surrounded by the people they loved," Pamela Olivo, acting executive director of the hospice, told *The New York Times*. Paul Armstrong, the family's lawyer, described Joe as a man of "deep faith, quiet countenance and principled courage."

By the time he was hospitalized, Joe had signed a living will—largely the result of laws passed in response to Karen's case—making sure to stipulate that if he was in a situation that was hopeless, he definitely didn't want any life-sustaining equipment, including even a feeding tube. And he didn't—thanks to his own courage in fighting for Karen and his work in establishing the hospice where he himself died.

The Quinlans' heart-wrenching situation—and that of many other families like them—inspired two decades of court cases, as well as state, federal, and local laws attempting to protect others from what they went through. Yet, sadly, these laws are in such disarray today—so checkered about what they mean and when they apply, so underused, or so poorly recognized—that families can still find themselves in the Quinlans' predicament with Karen.

Doctors don't always listen to patients' and families' wishes. End-of-life policies are implemented differently state by state, hospital by hospital, doctor by doctor, person by person. And because of the way medicine has changed both our living and our dying—and in so short a time—the kinds of decisions that need to be made aren't always addressed by the wording and format of the existing laws.

The issue still is: Who has the right to decide the way we die? We ourselves? Our families? The courts? Doctors? Hospital administrators? And how—and when—can those decisions best come into play? Where the power lies—and whether our wishes are therefore heeded—can still spell the difference between a good death and a prolonged, end-of-life ordeal.

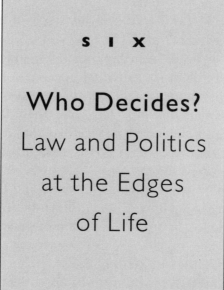

SIX

Who Decides?
Law and Politics at the Edges of Life

On Monday, December 17, 1990, Joe Foreman stood at the blackboard of a Sunday school classroom in rural, southwestern Lawrence County, Missouri. Foreman, a Presbyterian minister from Atlanta, was a minister without an official parish, but he was also a founder of the militant antiabortion group Operation Rescue.

Nearby was the hospital where thirty-three-year-old Nancy Beth Cruzan lay dying. With a fat piece of yellow chalk, Foreman drew diagrams of the hospital's entrances and hallways and rooms, strategizing, with the Operation Rescue veterans who kept arriving, a way to rescue Nancy.

Lester ("Joe") and Joyce Cruzan, Nancy's parents, and Chris, her elder sister, were camped out with her on a second-floor wing, in a private hospice room of the Missouri Rehabilitation Center, in the tiny town of Mount Vernon. Its population was a mere 3,400, so small that the first stoplights had been installed only the previous summer. But as the Cruzans took turns sitting with Nancy in her flower-wallpapered room, members of the national and international news media gathered outside her window. So did a highly vocal group of about a hundred right-to-life partisans, with Foreman as their leader.

A lot had changed in the fifteen years since Karen Ann Quinlan had gone into a coma similar to the one Nancy Cruzan was now in. The historic decision in the Quinlan case had shifted medical thinking and public opinion on end-of-life care and created important legal precedents. But that was only a local, New Jersey decision, not the law of the land. The spring before this crowd had gathered, Nancy Cruzan's case was decided by the U.S. Supreme Court, the first end-of-life case to have reached that highest federal level.

In the early hours of the morning on January 11, 1983, Nancy was driving home along Elm Road—an icy, two-lane country road southeast of Carthage—after working her late-night shift at the local cheese factory. Her old Nash Rambler must have gone out of control. State troopers found her lying facedown—injured, unconscious, and not breathing—in a ditch on the side of the road, thrown about 35 feet from her overturned car.

The first trooper to arrive thought Nancy was dead, but the paramedics who arrived next used CPR, got her heart beating, and started her breathing. They took her by ambulance to Freeman Hospital in nearby Joplin, where—according to medical records cited in the Supreme Court decision—admitting physicians noted that she was unconscious, with a lacerated liver, and an attending neurosurgeon diagnosed her "as having sustained probable cerebral contusions compounded by significant . . . lack of oxygen." Permanent brain damage, the court records note, generally results after six minutes without oxygen. Estimates were that Nancy had stopped breathing for some twelve to fourteen minutes.

Nancy was put on IVs. Several weeks later, on February 5, 1983, doctors surgically inserted a feeding tube (the procedure is called a gastrostomy) directly into her stomach through incisions in her abdominal wall. This was a far more sophisticated—and far more invasive—feeding machine than Karen Ann Quinlan had. Nancy's family had approved, wanting to do everything possible.

At first, there was hope. But, about three weeks later, when Nancy awoke from her sleep-state coma, doctors discovered that although she was physically awake, she was still cognitively unconscious and unaware. With that neurologically grim finding, her prognosis started to dim.

On October 19, 1983, after having been moved to two other hospitals for rehabilitation and even taken back home for a while, Nancy was transferred to the state-run Missouri Rehabilitation Center, a facility skilled in the long-term care of patients on feeding tubes and respirators. Nancy didn't need a respirator, but the feeding tube had to continue to pump artificial food and fluids directly into her stomach for her to survive. The formula needed to be experimented with to avoid gastrointestinal problems, and she required careful, highly skilled, daily monitoring. Done properly, doctors said, Nancy might live this way for another thirty years.

Like the Quinlans, the Cruzans—who were Methodists—hung on, praying for a miracle. But as Nancy's body bloated, as her eyes moved randomly around the room, open but not registering anything, as her limbs contorted and shriveled—as Karen's had—she also suffered seizures, bleeding gums, vomiting, and diarrhea.

"It took us three and a half years until we realized Nan's medical condition and how she wasn't going to get better," her sister, Chris, told me in October 1996. "Dad did a lot of reading and diagnosed it himself at first. At the beginning the health-care providers said, 'Try to get her to respond. Do everything.' So we did. Until we realized she *wasn't* going to get better. Then it was a matter of whether we would go on with this, allowing medical technology to maintain her, or let her go. Nan was independent, a fighter. She would not have wanted to be maintained."

By the middle of 1986, the Cruzans were finally given words for what they saw: Nancy was in a permanent, persistent vegetative state and would never recover. Four years after the accident, her parents came to a joint and painful decision—they asked the Missouri Rehabilitation Center staff to unhook Nancy's feeding tube. The center refused, its staff fearful they might be liable for murder. On October 13, 1987, the Cruzans took their request to court.

According to Donald Lamkins, director of the rehabilitation center at the time, Nancy was on Medicaid. The reimbursement regulations had recently changed, forcing him to tell the Cruzans that Nancy would have to be transferred to a nursing home, where there was less skilled care, because she was not being actively treated. "Joe said, 'No,' " Lamkins recalls. "He didn't think they'd take care of her as well as we would, which was probably true. I talked to Joe and Joyce several times and they were trying to figure out what to do.

"At the time," he says, "two doctors in California were charged with murder for taking a feeding tube out. They weren't convicted in the end but they were going through charges of murder. Well, I didn't want to stand trial for murder." Lamkins was also a devout member of the Church of Christ and opposed to removal of the tube on religious grounds.

At the time Missouri had no state law on the removal of feeding tubes. Like Karen, Nancy had told many relatives and friends that she would never have wanted to live if she "were a vegetable," but she had not put her wishes in writing.

The Cruzans contacted the American Civil Liberties Union (ACLU), which in turn referred them to William Colby, a young attorney working for a large Kansas City law firm and able to take on their case for free. Colby had at first argued with the nursing home that Nancy had constitutional rights to liberty and privacy, and the right—through her parents—to refuse unwanted medical treatment. When the rehabilitation center, including the physician directly caring for Nancy, still disagreed, Colby made the same argument in court.

The court appointed a guardian ad litem for Nancy to represent her interests separate from her parents, and to assess her medical and family situation, talking with her family and her friends. The guardian agreed with her parents that Nancy would have wanted the tube removed, so on July 27, 1988, Jasper County Probate Judge Charles Teel granted permission.

However, the rehabilitation center staff stalled. "It was agreed before the trial started," Lamkins says, "that whoever lost would appeal all the way to the state supreme court to make a really solid opinion. My personal opinion is that Joe got tied up in this thing. He liked the attention, but he also thought Nancy would want him to do this to help other people in her situation. By that time he'd met many others, and there was no law on this at all."

In fact, it was not Joe Cruzan but the state-appointed guardian ad litem who had said he would appeal to the state level—whoever won or lost—to clarify the law. "We had no desire to appeal after we won," Colby says, but the Missouri State Supreme Court "pulled up" the case from the trial court, allowing it to skip one court level. And on August 3, Missouri Attorney General William Webster filed notice that the state would oppose the Cruzans.

On November 16, the Missouri Supreme Court decided by a close vote of four to three to reverse the lower court's decision, and barred removal of Nancy's feeding tube. It cited the state's overriding interest in the protection of life, and set the most restrictive standards in the nation (only the state of New York had comparable rules), requiring "clear and convincing evidence" that refusal of medical treatment was what a patient who was not able to say so herself would have wanted. The Cruzan family was devastated. It had been nearly six years since Nancy went into her irreversible coma.

Unbeknownst to them, when the Cruzans found themselves at odds with the staff at the Missouri Rehabilitation Center and then with the state, they would also become the focus of a far greater and more organized opposition than the Quinlans had ever faced.

Whereas the Quinlans' local bishop had come to the Quinlans' defense—New Jersey's Bishop Casey even filed amicus briefs on their behalf in court—by the time the Cruzans began their fight, the pro-life arm of the Catholic Church had become more forceful in its opposition to the removal of life support. The Cruzans were also opposed not just by the rehabilitation center and by the Missouri state health department—which ran it—but by a newly potent, highly organized right-to-life campaign.

After the U.S. Supreme Court legalized abortion in 1973, the state committees that had been battling abortion on the grassroots level—many of them in connection with local churches and the pro-life arm of the states' Catholic conferences—joined on a national level to create the National Right to Life Committee, Inc. Its first mission statement, published in 1973, included opposition not only to legalized abortion but also to infanticide and euthanasia—which is what it considered the removal of a feeding tube to be.

"There's a link between the two," says Laura Echevarria, current deputy press secretary of the National Right to Life Committee. "Once you start discriminating against one human being—like an unborn child in the womb—you're open to discriminating against another. For the most part, society recognizes that a newborn is a human being, but because of the location, an unborn child isn't. Once you start doing that, with that kind of mindset, it leads to classifying people as not quite human. That can then include the disabled or the terminally ill."

Many other groups proliferated in the pro-life movement, Operation Rescue among them. Less visible in the national media have been the state-by-state political and legal campaigns, the best organized of which was at high tide in Missouri at the time of the Cruzan case.

Bill Webster, the Republican state attorney general, was the son of Missouri's undisputed kingmaker and power broker, Richard "Dick" Webster, whose ability to raise money on his son's behalf had set a new spending record in 1980 when young Bill was elected to the Missouri House of Representatives. Four years later, at age thirty-one, Bill Webster became the youngest attorney general in the United States and a leading voice in local conservative politics.

During the Reagan years, conservative Republicans held most of the executive branch offices in Missouri, including the governorship, having taken it from the largely Democratic majority based in the big cities of St. Louis and Kansas City. Bill Webster made aggressive use of his office to challenge liberal and pro-choice forces on many fronts—including school desegregation, abortion, and end-of-life law.

He reached his pinnacle in 1989 when, at the age of thirty-six, he argued and won the famous abortion case, *Webster v. Reproductive Health Services,* before the U.S. Supreme Court. It allowed states to impose restrictions on abortions, upholding a 1986 Missouri antiabortion statute, part of which prohibits use of public facilities and employees for performing abortions, but stopped just short of overturning *Roe v. Wade.* Webster's win over abortion advocates made him a rising star in the Republican national party, a position he clearly expected to consolidate in taking on the Cruzan case.

Another major player in both the Webster and Cruzan cases was attorney James Bopp Jr., general counsel of the National Right to Life Committee, Inc., and the founder in 1984 of the National Legal Center for the Medically Dependent and Disabled, with headquarters in Terre Haute, Indiana. The center received federal legal services Legal Aid funds from its beginning until the mid-1990s, when they were lost to congressional budget cuts, and has been involved in every major end-of-life case since its founding.

According to a 1996 mission statement, the center has aimed to "coordinate a nationwide campaign to thwart the legalization of assisted suicide and euthanasia [meaning withdrawal of life-sustaining treatment as well as any more active steps] through an aggressive and strategic plan involving litigation, legislative support, and the provision of technical support and resources." It prides itself on being "the only law firm that has been directly involved in the fight against assisted suicide, euthanasia, and similar efforts on a full-time, coordinated basis over the past decade."

While other groups representing the disabled claim that there is a cataclysmic difference between a disability and a persistent vegetative state, Bopp's group claimed that removing a feeding tube from a comatose woman such as Nancy was discrimination against the handicapped.

Many of the disabled fear government sanctions that would allow decreased treatment, especially based on criteria such as perceived "quality of life" and apparent "hopelessness" at what might or might not be the end of life. Their fears grow more profound as issues of costs are raised in connection with the kind of higher-intensity care those who are disabled often require.

Pro-choice proponents pointed out not only Nancy's hopeless condition but also the fact that her care cost taxpayers $130,000 a year. Nancy's condition was arguably not strictly terminal. The fact that she might not have wanted to live in the twilight zone in which she was living gave no comfort to those who are disabled and might not make a similar choice, and who feared that the choice was being made for them.

On behalf of the National Right to Life Committee, Bopp had filed legal briefs in nearly all of the major antiabortion cases since

1979. These included cases for fathers' and husbands' rights to prevent women and teens from having abortions, and cases against research involving the use of fetal tissue, even if that research might eventually be used to treat people suffering with progressive illnesses such as Parkinson's and Alzheimer's.

With Nancy Cruzan, this right-to-life campaign took a new and larger direction. As Nancy's case went from the lower trial court to the Missouri State Supreme Court, Bopp's group and other attorneys and supporters of the National Right to Life Committee and the United States Catholic Conference filed numbers of amicus briefs opposing the Cruzans throughout their struggle, some even attempting (unsuccessfully) to substitute their own members for Nancy's parents as her guardians.

The Cruzans found themselves in the midst of a nightmare, bereft at losing their daughter, yet having to fight bitterly even to allow her to die. Shocked and desperate after the Missouri Supreme Court overturned the lower court's ruling by just one vote, they finally appealed to the U.S. Supreme Court. On July 3, 1989, the same day the Supreme Court handed down its decision on *Webster v. Reproductive Health Services,* it also decided—against great odds—to hear the Cruzan case.

In all, more than fifty briefs were filed. National Right to Life and the United States Catholic Conference were among the opponents. On the Cruzans' side, amicus briefs were filed by the ACLU and the Society for the Right to Die, the American Medical Association, the American Hospital Association, and other medical and religious groups.

"I feel like a spectator," Joe Cruzan despairingly told a TV reporter from *Frontline* at the time, "like I'm sitting up in the bleachers in the poorest seats and two other teams are playing on the field, playing with my football, and there's not a darn thing I can do."

On June 25, 1990, the U.S. Supreme Court issued its historic, first right-to-die decision when it decided on the Cruzans' case. While the decision was immediately claimed as a victory by both sides, it was also a close vote (five to four), and it was limited in scope. The majority opinion, delivered by Chief Justice William

H. Rehnquist, was joined by Justices Byron R. White, Sandra Day O'Connor, Antonin Scalia, and Anthony M. Kennedy, but O'Connor and Scalia also each filed concurring but different opinions of their own.

Justice William J. Brennan Jr. filed a dissenting opinion, joined by Justices Thurgood Marshall and Harry A. Blackmun who had written the historic *Roe v. Wade* decision. Justice John Paul Stevens III, who was also opposed, filed yet another dissenting opinion. All or any of these opinions could be drawn upon for legal precedent in future cases.

Contrary to popular impression, the court refused to rule on whether Nancy's feeding tube should be withdrawn; the majority opinion simply affirmed the right of a patient to refuse unwanted medical treatment, including life-sustaining equipment like a feeding tube, while not labeling it a "fundamental liberty." It also supported the strict ruling of the Missouri Supreme Court that required "clear and convincing evidence" that this is what Nancy herself would have wanted, and said that Missouri could deny Nancy's parents or guardians the right to "substitute" their judgment for hers.

The dissenting opinions argued that refusal of such treatment was, indeed, a fundamental liberty, that the state of Missouri's ruling erred on the side of the "presumption of life," overriding whether the person living would have wanted such a life. They held that such a strict position did in fact deprive Nancy of exercising her rights and was therefore unconstitutional.

In effect, the majority decision simply threw the case back to the original Missouri state court to determine whether there was "clear and convincing evidence" that Nancy would want to refuse her feeding tube.

Five months later, three of Nancy's friends told Judge Teel's Jasper County court about conversations in which she explicitly said she never would want to live "like a vegetable" on medical machines. By then, her own doctor from the Missouri Rehabilitation Center, James C. Davis, M.D., who had opposed removing the tube three years before, testified that he thought it best to remove it now to end her "living hell." Nancy's court-appointed guardian ad litem agreed.

This time, the state did not argue, dropping out of the legal battle and, according to Lamkins, leaving the Missouri Rehabilitation Center without an attorney to represent it. "Bill Webster pulled some strings," Lamkins charges, "and got the state out of the case. He said the state no longer had any concern in it. I think he was afraid it would cost him votes since he was getting ready to run for governor. So when this went back to court, *nobody* represented us. The only attorneys in that court were Bill Colby, the Cruzans' attorney, and the guardian ad litem's. With those witnesses there wasn't even any cross-examination. I was in court, but I didn't even get to speak. How did it happen? Politics was involved. That's the way it works."

About a dozen right-to-life protesters staged a sit-in in Webster's office during the week that Nancy lay dying. "We're going to basically beg Webster to intervene for this woman," Randall Terry, a founder of Operation Rescue, told reporters. "I am outraged that he has not intervened. I have to ask myself, Do we have just another political opportunist here or do we have a true pro-lifer?"

In fact, the fortunes of Bill Webster had begun to turn sharply downward just before the Supreme Court's decision in the Cruzan case. Dick Webster died suddenly in March 1990, just three months before the court delivered its opinion. The younger Webster did end up running for governor in 1992, but he was defeated amid a campaign rocked by public exposés and scandal. A year later, he pled guilty to two federal charges of corruption, one for conspiracy and the other for embezzlement of public resources, and was sentenced to two years in federal prison, stripped not only of his license to practice law but also, as a convicted felon, of his voting rights.

On Friday afternoon, December 14, 1990, Judge Teel approved removal of Nancy's tube. After a three-year battle, the Cruzans had finally won the sad and dubious right to watch their daughter die. Doctors said that without her feeding tube, it would take about two weeks. At 2:30 P.M. that afternoon, the rehabilitation center finally, if reluctantly, took it out. And, that's also when Rev. Joe Foreman—and others in this gathering right-to-life storm—heard the news.

That day, Joe and Anne Foreman and their five children were driving from Des Moines to Denver in the 1985 two-tone Chevy van where they mostly lived. They doubled back and arrived in Mount Vernon on Sunday, December 16.

Before dawn on Monday, according to the *Washington Post*, some fifteen to twenty others had joined them—coming in mini-vans, with sleeping bags and tents and children in tow. By that afternoon, the group had not only transformed the Sunday school classroom into a war room, but they'd set up domestic headquarters at the Bel Aire Motel out on the main highway strip and organized a prayer vigil in front of the rehabilitation center. By afternoon, they were a hundred strong. That Monday, as well, right-to-life lawyers got to work, filing state and federal court injunctions with the state trial court, requesting that Nancy's feeding tube be reattached.

Two months before he came to Missouri, Joe Foreman had been in jail for five months, for trying to close down an abortion clinic in Atlanta. But things had become so polarized by the time the Foremans arrived in Mount Vernon that they'd stopped putting bumper stickers on their van because, as he told the *Washington Post*, "people tend to bash out your windows." Instead, they used a portable sign in their rear window that read ABORTION KILLS CHILDREN.

The Foremans now arrived with new signs saying things like: HOW WOULD YOU LIKE TO BE STARVED TO DEATH? and WHILE AMER FILLS THEIR GUTS ON AND BEFORE XMAS, NANCY LYES STARVED AND DEHYDRATED. They called this new campaign *antieuthanasia*. "The reason we hit this," Joe Foreman explained, "is because it's the next big step."

Wanda and Eugene Frye also arrived in Mount Vernon that Monday, coming by bus from Kansas City with abortion clinic arrest records of their own. Wanda was a licensed practical nurse. "We have a way of knowing when these things happen," she told me in 1997. "People who work in hospitals, doctors, nurses, they let us know. When we came down we had drawings of the place, blueprints of the hospital."

"We needed to find out just where Nancy was in the hospital," Foreman later told a reporter from the *Los Angeles Times*. "There were five or six scenarios. Somebody could go in and apply for a job. Or we could go in as gawking tourists and say something like, 'Is this the place they're gonna kill that girl?' Or we could go in as Christmas carolers. What we finally settled on was to have a couple go buy a poinsettia and take it in for the Cruzans."

Wanda told the group assembled at the church, however, that as soon as they found Nancy's room she could just push a feeding tube through her nose and into her stomach. That way, they could start feeding the comatose woman themselves. "I've dropped quite a few tubes," she'd said, "and I've never run into one I couldn't do."

Others agreed that *this* was just the right plan. All they had to do was find the room, then the men would block the doors while Wanda got to work. "God willing," she said, "then I'll drop a tube down her."

There was only one problem: If Wanda was nervous, if she jiggled, Nancy might have serious complications; in fact, she might even choke. "We decided that if the family was there and created a fuss," she later said, "we were simply going to step out in the hall and pray silently and abandon the force-feeding."

The next day, Tuesday, December 18, they put Wanda's plan into action, skipping the poinsettia delivery. According to Nancy's sister, Chris, "they faxed the media and the hospital saying they were going to storm the hospital." Lamkins says reporters' calls alerted him. Either way, the police and state troopers were there, already prepared.

Around nine in the morning, Lamkins was looking out his office window when a bus pulled up outside the hospital. Foreman, the Fryes, and some twenty-five others marched up to the hospital, through its back door, and up the stairwell to the second floor.

Wanda was wearing her nurse's uniform, with a stethoscope draped around her neck. The feeding tube peeked out of one of her pockets. Meanwhile, outside, amid the snow and cold, the prayer vigil heated up. Some protesters wore ski masks as they chanted loudly for feeding to resume for Nancy, "In the name of Jesus!"

The news media had gathered outside, and the *Frontline* reporters, the only ones inside with the Cruzans, had their cameras rolling. As the group ran up a back stairwell and neared Nancy's room at the end of a hallway, the state troopers stood guard at her door. Lamkins asked the protesters to leave, but they pushed past him. The hospital's chaplain stepped forward to meet them, suggesting they convene in the chapel. Realizing they'd never get into her room, some did move off to the chapel. But others used the tactics of civil disobedience—they dropped to the floor, took out Bibles and rosaries, and began to pray.

State troopers and sheriff's deputies lifted the protesters into wheelchairs, and rolled them out, into waiting hospital vans for the handicapped, and drove them to the local police station. When the police went to book them—on charges of trespassing—they all said their name was Nancy Cruzan. "Nineteen Nancy Cruzans because if it's okay to starve Nancy, it's okay to starve any of us," Anne Foreman explained of those who were arrested. "[It's] because," Joe Foreman added, "Jesus said, 'I was hungry and you gave me food, I was thirsty and you gave me drink.' "

"It has to do with life," Wanda, who has a Down's syndrome child, told me. "It doesn't matter whether you're talking about an unborn child or a person like Nancy. I believe that even people in that situation are valuable. When we take care of them, *we* become more compassionate caring for them."

Wanda said that while some protesters got out, she and several others were kept in jail for a week, ten of them in one area and more in another. "We weren't eating so I guess they got a little nervous. One woman was getting weak, so I guess we became a liability for them." Wanda says there was no bail or sentencing on the charges they faced of trespassing, but according to the Mount Vernon police, they all had to pay fines. The ones who got out went back to resume their vigil; by that time the hospital had locked all but a few, well-guarded doors. The protesters who stayed in jail were freed in a week, but by then, Nancy had died.

From inside her room, the Cruzans could hear Wanda and the others in the hallway and stairwell outside, braying, "Help me, Jesus!" and exhorting them not to starve Nancy to death. "I would have thought the protests would have bothered them," said Colby, their attorney, "but they were in so much pain from what would cause us all pain, having a child die. Really, that was their focus."

"We were all in Nan's room," Chris later recalled. "I would be leaning against the door and then Dad would, and then we realized they didn't care about Nan. They'd protest when the cameras were on. And then they didn't."

When the protesters were arrested, the Cruzans could still hear the prayer vigil outside. By then, the protesters had pitched tents and were living in the grassy area in the center of the hospital's main circular driveway. "It was December, cold. One day my dad went to a hardware store to buy a big thermos and brought them a pot of coffee. They didn't even know who he was," Chris said. "I thought the vast majority were there for publicity reasons. We're an ordinary, simple family, and we were doing the best that we could. We agreed the protesters were not going to turn our attention from where we wanted to be, and that was with Nancy."

While Lamkins and the hospital's staff had started the week opposed to what the Cruzans wanted to do with their daughter, by the end their sentiments had become more confused. "People inside felt they were under siege," Lamkins says. "But by this time the enemy had become the protesters and what they were doing."

Sheriff Doug Seneker headed up the security detail outside Nancy's door and later wheeled her body out to the waiting funeral home van. "It was really agonizing," he told me of those last ten days. "Most people around here thought that if she was going to be killed she should just be outright killed, but not slowly starved to death. You wouldn't do that to animals. [But] I've got six kids of my own and I would hate to have to be faced with a decision like Joe Cruzan had. He was an agonized man. I don't know what I would have done if it had been one of my kids in his kid's situation. Issues like these can't be seen in terms of black and white."

And that's also how Joe Cruzan saw it. "To some extent, I am antiabortion too," he told reporters, "but there's absolutely no connection between Nancy's condition and the unborn babies [the protesters] talk about. Nancy had no potential; she was just existing. . . . I would have gladly traded places with any one of them protesting down there. But I wouldn't have been out trying to influence their decisions. I'd be home enjoying my daughter."

Nancy died at 2:55 A.M. on December 26, 1990—eight days after the arrests, twelve days after the tube was removed, and eight years after she went into her coma.

"Her death was as peaceful as it could be," Joe later reported. "We spent every minute of her last twelve days with her. In many ways, it was more peaceful [than her life on the feeding tube had been], because she'd been having secretions, which always kept her gagging and choking. When they stopped the hydration, [the secretions] dried up."

She was buried several days later. On her gravestone is a poignant inscription: "Nancy Beth Cruzan, most loved daughter, sister, aunt. Born July 20, 1957. Departed Jan. 11, 1983. At peace Dec.

26, 1990." At the top is script that begins with the zigs and zags of a brain-wave scan; the zigzags form the words "thank you," and then they trail off, becoming a flat line.

When the New Jersey Supreme Court decided on Karen Ann Quinlan's case in 1976, it set in motion forces that have since shaped end-of-life politics, ethics, medical practice, and law in this country. By the time Nancy Cruzan died nearly a decade and a half later, not only were right-to-life protesters trying to unravel these policies, but the protection that the courts had intended to give patients and families was at the epicenter of a swirling battle.

Consent has a long basis in common law—on protections against assault and battery—but it became incorporated into medical case law in 1914, with Benjamin N. Cardozo's dictum in a New York lawsuit over unwanted surgery. "Every human being of adult years and sound mind," Judge Cardozo wrote in the case of *Schloendorff v. Society of New York Hospital,* "has a right to determine what shall be done with his body."

That patients also have a right to give *informed* consent to all medical treatments, meaning they must be fully briefed about the intent of treatments, the alternatives, and the risks and the benefits ahead of time, understand them, and agree to them, was incorporated into medical case law in 1957.

In writing his historic decision in the Quinlan case, New Jersey's Chief Justice Robert Hughes established four additional legal precedents that have since influenced court decisions in thousands of end-of-life cases—including that of the U.S. Supreme Court in the Cruzan case. They have also guided legislators in Congress and all fifty states in creating a new body of end-of-life law. The principles are as follows:

1. Patients have the right to refuse treatment even if this refusal might lead to death—based on the common-law protections against assault and battery and on the implied constitutional right of privacy.

While privacy is not specifically mentioned in the Constitution, it has come to be defined as a *liberty* interest, based on the Fourteenth Amendment, a post–Civil War amendment guaranteeing our right to equal protection and denying the government the right to deprive us of life, liberty, or property without due process of law. This right is in keeping with both the Declaration of Independence and the Bill of Rights. It was further protected in U.S. Supreme Court decisions, most notably with regard to bodily invasion in abortion cases like *Roe v. Wade*. This right was reaffirmed in a medical context with the Quinlan decision.

2. If patients are mentally unable to make treatment decisions, someone else may exercise their right for them. Specifically, Chief Justice Hughes held "that a decision by [the] daughter to permit a noncognitive, vegetative existence to terminate by natural forces was a valuable incident of her right to privacy which could be asserted on her behalf by her guardian."

3. Decisions that can lead to the death of a mentally incompetent patient are better made not by courts but by families, with the input of their doctors; *hospital ethics committees* should concur with doctors in order to be sure that diagnoses of terminal conditions or permanent vegetative states are correct, and to see that treatment is not only appropriate, but in keeping with what the family and the patient might want.

"Upon the concurrence of guardian and family," Chief Justice Hughes wrote, "should the attending physicians conclude there was no reasonable possibility of [the] daughter's ever emerging from her comatose condition to a cognitive, sapient state and that the life-support apparatus should be discontinued, physicians should consult with [the] hospital ethics committee and if [the] committee should agree with physicians' prognosis, the life-support systems may be withdrawn."

4. Decisions about end-of-life care should take into consideration both the invasiveness of the treatment involved and the patient's likelihood of recovery.

"Patient's right to privacy was greater than the State's interest in the preservation and sanctity of human life," Hughes concluded, "where [a] patient whose vital processes were maintained by mechanical respirator would never resume cognitive life, and the bodily invasion, involving twenty-four-hour intensive nursing care, antibiotics, the assistance of a respirator, a catheter and a feeding tube was very great.

"We think that the State's interest [against removal of treatment] weakens and the individual's right to privacy grows," he wrote, "as the degree of bodily invasion increases and the prognosis dims. Ultimately there comes a point at which the individual's rights overcome the State interest. It is for that reason that we believe Karen's choice, if she were competent to make it, would be vindicated by the law. Her prognosis is extremely poor—she will never resume cognitive life. And the bodily invasion is very great."

In 1976, these principles and precedents fell into an organizational and procedural vacuum. As we have seen, clear prognoses in cases of coma, particularly, were difficult to arrive at.

Justice Hughes had ruled that hospital ethics committees should be the key guarantors—by concurring with physicians—of proper prognoses. But he based this opinion on a law review article that greatly overestimated their prevalence. In fact, few such committees existed at that time. And, perhaps more significantly, there were as yet no legal ways for the prior wishes of comatose patients to be registered, or for a family member or other guardian to implement a decision for a loved one.

The Quinlan decision thus set in motion the development of a whole new body of laws that subsequently led to the U.S. Supreme Court's Cruzan decision and helped form legislation that has collectively come to be called *advance directives*. Together these laws would outline—jurisdiction by jurisdiction—how patients' decisions on their end-of-life treatment and care might be made, who might make decisions should the patient not be able to make them, and how these decisions might be implemented.

The first model living will was proposed in 1967 by Chicago attorney Luis Kutner, a member of what was then a tiny organization called the Euthanasia Society of America. The society was established in 1938 with the goal of giving "incurable sufferers" the right to die when they chose. By 1967, its goal had shifted to "champion the rights of dying people to control decisions about their own medical care" through education, lobbying legislators, and by passing out model living wills.

Subsequent changes in medicine, and the increased need for education and lobbying efforts, caused the society to reorganize into separate organizations, neither of which took on the now inflammatory term *euthanasia* in its name. Concern for Dying became the educational arm, and the Society for the Right to Die took on political work. In 1991, these organizations were rejoined as Choice in Dying.

In 1968, the year after the society began passing out its sample living wills, a bill allowing patients to make clear their future wishes concerning life-sustaining equipment was introduced in the Florida state legislature by Walter F. Sackett, M.D., a physician turned state legislator. It was defeated. In 1973 he tried again and was faced with intense opposition from the Florida Catholic Conference. The bill was defeated by a slim margin of six legislative votes, which scared the Catholic opposition—in the same year that *Roe v. Wade* was decided by the U.S. Supreme Court—and galvanized anti–living will efforts.

In the early 1970s California attorney Barry Keene joined the nascent campaign. Keene had befriended a neighbor who couldn't get doctors to stop treating his wife as she lay dying of cancer, and in 1972 his own family faced the same situation with his mother-in-law. She had actually signed a power of attorney that attempted to limit medical treatment, but Keene's family found there was no law requiring doctors to honor it.

When Keene was elected to the California state senate in 1974, one of the first things he did was propose a bill, called the Natural Death Act, to legalize living wills. It, too, was defeated.

Two years later, a few months after the New Jersey Supreme Court decided on the Quinlan case, Senator Keene introduced his bill again. It passed and was signed into law in September 1976. With the Natural Death Act, California became the first state to legalize a form of advance directive—a document for people to sign ahead of time stipulating how they want to be treated if they were terminally ill and could not express their own wishes. In 1977, forty-two other states considered similar bills and seven of them also passed.

That same year, the National Conference of Catholic Bishops issued a statement to the state Catholic conferences opposing both the new living will bills and the laws creating a brain-based definition of death, which had begun to be passed state by state. (Brain death still did not address the condition of *partial* brain death that Karen Quinlan was in.)

In its very divisions—Catholic against Catholic—the Quinlan case had foreshadowed a major new kind of battle. When the Supreme Court legalized abortion in 1973, conservative forces within the Catholic Church (particularly in the state committees) began actively organizing to reverse this decision. They were soon joined by conservative Protestants and fundamentalists, and together they forged the growing right-to-life movement that opposed not only those who were pro-choice on abortion but also those who were pro-choice for the end of life.

The newly formed National Right to Life Committee continued antiabortion campaigns and began filing amicus briefs in end-of-life court cases, but state living will legislation also became a new legal battleground.

In 1978 these battles were taken up on the federal level as well. The National Conference of Commissioners on Uniform State Laws is a national body that seeks to coordinate and make similar the law in all fifty states. That year it adopted the uniform brain-death statute as a model bill for all states. In 1984 it also drafted a uniform living-will law.

By then, the National Conference of Catholic Bishops had separated itself from the increasingly conservative National Right to Life Committee, withdrawing its total opposition to advance directives and drafting instead guidelines for a different kind of end-of-life law—called *health-care proxies* or *health-care powers of attorney.*

The National Conference of Catholic Bishops believed that living wills gave only the right to *refuse* treatment, but a health-care proxy could also grant the right to decide *for treatment.* With these documents, one specifies a person ahead of time to make treatment decisions should he no longer be able to decide for himself. States that adopted this version of an advance directive differed on whether this decision was to be made strictly as the loved one *would have decided,* or whether it could be in the loved one's *best interests.*

By 1987, forty states had legalized an advance directive of some kind; by 1992, all fifty states had done so. But as battles had raged in state after state, a national crazy quilt of end-of-life laws and court cases emerged.

Different state laws varied not only on whether they were living will or health-care proxy laws, but *when they applied* (for example, some states allow them to cover only the terminally ill; some include those in persistent vegetative states; some exclude pregnant women), *who could decide* for a patient not able to decide for himself or herself, and *how that decision might be made.*

The result was one of three possible kinds of end-of-life laws—all of which apply only when a patient is no longer legally competent to decide for himself. Two of the three require that a patient sign, *in advance* of a medical emergency, a document that will come into play at a time when he is not competent to make medical decisions.

With a *living will* a person specifies in writing what kinds of treatment are wanted and not wanted. Advocates say this gives individuals the most autonomy—most control over future treatment decisions. Those who see it as problematic say that one can't really spell out everything one will or won't need in advance, particularly as medicine continues to change so swiftly. Nor can one know in advance the particular medical situation one might be facing; a respirator, for example, might be needed to get over a rough case of pneumonia, but not if one has advanced lung cancer and recovery is hopeless.

A *durable power of attorney* or *health-care proxy* both require that one designate some other named person to make these decisions should the patient not be able to decide for himself. Advocates say this makes someone available to address the patient's *particular* medical circumstance at the time. Others still see problems, the largest one being that the law requires that a document be signed ahead of time. (There are also no uniform requirements that proxies are bound to follow the patients' wishes.)

The third kind of law—the *family consent* (or *surrogacy* or *succession*) *law*—requires *no* document to be signed prior to loss of competence. As of 1996, between twenty-four and thirty-six states (depending how various state statutes are interpreted) and the District of Columbia have passed family succession laws; these states have simply set up a system whereby particular family members, in a designated order of succession, are to be the ones to make treatment decisions for an incompetent patient. Such laws don't preclude living wills or health-care proxies, but if such documents have not been signed, patients are still protected.

Those who favor succession laws argue that they allow family members to make decisions *for or against* specific treatments—and for *a specific condition* at the time these treatments might be needed. Since there is no need to prove what the patient would have wanted, the family is spared the grief of a possible legal struggle during the most traumatic period of their lives. Detractors caution that in dysfunctional families, or where a life partner (say, in same-sex couples) might not agree with the next of kin, patients might *also* want to sign an advance directive.

The organization Choice in Dying—which has grown into a large, nationwide advocacy group—has been instrumental in campaigning for passage of all of these end-of-life laws and in sending out copies of living wills and health-care proxies—state by state—to those in need. (The National Right to Life Committee now also gives out a *Will to Live,* so people might detail what treatments they *want* at the end of life.)

Despite this effort, only 15 to 20 percent of all Americans have signed a living will or a health-care proxy. Arguably just a half to two-thirds of all states have surrogacy laws that would cover a patient—allowing his or her family to just decide on treatment—should no advance directive have been signed. This lack places the presumption on the side of treatment, which some of the Supreme Court justices who dissented in the Cruzan decision felt created an unfair legal weight.

When asked, two years after Nancy died, whether he thought living wills were a good idea, Joe Cruzan wryly said he thought they were necessary—but ridiculous. "I think the presumption should be that most people *wouldn't* want to live in a vegetative state for thirty years and they'd want the whole thing stopped," he said. "The people who would want to spend their last thirty or forty years that way, *they're* the ones who should write down in an advance directive that that's how they want to live." Fact is, he said, the way the living will laws are now written, someone as young as Nancy probably wouldn't have gotten around to signing one.

Despite the efforts of the National Conference of Commissioners on Uniform State Laws, laws still vary from state to state, even though there have been some attempts at between-state reciprocity. So if you sign a living will in Georgia—where living wills are legal—and you become ill and incompetent in New York—where they have not been given legal weight—it isn't clear whether your document can be implemented.

Like Missouri's at the time of the Cruzan case, New York law requires family members to present "clear and convincing evidence" of what the patient would have wanted. "[It's] an unreal standard," says one critic who believes that all states should just enact surrogacy statutes. "People don't talk like that. They say to their relatives or friends, 'Hey, pull the plug if I'm gone,' but they don't normally go out to look for forms to sign that say, 'I want to refuse artificial nutrition and hydration.' That's what's meant by 'clear and convincing evidence.' [Signing documents] is not how we live, and so people don't understand these laws."

Meanwhile, as the legislatures have continued to pass living will–type laws, case law—decisions made by courts across the country—has also grown as well. And it too has created a national legal crazy quilt of when and how these laws can be applied, meaning how—and by whom—decisions might be made at the end of life.

Between 1976 and 1993, lower trial courts have ruled on thousands of cases on forgoing treatment. The majority of them have cited *Quinlan* as a precedent and have decided in favor of the family, but their decisions are not binding outside their own county or state jurisdictions. By the beginning of 1997, about one hundred cases were decided by state appellate courts or federal district courts, in only twenty-five states and the District of Columbia. Those decisions, too, apply only in their jurisdictions in those particular states.

Thus many states and localities still have no applicable end-of-life case law, according to Alan Meisel, J.D., of the University of Pittsburgh Law School. The sobering fact is that although the New Jersey Supreme Court set patient- and family-friendly legal precedents in 1976, legal policy and its application in medical centers across the country are still so chaotic that what happened to Karen can—and does—continue to happen.

Nancy Beth Cruzan's case was the only one that has ever been decided by the U.S. Supreme Court, which would give it national application. And while that case reaffirmed that feeding tubes were to be considered like any other medical treatment, the rest of that decision was, as we have seen, more restrictive and confusing than most people think.

Chafing at the end-of-life restrictions in his own state, Republican Senator John Danforth of Missouri, then on the Senate Finance Committee, proposed the patient-friendly federal law, the Patient Self-Determination Act (PSDA), and helped shepherd it through Congress. It passed just after the Supreme Court's Cruzan decision in 1990, and went into effect in 1991.

The PSDA requires that all hospitals, nursing homes, and medical centers receiving federal funds—including Medicare and Medicaid funds—inform patients on admission that they have the legal right to make their wishes on care known to doctors and hospitals, according to the advance directive law of their particular state. But studies now show it isn't clear in the end that even all of these legal protections really matter.

Those who are among the minority of people who have signed an advance directive will no doubt be appalled to discover that patients who have signed such a document and those who have not end up being treated exactly the same way by their physicians.

The 1995 *Study to Understand Prognoses and Preferences for Outcomes and Risks of Treatment* (SUPPORT) of some 9,000 seriously ill patients at five major hospitals across America—described in Chapter 2—confirmed what several earlier studies had found: There were no differences in health outcome or medical treatment between those who had signed advance directives and those who hadn't.

Says Dr. Joanne Lynn, the SUPPORT codirector, "Those who had living wills or health-care proxies, or even do-not-resuscitate orders, were no more likely *not* to be resuscitated, no more likely *not* to have respirators or feeding tubes or antibiotics, than those who didn't." This was true even when patients had signed directives and discussed them with a nurse who had been specifically assigned to relay their wishes to their doctors, and even though the federal Patient Self-Determination Act had already gone into effect when this portion of the study began.

Why would a doctor ignore an advance directive? Some say research shows that patients often change their minds at the end, or that families don't necessarily choose what a patient might have wanted. It may be that what appeared to be a low quality of life at the beginning of an illness becomes acceptable once someone has gotten to that point, that it is often impossible to define when care becomes truly futile, or that the dying merely want to cling to any shred of hope they can find.

Dr. Lynn says, however, that all these answers are just rationalizations after the fact. Because few patients sign advance directives, because they only address very specific circumstances at very specific times, and because doctors ignore them anyway, all these documents and laws have turned out to be a public-policy failure.

"Perhaps the entire direction we have been taking has been absolutely incorrect and misguided," she says. "We might have to do something completely new, move in a completely different direction in handling issues at the end of life."

Though she still thinks people should sign living wills just to be safe, Dr. Lynn, in fact, has made it a point *not* to have a living will herself. As she wrote in an article entitled "Why I Don't Have a Living Will":

> On its face value, a "living will" purports to instruct caregivers to provide no life-sustaining treatment if the person signing it ever were on the verge of dying, with or without treatment, and were unable to make decisions for himself or herself. On the one hand, this is hardly a surprising instruction.
>
> However, many persons believe that they accomplish some very different ends by signing a living will. They believe they keep themselves from ever ending up like Nancy Cruzan or Karen Quinlan, or like a family member who had a particularly gruesome end of life in an intensive care unit. That belief is wrong. The public use of the standard living will is largely premised on an implicit promise that the document cannot ensure. Standard form living wills *should* have virtually no impact upon the care of persistent vegetative state patients, persons receiving vigorous therapy for potentially reversible physiologic imbalance, or persons with no clearly progressive and irreversible course toward imminent death, for none of these people clearly meet the requirement of dying soon irrespective of treatment. When people feel,

as they commonly seem to, that having signed a living will serves
to ensure that they will avoid medical torment of all sorts, they
are misconstruing the document.

"The main argument," she told me, "is that I want my family to be
able to live with their decisions *more* than I want my particular
decision. I wanted to disallow anyone from reading my writings
and deciding what I would have wanted. In fact I set up the standard for anyone who would overrule my family as being that of
abuse."

One technique that challengers have used to dispute end-of-life
decisions has focused on who should be the proper guardian
of an ill and legally incompetent patient. In general, these have been
attacks by outsiders against the patient's family and its designated
spokesperson.

Beginning with the Quinlan case, a string of cases were built on
opponents trying to appoint some other person as guardian to
make decisions that were different from what the patient's family
wanted—arguing in court, as they had in the Cruzan case, that the
family spokesperson was not a proper guardian because he or she
did not have the best interests of the patient in mind.

By 1991 these attacks on family members had reached such
heights of absurdity that the Indiana family of a forty-two-year-old
comatose woman named Sue Ann Lawrence, had to face a challenge in court from a former security guard at a massage parlor
called Eve's Garden of Eden, who claimed that because he was
disabled from a gunshot wound he was better able to know the
patient's best interests, even though he had never even met her or
her family. The former bouncer lost his bid for guardianship, but
not before James Bopp and other attorneys at the National Legal
Center for the Medically Dependent and Disabled succeeded in
having the feeding tube reattached that the Lawrence family already had won the right to remove. The Lawrences were still sitting
their horrible vigil when Sue Ann died of complications from the
reattached tube.

But the Indiana Supreme Court went ahead with an appeal
decision anyway: It ruled by a vote of four to one that tube feeding

was a medical treatment like any other and that it was therefore subject to the same grounds of privacy. Families did not need a court order, the judge stipulated, nor could outsiders like the bouncer qualify as "interested" parties. Still, the Lawrence family had to defend its decisions at one of life's most difficult times.

Julie Chase Delio, Ph.D., is another such family member whose experience is often cited. She had to face having her motives scrutinized and her family experience devalued when she fought in New York in 1987 to remove her comatose thirty-four-year-old husband Danny's feeding tube. Danny had suffered permanent brain damage as the result of a tragic accident during routine and minor surgery.

"I remember the loneliness you feel," Julie says, "when you look at someone you love and realize they aren't going to make it, that treatment should end so you can let them peacefully die. And you wonder if anyone else realizes that. And then you feel like such a monster, wanting someone you love to die." Thankfully, for Julie, Danny's mother agreed, and the State Court of Appeals finally granted her request, but not before a long and demeaning battle.

Julie had had to prove repeatedly that she wasn't Danny's enemy, that his death was not going to benefit her, that in order to protect Danny, the state or the doctors or the hospital didn't need to come between him and Julie and her mother-in-law.

"This was the sickest thing I ever saw anyone do to a person," Julie says, "being forced to plead for the death of my husband and having them dig into our finances (to see how I might have benefited), into our relationship, everything. I loved my husband. We had a wonderful relationship. He was my best friend. I give him all the credit for our winning this because it was his life force that kept me going when he couldn't anymore."

Julie was an assistant professor of medicine at SUNY Health Science Center in Brooklyn. Danny had had a doctorate in exercise physiology and before his surgery had worked in a hospital as well. She knew medicine and she had medical clout. But even she had difficulty.

"Before this, there was a long legal history of seeing the family with conflicting interests, but it was usually over money," says Robert Burt, J.D., an expert in end-of-life law at Yale University Law School, speaking on the legal assault on families in general.

"One member might be the heir to a fortune." Because it wasn't legally clear whether withdrawing treatment might constitute murder, those old laws of guardianship were painfully applied in these new circumstances.

It has not only been pro-life advocates who have used these tactics. Perhaps even more alarmingly, they are now being embraced in the context of talk about the "futility" of medical treatment, in arguments about medical cost cutting, and in growing pressure from health maintenance organizations and managed care.

Legal challenges may become as much of a problem for families who want to *continue* treatment as they have been for families who want to *refuse* it. Consider, for example, the case of Helga Wanglie.

On December 14, 1989, eighty-six-year-old Helga Wanglie tripped over one of the scatter rugs in her Minnesota home, fell, and fractured her right hip. Her family took her to their local hospital, North Memorial, where she was treated and sent to a nearby nursing home for rehabilitation.

"On January 1, 1990," her daughter Ruth later recalled, "I thought she looked so bad that I mentioned it to one of the nurses." Helga was taken to Hennepin County Medical Center (HCMC) in Minneapolis, where she was found to have developed respiratory failure and was put on a respirator. She was conscious through all this and recognized her family.

On May 7, 1990, she was transferred to Bethesda Lutheran Hospital in Saint Paul, which specializes in caring for respirator-dependent patients, in order to try to wean her from the respirator. During one attempt she suffered cardiac and respiratory arrest. She was found in the middle of the night, not breathing, with her eyes staring fixedly at the ceiling. No one really knew how long her heart had been stopped but she was revived with the help of electric shock from CPR.

After that, Ruth said, "We wanted her back in HCMC because of its closeness—about five miles—to our home, but Dad also wanted to visit her much more than he had been able to in downtown Saint Paul." Helga arrived at HCMC on May 31, 1990, back on her respirator. Doctors diagnosed that she was in a persistent vegetative state as a result of the heart attack, respiratory failure, and oxygen loss, all of which had caused brain damage and a coma. At the Wanglies' insistence—her husband, Oliver, their son, and their daughter, Ruth—she was given tube feeding, and treated aggressively for recurrent lung infections.

"When there was no improvement made in June and July," Ruth said, physicians at HCMC told her family that Helga's coma was permanent and irreversible, her condition hopeless, and told them they wanted to discontinue treatment. But the Wanglies disagreed, saying that Helga—the daughter of a Lutheran minister— would have wanted to keep on receiving treatment.

"All bills were covered by her own private insurance and Medicare," Ruth said. "We had one of the most expensive insurance policies out there. Most people wouldn't begin to pay the premiums we had chosen to. My mother had very strong religious convictions. If anything happened to her she wanted everything done to preserve her life."

The medical staff so strongly disagreed that HCMC's ethics committee got involved. It advised the hospital staff to follow the wishes of the Wanglie family and try to resolve their differences with them. "We agreed to a 'do not resuscitate' order," Ruth said. "We were kind of hoaxed, or forced into it by the ethics committee. I didn't really even want that, but we agreed." After several more ethics committee meetings it became apparent that the views of Helga's family and doctors were greatly divergent.

By December 1990, it was clear that these differences could not be resolved. Oliver Wanglie wrote the hospital a letter. "My wife always stated to me that if anything happened to her so that she could not take care of herself, she did not want anything done to shorten or prematurely take her life," he'd said, but the hospital responded "that it did not believe it was obligated to provide 'inappropriate medical treatment that [could not] advance a patient's personal interest.' "

On February 8, 1991, the hospital filed papers in Hennepin County District Court requesting that a conservator (or guardian) be appointed other than Oliver Wanglie. Doctors charged that he did not understand that his comatose wife would never recover and that she should not continue to be kept alive on a respirator. The hospital did not ask directly that the court allow doctors to discontinue treatment over the objections of Helga's family, but requested that someone other than her husband be appointed in order to make exactly that decision.

Oliver had been married to Helga for fifty-three years. They shared strong religious beliefs, among them a belief in the right to life. "My mother felt that one should let God take His course, not let man determine these issues," Ruth said. "We all knew that she wouldn't last long but this had to be a test case. We felt there was no human compassion shown to the family in this trauma."

On July 1, the court ruled that Oliver Wanglie knew his wife's views better than anyone else and was therefore in the best position—far better than any stranger—to make decisions about her care. Just three days later, Helga died of multiple organ-system failure—despite her respirator and feeding tube. But the legal point had been made.

This was a landmark case, the first time that physicians tried to argue *against* continuing treatment over a family's wishes. "The court noted that Mr. Wanglie had agreed with the physicians about every major treatment decision except for removal of the ventilation," one summary report of the case noted. "HCMC did not contest that Oliver Wanglie was competent to be the guardian of Mrs. Wanglie's estate or with regard to matters other than her shelter, medical care, and religious requirements. On those three matters, the court found that HCMC stated that he was incompetent because the hospital and medical team did not agree with him."

In 1996, when I asked Ronald Cranford, M.D., the assistant chief of neurology at HCMC, about the case, he said the staff felt "uncomfortable taking care of her. We didn't necessarily want to stop treatment on her, we just didn't want to take care of her. We tried to transfer her—that was lost here—but we couldn't find anyone to take her. She was in a vegetative state, on a respirator and [in her eighties]. We were getting dollar for dollar on her, so why not? Accept her care and the money, too. If we could have found someone [to take care of her], we would have worked with [them], but we couldn't. That's why we went to court."

Dr. Cranford said the basic issue is "Why do we in medicine continue treatment on a patient when it is futile? That is not a fundamental goal of medicine. . . . I've seen patients who were dead look better than her. We gave her maximal treatment for a year," he said. "It was kind of eerie for the doctors to take care of her for that year. Is this the purpose of medicine? Taking care of patients at eighty-five who should be allowed to die naturally?"

The fundamental question is who has the right to make our end-of-life decisions. "Our society is basically putting the burden of proof on family members to prove they speak in the best interests of their loved ones so we can certify them to act as guardians," says Arthur Caplan, Ph.D., director of the Center for Bioethics at the University of Pennsylvania Medical School.

"The common thread among [these cases] is that our society doesn't recognize intimacy or acknowledge the experience of what it means to grow up with somebody, marry somebody, raise somebody to adulthood, birth somebody, in terms of who is most appropriate to make decisions. We ought to have a system that makes it very, very hard to devalue these experiences and to take away the presumption of [family] decision-making authority over medical decision making."

Justice Hughes's decision in the Quinlan case also spurred the development of the new institution of ethics committees and, with them, the new academic field of bioethics. It gave patients and families a kind of ombudsman, and it significantly altered medical practice, especially the previously paternalistic and sacrosanct doctor-patient relationship.

In 1976, when Justice Hughes made his recommendations, not only did few ethics committees exist, but he did not envision the larger scope of such committees today. In 1983, the President's Commission for the Study of Ethical Problems in Medicine found that only 1 percent of all medical facilities in the nation even had such a committee. During the 1980s, many states passed laws mandating ethics committees, and in 1992, the Joint Commission on Accreditation of Healthcare Organizations (JCAHO), the organization that grants accreditation to hospitals, nursing homes, and other medical facilities, made it a requirement that these facilities have "a forum to resolve ethical issues." By 1993, the American Hospital Association estimated that some 60 to 85 percent of our medical facilities had ethics committees.

The new discipline of bioethics had emerged in the early 1960s, the result of advances in technology—the possibilities of kidney dialysis and later of organ transplants, beginning with the heart. Growth of the field was also fueled by exposés on abuses in medical experimentation on unsuspecting patients, by a growing civil rights movement, by the debates over abortion, by medicine's ability to save newborns that might have questionable qualities of life, and by genetic research. In 1969, the grandfather of modern bioethics think tanks, the Hastings Center, was established in Briarcliff Manor, New York; the Kennedy Institute at Georgetown University in Washington, D.C., the second giant in the field, began in 1971.

It was a 1962 article by journalist Shana Alexander in *Life* magazine that first brought the issues being debated behind closed doors into American homes. Alexander's article, "They Decide Who Lives, Who Dies," was about a committee in Seattle whose job was to select patients for kidney dialysis machines—which had just been made possible by the invention in 1961 of the arteriovenous shunt and cannula.

"It quickly became apparent," ethicist Albert Jonson has written, "that many more patients needed dialysis than could be accommodated. The solution was to ask a small group, composed mostly of nonphysicians, to review the dossiers of all medically suitable candidates and sort out those who would receive the lifesaving technology. Thus, the committee was faced with the unenviable task of determining suitability on grounds other than medical. Should it be personality? finances? social acceptability? past or expected contribution? family dependents and support?" Medicine had reached the point when life *could* be extended; the question was, for whom?

During these years, the view of the doctor as benign healer was also breaking down. New revelations about the underside of medical research suggested that patients might sometimes need protection from their own physicians. In his book, *Strangers at the Bedside,* David J. Rothman, Ph.D., director of the Center for the study of Society and Medicine at the Columbia College of Physicians and Surgeons, traced the long history of medicine's dark side.

The dubious precedent was set in November 1789, when the English doctor Edward Jenner tested his smallpox vaccine on his one-year-old son. While the baby suffered no ill effects, the unknowing subjects of later medical experiments were not always so lucky. Many tests that form the basis of modern medicine were performed on members of an underclass—children in orphanages, mentally retarded people, blacks, minorities, women, prisoners, students, and soldiers. Most had neither been told they were being used in experiments, nor had they given their consent.

In the United States, much of the impetus for this skirting of ethical decency came during wartime, the result, Dr. Rothman writes, of efforts to fight diseases that were threatening American soldiers. Among the first and most famous of such research projects was that led by army surgeon Walter Reed, M.D., who went to Cuba during the Spanish-American War to study the cause of yellow fever.

At first Dr. Reed had mosquitoes bite members of his own research team, but when two of them died, he turned elsewhere, demonstrating the stereotypical arrogance of physicians that has since sparked the social perception of the need for new controls. "[We] decided not to tempt fate by trying any more [infections] on ourselves," Dr. Reed wrote. "We felt we had been called upon to accomplish such work as did not justify our taking risks which then seemed really unnecessary." Instead, he used American soldiers and Cuban workers, many of whom were barely told of any risks, and who subsequently died.

Pressure for research and miracle cures reached a peak during World War II. In 1941, President Franklin D. Roosevelt created the Office of Scientific Research and Development (OSRD), with a branch for medical research, that gave $25 million in government funds to 135 universities, hospitals, research institutes, and industrial firms for studies.

"Because it was wartime," Dr. Rothman writes, "the agency underwrote protocols that [earlier or later, even] would have produced considerable protest." Typical were scenarios in which boys and girls aged thirteen to seventeen in Ohio Soldiers' and Sailors' Orphanage, patients at the Dixon (Illinois) Institution for the Retarded and in the New Jersey State Colony for the Feeble-Minded, and the primarily black poor at the Shreveport (Louisiana) Charity Hospital were given severe cases of dysentery through injection or otherwise, some in projects directly supervised by researchers from the U.S. Public Health Service. In Louisiana, among the 238 dysentery cases treated, 6 people died, including a twenty-month-old baby.

The one really positive prize in all this wartime research was the development and subsequent production of penicillin. Penicillin was indeed a miracle drug, and it served to silence many potential critics of the experimenters' methods.

After World War II, when the concentration camps were opened at Dachau, Auschwitz, and Buchenwald, the atrocities performed in the name of medical experiments by Nazi physicians were laid bare to all the world's horror. These physicians came before the international Nuremberg Tribunals in 1945 and 1946, out of which were developed strict international codes to regulate the use of human subjects in medical research. The first principle of the Nuremberg Code was that nothing should be done to human beings without their consent.

In 1966, Henry Beecher, M.D., a distinguished faculty member at Harvard University Medical School, blew the whistle on a sorry list of peacetime research projects that violated this principle. He published an article in the prestigious *New England Journal of Medicine* that cited twenty-two mainstream research projects, all of them morally suspect.

They were all supported by federal grants and were carried out at our best universities and medical centers, including Harvard Medical School, Memorial Sloan-Kettering, Case Western Reserve, Georgetown and George Washington universities, and the University of California at Los Angeles (UCLA). In one of these studies, mentally retarded children were purposely given hepatitis in order to determine its length of contagion; in another, live cancer cells were injected into twenty-two elderly and senile patients.

Yet, it was a 1972 news report in both the *Washington Star* and *The New York Times* that finally caused public outrage. "The experiment, called the Tuskegee Study, began in 1932 with about 600 black men, mostly poor and uneducated, from Tuskegee, Ala.," *The Times* reported, "an area that had the highest syphilis rate in the nation at the time."

From 1932 through 1972, when public disclosure forced the study to end, investigators from the U.S. Public Health Service had been studying—but never treating—these men in order to learn the long-term effects of secondary syphilis. The subjects had enrolled in the study having been promised that they would get free medical treatment. They showed up for medical examinations yearly and submitted to tests that included spinal taps, which are painful.

In the beginning, most were given the standard heavy metals therapy used at the time; some were given placebos. But when penicillin became available—the most effective treatment for this disease—rather than receive it, all these men were aggressively denied it. The Public Health Service went so far as to contact their draft boards to prevent them from being drafted so that they might not, even inadvertently, ever be treated. The reason given was that this might be the last time researchers could ever know the long-term effects of syphilis!

The exposés led to a series of 1973 congressional hearings, chaired by Senator Edward Kennedy, that in turn led to the development of criteria to require informed consent from patients involved in medical research and to the establishment of local institutional review boards (IRBs)—committees of peers that would examine, approve, and monitor all research that involved human beings.

Institutional review boards are still required in all medical centers and research institutions where medical research that uses human beings is being done. These federal regulations brought in outsiders to oversee medical practice, setting the stage for the ethics committees that soon would come. Among those who would sit on them were philosophers, lawyers, and clergymen—the group of people that we now call bioethicists.

"Medical practice has become radically transformed, often obliterating the vital distinction between therapy and scientific research," Jay Katz, M.D., an esteemed ethicist and physician at Yale University Law School, wrote in 1995. "Thus, the increasing use of human beings as means for the ends of others can undermine basic democratic values of citizens' rights to autonomy and self-determination."

Today, newer issues and revelations continue to fuel tension between patients and physicians—disclosures of radiation testing on U.S. citizens during the Cold War, for example, even within our most prestigious hospitals, or, partly because of Tuskegee, the extended distrust of physicians felt in the black community, particularly over issues relating to AIDS and taking organs for transplant.

However, rather than tighten controls, in November 1996, on the fiftieth anniversary of the Nuremberg Tribunals and Codes—

and while physicians worldwide were in Germany marking this historic event—the Food and Drug Administration announced that it was lifting the five-decade-old U.S. ban that required patients' informed consent in medical experiments in specific circumstances.

"The patients must have a life-threatening condition, like a severe head injury," *The New York Times* reported, "and must be unable to say whether they want to be part of a study. They would be selected only if it was not feasible to obtain consent from a relative." This would mean that in emergency situations—heart attacks, strokes, head injuries—experimental treatments might be used *or purposely withheld,* depending on whether a patient was assigned to an experimental group or to a control group.

The lifting of this ban has since provoked an ethical and legal furor within medical circles, as the bedrock of informed patient consent was being seriously challenged in the name of medical progress. Some doctors argued that these changes were required so that medical research, particularly for head injury patients, could go forward, but others, like ethicist Jay Katz, saw this change as egregious and horrifying.

"The new regulations send a dangerous message to the research community," Katz told *The New York Times,* speaking from Germany where he was participating in the Nuremberg anniversary discussions. "That message ... is that it is more important for research to proceed than it is for patients to have an opportunity to agree to be research subjects."

What we are seeing now is the patient caught in the vortex of a heated, bloody battle—troops with conflicting interests fighting over the body in the bed—not only for the way treatment occurs but for physical and political control in sickness and at the end of life. The question still remains—two decades after Quinlan—who has the power to decide? Patients and families? Or medical institutions and physicians?

While medical science has since grown more clear on comas and persistent vegetative states—issues that end-of-life experts focused on during the 1970s and 1980s—continued medical success has caused newer conditions of chronic dying to be a far more common circumstance. These conditions include progressive degenerative illnesses such as Alzheimer's, Lou Gehrig's disease, and multiple sclerosis, as well as slow declines from cancer or heart disease—conditions that medicine is far less certain about in determining when treatment is hopeless, when the condition is truly terminal, and in what length of time.

In fact, now that we have this new body of end-of-life law, ethics, and practice, more Americans are finding that these laws do not address the issues raised by their particular conditions. Questions patients and families face today are not just about when a person is competent or on a machine from which he or she might be disconnected. They are about when to stop chemotherapy or dialysis, when to give ever higher doses of drugs that might create comfort but foreshorten life. These situations are not addressed by living wills, health-care proxies, or surrogacy laws.

Medical progress has now made it difficult for anyone to die without a specific decision being made to withhold or withdraw treatment. Indeed, the American Hospital Association estimates that 70 percent of the 6,000 or so daily deaths are "somehow timed or negotiated, with all concerned parties privately concurring on withdrawal of some death-delaying technology or not even starting it in the first place."

Often the medical issues that enter into such a choice may indeed be difficult for a layperson to comprehend, and the burden of such a choice difficult for a family member to take on. There are also cultural and class differences that make such discussions difficult. And the language we have come to use in talking about the withdrawal of life-sustaining treatment isn't as sensitive or clear as it might be, particularly in a time of great family crisis.

Physicians today have come to use code words like *quality of life* or *futility of treatment,* but when one is talking about one's own mother or a dying child, or when one is confronting death oneself, what do such terms really mean? For example, when a poor black family is told by a team of mostly white physicians that it is futile to treat their baby or that the quality of life expected is poor, what they may be hearing is that no matter how sick their baby is, the deciding factor for the doctors is that the baby is black.

These days, the banner of costs is also frequently waved. States like Oregon are implementing medical rationing, while health maintenance organizations are threatening all the gains made in patient autonomy and decision making with strict regulations on treatment, payment, even financial incentives for physicians to undertreat.

The bottom line is that more than twenty years after *Quinlan,* and seven years after *Cruzan,* families and patients are still not the ones making most of these difficult decisions. Even though case after case has wound through state and federal courts, even though we now have new laws in all fifty states, even with the PSDA enacted by Congress—and even though these new laws all reaffirm a family's right to speak for a loved one, whether treatment is given or withheld is still most often the decision of the treating physicians.

In the summer of 1996, Joe Cruzan committed suicide. Some press reports speculated that he had decided at the end what he'd done for Nancy had been wrong, but that's not how the family felt.

"One of the things people don't realize is how long [Nancy's situation] took," their daughter, Chris, told me shortly afterward. "I have two daughters; they were small children at the beginning and they were teenagers at the end. People's emotions are so complex. All of this with Nan had a tremendous impact on all of our lives, but to pick out one thing and say this is the reason [he committed suicide] is hard."

No one doubted, however, that it was the combination of Nancy's death, she said, "and all we went through with the courts and the protests. Dad was always a person who would fix whatever was wrong, a simple man, an independent, stoic, strong-willed man. But those qualities that helped him keep going to do what he thought was best for Nan worked against him once she died. He kept his grief bottled up inside and in the end, it just got to be too much for him.

"I don't think he ever got over that initial loss of her in the accident. Then added to that, it was eight years from the initial loss to the funeral. Dad went into it at middle age and he came out of it facing retirement. So he came out without a whole lot left to give. It's sort of like a battery. Like there's only so much, and then it's used up."

Chris says, however, that of the basic decision to let Nancy die,

Joe never had any second thoughts. "He didn't *ever* think that he'd made the wrong decision, but these things are not all black and white," she said. "There are grays. You miss a child when she's died. And you also want to do the right thing by what you think she would have wanted."

Bill Colby, the Cruzans' attorney, gave one of the eulogies at Joe's funeral. "The psychiatry books are filled with analyses which tell us that a parent who loses a child suffers the single greatest trauma a human being can experience," he said. "It is well documented that many parents never recover.

"But there is no book to tell us the depth of wound suffered by a parent who loses a child to permanent coma, stays with that child night after night, year after year, and when recovery does not come, that parent must then fight a highly public battle to free that child from unwanted medical technology, with the ultimate outcome, seven [nearly eight] torturous years after the accident, of 'winning' the right to allow that child to die.

"Joe's clear focus never strayed from his family and doing what he knew was right for the daughter he loved. The one constant that stayed with Joe, and all of the family throughout the public battle, was the firm conviction that they had charted the course in their case for Nancy that Nancy would choose for herself if she could. He counted the final authorization to set his daughter free from her medical prison as both his greatest and saddest accomplishment in life."

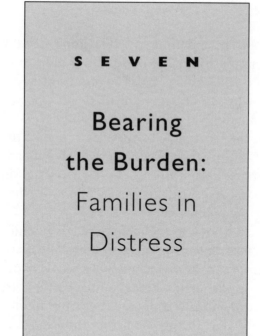

SEVEN

Bearing the Burden: Families in Distress

The way families are organized today is totally new, and not just because we live in an age of high divorce, single parenting, or same-sex marriage. Twentieth-century medicine has reshaped our lives, shifting the likelihood of death from an event that may come at any time to one that occurs mainly in old age. And that age is continually going up.

This shift has created new generations, giving American children not only the gift of living grandparents, but often, of living *great*-grandparents. It has also given those children's parents new generations to care for.

For those born in the mid-1990s, life expectancy has soared to seventy-seven years of age, and it isn't uncommon for people born early in the century to live well into their eighties and nineties. Indeed, this older segment of the population—those golfing in Arizona or Florida or traveling with elderhostels, as well as those who are poor and living tucked away in apartments or nursing homes—is the largest growing segment in the nation.

In 1900, only one household in sixteen included someone over sixty-four. Today the figure is one household in four. More than half of all midlife adults (people between fifty-three and sixty-one years old) still have one or both parents alive, and nearly three-quarters of them also have at least one child and one grandchild. Until the mid-twentieth century, most people did not live long enough to become the senior member of a four-generation family.

Nineteenth-century families were large in size, but households were filled with children—from four to eleven in a family—rather than grandparents. Most parents were young, in their twenties and early thirties. By the time they were in their thirties, their own parents were usually dead. In these large families, some of the youngsters were the biological children of the resident couple; others were stepchildren, the children of relatives or close friends who had died, apprentices, servants, or boarders.

In some ways, those families were not unlike separated or remarried families today, but they were reshaped by death, not divorce. While "family values" critics claim that divorce or single parenting are destabilizing the "traditional" family, the good news is that families today are perhaps far *more stable* than ever before, largely because we are no longer as afflicted by early deaths and can count on multiple living generations.

But the same medical advances that have given us this new, multigenerational stability have also created unprecedented burdens. Reproductive technology now allows us to postpone parenthood to an age when death was common at the turn of the century. And this new control of reproduction has allowed women—who have always been the primary caretakers—to work away from home. We've reduced the dependency of the young, but we have added a huge burden at the other end of life—with fewer people at home to give the kind of care that families have traditionally provided. Moreover, as the birth rate continues to drop, fewer children are available to care for these additional generations of the elderly.

"Family values" moralists notwithstanding, sons and daughters today are just as faithful caretakers of their frail, elderly parents as sons and daughters were in the past. In 1993, two major studies reported that the great majority of Americans are taking care of their own—in their homes and apartments, and in those of their loved ones, in every city and suburb and town across the country.

A study by the National Institute on Aging surveyed nearly 13,000 Americans aged fifty-one to sixty-one and found that most were in very close contact with their aging parents. Some 85 percent of the elderly parents saw or spoke with their midlife adult off-spring from two to seven times a week. The adult children did everything from providing financial help to cooking, shopping, taking them to doctors or other appointments, arranging caretaking, and caring for them themselves.

The second study, conducted for the American Association of Retired Persons, concluded that "the predominant pattern in the American public's behavior and feelings is that of very tight-knit and bonded family relationships."

These families are also caring for elders who require more intensive, sophisticated care than in the past. When people survive longer, they run a higher risk of Alzheimer's and other degenerative diseases. Indeed, Alzheimer's is the fourth leading cause of death, killing 100,000 people a year. Studies show that "more than 90 percent of Alzheimer's patients develop the disease after the age of 65," one 1995 report read, and "about half of everyone over the age of 85 is afflicted."

Americans have traded the stress of constant and capricious loss from death for the emotional and financial stress of long-term, high-intensity caring—yet another double-edged gift of medical miracles. We are given the option of "doing everything possible" for a loved one, yet to do so can have catastrophic family consequences and is pushing some American families to the brink of collapse.

In 1990, a man whom I will call D. Hale Cobb III died at the age of seventy-two of Alzheimer's disease. Hale had been the chief financial officer of a large corporation, known around New York City for his hilarious sense of humor and his flaming red hair. But over the previous eight or nine years, Hale had slowly begun to lose his mind. During his final two years, he was unrecognizable as the man he had once been: wheelchair bound, incontinent, tending toward violent words and behavior, howling at lights and at the moon. He recognized only his wife, Sally, and then just intermittently. It was as if he'd been invaded by the Body Snatchers; he looked the same, but an alien had entered the family home.

Alzheimer's is a progressive neurological disorder that slowly disables the brain, first eroding memory, then slowly wiping out other brain and bodily functions until death occurs. It is incurable, and its timetable is both slow and unpredictable.

In 1976, shortly after Hale took early retirement from his corporate job, he'd had a severe gall bladder attack. A year later, he developed prostate cancer. Both times he'd had emergency surgery and both times he'd needed Sally to take care of him afterward. But in 1983 or 1984, there was something else, something subtle.

Hale's son and three daughters, and his stepson and two stepdaughters, all noticed the change separately—it took two years before Sally could admit it. She made excuses, trying to convince herself that Hale was merely aging.

At that time, Hale was around sixty-five. Sally, his second wife, was in her early fifties, and they had been married fifteen years. Hale's first wife had died of cancer years before; Sally's first husband had died in a disastrous boating accident. Sally was still working in the public relations department of a museum, a job she loved.

"In retrospect," Sally says, "I think that's when he must have begun getting sick. He pressured me to stop working. He was already becoming forgetful, and he wanted me home more, he felt better with me around the house."

It was the little things at first. Hale misplaced his glasses. He lost his keys, his scarves, his umbrellas. He repeated himself, told the same jokes, asked the same questions over and over. He forgot phone numbers, addresses. He forgot words in the middle of sentences. Soon he began to lose socks or shirts he'd just taken out of drawers. Then he made lists to remember things, and he started to lose the lists.

By early 1986, it was hard even for Sally to toss off his memory loss as aging. He'd begun to lose things he'd spent his entire career carefully guarding—his appointment book, his checkbooks, his financial statements, his wallet, even some valuable bonds he'd just taken out of the safe deposit box. By the end of the year, he was forgetting to take turns on his regular routes. He drove down wrong streets, got on wrong trains. He became disoriented, lost his way home from the local store in their suburban Connecticut neighborhood.

Sally put off asking Hale not to drive for fear of hurting his manhood. But in late 1986, Sally discovered that he was paying their bills many times over; they were losing thousands of dollars each month. Sally began paying the bills herself. Then he got lost on their regular drive to their country home in Vermont. Finally, something happened that was hard to miss—Hale ran over the neighbor's dog. Sally worked up the courage to take away his car keys and hide them, knowing he never would find them.

One spring night in 1987, Hale's granddaughter got married. It was a large, very elegant garden wedding held in a large home on the shore, with lawns that rolled down to the Long Island Sound. Many of Hale's former business associates were there. As they sat down to a formal dinner, at a table set with crystal and china under a white tent, Sally tried to pretend everything was okay as Hale began to drool and curse and make inhuman noises. He was unable to cut up his meat and began throwing his peas at the guests.

"After dinner," Sally says, "when he started ranting at a man who'd been his longest, closest friend, I realized completely how sick he was. We had had a lot of friends, but after that they started going away. I also realized that our youngest grandchildren stopped wanting to come to visit." They said they were scared. Sally was devastated.

Soon after that, Hale began having trouble walking and needed a cane. Then he began waving his cane at her and threatening violence. Sally knew she needed help, and she began to confront the realities of her situation.

Sally wanted to hire an experienced nurse, but she soon discovered that their health insurance (a policy that at the time was actually the very best there was) and Medicare would cover the cost only if Hale needed *skilled nursing care*—help with such things as IVs or catheters—rather than *custodial care,* which is how they defined the day-to-day assistance Hale needed.

In August 1987, Sally hired round-the-clock nurses from a local registry and paid for them herself. "I had two people every day," she says. "One from 4 P.M. to midnight at $140 a day, and the other from 8 A.M. to 4 P.M., also for $140, so it was $280 every day. From August 4, when they started, to November 7, 1987, I spent $17,560." The Cobbs weren't poor, but when she got a financial consultant to help her sort out their expenses, Sally realized she couldn't afford a private nurse for very long. She looked around for a less expensive solution and settled on a live-in aide.

The first two aides, hired from home-care agencies, were disasters. One was verbally abusive to both Sally and Hale, and Sally suspected the second one of stealing. The third, the one she finally hired, was the aunt of Sally's cleaning lady—a kindly woman with no citizenship papers, but a big and willing heart. Sally paid her room and board and $300 for five days a week. On the weekends she hired a second aide for $160 for each two-day shift.

Ironically, when Hale was in his prime, he'd considered himself wealthy and had been proud of his financial success. He'd wanted to provide for Sally, to leave money to each of the children and grandchildren, to leave a small amount of money to the museum where Sally worked. And yet, even with their substantial investments, Sally would not be able to afford long-term care for any prolonged period of time. Their children also worried that the costs of Hale's care might be so great that Sally might use up their joint marital assets and then find herself with little to live on in her own final years.

They went to an attorney in a new, specialized field called *elder law,* who told them that Medicaid—the federal medical funds set aside to cover indigent Americans—would cover Hale after he had "spent down" all but a designated amount of his savings (their home was exempt). In order to retain any funds for Sally, however, they would have to legally divide their assets—half to Sally and half to Hale—no later than two years before Hale might need nursing home care. (This regulation was obviously designed to *prevent* people from going on Medicaid.) Failing that, Sally could divorce Hale and divide their assets that way.

Sally was horrified. Hers was a generation of women who stood by their men. She would never divorce Hale, but she was finally persuaded to divide their assets. The lawyer told her to spend money on Hale's care only from the share that was his. But she didn't always listen and spent hers too, feeling the need to protect him. In any case, Hale needed nursing-home care before the two-year waiting period was up.

By New Year's of 1989, Hale was having crisis after crisis. The prostate cancer returned. He began having kidney stone attacks, the beginnings of heart failure, pneumonia. Each time, the family doctor put him into the hospital and aggressively treated him. Not everything was covered by health insurance or Medicare. So Sally paid. There were deductibles, medications, papers to fill out, insurance clerks to call. And call. And argue with. Sally grew more exhausted, and though she refused to talk about it, their sons and daughters began fearing that Hale would soon need a nursing home and that Sally's health might also give way.

By the spring of 1989, Hale began waving his cane not only at Sally but at their children and the older grandchildren, threatening violence, yelling obscenities, and throwing food at them. He smashed the downstairs TV. He tried to hit the aide and cursed at her. He tried to hit Sally. And she tried to deny it. She'd say "He didn't mean it," or "He's sick." She tried to be brave. But to watch Hale was to wonder at what point a human body ceases to be truly human.

By summer, he could no longer walk even with the cane or with a walker and he couldn't get up or down the stairs. He would fall in a ball onto the floor, and just lie there, howling, in a rage. Sally was athletic. She rode horses three times a week and swam on the days in between, but she permanently injured her back trying to lift him. Day and night he wandered around the house. He opened doors while she slept and wandered out. She stopped sleeping, afraid he'd get lost or fall in the nearby lake or get hit by horses along the horse trail near their house. Then he became incontinent.

He'd urinate or defecate wherever he went, whenever he felt the need. Sally didn't want to wound his pride by buying diapers. She and the aide decided they would take turns sleeping. They followed him around, brought him back, cleaned him up, cleaned the rug, wiped the floor. The doctor began to prescribe sedatives to quell his rage, but his cursing and violent threats continued. Sally was scared that anyone should find out about the abuse, although now only a handful of friends dared visit.

Still, each time Hale became physically ill his doctor called in specialist after specialist to treat him, just as he might have if Hale had had any real hope of being cured. Gastroenterologists, cardiologists, internists, surgeons, oncologists, urologists. These doctors said his prostate was fine, though it seemed as if they were treating him for cancer. No one ever mentioned the C word. Even more important, none of these doctors acknowledged the fundamental truth: Cancer or not, Hale Cobb had lost his mind.

Only that summer did *any* doctor admit that he probably had Alzheimer's. But the Cobbs' children knew all along. They also knew that Hale had always said that if he lost his mind, he would never want to live. Even now, whenever he could manage a coherent sentence he would say, "I want to die," but his doctor only began to give him antidepressants.

As Hale's physical ailments became more frequent, his children began to ask his doctor: "What's the point of aggressively treating one illness after the next? What is he coming back to? If he's cured of this, won't he still be a man without a mind? Isn't pneumonia supposed to be an old man's best friend?"

Sally was more hesitant. She, too, knew that Hale never wanted to live like this, but she was of the generation that venerated doctors. She'd always thought that one should care for one's spouse as much as one possibly could. Yet Hale seemed to be suffering needlessly.

Hale's doctors weren't hesitant at all. Whenever his family asked them to stop aggressive treatment, to stop scheduling surgeries for heart problems or fighting pneumonia, the family doctor—and the specialists he brought in—accused them outright of wanting to murder him. One doctor finally asked his incredulous wife directly, "What? Are you trying to kill your husband?" Sally just cried.

Before Hale's first wife died she had begged doctors to stop treating her cancer once she saw that the treatments were hopeless. After she died, Hale told anyone who would listen that he'd made a big mistake letting those useless treatments go on, and said that if this kind of thing were to happen to him, please, just let him go. But Connecticut did not have a living-will or health-care proxy law until 1991. By that time, Hale had already died.

One night in the fall of 1989, Sally woke up terrified. Hale had gotten out of bed and collapsed unconscious on the bedroom floor. Frantically, she called 911. The ambulance came for him. Once he was in the emergency room and admitted into the hospital, doctors went full tilt to save him. State and federal law required them to do so.

Sally hadn't known all that, but if she had it wouldn't have mattered anyway. As with most caregivers, her middle-of-the-night instinct was to call 911. She didn't realize that if she called, doctors would "do everything possible" to save him, even if "everything" wasn't really what she wanted them to do. And if she had realized, she would have called anyway. She could not have sat and watched Hale die on the floor.

This time Hale's sons and daughters made a special plea. Among them were a psychiatrist, a media executive, a college history professor, a special education teacher, a Wall Street analyst. They were PTA presidents and Ivy League graduates, professionals who were married to professionals; they were accustomed to making the system work for them. They asked the doctor not to give Hale antibiotics, not to do any surgery, not to give him fluids. They wanted Hale just to have pain medications to keep him comfortable and let him go. But his family doctor and the specialists he enlisted refused.

These adult children insisted that if things kept on, Sally might be so worn down that she would be the first one to die. They saw Hale's medical treatment as no different from physical abuse. One son, speaking on behalf of Hale's family, threatened to sue the doctors and the hospital for physical and emotional assault and battery, but he and his siblings backed down when they realized that Sally was too distraught to withstand a trial.

Demented as he was, Hale tried to pull out his own IV and catheter tubes. His children and stepchildren and their spouses all thought he was trying to make his wishes clear in whatever way he could. The hospital staff tied his arms to the bed. Finally, Hale was medically stabilized. His doctor told Sally that it was time for a nursing home. Hale had always told everyone he never wanted to go to a nursing home, that he hoped he would die long before that.

Sally was torn. She wanted to take care of him, but she wasn't physically able to anymore. Hale had been a dignified man, and now everything about his condition was so undignified. It was as if the real Hale had actually died years before. The doctor gave Sally some Valium to calm her down. Then she said she'd look around.

It took time to find Hale a nursing home bed. Sally said that she'd consent to a home only if they could find a place nearby, so she could be with him every day. She didn't want him to go; she felt guilty, responsible, dutiful. Finally she reasoned that he'd only be sleeping in the home, that *professionals* would be caring for him, and that she'd be with him all the time anyhow, just as before.

Meanwhile, the family was told that Hale had to leave the hospital. He had used up the Medicare days allotted for intestinal bleeding, and there was nothing more they could do to treat him. Since he didn't yet have a nursing home room, he was taken by ambulance from the hospital back home, and put to bed in his and Sally's room.

That's when all five of Hale and Sally's daughters and stepdaughters and one daughter-in-law decided to come—from Maryland, from New Hampshire, from Texas, from the suburbs of Chicago and New York. They came together as women—without their husbands and children—for the first time in many, many years.

They spent nearly a week spelling Sally in caring for Hale, sitting up late together in the living room, and spending long hours talking around the old, round kitchen table. The normal issues in their lives seemed to evaporate as they focused intently. They realized how very desperate Hale's situation was and the enormity of care that Sally had been trying to provide. Finally, a consensus among the daughters, at first emotional and unspoken, boiled to the surface. It was as if in this state—all female, all daughters, all unleashed from the moorings of what others might say is just or right—a higher sort of rightness took over.

The night before he was to go into the nursing home, Hale lay under a cream-colored down comforter in his and Sally's antique, four-poster bed, moaning in apparent pain. He recognized no one. The daughters called another doctor for advice, a friend of the family who was a hospice physician. He had told them that in hospice it's common to increase the pain medication when it's clear that someone is in terrible pain and ready to go (though he didn't say whether that meant "ready to die" or psychologically ready). They thought Hale was as ready as anyone, and they decided to help him.

They called Hale's own doctor and asked him for pain medication. He told them he would write a triplicate prescription for Demerol and they should come pick it up. "How many of these pills would be so much that it would kill him?" they asked. And the doctor told them how much was too much, so they'd "be sure not to exceed that dose."

Hale had always loved homemade applesauce. While one daughter went to the drugstore to fill the prescription, another stopped at a local gourmet shop and bought organic Granny Smith apples. The daughters and the stepdaughters and the daughter-in-law gathered downstairs in the kitchen. They peeled and cored the apples one by one, cut them into one-inch chunks, and boiled the chunks with lemon juice, sugar, cinnamon, nutmeg, and a little vanilla. Then they dumped the entire bottle of Demerol onto the butcher block counter, mashed up the pills by grinding them between two spoons, scooped up the powder with a butter knife, and blended it in with the applesauce, stirring constantly.

They wanted to be sure the mixture wouldn't burn Hale's lips, so they waited until it cooled slightly. Then two daughters sat on either side of their father in the bed, and two stepdaughters sat by his legs. One daughter and the daughter-in-law took turns stirring the pot down in the kitchen, to keep it warm—the way Hale liked it—and to maintain its potency. They shifted positions, all of them switching off with each other. Hale's head rested on three pillows, his thin face surrounded by 330-thread-count linens trimmed in delicate lace. They kissed and stroked and talked to him. His own daughters talked most—of their childhood, their mom, how much they loved him. All of the women told him they loved him. He didn't know who they were, not even his own daughters, but he seemed comforted.

Then his daughters explained what they were about to do and Hale began to open and close his mouth. There was something there inside his brain, but it was hard to tell what. Suddenly he whispered. "Go," he said, "I want to go." He opened his mouth like a baby wanting to be fed. Those were the last intelligible words he ever said.

One daughter, then another—daughters and stepdaughters and daughter-in-law—began spooning the drug-laced applesauce into his mouth. Sally stayed on the third floor, collapsed in sleep in one of the guest rooms, knowing, but not really wanting to know, what they were doing. Hale wasn't able to swallow very well by then, so the applesauce began dribbling out the corners of his mouth, down his cheeks and chin. They worried that he'd choke. They sat him up. They wondered why they were worried, when what they wanted was to help him go. All six of them cried and cried.

They stayed up all night, and by morning, Hale was still breathing. As the nursing home attendants came in with their gurney and wheeled him off, they were consumed with a terrible feeling of defeat. They felt they'd let him down. Luckily for them, no one did any blood tests when, in late October 1989, D. Hale Cobb III was admitted.

That had been Hale's—and the family's—last best chance. Once Hale became a nursing home patient, he could no longer have his own family physician. When Hale entered the home, he was assigned one of their doctors. Sally was asked if she wanted a doctor who would "do everything possible" for him. She said yes.

She didn't understand medical euphemisms. The new physician was even more aggressive about prolonging treatment than their family physician had been. To Sally and the children, "doing everything possible" meant taking good care of Hale and keeping him free of pain or other uncomfortable symptoms. But after they realized that wasn't what the doctor intended—that he'd meant far more than that—they were not permitted to change physicians.

Hale stayed in that nursing home—an expensive private nursing home in an exclusive Connecticut neighborhood—for ten months. Medicare and the health insurance policy that Hale and Sally had both had a per diem coverage; even together that rate was far lower than what Sally had to pay.

Hale recognized no one. The only thing he could still do was sing old songs with Sally. She liked that, because it made her feel the warmth of still having a spouse she loved. They would sit holding hands as they sang. For some reason, the memory of old songs was the only part of Hale's brain still alive. The rest of the time he was nearly an animal.

He was often strapped to his bed or his chair. He was diapered. He cursed and yelled and wailed. He was more violent than ever. Each time he got ill, they'd rush him to the hospital to be treated. It was always the same thing: antibiotics, fluids, heart medications, whatever they needed to do to keep his body alive, despite what Hale's family might say. And then they'd return him to the home, always worse than when he left.

In September 1990, Sally's brother persuaded her to visit him and his family in Maine for a weekend. They'd tried to get her to visit for two years but she'd felt guilty about leaving. Hale had just been sent to the hospital for pneumonia, treated, and returned to the nursing home—this time nearly unconscious, almost totally unable to swallow, and with tubes coming out of veins in his legs and arms. This time, in her exhaustion, Sally said yes.

While she was in Maine, Hale's son came to see him, as he'd promised, so Hale wouldn't be alone while Sally was gone. Hale died during the night, after his son spent the day with him, holding his hand as he lay in bed.

The morning of the funeral, as the children gathered around the kitchen table again—this time with Sally—they got into a big fight. Feelings that had been building all those years Hale was ill finally burst out. Hale's children accused Sally of holding on to him longer than she should have. Sally said she loved him; she hadn't known how to get the nursing home to stop treating him; she couldn't *not* rush him to the hospital whenever he got sick.

His children said they did not understand why Sally had a physician who was as aggressive about treating Hale as the nursing home's doctor was, nor why she couldn't just change doctors. They accused her of being selfish in wanting Hale to continue being treated.

Sally's own children were angered both by these attacks on their mother and by the physical and emotional toll the whole situation had taken on her.

And the financial burden had been staggering. By this time, Sally had spent what would have been Hale's entire share of their joint marital investments on his care, except for his portion of the house where she still lived. During his final year and a half, Sally had also spent $100,000 of her own assets on his care. The nursing home alone cost $72,000 a year, not including many doctors' bills, which somehow didn't seem to all be covered, nurses' aides and private nurses whenever he went into the hospital, since she felt the regular nursing staff needed help with the intensity his care required.

In the end, it wasn't clear what was or wasn't covered by Medicare or the private health insurer. The mountain of paperwork required for reimbursement simply overwhelmed Sally. She worked at it diligently, but she probably failed to claim some reimbursements that might have been covered; her health insurance would pay after Medicare covered a portion, and after the health insurance sent a check, she often would have to file multiple appeals. Weary and under stress, Sally filed claims; but she also just paid.

"I foolishly listened to Hale when he kept pushing me to stop working," she says, "and I lost a lot of money because of that. If I'd worked five years more I would have had a much better retirement package and I could have built up our savings even more." But by then, the Hale she had known was gone, and their investments were mostly used up. He'd wanted to leave his wife and his children well off, but now his children would get nothing, and Sally was left with little more than their home when he died.

Instead of a legacy of wealth, Hale's long and frightful dying process left his family a legacy of sadness. The resentment Hale's children felt toward Sally for what they believed was her role in extending his life into indignities he'd never wanted created a permanent rift that has carried on to the grandchildren as well. Sally's children are equally as angry at Hale's children. They are all still polite to one another, but in the end Sally was left grieving not only the loss of her husband but the loss of family closeness and of the solid financial base that she and Hale had spent a lifetime building. The way Hale died left his wife in financially reduced circumstances and ripped apart the family support she would need for her own aging.

Even families with the best intentions and the greatest resources find themselves exhausted trying to tend to the rigorous needs of the dying. They need help in making good medical or care decisions, they need help interacting with physicians and sorting through their treatment options, and—when they do make tough decisions—they need the power to implement them.

Rather than helping families, both the medical and legal systems tend to construe family concerns as a conflict of interest with the care of the patient. Medical care is primarily patient centered, and should the family disagree with the treatment decisions that are made, the family is often suspected—sometimes even accused—of abuse.

Yet in looking at the Cobbs, it is not so clear who was the abused and who was the abuser. Hale and Sally were both abused by a medical system that refused to acknowledge the impact of extended—and hopeless—care imposed on both a terminally ill patient and his family against their wishes. Was the family wrong in trying to help Hale hasten his death? But what, then, of the doctors who kept on treating, ever prolonging the inevitable, while Hale suffered and his family did the caring?

Now that life can be almost mercilessly extended, we are finding that we have failed as a nation to assess adequately the goals of modern treatment—when treatment makes sense, when it undermines the well-being of both patient and family, and what happens then. There is no cultural agreement about when treatment should stop, and no good social provisions for long-term care.

At the very same time that Hale was in the nursing home, Jean Elbaum, who was comatose, was in a nursing home in another suburb nearby. For two years, Jean's husband, Murray, tried to have her life-sustaining equipment shut off. Since she had not put her wishes about medical treatment in writing, the nursing home refused to do as Murray asked. Finally Murray won his case in court, the year before Hale died. But a second court ruled that he must pay the $100,000 the nursing home charged during the time he had tried to force it to stop his wife's treatment.

Individual families are heroically caring for their own, but they need informed, sensitive help, much like the patients these families are caring for. The ethics of caring—the idea that everyone should focus on the comfort of the sick person—do not acknowledge family members' strong emotional bonds with one another, and how they might interpret what they need to do as a result of these bonds. Nor do they acknowledge the sacrifices that medical success demands.

Nearly two decades ago—as illness began to be prolonged—the grassroots phenomenon of support organizations and self-help groups for patients and caregivers began to appear. The fact that these groups are mushrooming throughout America in itself is a clue about the magnitude of difficulties that families and patients face with illnesses that entail long-term declines.

Today such groups have formed to deal with almost all of the illnesses that Americans now die of. Patients and families across America can attend support groups for cancer, AIDS, Alzheimer's, Lou Gehrig's disease, multiple sclerosis, kidney, heart, and lung disease. They provide information on treatment and research; on how to communicate with physicians and caretakers; on what to expect and how to go through diagnostic and treatment procedures; and they offer psychological, spiritual—even physical and financial support—as well as counseling and therapy on coping with illness, decline, and death, and on the extreme burdens of caretaking.

"We know from experience," says Diane Blum, M.S.W., executive director of Cancer Care, Inc., "that information is a powerful tool that can help people cope with a cancer diagnosis and improve the quality of care they receive." The important role these groups play cannot be overrated, given studies that now show just how terrible the impact of extended dying has been on American families.

Recall the SUPPORT study that examined the cases of some nine thousand people who came into emergency rooms throughout the country with five major illnesses, including heart, kidney, lung, cerebrovascular disease, and cancer. These patients (nearly five thousand of whom died) and their families were followed from the time they were admitted until they died, or until the six-month follow-up period had ended.

Dr. Joanne Lynn, SUPPORT's codirector, says that researchers learned that treatment decisions are in fact made not by the patient alone but by whole families, in consultation with their physicians. These decisions—and even those portions of treatment decision that the patient might make by himself—are most often arrived at with the entire family's well-being in mind. They are not, as doctors and lawyers have long believed, simply patient centered.

Among the study's major findings was the enormous impact of illness on American families. Most important, researchers found that the consequence of serious illness and its medical treatment—the long-term care that may be needed after a patient is over an initial crisis—can have a major, and sometimes catastrophic, impact on the patient's entire family, even putting other family members dangerously at risk. In looking at the impact of serious illness on 2,661 of the patients who survived long enough to return home, the SUPPORT study researchers found that for 55 percent—or more than half of them—the family unit as a whole experienced one or another very serious problem, or a whole complex of problems, as the result of that one member's illness. Three-quarters of all these patients lived more than six months, so the time during which these problems occurred was considerable.

The serious adverse effects on the families included the following:

· In 34 percent of all the families studied, the patient was so impaired that he or she required a large amount of caregiving assistance from another family member.

· In 20 percent of all the families in the study, someone had to quit work or make a major life change to give the care needed.

· For 29 percent, a major source of family income was lost; in 31 percent of the study's families, most of the family savings were spent. (The study didn't address the debts that remained or whether families were forced, as some are, into bankruptcy.)

· For 17 percent of all the patient families, the cost of the illness caused a major change in family plans, including moving to a less expensive home, delaying medical care for another family member, or altering someone's educational plans.

· For 12 percent, another family member became ill or unable to function normally because of the physical or emotional stress of one family member's illness.

The SUPPORT researchers point out that their data merely confirm other studies: One study of four hundred cancer patients found that 90 percent of them were dependent on another person for assistance with personal care, shopping, or transportation, and that their caregivers reported a similar loss in savings and having to go into debt.

A second study, of heart bypass patients, found that a third of their spouses reported "severe anxiety" and nearly half said their financial situations were "highly inadequate." A third found that spouses of patients with Alzheimer's disease had poorer mental and physical health than the general population.

National attention has been focused on the lack of health insurance and the financial pressures that uncovered medical care inflicts on families. But 96 percent of the patients in the SUPPORT study *were* covered by health insurance or Medicare. Acute medical care was not what created financial burdens. Rather, what was devastating were the home-care costs—which were not covered by Medicare or by other medical insurance—the financial, emotional, and physical costs of providing the additional daily care that seriously ill and dying patients required once they were out of the hospital.

In fact, when researchers looked further, they found that while many patients might opt against choosing life-prolonging treatment so as not to burden their families, those patients and families who chose treatment aimed at "comfort care" rather than "life-extending care" experienced the greatest economic hardship. Researchers attributed that to the relative lack of home-care coverage in our medical care system, which favors in-patient acute care.

Although families bear the impact of extended treatment most heavily, they have had to fight to influence treatment decisions. And instead of establishing support systems for beleaguered families, our society has brought forth phalanxes of lawyers, ethicists, physicians, and social commentators who threaten—as we have seen—to put limits on the kinds of medical choices families can and cannot make, and to monitor them if they suspect abuse of services or even of the patients themselves.

Interestingly, while some other researchers suggest that relatives may not be the best decision makers because they might have a financial interest in one decision or another, the SUPPORT study found that the possibility of economic hardship identically affected the preferences of the patients and the family surrogate, and had nothing to do with any disagreements about the goals of care.

"Families are those who grieve for the patient's suffering and death, who have a history of making decisions that account for the well-being of all concerned, and about whom the patient most likely would have had the most concern," Dr. Lynn says. "Somehow to imagine that the society could, or should, set up systems that remove the family from decision making is almost outrageous."

Although some fraction of American families may be downright abusive, even healthy families aren't well served by the current, unrealistic medical model: "We must save the patient; it's not our concern whether the family has the resources to give him long-term care." *Patients' rights* and *legal protections,* Dr. Lynn concluded, are not the real concerns of healthy American families.

Among the more astounding findings she cites come from the work of her colleague David Reiss, M.D., a psychiatrist at George Washington University Medical Center. In examining the long-term survival of kidney disease patients in a dialysis program, Dr. Reiss learned that those patients who came from the healthiest, most intact, best educated, most supportive families were the ones who survived the shortest length of time. In fact, strong family bonds almost predicted short survival.

Their shortened survival rates were the result, it seems, of their noncompliance with their doctors—specifically, their refusal to keep to the diets prescribed. "As best as we could determine," Dr. Reiss and his colleagues wrote, "none of the deaths was an explicit suicide." Yet these patients were dying, and dying faster as a result of something they themselves chose to do. Without stating it—perhaps even without realizing it—the ill person merely took matters into his or her own hands in order to preserve the health of the family unit.

Intrigued by Dr. Reiss's findings, other researchers have since studied patients with ailments that require someone in the family to spend long periods in high-intensity caretaking. The healthiest coping mechanisms of families in the past may no longer work today, these researchers concluded. The crucial distinction is between short-term and long-term care. While nearly all families are able to spring into action for one member in crisis for a short period of time, most families find it difficult to concentrate all their physical and emotional resources—especially without supportive and financial long-term care assistance—on one person month after month, year after year.

A growing number of medical researchers and counselors have now begun to create programs to help patients and their families differentiate between the demands of an acute phase of an illness—say, when a person has an immediate medical crisis that lands him or her in an emergency room or an intensive care unit—and the kind of care that's needed for coping over the long haul of a chronic disease or terminal decline. (It's the difference between the energy requirements of a sprint as opposed to a marathon.)

Partly from the knowledge culled from medical programs like Dr. Reiss's, partly from the extensive help provided over the last two decades by self-help groups like Cancer Care, partly from the development of new medical fields such as family therapy and psycho-oncology, a new group of professionals has also begun to emerge with expertise on the psychosocial dimensions and family dynamics of illness and dying. They also have developed sophisticated knowledge about the psychological trajectories of disease-specific modern illnesses.

Froma Walsh, Ph.D., is the codirector of the Center for Family Health at the University of Chicago, a faculty member at the university's school of medicine, and the coeditor of *Living Beyond Loss: Death in the Family*. She has found that today there seem to be three different trajectories of illness.

"The first," she says, "is a steady downhill course that is only a matter of time from diagnosis to death. The main concern families have here is how to postpone death as long as possible." In a way, this faster trajectory is easiest to handle.

"The second illness trajectory is a steady, chronic course that may not progress toward death quickly, like Alzheimer's, an illness that challenges the caregiver but is no more likely to cause death than something else that may happen to any other family member," Dr. Walsh says. "Here the family is focused on taking care of the father, for instance, when the mother dies. They may be almost burned out from taking care of one family member, so they can't focus on another, because they have no energy left."

In this kind of trajectory the family needs to learn how to put what Dr. Walsh calls "boundaries around the illness" in order to keep the health of the entire family intact. That means that dialysis patients, for example, are encouraged to arrange for these treatments themselves—with a set schedule and reliable transportation—and their families are helped to continue their normal life, with the patient (and his or her care routine) incorporated among the many other dimensions of family life.

Indirectly, this also benefits patients because they are more able to live whatever time is left as *persons* rather than only as *patients*, and they are less likely to be resented by other family members.

The third course of illness resembles a roller-coaster trajectory. "There are all these life-threatening episodes," Dr. Walsh points out. "The patient can die at any episode. That makes it hard, because often you can't be admitted into a hospice program because it's not clear whether the person will live or die. The family members feel high anxiety, and they worry. If they upset the patient, they could precipitate a crisis or the person could die. So they have to live with the constant threat of loss, that at any moment this ill family member could die." This is the one that seems to be hardest for families to handle.

Living with a mastectomy, a colostomy, a heart or a lung condition can bring new vulnerabilities, emotional explosions, and physical and sexual adjustments. Sleep disorders can affect not only couples but whole households. Ill children can create jealousies and tensions for healthy siblings. Trouble can appear in the form of depression, anger, substance abuse, or in resentments over rehabilitation. Most critically, the ill person is different from the way he or she was before, and it takes effort for both the patient and the family to readjust.

In these circumstances, tyranny, gender politics (since women are often the caregivers), abuse, or emotional scapegoating can emerge. People often think of caregivers tyrannizing patients, but more often it's the patient who becomes unreasonably demanding, producing a family cycle of anger and guilt.

As the illness goes on, dysfunction can increase exponentially. Sometimes, outrageous behavior may be a patient's desperate move to have some minor semblance of control in an out-of-control experience. Giving the patient any kind of control—even if it's over pain medications or who can come into the room—can help reduce tyrannical behavior, since it's the feelings of total dependence that often increase patients' frustration and anger.

With violence and abusive behavior, however—most particularly when it is the result of Alzheimer's or another form of dementia—boundaries need to be set to protect the rest of the family, and it is crucial to address the caretaker's needs as well.

To do so, Dr. Walsh says, may require reorganizing the family as a unit. Work may need to be shared in different ways; more people may need to contribute financially; someone new may have to learn to take over as parent. More home care might be needed, or help from a day-care center, nursing home, or rehabilitation center. The patient may be asked to do more for himself. Or he may need to enter a nursing home or a hospice program.

Illness trajectories can quickly change. Once the patient and family have adjusted to one level of illness and disability, they often find that the illness changes drastically, seemingly overnight, or spirals quickly downward. Families are forced under these conditions to learn a new kind of flexibility, to move from learning to take an illness in stride, to making full use of the little time left, to preparing for imminent death.

"Nothing is harder on families than death," Dr. Walsh says, "because it brings up feelings that are not all nice. Unless you can talk openly about this, it really shuts communication down. [Family members think] that they are not allowed to have days where they're frustrated or overwhelmed or angry about what this illness is doing to their lives. And then [their anger or frustration is] compounded by guilt. After all, a parent or a partner or a child is dying, so what right do they have to these feelings? Sometimes there's a sense of, 'Well, I'm not the dying person, so every [other problem] is kind of minimal, so I should be stoic and just accept it.' Well, where feelings don't get expressed in a relationship or are taboo, they can come out in behaviors that are dysfunctional." Families that can talk these normal feelings through can come out of the long illness and death of one of their members still healthy and intact.

The lack of available home care, lack of finances to cover it, the sorry state of nursing homes, and the relatively high cost of insurance for long-term care weigh heavily on families. For patients who qualify for it, hospice can be a miracle. But hospice isn't for everyone. Aside from the need for a primary caretaker and a six-month diagnosis, there must be space in the home where a person may peacefully die, and the home must be stable enough to bring opiate drugs into it.

The sad secret that many don't want to admit is that care at home, wonderful as it can be in helping a patient to a good death, is hard on families. Home care may allow for those close, intimate, late-night times with the dying family member, for opportunities to resolve unfinished business, often with skilled counselors to help. But there are also the difficult times: changing diapers, losing sleep or feeling intense anxiety because the patient is in pain or can't breathe, having strangers in the house—even giving up a certain amount of family and patient autonomy to them—having to remember to give many different kinds of medications on a complicated schedule, doing sometimes gruesome tasks, or just plain exhaustion and fear. Lacking help to make adjustments, not having enough information on treatment decisions, and not knowing what to do when a new illness plateau arises can leave families and patients overwhelmed.

These are tough decisions. If patient and family issues are addressed all along, if families know what to expect in a particular illness trajectory, if they have guidance in knowing what decisions might be required of them and preparing ahead of time, a more sane—and family-friendly—illness environment might appear.

"Healthy families aren't distinguished by an absence of problems," Dr. Walsh says. "It's how they mobilize with the problems. At the time of illness and loss there is a flexibility, a shifting of burdens and roles so that no one member is overly stressed."

America at the end of the twentieth century is a nation of blended, multicultural families, or "families of choice." Physicians and counselors are just beginning to consider how these new family structures might affect care of the dying.

Barbara Koenig, Ph.D., is an anthropologist and executive director of the Stanford Center for Biomedical Ethics in Palo Alto, California. The rise of modern bioethics, with its emphasis on individual rights, she says, has failed to take into consideration our nation's cultural diversity.

"We tend to be very individualistic, and there is the assumption that everyone wants to be very aggressive about making decisions, talking openly, planning, making wills, being sort of very hyper-rational about it," Dr. Koenig told a *New York Times* reporter in 1995. "The bottom line is, the United States is aberrant in being so open about death."

American families in fact have widely different views on such crucial issues as the nature of death, necessary rituals, expectations of an afterlife, whether folk medicines or faith healers need to be involved in the medical process, whether or not the patient should even be told of a poor prognosis, whether the patient or the family should be the primary decision maker, and who in the family should make decisions.

It should be no surprise that Chinese, Irish, Italian, Lebanese, Japanese, Vietnamese, Haitian, Russian, Korean, and German-Jewish families do not function alike, either in sickness or in health, nor do people from within those cultures necessarily function similarly from one generation to the next, particularly if one of them is the immigrant generation.

One study of eight hundred elderly patients at the University of Southern California found that Mexican and South Korean immigrants were far less willing to make medical care decisions than were either white or black Americans. While 87 percent of whites and 89 percent of blacks felt a patient should be told they had metastatic cancer, only 65 percent of the Mexican-Americans and just 47 percent of the Korean-Americans did. And while 65 percent of white Americans thought a patient should decide about the use of life support equipment, only 28 percent of the Koreans did. (The majority thought the family should.)

Medical social workers have found that Haitian families believe that even talking about death brings on bad spirits. Korean-Americans, Japanese-Americans, and Mexican-Americans give more weight to the decision making of the family than to the patient. Some ethnic groups, such as the Japanese, consider it cruel even to tell the patient that he or she is dying; the family must make the end-of-life choices. And many Asian cultures feel it is bad luck for people to die in the home.

Professionals who deal with these issues—psychiatrists, psychologists, social workers, chaplains, hospice counselors, leaders of support groups, and so on—need to consider this large variance in the way that modern families are structured and how they make family decisions.

Programs that can facilitate culturally diverse medical decision making have begun to be implemented in many medical centers around the country. Among the most successful is an educational effort called Decisions Near the End of Life, which is led by Harvard-trained psychologist Mildred Solomon, Ed.D., and jointly run by the Educational Development Corporation, in Newton, Massachusetts, and the Hastings Center.

As of 1996, the Decisions staff was running programs at 175

hospitals and nursing homes nationwide, helping health-care professionals think more deeply about the experience of dying, develop culturally diverse ways to communicate with families who are undergoing a loss or are grieving, and guide these families to better decision making.

Dr. Solomon cites as an example a hospital that serves primarily a population of Cambodian immigrants who look to their tribal leader for help and empowerment in medical decisions. The problem was, the leader wasn't always there when crucial decisions needed to be made. Instead of fighting against this cultural belief, the hospital went to the tribal leader and asked him to empower bilingual Cambodians to work with the hospital staff and act as his on-site substitutes. Once he agreed, the care and decision making went more smoothly.

In another program, in the Southwest, Native American medicine men and medicine women were enlisted to work in hospitals so that Native American cures could be utilized as an adjunct to Western medical treatment.

Families in which there is conflict—particularly over who has the right to decide on treatment—pose a special challenge. Culturally and racially mixed marriages, for example, divorce and remarriage or same-sex relationships can complicate families and may cause family strife to quickly become bitter and complex. "It's important in the dying process," says David Brennan, M.S.W., a social worker and bereavement counselor, "to try to reduce these conflicts [and to include in the dying process] the communities that people are now knitting together."

Brennan, who worked at The Hospice at Mission Hill in Boston (which largely served an AIDS clientele and has now closed), and Tom Grothe, R.N., a nurse at Coming Home Hospice in the primarily gay Castro district of San Francisco, deal daily with AIDS. Such hospices see gay families, poor families, Hispanic and black families, birth families, families by marriage, and families of choice. All of these families—and the patients themselves—are coping with what therapists who see them now call multiple grief.

These communities must deal not just with individual loss but with multiple losses—one death on top of the next, friend after friend, sometimes at the rate of five or more a week. Grothe says each person he sees in his hospice now may know one hundred or more people who have already died. Indeed, the extent of pain and disruption that the AIDS communities—gay and straight, mainstream and minority—are experiencing today is precedented only by periods in history where there have been wars or vast epidemics.

Grothe says that San Francisco gays, for example, have now lost their entire sense of community to AIDS—along with their artists, their spokesmen, their singers, their dancers, their caregivers, and their lovers.

In the Boston community where Brennan worked, fathers and mothers with AIDS in minority families die, leaving children—some of whom have AIDS—to be cared for solely by aging grandmothers or aunts.

In communities like these, people are suffering from deaths still unmourned as they themselves are dying, approaching each new death—including their own—with fresh visual memories of those who have only recently died. They are dealing with a kind of multiple grief that is rarely seen outside of battlefields. It's a grief that permits little time for sadness or mourning, a grief that causes numbness, from which it is hard to recover and is carried to the funeral of every friend or lover who succumbs.

Those who work with the gay community find that multiple losses are too much to handle by working each grief through, as one might when deaths come one at a time, some years apart. Instead, mass rituals, like memorial services, are used to mark a whole community's grief, to shape this grief so it can be vented in very particular times in particular ways, so that it doesn't paralyze people every day, day after day, year after year.

Just as therapists like Grothe in the gay community have learned how to help its members cope with frequent loss, therapists—like Froma Walsh and Mildred Solomon—are helping modern, blended, multicultural, multigenerational American families of all kinds. In the process, they are helping these families not only to shape their ways of coping with modern dying, but to build better memories of death for the generations to come. In so doing, they are creating an entirely new culture of caring and dying.

EIGHT

Hospice: The Birth of the Modern Art of Dying

One night at the inpatient unit of Cabrini Hospice in Manhattan, Sister Loretta Palamara walked into a room to sit with a patient. "Joseph was actively dying," she later told me. "A young doctor—a new resident—was standing near him. Joseph had signed papers requesting no treatment. The young doctor didn't know what to do, since medically he'd done everything he *could* do."

Sister Loretta pulled a chair up next to Joseph's bed. "I began stroking his arm and talking to him gently," she said. "Then the doctor saw a pack of cigarettes on the TV and asked if he could take one. They were Joseph's. He wouldn't be needing them anymore, so I told him okay, I didn't think he'd mind."

"The doctor went out into the hall, smoking and pacing," Sister Loretta said. "He kept looking back in. Then he came back and sat there as I sang softly to Joseph and told him, 'Look for your parents. They're going to show you new playgrounds.' Boy, was I nervous. I'd never had a doctor watch me before. But I kept on.

"All of a sudden, Joseph smiled, tried to sit up, and held out his arms. 'Sister,' he said, 'I see them!' I asked who. 'My parents,' he told me. 'And they're just as beautiful as you said.' And right after that, he died."

Just then, the doctor's beeper went off and he started to run out of the room. Sister Loretta asked if he wanted the cigarettes, and he called back that he didn't smoke.

She sat with Joseph about ten minutes longer, still stroking him. Then she went to find the young doctor. "I wondered how he was, because he seemed so nervous. 'I know you've seen death before,' " she told him.

" 'Sister,' he said, 'I've seen deaths, but only in emergency situations. It's always been so frenetic and violent. Never so peaceful like that. You know, if people have to die, everyone should be able to die like that.' "

In hospice circles, Sister Loretta—a nun of the Mother Cabrini Order and Cabrini Hospice's spiritual counselor—is known to be particularly gifted at helping people die peaceful deaths. She estimates that she's been with more than one thousand people as they have died.

When she told me about Joseph, I had just begun to spend a month following her on her rounds at Cabrini Hospice, nearly camping out at her hospice, trying to learn what she does. It was she who first introduced me to Peter Ciccone, who was an inpatient at Cabrini Hospice at the time, and it was she who helped me understand what was happening to Peter in those months as he slowly grew paralyzed with the AIDS virus, and when he finally died.

Sister Loretta tries to talk with each patient in his or her own symbolic or spiritual language, I found, to communicate so that anyone—no matter what his or her religious or spiritual conviction—can hear the metaphoric language of transcendence that seems to occur near death.

One reason she may be so good at what she does might be because she grew up in Hollywood, one of two child-actress twins whose mother was also a screen actress, and she learned to communicate—body and soul—in big-screen, living color. Though she weighs close to three hundred pounds, she is not averse to dressing up in a clown outfit, planting kisses on cheeks, or sharing candy hearts with a dying patient.

But there is also another reason behind Sister Loretta's commitment. When she was twenty-five, she nearly died when she was hit by lightning as she was trying to close a window for an elderly nun in her convent. The lightning bolt seriously damaged her metabolism—which is why she is now so large (she gained one hundred pounds in a single year).

In 1969, eleven years later, when she was thirty-six, she almost died again from an embolism that doctors said was caused by complications from the continued weight gain and from the lightning. Lying in her hospital bed, she had a classic near-death experience, feeling herself traveling through a tunnel, experiencing a deep sense of absolute peace, seeing a bright light emanating an intense kind of love, and finding the elderly nun—who had since died—coming to greet her, telling her to go back, she had a mission to do, that it wasn't yet her time.

Only later did Sister Loretta realize that her mission must be to work with the dying. She is now dangerously rotund and has to walk very slowly, stopping to catch her breath every few steps. She is always on the brink of ill health, but she uses these experiences as her guide, as her way of understanding that heightened kind of sensory feeling that seems to occur as people near the end of life, and in being able to communicate in that symbolic language of death and dying.

In helping people die, Sister Loretta says that intimacy and touch are what counts, even if offering that means becoming as exposed and raw as all of us eventually become in the process of dying. In the end, love is what matters—a heart connection so real that no one feels afraid to delve into emotional business left unresolved, to share a very basic human connection of spirit, or feel alone as one dies. Sharing that experience is a need—and giving it is a skill—that the mainstream medical establishment hasn't adequately acknowledged.

t is April 23, 1992. At Cabrini's inpatient unit, fifty-nine-year-old Audrey Hill is "actively dying." She has lost sixty pounds and is as thin as a starving prisoner of war. Cheeks caved in. Eyes bulging. Great gaps in her mouth where caps have fallen off her teeth. Lips pursed. When I walk into her room, she is lying in bed, clutching a soft stuffed rabbit.

This is my first day trailing Sister Loretta. When she introduces me, Audrey looks up from her pillow, and smiles with incredibly warm eyes. She sticks out her hand and says, graciously, "Hello, I'm Audrey." Her breathing stops often, for great lengths of time, making it seem as if there will be no more breaths. Then, casually, she takes another. Sister Loretta pulls up a chair for me to sit beside Audrey and leaves me to stay alone with her in her room.

Audrey's eyes keep rolling up in her head. Sometimes she stares at nothing. Then she comes "back." And smiles at me. She says that when she's "away" it's "like sleeping." It's easy to fall in love with Audrey. She is grateful for very small things—sips of water from a cup held by more steady hands, a pillow fluffed, someone to hold her hand—so full of compassion and humor. When she comes back after one of her lapses, she strokes my hands, as if to calm me, and says, "Tell me about your loves." Audrey seems to spread love all over the room.

I later learn that this intimate, intense kind of love—a love that feels as personal as staring into someone's eyes at the heights of passion, a love that includes forgiveness as much as immense compassion and giving—is the kind of feeling expressed by many people near death, even those who weren't nearly so loving beforehand. It's as if something inexplicable happens to transform them. Their bodies might be fading, but at the same time, there is an elusive coming alive from within, a heightened intensity of life and of spirit that seems to bloom even within the physical process of dying. It is this spirit that hospice aims to encourage.

Audrey tells me she knows she is going to die soon. Yes, she's afraid of being abandoned, but she's also afraid of burdening her children. Tears slip quietly from the corners of her eyes. "You think about things you could have done," she says, "things you might have wanted to do or say, but then you realize you've run out of time."

Audrey didn't die that April day, but in June, two months later. Her story, the story that brought her to Cabrini, illustrates what makes hospice so special, and what can make dying a time of psychological and spiritual growth in the very midst of sadness and loss.

Before she became ill, Audrey's twenty-nine-year-old son, Jonathan, later tells me, she had been "a moderate success by anyone's standards." Essentially, she was a workaholic, a career woman, raising two children, now adults, working eighteen-hour days as the founding president of a corporate travel company. Her husband had died of cancer ten years earlier. She herself was diagnosed with inoperable cervical cancer in January 1991. By February she was given only forty days to live.

Audrey's chances of survival were small, so she made the crucial decision that she'd rather have help with her pain than prolong her illness with torturous treatments. She called Cabrini Hospice nearly right away. Jonathan got a larger apartment so she could move in with him, and Cabrini sent home-care aides, nurses, a doctor, pain medications, a hospital bed. But it also sent social workers, music and art therapists, and teams of volunteers. Audrey didn't die, as doctors expected.

"She's said that except for the fact that she's dying, this has been the most terrific time of her life," Jonathan says. With her pain controlled, she was able to continue working until June 1991. After she stopped, she began cooking, doing needlepoint, learning to play the guitar from the music therapist—things she had never had time for. She also held late-night salons with her friends, having philosophical discussions on dying, reading and discussing, among other things, the books of Elisabeth Kübler-Ross. But her health steadily declined; she had a stroke, she broke her hip, she entered a roller-coaster time of last breaths and revivals.

Audrey became incontinent at the beginning of April 1992, and her pain grew more severe. She'd come into the inpatient unit for a urinary catheter and a readjustment in pain medications. It seemed the end was near. On the day I met her, she'd had a serious decline. Yet something—no one could figure out what—was making her hang on.

When someone as sick as Audrey resists death, Sister Loretta later tells me, it's often because of some unfinished business. The dying person might be waiting for something—say, the birth of a grandchild or to see the wedding gown of a child about to be married, or to hear something as simple as a last "I love you" or "I forgive you" or "I'm sorry."

She views her job as helping patients by figuring out what's keeping them and helping them to resolve whatever that is, helping them to tie up, so to speak, the various strings of their lives. "Usually, if you find the right thing, people will go on the spot," she says. "You have to stay open to find out what that thing is. If you're filled with judgments, you won't find anything. But if your heart is open, you will."

By the time she died, Audrey was back home, spending her days in a hospital bed in her son's living room. Each day, while Jonathan went to work, her twenty-six-year-old daughter, Margaret, and Margaret's two children came over. Friends came by, and in the evenings there would be the salon. Audrey lay in the center of it, beaming.

Then something began to change. She started sleeping more. When she awoke, she'd say she was getting ready to go on a journey, packing her bags, getting her ticket, things she knew she needed from the travel business. Sister Loretta encouraged Audrey's children to respond to her in the same metaphors, to speak of helping her to pack and to travel. Then Audrey said the words that revealed what had been keeping her from dying: She told everyone she was waiting for her dead husband to come and get her.

Soon, Audrey began to smile in her sleep. She held Jonathan's hand. She told Margaret and her grandchildren she loved them. She'd listen to music and talk to friends, but she was waiting. Listening. Looking at the ceiling or the wall. Then one day she announced that her husband had come, that he was here, now, in the living room with her. She grew enormously calm. She began talking to him as if he were sitting on the couch, standing near. Her four-year-old grandchild came in and pronounced the room filled with people—ghosts that no one else could see. Audrey just smiled.

A few mornings later, while Jonathan was at work and Margaret hadn't yet arrived, while Audrey and a friend were watching a movie on TV, Audrey just quietly died. The friend stood up to change the channel, and when he looked back, Audrey had gone.

Sister Loretta says that Audrey, like many dying patients, had chosen a time when it was easier to leave than if her whole family was standing by. "I feel like I'm a midwife, like I'm pushing new life," she said. "But instead of saying, 'Push, push, push,' I'm always saying, 'Go toward the light. Look for your relatives and friends.' " And that's probably just what Audrey did.

▪   ▪   ▪

In America, hospice has pioneered a new approach to dying. The "hospice philosophy," as its adherents call it, focuses on this sort of psychological care, rather than solely on medical treatment. Yes, hospice practices palliative medicine, but it also attempts to help patients and families bring emotional closure to life, and to consider how a transition might best be made from this life to whatever might (or might not) lie next.

Since 1974, when hospice began in this country, it has brought Americans back to a familiarity with dying that once was there when death occurred mainly at home. With it has come a renewed intimacy with the psychological and spiritual aspects of dying and a knowledge of how to make peace both with life and with death.

The hospice philosophy has also begun feeding back into medical institutions, in the same way that the home-birthing process fed back into obstetrics two decades ago. And, as with birth, new kinds of midwives have since appeared—therapists, social workers, psychologists—who are influencing even more traditional hospital care.

The modern hospice movement began because of the zeal of an Englishwoman named Cicely Saunders, a nursing student during World War II who saw much suffering and death. She realized that what mattered most at the end of life was pain control, dignity in dying, and help addressing the psychological and spiritual pain of death itself. By the time she returned from the war, Saunders understood what she wanted to do with that knowledge.

First she got a degree in social work; next she got a degree in medicine. Then she began working in hospices around London, which at the time were places where nuns took care of the dying— rather like the refuges run by Mother Teresa in India. Dr. Saunders wanted to combine the idea of caregiving with the best of modern medicine, and particularly with the best pain medication she could find. She discovered a blend of heroin or morphine, cocaine, alcohol, and antinausea medication—named "the Brompton Cocktail" after the British hospital that created it—and pioneered in giving pain medication in steady doses around the clock, so pain never had a chance to peak.

In 1967, Dr. Saunders began her own hospice in a suburban

section of London. She called it St. Christopher's and housed it in a sprawling old home surrounded by gardens and stone walls. It had a chapel, a child-care center, a room for afternoon tea, a bar for night discussions, and space where dying patients could spend time with their families and friends.

The first goal for staff at St. Christopher's was to be sure patients got their pain—or other uncomfortable symptoms— under control. Then they went on to their next mission—to help the terminally ill do what Dr. Saunders considers to be their own, "real" work of dying. That, Dr. Saunders says in her lectures today, means coming to terms with "who you are, what the world is about, and what your place in it somehow is—the search for meaning." She believes a good hospice provides an environment where people can discover that wider view of life—through art, music, love, relationships, family, beauty, or religion.

During these same years, Elisabeth Kübler-Ross, M.D., a Swiss-trained physician, had begun what would become her famous Death and Dying Seminar at the University of Colorado's medical school. She would ask dying patients to come to a meeting with her medical students to describe what they were experiencing emotionally and to talk about what physicians might do to improve medical treatment and care for the dying. In essence, she asked the dying to teach her students.

Later, she brought her work to Billings Hospital, associated with the University of Chicago's medical school, and developed insights that would forever change our psychological thinking about death.

In 1969, Dr. Kübler-Ross's book *On Death and Dying* catapulted the previously taboo subject of death into modern public debate. From studying her own dying patients, she posited that from the time people receive a diagnosis of a terminal illness until they die, patients go through five emotional stages: denial, anger, bargaining, depression, and acceptance. Each stage involves specific emotional tasks. Dr. Kübler-Ross also believed that helping someone through the passage from health to illness to death is an art that can be learned. Teaching that art became her life's work.

Since Kübler-Ross's first book was published, a generation of counselors has relied on her system of stages in work with the dying, but many have misinterpreted what she wrote, expecting these stages to come in lockstep sequence. Instead, Dr. Kübler-Ross saw them as fluid, back-and-forth swings. In what order people pass through these stages, she believed, is up to them, nor do they necessarily have to go through all of them. Nor does one lead inevitably to the next.

Starting with her 1974 book, *Death: The Final Stage of Growth,* Kübler-Ross also began to suggest something more, however. What she saw earlier as five stages might be jointly called *resistance.* After that, although there may be some overlap with the last of those stages, are two additional stages in dying: a stage of life review, known as *finishing old business,* and a stage that might best be described as discovering total truth, or *transcendence.*

Finishing old business is learning to finally drop one's emotional baggage of jealousies or resentments and make an intimate, heart-to-heart connection through love. It is from this bond of openheartedness, she suggests, that transcendence, or psycho-spiritual transformation, can emerge, becoming a kind of love that is not just one-on-one, but universal, encompassing the vastness of life and humankind.

Today, many hospice workers, like Sister Loretta, have become as comfortable with such ephemeral goals in their work with the dying as they are with their basic mission to ease physical and psychological suffering.

The first hospice in America drew on the pioneering thinking of Cicely Saunders and Elisabeth Kübler-Ross through the work of Florence Wald. In the mid-1960s, Wald was dean at Yale University's school of nursing, part of the high-tech Yale–New Haven Medical Center.

Wald had watched as medicine moved from a focus on people, as she put it, to a focus on their diseases. This was of particular concern to her because of her responsibility to train future generations of nurses. It disturbed her deeply that neither death nor the impact of treatment on patients and families was even talked about. "Communication was lacking between caregivers and patients," she says, "and the way decisions were made excluded patients."

Wald sought new solutions in the work of Drs. Saunders and

Kübler-Ross; she asked them both to speak at Yale. Then in 1968, she took her entire family to London and spent a month of her summer vacation at St. Christopher's nursing the dying— something she hadn't done in years.

Back in New Haven, she couldn't stop talking about this wonderful work, sharing her enthusiasm with friends and colleagues, even when she'd meet them on the street. Among those she happened to run into were two doctors and a minister who were as concerned as she was about aggressive medical treatment. They began meeting at her kitchen table in Connecticut and others soon joined them. So it was that in Branford, Connecticut, in 1974, the first American hospice was born. Wald resigned as dean of the school of nursing to focus solely on forming this hospice and, ultimately, reshaping the care of the dying.

The Connecticut Hospice began by offering home care. Eventually, Wald and her co-founders also built an inpatient residence, but as the hospice movement has grown in America, it has commonly emphasized—as Wald's hospice (and Cabrini) does—care and medical support in patients' homes rather than in residential facilities. Here, as abroad, hospice care always tries to put the focus on humane dying. The secret is assuaging pain so that the patient's real work—the psychological and spiritual work of dying—can go on.

Whereas Dr. Saunders relied heavily on the Church of England, hospice in America became infused with a larger, more diverse spirituality. Good hospices here seem to be able to assist in life closure no matter what the religion (or lack of religion) of the dying patient. Using whatever belief system the dying person might have, good hospices seem to be able to pay attention to the mind, the body, the family, and—just as significantly—to the spirit.

In addition to regular medical charts, Sister Loretta keeps note cards on all her patients, jotting down names of their immediate families, what religion they are (if any), what these dying people consider important in life—music, art, special events—and the names of those close to them who have already died. That's how she knew that Joseph's parents had died when he was a child and that Audrey's husband had died before her. All this plays a part in helping the person die well, she says, since for all of us, death occurs within the context of our total lives.

Audrey and Joseph had both "chosen" a time to die, she believes, when it was easier to leave than if their whole families had been standing around. But there is work to be done in order to provide an environment in which the dying might have so calm a departure. That work has now become part of hospice lore.

Hospice workers often talk about "finishing old business," which is helping patients face their own psychological baggage (those things left undone or unsaid), and releasing them from its burden. Discovering what is keeping someone from going often takes psychological probing, some luck, and a lot of skill.

"Sometimes I'm flabbergasted to discover what it is that keeps people from going on," Sister Loretta says. Once, some years back, a Jewish patient at Cabrini went into a coma on Yom Kippur and hung on by a thread for ten days before she died. Her children hovered around her. Around midnight one night, when they were exhausted and punch-drunk, Lisa (not her real name), a daughter in her late twenties, came out of her mother's room and told Sister Loretta that she'd run away from home when she was in her late teens, and for eight years no one had known where she was. Even though she'd come back and taken care of her mother for the past three years, she wondered if those lost years had anything to do with her mother's not wanting to let go.

"I took her by the shoulders and I said, 'Did you ever apologize for not telling anyone where you were?' " Sister Loretta says. "She said, 'Well, I came back and took care of her!' And I said, 'Did you say you were sorry?' She hadn't. So she went back into the room and stood by her mother's bed and said, 'You know, Ma, you were so difficult, and the more you were, I was, and we tried to hurt each other, and I couldn't stand it anymore, so I ran away. But as I grew up I realized how hard this was on you. And it was hard on me, too. I never apologized, but Ma, I'm sorry.' "

Then Lisa came out of the room and told Sister Loretta she'd never felt so free in all her life; she felt as if bricks had come off her shoulders one by one. An hour later, her mother died. The mother had hung on to give Lisa a last gift. Perhaps she waited to die so that, in that period of Jewish atonement, Lisa could say what she needed to say in order to lighten her grief later on, set her free from unnecessary guilt. Or maybe she simply needed that acknowledgment to know that things were right between them.

True, Lisa's mother was in a coma, but Sister Loretta believes that patients in an end-of-life coma have the capacity to hear and respond in this way. One comatose woman hung on, she says, until amends were made—at her bedside and over a period of many days—between her daughter and the estranged, formerly alcoholic father who had abandoned her.

"Another time, Vinnie [also not his real name], an alcoholic gambler who was Catholic, kept hanging on and not dying, gasping for air for ten days," Sister Loretta recalls. "Then his cousin Tony came in and told me that Vinnie's nickname was Stash, because he gambled so much he hid money all over the place. Once he even went to the track straight from a bed at Sloan-Kettering. I realized he was hanging on because he didn't know where to go. So I leaned over—I could feel his stubble on my face—and I said, 'I know you've gotten some mud on your face, but don't forget that there's a heavenly father up there and he loves all his children and is able to forgive.' " Just after that, the cousins came in and started telling jokes about his days as a bartender—how much fun he was. Sister Loretta sat next to him, stroking his arm and listening, telling him it was okay to go. And he died in the middle of their stories.

The recognition that a dying person needs to finish old business has since spread from the hospice setting to therapists, social workers, nurses, and counselors working with patients in a variety of medical environments. Like hospice workers, these caregivers have come to see that even children will hang on until they've tied up loose ends, or even until parents give them permission to die. But sometimes they hang on so long that it's sheer torture for everyone.

Penelope Buschman, M.S.W., is a clinical specialist for child and adolescent psychiatric nursing at Columbia Presbyterian Medical Center in New York City. "A child," she says, "needs to have the information on dying that he's asking for so he has time to make the plans he wants to make. I had a little eleven-year-old girl with a brain tumor who asked the night nurse at two o'clock in the morning to call her family. She had made out her will, and she wanted to talk to each member, her siblings and her parents, going over what things she wanted to give each of them. She died the next day. She had certain work she had to complete, and she knew the time frame involved. Fortunately, she was listened to. I think children do have a sense that they are dying, so honoring their requests is very important.

"Another little girl, Elizabeth, who was also eleven, had become almost mute. She said, 'I want to be able to tell my mother how lonely and scared I am. I know I'm going to die, and I want to talk about it. She keeps wanting to cheer me up and say I'm not going to die.' I told the mother, 'Elizabeth wants you to just listen to her and not respond by covering it over, because she has some very important things to say.' So the mother just listened and held her child, and Elizabeth died soon afterward."

If the child is having difficulty letting go, Buschman, like Sister Loretta, tries to find the problem. When children hang on, she says, sometimes it's because they are worried about what will happen to their parents without them. They feel protective—especially children of single parents or those in difficult stepfamilies. They need to be told the parent will be okay, that it's all right for them to go.

Genevieve Foley, R.N., and Stephanie Vitalano, R.N., psychiatric nursing specialists at Memorial Sloan-Kettering Cancer Center's pediatric unit, do similar work. Because parents often have so difficult a time with the death of a child, they say, children tend to be closer to their nurses than adult patients are, and when they grow nearer to death, they often want to spend only short reprieves at home and to die in the hospital with their nurses. They feel safer—and also, the amount of time these children spend in treatment, and the nurses and doctors they spend that time with, competes in their short lives with the time they've spent with their families.

Often, kids also find it easier to talk about dying with their health-care workers than with their parents because they can get straighter answers. But it is also because counselors and therapists have acquired new skills—music and art therapy, guided imagery, play therapy—that makes them more able to give their patients support.

"Sarah [not her real name] was eight years old," Vitalano says. "She'd been sick with leukemia for three years and had spent a good majority of it hospitalized. She was here for six months straight, so she was very attached to us. Her mother didn't spend so much time here. Sarah knew her mother denied that she was dying, so she tried to protect her. We talked about it through storytelling. We talked with her bear."

She and Sarah would pass the bear back and forth and talk about what was happening to it as they each acted things out. "I had the bear driving and hitting a brick wall. I then passed the bear to her and asked her, 'So what happened to the bear?' " Vitalano says. "Sarah just said, 'The end.' That was it. She felt very protected, though, and felt that Jesus was taking care of her."

Sarah's mother had been a single parent, and Sarah was her only child. "There was a new stepfather," Vitalano says, "but Sarah wanted to be here in the hospital. She felt safer because there were more people to take care of her. When she actually died, her mother wasn't here. She was at church." That story seems to be fairly typical—a mother having so hard a time that she can't be there, the child growing close to the staff, taking care of her own need for comfort but also protecting her grieving mother's inability to cope.

Diane Haug, M.A., a former therapist in a children's cancer center in Texas, has noted that even when parents are willing to be there at the last moment, children sometimes seem to find it easier to keep them out.

"Children have the potential of moving through their dying process with unbelievable grace and equanimity," she says, "but one thing they do need is one person who can help them move through this without the attachments a parent would have in longing for things to be different. It can be the cleaning lady—and often it is—who can be there with them and is not resisting what is happening to them and their experiences. Kids want to talk to someone, and unfortunately, it can't always be their parent." A child's death is outside the natural order of events, the most painful kind of loss—so terrible a loss that without meaning to, a parent can hold a child back.

Young children are usually unafraid of dying, but if the mother hasn't resolved her own unfinished business with that child, her guilt later on can be overwhelming. Therapists try to help parents work through their emotional pain beforehand. The signs that death is approaching are usually ample, if the parent is helped to recognize them.

"About four to six weeks before they are dying, people start divvying up their possessions," Vitalano says. "Sarah gave me a picture of her. It said, 'I love you. Sarah.' She'd been very possessive, and that changed. She also became gentler. Before, if you called on the phone late, she'd give you a lashing. Then she began to be more forgiving. We'd play, go to the chapel so she could play the piano. And she began writing little letters to Jesus. She hadn't done that or been religious before. She wasn't asking him to help, just telling him she loved him.

"She really protected her mom and gathered other people she needed around her. In that period, at the very end, her mother began visiting her more because it was easier, because Sarah was so loving at that time." Soon Sarah also began talking of seeing her father, who'd died three years earlier. She hadn't talked about him before, but now she would say she saw him. It gave her—and her mother—comfort and relief.

"In the last few days before they die, or when they rally and have a really good period of quality time, say, about a week with their family before they die," Vitalano says, "most every child talks about seeing someone waiting for them when they die. And then, they die."

Adolescents and young adults seem to have a harder time than younger kids. Children don't really understand death until they are around five, because they don't yet understand time or permanence—the permanent quality of death as opposed to, say, just sleeping.

Children between about five and thirteen have a better understanding of the permanence of death, but less fear than they will have later. Perhaps it is because their identity is not yet fully formed. Teenagers both understand the permanence of death, grasp what that means for their future, and are more firmly rooted in who they are. They fear leaving. They fight harder, struggle more, and then, when it's clear they are dying, they want it to be over more quickly.

"One fourteen-year-old," Sloan-Kettering's Genevieve Foley says of a patient of hers, "said, 'If I'm going to die, tell me, because I have things I have to do.' We did, finally, and he said, 'Thank you. I know. That must have been hard for you.' And then he called in his brothers and sisters and it was like he was making up his will. He divided his possessions and he died totally at peace." The sibling bond is generally strong, and children of all ages need to be included in saying good-bye to the dying family member.

Near the end, children might have anxiety, though—fear of dying in their sleep, fears of leaving their families. They might need to be held, sung to, stroked. Young children, kids under the age of six or seven, aren't able to be as direct as someone eleven or older would. Just as Sarah was able to work through fears of dying by playing with Stephanie Vitalano and her teddy bear, therapists like Diane Haug use drawings, artwork, poems, dreams, and story-telling.

"Jennifer was a four-year-old who was dying of an abdominal tumor," says Haug. Her belly was filled with this tumor. In the last three months of her life, her artwork shifted significantly. This is all symbolic language. I asked her to draw her family. On one side she drew her family and on the other side of the page was her body. Raining down on her family was just a cloudburst of tears, but raining down on the side of the page over her body were halos of light and rainbows. That's the kind of imagery younger children can really share with their artwork. They know a lot more than you'd expect."

To respond, Haug doesn't try to push them. She says she just repeats back what she's seen: " 'Oh, I see tears above your family; I see rainbows around you.' And if you get it wrong, children will be sure you get it right and that you understand, not directly, but within the framework of their symbolism, within what is develop-mentally appropriate for their age. They might say they see them-selves as angels, or that Grandma is there beside them."

Kübler-Ross's stage theory of preparation for death was eagerly embraced partly because the public had already absorbed one of the key ideas of post-Freudian psychology: Life is a continuous process of psychological growth. But the seeds had also been planted in psychological theory for her notion of transcendence at death.

Throughout the 1950s and 1960s, giants in the emerging field of humanistic psychology—Carl Jung, Gordon Allport, Carl Rogers, Rollo May, Erik Erikson, Abraham Maslow—argued not only that human beings are essentially good (differing somewhat from Freud's view), but that we are propelled forward by a desire to grow and to know. They suggested that the human life cycle is a kind of urge toward heightened health, the kind of megahealth that was variously called by this new, humanistic wave of psychologists *peak experience* or *self-actualization*.

It was during the late 1950s and early 1960s that Dr. Erik Erikson proposed his now famous theory of the human life cycle as an eight-stage task theory of growth. These stages begin with the first—*trust v. mistrust*—in which, to remain healthy, the infant must successfully resolve the tension among learning to trust himself, his caretakers, and his environment. Erikson's last stage, however, determines successful life closure; here the tension must be resolved between *ego integrity v. despair*. At the end, we have to learn how to make sense of the whole of our lives and of the legacy that we have left that might survive beyond our physical beings.

At our best, Dr. Maslow said, we might have peak experiences that border on ecstasy or mysticism. More significantly, these experiences might occur as we near death. Underlying all of life might in fact be an urge toward transcendent growth in which we might discover a connection to a larger, more cosmic awareness or intelligence.

In 1963, Robert Butler, M.D., director of the International Leadership Center on Longevity and Society at Mount Sinai School of Medicine in New York and former director of the National Institute on Aging, wrote that he saw in his geriatric patients an urge toward a process that he called life review, a taking stock and reintegrating. Dr. Butler proposed that this life-review process actually be used as a therapeutic tool to bring about life closure. That tool has since been taken up by the developing hospice movement and is used in nursing homes and by psychologists and social workers nationwide.

In 1996, in a chapter on "Life Review" for the *Encyclopedia of Gerontology*, Dr. Butler included that transcendent dimension of the spirit that Dr. Kübler-Ross, Dr. Saunders, and other hospice workers had found. He even suggested that memory itself—in the process of life review—might be an important trigger for biochemical and neurological changes in the brain, changes that might lead at the end of life to ecstatic and mystical experience.

And, in fact, that is just how some hospice physicians have begun to work. Ira Byock, M.D., is a former hospice medical director, the current director of the "Quality of Life's End Missoula Demonstration Project," and the Robert Wood Johnson Foundation's new $12 million "Promoting Excellence in End of Life Care" program, with headquarters in Missoula, Montana, as well as author of the book *Dying Well,* and president of the Academy of Hospice and Palliative Medicine. He advocates using the process of life review in a direct effort to elicit that transcendent dimension with his dying patients.

Like many other physicians in their mid forties, Dr. Byock is a child of his time. He grew up in college on the developmental psychology of Dr. Erikson and the transpersonal psychology of Maslow. He went to medical school at the University of Colorado Medical School in Denver, taking the death and dying seminar that was still given there even though its founder, Dr. Elisabeth Kübler-Ross, had left.

But he was also influenced by another stream of American psychological thought, with origins in the East. Dr. Byock attended Naropa Institute in nearby Boulder, a college run by Tibetan Buddhist teacher Chögyam Trungpa, Rinpoche, at which many teachers from Christian, Buddhist, Hindu, and other Eastern traditions also taught.

And he drew on the psychospiritual approach of medical philosopher Eric Cassell, M.D., author of *The Nature of Suffering* and a professor of internal medicine at Cornell University Medical College in New York. "Suffering occurs not merely in the presence of great pain, but also when the intactness of the person is threatened or sundered," Dr. Cassell wrote, "and remains until the threat is gone or the intactness can be restored."

If a person's sense of self can be reorganized around something else—something larger—suffering can cease, even in the midst of pain or the progressive losses endured as we decline in chronic illness. It can also cease as we learn to view life as larger than our mere bodily selves, when we can see ourselves in a timeless, transcendent dimension, as a life of the spirit.

This is the kind of talk that a newer, younger group of physicians like Dr. Byock now use. Synthesizing the ideas and methods of all the specialists he studied with, Dr. Byock has created a systematic way of his own to help patients *grow at the end of life* by tapping into their memory banks of stories.

By recording these stories; by eliciting from them the wisdom generated by the experience of their own lives; by giving patients a sense of their own transcendent dimension by making them aware of having a past, a present, and a possible future—a legacy of a life story to leave for their loved ones—he is trying to give his dying patients a sense of an emerging soul that can survive beyond. Dr. Byock talks about this sense as spirit, and he considers it a mark of his own success if his patients can die *well,* in their own unique ways, if not in their bodies then in their minds.

In his lectures, Dr. Byock calls his system "Beyond Symptom Control: Growth at the End of Life," saying he is trying to utilize these memories to elicit a feeling of ecstasy and wonder. As we near death, our multiple spheres of personhood come apart, he says. We are no longer who we thought we were but a collection of parts— body parts barely functioning, floating memories, not the personality we were nor the professional, the doer, or the actor. We are all of them, and we are also something more.

Among the major findings of the SUPPORT study of hospitalized patients in America is how different the progress of death is from one illness and one patient to the next, and how varied and inexact are doctors' abilities to predict when an illness is really terminal, with what degree of certainty, and in what length of time.

People with congestive heart failure, for example—the most common cause of death in America—may live a severely impaired existence for one or two years at the end stage of their illnesses, but they often live longer than their doctors expect.

Like AIDS patients, congestive heart failure patients often have crisis after crisis, each controlled by emergency treatments and medications, while becoming progressively weaker. Yet, during that time they could die at any moment; medical management of fluid buildup in the lungs means that death from congestive heart failure now comes as a result of arrhythmia, an instantaneous and unpredictable electrical misfiring in the heart.

The SUPPORT study indicated that, on the other hand, people

with multiple organ system failure tend to die sooner than their doctors expect. The illness-to-death trajectory of those with chronic obstructive lung disease, cirrhosis, or coma were all different from one another, nor did they match their doctors' prognoses.

These findings led researchers to suggest that it is really quite difficult to assume—as many in the hospice community and among the lay public do—that there is a time for cure, and a time when a patient may be clearly classified as dying. Whether or not their doctors were right, were deluding themselves, or being overly aggressive in their treatment, most patients in the study died while their doctors still thought they might recover—which meant that many would never have been referred to hospice, even on the very day they died.

"This finding implies that in the face of serious illnesses it may almost always be necessary to develop parallel streams of plans," researchers wrote, "one [plan] which facilitates discussion about death and optimal support of the patient and family through death and bereavement; and a second [plan] which provides maximal efforts to restore physiologic balance. . . . The common teaching that one can find a time to shift from aggressive treatment to death-accepting care may be misleading: both may have to exist simultaneously."

Cancer was the one illness where researchers found a major exception. Perhaps because it has been best studied, or perhaps because its end stage is more predictable and clearly defined, physicians could tell with more certainty when a patient was terminal and roughly—though not with the high degree of accuracy many laypeople expect—how long he or she had to live.

Rather than seeing cancer as an aberration, researchers suggested that it might soon become possible to conduct similar end-of-life studies for the range of other illnesses of which Americans now die.

Two decades of referrals of cancer patients to hospice has allowed hospice workers to develop highly astute predictive skills in the absence of aggressive end-stage treatment. As I followed Sister Loretta on her rounds, she showed me the signs that said death was near: problems with swallowing, breathing changes, skin mottling, body-temperature changes, blood pooling in the back, a slight forward jut of the jaw.

Many health-care workers say they find it helps to tell patients and families as much as possible about the final process of their particular disease. Should a family opt to have the patient die at home, they need to know what to expect physically, what they should do or not do in responding to various symptoms of dying, when to call 911, what the legal responsibilities of these help agencies are when someone calls, and when not to call but to call hospice instead. Such information is provided in booklets supplied by most local hospices or from the National Hospice Organization.

"[In the days] when Grandma died at home," says Barbara Karnes, R.N., a former hospice director from Stilwell, Kansas, "we learned how to die and we learned how to grieve. Today Grandma lives in a senior citizen high-rise and when she gets sick she goes to a hospital and from there to a nursing home, and then, lo and behold, she's dead. And we didn't learn how to die and we didn't learn how to grieve. So we approach the most normal and natural experience of our lives totally unprepared.

"There are really just two ways to die," she says, "gradual and fast. Fast is getting hit by a truck, having a heart attack, or suicide. It's harder on the survivors than on the person who's died. We're left with lots of unfinished business, with questions and no answers. Grief from past deaths further complicates our grieving. But gradual death, if we take the opportunity, gives us the chance to try to say a proper good-bye. Gradual death also happens in two ways: In old age, when our bodies just wear out. And through disease, which is a way the spirit decides to get out of this body."

Karnes lectures on the dying process at national hospice conferences and has written her own booklet, *Gone from My Sight: The Dying Experience.* "The three things I look for when I first go in to see patients to see whether they are dying," she says, "are whether they are eating less, sleeping more, and withdrawing."

Two to four months before people die, she says, their eating habits change. They might first stop eating meat, then chicken, and then fish. "It's not that they don't *want* it," Karnes explains, "they *can't.*" Those are the words the dying use: *I can't.*

After that, it's fruit and vegetables, even ice cream, and then liquids. "The one thing it's hardest for families to understand is that it's okay not to eat," Karnes says. "It's part of the dying process. It's not starvation. The person died of cancer, or whatever, and not eating is part of the process."

The problem in families is that food is used as an expression of love and caring. "The bottom line," Karnes says, "is that we eat to live, and if the body is preparing to die, it doesn't want the food, it doesn't want the grounding or the energy that food brings. It's preparing to shut down. If a person hasn't entered the dying process, he or she feels hungry, so the person may need a gastrostomy or a feeding tube. If they have entered the dying process, they aren't hungry. They don't want food, so don't push it."

Forcing a person who is dying to eat can cause severe complications, such as aspiration pneumonia—when food or liquid a person is unable to handle simply goes down the wrong pipe. Even a standard IV can cause ill effects. When a person's kidneys can no longer adequately process fluids, the excess fluid collects throughout the body, and it can cause highly uncomfortable congestion from fluid buildup in the lungs. Cutting down on IVs also allows doctors to reduce the uncomfortable accompanying need for oral and respiratory suctioning.

People fear their family member will be dehydrated. They *will* be dehydrated, but those who want artificial hydration or nutrition don't realize its downside. "When we pump in that fluid and their kidneys aren't working properly we may see water coming out of their skin. Well, it's like a sponge. If it can't get rid of the water it oozes out," Karnes graphically explains. "That's how a person's body feels if you're pumping in the water and they're not peeing it out."

Dehydration, in fact, is the body's natural way of shutting down; the electrolyte imbalance that builds up allows dying patients just to drift off into a painless sleep rather than to fight for breath as the lungs fill with fluids. "The body's normal and natural way to die," Karnes says, "is by starvation and dehydration. It's the body's way of anesthetizing itself."

The issue of whether or not to give artificial nutrition and hydration is controversial, dependent on each family's cultural values and each patient's needs. But, in fact, Karnes's descriptions are confirmed by research reports published by the federal Agency for Health Care Policy and Research. Unless there are extenuating circumstances, these reports suggest—say, the family is profoundly committed to their loved one's having such interventions—it is more comfortable near the end for the person dying to go *without* having artificial fluids.

Two to four months before death, sleeping patterns also begin to change. "First patients will take an afternoon nap," Karnes says, "then a morning nap, too, then they're asleep more than they're awake, and their world and reality change. Their dream world becomes more their world than their waking world."

Indeed, this may be why we hear reports of dreamlike visions among the dying, or visitations from dead relatives. Yet, if family members don't understand this special time, they may feel tremendous fear and concern and even try to persuade the dying that they are wrong.

"Now, a person is asleep more than awake. This world is not their world," Karnes explains, "and they will begin to talk about things that don't really make any sense to this world, because everything to them is a dream. If pain isn't an issue, you can go in, wake them up, talk to them. When you leave they'll go back to sleep and not really know if they dreamt your visit or if you were really there. This is also a time that a person says, 'You know, I had the nicest talk with Mom last night. She came and sat on my bed and we had so much fun.' And Mom has been dead for ten years."

In my own experience with dying people, I have noticed a strange distinction at this point. Those who have visions and are not yet actively dying—say they have them from a reaction to a drug like Demerol—people their visions as much with those who are still alive as with those who are dead. But when their visions are peopled entirely with those who are dead, they are very likely on their way.

Like a growing number of others who work with the dying, Karnes believes that these visionary relatives or friends help patients move from this world to the next, that we don't die alone. She describes this state of consciousness as if it were a double vision, a double exposure on a film, since both worlds seem to be there for the person simultaneously and it's hard for them to know which is which, who is in which world. If family members panic in response, they will either cause fear or simply make the dying refuse to talk about what they are experiencing. "The language of the dying is symbolic," she says. "If you listen they tell you what the other world is like because they are a window into that other world."

Two to three months before death, people start to withdraw

from the world, to want to see fewer and fewer people, to go completely inside themselves. "They are taking all their memories and packing their bags," Karnes says, "taking these bags of memories with them." About one to three weeks before death occurs, the labor of dying—like the labor of childbirth—actually begins. This, Karnes says (using an image made popular by Dr. Elisabeth Kübler-Ross), is like a caterpillar trying to get out of the cocoon, to fly free from the body like a butterfly.

Three things determine how difficult our labor of dying will be, much as they do when women give birth: how much our pain is controlled, how much fear we have, and how much unfinished business we are troubled by. "The key thing that tells me that [the] labor [of death] has begun," Karnes says, "is that people start sleeping with their eyes and their mouth partly open. It takes energy to keep your eyes and mouth shut and a person is losing energy. The other thing you'll see is random hand movements, picking at the air or their sheets, or taking off their clothes. They are often restless and agitated. They are getting ready for a trip.

"And then," Karnes says, "you start to have breathing changes, puffing, or start-and-stop breathing. About one to three weeks before death, nothing seems to work right. They may be hot or cold. Or part of their body is hot and another is cold."

What's happening is that the metabolism is failing to work and the body's inner thermostat is going haywire. People may not be able to swallow anymore. They begin to say how tired they are, how utterly, totally tired, so tired they can't even move their legs or their arms. Their bodies are just slowly shutting down. "This is how people die," Karnes says. "It's all normal and it neutralizes the fear to know ahead of time what's going to happen."

About a day or so before the end, aside from these breathing changes, the skin starts to look mottled. The blood pressure is dropping and circulation is being cut back so the body can concentrate on getting blood to the brain and the vital organs. Blood also begins to pool in back and is visible as blotches when a person is turned over.

Shortly before death, the body's natural anesthetic kicks in. Breathing has already begun to slow, and the dying person has grown sleepier and sleepier. By now, Karnes says, maybe hours to minutes before the end, most people begin not to respond to the world around them. They are quiet and still, as if asleep but with their eyes partially open. Breathing slows even more. They might look at those who are nearby, and seem to be seeing right through them. Or, they might begin staring at empty places in the room and reaching out to unseen others.

Just at the end, breathing changes so that the jaw juts forward just slightly. As Karnes describes it, the dying seem to be breathing like fish. And then there is a slight change of facial muscles. And they are gone. The strange thing, though, is that there still might be another breath or two, a sigh, the body finally giving out. Letting go.

By all reports, the last sense to go is hearing. Through all this process, lightly touching, stroking, soft light, soft music, and soft words can help a person relax and move through this experience. And the words most useful then are: *I love you. I understand you have to go.*

"When a person is really scared and restless," Karnes says, "it helps to hold her hand and talk her through." That's what Karnes did with one of her first patients.

"I walked in and realized Bonnie was dying. She wasn't responsive but she was very agitated," Karnes says. "I thought she was scared, so I took her hand. I sat down next to her bed and talked to her softly. 'Bonnie, you're dying,' I said. 'This is what it's like to die. I want you to relax. I want you to be like a log that floats downstream. I want you to go with whatever comes. Just let go. Let go of all your insecurities, your mistakes, your fears. I want you to take only the good thoughts with you. Remember that you are a beautiful child of God and that you've always done the best you could. I think we're far harder on ourselves than God would ever be. Take only the good with you, Bonnie, and relax. You can get out of your body just as easily as you can get out of a pair of shoes. But if you're afraid, if you don't know what to do, then stop a minute, say, "Help me. I don't know what to do." And there will be a spiritual presence there to help you. Go with that presence, Bonnie, you're doing such a good job.' " And Bonnie, she says, grew quiet and died.

Bonnie would have died whether Karnes was there or not, since death is just as natural a process as giving birth, and neither can be easily stopped once it is in progress. But, like most hospice workers, Karnes feels that such guidance eases the passage.

Today, many hospice patients will hear some variant on the

phrases Sister Loretta uses: "Go toward the light, look for your relatives and friends." Karnes may have talked to Bonnie about God, but she tailors her guidance to the individual. "It depends on their belief system," she explains. "The key is relaxation. I've walked people through a mall with a light at the end because these were people who liked to shop."

Talk about "the light" has become so ingrained in hospice lore that it's hard to remember how new it is. In the past, people might have mentioned Heaven or God, but no one ever talked about "the light." In fact, it emerged during the 1960s and 1970s, in conjunction with major changes in medicine.

Between 1959 and 1960, psychologists Karlis Osis, Ph.D., and Erlendur Haraldsson, Ph.D., began to collect the observations of 640 doctors and nurses of what occurred as some 35,540 of their patients died. From 1961 to 1964, they collected a second set of responses from more than 1,000 health-care workers—reporting on some 50,000 patient deaths—in New York, New Jersey, Connecticut, Rhode Island, and Pennsylvania. Between 1972 and 1973 they also did a smaller study in India to compare patients dying in each of these two cultures.

Their studies of dying patients were then compiled in their important book, *At the Hour of Death*. Drs. Osis and Haraldsson reported that for a significant portion of these patients there was a rise in mood and a noticeable feeling of peace prior to death. In addition, a second significant portion had one or another kind of vision.

Some 84 percent had visions of dead relatives who had a close relationship to the patient (23 percent said it was their mother; 18 percent said it was a spouse), and most patients reported that this vision was "coming to take them away."

The rest reported apparitions of various kinds. Patients labeled them anything from angels to beings of light or some form of spirit guide. "On the whole," the authors wrote, "Christians tended to [see] angels, Jesus, or the Virgin Mary, whereas Hindus would usually see Yama (the god of death), one of his messengers, Krishna, or some other deity."

Dr. Osis estimates that in total, probably a third of all the patients had what these two researchers ended up calling "deathbed visions." He suggests one use caution in interpreting these numbers, however, since not everyone was conscious at the end and, in fact, he doesn't really know what percentage of all the patients the health-care workers in his study reported on were even conscious or not.

Drs. Osis and Haraldsson were far more interested at the time in the fact that reports of these visions appeared at all, under what circumstances they appeared, and in their content. The real issue is that the existence of these visions *had to be shared* with a health-care worker even to make it into the study, and at the time—as opposed to now, when such visions are daily tabloid fare—visions at death were rarely discussed, and particularly not with doctors or nurses.

Researchers found that patients with slow, chronic diseases—such as cancer—more often tended to report seeing visions than those with faster-killing diseases, such as heart attacks. Those who knew their physicians better and longer tended to report these visions more frequently, probably because, the authors surmised, they had more time to learn to trust their doctors and nurses with stories of such unusual occurrences. Taking medications or not seemed not to matter, which led these doctors to conclude that these visions were a separate phenomenon from possible drug side effects.

"If you believe in an afterlife," Dr. Osis told me, looking back on his research almost twenty years after his book first appeared, "it's probably a quite difficult moment to get from one world to another, so the relatives come to help. In my old age, when death is a much more immediate possibility, I think I have made up my mind that there is something after death. Now the nature of this, I'm not sure, but it is archetypal, maybe a being of light, but the splendor that will come with dying I think will be great." After studying similar events at the edges of life, Dr. Osis is not the only researcher to hold such thoughts.

In 1975, Raymond Moody Jr., M.D., a psychiatrist, published *Life After Life*. The book was a series of stories about people who had been clinically dead—say, because of a heart attack or an accident—and had been revived. These people reported with wonder that while they were "dead," they'd had strange experiences. Dr. Moody was the first to label such accounts "near-death experiences" (or NDEs).

Moody's book, which became a huge best-seller, was embraced not only by the popular press but also by cardiologists and paramedics—who had brought patients back from the brink of cardiac arrest with modern resuscitation equipment—and by emergency or operating room medical personnel and nurses. It was also picked up by hospice workers, some of whom began to recognize these experiences as descriptive of what some of their dying patients hinted at as they teetered between life and death.

The people Dr. Moody wrote about in *Life After Life* recounted joyous meetings with dead relatives or spirits who came to guide them. They told of a sensation of traveling at what felt like the speed of light, covering vast distances inside a dark tunnel that was so huge it seemed as if they were inside a tornado. They talked of seeing their whole lives portrayed before them at high speed, a kind of fast-forward life review. And nearly everyone said they'd encountered an intensely brilliant, absolutely magnificent, immensely powerful and loving light.

"The light immediately communicated with me—by telepathy—but instantly and clearly," one man who'd had an NDE explained to me. "The first thing I was told was 'Relax, everything is okay.' Now I've been told in other situations—'Relax, it's okay'—when it isn't. But in this situation, it's the most comfortable feeling you could ever imagine.

"For the first time in my life I felt absolute, unconditional love. It can't be compared to the love of your wife, or the love of your children, or a very intense sexual experience. It couldn't even begin to compare to all of them combined. If you could imagine what pure love could be, that's the feeling you get from this pure white light. It's extremely emotional and so beautiful. I also realized this light had total knowledge.

"I had always wanted to know," he said, "when a person dies, is there an afterlife? A heaven, if you will. A god. Well, there is absolutely no question in my mind now that the light is the answer. Upon entering the light—you might not refer to it as the light—but it is total, pure energy, total knowledge, total pure love. Everything about it is the afterlife."

In Moody's and later accounts, NDEs were experienced by a range of Americans—from housewives to plumbers, to businessmen to Vietnam vets. Even children—untutored in the popular accounts and naive about the negative reactions that such stories might provoke—reported similarly exhilarating events. Most astonishing was that even though not every account contained *all* these ingredients, the accounts were remarkably the same, whether one heard the tale from the smallest child or the oldest adult, whether from Americans or from people around the world. For children and adults alike, these experiences seemed to eliminate forever any fear they might have had about dying.

While NDEs might resonate with traditional religious teachings, they are hardly describing the heaven or god that most religions envision. Still, George Gallup Jr., of the Gallup Organization, estimated in his 1982 book *Adventures in Immortality* that 15 percent of Americans had come close to death, and 34 percent of those reported having NDEs, or about 8 million people. By 1993, the Gallup Organization reported in its *Religion in America* survey that 12 percent of Americans had now had a near-death experience, or roughly 13 million people, enough to populate a city.

By the late 1980s, stories of NDEs had become staples of tabloids and talk shows. By 1990, the International Association of Near-Death Studies (IANDS) was formed, an organization of those who had had NDEs or were interested in research on the phenomenon. That organization began to publish a *Journal of Near-Death Studies* and set up a network for local and regional conferences and NDE support groups. By the early 1990s, personal NDE stories were regularly appearing on best-seller lists. Ironically, the high-tech emergency room, operating room, and the CPR "crash cart" may have created what has become our most ubiquitous modern-day mystical experience.

Psychologist Kenneth Ring, Ph.D., is a University of Connecticut professor and author of *Heading Toward Omega,* a later report on NDE research. "The most common words used to describe it is an overwhelming, absolute peace," he says. "One woman said, 'If you could take the thousand best things that ever happened to you in your life and multiply them by a million, then maybe, with the emphasis on the word *maybe,* you could get close to this.'

"Another man wrote, '*PEACE!!*' But to give you an idea of

what this peace was, he said, 'You'd have to write each letter a mile high in soft, glowing colors.' So the quality of peace that attends the experience of dying is beyond imagination for anyone who hasn't had this experience.

"Almost invariably," Dr. Ring says, "not only have they come to believe, but they know with a deep inner certitude that there is some form of conscious existence after what we still here call death.

"What we have in the contemporary NDE," he says, "is a modern version, cloaked in the symbols of our own time, of the ancient mystery teachings concerning life, death, and regeneration." Near-death experiences, coupled with the symbolic and uncanny experiences hospice workers and families see with patients dying quiet deaths at home, have given Americans a modern spiritual vision, providing hope to those who are terminally ill—whether or not they are religious—that something magical can happen at death.

Though NDE stories are no doubt comforting to those who believe in them—convincing many even of the factual existence of an afterlife—some physicians and social scientists who have studied them remain convinced only that peak experiences occur near death. They view these experiences purely as phenomena of brain chemistry or physiology.

These peak experiences, they say, can be elicited throughout our lives by many other kinds of intense events—among them drug-induced psychedelic experiences, profound religious experiences, certain yoga or meditation practices, and intense physical or psychological trauma.

Medical and psychiatric researchers offer an assortment of physiological reasons why NDEs might occur. Some say that in crisis or during trauma, endorphins are released, numbing all pain and giving a feeling of great euphoria. Others say that when particular brain centers are stimulated, a whole array of experiences are triggered—including depersonalization; involuntary memory recall; intense emotions like euphoria; auditory, visual, or kinetic hallucinations; and even out-of-body sensations. Some researchers locate this trigger in the brain, in the right temporal lobe. Others say that the visual sensation of the tunnel and the light come as a result of the excited, random firings of the optic nerve or something else occurring in the visual cortex.

Metabolic or electrolyte imbalances or oxygen deprivation can also cause hallucinations, as can various kinds of medications—although it should be noted again that not all those who have had NDEs were taking medication.

Daniel Dennett, Ph.D., director of the Center for Cognitive Studies at Tufts University and author of *Consciousness Explained,* says these experiences we call NDEs can all be explained by the physical effects of the dying brain—that they are the brain's biochemical way of dealing with traumatic stress.

The remarkable thing is that neither scientific study nor skepticism matter at all to those who have had an NDE—or to those who are terminally ill or dying. What they—and their doctors—say for sure is that something mystical can occur at death. These stories are bringing a new kind of hope to the terminally ill.

I ndeed, so many hospice patients seem to have these kinds of experiences that NDEs and deathbed visions have now been more officially incorporated into hospice work, into the hospice philosophy, and into work with the dying even in mainstream medical institutions.

Pamela Kircher, M.D., at the time a hospice doctor at the Texas Medical Center in Houston, took an informal survey at a 1992 meeting of the National Hospice Organization, giving the one hundred hospice nurses, doctors, social workers, and administrators who came to a workshop she gave on NDEs a questionnaire to fill out.

Seventy-three percent of them responded. Of these, 73 percent had had a patient tell them about having had what seemed to them like an NDE or visions; 75 percent felt that hospice patients frequently have such experiences; and 77 percent thought these visions were helpful to patients in the last days of their lives. Further, 60 percent thought these were not a form of hallucination but an actual experience, and that medications did not increase the probability of their occurrence.

In 1989, Maggie Callanan, R.N., then a hospice nurse in the

Washington, D.C., area, attended the first annual IANDS national convention. She was struck by the similarities between NDE stories and some of the observations she had made of dying patients.

After the conference, Callanan went home and talked with her friend and fellow nurse Patricia Kelley. They decided to go through all their patient records and notes one by one. From this material came their book *Final Gifts,* which gives caregivers and families a better understanding of the symbolic language used by dying patients.

Callanan and Kelley coined the term "nearing-death awareness," observing that their patients lived in two different worlds at the same time. They seemed to be getting ready—as Audrey Hill was—to travel from this world to another, and they seemed to be communicating two kinds of messages. One, it seemed as if they could choose (within a certain time frame) when it was that they would actually die. And two, they let their family members know through the metaphors of travel, such as Audrey used, that their relatives were waiting, that they are getting their tickets or packing their bags.

If patients were afraid, Callanan and Kelley found, they could be calmed when others entered into their conversational framework, using the same metaphors that the dying were attempting to speak. If a dying person says he "can't find the map," these nurses wrote, those close to him might respond: "I know you'll find the map yourself when you're ready."

"I personally have come to see their confusion as *my* problem," Callanan concludes. "Get into the metaphor with them, [but be] honest. If someone says, 'Do you see that angel sitting at the foot of my bed?' I will say, 'No, to be truthful I don't, but I can see that *you* do, and that it brings you great joy, so I'm very glad for you.' How do you help the dying? Open your hearts to the possibility that [they] are true prophets."

NINE

New American Sacred: The Return of Prepared Dying

t's the morning of May 26, 1987, at Karme Choling Buddhist Meditation Center in Barnet, Vermont. The rain is falling erratically—sometimes heavily, sometimes gently—but it doesn't daunt the people walking slowly through the woods behind the main house, up the hill, along a muddy dirt road to the meadow.

On the left, just where the trees end, as the meadow opens up and the dirt road continues over a tiny rise, is a site littered with construction equipment—trucks, wheelbarrows, and cement mixers, all incongruous in these woods. If you go up the road slightly and look over the rise, you can see what the equipment was used for. Across the meadow is a giant cement structure resembling a small nuclear power plant, with a rounded steeple at the top, its center open to view through windowless holes on all four sides.

This *purkhong*—or fire pit—has been built for the cremation of the Venerable Chögyam Trungpa, Rinpoche, an abbot in the

Kagyü order, one of the four ancient schools of Tibetan Buddhism. Officially, he was the Eleventh Trungpa Rinpoche, since according to Buddhist teachings, abbots and high lamas are reincarnated again and again.

Buddhism holds that it is partly the way in which one prepares for dying that determines enlightenment—a concept, like "the light," that to Christians might be understood as finding God—and the way one is reborn. Some of these teachings on the art of dying are contained in the classic text the *Tibetan Book of the Dead*. Chögyam Trungpa, Rinpoche was a master teacher of this book and these teachings.

Rinpoche is a Tibetan honorific, like *Reverend* or *Rabbi,* and means "precious one." This particular Rinpoche was also a *tulku,* akin to a saint, and had—as is traditional in Tibetan Buddhism—already been reincarnated ten times, going back to 900 A.D. In this lifetime, and in each but the first three of his lifetimes before, Trungpa Rinpoche was the supreme abbot (like a Catholic cardinal) of the many monasteries in the eastern part of Tibet, known as Kham.

Those in the Trungpa line were all expert in the *Tibetan Book of the Dead.* "I received this transmission at the age of eight," Chögyam Trungpa wrote in the preface to one English edition of this text. "[I] was trained in this teaching by my tutors, who also guided me in dealing with dying people. Consequently I visited dying or dead people about four times a week from that time onward. Such continual contact with the process of death, particularly watching one's close friends and relatives, is considered extremely important for students in this tradition, so that the notion of impermanence becomes a living experience rather than a philosophical view."

In 1959, when the Chinese invaded Tibet and began destroying its monasteries, the Eleventh Trungpa Rinpoche disguised himself and escaped on horseback. With a small party of monks and attendants, he rode over the Himalayas, entered India on foot, and from there eventually brought these teachings to the West. In 1970, he founded Karme Choling in Vermont, the first of some fifty meditation centers he built throughout North America and Europe.

Over the next twenty-five years, these centers attracted many of the best and the brightest—poets including Allen Ginsberg (who took Trungpa Rinpoche as his spiritual teacher), novelist William Burroughs, musician John Cage, performer Meredith Monk, New Age spiritual teacher Ram Dass (Richard Alpert, Ph.D., former Harvard psychology professor), and hospice doctor Ira Byock.

On that May morning in 1987, some three thousand of these Westerners slogged up the wet hill toward Trungpa Rinpoche's cremation site. Over the rise, inside the *purkhong,* wood was already stacked several stories high. Encircling the *purkhong* were tents strung with hundreds of colorful flags—blues, yellows, oranges, reds. Inside the tents stood row after row of chairs for the visiting dignitaries.

His Holiness the late Dilgo Khyentse, Rinpoche, head of the Nyingma school, the oldest of the four ancient schools of Tibetan Buddhism, had come from Nepal to preside. A near battalion of maroon-and-gold-robed monks came as well, representing the various schools. They'd traveled from monasteries in India, Bhutan, Sikkim, and Nepal.

In the West, Chögyam Trungpa, Rinpoche was controversial. He came from the *crazy wisdom* Buddhist tradition of "mad" yogis who for centuries have believed that it is exactly those times when the ego is least in control that the most can be learned about consciousness and mind. In keeping with the reputations of his forebears, he was known for his brilliance and outrageousness, his profligate drinking, and his active sex life. He died in Halifax, Nova Scotia, at the age of forty-seven of liver disease and complications of a stroke.

In Buddhist circles, however, Rinpoche was regarded as a particularly great and enlightened teacher. Grand and extensive rituals unique to teachers of his high rank—based on instructions given by Khyentse Rinpoche before he traveled to Vermont from Nepal—were followed in preparing his body after death.

Trungpa Rinpoche's corpse was placed sitting up in meditation posture on a raised, ornate shrine, and for the next few days, hundreds of mourners filed by to meditate with him. After a week, he was moved from Halifax to Vermont. Lamas expert in the practices surrounding dying came from the East to chant and pray, and to show his closest students how to pack and repack his body in special salts, mummifying it in the ancient way.

Specific ceremonies were held during each of the forty-nine days after death, and during that time, Rinpoche sat encased in these salts inside a huge ornate box in the center of Karme Choling's main meditation hall. Those who meditated there described his energy as seeming to fill the entire space, but the day of the cremation was the most powerful of all.

By noon, those thousands gathered in the upper meadow included reporters from *The New York Times* and *Time,* and a photographer from *Life.* I was among them. Some stood on the grass, fifty deep; others sat on the chairs in the tents. It was a festive occasion. Since Buddhism views death as an opportunity for enlightenment, that's exactly what was expected of a teacher who was apparently enlightened already. Yet no one—at least none of the Westerners—knew exactly what would happen.

A lone bagpipe sounded down at the main house, signaling the start of the funeral procession. The crowd hushed. From the moment the bagpipe wailed, the rain slowed. Led by the bagpipe player, the procession wound slowly up the narrow, muddy road. As the bagpipe moved closer to the top, the rain gradually stopped altogether, becoming a thick, low-lying fog. By the time the procession reached the top of the rise, the sun had begun to shine through the fog.

As the procession made its way through the parting crowd, Rinpoche's now mummified body could be seen sitting in meditation posture inside an ornate, small, opened box that was painted gold and lined in silks. The box was carried—like a handheld rickshaw, resting on two long poles—on the shoulders of pallbearers. Their teacher was dressed in his most elaborate gold robes, a ritual crown anointing his head.

At the *purkhong,* pallbearers hoisted him up through the center, seating him in the open portion of the steeple. By now the sun was shining brightly, the sky clear and totally blue behind him. From the meadow, Rinpoche could be seen through the openings, sitting tall, framed by the sky on all four sides.

Monks began to blow traditional Tibetan horns and to ring prayer bells, as one monk—traditionally one who had no connection with the teacher who had died—rose from his chair, walked toward the *purkhong,* and lit a flame. As the wood caught, Khyentse Rinpoche began to chant, some fifty monks and hundreds of American Buddhists joining with him.

Soon flames leaped up toward Trungpa Rinpoche and completely enveloped him, dancing off his body, shooting from his head, gobbling up his crown. Black smoke swirled up into the blue sky, concentrated in one long line. Like a dark rope dangling between pyre and sky, the smoke seemed to join heaven and earth.

Suddenly three black birds gathered overhead, and slowly, quietly, began circling that rope of smoke. As they circled, a huge rainbow appeared—not stretching from one end of the mountains to the other, but a circular rainbow, a halo that completely surrounded the sun, wider and with more bands of color than most people had ever seen. As the fire died down, a dramatic succession of rainbows began to dot the sky.

The mourners stopped talking and stared, awestruck. It is said in the Buddhist scriptures that these are exactly the signs that appear when great teachers die. Some texts even describe the phenomenon of having mastered the art of dying as becoming *a rainbow body*. But this was Vermont in 1987, and though these Americans considered themselves Buddhists, they were not prepared for ancient signs and symbols.

After the fire and the smoke died down—and the rainbow had disappeared and the birds flown off—it began to drizzle again. Slowly, people filed down the mountain. Going up, they had laughed and talked, but going down there was silence. This was a crowd that was shaken. On this mountain meadow signs had appeared that were as auspicious to Buddhists as the Star of Bethlehem has been to Christians or the burning bush to Jews.

All of the world's cultures and great religions have considered dying well an art to be learned, an art essential to a good passage into some next life. In fact, nearly every culture before our own secular age has had instructions on the art of dying.

Judaism's mystical teachings on dying and the journey of the soul after death are contained in the esoteric texts of the *Kabbala* and the *Zohar*. The shamanistic rituals of Native American, African, Aborigine, and Latin American cultures are passed down in oral traditions. Asian and Middle Eastern cultures all had sacred rituals and teachings on dying, such as the *Tibetan* and *Egyptian Book of the Dead*.

Modern scholars like Stanislav Grof, M.D., a psychoanalyst, and Joan Halifax, Ph.D., a medical and cultural anthropologist, co-authors of the book *The Human Encounter with Death*, and Carol Zaleski, Ph.D., a professor of religion at Smith College and author of *Otherworld Journeys*, say that the chief purpose of all these religious texts and rituals was to help people consummate a life well lived with a death that was transcendent.

During the Middle Ages, when the plague swept Western Europe, sacred Christian teachings on dying (called, as a body, *ars moriendi*, or "the art of dying") began to appear, spreading the previously secret exhortations of the clergy to the populace during a time of tremendous need. These were stories and pictures of the visions of notable saints as they died—or, if these saints had survived near-death ordeals, visionary accounts of the transformative ways their ordeal had affected them.

The teachings of *ars moriendi* were intended to be used as instructions about repentance, the afterlife, the war for the soul between heaven and hell, and about how the dying person could use prayer and gain forgiveness. Dying well meant both lessons on what to do on one's deathbed and instructions on handling an afterlife.

In order to prepare, most religions have used rituals or ceremonies that had ecstatic components to help believers achieve the kind of consciousness change it was always thought that human beings would experience at death. Philosopher William James has described some of these components in his classic *The Varieties of Religious Experience*. Among the many are Catholic vespers, and intense singing, prayer, and meditation; Muslim Sufis, with their whirling dervish dance practices; and Central and Native American shamans, who use guided dreaming, peyote ceremonies or the taking of other psychoactive chemicals and plants, and sweat lodges to induce visions.

The long, dark, isolated retreats of Hindu yogis or Buddhist monks, or the ancient Egyptian practice of temporarily entombing priests alive to produce states of near asphyxiation, all provoke what can only be described as classic near-death experiences. The adept is supposed to return from these experiences to share the knowledge learned and the visions seen.

Not only was this knowledge essential for the transition into an afterlife, but it affected the quality of the passage itself. Preparing for death nearly always included hearing vision stories, or "practicing" this altered state of consciousness ahead of time by inducing nonordinary, ecstatic states similar to those anticipated at death.

Over the past century, however, as death came under the province of science and medicine, as the power of the more mystical branches of traditional religions has begun to wane, as American religions have grown more concerned with secular matters, these lessons on dying well have drifted into obscurity.

Of course, orthodox traditions continue to exist. When the Grand Rebbe Menachem Mendel Schneerson lay dying at the age of ninety-two—of complications of a stroke—the Lubavitcher followers of this Hasidic Jewish leader davened and prayed continually as he spent four months in Beth Israel Hospital in New York on life support. When Cardinal Joseph Bernardin of Chicago was dying of pancreatic cancer, he said that he'd learned once again to trust in God through prayer.

While Gallup surveys report that a high percentage of Americans believe in heaven and consider themselves religious, baby boomers have tended to lose this connection with mystical Judeo-Christian traditions, either because they moved away from their childhood faiths or because the mainstreams of these religions themselves had lost their traditionally mystical base in efforts at reform or Americanization. Yet, as the dying process has grown more prolonged, this secular generation is looking for new answers in its own way.

For a growing number of Americans, Trungpa Rinpoche's death underscored exactly what he and a growing number of other Tibetan Buddhist teachers had taught them over the past two decades—that Buddhist teachings can lend powerful help in getting ready to die. And, indeed, Allen Ginsberg used these teachings when he himself died in the spring of 1997.

Among the numerous teachers who had begun to teach Buddhism to Westerners were Tibetans Geluk Rinpoche and Dilgo Khyentse Rinpoche, as well as Sogyal Rinpoche, Chagdud Tulku, Rinpoche, Americans who were ordained as Buddhists, such as Columbia University professor Robert Thurman, Ph.D., and the Dalai Lama himself. While many of their teachings on Buddhism remain rather esoteric, Sogyal Rinpoche's book, *The Tibetan Book of Living and Dying,* published by HarperSanFrancisco in 1992, became so popular that by 1996 it had sold over a quarter of a million copies and was on national best-seller lists.

Tibetan Buddhism is a religion with a complex philosophy on how to live life, how to prepare for death, and, since it embraces reincarnation, how to make one's way after death in a greater realm of the spirits so that one might have an auspicious rebirth. The classic *Tibetan Book of the Dead* is an enormously elaborate set of instructions to be learned ahead of time and to be read to someone after he or she has died. It contains detailed descriptions of various visionary realms that appear as the spirit leaves the body and passes through an in-between time (known as the *bardo*) from death to rebirth.

The text itself is a guidebook on how to choose a path through these realms. While the beginning stages sound much like modern descriptions of near-death experiences, the later horrors that can arise—if one makes incorrect choices or allows spirits' tricks to lure the unknowing down a wrong path—are much like descriptions of purgatory.

Although the *Tibetan Book of the Dead* is perhaps the best known of Buddhist texts, it is not what Buddhist teachers generally taught to their Western students. Used most often were the kinds of meditation practices that Sogyal Rinpoche describes. *The Tibetan Book of Living and Dying* outlines the Buddhist psychological path, giving instructions on how to handle one's mind and emotions through daily meditation practices and to use these practices as preparation for both life and death. But Sogyal Rinpoche also gives often-secret practices for controlling bodily energy so that one can move this energy out of the body at will, directing how consciousness leaves the body even at the moment of death.

Rather than remaining a dusty body of strange-sounding, esoteric instructions, many of these ancient Buddhist teachings have turned out to be as applicable to death at the end of the twentieth century as they were in the ninth century and earlier, when many of the texts were apparently first written. That is why they are experiencing a growing popularity today, albeit a popularity domesticated specifically for Americans.

Chögyam Trungpa's heir, Osel Tendzin, was an American from Passaic, New Jersey, who was born Thomas Rich and given his Buddhist name when he was enthroned as Trungpa's Vajra Regent. Tendzin was a controversial teacher himself who died of AIDS in 1990. Before he died, however, he helped many of his students with specific instructions on dying, as he himself had been taught.

"You and I and all of us have traveled this path before, and we will travel it again," he wrote to Judith Hardin. "Sometimes we live a long time, and sometimes a short time. It's what we do with our time now that's important." He told her, as Rinpoche had told him, to consider every moment to be meditation practice, and especially "those moments of panic and impending death.

"When you begin to feel the panic," he'd said, "dive into it with full awareness [and] allow the thoughts to flow freely, disregarding whether they are positive or negative. When the mind begins to settle, see how everything is based on accepting and rejecting, good and bad, pleasure and pain. And also see how awareness transcends all of these. Continue to do this whenever panic strikes. This is the best preparation you can make for death."

Buddhist teachings are founded on the concept of impermanence, that the only thing in life that is certain is change, and that death is merely the greatest change of all. In meditation practices, one can observe this minutely by seeing that one's thoughts and daily concerns change, even moment by moment.

But one also begins to perceive a continuum of consciousness behind all that change, the consciousness that lies behind the one we are generally aware of. Some might call it "the Watcher" or "the Witness." It's the part of us that stays up all night, that knows in the morning whether or not we have dreamed, and what the dream was about. Buddhists might call it "big mind." (Christians might call it the mind of God within each of us.) This is the awareness, they say, that will survive death. This is the consciousness Tendzin was trying to tell his students to pay attention to.

There are two aspects in preparing in advance to manage this consciousness at the moment of death. First is to recognize and grow comfortable with it beforehand to allow a glimpse of the mind that will endure. Second is to create a powerful imaginary image—vivid, dreamlike, seemingly real—and try as much as possible to merge one's mind with this image. In a way, this is an organized teaching on how to create a powerful dream, hallucination, or vision—much like those who have NDEs report—and then to practice a way to walk directly into it.

There are many meditation instructions for this that these different Buddhist teachers teach, Tendzin told Judith to use an advanced meditation practice called *Vajrayogini,* after the name of the deity in the visualization involved in this particular practice. This was a meditation practice that Trungpa Rinpoche had taught Judith before he died, and now Tendzin told her to practice it as much as she could.

Vajrayogini practice requires specific instruction from a teacher, since there are secret aspects to it. Basically, though, one imagines a deity named Vajrayogini, a passionate, fiery red goddess with long, flowing hair. She is pictured in Buddhist deity paintings as standing in a dancer's pose, with a crown on her head and one leg up, seeming to sway to and fro.

After beginning a simple meditation in which Judith was to notice her thoughts and settle her mind, she was to picture Vajrayogini, and then begin to try to feel her enormous energy, feel her power, her intensity, her compassion, her love, her confidence, her blessings. It was an empty dream image, very spacious and colorful, but a being at the same time. She was to try to merge her mind with this image, become this image, and later in the practice, to dissolve her mind into space as this image later dissolved in her thoughts, becoming like a rainbow light.

Osel Tendzin once described the effects of the practice like this: Crystal-like. Sparkling. Groundless. Energy. Like fire. Vast. This is like the mind of the Buddha, the Watcher. This was exactly the same, powerful feeling that he said Judith would feel at death. If she practiced it daily, then it would come as no surprise as she died.

"Consider [this mind of the Buddha] as inseparable from your mind and experience that in the form of warm, bright light," Osel Tendzin wrote her. "And consider [Vajrayogini] to be inseparable from your body, so that in your waking hours you develop a strong identification with [her] power, which can be liberating at the moment of death." As she practiced, she was trying to form a habit so strong that she'd instinctively know what to do as she was dying. Out. Out. Out. With each breath, she'd let her mind float out into a greater sense of space.

It was to help her practice her own ability to push her mind out of her body, first into a powerful dreamlike visualization, then to trust that it was okay to dissolve her mind with that visualization, out, out into space. And that's what it would be like to die.

In a simplistic way, it is like Lamaze breathing for childbirth. Meditation would help during the dying process, and at the moment of death it would give her something to focus on in order to move her consciousness out of her failing body and into whatever lay next.

Through an ancient Eastern tradition brought to the West and repackaged for a new and secular generation, Tendzin was teaching something similar to what devout Jews learn through davening and praying, and devout Christians learn through a lifetime of prayer or Holy Communion—to merge one's mind with God, or the blood and body of Christ, and at death, to receive blessings and grace.

But there is something more. Baby boomers are also drawing on their generation's own experiences in a search for spiritual guidance at death. In the process they are reexamining transcendent moments of all sorts. For them, this can, of course, mean meditation and prayer, but it might also include music, art, dance, diet, intensive psychotherapies, dream work, hypnosis, even psychedelics or hallucinogenic drugs.

It is April Fool's Day, 1995. In the grand ballroom of the Crown Plaza Hotel in New York City, Rachel Naomi Remen, M.D., is addressing an audience of nearly one thousand people who have come to a conference called "The Art of Dying." There are doctors, nurses, psychologists, social workers, hospice medical workers, and volunteers. There are caretakers of those who are dying of many different diseases. There is a sampling of American Buddhists and Hindus, as well as of Catholic priests and nuns, Christian ministers, and Jewish rabbis. And there are dying patients themselves. In a word, this audience is a cross-section of late-twentieth-century Americans.

"I have come to deliver a simple message," Dr. Remen chides good-naturedly. "You don't have to be a Tibetan Buddhist to die well." And yet, she says, one can't help but notice a sense of mystery surrounding death, most especially as dying moves once again into family homes.

In the recent past, before hospice, you never saw death unless you were a physician, Dr. Remen says, and even many doctors haven't experienced death at the moment it occurs. They are there before death. Or after, to sign a death certificate. But the moment of death is a stunning time. You are in the room with someone. And then suddenly you are alone. There's a feeling of awe you may never otherwise experience. The modern dying process, she says, is bringing mystery alive again in people's lives.

Dr. Remen is a psycho-oncologist. She trained at Stanford Medical Center and Cornell Medical School as a pediatrician. Now she is on the faculty of family and community medicine at the University of California San Francisco School of Medicine, and is the co-founder and medical director of the Commonweal Cancer Help Program, in Bolinas, California. She also runs her own Institute for the Study of Health and Illness, training other physicians to care compassionately for those facing life-threatening illnesses.

In all this, Dr. Remen takes the psychological work already begun by hospice a step further. She not only sees death as a natural part of life, but she views the very process of dying as the great opportunity for each of us to make our life journey whole.

Because most Americans now die in hospitals, isolated in sterile, institutional environments, many lose touch with the more transcendent dimensions of dying. And while we might be involved with the care of a loved one at home, we are often so scared and overwhelmed by their physical needs and by their loss that we, too, might fail to notice this spiritual dimension.

Yet, she says, transcendent moments themselves are crucial. In fact, they might well be *the* most crucial experiences of our lives, the critical psycho-spiritual work we each need to do *in order* to finish our lives well. She views her job as helping people explore their own memories of transcendent moments throughout life so that they might consciously use these memories to put them in touch with what they might experience as they die. She also trains physicians to be aware of life's sacred dimensions in order to better help their patients. That is what she is here at this Art of Dying conference to impart today.

Dr. Remen begins with the story of the death of the father of a colleague of hers, which occurred when this fellow-physician was only fifteen years old. The father had been suffering from Alzheimer's disease so severe he was unable to speak at all for ten years. One Sunday, Remen's future colleague and his seventeen-year-old brother were staying with their father while their mother took a much-needed afternoon away.

Suddenly, as they were watching a football game, the old man had a heart attack. Kneeling near his dad, the future doctor yelled to his older brother to call 911. But as the brother went to grab the phone, the father spoke for the first time in a decade. "No, son," he said. "Don't call 911. Tell your mother I am okay. Tell her I love her." With that, he died.

An autopsy was performed and the man's brain was found to be almost totally destroyed by his disease. There was no physical way he could have said those words. "Now, I ask you. Who spoke?" Dr. Remen says. "Awe is the only possible response to events like these. Not to acknowledge such mystery is to miss something important in life and death." Doctors, families, and health-care workers need to pay careful attention. To do so can provide those who are dying the opportunity to become whole at the end of life.

"Our wholeness emerges when we let go of the ways we have changed who we are throughout life," Dr. Remen says, "when we truly remember ourselves. And often we remember ourselves in times of loss. That's when the authentic pattern of who we are emerges most clearly. [Yet] there is no right way to die, just as there is no right way to heal. Our deaths are as individual as our fingerprints. They have very deep meaning, and arise from our own personal story. We die in our own way. But the way in which we die can show us the meaning in how we have lived and help us resolve the [riddles] of our lives."

For Dr. Remen, as for Sigmund Freud before her, meaning is carried in the unconscious rather than in the conscious mind. She helps her patients to connect with their own life's meaning through stories like the one she has just told, and she also uses the ways of modern psychology to elicit the wisdom of the unconscious mind—memories, dreams, poetry writing, artwork.

"I ask patients and students to explore their own experiences of the sacred," she says. "What would you call a sacred moment in your life? What allowed you to have that experience? What are your experiences with death? What are your ways of dealing with loss? What are your inner experiences? Your dreams? What are your regrets in life? What are the things you need forgiveness for? Who are the people you haven't forgiven?

"We talk about unfinished business, [but we also talk about] dreams and experiences. The closer death gets, the more the mystery shows itself. When people die they experience this mystery in a very personal way."

Although Dr. Remen has not studied Carl Jung's work, she seems at times to echo his notion of a collective unconscious. She maintains that there is a larger human memory, or a universal wisdom that speaks through all of us. It shows itself when we least expect it. At death the teachings of those who are dying can also help those around them tie up the puzzles of their own lives, if they are ready to listen or notice. That lesson was brought home to her personally when her own mother died.

"When she was eighty-four years old, my mother had open heart surgery," Dr. Remen says. In her book, *Kitchen Table Wisdom,* she describes how difficult this surgery was, how her mother lay unconscious for a week, breathing with the help of a respirator. Finally she regained consciousness, but she did not recognize Dr. Remen—her only child—and began hallucinating. The nurses called it "intensive care psychosis" and said it was often an affliction of the hospitalized elderly.

"After her surgery," Dr. Remen says, "my mother saw birds in her hospital room, birds that weren't there. And she started talking about things in her childhood, about her own mother, who was full of *che-sed,* a Hebrew word that translates as loving-kindness. I was named after her, Rachel, but until then, I'd always used my middle name, Naomi.

"The nurses started correcting my mother when she talked about the birds, but I didn't," Dr. Remen says. "One day I came in and began to sit in a chair and my mother told me, 'Don't sit there. I have a visitor.' So I pulled in another chair. Mom turned to the first chair with great tenderness and said, 'Rachel, I'd like you to meet Rachel.'

"My birth name is Rachel Naomi. My mother told her mother she'd named me Rachel—after her—but she apologized about calling me Naomi, telling her my father had wished it. That name was after his father, Nathan. She also told her mother about my childhood, her pride in the person I'd become, and they talked about people I'd never met—my great-grandfather David and his brothers, my granduncles, who were handsome men and great horsemen. Finally she closed her eyes and said, 'I'm glad you are both here now. One of you will take me home.' "

Her mother died shortly afterward. Dr. Remen was late getting to the hospital that day. She'd stopped to buy irises, her mother's favorite flower, but all she could find was a small bunch of iris buds, tied together with string. Her mother was dead by the time she got to the hospital and Dr. Remen left the flowers on her bed. They lay next to her, from the hospital to the funeral parlor, three thousand miles away.

"By the funeral, they had been out of water for four days and had traveled from California to New York," Dr. Remen says, "but when I arrived, the irises were in full bloom, tied in their string, lying on the top of my mother's casket, infused with some incredible purple light." Dr. Remen now goes by the name Rachel.

The dying process can teach us to open to the mystery of life. "I've shown up and had someone say, 'My husband is talking to someone who isn't there. He's hallucinating.' Well, what if it's not a hallucination?" Dr. Remen says. "I might first ask how the experience affects the person who's having it. If the response is awe, I'd say it's mystery. We make everything into pathology. If my mother was afraid of her vision she might have needed medication, but that vision made her death sacred for her and for me."

One of the gifts of the dying is the ability to shift reality enough to make us realize that there may be more to life and to survival than the mind thinks. The task of dying is different for all of us, but in the process, we may learn to view life as a journey of the soul. Dying itself is an opportunity to complete that journey well. "Life is a spiritual path," Dr. Remen says, "and death may be the experience of the soul that integrates and clarifies it."

■   ■   ■

Modern pharmacology's ability to synthesize psychoactive drugs has made the psychedelic experience—one that can encourage memories to arise as well as induce and mimic an ecstatic, mystical state—a common and widespread phenomenon for many Americans, and especially for the baby boom generation. Now, some are beginning to regard these drug experiences as a way to prepare for the shift in consciousness that may occur in dying.

For many, the first glimpses of the transcendent power of dreams or controlled images arose with psychedelic drugs. And so, many therapists and physicians are now beginning to consider using these drugs as a means for helping patients prepare for death. In a way, it is utilizing what many baby boomers have already learned about merging with dream images or using controlled hallucinations, taking that to a next step for use in a far more disciplined and traditionally organized way.

Such preparatory, visionary experiences were once practiced only by Native American or Aborigine shamans or medicine men, within sacred ceremonies, and by non-Western cultures that incorporated as part of their social milieu the nonordinary states of mind that psychotropic plants can create.

The modern synthesis of plant medicines into psilocybin or LSD (lysergic acid diethylamide), however, removed the religious moorings from these experiences, opening them to potential abuse as party drugs. At the same time, it introduced vast numbers of people to altered states of mind that previously had been known only through religious rites and visions.

During late 1995 and 1996, those who could tune in to the Internet could read the daily logs of 1960s acid guru, Timothy Leary, Ph.D. In the 1990s, Leary was detailing his experiences in a diary he kept on his home page as he died of prostate cancer. He said that death was the ultimate altered state of consciousness of life. His way to get ready was to use his standard candy store of drugs.

"Between April 14 and April 21," according to *The New York Times,* and to Leary's diary, "his 'average daily input of neuroactive drugs' included 50 cigarettes, a joint of marijuana, two lines of cocaine, 12 balloons of nitrous oxide, 0.45 of a cubic centimeter of ketamine and assorted other intoxicants."

He died ecstatic, at home in his bed, just after midnight on May 31, 1996. The night before, *The New York Times* reported: "Tim told us, 'Don't let it be sad. Buy wine. Put soup on the stove.' Tim loved life." His last words were: "Why not? Why not? Why not?" And that was the story of his life.

Leary's method was actually based in research that began when his acid days first started. In the early 1960s, he and Richard Alpert, Ph.D. (who changed his name to Ram Dass, the name given to him by his Hindu teacher, the late Neem Karoli Baba) were both psychology professors at Harvard.

They began experimenting with LSD in order to understand the mystical/ecstatic potential of the human brain, and to study how these mind-altering drugs changed consciousness. (Both were later fired by Harvard for sharing their stash of psychedelics—which they had a research grant to use—with undergraduates.) On their research team were writer Aldous Huxley, the famed author of *Doors of Perception,* and Eric Kast, M.D., who did some of the early work using LSD with the dying.

At the same time, psychoanalyst Stanislav Grof, medical and cultural anthropologist Joan Halifax (an expert on shamans), and other clinicians and researchers began to use LSD in counseling dying patients at the Maryland Psychiatric Research Institute in Spring Grove. They, too, were influenced by Huxley.

In his seminal novel *Island,* Huxley had written about mescaline—another psychedelic—and described it as *moksha,* a Hindu term for enlightenment. When his wife, Maria, died of cancer in 1955, Huxley gave it to her, and said that it—and hypnosis—had helped her get into deep trance states as she was in the process of dying. Near the end, it helped her move more easily, he'd said, into a mystical state of consciousness that became death.

He kept telling her to go toward the light and the drugs helped her do that more easily. After Maria's death, Huxley began experimenting with LSD himself and found he could elicit the same state, apart from the dying process. Later, when he was dying in 1963, he asked his next wife, Laura, to give him mescaline so that he could also merge with that light.

Huxley was introduced to this idea through the work of Albert Hofmann, Ph.D., a Swiss chemist working at Sandoz Pharmaceuticals labs, who had inadvertently synthesized LSD while looking for a medication to improve blood circulation in the brain. Soon he realized that its mind-altering properties were similar to those caused by the kind of plants used worldwide by shamans in religious and healing rituals.

Like narcotics, hallucinogenic drugs have gotten a bad reputation. They are potent—and therefore they have been deemed illegal by federal agencies, which may have overreacted in claiming that they have no medical use. In the 1996 referendums in California and Arizona—which many saw just as referendums on the medical use of marijuana—voters in Arizona in fact passed a bill that would allow LSD (and all Schedule I drugs, including heroin and marijuana) to be used for medical purposes. Like opioids, psychedelics can—and have—been used responsibly in medical environments.

Among the most interesting work has been their use with the terminally ill in the work of Grof and Halifax. During the 1970s, with the FDA's research approval, they were using LSD in therapy sessions to treat alcoholics when a woman named Gloria, who was a part of their research team, found she had advanced breast cancer. She was so anxious and depressed about her poor prognosis that she asked whether she could try therapy sessions using LSD. The team agreed.

These sessions usually lasted from six to eight hours—the length of time the drug is active in the body—with two or more therapists working in tandem with the patient the entire time, attending to what came up for that patient from her subconscious, and helping her work it through. Since the drug was pure—not a street drug formulation—toxic residues were nil, so the legendary "bad trips" were avoided.

In their book *The Human Encounter with Death,* Grof and Halifax wrote about how Gloria described her experience. "Mainly I remember two experiences," Gloria said. "I was alone in a timeless world with no boundaries. There was no atmosphere; there was no color, no imagery, but there may have been light.

"Life reduced itself over and over and over again to the least common denominator. I cannot remember the logic of the experience, but I became poignantly aware that the core of life is love. At this moment I felt that I was reaching out to the world—to all people—but especially to those closest to me." As she came out of the experience, Gloria said she never felt such joy and incredible love for her coresearchers, her parents, her husband, and her family. Her depression and fatigue lifted. She felt at peace, and she died that way five weeks later.

The Spring Grove team began to focus almost exclusively on LSD therapy with terminal cancer patients, trying to work in ways similar to how many counselors use NDE narratives with dying patients today—helping patients quell fears of dying and taste the sort of experience that might accompany death. Their work was also similar to that of shamans and medicine men (and women), who use peyote rituals, vision quests, and sweat lodges as guides toward their own deaths.

By the end of the 1970s, the political climate had changed and the FDA did not renew the Spring Grove group's research authorization to use LSD. At that point, however, the team had already worked with more than two hundred patients and had built an impressive body of research on the psychology of dying.

Since then, psychedelic work with the dying has nearly stopped. Today, however, some researchers are attempting to resurrect it once again, this time using not only LSD but also shorter-acting hallucinogenic drugs, such as psilocybin, ibogaine, DMT (N, N-dimethyltryptamine), ecstasy (3, 4-methylene dioxymethamphetamine, or MDMA), and ketamine, which might be easier on dying patients.

Among the front-runners in this research are Rick Strassman, M.D., associate professor of psychiatry at the University of New Mexico Medical School in Albuquerque; and Charles S. Grob, M.D., associate professor of psychiatry at the medical school at the University of California in Los Angeles (UCLA), and director of childhood and adolescent psychiatry at Harbor-UCLA Medical Center.

Rick Doblin, president of the Multidisciplinary Association for Psychedelic Studies, based in Charlotte, North Carolina, and Ethan A. Nadelmann and his Lindesmith Center in New York City, a think tank on drug policy, also report an upsurge of interest elsewhere.

While some of this research is aimed both at boosting the failing immune system by decreasing psychological stress and pain, particularly with terminal cancer and AIDS patients, it is also aimed at helping those who are dying more easily—and quickly—open up emotionally, resolve personal and family issues, and experience ahead of time the kind of transcendence they might face at death.

Researchers say that ecstasy is a drug that, if properly used, can enhance openness, intimacy, and empathy. In research trials it seems to be helpful as an adjunct in speeding up the process of finishing old business with family members. Psilocybin, on the other hand, can create visionary, cosmic-consciousness feelings. Both of these drugs seem to have the potential to replicate an NDE.

One of Dr. Grof and Dr. Halifax's patients, a twenty-nine-year-old African-American man named Dean, was dying of kidney cancer. In the course of many therapy sessions, LSD was used during three sessions. During those times, Dean had experiences of the light, of a life review, of euphoria, and of the merging of his consciousness with a more universal consciousness.

Shortly before he died, Dean got uremic poisoning and was in and out of a coma. "I was saying to him, come out of the darkness into the light, don't be afraid, go into the light," Dr. Halifax says. Dean didn't die right then. When he became more lucid, he reported that as he was fading deeper and deeper into his coma, he experienced exactly what Dr. Halifax had been describing. He also said that it was no different from what he'd already experienced in the LSD sessions.

"He did see the light and he went toward it," Dr. Halifax says. "He also said there was a moving picture on the wall across from his bed and he saw all the faces of people he'd killed in the war, plus all those he'd beat up on as a child. When he came back, he said, 'I won't have to go through that again.' And he died an extremely peaceful death a month later."

Dr. Grof has since created a kind of hyperventilation breathing resembling yoga breathing techniques—which he labels *Holotropic Breathwork*—in lieu of psychedelics. He also uses music, yoga exercises, expressive painting, and dancing, and makes use of past-life regression and deep therapeutic states.

Dr. Halifax uses various forms of meditative contemplation, most of them based on Buddhism, and runs a center called Upaya, in Santa Fe, in which she works with the dying. Through a project called "Being with Dying," she trains people to work with the terminally ill; she also helps caregivers with stress, and in managing their own spiritual and psychological issues related to a loved one who is dying.

"The LSD project took my breath away," she says. "I began to understand dying as one of the three most intimate events of our lives—sex and birth being the other two. Now I continue the work without using LSD as an adjunct. The dying process is developmental. It is the last stage of our life. It involves a transformation of the mind, an altered state of consciousness." Both she and Grof still counsel the dying by preparing consciousness for death ahead of time.

"Other cultures had the idea that death is not the end of consciousness," says Dr. Grof. "It goes on. And they had maps of these states and support systems. They had experiential training for dying, rites of passage that provided death experiences, whether with psychedelics, dancing, or drumming. People had death, rebirth experiences, a chance to prepare for death all their lives. So now we have lost this. And we have a materialistic science that says there is no consciousness that lives on."

Holotropic Breathwork can be used in lieu of psychedelics, he says, because it "[can] take people into similar places." Ideally, however, he would like to have a range of psychological tools to draw on—with psychedelics as part of it—so that the kind of therapy and preparation for dying could be matched to a patient's need, depending on the particular patient—his or her strength, experience, and physical condition.

"If you have an opportunity to practice nonordinary states, it takes away the fear of death," Dr. Grof says. "[But] we have a culture that is not only unused to mystical experiences, it denigrates them; in fact, it even confuses them with psychoses. We have a Bible in every hotel room, yet all the experiences described in the Bible would be seen today as psychotic, pathological. We don't have a mainstream religion where people could have a powerful religious experience. There were mystical traditions in every religion, and now we are talking about using them again in preparation for death."

It should be no surprise that the early 1960s explorers of psyche-delic drugs eventually turned to Eastern religions. While psyche-delics could offer glimpses of the sacred, they offered no way to remain in touch with it. Meditative and prayer traditions, on the other hand, offer steady contact with the sacred. They also provide developmental stages—appealing to Western psychologists—to move through.

Many of those doing trailblazing work in both areas lectured at or attended Chögyam Trungpa, Rinpoche's Naropa Institute, cross-fertilizing thinking from one to the other. Beginning during Naropa's first summer, in 1974, not only was Trungpa there, but so were Dr. Grof and Dr. Halifax, as well as Ram Dass and his colleagues Stephen and Ondrea Levine. Since then, Ram Dass and the Levines have become among the most influential thinkers in altering the American culture of dying.

After he was fired from Harvard, Ram Dass took his personal studies elsewhere. Aldous Huxley had showed him a copy of the *Tibetan Book of the Dead*. Realizing the similarities between the drug experience and the after-death experience described in this text, he went to the East, looking for a teacher. He traveled to India in 1967, and ended up studying with the late Neem Karoli Baba (also called Maharaji), whom some considered a Hindu Indian saint.

By the time he returned, Ram Dass had also learned enough of Buddhism to realize that the state of mind he'd discovered on psychedelic drugs was similar to the descriptions of the stages the mind-spirit would encounter after death that were found in the *Tibetan Book of the Dead*. He and Leary (and another researcher, Ralph Metzner) wrote a book, *The Psychedelic Experience,* based on that text to describe the travels of the conscious mind while on drugs. He also wrote *Be Here Now,* which was perhaps *the* seminal spiritual book of the boomer generation.

What isn't as well known is that Ram Dass came back from India not only having found a Hindu guru but also having learned from him how to work with the dying. He has since spent the past three decades using what he learned, sitting with the dying, watching, helping, learning. Employing a variety of meditative, breathing, and psychedelic methods, Ram Dass has run workshops, set up hospices and homes, and counseled those who are dying of cancer and AIDS.

In 1976, he founded the Hanuman Foundation Dying Project. With Stephen and Ondrea Levine as codirectors, he began giving workshops in Santa Fe and in the San Francisco Bay area to help those who were dying make a more spiritual journey of their deaths.

Two age-old premises underlie their work, premises that by now are familiar in this book: Death is not an end but a transition; and we can learn to make that transition well. They, too, aim to use altered states of consciousness *ahead of time* so that the dying person might more easily—and quickly—resolve personal, emotional, and family issues and might grow comfortable with transcendent feelings. Much of their work—which uses meditation—also aims to reduce panic and fear and prepare the patient for what he or she might feel at the moment of death.

To Ram Dass, dying is an opportunity to open to the intuitive qualities of the human mind—to what he calls the soul—and to use these qualities to connect with what Carl Jung called the collective unconscious.

On this spring day in 1992, when I heard him lecture at a conference in New York called "Conscious Aging," Ram Dass looked like what in fact he is: a retired professor living in California. He no longer sports the long beard and white robes of the 1970s. His short white hair reveals a bald spot, he is clean-shaven except for a small mustache, and he is dressed in a salmon-colored V-neck sweater over a button-down shirt, with greenish-khaki pants and penny loafers.

"I am one of the few people who gets thrilled to be with people dying," he tells his audience, which consists largely of more than a thousand psychotherapists. "It's such a grace for me because I know I am going to be in the presence of truth." That's because the dying, he says, exude an intense feeling of love; he learned how to recognize that space, he says, from psychedelic drugs.

"Most of our images of love have to do with romantic love," he says. "We give lip service to the fact that there is another love that's not interpersonal. We call it God's love. Or whatever. But to be with someone who is dying is to feel it. Sitting with someone who is dying is so intimate a human contact that we are floating. That's how grief gets transformed into a living, loving space. And it transforms the pain."

To help someone get ready, to be with him as he dies, he says, is to learn to be able to switch channels, as if on a TV, in order to tune in to a more vast space. He first got a glimpse of how to do it back in 1963. "I was helping my stepmother die at sixty-nine. She'd developed cancer. We were good buddies. My father was eighteen years older than she was, so I went to the doctors' with her, got the reports and all. She was a tough, poker-playing, willful New Englander with a stiff upper lip. My job wasn't to say, 'Hey, Phyllis, you should open to this.' So I was just with her. We lay on the bed, talked, and I would hold her. But the pain of the cancer ate away her will."

Four days before she died, he says, she gave up. "Now we see giving up as bad, losing the will to live. We keep encouraging people to keep fighting, denying death. I saw my mother dying, completely surrounded by deception. People would say, 'You look great,' and leave the room and say she wouldn't last the night. She was alone with the denial."

With his stepmother, it was far more truthful and real. "When Phyllis surrendered it was like watching the egg breaking. When she gave up it was like some being emerged that she'd been her whole life. It was so amazingly strong. She went into another plane where she was just 'being' with me. And dying was just happening.

"At some point she said, 'Richard, sit me up.' She took three slow, deep breaths, and she left. I now read Buddhist texts, and the way in which conscious lamas leave their bodies is they sit up, take three breaths, and leave their bodies. Now who was she? How did she know?"

In setting up the Dying Project, he wanted to train people to work with the consciousness of dying. "People come who want to do spiritual work, to use their death as a vehicle for their own awakening," Ram Dass says. "The more you are aware of life the more you see the release at the moment of death as taking off a tight shoe. It's an opening, an expanding, a speeding up of awareness, and a slowing down of bodily process. It takes preparing."

Most of us operate daily on just two channels—the physiological ("I'm fat, young, old") and the psychosocial ("I'm powerful, neurotic, a lover/mother/daughter"). "Channels one and two only let us see death as fear," he says. "They don't let us see death as change, without fear. But if we can change the channels, we might find we can connect, soul to soul. The intimacy of just being there, openhearted, with someone who is dying allows a shared consciousness that is so great that one can't help understanding the message of the human spirit, which is love." In helping people prepare, the main thing that he tries to communicate is that we are *not* our bodies. Who we *really* are, our spirit, might move—whole and complete—into a different plane.

S tephen and Ondrea Levine have written more than six books on the specific philosophy and techniques they use to aid the dying. This meditative style has since found its way into mainstream medicine in work with ill patients in hospitals, into nationally distributed guides for the management of pain in cancer and AIDS patients, and into the literature and workshops of established self-help groups such as Cancer Care.

The hospices and hospitals that use meditative techniques like the Levines' also use them as adjuncts for their pain patients. The benefits they focus on are relaxation and reduced panic and fear, both of which can break pain cycles in which psychological distress compounds physical pain.

Stephen first met Ram Dass in the late 1960s, when he was the editor of the *San Francisco Oracle,* a popular underground paper during the Haight-Ashbury days. Stephen had a familiarity with drugs himself; he was a recovered heroin addict who had turned to Buddhism.

"It was in 1964 when I stopped smack," he says. "I had dabbled with Buddhism before drugs—since 1957, when I was nineteen— but that day I was in my car and I literally pulled over to the curb because I suddenly realized I wanted God more than the shot I was on my way to get. The smack was part of my spiritual search but it didn't work. I've been clean now for nearly thirty-five years." The teachers he found were in the Theravadan tradition, which comes out of Burma, Cambodia, and Thailand.

By 1975, he and Ram Dass were teaching spiritual workshops together, to one of which came Dr. Elisabeth Kübler-Ross. At that time, Dr. Kübler-Ross's center, Shanti Nilaya, was located in California. She invited Levine to be a meditation teacher in her workshops with the terminally ill.

Melding what they'd both learned about dying from Kübler-Ross with their training in Eastern spiritual traditions, Levine and Ram Dass began to map out a path for *conscious dying*. Their work has since helped shape an entire next generation of midwives to sit with the dying.

In 1976, at his first workshop with her, Elisabeth took Stephen (as both of them like to be called) on a lunchtime jaunt—to see a woman who was dying in a local hospital. As he stood in the doorway, terrifically pleased that he'd get to watch what she did, Elisabeth pulled up a chair close to the bed, and told him that's where he should sit. Stephen was terrified. Meditation techniques aside, this was the first time he'd practiced his methods with someone who was actually dying. Instead of letting him watch her, Elisabeth turned and told him this chair was for him and sat at the foot of the bed.

Gathering in his terror, he decided to just sit and be silent. Then the room slowly grew calmer. The woman, he says, began to show him what was needed, giving him the space and time to just be. Soon he focused his mind on a place near his heart, that place we all feel when tears are about to come, and he found himself breathing from that spot, breathing in her pain, and breathing out toward her from that spot. Soon, from the silence and from the heartfelt pain they both shared, grew an intimacy between them of softness, of sadness, of deeply felt connection and compassion.

"This was a woman who had one of the first bone marrow transplants," Levine said, "and in those days they bored a hole in the bone rather than injecting it into the blood. She didn't want it a second time and died the morning they were going to do it again."

In late 1976, humbled by this and similar experiences, Levine—with his wife, Ondrea, and several others—helped Ram Dass start the Dying Project and the first Dying Center, in Santa Fe. Among the most important things he learned was that sense of heartfelt quiet and compassion first taught by that one dying patient. Love, Levine says, echoing Ram Dass, is all that matters at death, but he has since expanded on his first lesson, creating guided meditation techniques to help patients cope with pain; to help caregivers reach that shared, heartfelt intimacy; and to help the dying move psychologically through death.

From 1979 to 1982, the Levines also ran a free phone line that they maintained twenty-four hours a day to talk to the dying and help them through death with their growing body of guided meditations. Since those years, their books and workshops have given counsel to thousands of patients and caretakers nationwide about how to use meditative techniques to manage pain, and guided imagery to quell fear in the active transition to death.

In October 1993, I went to the Boston Marriott Hotel, on the Cambridge side of the Charles River—in the very shadow of Harvard, where Ram Dass used to teach—to attend one of Stephen and Ondrea Levine's "Conscious Living/Conscious Dying" workshops. Over five hundred people—including the terminally ill and their caretakers, as well as doctors, nurses, and therapists—filled the grand ballroom, at $140 each for the weekend. (In 1997, they were still doing these same workshops, as well as a new one, based on their latest book, called *A Year to Live*.)

Onstage, Ondrea—intense and waiflike, with long, dark hair— sits in meditation posture in a straight-backed chair, eyes closed, silent. Stephen, scraggly-bearded, sits in a chair beside her, speaking for both of them. He says Ondrea is demonstrating *being*, which is how we can best be with the dying. He says she is trying to breathe through her heart, feeling the pain in the audience, and trying to send back love. Totally present. When she has something to say (and that something is usually important, I learn), she will come out of her meditation and say it.

"People always have Column A, which is reasons to live," Stephen says, "and Column B, which is reasons to get out. We're so tired and so used to common, ordinary, everyday grief [that] we ostracize our pain. At the moment we most need compassion for ourselves, the mind responds by anger at our pain. It's a distancing experience that won't help you heal. . . . It's tragic that so many people on their deathbeds are so willing to die. It's because they haven't paid attention to their lives."

A terminal diagnosis, he says, is an opportunity to learn to pay attention; pain can be a way to practice forgiveness and mercy toward ourselves. We suffer because we try to push away what is going on, and by doing so, pain only looms larger. Dying, in fact, *is* a process of progressive loss, but rather than meet it with self-pity ("Oh, I can't play the violin anymore"; "I can't walk"; "I'm no longer able to control my bladder"), Levine suggests learning to *open* to what's going on, and in the process, learning to feel the human connection within ourselves and with everyone around us. Even though he is a recovered addict himself, he *never* suggests that anyone forgo opioids like morphine, but he does tell those in pain to learn to use meditation to *soften around it*, to use the pain as a way to wake up psychologically.

"Death isn't the enemy," Levine says. "For individuals in terrible pain it is merciful. If you didn't have death as your security, who would leave their house? *Anything* could happen, and then you'd have to live with it for five hundred years." Getting out of a body that is in pain or can no longer function is not only a merciful gift but a shared, human condition. Recognition of this fact is the quickest way to make a heart connection.

We sit there, as he tells us what to do, those of us who can, in our straight-backed chairs, eyes closed, looking just as Ondrea does: Quiet our minds. . . . Pay attention to our breathing. . . . Breathe in . . . breathe out . . . breathe in . . . breathe out. . . . Imagine when we breathe in that we are taking in dark, damp, blackness. As we breathe out, we are sending out light, clarity, goodness. . . . Breathe in . . . breathe out. . . . Think of someone we love who is ill. As we breathe in, draw in their fear, their uncertainty, their pain, as that blackness. Imagine that it is coming from a point in their heart. . . . As we breathe out, send back, to that point in their heart, our light, our clarity, our strength, our fearlessness. . . . Breathe in . . . breathe out.

We do this for ten minutes maybe, and then we go back to just quiet mind. I find when I open my eyes my mind is still, but there is a deep, vulnerable, very open feeling in my heart. (Months later, when I am sitting with a dying person, doing this quietly to myself, sending out thoughts of light and life, I find that he is indeed calm and relaxed himself.)

"One of the worst abuses we can do to other human beings," Stephen says, next morning, "is make them feel they need *you* to discover their true natures. It's a damnable lie." Instead, he says, it's better if they have tools they can use for themselves, because we might not be there to help if they suddenly find themselves alone in the midst of active dying.

Now he tells us to lie on the floor, each of us with a partner. One of us is the *breather,* the person who is lying on the floor, and the other is trying to tune in to that person's pattern of breathing, trying to match his or her breathing with that other person's. At the end of each out breath, the person matching his breathing to the other's says "Ahhhhhh." Stephen says this exercise is called the "Ahhhhh breath."

"You can use this Ahhhhh breathing to slow down someone's breathing," he says, "so if they are having an anxiety attack, going *Ah/ah/ah/ah/ah/ah,* it can calm. Start with them, with their rhythm, but then begin to slow them down once you're tuned in."

By the time Holly, my partner, and I finished breathing, I realized I had rarely felt so alive. That, Stephen says, is "being present" to what we will probably feel at death.

He also says that dying feels like a process of melting, a very American metaphor for the physical process of death described as well in ancient Buddhist teachings. First comes the *physical* melting, as the body slowly loses its ability to move, digest, regulate temperature, even breathe, he says. Then there might be that initial moment of pain, or panic or fear. But *after* that moment comes a *psychological* melting, a feeling nearly like falling—or walking—*into our own dreams.* And in that process, as we begin to feel lighter and lighter, comes a final, incredible feeling of joy and peace.

This kind of thinking actually fits well with orthodox Western religion, but I did not understand just *how* well until my husband's uncle, an elderly, devout Irish priest, died. Father Tom Sheedy, a kindly parish priest, took lifelong comfort in the rituals of

Catholicism, and he used those rituals to help him spiritually as he died.

On Sunday evening, October 3, 1993, Father Tom, age eighty-eight, was sitting at home in the study of the rectory he shared with Father Vincent Keenan, age sixty-nine, in Pass Christian, Mississippi, at Our Mother of Mercy Catholic Church. They were watching the last game of baseball season, each in his own reclining chair. Father Tom was a Mets fan, born and raised in Yonkers, New York, and the Mets were playing the Florida Marlins, so he could see it on local TV.

When he was in his twenties, Tom Sheedy was an accountant on Wall Street. Each day he took the train downtown from Yonkers, where he lived with his family. On the North Hudson line, he had to pass through Harlem day after day. Poor as the Sheedys were, he realized that life for those who were black and living in Harlem was far worse.

Tom Sheedy was as Irish as they come. His mother, Bridget, still spoke with a brogue. His father, Patrick, would send him to the corner bar to bring home milk bottles filled with whiskey. But when the stock market crashed in 1929, he decided that some things in life were more important than his job. He saw life in Harlem getting worse, so Tom Sheedy did an unusual thing for the time—he *quit* Wall Street and decided to enter the priesthood. He wanted to become a member of the Josephite Order—founded in England and dedicated to helping poor blacks.

After he was ordained in Baltimore in 1941, Father Tom was sent to small black parishes throughout the South: Okeechobee, Tampa, Pascagoula, Memphis, Biloxi, Gulfport, Napoleonville, and New Orleans. He saw the rise of integration, the sit-ins, voter registration, but politics wasn't his thing. God was. Father Tom was a spiritual man, and no matter who was around, he would say Mass each day. In fact, he'd go into a church three times daily to sing vespers, even if he had to sing by himself.

At the all-black Our Mother of Mercy Catholic Church, in Pass Christian, Father Tom was officially in semiretirement. Father Keenan was the head priest, but actually, *he* was the one who wanted to retire. Yet that night, as they watched the game, Father Tom started to worry. In three weeks he would be eighty-nine and his driver's license was about to expire. Because of his age, he'd need to have an eye test to renew it, and he was afraid he wouldn't pass. There was a hole in his vision, a dot of nothingness in the middle of his left eye. Doctors had given him medicine, which he sometimes forgot to take; they said the dot was a blood clot ready to burst. So he worried. He needed to drive to get around.

Father Tom couldn't help noticing, caring, getting involved. He baptized the babies, married the young and the old, presided over funerals, talked with anyone having problems. He gave money to anyone who needed it, heard problems of divorce, of drugs, of sadness and illness and death. And he could do the best imitations of Jimmy Durante and Al Jolson east of the Mississippi—and probably also west.

"He was a showman, and he'd entertain all the priests and nuns when we met," said Father Keenan, "and he made the parishioners everywhere laugh." They loved him at Our Mother of Mercy, a white priest in an all-black church. And they also loved him down the block and around the corner, in Saint Paul's Catholic Church, the mostly white church in town.

But things weren't all well with Southern churches. Father Keenan said they had to send for priests and nuns to come to Mississippi from Ireland—rather like coming to do missionary work. That's because the order of Josephites was dying out. "No one wants to be a priest anymore. There are only thirty-five Josephites left under sixty-five years of age in the entire Western Hemisphere," he said. To help Fathers Keenan and Sheedy, the order had assigned them Sister Martina Fox, an Irish nun. A sprightly, cheerful person, each morning, afternoon, and evening, she would be there to say prayers with Father Tom.

On Tuesday morning, two days after that Mets game when he worried about his vision, Father Tom went to visit the residents of the Miramar Nursing Home, something he did twice a week. This is part of the reason he had to drive. To get there, Father Tom had to back out of the rectory driveway, go past the railroad tracks, turn right down the hill, stop at busy Route 90, hang a right onto the highway without the benefit of any traffic light, and drive about two miles to the nursing home.

Route 90 runs along the Mississippi Gulf, the main scenic highway to New Orleans. Until recently it's been long and lazy, winding past miles of verandas with ceiling fans on their porches.

But during the late 1980s, gambling casinos came to the Gulf, and with them high-speed traffic.

Once a week, when he was at the nursing home, the nurses would force Father Tom to hold out his arm so they could check his blood pressure. Too high and they'd chide him, make him take his medicine. They told him to mind that hole in his bad eye. That day his pressure was okay, but they told him they worried, too, about the high-speed drivers.

When he got home for lunch, Father Keenan and Sister Martina had a surprise. The day before had been Father Keenan's day off. He went to New Orleans, and on the way back he stopped at the supermarket, saw a great ham roast, bone and all, and bought it. Father Tom loved ham roasts. And he also bought Father Tom some ice cream, his favorite—vanilla. Father Keenan decided to roast the ham for Tuesday lunch, invite Sister Martina, and celebrate Father Tom's birthday—even though it was three weeks early. "Who knows," Father Keenan told him. "On your birthday I might not be here."

So that Tuesday, when Father Tom walked in from the Miramar Nursing Home, Father Keenan and Sister Martina sang "Happy Birthday," sat down to lunch on ham, and even had him blow out the candles on a ball of ice cream in a dish. The fact is, he didn't have ice cream much anymore, didn't eat as much as he had altogether, because he always felt full, but never really much talked about it. He'd say he was on a diet, but it would turn out eating hurt a painful spot in his stomach.

That night, Father Keenan had on a sitcom. Halfway through, Father Tom got bored, so he went into the living room and sat in the recliner there while he listened to the news on CNN. Then he went to bed.

Father Tom's room was right next to Father Keenan's. They shared a bath, the sink filled with tiny pieces of used-up soap all lumped together in hopes of making one bar to save money. The parish was poor and they didn't want to be a burden. Already this year Father Tom had had to buy a new hatchback Toyota Tercel to get around because his old car had broken down.

In his room, stacked on the floor, were several years' worth of Church journals, most arguing the pros and cons of life-sustaining medical treatment. Father Tom had been one of seven children.

Two of his siblings were still alive well into their nineties, but his sister Peggy had been in a Yonkers nursing home on a feeding tube, in a coma—after she'd had a stroke—for the past six years.

Each year he went north to visit the family, and each year he wondered when she would die. Each time he visited, Peggy was curled tighter into the fetal position, growing skinnier. He'd wanted the tube removed—especially after the Church decided it was okay—but he couldn't bring himself to be the one to say it.

Wednesday was his day off. As usual, he was going to visit a priest friend at a parish in Biloxi, but this day a woman at the Miramar Nursing Home was celebrating her ninetieth birthday. Father Tom went to her party a little before noon, then he drove home, had ham leftovers, and set off for Biloxi. He hated wearing his seat belt. It pressed on his stomach just where it had begun to feel a little sore. So he decided to skip the belt.

Just after 1:00 P.M., Father Tom drove out of the rectory drive-way, past the railroad tracks, down the hill to Route 90, and stopped, since there is no traffic light. To get to Biloxi he had to turn left, crossing the two-lane highway going in the direction of New Orleans, onto the two-lane highway going down the Gulf coast to Biloxi. Cars were speeding, entering, leaving, rushing, turning, since it was still lunchtime.

Father Tom began to turn left. He never even saw the brown Chevrolet that came up on him at high speed, just in the spot in his vision where he had that large dot. It hit him broadside on his door. The man from Frankeye's Wrecker, who later pried him loose, said it dented his car from the beginning of the driver's side door back to the rear, sending the metal door eighteen inches in on Father Tom. A seventeen-year-old girl was driving. She belonged to a parish in neighboring Bay Saint Louis.

The ambulance came. Someone went to get Sister Martina. She followed Father Tom's ambulance in her car to Memorial Hospital in Gulfport. Shortly after they reached the hospital, Father Tommy Conway, a young Irish priest, arrived from Gulfport, and Father Keenan came.

By then Father Tom was conscious. The doctors asked his name, his age. Sister Martina started answering for him, but he kept correcting her. Since they'd already celebrated his birthday, she said he was eighty-nine, but he said no, he wasn't eighty-nine *yet*. He was still eighty-eight. Father Tommy helped him get on a gown. A few minutes later, he asked Sister Martina where his pants were. She told him he didn't need them, but he persisted. He said his money was in his left pocket and she should get it to keep it safe. Then he went to X ray.

They said he had blood in his urine and was bleeding internally. He had some broken ribs, his pelvis was shattered, his bladder, a kidney, and one lung had been punctured. They also found a massive tumor on his abdomen, right where it hurt when he put on his seat belt, and another one in his kidney. On his death certificate it would say he had kidney cancer. Then Father Tom started sweating profusely, got extremely white, and felt chilled. He turned pale and became unconscious; it seemed as if he was going to die right then.

But then he came back. Father Tom was lying in bed, covered, when he turned to Sister Martina and first said it: "If I'm not going to make it, make sure they just let me go." He was thinking about his sister Peggy. He told her—and the doctors—he didn't want to be put on any machines. He said it again and again, anytime anyone came to ask him. No respirator, no nothing. Sister Martina nodded. When Father Keenan came, he told him, too. He made them both agree, and they did. And they told that to the doctors, many of whom were in Father Tommy Conway's parish, and so they listened. They also didn't take him to surgery, since he was in shock and was unlikely to come out of it. Father Keenan called Father Tom's family.

Sister Martina asked if he were in any pain. "Oh boy," he said, and pointed to his chest. So they gave him a shot of Demerol. Later on, the pain came back, so they gave him another. Around 2:00 A.M., Father Tom went to sleep and never really regained consciousness. But before he drifted away, just after he came out of X ray, something extraordinary started to happen.

When Father Tommy Conway arrived, he asked Father Tom if he wanted to be anointed; he did, and received the last rites. Then, as if by instinct, Sister Martina began praying with him. She told him she'd say the prayers out loud and that he could follow along, but that he shouldn't talk. He asked if she meant he should say them in his mind, and she said yes.

So she started saying all the prayers she could remember. She thought of vespers and began singing them, the prayers Father Tom had said every day. She read out loud from her prayer book.

"I tried to keep his mind turned toward God," Sister Martina said, "to open communication between him and the Lord. This was a man who'd prayed daily three times a day plus services most of his life, so it wasn't really hard."

Doctors and nurses gave them privacy. When the nurses asked if she'd like to play music, she said all he'd ever done in his life was watch TV and pray, so she didn't want to clutter his mind—maybe the music she chose might distract him. She said the Psalms, she tried to sing the melodies, she thought of every prayer she'd ever known since her convent days. And she sat in a chair by his bed all night, covered over—praying—with two blankets on top of her.

At one point, Sister Martina said, Father Tom got scared. So she told him God had a room for him, "a mansion in heaven." Father Tom opened his eyes, smiled. He asked her, "How do you know?" They laughed; he stopped being scared. Mostly, he moved his lips silently when he could. And he listened. And prayed in his mind. The doctors would check every now and then and ask again if they were sure they didn't want anything done. And Father Tom, Sister Martina, Father Tommy, and Father Keenan would tell them no. When Sister Martina grew sleepy, Father Tommy took over. He, too, said prayers, and he told Father Tom it was okay to let go.

Around 5:00 P.M. the next day, Father Tommy noticed Father Tom's breathing had grown very shallow. His urine bag was empty, indicating his kidneys had failed. Soon he took a long time between breaths. And then there were no more breaths at all. "It was very peaceful," Father Tommy said. "His eyes had been half open all day, so I closed them with my two fingers."

"This is how people die in Ireland," Sister Martina later said. "No machines. Surrounded by families and people saying prayers. But here it's very unique. It was extremely peaceful. They didn't rush around trying to treat him, and they consciously controlled his pain."

When Father Tom died his face was astonishing, so peaceful, with a big, warm smile. On Wednesday evening, October 13, black parishioners gathered at Our Mother of Mercy. Father Tom's body was lying up front, still smiling. Some said he seemed as if he were surrounded by an army of giant angels. Gospel singers sang "Amazing Grace" and "Danny Boy." And seventy priests, who'd come from all over the South, and all the parishioners filed by.

On Thursday, they held the funeral mass at the mostly white St. Paul's around the corner, this one bigger and packed full. More priests came. The mayor of Pass Christian. Black and white people together. They sang "When the Saints Go Marching In," they sang "A-Men." The local archbishop spoke. Nearly a hundred priests gave Communion. Father Tom's casket was now closed. The angels seemed to have gone. Father Tom, some said, was already with God.

They carried his casket into a waiting hearse and the black parishioners and the hundred priests and the white parishioners from Saint Paul's, and the mayor and the Irish missionary priests and nuns walked following the hearse, past the poor houses of Pass Christian, past the white clapboard Our Mother of Mercy, across the railroad tracks, singing "When the Saints Go Marching In." There, they buried Father Tom in the church's graveyard. A year later, the parishioners would buy a stone that said, HERE LIE PRIESTS FROM THE JOSEPHITE ORDER. And there would be room for all four of them in that Mississippi area.

"The most interesting thing about Father Sheedy's death," said Larry Killebrew, M.D., his medical team leader, "was that when he first came in, he was struggling and his blood pressure was dropping. But when Father Tommy and Sister Martina came in and started saying prayers with him, his blood pressure stabilized and his heart rate went right down."

Father Tom had pelvic fractures and blood in his urine. "He was fully conscious and told us that he'd had a sister on life support for some time and he made it very clear he didn't want any intubation, no ventilator, or anything. He wasn't a real good surgical candidate because there was a lot of bleeding. We tried to get him stabilized. Maybe times have changed. Maybe it's me. But the farther you get away from academia and more into the trenches, the more you see how to do what you *should* do rather than what you *could* do."

Father Tom died a good death. He was lucky. He had the power to take charge of his own death, the people willing to help him, and the psychological and spiritual skill to know how. Father Tom died in his own way, going directly toward his own view of God.

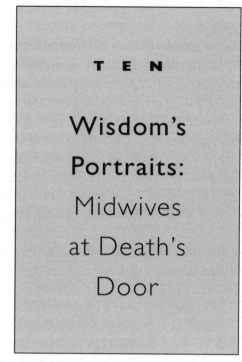

TEN

Wisdom's Portraits: Midwives at Death's Door

D r. Elisabeth Kübler-Ross is sitting on a log outside the door to the main kitchen at the Elisabeth Kübler-Ross Center, chain-smoking, brown-and-gray-streaked hair bobbing as she talks, telling me about her first lessons in death.

Elisabeth was born on July 8, 1926, in Zurich, Switzerland, one of triplet girls. Her parents thought they were being fair, taking turns, but they actually couldn't tell two of these daughters apart. The one sister who looked different always ended up on their mother's lap, the other—the one who looked identical to Elisabeth—on their father's. Elisabeth was the odd sister out, so she befriended the family rabbits. The only problem was, every once in a while her father told her to take one to the butcher to prepare for Sunday family dinner.

One rabbit, Blackie, was Elisabeth's favorite. She saved it to the last, but one Sunday her father told her it was time. Tears streaking her face, she cradled this rabbit all the way to the butcher's. But the worst was yet to come. Afterward, he handed her back the meat wrapped in paper. "What a shame," he told her. "This rabbit was pregnant. If you'd waited just a few more days you would have had a lovely new batch of babies."

Elisabeth puffs hard on her cigarettes as she tells the story, some sixty years after it occurred. She says it took her until her early twenties to understand both the pain and the transcendence of what can only be described as the circle of life.

She'd experienced illness and death early, setting her on what became her life mission. At five she was hospitalized with pneumonia and not expected to live, but the little girl in the bed next to her died instead. A short time later, a beloved neighbor died, but not before she was called to his side so he could tell her good-bye.

At thirteen, one triplet became ill with what probably was polio, causing her to be crippled and frail for much of her life. Elisabeth vowed to become a physician. That same year, World War II broke out, with the news—which Elisabeth heard over the family's new radio—that Germany had invaded Poland. Elisabeth vowed that when the war ended, she would use whatever medical or other skills she then had and go to help the people of Poland.

She was nineteen when the war ended and had become an independent, rebellious child, rejecting her father's plan for a traditionally feminine, comfortable life. By then she'd already gotten a job in a local hospital as a laboratory assistant and, nearly alone, had organized a medical relief program at her hospital for the teeming refugees coming over the Swiss border to escape the Germans. After the war ended, she joined the International Voluntary Service for Peace to help rebuild war-torn Europe and to try to keep her vow to make her way to Poland.

Packing syringes, some medical supplies, and a few clothes in a backpack, Elisabeth hitchhiked across Europe to those places the Voluntary Service sent her. She worked as a cook for the Voluntary Service in towns its crews were helping to rebuild, and she ran medical clinics in refugee camps. Finally, she was sent to Poland.

Elisabeth was among the first people to enter Maidanek, a German concentration camp in Poland—"one of the worst concentration camps," she tells me, "where nearly a million children died." There she wandered around, trancelike, nearly by herself. In one abandoned railway car she saw so many shoes—once worn by both adults and children—that they had become matted together by fungus. Another railway car was nearly filled with human hair.

Her mission may have begun to unfold when she made her way into the crumbling barracks. There she found—scratched on the walls with tiny fingernails, next to little bunk beds, besides messages of love to mommies and daddies—hundreds and hundreds of butterflies. She says she wondered for a long time what those butterflies meant.

Elisabeth went back home, got a medical degree, married Manny Ross, an American physician, and moved to the United States with him. Serendipity put her into a psychiatric residency, and she eventually became known at Billings Hospital in Chicago for her work with the dying.

After years of treating dying patients, she finally understood the butterflies: At death, she says, there is a metamorphosis of the human spirit, much like a butterfly breaking free of its cocoon. Our great task is to learn how to understand this transition well enough to lend a loving hand.

I t was the end of May 1993, and I had waited two years to attend Kübler-Ross's five-day, internationally renowned "Life, Death and Transition" workshop. There were long waiting lists. When she lectured, two or three thousand people showed up, and it was hard to get anywhere near her. She'd already suffered two strokes and wasn't always leading these intensive workshops herself anymore. Nor, when she was, were they always at her center, in rural Virginia, where she now lived. I wanted to come to this center, with Elisabeth.

She had been blunt about the conditions under which I could attend. I had to pay, like everyone else, $350 for the entire five-day week, room and board included. And I would have to come not as a reporter, but as myself. She was sure I'd had losses and deaths in my past, she said, and I should plan to think about them. After the workshop, I could write about my own experience, or about her, the workshop, and the center, but not about anyone else.

I headed out of New York City on a Sunday morning, going south down the New Jersey Turnpike, turning west at the Pennsyl-

vania Turnpike, then south again, on through Harrisonburg, over
the majestic, bluish-green Shenandoah Mountains. On Route 250,
I finally amble through the tiny town of Head Waters, with its one
general store, one church, and one phone booth. Then I turn right,
along nearly deserted Route 614, for 7.2 miles, nearly to the West
Virginia border.

There, by a small dirt drive to the left, is a pockmarked wooden
sign that reads THE ELISABETH KÜBLER-ROSS CENTER. The next drive
over is the adjacent Healing Waters Farm, where Elisabeth lives in a
rustic log cabin, amid the notes and letters of a lifetime of work,
where she grows vegetables, and where her sheep, cattle, and ten pet
llamas roam. For ten years, in this rustic conference center on a 260-
acre farm that Elisabeth bought from Raymond Moody—the father
of the NDE—she has trained heath-care workers in the dying process and helped the terminally ill and their families prepare.

Up ahead, I can see the main building. It is clad with vertical
wood siding, cedar perhaps, and constructed in an octagonal shape.
A large wooden porch encircles the front of the building, and big
white French doors mark the main entry.

There is no staff there when I arrive, only a sign to "help yourself"
to chicken soup and cheese sandwiches, and another to please con-
serve electricity. I later learned there isn't much staff at all. The windows on the second floor, overlooking the front porch, are those of
the women's dorm, where I am headed. Twenty neatly made bunk
beds encircle a huge round room, their feet pointing toward the center. I choose a bottom bunk bed near a window. The sun lights up this
dorm, coming from different angles from sunrise to dusk.

This conference center is beautiful, with a quality of primordial
peace, yet it is startlingly austere. I'm shocked every time I put my
used food tray—breakfast, lunch, and dinner—in the cafeteria-
style, chrome slot and look through. There is the world-famous
Elisabeth Kübler-Ross, scraping the old food off my dishes, piling
the plates and silverware and glasses into a dishwashing machine.

Elisabeth runs this center nearly alone, just as she did her
European camps for refugees after the war. She especially loves to
bake, and makes great desserts, mostly shortcake and different
kinds of pies—rhubarb, apple, strawberry. She uses recipes her
mother gave her when she was a child. Her mother also taught her
to knit, and she's always knitting—scarves, little booties, sweaters,

blankets—things she will sell at auctions or in her little store here at the center.

A workshop staff of five therapists ("trainers") will soon arrive, but the only full-time person besides Elisabeth herself is her assistant, Debbie—a combination secretary, cook, laundress, and all-around helper. Keeping staff light allows Elisabeth to give financial aid to those who are terminally ill and can't otherwise afford to come.

When I walk through the main building, one of the first things I see is a striking sculpture, *Angel of Death,* by Melinda White, a Vermont artist. It takes up the rear of the dining room. Lying on what is obviously her deathbed is a figure of papier-mâché, human-size, skeletal—probably old, but it's hard to tell—covered by a burlap blanket. Leaning over her right shoulder, looking into her face, is a human-size angel with big wings.

Looking at the dying figure from her left side—the side opposite the angel—I see that her face is contorted in what could be agony. But looking at her from the right, on the side of the angel, I see her looking up with a blissful smile, her eyes riveted on the angel's face. From this angle, death looks majestic and joyful. The most important thing Elisabeth will teach us is about angles: If we can shift our angles at death, she will say, slightly alter and expand our view, we will better learn to see the unimaginable mysteries that lie at the edges of life. The workshop is scheduled to begin at 10:30 the next morning.

E lisabeth Kübler-Ross was arguably the first of a growing cadre of professionals who might be called modern midwives to the dying. These are the psychiatrists, physicians, psychologists, social workers, therapists, religious advisers, and nurses who help the dying through the psychospiritual passage of late-twentieth-century death.

Some are affiliated with hospitals or hospices. Some are leaders in the network of disease-specific self-help and support groups—organizations like Cancer Care and SHARE (a national support network for people with cancer). Some are members of associations formed for people with every condition from Lou Gehrig's disease to multiple sclerosis to heart, lung, kidney, or Alzheimer's disease, as well as groups like the Gay Men's Health Crisis and God's Love

We Deliver, both in New York, and Shanti and the Living/Dying Project in California that succor AIDS patients.

These modern-day "midwives" help patients and families through the whole course of an illness, from diagnosis through treatment through decline to death, and even afterward, helping surviving family members with their bereavement. But this isn't exactly a profession one can plan for. Many of these are people who—like Elisabeth herself—were in some way *called*.

On Monday morning, the first day of my workshop, twenty-five people (plus the trainers and Elisabeth herself) gather in a large upstairs meeting room. They are teachers, housewives, executives, therapists, nurses, gymnasts, plumbers, politicians. They have come from as far away as Hawaii and Switzerland.

Some in our group have terminal illnesses, but only one is clearly near death—a young woman in her mid-twenties who is dying of a hereditary degenerative disease. She has come with a private nurse, and even with her electric wheelchair she can barely move around. And yet she's warm and engaging and tries to participate in everything, even when she's clearly struggling to stay awake. Several of the attendees have recently helped someone they loved through the dying process. Others have lost a loved one long ago and are still grieving. I soon discover that I am, without knowing it, still in mourning myself, the victim of unresolved grief from a death gone bad long ago.

We start each session by singing from a song booklet on which Elisabeth has written, "Nothing creates greater positive energy faster than singing! Here are some of my favorite songs." They are old camp-meeting songs: "Michael, Row the Boat Ashore," "Danny Boy," "Amazing Grace," "This Little Light of Mine," "You Are My Sunshine," "He's Got the Whole World in His Hands," "Rise and Shine." They are cheerful, powerful songs. We grow close.

"It isn't an accident we're here," a trainer named Sheila tells us at the start. We introduce ourselves. This day, Elisabeth says, is "Baloney Day," the day we *say* why we're here; she says we'll find out the *real* reason later. To help us find out, we are to draw a picture. Crayons are plopped on tables in the cafeteria. We're to take some drawing paper, choose any colors we want, and go to it. It's been years since most of the people in this room drew anything.

I draw two stick figures, me in colors I later learn are depressed, and my husband, I think, in happy yellows and oranges. I am just starting this book, and—no surprise to anyone but me—I happen to put a thought bubble over my head containing a book with two blank open pages. I later discover that this might actually be two coffins—my husband's and mine—and what *really* might be going on is my own fear of dying. Or it could be memories of my long-deceased father and sister; those memories, I learn, have continued to affect me.

She asked me—as she asks everyone—to bring photos, diaries, letters, memorabilia about people we loved. I dug through old boxes and stuffed a suitcase pocket with pictures of my sister and father, letters each of them had written to me. I hadn't thought of those letters in years.

That first evening, the trainers go over our drawings. Like dreams, they say, drawings are a window into our unconscious, our souls. They can tell us—and those trying to help us—not only how we are coping with dying, but what our illness feels like to us, even whether our subconscious believes that the particular medical treatments planned for us by our physicians will have success in producing a cure.

We look at our drawings—at the emotional feeling, at color, shape, positioning on the paper, what is put in and what is left out. Elisabeth divides drawings into four quadrants. The *past* is in the lower left, the *near future* in the lower right, the *present* in the upper right, and the *far future* in the upper left. In my drawing, that's where my blank book is. The unconscious, Elisabeth says, knows more about us than we think, and we can see what it knows by putting it on paper. The closer we get to dying, the clearer the subconscious imagery in the drawing becomes. A child with leuke-mia, she says, drew a purple balloon going up into the sky in the top left quadrant, and she knew he knew—though maybe not consciously—that he would die.

A man who was a Quaker refused to have chemotherapy for his cancer. When Dr. Kübler-Ross questioned him, he told her that his doctor had said that chemo would kill the cancer cells, and he took seriously the commandment "Thou Shalt Not Kill." She asked him to consider whether there was a way to just get the cancer cells to *leave,* rather than killing them. The man soon came back with a drawing of dozens of tiny little gnomes, each carrying off a cancer cell. The man then agreed to treatment. Since he viewed his cancer like this, she knew it would go into remission. And it did.

On day two, after we sing, Elisabeth introduces another quadrant theory, this one related to personality development. As babies, she explains, we relate primarily through our physical quadrant, focusing on getting around, learning about life here on earth, learning where to pee, and so on. At six months we begin opening up what she calls our *emotional* quadrant. By age six, if all goes well, we start to explore our *intellectual* quadrant. Then as we grow older, a *spiritual,* or *intuitive,* quadrant opens up, which is the most important, the whole point of our being on earth. This quadrant grows larger and wiser as we age and as we grow nearer to death.

By the time we die, she says, we are functioning almost entirely from that intuitive, spiritual quadrant; this is the quadrant that teaches us what life as human beings is all about and that allows us to move into what she calls the next realm, the quadrant from which mystery can occur. The approach of death inevitably makes the spiritual quadrant take over, even if you're very young. That is why, she says, dying people—even small, dying children—are so intuitive, so in touch not only with their own unconscious but with a seeming pipeline into some higher consciousness. It's why the dying often seem so enormously wise.

She was the first to suggest that dying patients inevitably communicate from this quadrant, and that we can glimpse it—and help them—if we understand their symbolic language.

Critics say that Kübler-Ross has grown stranger as she has grown older; they are dismayed by her lack of scientific method, by her talk of "the light" and near-death experience, by her insistence that she "knows" there is someplace we go when we die. This view is based, she says, on reports of patients who have recounted events seen from a point outside of their bodies in that time when they have "died," and that they can even accurately describe medical procedures done to them during that time when they had no prior medical experience.

In fact, Elisabeth has always talked like this. She says that, over the years, more than 20,000 patients have told her about having near-death experiences, many with out-of-body components. Moreover, she says, nearly as many of their relatives or close friends had simultaneous ESP or dream experiences about them at the very time they died.

By expanding on her quadrant theory and by using her stories of near-death experiences and dying, Elisabeth is able to explain— even to very young children—what death is like. In doing so, she eases her listeners' fear. She does it now for us, on day two. "The language of the dying patient," she says, "is the language of the spiritual quadrant."

We are in the large room above the dining room and the *Angel of Death* sculpture. This room is lined with Elisabeth's favorite toys. She uses them to help people get in touch with their unconscious, and she uses them—as she does now—to demonstrate her theories of death.

My particular favorite is a stuffed red caterpillar. It's a weird, foot-long thing with a zipper on its belly. Elisabeth holds it. She says that our spirit is like this caterpillar. She passes it around so we can feel it. That's who we are in normal, healthy, human form—a caterpillar, she says. When we are sick we become cocoons and start cooking, preparing for our transformations. Metamorphosis is happening, a metamorphosis of the human spirit. When we die, our transition is complete.

She takes back the caterpillar, zips open its belly, and turns the toy inside out. It instantly becomes a huge, gorgeous, colorful butterfly. What happens at death, Elisabeth says, is a release, a transition, a transformation of the spirit. We instantly fly free, a butterfly of the spirit.

"Anyone who has had a genuine NDE is not afraid to die," Elisabeth says. "What they come back to say is that life is about learning unconditional love." The rest of her workshop is about resolving unresolved emotions in each of our own lives—emotions, she says, that prevent unconditional love. These emotions have to do with loss and grief. Finishing *this* old business will help us both to live well and to die well in the future.

There are single-bed mattresses stacked up against the wall, and now we use them, each of us working with a trainer in front of the whole group. The singing, the drawing—something—has made it intimate enough here for people to get up one by one and work on their most private stories. We are trying to get at primordial emotions here: at pain, sorrow, grief, anger. Almost everyone seems to have anger—rage, in fact—blocking his ability to love. Almost everyone ends up working with this anger, taking great stacks of the Harrisonburg, Virginia, and Staunton, Virginia, phone books, the fattest ones around here, and beating them to shreds with cut-down black rubber hoses.

As we move around the group, one story seems to weave into another: mothers who have lost children, children who have lost mothers, husbands who have lost wives, wives who have lost husbands. We are dealing with those who have gone and with the pain of going ourselves.

We scream—coached by trainers—at photos of people who have hurt us. We tell them how we feel. We tell them we love them. We hold dolls or pillows representing lost loves. We hit the telephone books with the black hoses, getting at ever-deeper rage. We hold on to pillows and sob.

Elisabeth says that for those who are dying or coping with grief, tools for finishing old business will allow us to move more quickly toward forgiveness, toward unconditional love for those around us, toward the deeper love of "the light." She is giving us the tools for an easier dying.

I am the last one to go. I sit on the mattress, put a pillow in front of me, and spread out my little pictures. I had thought I wanted to talk to my father, to tell him how angry he made me that he'd died. But I realize I want to talk to my sister instead. I clear all the other pictures away. I tell her I never knew she was dying, how lonely it must have been, how no one ever talked to her about it, and how mad she made me when she'd tease me, knowing I was not allowed to fight back, how shocked I was she was gone, how I never knew how she died, how I wondered if she were in pain. Was it terrible? How sorry I was. And I missed her. I missed not having someone to share growing up with.

And then I realize I am shaking. I am angry at her, too, for dying, angry that my life had been so changed by her death. I take the phone books from Harrisonburg and a black piece of hose and start beating them. I go through three books, sobbing all the while. I had no idea these feelings were in me, no idea I could do such a thing, especially in front of a group. When I am calm, I hold the pillow, first with the photo on it, and tell my sister I love her and miss her. Then I remove the photo and cradle the pillow as the raw, wounded child I was. The trainers coach me through all of this, and now they tell me that I should hold that child as long as I need to, that it is someone worthy of love.

Part of me thinks all this is stupid. But then there is that other part. And that part feels the way we all feel when we are children and cry longer and harder than we'd ever imagine we could cry, and then afterward, as we are gulping to catch our breath, there is that cleansed feeling, and somehow, being drained, maybe, there is a lightness. Somehow, it feels finished. Cathartic.

I realize I am still angry at my father for not telling me my sister was dying, though, and for dying himself, but I also realize that— trite as *this* sounds—he did the best he could. I feel all this deep inside my body, not only intellectually. I also realize that he wasn't a giant of a person, and he was only forty-six when he died.

Now, after beating those phone books, I somehow feel flooded with love—for my daughter, my husband, my mother, my step-children, my friends, the people still alive whom I love. I feel I could forgive my father. But mostly, I feel a certain communion I'd never had with my sister.

That night, we have what Elisabeth calls a pine cone ceremony. She has told us to look during the day for a pine cone that feels like us and bring it to the ceremony, that there will be a fire and we are to think of what we would like to leave at the center emotionally—something we don't need anymore—and invest the pine cone with it, then throw it into the fire. I'd be lying if I didn't say there was a part of me that was cynical—all that sixties, hippie-dippy stuff, I thought.

But during the day, I discover on the ground a very deformed, mutilated pine cone, small, missing some of its little flares, a bit misshapen and shriveled. I can't say why, but it reminds me of myself, and this is the part—that view of myself—that I want to leave at the center. I feel as if something happened on the mattress that might now allow me to leave a shriveled view of myself right there in that ceremonial fire. None of this, I should say, was really all that conscious.

At the ceremony, I find myself seated next to the woman who is dying. I like her and she likes me. We have become friends. As Elisabeth lights the fire in the huge central fireplace and everyone starts to sing, a man comes in who hadn't been at our workshop; the young woman tells me it is her friend Steve. She says he'd spent a lot of time with Elisabeth and often comes to help at her workshops. She says he recently had a second kidney transplant. She asks if I mind if he sits with us. Of course I don't, and she motions for him to sit between us.

As I sit there, deformed pine cone in hand, I ask Steve about his kidney transplant. He tells me he needed a second one because his first one, done twenty-seven years ago, had failed. That first one had been donated by his father, who had recently died—but not because he was missing his other kidney. Steve wants to be here tonight to think about how grateful he is and how much he loved his dad.

I asked why he needed the first transplant. And Steve tells me this: When he was a child he'd gotten a strep throat. Somehow, they didn't give him antibiotics, and it went into his kidneys. He got nephrosis. Most of the other kids ended up dying if they had nephrosis, but he was one of the first people to try dialysis, and then one of the first to have a kidney transplant. He must have seen my astonished face because he listens intently as I tell him that my sister had had nephrosis, that she had gotten it exactly as he had, but that she was one of those kids who had died.

Steve looks at me. He says, "I want you to know one thing. She had a very gentle, easy death. From watching what happened to the others, from being in beds next to them when they died, from having my own kidneys fail, what happens is that the toxins slowly build up. And you get sleepier and sleepier. And then you just drift off, asleep, and go into a coma. While you are asleep, the body shuts down and you die, probably of cardiac arrest. I was brought back, but I know myself, from having gone through it, from lying next to those who weren't brought back, it was a very easy death. I want you to know she didn't suffer. There wasn't any pain. She wouldn't have felt anything. She just drifted off and went to sleep."

I start to cry. Just slightly. I realize that that is exactly what I needed to know. I feel a huge wave of relief. Some of my sadness must have come from guilt, some from fear. But some had also come from not knowing.

And then it is my turn. While we had been whispering, others had gone before me, telling their stories, and throwing their pine cones into the fire. So now I stand up, pine cone in hand, in front of the big brick fireplace in the dining room, with the fire roaring crisply behind me, and look around at those people I'd spent the week with. I feel like I love them more than anyone. I look at Elisabeth, that wiry, chain-smoking, short, blunt little woman who can tell immediately, and instantly lets you know it, when you are being a *phony baloney*. I feel so much love for her.

I say: "I am throwing this *deformed* pine cone into the fire." I say: "I am leaving behind the guilt I felt about these deaths, the anger, the sense that I had been maimed." I say: "I feel I've been given a great gift being here. I have been given the gift of my life." Before I start to cry again, I turn and throw my pine cone into the fire.

That night, the last night we are together, we all sing one last time. Steve plays a terrific guitar, so we sound better than ever. And then we have an auction, Elisabeth's standard end-of-workshop event, to raise money for the center. She and her assistant Debbie trot things up from her little shop on the floor below—the scarves and booties she has knitted, some posters and T-shirts, and some surprise gifts that are wrapped.

Things are held up and sold. Then Elisabeth holds one poster high. It is a picture drawn by a little boy shortly before he died, a huge, colorful drawing. "People who are dying," she says, "use their own language. They are our teachers. And the best teachers in the world are dying children. They will teach you everything you need to know about dying. They use two languages: The symbolic verbal and the symbolic nonverbal. It's just the way Jesus used parables. Why? Because very few people were ready to hear his teachings. Yet they had ears to hear and eyes to see.

"The same is true for dying children. They know adults are phony baloneys about dying. They say, 'Eat your chicken soup and you'll get well,' but they know from their spiritual quadrant they are dying. Nurses and doctors run away. But maybe a cleaning person or an orderly comes in. A child can smell who can hear. And that person sits on the bed and says, 'You're trying to tell me something.' And the child gives twenty different stories until the person gets it. They just need one human being who can hear: 'I'm dying and I know it.' That's the symbolic verbal."

She holds this poster up high, a child's symbolic drawing about dying. Across the top this child wrote: "To Mommy, From Cory," but mostly, the letters are in the top left quadrant, the one that is the *far future*. Also in that quadrant is a huge, medieval kind of castle, made of squares of orange and red and yellow, with five pointy turrets, some with blue, black, and purple squares, some with orange and yellow. Next to the castle, kind of on the side, but right in the center of the picture, is a tinier castle, all in red, only I didn't notice it at first.

A rainbow road marches straight up to the castle gate, straight from the *past* to the *far future,* covering the whole left side of the page. On the right, the *present* and *near future,* are stars, suns, oranges and yellows and reds, some of them with big faces smiling. This picture looks very happy. "I asked Cory what this castle was," Elisabeth says, "and he told me, 'It's God's summer castle.' Then he asked, 'What happened to Quasar?' I asked who Quasar was, and he told me it was his dog who'd died two weeks before that."

In the weeks before Cory died he'd often called Elisabeth on the phone. One day he asked whether dogs go to the same place as people when they die, whether dogs have souls. "I said I didn't know," Elisabeth says, understanding that he was asking if Quasar would be there when he died. "But," she continued, "say to God you *need* to see Quasar and if you tell him, he'll be there." She also says she told Cory that she didn't really know how, but if he wished hard, he would find anything he would really need. Then she'd crossed her fingers, hoping that what she'd said was really true, that she wasn't just being an old, adult phony baloney.

Just ten minutes before he died, Cory became very excited and asked his mother to call Elisabeth again. She'd put the phone by his ear. "Elisabeth," Cory had told her, ecstatic. "He's there."

"Who?" she asked, forgetting.

And Cory said: "Quasar, stupid! I even saw him wiggle his tail."

After Cory died, Elisabeth happened to pull out his drawing. When she looked closely, she saw the little red castle in the middle, right next to the big one. "If I'd known," she says, "I would have seen that tiny little dog castle on the side." She would have known for sure that Cory knew he'd see Quasar when he died and she didn't need to really cross her fingers.

I decide I need a copy of Cory's castle—to remind me that larger things than we know might occur at death—and buy it. Elisabeth signs it: "Love, Elisabeth K. Ross."

I suddenly feel flooded with happiness. I decide I want to give more to the center, so I spontaneously bid on one of the wrapped surprise gifts, getting a small box for $50. Then, I'm furious when I open it. Inside is a cheap, crummy, fake pearl necklace I think I'll never wear. I'm mad I spent $50, and I immediately mope in disappointment, forgetting all those forgiving, loving, wonderful feelings.

But as I am leaving, the ill young woman maneuvers her electric wheelchair to come up beside me. "You know," she whispers, "I bet you opened that box and thought, 'Damn, a crummy little fake pearl necklace. Just what I don't need.' But I thought I'd tell you: That necklace is the only gift Steve brought with him. It may not be what you'd wear, but it came straight from his store." And she smiles. I look at it. I look at her. I kiss her. I put it on. I realize that, in fact, I got exactly the gift I needed. That message I got from Steve, and now this necklace, feel to me like real gifts, from some larger view of life than I had been able to see.

A round noon, on Thursday, October 6, 1994, someone set fire to Elisabeth's log cabin while she was away. It burned to the ground with all her belongings—the manuscripts of all nineteen of her books, countless art objects she had collected, including gold and silver thimbles for sewing and antique Christmas ornaments, and unanswered letters from nearly a quarter of a million people asking her questions about dying.

Officials who investigated said that most likely the cabin was destroyed by a fire set by arsonists. The same day, one of her ten pet llamas was killed by a high-powered rifle as it grazed in her field.

The trouble had started soon after Elisabeth bought the farm in 1984, when her neighbors learned that she planned to use it to care for between twenty and forty infants with AIDS. In a town of 2,800, some 2,000 people signed a petition against her. Some began shooting rifle bullets into her windows; those bullets were the cause of the pockmarks on the wood sign at the turnoff to the farm.

After the town stopped Elisabeth from getting the permits for the AIDS babies, she'd decided to use the building she'd already constructed as a dormitory and conference center. And among those who came were people with AIDS. Elisabeth made a point of not asking the health status of those who came to her workshops, since sanitary precautions were in place, but some of the townspeople were so afraid of AIDS that they wanted to shut the center down entirely.

Elisabeth had suffered two strokes. Her husband had already died. In 1995, after her home was destroyed, Elisabeth had a third stroke, and at the age of sixty-eight, she left her Virginia center and moved to Arizona to be near one of her two grown children.

That August I called the center to see how I could get in touch with her. The answering machine gave me this message: "The Elisabeth Kübler-Ross Center is closed," a woman's voice said. "There will be no more of Elisabeth's workshops. There will be a final newsletter mailed out in late July. If you would like a copy and are not already on the mailing list, please leave your name and address. Thank you for your loyal support of Elisabeth, her work, and her center. May God bless you."

The American past provides models for midwives coping with protracted dying. Tuberculosis most closely resembles today's chronic illnesses. The disease took years, even decades, to take its slow and fatal course, which consisted of a series of acute attacks and long remissions that devastated the body but rarely affected the mind. It is estimated that it may have caused one death in five in New England communities during the 1800s.

Sheila Rothman, Ph.D., a research scholar at the Center for the Study of Medicine and Society at the College of Physicians and Surgeons at Columbia University in New York, has studied one particular community by poring through letters, diaries, and other written records. She found that just as this community had midwives for birthing, they also had midwives for dying. Instead of denying death, families used it as a way of talking about love, family, spirituality, and the purpose of life. They also created social structures that helped the dying person go more easily, that helped families manage pain and grief, and helped survivors move on.

The community Dr. Rothman studied was a homogenous group of Evangelical Christians. "Their religion required them to keep notes about how each person died," she says, "so they could tell their families how they had made 'the passage.' And they lived in close-knit communities, so people could see others growing ill, the men and women with 'emaciated forms, sunken cheeks, hollow eyes, and sepulchral coughs' visiting their neighbors, receiving callers, and coming to church on Sunday.

"In this way," she says, "the entire community came to know the markers of the disease, and its course up to and including death. They died at home, but gender was very important. Men and women had special obligations and died in different ways. In fact, they were *expected* to die in different ways."

For women, dying centered around family and home. Their religious vision was of a heaven in which families—especially parents and children—would be reunited. On Sundays, after church, whole families would trek to the cemetery to visit those who had died. They would use this time as an opportunity to talk about death and God, and about how dying was an opportunity to be "awakened."

Most poignantly, women consciously trained their children to be good orphans so they'd be welcome guests in others' homes, so relatives would want them and they wouldn't wind up in institutions. In fact, it was a mother's duty to prepare her children for their own deaths, and for the deaths of parents, aunts, uncles, sisters, and brothers.

Mothers died at home so they could be with their children as long as possible. In a woman's last week, there were constant guests in and out of the home. Certain neighbors were either specially asked, or volunteered, to sit with the dying person, taking turns during the days and the long, scary nights. They came to be known as "watchers." They were used to shifts like this, since many had been called on as midwives in earlier times, when the dying women were giving birth.

On their "watches," they prayed and sang with the dying person, giving her medicine—herbs, natural opiates, or whatever— holding her hand, sitting with her while she slept, talking with her when she awoke, their presence alone reducing the fear. "Yet the dying person was in control," Dr. Rothman says. "Gifts were given and you planned your own funeral service."

Men, on the other hand, died away from home, told by their

doctors to travel to warm climates for their health (sunshine was thought to be the cure), or to switch professions so they could be outdoors. Many men from this community went to Cuba. There they formed communities, cared for each other, and sent messages and letters back home. When death seemed near, the family was told to come, and another watch began.

Faith supposedly helped them bear pain and discomfort; they appeared to die without despair (but then, maybe they left despair out of their accounts for posterity's sake). The accounts they wrote of dying were meant to be passed on to children; parents were expected to be models of bravery, examples for their children of how to die well. It was social custom that got them through.

Today there are new customs, new watchers, particularly for communities coping with AIDS. Here are some portraits of modern-day midwives doing new "watches" for the dying.

You hear her shriek in Brooklynese before she comes in—a loud, shrill, street shriek. "Heeeey! You're all here! I hope it's worth it!" It's *darshan* (the Hindu word for public teachings from a guru) every night where Ma Jaya Bhagavati lives, in Sebastian, between Orlando and Palm Beach in central Florida, and the room is filled with people sitting on the floor. Those who lived there call it Kashi Ashram, but everyone else calls it the Ranch.

Some of them have been with Ma for seventeen years; they cleared her land and planted the lush flowers and the trees chosen for their fragrance. Others are children who've grown up on the Ranch or who go to the private school the Ranch runs. Still others have come to see this teacher for a day, for a week—as novelist Paul Monette did in the time before he died—or come regularly, one day almost every week—as Kimberly Bergalis did for two years before she died.

Most Americans who remember Kimberly think of her public advocacy. Only twenty-three when she died of AIDS, which was allegedly given to her by her Florida dentist, David Acer, D.D.S., she testified before Congress nearly on her deathbed, hoping to bring HIV testing to the medical community. Fewer people are aware of Kimberly's private journey toward death, with Ma as her guide. Ma has helped so many other AIDS patients die that the pond on her ranch is muddy with their ashes.

Ma was born Joyce Green, to an Orthodox Jewish family in Brooklyn, and grew up hanging out with the homeless people who lived under the boardwalk, near the amusement park in Coney Island. The state of her health seemed precarious, which began the long story about how she'd become a spiritual teacher in Florida.

According to Ma, there was something wrong with her pituitary gland. Although it has since healed, she claims she has actually died seven times, and once she woke up in the morgue in Bellevue Hospital in New York with a tag on her toe. During at least three of these episodes she seems to have had what sounds like a near-death experience.

Ma was a housewife, married into an Italian family in Brooklyn, when she first discovered the spiritual. She wanted to lose weight, and a friend told her that yoga would be good. So she went to a yoga class and there she was given a mantra. The teacher told her to say her mantra each day, but she figured she'd lose weight faster if she said it all night, too. So, after her first yoga class, she spent the night in her bathtub, repeating her mantra again and again. In the morning, she had a vision—she saw Christ in the hallway. Her husband told her that if she wanted to see Christ, he'd take her to church. But she told him, "Why go to church when I can see Christ right here in the hall?"

A few nights later, she sat in the bathtub and did her mantra again. By morning, she says, an old Indian man was sitting in her bathroom wearing what she thought was a diaper. She says he turned out to be Nityananda, a great Hindu teacher, and later she also saw Neem Karoli Baba, Ram Dass's teacher. She also claims she saw Swami Muktananda in her backyard. Ma says these teachers have stayed with her and taught her a spiritual path, but a tempest has gathered around her. Some of her students say that Ma does not always tell the whole truth.

I came to Florida after hearing about Ma from an old college friend. At the time, he was one of Ma's chief advisers. He has since left her community, disillusioned. Ma is controversial. Like my friend, others of her students have left—including Ram Dass—but the controversy seems to stem not so much from the fact that she is enormously psychic, which it seems that she is, but how she uses that ability. Despite these controversies and defections, no one disagrees that Ma seems to spread magic. Nor does anyone dispute that she's intense, passionate, compassionate, dedicated, and profoundly skilled in helping the terminally ill die.

After she had her bathtub vision, Joyce (the name Ma would come later) studied with spiritual teachers in New York. (No surprise, her marriage also broke up.) In 1977, she went to India to study with Hindu teachers. One of those teachers gave her her Hindu name, and another—a woman named Hilda who taught for some time in New York City before she, too, died—told her to go to Florida. That state now has one of the highest incidences of AIDS, ranking third after New York and California; Ma always intended to work with the dying.

These days, she travels her eighty-one-acre Florida ranch in a golf cart. At the Ranch's center is the pond that Ma has named Ganga, after the Ganges river in India where the ashes of the dead are put. "This is my Ganga," she says. "The ashes of my dead are here."

In Ma's house, hundreds of photos line her walls. They are white, black, gay, straight, young, old—many near small boxes she says contain some of their ashes. She says prayers for them all.

Encircling the pond are six shrines—a Jewish shrine, a Buddhist temple, three Hindu temples, and a Christ Garden, where Kimberly Bergalis prayed. Elsewhere there is also a garden and shrine for Mary, and many outbuildings where people live, work, and go to school.

On this spring night in 1995, we all leave our shoes outside the main building near Kashi House, where Ma lives; we await her arrival, meditating. Then that shriek, and in comes a veritable cross between a drag queen and Auntie Mame—Ma dressed tonight in a long beige vest over a T-shirt and leggings. She walks with a swagger up to her raised sofa, tattoos peeking out one long sleeve, bangle bracelets clashing like cymbals.

Sometimes she wears a sari. Sometimes she dresses in long, flowing black. A diamond pierces her nose. Seven or so earrings pierce each ear; two of them hold big diamonds, others hold long, dangling gold pieces. A gold necklace—reminding her of a particularly close student who'd died of AIDS—that says "Brooklyn" (his name) rings her neck, as does another necklace with a *phurba*, a Tibetan religious piece used to gather wrathful energy for healing.

Just this week she has had her black hair cropped—"by Julia Roberts's hairdresser," she says proudly. With her tanned skin, she looks a lot like Joan Baez—same age, too; Ma is in her mid-fifties. She has three lipstick-red stripes over her third eye (the spot between her eyebrows said to open to spiritual energy). She keeps up a jangle of remarkable chatter—especially remarkable because it was so wide-ranging and informed, and she'd left school when she was fifteen. Her smile and her humor are infectious. It's easy to love her.

Before she starts her talk, the youngest children go up to kiss her. Some have been adopted by the people here tonight; some are AIDS babies. Then she puts on her glasses—black, with rhinestone trim, so she looks rather like Elvis in his Las Vegas days. "This whole evening," she says, looking around the room, "is once again about how to die."

I t's a Thursday, so Ma has already been on her rounds since ten in the morning. I have spent this entire day following her. She sets off with an entourage, after she has worked out on her outdoor deck on her exercise equipment and done aerobics to Susan Powter's videotape. Around ten, we leave the Ranch in the Ma Mobile, a deluxe, one-bedroom RV van. We are headed to see the terminally ill—to county homes where the maimed and the dying are warehoused, to nursing homes, rehabilitation centers, homes for AIDS babies, and AIDS victims—black and Hispanic and white, gay and straight.

To Ma, there are no "throwaway people," as she says. She aims to take care of the downtrodden, people that most mainstream support groups or religious organizations or hospices or hospitals would rather forget—prostitutes, gamblers, drunks, the poverty-stricken who wind up inside the county homes. She also cares for regular folks—the old *yentas* from Brooklyn, sent by their children to the poorest nursing homes, Miami matrons, old men, gay men, druggies, tiny AIDS babies, some of them cringing in terrible, untreated pain.

The van is stacked with goodies for the staff and patients at all of these places—brownies, cookies, chunks of cheese, oranges, apples, bananas, and grapes. Hundreds of little plates of food, made at the ashram over the past several days. When Ma comes to these homes with her food and her entourage, she trails behind her a trove of sassy, slightly off-color jokes. She's an energy vortex, wearing Red perfume—"A lot of my people are blind, so they know me that way," she says—spreading humor and laughter in these houses of death. Ma saw her own mother die of cancer in a Brooklyn poorhouse. To her, death is normal; it's how the dying are cared for that is barbaric.

At Hope House, which is a suburban-style residential home for AIDS patients, John—who, in black tie, went as a part of Ma's entourage to an AIDS fund-raising party hosted by Marla Trump at Mar-A-Lago—tells Ma that the Hope House residents have decided to plant a memorial garden out back. "Each plant," he says, showing her several, "will be a memorial to every resident who lives here, a living testament to the dead."

At the Palm Beach County Home, next, they stand outside the building and near their rooms, waiting for the Ma Trolley to bring food from room to room. There is Vinnie, who was paralyzed from the waist down in a car crash and can only lie flat on his stomach on a gurney. Ma tells him he can have anything he wants but a woman. Vinnie laughs and says that a woman is all he wants.

In another room, music is playing, and she gets the disabled residents to lift themselves out of their wheelchairs with their hands, shaking and yelling "Boogie down!" She feeds a large black man named Fred, who was paralyzed from the neck down when he tried to break up a fight between two brothers and got kneed in the back by one of them, breaking his spine. And she is alert to the pain of Laura, whose boyfriend shot her in the head and left her for dead. Laura is in a wheelchair, trying to come back. She tells Ma that she feels life in her paralyzed arm; she wants Ma to feel it and heal her.

Ma is street folks, and so are the people in these homes. Few will ever leave. Yet they smile when they see Ma. People young and old, conscious, subsisting on loneliness and feeding tubes. We go to a group home for AIDS babies, and there in a stroller sits two-year-old Travis, whose mother has just abandoned him. He has neuropathic pain so severe he only sits and stares, yet the home is not able to get him any morphine. Ma just gently picks him up and holds him; he nestles quietly into her breast.

For those who are conscious, Ma gives them spark. But when

they look as if they are near the end, Ma looks into their eyes. She tells them to look into hers, if they can. She says she breathes in their pain. She looks deep into their eyes . . . intimately . . . intensely. Then she touches them on their third eye and on the top of their head, to open them, she says, "and to get them ready for death." She does this with a man named Hermie, who, as she walks in, is curled up in fetal position, actually seeming to be having a stroke before our eyes, with no one in attendance, and she does it with the babies in the AIDS nursery. Each of the patients seems to take it in completely, and grow calm.

"I work with the prostitutes and the junkies," Ma says, "so if they ask about God, I'll talk about death in that way. Or I'll talk about love to someone who doesn't understand that well. Because death is love. But, if they ask, I'll also explain the dying process. I explain how the soul rises out of the top of the head. I explain, 'Go into the brightest light you can find and merge with it, and then the soul is released. It's the higher mind.' And I teach them detachment, to focus on this core mind. Nityananda [one of her teachers] called it the heart space over the head. I've seen that space become so bright in the dying process that I, who teach them, am in awe." (She is saying that the core space is the space at the top of your head that the soul exits from.) She wants to give a simple message: There is life until the end, and in death there still is hope. But it helps to learn how to get ready.

Tonight in her *darshan,* she is introducing us to the state of mind we will experience as we die. "I am going to bring you into a meditation and have you understand the very essence of death, as I have done so many times," she tells us. "I want to explain the process. If you understand about death as children—and I'm talking to my children's section over there—you will not fear death as you grow old." These children with AIDS—and those who just live at the Ranch—can live life more fully, she says, if Ma's darshans can eliminate their fear of death.

"Sit up straight and close your eyes," she says. "Picture yourself however you want to be at your death or when [the body is disposed of], whether it is under the ground, whether it is on a funeral pyre. But first, go back to an hour before death. This is a wondrous moment. You are making yourself acquainted with the great essence, with what is.

"An hour before death you are aware. Perhaps you are very old, perhaps you are very young, but you are aware. There's a final moment, the upward wind of life, the caressing of God's breath inside of you; the Buddha essence begins to rise from the feet, so you feel your feet getting cooler, cooler. Your knees becoming cooler, cooler. Your thighs, your pelvic area, your hips.

"Your heart is beginning to beat fast in anticipation of the moment when it will not be," she says slowly, as the group—maybe a hundred of us—sits quietly on cushions on the floor and listens, eyes closed. "Each beat feels like a thunderous sound. If you are prepared, the sound will bring you bliss. If you are prepared, the sound will bring you joy. *Boom . . . Boom . . . Boom . . . Boom . . . Boom. Boom . . Boom . . . . Boom.* It is irregular. You can hear voices. Where are they coming from? They are the ones you love. They calm you, for they, too, have been trained in death.

"Begin to rise up," she tells us. "Up, up, up, up, out of the heart space, into the throat. You try to speak; your tongue turns up—a great moment of joy. 'I am okay,' you want to say. 'I am fine. I am with God. I am with the Buddha. I am with Padmasambhava. I am with Shiva. I am with Kali.' " (These are Buddhist and Hindu names for the divine.)

"The breath is leaving the throat area. You do not gag, for you are relaxed. You are joyful. I will take you into death now. Sit straight.

"There are a few minutes left. You want to whisper, 'I love you,' or 'All is forgiven.' You can't; there is no more voice. Your eyes turn up. First, there is darkness, wondrous, wondrous, sweet-scented lotus darkness. You wonder, 'Am I dead?' But no, there is slight sound. It is your loved ones. You go further, deeper. You reach the top of the head. There is no gravity now. There is no body. Remember, you must rest in the very essence of your true mind. All thoughts cease."

I am sitting beside Ma tonight, eyes closed, trying this myself. At this point, she leans over and touches the spot where my third eye is supposed to be and a point at the top of my head, which is called the *bhramarandra* in Buddhism. As she does, all of my consciousness focuses there, in those spots. And there is a kind of sensation of light and a very great lightness of mind and a calm.

"You feel," she says, "a slight wind. It is the breath. 'Am I dead?'

You are so excited. You breathe in. Gently now, breathe in. You breathe out. You hold the breath out—hold the breath out, and what a shock, you breathe in again. But you don't breathe in as deep, and you breathe out. Hold the breath out—and you breathe in again. You can almost feel yourself rising, rising, rising. It's a different type of excitement—and you breathe out—and you breathe out and your mind breathes out for you. And when the breath wants to come in now, at this moment, let it; otherwise, pay no attention.

" 'Am I dead?' and the light draws you into it. All the rainbow colors—it is so vivid, so clear—you are light, you are the rainbow. 'Am I dead?' and in that moment there is a holy being. Perhaps the Buddha, perhaps the Christ, perhaps Mother Kali, perhaps Hanuman. 'Am I dead?' And the holy being turns to you with the brightness of a billion suns and takes your hand.

"You are dead. You are ecstatic. There are a few threads attached to the body. Those around the body begin to rub the body with oil and place flowers, and after a while the threads are cut. 'I am dead!' [Long pause . . .]

"There is no breath. There is only lightness. There is no fear. There is only joy. 'I am dead. It is over.' And there is the holy being. It is the Buddha. It is Christ. It is Shiva. Take me. And you recognize your own, and you become your own. And you are taken to the funeral, the funeral pyre, the coffin, the tomb. There is my old cloth. There is my old me, and you watch the pyre being lit, and you are no more.

"Oh, but you are. Oh, but you are. You are free of pain. You are free of envy and jealousy. You are free—way over the head now, concentrate way over the head—way over the head, and be in the silence of remembrance. Feel, see, be the light as the [funeral pyre] fire consumes your body. As the flesh melts, the bones melt, the marrow melts, and the ash mixes with the ash of the wood. You are free.

"Gently be reborn into this body for this moment. Breathe into your heart. Keep your eyes closed and exhale gently. Breathe into your heart and exhale gently. Open your eyes.

"Were you ever dead before? Will you be dead again? Of course. Will you be reborn again? Most of you claim you will. Will you ever serve again? Again, again, again. I use the word *again, again, again.* You have been there. We all have.

"Why not, my children, get it right? Why not walk with death every second so you never forget how to live? Why not be prepared so you never forget how to die? Death lives here at Kashi Ashram; so does birth; so does life. Befriend death and you befriend yourself."

Therese Schroeder-Sheker, founder of the Chalice of Repose, is ethereal-looking, even today, in her mid-forties. Her long brown hair streaked with gray envelops her face and falls way down her back, stray wisps framing her in a whitish light, especially as she leans over, playing her harp. Her smile is soft. Her voice is lyrical. At college she'd studied medieval music. She played the harp, and she still does. But these days, Therese plays her harp and sings for the dying in the hospitals, hospices, and nursing homes in Missoula, Montana.

While still in school more than twenty years ago, she got a job as a nurses' aide in a geriatric home near Denver. On her first day, she got a lesson on death and dying.

"They took all the nurses' aides and taught them the same thing, and this is what I learned," Therese says. " 'When *they* die'— that's how the staff called people there—'*they* will urinate and defecate all over the place.' My job was to clean it up as quickly as possible, get the body into the body bag, and *ziiiipppp!* it up as soon as possible, because the empty bed costs money. So you have to get them out of the bed and clean it up as soon as possible. Death is a fiscal problem." Dying people, it seemed to Therese, were being treated like inmates or animals.

After a few deaths, she wanted to quit. She was most upset at herself, for she, too, had started to look on dying patients as problems. Still, almost right away, she began making friends with some patients at the home, and that is what temporarily held her.

One night, a woman she was especially close to called her to her bed. "Dearie," she said, "will you come back and spend time with me this evening?" She wanted Therese to say the rosary with her.

Therese said she had to study for a course at school. But the woman persisted. "That's okay, dearie," she told Therese, "but if you don't come to say it with me tonight, I probably won't be here tomorrow." Therese stopped. She realized that the woman was telling her she was going to die. That night she returned, and she and her patient shared stories about their lives and said the rosary. Then Therese went home. When she got to work the next morning, the woman's bed was empty.

She was devastated. After work, she went to talk to a friend, a priest. Once again she wanted to quit. She was afraid she'd turn into a hard-boiled nursing-home worker. The priest looked at her hard.

"Go back and protect them," he told her. "Be there for them in a new way." Therese had never been religious. Her mother was Irish and a dreamer. Her father was a skeptical scientist. Some of the residents of the home were Jewish; others were not. "Can you empty your heart so you can be with them?" Therese said the priest asked her. "Can you read to them from the Torah or find a text from the Gospels? Just don't ring the buzzer so quickly [for the nursing staff to come in] after they die." So she went back to work. That's when a patient she calls David showed her something new.

"He was an emphysema patient—an old buzzard who would throw bodily fluids and lumpy things at us," she says, too modest to use the words *urine* and *feces,* "and grab body parts. One day, I went in and I heard a death rattle. David was drowning in his fluids. At the time, many of my friends were pregnant with their first babies. I'd learned a lot about midwifery, and I'd heard about the gravity position. So I went in, closed the door, and touched him. I realized that suddenly everything had changed with him. I started singing Gregorian chant. And then I got in bed with him, and held him in the midwifery position."

Therese sat behind him, straight up in the bed, her butt where the pillow would be, cradling David against her from behind, her head and heart lined up with his. He was sitting up slightly, which made his breathing easier, leaning his head against her, her legs crossed, Indian style, underneath his back and waist. She sang softly while she held him and rocked him gently, making her way through the entire *Mass of the Angels,* the *Adore Te Devote* of Thomas Aquinas, the *Ubi Caritas,* the *Salve Regina,* and the *Mass of the Blessed Virgin Mary* before he died.

"Although his lungs were really disintegrating, his breathing took on a new form. He'd been thrashing and struggling, and I realized that his thrashing had turned to peace and his breathing had synchronized with the music. And he died peacefully. I felt him go from warm to cold. And I went home and knew something very important had happened in my life. That was twenty-three years ago. The women around me covered for me that day, but things have changed and are very different today." Where she works now she no longer has to conceal what she is doing.

Therese eventually quit the geriatric home, went back to her music, and became a concert harpist. One day she happened to hear Frederick Paxton, a professor of medieval music at Connecticut College, talk about the death rituals of the Cluny monks, an eleventh-century French order. They were skilled in palliative care several hundred years before hospice began. In addition to their special herbs, they used music to assist what they called "a blessed death." Paxton was talking about their music, called "infirmary music," and their rituals, called the "Cluniac customaries." Therese knew that she was hearing about her future life's work.

Later, she and Paxton sorted through the Cluny manuscripts, translating and scoring the music for modern times. In the process, Therese came to the realization that the Cluny monks altered the music in accordance with the person's illness, synchronizing the music to the dying person's breath (this was one aspect of what she came to call "prescriptive music"). By doing so, they not only helped calm the patient but tried to lead the soul out of the body, hoping it would follow the musical notes upward toward God. This, Therese realized, was what she wanted to do.

"There had been a Western tradition of death preparation," Therese says. "People don't understand yet that there were parallel tracks for conscious dying in the Western monastic world and in the Buddhist tradition." Therese took on, as her life's work, the reintroduction of prescriptive music into a Western medical setting.

In the early 1990s, Lawrence L. White Jr., president of Saint Patrick's Hospital, helped to bring her to Missoula to help dying patients. In 1992—working by then with hospice at Missoula's two hospitals, and through the University of Montana—Therese founded the Chalice of Repose's clinical practice and school. This is both a degree program in special clinical training using music thanatology—offered through the medical school—and a clinical care team that does its unique brand of spiritual/clinical work wherever patients die.

In the spring of 1994, the Chalice of Repose graduated its first class of eighteen students, trained by an interdisciplinary faculty of thirty people from the medical sciences, the arts, and the human-ities, as well as by Paxton and Schroeder-Sheker. The newsletter of Saint Patrick's Hospital, where the program is housed, dubbed it "the world's only course in musical sacramental midwifery." Though some health-care workers look askance at their methods, the first Chalice workers are known in Montana for their clinical responsiveness as well as for their otherworldly work.

Each of them has a beeper and a small harp. When a beeper signals them, they grab their harps and go off in teams of two to play prescriptive music at the bedsides of the dying—in Missoula's hospitals, in a nursing home, in a hospice patient's home, or in a hospital burn or intensive care unit. Their presence, they have found, is particularly soothing when a respirator or other piece of life-support equipment is shut off; their music fills the room as the noisy machine suddenly becomes silent. Just as Therese first did years ago with David, Chalice workers surround the dying patient with the Cluny monks' music, synchronized to calm the person's breath. They now use other music as well.

"People know when they are dying," Therese says. "When Cluniac monks or nuns knew that their time was near, they directed their monastic dying. It was the dying person's privilege and re-sponsibility to say: 'The time is near' and to ask for forgiveness. And in the Cluniac infirmaries, from the time a person would say, 'My time has come,' he was attended by two people day and night who sang to him until [he died]. It had to do with unconditional commitment to the relief of pain. They had their pharmaceuticals [grown in the monastery's garden] and used them and music to relieve pain." The music was also to help the patient's mind and breath out of his body, to help the soul leave the body.

"There is a big difference between music for the living and the dying," Therese says. "Prescriptive music can have many applica-tions. When we use it with the dying it has to do with helping people unbind from the body, so we provide a lot of music outside of time—Gregorian chant, Hebrew cantation [Chalice workers don't use only Christian music]. We have certain music that can heat or cool metabolic or respiratory systems. It has to do with inhalations and exhalations, so we focus on the respiratory system of the dying person. We start a new phrase of music only with their inhalation, and connect to that."

They also talk to the patients and family members ahead of time, taking a kind of musical history of each patient, trying to learn what music was important to him or her at various times in the person's life, in order to use that music during the period prior to active dying to elicit old memories and work them through. "We use the music to reconnect them with that part of their lives from which they have been disconnected," Therese says, "to help them reconnect and finish business, giving them and their family members permission to let go and die in peace."

On Father's Day in Montreal, we are sitting in a sun-drenched room listening to a different kind of music. In one corner, a young French volunteer named Caroline, with a voice as pure as Judy Collins's, is strumming a guitar, singing lyrical songs— "Kumbaya," "Puff the Magic Dragon," "Suzanne" (the Leonard Cohen song), "Where Have All the Flowers Gone?" and songs in French, since this is a bilingual country.

Families sit in small clusters throughout the rest of the room. Nurses have wheeled in hospital beds and recliners. A man who seems to be in a coma in one bed is connected to an IV line. A woman who is parchment thin fades in and out of sleep. A man sitting on a recliner gently holds his wife's hand. A woman with a turban hiding her wispy bald head cradles her grandchild on her lap. These people are all dying. But for now, they are each the nucleus of their own family unit.

During one song, a daughter takes tissues from the hand of her dying father to wipe her own eyes; a mother goes to bring her dying child some vanilla ice cream. They are all an audience of love, sharing what may be their last, most magnificent concert together, feeling the joy and warmth of a song and a summer day.

This is the day room in the Palliative Care Unit at the Royal Victoria Hospital, part of prestigious McGill University. It is the way it is because of one man—Balfour Mount, M.D., its founder and director, a handsome, soft-spoken man in his mid-fifties.

Mount is a man who seems as if he has been inspired when he talks—humbled, made raw, on a mission. And indeed he is. He is also one of the most respected physicians in palliative-care medicine, a field he helped create nearly twenty years ago. Today, Dr. Mount's way of incorporating palliative care into the Canadian medical mainstream has become a beacon for physicians worldwide who are concerned with improving care of the dying.

Mount was born into a family of medical high achievers. His father was a distinguished Canadian neurosurgeon, his mother was a nurse, and his older brother was also a physician. Mount was likewise destined. He went to medical school at Queen's University, then to McGill as a medical intern.

While he was there two things happened: First, he decided to specialize in cancer, urology in particular. Second, he learned he had testicular cancer—exactly the specialty he'd intended—which at the time had a survival rate of just 30 percent. "My chances looked slim," Dr. Mount says. "Then I went to Memorial Sloan-Kettering for surgery."

Not only did doctors there save his life, but they later trained him to become a surgical oncologist specializing in urology. When he returned to McGill, he immediately gathered acclaim as a surgeon, and became among the first oncologists there to use advanced chemotherapy techniques to cure cancer.

The problem was, now that his patients were living longer, he realized—having been a seriously ill patient himself—how lacking the medical system was in caring for the terminally ill, and how utterly ill-equipped it was to provide quality care for the dying. He started looking for solutions by examining the problems, beginning at the Royal Vic.

"In 1973 we did a study at this hospital, looking at attitudes toward death among doctors here," he says. "By the end of that summer I was convinced there was a very serious health-care problem at this institution, and this is a good one. We found that dying patients and families had unmet psychosocial and physical needs, that their pain was unmet by the health-care system. The dying are alien to our Western health-care system, which is set up to cure. They make health-care workers feel like failures."

To find some answers, he decided to go to London to talk with Cicely Saunders about hospice, and he came back impressed and inspired. But he also realized that since most people die in hospitals, the freestanding hospice program that Saunders ran was not what he had in mind. He wanted a plan for his hospital, yet the hospice solution just might be made workable within a hospital setting.

Mount asked his hospital to give him two years to set up a pilot program. "My reputation was based on great success with radical surgical procedures and oncology. I was the first to use cysplatin [a chemotherapy drug] here, so I had clout," he says. He proposed to add a palliative-care unit to the hospital, as well as home care and a follow-up bereavement component for families. By 1974 he had established such a program at the Royal Vic, thereby making it the first teaching hospital in the world to establish its own hospice and palliative-care unit.

But Bal Mount wasn't content to just focus on pain or relief of symptoms; he wanted to add a spiritual dimension to treatment within a modern hospital complex, which would mean retraining medical personnel in how to care for the person who was dying. If doctors see their mandate as *fighting disease* rather than *relieving suffering* they will always fail, he believed, but if they see it in a broader sense, with a mandate of *healing*, they will have a different kind of success. This kind of success meant creating a period of dying in which the dying person could rise to his greatest heights, whatever that was for each person, and come to the end of life perfectly well.

By 1974, Mount had persuaded the hospital to begin. In his plan, as soon as a patient was diagnosed with a terminal illness, palliative care would be integrated into physicians' plans for treatment. Care would proceed along two tracks—successful cure and a plan for a peaceful death. As death came closer, palliative care would increase, while aggressive treatment might slowly decrease. The goal was not necessarily *fighting disease*; rather, it would be *relief of suffering*, but the key element was the relief of suffering *however the patient defined it.*

"If you see it in the broader sense, our mandate is *healing,*" he says, "but healing doesn't necessarily have to do with just the physical body. If one has a broader idea of what healing and wellness are, all kinds of people die as well people.

"The health-care system fails to meet patient needs out of extraordinary demands," Mount says. "Health care has come to be seen as fighting disease. It's hard for a world-class cardiology surgeon, for example, to stay world-class, not [to mention asking him] also to be a psychologist and a priest. But someone has to do that and that is the challenge." Proving this became Bal Mount's medical mission.

The person most responsible for teaching this vivid lesson was a young man in his twenties named Chip, whose photo he keeps near his desk. Chip appeared soon after the Royal Vic's program began. He was from a wealthy Canadian family; he was handsome, athletic, absolutely destined for great success. Until he got cancer.

"I thought I'd cured him, but he finally died of his disease," Dr. Mount says. "He was an extraordinary physical specimen, but that part of him just fell apart, yet he just grew in terms of his understanding of spirituality. Before he died, he said: 'This past year has been the most important year of my life.' "

This kind of wellness and dignity has to do with the health of the body, the mind, and the spirit, and with the interaction among them. At death, Dr. Mount says, people have a need for a transcendent dimension, a need to connect with something larger than themselves.

"Body, mind, and spirit each contribute to our sense of ourselves, and as caregivers we have to be able to be comfortable with and speak the language of each of them. In the early twentieth century it was sex that was repressed. Freud had to open that. In the closing years of the twentieth century it's time to reexamine the spiritual dimension of personhood.

"The mind has a major role in defining the person and in defining levels of pain," he says. "I would submit that we diagnose ills of the body with some skill, that we diagnose ills of the mind with less skill, and we diagnose ills of the spirit with little or no skill at all, and that we often ignore the impact of each of these on the others."

The spirit is the essential self, the part of Chip that could grow while the body and mind were crumbling. It is the part of us that is concerned with values, faith, meaning, the part that Dr. Elisabeth Kübler-Ross says just expands exponentially as we near death. "Whole-person care," Dr. Mount says, which are his words for the total care of body, mind, and spirit that he posits is required to treat the dying, "has to do with examining ourselves as family, caregivers, loved ones, and friends."

Dr. Mount discovered medicine's mind-body dimension by paying attention to his own patients. "There was one particular patient," he says. "I did a radical cystectomy [removal of the bladder] a day or two earlier on him. That day I was in the operating room. I hadn't seen him since I took out his bladder and rearranged his body. I just didn't have the time. As I passed his room I was flying. And our eyes met. First, I felt terribly guilty, knowing I hadn't seen him and how much he probably wanted to talk. But I also realized that had he been in palliative care, I *would* have seen him, because his needs would have been different. When he was in that bed I thought of his electrolyte balance and metastases, not him, his state of mind."

Mount kept his post as professor of surgery at McGill University's medical school, but he also began to write about treatment for patients like this, about palliative care, and about wellness. He began to make films of his dying patients in their last months and days to show the life that blossomed from within when there was no other hope but death.

He started to teach what he was learning from his own dying patients: He organized what became an annual international congress on the care of the terminally ill; he invited physicians from all over the world to spend a week or more in training at his palliative-care unit; and he began a division for palliative-care medicine within the medical school itself. He wanted to teach new standards of care for the terminally ill that made centers that helped them through the final stages of life "monuments not to the incurability of some diseases but to the dignity of man."

Whole-person care, he teaches, includes learning how a patient defines personhood, who that person really is. That means taking the time to talk with him or her. It means establishing an honest, level playing field for communication so that the doctor and patient are in a two-human-being relationship that can examine ultimate questions of life.

Whole-person care also means setting diagnostic and therapeutic goals in terms of the *patient*, not the disease, he says, and focusing on the function the person has in terms of decreasing resources, not on length of life. It means increasing a person's coping ability by decreasing uncertainty, by granting respect, by letting people know what is likely to happen, so they can prepare.

It means helping them do so by controlling their pain and other symptoms, by helping them assess the meaning of their illness for them as human beings, and helping them resolve difficult issues— for instance, "Who is going to take care of my handicapped daughter?"

It also means exploring what other family members bring to the experience: What death means to them, what *this* patient's death means, and what their emotional abilities and resources are in the process of physically caring for someone dying.

For doctors or nurses, it means assessing and using sources of meaning *for that person* by being human themselves, by taking the time to find out who the patient is, what he's accomplished in life, what meaning life still has for him, what legacy he leaves, and how he can find a context for deeper meaning.

Whole-person care also means helping dying patients look for a new kind of hope—hope in the absence of pain, hope in good symptom control, hope for someone to be there when they die, hope for days like that day at the Sunday concert.

And it also means helping the dying person set certain long- and short-term goals that provide her with a way through, that allow a way for a patient to heal her spirit and move from self-centeredness to a focus outside the self, whether through art, music, religion, meditation, poetry, children, or gardens.

"Whole-person care," Dr. Mount says, "has to do with examining ourselves as family, caregivers, loved ones, and friends. Only if we are consciously on the path ourselves, looking at our own woundedness and loss, can we meaningfully share the burdens of our fellow travelers and assist them on their way."

ELEVEN

Dr. Kevorkian's Challenge:
Two Deaths in Michigan

When they met in 1988, Heidi Fernandez told me, she thought Tom Hyde was one of the sexiest men alive. Six feet tall, with a lean, muscular body, he was a landscape designer by trade, a man who could shinny up trees and entertain friends by doing inverted headstands on the arms of chairs. The sexual magnetism between them was so strong that they'd pull over to the side of the road around Farmington Hills, Michigan, roll up the top of her white IROC convertible, and steam up the windows.

By 1991, Heidi and Tom had moved in together. Neither of them particularly wanted to get married, but they were both hungry for family. Heidi had lost both her mother and father; Tom had lost his father and, though he had a son from an earlier marriage, he was divorced and his former wife had custody of their child. So as Heidi remembers, when she became pregnant, "Tom was just ecstatic." Heidi was thirty-four and Tom had just turned twenty-nine.

But in February 1992, when Heidi was about five months into the pregnancy, something odd started happening to Tom. As they lay in bed, a muscle in his chest, his shoulder, his right arm, would start to ripple. "We laughed about it," Heidi said. "But now I know it was probably the beginning of his disease."

On Mother's Day, May 10, Heidi gave birth to Carmen Denise Fernandez-Hyde. While she was still in the hospital, two more puzzling things happened to Tom. Carmen was born premature, so her room wasn't quite ready. As Tom tried to hoist himself through the attic hole in their baby's room to get down Carmen's crib, his right arm buckled and he dropped from the ceiling opening down onto the floor.

More troubling, the day after Carmen's birth, he showed up drunk at the hospital—at least Heidi assumed that was why he was slurring his speech. Tom swore he wasn't drunk. On his way there, he said, he'd stopped at their favorite take-out place to get her some food, and the restaurant owners gave him a margarita to celebrate his new fatherhood. "Heidi," he told her, "I only had one drink, and I didn't even finish it."

A week later, Tom returned home from work early. Heidi was on maternity leave from her computer graphics job. "We were totally taken with being new parents," she recalled. "It was a beautiful day. [When] I saw Tom coming up the walk, I thought, 'Oh, he's coming to check up on me, to see whether I'm taking care of Carmen okay.' But something about it seemed strange. I said, 'Tom, what are you doing here?' And he suddenly just started sobbing."

Tom said he'd dropped his hammer at work. He literally couldn't hold on to it; his hands had lost their strength. As he cried, he told Heidi he'd been falling down. There were times over the past few months when he'd fallen off his motorcycle because his leg wouldn't hold up the bike, when he'd fallen down a flight of stairs or toppled off boards at work. His speech was often slurred, as it had been that day in the hospital when she'd thought he was drunk. When he dropped the hammer, he'd finally admitted to himself that something was seriously wrong.

"We didn't have our own family doctor, because neither of us ever got sick," Heidi said, "so I called my sister to ask for the name of a doctor her husband had seen." About 11:30 in the morning on the day of his appointment, Tom called Heidi from the doctor's office to say he was being sent to nearby Bottsford Hospital for a CAT scan. That was the beginning of months of fear and uncertainty. Tom was tested for head injury, stroke, pesticide poisoning, Lyme disease, multiple sclerosis, anything that would explain what was happening. "We prayed it would be Lyme disease," Heidi said. "I don't mean to say that Lyme disease isn't bad, but it's something that's treatable."

May turned into June turned into July. The tests continued. As Carmen began to smile, wave her arms, hold up her head, Tom grew weaker and weaker. "By July, his chest muscles, his biceps were always rippling even when he wasn't moving," Heidi said. "They had rippled once in a while but now it never stopped. We tried to make jokes. Tom's leg would jump up and down and I would sit on it, bouncing. Then his whole body started getting stiff and I'd accuse him of being a clod. He'd walk across the room and shake and drop his coffee and I'd say, 'Don't stain the carpet!' I'm so ashamed for saying that now."

On August 6, Tom took Carmen to a baby-sitter's and drove to an appointment at the Michigan Institute for Neurological Disorders. Heidi had gone back to work at the computer store. "He called me just before lunch," she said. "His voice sounded awful, but he said we'd talk when I got home. I told him, 'No, come down here and let's go out to eat.' When he drove up, I went outside to the parking lot. He was sitting in our Toyota pickup, hunched over the steering wheel, his head on his arms. . . . He said, 'They told me I have amyotrophic lateral sclerosis.' I didn't know what it was, but I heard 'sclerosis,' and thought, 'That's not good.' Then he told me what it meant." Heidi could barely repeat what he'd said. "Babe," he'd sobbed, "they say I'm going to die."

Tom's illness is also known as Lou Gehrig's disease, after the baseball immortal who was felled by it. Its cause is still unknown, but its deadly progress is not. Amyotrophic lateral sclerosis (ALS) is a neurological illness that slowly eats away nerves and atrophies muscles. Its victims eventually become completely paralyzed and cannot swallow or breathe. Nature, in her cruelty, has decreed that through all this the sufferer's mind remains completely clear.

That day they thought they'd learned the very worst. But what neither of them knew then was that just eleven months later, Tom's body would have deteriorated so badly that he would fear living more than dying, and that he would beg the notorious retired Michigan pathologist Jack Kevorkian, M.D., to help him die.

On August 4, 1993, thirty-year-old Tom became Dr. Kevorkian's seventeenth and youngest patient, the first after a new Michigan law banning assisted suicide officially went into effect, and the first for which Kevorkian would go on trial.

In November 1993, during the pretrial hearing in Tom's case, I went to Michigan to meet the man called Dr. Death. I also wanted to learn why someone would be so desperate that he or she would seek his help, desperate enough to want to die in the back of a rusty van with the help of a makeshift machine.

In that Detroit courtroom when I first met Dr. Kevorkian I also met Heidi Fernandez and Carmen, and many family members of other patients Kevorkian had helped, all of them wearing buttons that read *I Back Jack*.

During the following year, I talked with Heidi extensively on the phone and visited her and Carmen at their apartment in suburban Novi, Michigan. I also subsequently talked in depth with the families of six of Dr. Kevorkian's other patients.

In addition, I visited hospitals and hospices in the Detroit area; interviewed physicians, psychologists, social workers, and nurses; and attended public hearings of the Michigan State Commission on Death and Dying—set up by the legislature to determine the state's long-term stance on assisted suicide and evaluate the law under which Dr. Kevorkian was now being tried.

I was interested in the medical and legal environment in which these assisted suicides were occurring, how the cases arose, how the professionals in that community felt about them, and what impact they were having on subsequent medical practice.

In November 1993 I also met thirty-two-year-old Glenn Leung and his family. Glenn was also coping with ALS. He and Tom had the same medical doctors during their illness and the same hospice doctors—even the same hospice aides—as the end approached. Both were cared for at home by a young working woman with a small child. Both lived in the suburbs of Detroit near Jack Kevorkian.

Tom ended up calling Dr. Kevorkian, and got his help. Glenn carefully considered it, and then changed his mind. Why, I wondered, would one person want help in dying and another be willing to go to the end of the same terrible disease? What are the personal and medical issues that weigh on such a decision? What kind of care or lack of care can affect such a decision one way or another? Is a request for death the result of depression or a rational choice? How do family dynamics come into play? What made the difference in the decisions of Glenn Leung and Tom Hyde?

Jack Kevorkian catapulted into the news during the summer of 1989 as the doctor who had invented a suicide machine. The media portrayed him as a crazy scientist, a skinny, graying, bespectacled man posed with a curiously medieval-looking contraption on which hung three upside-down bottles with dangling tubes.

By June 1990, when Dr. Kevorkian helped his first patient die— a fifty-four-year-old Portland music teacher and Alzheimer's victim named Janet Adkins—Dr. Death had become a household name. Since that time, law enforcement agencies have tried to jail him, professional medical associations have denounced him, and lawmakers have attempted to stop him with legislation. And yet a near-avalanche of terminally ill patients and their families have embraced him not as a villain but as a hero.

Not since Karen Ann Quinlan first appeared in the news had the grim reality of modern dying been made so visible. Dr. Kevorkian and Janet Adkins were launched center stage in a changing world consciousness, placed squarely in the middle of a shifting medical and legal map. Assisted suicide has become the great emotional and ethical divide at the end of this century, a flash word for either fury or relief, but destined to be the most controversial pro-choice v. pro-life issue of the next several decades.

Jack Kevorkian, sixty-two when Janet Adkins died, was born on May 28, 1928, in nearby Pontiac, Michigan, one of three children of Armenian immigrants living in what then was a busy industrial town. Jack, the middle child and the only son, apparently was brilliant in school, skipping sixth grade, and getting both his bachelor's and medical degrees from the University of Michigan in just seven years. Later he trained as a pathologist, a specialist who analyzes tissue cultures.

Kevorkian was thirty-three when his father died of a heart

attack. Several years later his mother died of bone cancer. She was constantly in pain, but only later did he learn her pain was so great that his sisters, Flora Holzheimer and Margo Janus, secretly asked her doctor to help her die. The doctor had refused. By the time they told their brother, Kevorkian had already become interested in assisted suicide.

That passion had its start when, as a medical intern, he was confronted with suffering so unthinkable that he could never forget it. As he later wrote:

> The patient was a helplessly immobile woman of middle age, her entire body jaundiced to an intense yellow-brown, skin stretched paper-thin over a fluid-filled abdomen swollen to four or five times normal size. The rest of her was an emaciated skeleton: sagging, discolored skin covered her bones like a cheap, wrinkled frock.
>
> The poor wretch stared up at me with yellow eyeballs sunken in their withering sockets. Her yellow teeth were ringed by chapping and parched lips to form an involuntary, almost sardonic "smile" of death. It seemed as though she was pleading for help and death at the same time. Out of sheer empathy alone I could have helped her die with satisfaction. From that moment on, I was sure that doctor-assisted euthanasia and suicide are and always were ethical, no matter what anyone says or thinks.

Although Dr. Kevorkian had a long career in hospital pathology labs in Michigan and later in California, that image always stuck with him. He was forever doing research on the side, intent on understanding the physiology of dying. He wanted to find a way to know the exact time of death by examining physical reflexes in the eyes (so doctors would know the exact time when organs could best be taken for transplant); he wanted to experiment with direct blood transfusions from cadavers to learn how to save lives on battlefields; and he was fixated on achieving legal changes allowing criminals on death row to choose death by anesthesia so that they, too, could donate their organs for transplants.

He was also always committed to finding ways to help hopelessly ill people have some choice about dying pain-free deaths.

"They say," he told me that first day I met him in November 1993 at the Detroit courtroom hearing for Tom Hyde's trial, "that *virtually all* deaths can be pain-free, but that doesn't mean *all*. What about the rest of us?"

By 1986, he had retired, moved back to Michigan near his sister Margo, and began living on a pension, and later on Social Security. That year he heard that assisted suicide and euthanasia were practiced in the Netherlands; they weren't legal there, but, oddly, officially condoned by both the government and the Dutch Medical Society, under certain strict conditions.

The next summer he went to Holland, returning enthusiastic to try what the Dutch were doing. He began to look for a way to operate openly at the edge of the law. While *euthanasia*—which meant direct help, by giving a lethal injection, for example—might carry charges of murder, *assisted suicide*—which is helping someone else by prescribing or making available lethal medications they take on their own—probably would not. At the time, thirty-two states had laws that banned assisted suicide; the others (including Michigan) had no laws that specifically addressed it.

Kevorkian also found that a grassroots movement for assisted suicide had begun in the United States. It was led by Derek Humphry, a former *Los Angeles Times* reporter, who co-founded the Hemlock Society in 1980, a group that advocates the right of terminally ill patients to choose the time and manner of their own deaths. Humphry would later publish *Final Exit*, the 1991 best-seller that gives detailed instructions for "self-liberation." At the end of 1987 and the beginning of 1988 he was organizing a campaign to legalize euthanasia and assisted suicide by putting referendums on state election ballots, beginning with California.

Kevorkian offered Humphry his services, telling him he'd open a California clinic to which terminally ill patients might come for assistance in dying. Humphry declined this offer—saying he preferred to try to change the law rather than to break it.

The 1988 California campaign failed to get enough signatures to put a referendum on the ballot, but by that time Dr. Kevorkian had already begun working on an idea for a suicide machine, sitting in his second-floor apartment and lab, at 223 South Main Street, above suburban restaurants and shops in Royal Oak. The lab overlooked the parking lot where he usually parked his rusty white 1968 Volkswagen van. Across that lot was the Royal Oak Police Station, where he was later to be taken quite often.

Press reports portray his lifestyle as stoic, underscored by his single mattress on the floor and his Salvation Army furniture. He is notoriously thrifty, but things are not all as they appear. When he moved back from California—where he'd worked before he retired—the mover lost a shipment of his *real* furniture, including his harpsichord and his organ. Dr. Kevorkian never married, which he calls "the biggest mistake of my life."

He has a warm, zany sense of humor, exemplified by a diet book with limericks he once wrote. He has painted a large collection of abstract, sometimes macabre oils, many of which have been shown in art galleries. He is an accomplished classical musician (a CD of him performing his own music was released in May 1997) who plays keyboard and flute, and he is interested in film. (One reason he'd gone to work in California was to try to make a full-length Hollywood film based on Handel's *Messiah*.)

By March 1989, he'd developed a regular routine in which he rode Margo's bike to read in the Royal Oak Library. That month he came across an article in the *New England Journal of Medicine* that elated him: "The Physician's Responsibility to Hopelessly Ill Patients," co-authored by twelve distinguished physicians from institutions like Harvard and the Mayo Clinic. The article focused on end-of-life care for dying patients, reiterating the need to control terminal symptoms and pain, and the legality of withholding and withdrawing burdensome treatment. Then it said something more: All but two of these doctors agreed that "it is not immoral for a physician to assist in the rational suicide of a terminally ill person." It was the signal Kevorkian had been looking for.

That summer, a thirty-eight-year-old man named David Rivlin, a quadriplegic who had severed his spine in a surfing accident when he was nineteen, engaged an attorney to go to court for him to request the right to be disconnected from his life support. On July 20, his request was granted. Rivlin lived in a nursing home in Farmington Hills, breathing with the help of a respirator. Dr. Kevorkian set to work.

Sitting at his kitchen table, he sketched a design for a suicide machine that Rivlin could operate with his clenched teeth. Kevorkian would insert an IV in a vein and start an intravenous drip of saline solution. Then Rivlin would activate a device—making it assisted suicide rather than euthanasia—that would start a second solution flowing. Kevorkian planned to use thiopental, an anesthetic that causes unconsciousness in seconds. A minute after the patient hit the switch, a timer would automatically start a third solution flowing, a mix of potassium chloride and succinylcholine, causing nearly instant but painless death from a heart attack.

Dr. Kevorkian found parts for his machine at local hardware stores, medical supply stores, garage sales, and flea markets. He tried a motor from an electric toy car, another from an old clock, electrical switches, and standard tubes and vials. When he finished building that first suicide machine, he went to see Rivlin, but Rivlin rejected his help.

Instead, Rivlin decided to be moved from the nursing home to a friend's house, where Dr. John Finn, the medical director of the Hospice of Southeastern Michigan (now renamed the Hospice of Michigan), supervised his death. "I could be with him and his family," Dr. Finn later told me. "I didn't give him doses that would kill him. I just gave him morphine and Valium so he would be unconscious and not gasp [when the respirator was turned off]." Art Humphrey, a Detroit television reporter, later confirmed that Rivlin's death came quickly and peacefully.

What Finn did for David Rivlin is considered legal and ethical by the American Medical Association, by the courts, and by medical ethicists. But not all physicians feel comfortable doing so when the patient is conscious and makes such a request yet—like Rivlin—is not terminally ill. Still, the courts have granted patients the right to refuse unwanted treatment such as the respirator, and Dr. Finn agreed to help.

Kevorkian, however, was left with his machine. He tried to place an ad in the *Oakland County Medical Society Bulletin* in search of terminally ill patients, but it was rejected. An acquaintance wrote an article about him in a local weekly paper, and then a local TV station put him and his machine on the air. He started getting calls from everywhere—victims of multiple sclerosis, cancer, Alzheimer's. National and international newspapers, wire services, radio shows, picked up the story. And so did Ron and Janet Adkins, a well-to-do couple in their fifties who lived in Portland, Oregon.

Ron Adkins ran his own investment firm; Janet taught English at a community college and piano lessons at home. They'd been married for thirty-three years and had three sons in their late twenties. Janet was a bright, funny, intelligent woman who read philosophy and politics, and knew the literature of death and dying. She'd read the books of Elisabeth Kübler-Ross. She believed in reincarnation. They were members of the Unitarian Church and of the Hemlock Society, the organization cofounded by Derek Humphry.

Janet and Ron had met while she was still in high school; they played music together in the same band. Music had been her life, but sometime in 1986, Janet began to falter while sight-reading piano music. Now when she and Ron played after dinner—she on the piano, he on the flute—she found she couldn't keep up. At first she thought she needed new glasses. Then she learned the truth.

On June 12, 1989, doctors told her she had Alzheimer's disease. "Right then," Ron told me, "they laid it out how it would progress. 'Eventually Ron will pick out your clothes, eventually Ron will bathe you, eventually Ron will put on your diapers.' It was devastating. We went out and walked along the river. Beyond the tears, there was no question what she was going to do. Years before we had decided that if we ever became terminally ill, we had a right to decide if we wanted to *exit* [Humphry's term for *rational* suicide] while our dignity was still intact. Also, within the Unitarian faith, there is no problem with this. . . . Her mind was her most important item, and here it was going to be taken away."

Janet wanted to think about how she would die while she was still coherent enough to make a plan. "She thought about jumping out of our tenth-floor apartment building, or jumping into the river," Ron said. "Then we thought of pills, but we had no means. We tried to find a doctor who would give us some, but they all said no. She just thought it was so unfair, as did I, to be led by medicine men to the door of death, and then they abandon you. You're on your own. Get yourself a gun and shoot yourself."

In September 1989, as Janet thumbed through a copy of *Newsweek* magazine, she read about Dr. Kevorkian and his suicide machine, and she asked Ron to call him. He got in touch with him through the Michigan chapter of the Hemlock Society. Janet, who'd read about assisted suicide in the Netherlands, was comforted to hear that Dr. Kevorkian was going to do it with the same kind of drugs, and that a doctor would be there, that she wouldn't have to do it alone. Dr. Kevorkian also conducted himself very professionally, Ron said. He asked for Janet's medical records, he consulted with her physicians, he talked with Ron and Janet several times.

Then they heard of an experimental drug program for Alzheimer's at the University of Washington; Ron, the couple's sons, and Dr. Kevorkian encouraged Janet to try it. And beginning in January of 1990, she did. Within three months, it was clear the program wasn't working.

Janet knew what would come next. Her regular doctors concurred; her mind would steadily and surely deteriorate until there was little left. Janet did not want to go to the end of this disease. But all end-of-life law stipulated—and Dr. Kevorkian stuck by it—that she must make her choices clear while she was still considered "legally competent." If anything, she had to err on the side of getting his help too early, before it was too late.

In early April, the Adkinses called Dr. Kevorkian and set a date. Janet wanted time to tie up loose ends. She asked the family therapist who had been working with them all year to spend the weekend with her, Ron, her mother, and their sons, helping them come to some family closure. Janet's plans were never a secret.

On Thursday, May 31, they met with their minister to finalize her memorial service. On Friday, June 1, she, Ron, and her best friend, Carroll Rehmke, flew to Detroit, checked into a hotel, and met with Dr. Kevorkian and his two sisters, Flora and Margo. Then they spent the weekend as tourists, shopping, going out to eat, going to a concert.

On Monday morning, June 4, 1990, Janet said good-bye to a tearful Ron and Carroll (Dr. Kevorkian didn't want them to go to avoid the risk of their prosecution), got into a car with Flora and Margo, and drove to meet Dr. Kevorkian at Groveland Oaks County Park, a wooded public campsite. There she became his first patient, dying in the back of his van.

Much has been made of this van, but it wasn't Dr. Kevorkian's first choice. He'd wanted help in dying—he called it *medicide*—to be medically dignified. At first he tried to find a doctor's office to use, but once he said what he planned, everyone he asked declined.

Then he tried rented space, dentists' offices, hotels. He even tried to rent an ambulance. After that, he tried friends' homes, but once he told people what was planned they declined. A few days before Janet's death he was still searching for a place, frantic. Janet got on the phone and told him the van was fine.

At the campsite that Dr. Kevorkian finally used (he needed electricity for that first machine), Janet lay down inside the van on a bed made with clean sheets and a pillow, hidden behind windows draped with curtains that Dr. Kevorkian had sewn. At first, he had trouble finding her veins, then he broke one of the bottles with the drugs and had to go home for more. Finally, Janet activated his makeshift machine and died. As a believer in reincarnation, she felt sure she'd be around again. "Thank you, thank you," she said as she hit the switch. Dr. Kevorkian told her: "Have a nice trip."

With that, Janet Adkins, Jack Kevorkian, and assisted suicide rocketed to national and international notoriety. (Ron Adkins says none of them had expected that this would occur.) Michigan authorities, not knowing what else to charge him with, charged Kevorkian with murder. A judge declined to hear the case for lack of evidence of murder, as did judges presented with similar charges in the next fifteen patients that Dr. Kevorkian helped.

After Janet Adkins's death, Michigan authorities confiscated Dr. Kevorkian's suicide machine. On February 5, 1991, a Michigan judge returned the machine to his attorney but barred Kevorkian from using it, from obtaining drugs needed for the procedure, and from helping others commit suicide. He went back to his lab and designed another, this one able to function without electricity and using a different, faster-acting combination of drugs.

But he also worried about terminally ill patients who might have fragile veins.

Sitting in his apartment, now drinking out of coffee mugs bearing the logos of local TV channels that had been left behind or given as gifts by news crews, Dr. Kevorkian designed a different, second device, this one utilizing carbon monoxide. Medical tubing would bring the gas from a canister to a surgical mask that could be put over the nose and mouth. Near the mask, the hosing could be blocked by a paper clip. From the clip hung a string. When patients were ready, they simply had to pull that string, releasing the flow of gas. Unconsciousness would come swiftly; death would be painless within five minutes.

On October 23, 1991, Kevorkian defied the court order and used both new machines for the first time, assisting in a double suicide in a cabin in rural Bald Mountain State Park. That day he helped fifty-eight-year-old Marjorie Wantz, who suffered severe pelvic pain that doctors—including Dr. John Finn—had been unable to diagnose or treat, and forty-three-year-old Sherry Miller, a divorced mother who had hopelessly deteriorated from multiple sclerosis. Sherry was the first of Dr. Kevorkian's patients to use the new carbon monoxide device, since he had trouble putting an IV needle into her fragile veins.

In a swift emergency move, the state Board of Medicine, the professional licensing body, voted unanimously on November 20, 1991, to suspend Dr. Kevorkian's medical license in Michigan, an action the Board had considered after Adkins's death but tabled because of the court order. This meant Dr. Kevorkian could no longer get the necessary drugs for his first machines with their bottles of lethal prescription drugs. Since no license is needed to buy carbon monoxide gas, this second device now became his method of choice.

To stop Dr. Kevorkian, the Michigan State Legislature passed an emergency bill in fall 1992 temporarily banning assisted suicide for fifteen months (while the Commission on Death and Dying created at the same time studied the issue) and making it a felony punishable by four years in jail and a fine of up to $2,000. On December 15, Governor John Engler signed it into law, scheduled to go into effect on March 30, 1993, but Dr. Kevorkian only quickened the pace of his assisted deaths. Distraught lawmakers pushed up the effective date of the new law to February 25, 1993.

In fact, legal maneuvering delayed its implementation until late spring; during that time Kevorkian's medical license was also revoked in California. Legal efforts against him—and against assisted suicide—neither started nor ended there. But they came to a head when Tom Hyde died.

One night, a few weeks after Heidi and Tom learned he had ALS, they were lying in bed on their screened porch, watching fireflies. "I said, 'Did you know this was serious?' " Heidi recalled. "And he said, 'Yeah.' So I said, 'Why didn't you tell me?' And he said, 'I tried, but you didn't want to believe it.' And I didn't. Oh God, if you could know how I did not want this to be a bad thing. I made excuses. The rippling was because he was working too hard; same with the falling. I'd make excuses because I didn't want to think anything bad was happening to him. But he knew."

Heidi tried to keep going by imagining that if she just found the one doctor who could help him, if she just got him the best medical care, if she took him to the best specialists, if she paid all his bills because Tom had no health insurance, well, maybe, just maybe, he wouldn't die. She kept copies of his medical records, read studies on ALS at libraries, nearly *willed* his disease away. But ALS is incurable.

By mid-September 1992, Tom had to stop working. He became Mr. Mom, staying home with Carmen, and he loved it. Sometimes they played outside. When the sun was warm, he'd take off his shirt and Carmen would cling with her little fingers to the hairs on Tom's chest, sleeping, snuggling, growing.

By the end of September, Tom needed a cane to walk. His arm muscles shrank, his chest grew hollow. He went to Florida, where his family now lived, to tell his mom, stepfather, two brothers, and a sister about his illness. While he was there he grew so weak that he could no longer support himself with a cane; he fell down the patio steps. In October, Tom, Heidi, and Carmen moved to an apartment for the handicapped in the suburb of Novi. One consolation: Tom was closer to his thirteen-year-old son, Joe, who would sometimes visit.

At Christmas, Heidi and Carmen went to Florida with Tom, and met his family for the first time. Before they left Michigan, he and Heidi talked about getting married. But the next month Tom was to begin receiving disability payments from Social Security, and his caseworker told them that if they married, his benefits would be drastically cut. Heidi's salary would have to be factored in. They decided not to marry, but Tom gave Heidi an engagement ring. In Florida, Tom's mother and his twenty-two-year-old brother, Sean, were shocked at how much Tom had deteriorated between the two visits.

In January, Medicaid began to pay Tom's bills. His decline grew more rapid, but Heidi thought she might have discovered a miracle. Doctors at an ALS clinic, led by Dr. Daniel Newman at Henry Ford Hospital in Detroit, were beginning trials of an experimental drug. "Tom always knew he was going to die," Heidi said, "but I never gave up hope. He agreed to go there for me, but he made me promise that if I saw them poking and prodding him like a guinea pig more than he was able to stand, I'd stop."

That month, Heidi also wanted to make day-care arrangements for Carmen, but Tom kept saying he was fine, he wasn't ready to give Carmen up. "Tom did not want to give in to this disease," Heidi said. "But he would be terrified each night when he went to sleep, wondering what bodily thing he wouldn't be able to do when he woke up the next day. Overnight he went from being able to move his hands to waking up and finding them clenched and unable to move. That's how fast this disease moved."

Then one day in February 1993, the same month the new law criminalizing assisted suicide was to go into effect, Tom was forced to face reality. He called Heidi at work, hysterical, saying he'd dropped Carmen's bottle; his hand couldn't hold it. He couldn't change her diaper. He felt she wasn't even safe in his arms. That day was when life, for Tom Hyde, came unraveled.

Heidi found day care for Carmen, and from then on, Tom had to stay home alone. He went from a cane to a walker to a reclining chair in the living room; then he began using an electric scooter. He developed trouble eating and swallowing. There would be scenes: Tom would take maybe an hour to eat. His food would get cold and he'd ask Heidi to heat it up again. He'd yell. Once, in his frustration, he threw the food on the floor. He'd choke; she'd have to use the Heimlich maneuver. He'd choke on his own saliva. He began needing help with bodily functions, since he couldn't get to the bathroom in time and he couldn't get his pants down. The pain from the constant muscle spasms grew terrible.

ALS doesn't kill all the nerves and muscles at once. Usually the first to go are the neural pathways that send messages between the brain and the muscles, but they slowly shut down, bit by bit. That means the muscles don't lock and unlock smoothly, so they cramp and spasm with excruciating pain. At first the nerves serving large muscle groups die—arms, legs, mouth, tongue. Next are those that control swallowing, breathing. As each of these neural pathways shuts down, there is pain.

His doctors gave him medicine—minimal doses of the muscle relaxants Valium and Lioresal—but since the side effects of these medicines (and of anything stronger, say, morphine) could interfere with his respiration, and since with this disease, respiration becomes a problem, doctors refused to give him anything more, for fear the medicine would kill him. But Tom was terrorized by the pain.

At Henry Ford Hospital, doctors in the experimental ALS program did test after test, trying to determine whether to accept Tom for their drug trial. In mid-March, Tom's brother Sean came up from Florida to help. On May 4, 1993, Heidi came home from work after picking up Carmen at day care, and found Tom lying on the floor with Sean sitting helplessly nearby. Sean said Tom had had a terrible episode of breathing trouble. Phlegm had lodged in his windpipe and he couldn't cough it out; his chest muscles didn't work. He'd fallen on the floor gasping. Heidi called the hospital and Tom was admitted.

He was released the next day, but as Heidi wheeled him out, a doctor took them aside. He explained that ALS was beginning to affect the muscles surrounding Tom's lungs so he was no longer eligible for their experimental program. The only thing they could recommend was hospice. For Heidi, those words were the end of all hope. Tom had, at most, just six months to live.

"Tom didn't want hospice," Heidi said. "He was so independent. It was hard enough for him to let me help him. Tom was very proud. He couldn't bear being dependent, and he didn't want strangers taking care of him in his own house."

But the final straw, for Tom, was watching Heidi and Carmen bending under the increasing burden of his illness. In early June 1993, Heidi wrenched her back while she was trying to pick him up in the shower, so she had to go on disability herself. Tom began having more terrifying breathing episodes. He would gasp for air and fall over, terrified; Heidi could no longer lift him. She'd put pillows around him on the floor, trying to keep him comfortable until help came. Tom would become hysterical, and Carmen, seeing her father try to crawl, seeing him lying helpless, moaning and gasping for air, would become hysterical, too. Tom told Heidi he didn't want hospice care. He wanted to die.

First, Tom asked his good friend Wayne, a fishing and hunting buddy, to take a gun and shoot him. Wayne refused. Then Tom gave Heidi's friend Sandi a list of lethal drugs and asked her to try to find them. She refused. Then he asked Heidi to help him die. "I love you," she told him. "Does it make any sense that I'd want to help you do that?" They fought and fought, but she kept on refusing.

In the beginning of May, Tom's stepfather had died in Florida after a long illness. In mid-June, Tom persuaded his brother Sean to drive him down there in the hope that there might be enough morphine left in the house from his stepfather's hospice care for him to kill himself. By then, Tom was so angry at Heidi for refusing to help that his farewell words were "Fuck you!"

When he got to Florida he found no morphine. Inconsolable, he called Heidi back in Michigan to beg her to find the address of Dr. Jack Kevorkian. Of course, he'd seen him on their local news. "This was the last thing I wanted to do," Heidi says. "Both my parents were dead. Tom was the love of my life. But I told him I would do whatever would make him happy." She found Dr. Kevorkian's number and address in the phone book.

On June 22, 1993, with Sean watching and his mother nearby, Tom spent several hours typing Dr. Kevorkian a letter from Florida, slowly, laboriously, with the little muscle control he had left.

> Dear Dr. Kevorkian,
>
> I open this letter by applauding you and the outstanding work you have been doing. . . . I am a thirty-year-old male diagnosed with ALS, Lou Gehrig's disease. . . . My wife has reached, or nearly so, her emotional, physical, and financial limits with working full-time, being my caretaker, and dealing with a toddler. . . . I am no longer ambulatory, speech is all but unintelligible, respiratory muscles weakening dramatically, eating and swallowing difficult, and aspiration is imminent. I will not be catheterized or diapered, and if the progress continues at this rate this will soon be necessary.
>
> The degradation has gone far enough. There is no quality to my life. I frighten my daughter. I see fear and pity in my son's eyes.

They don't need to be exposed to that, especially my boy. He will remember. I've made my peace and I just wish to die with the little dignity I have left, with as little mess as possible. . . . We lack knowledge, access to equipment and pharmaceuticals. . . . Can you please help me with this, or at least counsel me in this matter. Time has now become an issue. I greatly appreciate all consideration in this matter.
Cordially, Thomas W. Hyde

Tom's mother mailed the letter, and Tom flew home. Heidi had told him her condition for him to come home was that she get hospice to help, and Tom reluctantly agreed. Nine days after Tom typed his letter, Dr. Kevorkian called. That night he came over with his sister, Margo, and his assistant, Neal Nichol. Carmen was already asleep. Margo explained that for legal reasons she would like to videotape Tom requesting Dr. Kevorkian's help.

On camera, Tom spoke slowly, barely audibly. Most of the time he needed Heidi to translate, and he nodded to show he agreed with what she was saying.

"Tell us what you want," Dr. Kevorkian said. Haltingly, Tom replied: "I . . . want . . . to end . . . this. I . . . want to . . . die."

Heidi read him the legal agreement that Dr. Kevorkian gave them. It stated that it was Tom's wish to die and that no one had coerced him. He nodded and immediately signed. Heidi sat next to him, alternately translating for him and crying, wiping her own eyes, then handing him pieces of tissues and paper towel for his. Neal told them that the doctor's services were free. At the end of the tape, Tom and Heidi fell into each other's arms, sobbing.

"That night Tom looked at me and said, 'Let's get drunk,' " Heidi later told me. "After he got sick [with ALS] he didn't drink because liquor made him weaker, but that night he wanted to. He was like a new man when Jack said he'd help him. So I brought out some rum, and I just ended up sitting on his lap as we drove up and down the sidewalk on his electric scooter, having a great old time. We didn't know Jack Kevorkian before that day, but he was like a god to us."

Kevorkian had told Tom and Heidi to enjoy life, and when things got too rough, to call him. Meanwhile, they had become clients of the Hospice of Southeastern Michigan where Dr. John Finn was medical director—the largest hospice in the Detroit area, with one of the most skilled staffs in the nation. A volunteer came in the mornings to give Tom his bath—the hardest part for Heidi since she'd hurt her back. "Hospice called all the emergency people—911 and the police," Heidi said, "to say that if he died they'd take care of it. He got 'do not resuscitate' forms signed, and they said that if he fell, they'd come to help him off the floor."

Soon he was falling a lot. And one day, when no one was in the house, Tom had a bowel movement outside before he could get to the bathroom. When Heidi came home, she discovered he'd been trying to wash down his legs in the backyard with a hose. After that, Tom said he was ready.

They set a date with Dr. Kevorkian for August 16, about a month away. Heidi and Tom decided to get married on August 8. They bought wedding bands. Then Tom grew sicker. Doctors were saying he might need to be put on a respirator or a feeding tube imminently. He refused. But his greatest fear at that point was that Heidi would wake up or come home to find him dead. "He was convinced I wouldn't be able to handle it," Heidi said. "Or having Carmen see him dead. He was so afraid for her to have to see him suffer. So even after Jack had set the date, Tom asked him to move it up."

The revised date was August 2. Then Tom realized his Social Security check wouldn't come until August 3. He tried to arrange for Heidi to sign it instead of him, but the paperwork couldn't be done in time. He panicked. Heidi told him she didn't care about the $500, but Tom did. He nagged and nagged Heidi to call Dr. Kevorkian again to arrange a delay.

On July 31, Margo called to see if Dr. Kevorkian could change the date to August 3, and Heidi mentioned Tom's concern. Margo checked with the doctor and got back to them: "He doesn't want you to lose that money, so he'll do it instead on August 4." That meant there were just three days to go. Heidi and Tom told their families and close friends.

She wanted to get married right away, but Tom hesitated, worried that she'd become responsible for some IRS bills he owed. So there was no wedding—but by the time he died, he'd given her both an engagement ring and a wedding band.

On August 3, the Social Security check arrived. Heidi, Carmen, and Tom piled into the car and deposited the check in the bank. Later they drove with Tom's sister, who'd come up from Florida, and his friend Wayne's family to spend the day in the woods around Proud Lake.

Tom wanted his favorite dinner that night—sloppy joes. It took him about an hour and a half to eat. "Then we went to bed," Heidi told me. "We put Carmen's crib in our room, but Tom said, 'I want the baby with us.' " Heidi put Carmen between them, and Tom kissed her and just looked at her for an hour or so.

Finally, after midnight, Heidi put the sleeping baby back in her crib. Then Tom and Heidi made love. This had been possible for them all along, despite Tom's physical deterioration. It was one normal thread in their relationship, one of their last ways of communicating. "People think ALS is a devastating disease," Heidi said, "but we could still have sex, and we did that night before he died. That was one muscle that still worked, but it's very different having sex with someone who you know is going to die the next day. Then we hung on to each other. When he died I lost the person I'd most clung on to in all the world."

On Wednesday, August 4, 1993, Heidi got up at a quarter to five. Neal Nichol and Dr. Kevorkian's sister Margo were coming at 6:30. "Tom wanted coffee," Heidi said. "I don't know what I was thinking, but I made so much I had to put it in pots and pans all over the apartment. I only have a four-cup coffee maker. Then I got him up at 5:30, got him dressed, put him in his walker, and went back to the kitchen. When I looked back he wasn't there. I found him leaning over Carmen's crib, looking down at her, crying."

When Neal and Margo arrived, Heidi put Tom in his wheelchair and wheeled him out to Neal's waiting car; Dr. Kevorkian was meeting them elsewhere. Heidi had wanted to be with Tom when he died, but under Michigan's assisted suicide ban, anyone present at the event would be liable to prosecution. Tom was wearing Heidi's favorite gray sweat pants and T-shirt; he'd asked if he could wear her clothes so he could feel that she was near. Heidi did the same, putting on Tom's khaki shorts, his socks, and his favorite shirt.

"We said a hundred times, 'I love you, I love you,' looking into each other's eyes," she said. "I put him in the car, steadying him, lifting him up, putting his hands up on the door so he could hold on. It was so normal, everything we always did. I was thinking he's just going on a vacation. Then I gave him two Valiums in an empty film container and water in Carmen's Ninja Turtle squirt bottle to relax him when he got there. And they drove away. When I couldn't hear the car anymore I went back inside."

Neal drove Tom to meet Dr. Kevorkian in Royal Oak, where they moved Tom to the bed in back of the doctor's van. Dr. Kevorkian claimed at his trial that the suicide took place in the parking lot behind his apartment, in full view of the police station. But earlier, his lawyer told the press that it had been on Belle Isle, a beautiful, wooded Detroit park where Dr. Kevorkian eventually turned himself in to the police.

Dr. Kevorkian testified that this is how Tom died: With one finger on his left hand, he pulled a string attached to a paper clip that was connected to a canister of lethal carbon monoxide. As he pulled the string, gas flowed through a tube into a mask that covered his face.

Margo had stayed with Heidi. "Carmen woke up at 8:30 and I called my sister to ask her to come get her," Heidi told me. "Then Jack called at 9:08 and said, 'Hello, this is Dr. Kevorkian. Everything's gone fine. Can I talk to Margo?' Margo took Carmen and held her while she talked to Jack. I remember I ran into the bathroom and just screamed. I just fell on the floor and howled. I didn't even recognize my own voice. Just after that a swarm of reporters showed up, with microphones and cameras, with TV cameras pushing into my windows."

Later that day, Heidi went to the coroner's office to identify Tom's body. She wore his baseball cap and his sunglasses, just to make him feel close. Instead of seeing Tom's body, she was shown a black-and-white image of it on a TV monitor. She said he looked as if he were asleep, with a kind of smile on his face. Afterward she stood beside Dr. Kevorkian, at his request, at a press conference. Once she got home again, she didn't go out for five days. During that time, she read and reread a letter Tom had given her just before he left.

> I want you to know how much I appreciate everything you have done for me and for us. All the hard work and heartache. I'd have never made it this far without you, my babe. I love you two more than anything. Please love and care for our precious little girl with everything you have, for both of us. I'll love you forever. Be happy for me. I am. . . .

■   ■   ■

When Tom died, hospice staff members were in the middle of planning his scheduled August 8 wedding: rings, minister, music, flowers. Some were so taken aback by his death that they felt betrayed. Others said they might have made a similar decision themselves. But Tom was the third of their patients to end life with the help of Dr. Kevorkian, and morale was beginning to fray.

"I have to practice with Dr. Kevorkian in my backyard," said Dr. Finn, the hospice's medical director. "I hate coming home each night to turn on the TV and maybe find he has killed another of my patients."

Dr. Finn supervises the care of some seven thousand patients a year. He is among the most forward-thinking, sophisticated pain specialists within national hospice circles. In 1994, Dr. Finn was appointed the educational director of the Academy of Hospice Physicians (now renamed the American Academy of Hospice and Palliative Medicine).

His skill is motivated partly by his own personal tragedies. Both his parents died in unremitting pain. He had also faced the nearly unthinkable death of his two-year-old daughter, Rebecca. Her appendix had burst and Rebecca had swiftly developed peritonitis. She was placed on a respirator but went into shock, suffered brain damage, and was declared clinically dead. Dr. Finn himself turned off her respirator and cradled her in his arms as she drew her last breaths.

Dr. Finn was an oncologist, but after Rebecca died he decided that field was "too aggressive" and chose hospice medicine instead. He went to London to study with physicians working with Dr. Cecily Saunders at St. Christopher's Hospice, and came back well ahead of most other American physicians in his understanding of terminal treatment.

He also began to think it might be time to prepare for the legalization of assisted suicide; he knew that while sophisticated palliative care can manage a peaceful death for most patients, it can't for some small percentage of them. In that, he also saw an expanded role for hospice. He felt that hospice should take the lead in developing expertise in handling terminal diseases in addition to cancer—the primary focus of hospice at that time. Heart disease, lung disease, AIDS, muscular dystrophy, ALS, Alzheimer's, all require disease-specific symptom and pain management over months, or even years, before death.

Other Michigan doctors were also beginning to change their thinking. As they cared for their dying patients, they could hardly ignore Dr. Kevorkian's challenging presence. The month before Tom Hyde died, members of the Michigan State Medical Society voted to revise their position on assisted suicide. In doing so, they broke ranks with their parent body, the American Medical Association, which remains firmly opposed to assisted suicide. Michigan's new no-position position created a furor within the AMA, becoming a chapter essentially admitting that the best of American end-of-life medical care might not be good enough. (The chapter reversed its position in the spring of 1997.)

"The bottom line we get out of the public reaction to Kevorkian is that the issue is control," said Howard Brody, M.D., the Michigan medical society's spokesperson. " 'Will my doctor allow me a reasonable amount of control over my dying, or do I feel that the only way I get control is to find Dr. Kevorkian and get hooked up to his machine?' "

Dr. Brody was also appointed head of the Michigan Commission on Death and Dying, set up by the legislature when the state's 1993 law went into effect, representing the entire range of public opinion in Michigan and intended to advise the legislature on whether that law criminalizing assisted suicide should become permanent. After more than a year of research and public hearings, a split commission voted that assisted suicide should be made legal.

At the Hospice of Southeastern Michigan, staff opinion remained divided. Joan Hull, Ph.D., the staff psychologist and a religious Catholic, wrote up a suicide emergency protocol that stipulated what staff members should do if a patient asked for help in dying or, worse, if a patient was found trying to contact Dr. Kevorkian. She also compiled a sheet to be distributed to such patients describing Dr. Kevorkian and his techniques. Among other things were warnings that Dr. Kevorkian was not a physician licensed to practice in Michigan, that the police and press would be involved, and that carbon monoxide poisoning is "probably not painless." The sheet suggested discussing assisted suicide with hospice staff members. Assisting in a suicide wasn't something they did, of course, but the hospice saw this as a flag that a patient or family needed more psychological or physical care.

Other hospice staff members focused on Dr. Hull's broader intention—to open up discussion with patients and to assess them for depression or inadequate symptom control. They wanted to let patients know that in appropriate cases, terminal sedation to unconsciousness, using narcotics, barbiturates, even anesthetics, is ethical, legal, and possible. The hospice had begun to create model care programs for patients with diseases other than cancer, those in difficult circumstances like Tom's.

"When you're confronted with death," said Carolyn Fitzpatrick-Cassin, the president and CEO of the Hospice of Southeastern Michigan, "the issues become far more complex. What is quality of life if you're no longer an active professional? What is suffering? What is debilitation you can live with and can't live with? What can we do to help you and what is it that medicine can't yet provide?"

The patient in most distress is not the end-stage terminal patient, Cassin has found, but the one who is chronically ill—the one with MS, ALS, Parkinson's, or Alzheimer's disease—the illnesses of decline. "We think we're able to have success with almost all kinds of physical pain in almost every disease category by the use of narcotics and a variety of medications used in a different way than they were originally intended," she said of her hospice. "We can control almost all physical pain—if that's the issue for someone—if we use terminal sedation, and we estimate it will [apply] to only one percent of patients who are very much in the last few hours or days of life."

But physical pain is not by itself generally the primary reason people ask for help in dying. "The other kind of pain, that is harder to get at," Cassin said, "I would put in the category of suffering—despair, hopelessness, anticipatory grieving, loss of control, not having control over one's life anymore, and an altruistic concern about sparing their loved ones. And some people's lives have just lost meaning at this point because they've said their good-byes and have the feeling of wanting this to be over. That's what hospice does best.

"The medical community [as a whole] will over time learn to control physical pain, but the suffering, the social and family support, the psychosocial suffering is the big gap in the health-care system, and it is where we need to place our energy," Cassin said. "These are the people who seek assisted suicide. So what percent of those people can't we help? We don't have good data on this."

Unfortunately, these are just the kinds of patients that federal health-care policies have tried to keep hospices from treating; regulatory fraud prevention programs (like Medicare's Operation Restore Trust) have tried to get money back from hospices for patients surviving longer than six months. For patients with chronic, eventually terminal illnesses, there are few good long-term care alternatives.

"Chronic disease patients want hospice because they think we can help but we can't," Cassin said. "We can only take those with six months to live and when we get there we have to discharge them because they aren't going to die, for example, a post-polio patient we're discharging now. This is a person who has talked with Dr. Kevorkian and if I were in that situation I would too. It's hard for people to get through years, but months is easier. We think hospice should be the place to care for anyone who is terminally ill."

The vast size of Cassin's hospice allows her to juggle some funds—partly with the help of payments from patients who are not on Medicare or Medicaid, which means she can care for some patients for longer periods of time—and her hospice's particular expertise allows good control of pain and good palliative and supportive care. But still, she's seen this desire for help in dying among some patients.

Cassin recalled in particular one seventy-year-old woman, Marguerite Tate, who had ALS and was among the first patients to prompt this hospice to create different programs for people with different illnesses. On December 15, 1992, Tate became Dr. Kevorkian's seventh patient. Like Janet Adkins, she was an accomplished musician and lived in despair at the end of her life at the physical losses she continued to suffer.

Tate was wheelchair bound by the time she died, unable to move well or speak; once a pianist, she now communicated by tapping letters with one or two fingers on a keyboard designed for the severely disabled. She had begged Kevorkian to help her and even went with him on TV appearances to explain why.

"She was on our hospice program for eight months, and she told us when she came on that she wanted control at the end of her life," Cassin said. "I feel confident that, in the end, she made the right decision for her by going with Dr. Kevorkian. How painful it was for her to lose those things in life that had meaning for her, that had made life worth living, that allowed her to function. We did help her, but for her, she had had enough. It drew for me this picture that there are some times when we *can't* help. This was a dignified, wonderful lady. I could understand her choice."

When Marguerite died, Cassin and Dr. Finn began to step up their efforts to create programs for patients who were at high risk for suicide, patients with illnesses other than end-stage cancer. With Tom's death, the hospice strengthened these efforts even further.

Glenn Leung—the thirty-two-year-old ALS patient I was introduced to when I first went to Michigan and met Heidi and Carmen—became one of the first patients to receive their newly designed, high-intensity kind of care, with aggressive attempts at symptom management and with the goal of creating an alternative for patients who might otherwise look for help from Dr. Kevorkian.

Glenn Leung was half Irish and half Chinese. He could eat with chopsticks before he learned to handle a fork or a knife, but in 1990, Glenn suddenly began dropping things, too. For him it began with food.

Earlier that year he had taken a leave from law school and moved from Michigan—where he'd grown up, gone to college, and now law school—to Atlanta. His parents had divorced and two of his close friends had died. He still had lots of friends in Michigan, but he wanted to be near his sister, Sharon, and her husband, Pat, who'd gotten him a job at the Ritz Carlton Hotel. But soon he was not only dropping things when he ate but he was also dropping things at work. Glasses. Dishes. Whole trays.

Like Tom, Glenn at first thought these were accidents, but about six months later, he got scared. Baseball was Glenn's first love. "I was getting ready for my regular softball game. I put my mitt on my left hand to warm up by smacking the ball in it and I couldn't hold it," he told me. "At the time, I was frightened. But I had no idea what it was, the magnitude of it. So I went to the doctor, and he sent me to a neurologist."

Finally, on April 4, 1991, after months of testing like Tom went through, a specialist at Emory University Hospital told Glenn he had ALS, that he would die like his baseball hero Lou Gehrig. "I walked out onto the campus," Glenn said. "At that time of year it's spring in Atlanta. All the flowers, the grass, the dogwood. It may sound like a cliché, but I noticed every single color. It was all like crystal, crystal clear. I didn't have many physical problems yet. But I'd asked the doctor how long I had to live. And though the doctor wouldn't come right out and tell me, he said he thought I'd have about four years. Then there would be a total system failure.

"I just broke down and cried. In the weeks afterward, I began having problems with my legs. One day I was crossing a busy street. A car was coming at a good clip and I couldn't move fast enough to get out of the way. The car didn't hit me, but it did hit emotionally how bad it was getting." He knew he needed help.

By then, Sharon and Pat had moved back to Michigan, and Sharon had just given birth to their daughter, Emelia. Shortly after that, her marriage broke up. Sharon, who worked for the Bose Corporation, had a small home of her own, with her office upstairs. It was a little white clapboard house with blue shutters in the Detroit suburb of Royal Oak, where Jack Kevorkian lived.

That spring, Glenn came to celebrate Emelia's first birthday, and they went to a Chinese restaurant. It was when Glenn made a mess of the rice that Sharon knew something was wrong. "When he drove me back to my house he said, 'Pinch that flesh between my thumb and forefinger.' All the muscle was gone. I just felt my fingers and skin," Sharon said. "I think I had some concept it would be massive, but you don't realize all at once how much support you might need." From the start, though, it was understood that he would move in with her. He went back to Atlanta, packed up, drove back in his car, and moved into a second bedroom in Sharon's house on Cherry Street.

Glenn saw the same doctors Tom did—Louis Rentz, D.O., at the Michigan Institute for Neurological Disorders, and Daniel Newman, M.D., at the ALS clinic at Henry Ford Hospital in Detroit. "In August 1991, when I first came to live with Sharon," he said, "I could walk freely, use the bathroom without assistance, I was social, going to sports events with friends. But by the beginning of 1992, I couldn't get out of bed by myself, and I needed help getting dressed and with feeding."

Sharon would sit both Glenn and Emelia at the table, feeding one, then the other. Then in May 1992, she called the Hospice of Southeastern Michigan for help. Once he joined hospice, its medical director, Dr. Finn, came to see him, as did psychologist Dr. Hull, social worker Judy Kelterborn, M.S.W., volunteer coordinator Dave Turner, and a battalion of nurses, aides, and volunteers. Along with them came a hospital bed, a reclining chair, and special equipment. Sharon and Glenn lost their privacy to well-meaning strangers. Glenn was appreciative, but he was soon confined, tethered like a Siamese twin to his Sony four-foot color TV screen.

"I started to realize," Glenn told me later, "that I wasn't just sick, but slowly dying. I'd practice, pretending I was on my last few breaths. I hoped it would lessen my anxiety, but practicing it made me realize the actual event will be different. I also learned that until I actually get to a physical change there's no real way to visualize it or know how I'll feel then, even though it's been explained to me."

Visualizing his death filled him with sadness and fear. As his body shut down, bit by bit, his mind went on overdrive. Friends started mattering to him more. He began appreciating how loving and kind people were, even strangers. "I started to realize what was important in life, and though I couldn't change my own life, I started trying to communicate to people. I wanted to say how much of a miracle the human mind is," he said, "and that the human body is a miraculous machine in itself. Now my mind is as sharp as it's ever been, but it's harder and harder to share, harder to communicate all the time. The real Glenn Leung gets harder to share, and further and further inside." He felt he was in a rush for time.

By the time I met him, Glenn was spending most of his days in the recliner, like an immobile piece of furniture in front of the TV. He could move only a few fingers. And when he spoke, he had to struggle . . . to . . . say . . . each . . . word. Saliva drooled down his chin. He couldn't control his tongue or use his hands to wipe his mouth, and it was difficult for him to swallow. He was reduced to a diet of pureed meat and vegetables and mashed potatoes. He needed total care.

But he could still finger the remote control for the TV. He watched endless sports—football, baseball, E-Span. Exercise programs fascinated him. Muscles he had never noticed before seemed to lurch out from the screen—hands do so much, he thought, feet, legs, fingers; he even started to notice what people could do with their faces and tongues.

Glenn particularly noticed the women in the aerobics classes. He still felt sexual desire, but there was nothing he could do about it, even for himself. "I think of sex every day," he said, "but I'm not married and I don't have a girlfriend." Having sexual urges with no way to relieve them made him anxious and sad.

Volunteers and aides from the hospice learned how to feed him. They also learned how to help Glenn get to the shower, sit him on a stool while they bathed him, help him hold up his body enough to be soaped, and hold the urinal as he peed. He had to learn how to accept such intimate help.

"I had a hard time getting over a feeling of hopelessness," Glenn would later tell me. "When you're healthy, even on your worst day, when you go to sleep and wake up there's some new hope that maybe tomorrow or next month or next year, things will be better. But now I realized every day was the best I will ever be."

Soon he was a prisoner to whatever TV channel was on, since he could no longer even use the remote to channel surf. He studied the TV program guides each night so that Sharon could set the TV channel for the following day. He learned to plan naps around the programs he didn't want to see, but he was always awake for the news. And in Detroit, Dr. Kevorkian was often the lead story on the TV news.

On December 15, 1992, there had been another double suicide: sixty-seven-year-old Marcella Lawrence, who'd had intense pain from heart disease, emphysema, and arthritis in her back, and Marguerite Tate—Cassin's hospice patient whom Glenn also knew—both died inhaling carbon monoxide at Tate's house. That very day, just hours after those deaths, Michigan's Governor Engler signed the legislature's bill banning assisted suicide into law. "I want to sign it today," he angrily told reporters, "to protest what Dr. Kevorkian has done."

As Glenn watched the news, as he saw bodies being wheeled out of homes and secluded cabins, and unloaded from Dr. Kevorkian's ubiquitous white van, he also saw images of politicians, critics, theologians, all furious, saying the new law would soon stop Jack Kevorkian. Seeing those bodies didn't make him panic. But listening to the politicians began to terrify him. He wanted to be sure, if he needed to, that he'd be among the few that Dr. Kevorkian could help.

In February, when the new law was to go into effect, Glenn started planning his funeral, picking his pallbearers, thinking night and day of Jack Kevorkian. He asked Sharon to find him. He didn't know that Dr. Kevorkian's number was right there in the Royal Oak phone book, but he did know from seeing it on TV that he lived just blocks away.

Sharon was frightened and never tried to find Kevorkian. Instead, she called Glenn's doctors: Dr. Rentz, at the Institute for Neurological Disorders, and Dr. Finn, at hospice. They both came to talk with Glenn and what they said changed his mind about assisted suicide. "Dr. Rentz told me there is a big difference between dying naturally and taking your own life," Glenn later told me, "and he explained that any life, as long as you can find some meaning, is better than death. When he told me that I felt it was true because I could still watch TV or movies or do a lot of things that many people could never do. I realized that even though I'm very sick now and declining, I'm still able to get some enjoyment."

"That he was losing control of each part of his body, of everything in his life, was hard for him," Sharon later said, "but Dr. Rentz said Glenn could still control things by choosing not to eat or have a feeding tube, that that is a natural way of not keeping things going, a way of keeping control. Neither of us had thought of that before. We realized Glenn didn't need carbon monoxide. He could just have a choice at that point."

Dr. Finn also assured Glenn that when the time came, he could go into the hospital and have as much sedation as he needed. He said he would use narcotics, barbiturates, put Glenn in a coma, without food and water, and "let nature take its course." Dr. Finn was talking about unconscious, terminal sedation. These promises made Glenn relax. Yet for various reasons—some having to do with Glenn, some with his doctors, some with a lack of communication—that's not how it worked out.

Dr. Rentz's words stuck in Glenn's mind: "suicide was tantamount to giving up," and "every moment of this life is so much better than having no life at all." Those around Glenn described him with words like *courageous* and *brave*. Glenn began to view this disease as intense, terrifying, a sports rookie version, maybe, of *Glenn's Excellent Adventure*. He didn't quite say it, but he intended to become the Clint Eastwood of ALS.

"I've been very consistent about no other aggressive means to prolong my life, no feeding tubes, no respirator," Glenn said. "Sharon has a durable power of attorney." But in fact, beyond this position, Glenn had no bottom line—no agreed-upon point where he would take Dr. Finn's offer of help. Nor did he know how he would make such a decision.

Glenn was on Valium by the summer of 1993, something for muscle spasms, and antibiotics when he needed them, lowering the possibility that he might die of infection before the disease ran its course. Hospice brought a commode, a Hoya lift to move him out of bed, plastic urinals. Glenn could do less and less. His muscles didn't move, but he could still feel every little sensation. Itches. Pain. Discomfort. He couldn't do anything about them, though, and he was less and less able to speak, to tell his aides how to move him or when the way he was moved caused him pain. His inability to speak made him terrified of being moved the wrong way, of being powerless to let him or her know. Glenn felt he was encased in a casket of flesh.

Dr. Hull began to introduce spiritual concerns into their talks, but when she did, Glenn just stopped wanting to see her. He thought what she was saying about religion and God was baloney. He was distraught, though, since he had less and less function every day. Hospice workers and visitors came, but there were gaps of one, two, or three hours when Glenn was alone. In August, after Tom died, Tom's aide, Kelvin, came to work on weekends with Glenn.

"I knew I needed their help," Sharon said, "but at first you're afraid because you feel kind of weak yourself, and then you're embarrassed. Glenn resists things until the bitter end, and sometimes I get scared. But when we get to a point, we try to cross it together. I say, 'I can't do this anymore, and what do you think?' He tries to stretch things out because he doesn't want to recognize he's lost another thing, but I have to try to be clear what I can and can't do and try to talk with him."

Glenn was so opposed to being bedridden that hospice made a special exception from their usual practice by assigning him two aides at a time. Together they could lift him, and with the Hoya lift, he could continue to get out of bed.

In November 1993, Glenn was still easy to be around. Friends came to visit, his smirky attitude making him likable, the fact that he joked, even though he could hardly speak, that he still thought of himself as a guy's guy—watching the games while wearing a Detroit Red Wings T-shirt, though a *Field of Dreams* afghan covered his legs. He and Dave Turner, the volunteer coordinator, were the same age, thirty-three, and they talked a similar "guy" language. "Hey Dave," Glenn would quip. "You'd better get to my funeral early because it will be packed. There'll be so many babes there, you won't be able to find a seat."

By December, Glenn could speak only a few words, with great pauses in between, working his mouth as best he could. It was so hard to understand him that he needed Sharon or Dave to translate. Practically the only thing Glenn could move were his eyelids and his mouth, but his mouth didn't stop talking much at all. "Since I speak so slowly now," he said, "I find I'm thinking slowly. I don't want people to think I'm losing my mind, 'cause I'm not. So every once in a while when I realize my mind's going slow I just tell myself: 'Hey, move it!' "

By the end of December, since he was paralyzed from his neck down, Glenn could eat only liquids and purees, and a froth of mucus formed whenever he tried to breathe or speak. He couldn't hold up his head and needed a towel behind his neck, folded twice, to help him breathe. His wire-rimmed glasses slipped over his eyes, so he needed someone to adjust them. With a neck collar on, he couldn't talk. All this positioning was important, since he had to sit as he was placed until someone showed up later to move him.

By the beginning of January 1994, Glenn was focused almost exclusively on getting through his daily routine, the physical functions of keeping his body alive. I went to Michigan at the end of the month. Glenn was nearly impossible to understand. Sharon told me she'd learned to read what he wanted by his eyes. They'd long ago crossed some border of intimacy as brother and sister. When Glenn had to pee, others left the room. Sharon had to adjust Glenn's body exactly right, scoot to the edge of the chair, knees up, legs apart.

Then she had to put his penis into the urinal and hold it between his legs. Since the muscles that expel urine were also affected, she might stand and wait, holding it, for nearly twenty minutes. He concentrated hard. She concentrated hard. It took maybe half an hour. She wanted him to get a catheter put in but he refused.

By spring, Sharon was running out of steam. She told me in one of my regular phone calls that she'd read books about dying. She decided maybe Glenn needed closure, so she told him he'd given her and Emelia a real gift, a legacy, that he'd been brave and courageous, that it was okay to go, that she'd be okay. She started to cry. She really meant it. She also loved Glenn, and didn't want him to leave her, either. No matter; Glenn said he wasn't ready to go anywhere.

Judy Kelterborn, the hospice social worker, had long been the person campaigning for hospice to skirt the normal rules and add more aides for Glenn's care schedule. Her grown son had drowned and Glenn reminded her of him. "Glenn was a phenomenal person," she later told me. "His philosophy after he got sick was that if he could change things, he would go back and be kinder to people and smell the flowers. He was so kind, he'd say thank you for taking the time to come to meet me. It was horrible watching this wonderful person just close up because of his physical condition." She wanted Glenn to stay alive as long as he could, and began to get mad at Sharon. Sharon told me she was "maxed out," but Judy said Sharon was "selfish."

By July 1994, stress was causing Glenn's hospice aides and volunteers to quit or ask to be reassigned, leaving Sharon frequently on her own. "One of Glenn's big fears was when he'd be trapped inside himself and now he is," Sharon said. "He can't do anything. I'd always said, 'I'll do whatever you want me to do,' but now I feel mean. I just feel, 'Look, I can't do this anymore.' Glenn has made his own decisions, but he's done it in a vacuum. We have hard choices. If the help doesn't show up, it all falls on me. I can't do it. I just can't. Then in the next breath I feel so guilty, because in the beginning I said, 'I'm here for you.' Now this is our whole life. It's gone on longer than anyone imagined."

Sharon was only twenty-nine years old. Emelia needed her. Her pressures at work had increased. She rarely went out. Hospice staff members suggested giving Glenn a little morphine at night, just .25

mg, enough to let him and Sharon get some sleep. Otherwise, he was awake a lot, calling her, asking her to reposition his shoulder, his leg, his arm. He refused, thinking the morphine meant the beginning of the end.

Glenn also refused a feeding tube, even though he was constantly choking. "He doesn't want to go violently," Sharon said. "In his disease, the only way that will happen is if he chokes to death. Well, he keeps pushing himself to eat, so it's up to him. He's the only one to decide not to eat anymore, or to have a tube."

Over the summer, Sharon tried to tell him what she read in Sherwin Nuland's best-seller, *How We Die*. If he stopped eating he would go in his sleep; he would simply be weaker and weaker, it wouldn't be violent, choking or gasping for air. He could also die of pneumonia. If his urine was dark, maybe his kidneys were beginning to shut down. An aide told him that was a warning sign, so he got scared. Glenn didn't want to die.

He asked Sharon where the food and liquids go if they aren't going out. "Well, I said for one thing you aren't taking in much liquids, and for another, it could go elsewhere and back up." She started checking his arms and legs. They didn't look swollen. "But of course they are raised," Sharon fretted, "so maybe it's going into his lungs. Maybe he'll get pneumonia."

Hospice suggested that he go into a nursing home for a five-day respite program so that Sharon could regroup. Glenn said he wouldn't go. He didn't want to be in a nursing home. He didn't want to be with old people. He didn't want to be with young people with AIDS. He wanted to stay home.

Sharon was desperate. She wanted to do what Glenn wanted, but she also worried about Emelia needing her. She tried to persuade Glenn to get a catheter. He finally agreed to go to a nursing home for five days, came back with a catheter, and said it was absolutely terrible being there. Mostly, they couldn't understand him, but he wanted to keep the catheter.

By now, Glenn seemed to be holding on by sheer willpower. "I went on vacation three weeks ago and said good-bye," his translator Dave Turner told me in mid-August. " 'Well, if you're not here when I get back,' I said, 'I'll see you on a baseball diamond somewhere else sometime. I'll be in center field.' Glenn smiled and said he'd be in left field. But as far as hospice workers are concerned,

Glenn is already in left field. He's struggling to hold on to life more than anyone we've ever seen."

Dave was at Glenn's house from 1:30 until 4:00 in the afternoon, most of that time trying to feed him. "You know how it feels when you get something down the wrong pipe?" Dave said. "Well, that's how it is for Glenn with every mouthful. He can't get his tongue to work like we do, so he can't get the food to go in the right place, so he chokes with every bite. And it also runs out his mouth all over his face. It's terrifying to feed him and it's very hard on the volunteers, physically and emotionally, because with your left hand you have to hold his head in just the right place, because he can't hold up his head. Then you have to spoon it in with your right hand. And then it runs all over his face, so you have to wipe him and then he starts to choke and you feel at each spoonful this could be it and you've made him die. I've told him how hard it is on us, but he still insists on being fed. I don't even think he's a candidate for a feeding tube anymore because I'm not sure his body could stand it." Sharon was amazing, he said. She just kept trying to help him.

Dave thought that if Glenn believed in an afterlife, if he didn't feel that death was the end, he wouldn't be struggling so. The people who have the hardest time dying, he told Glenn, those who struggle to stay alive the most, are those who don't believe in an afterlife. Glenn didn't respond to this but he began to ask Sharon to put on the video of the movie *Field of Dreams,* time after time after time.

What Ray Kinsella, the movie's corn-growing, baseball-loving hero, learns is that Heaven is a place where dreams come true. It's the dream that counts, like a dream of playing ball with the greatest ballplayers of all time. And in this afterworld, all those players—even Lou Gehrig—would be young and whole again. Perhaps death and the afterlife would feel to Glenn just like melting from the playing field into the surrounding field of corn and dreams.

By the end of August 1994, as Glenn watched those baseball greats playing ball in an all-star afterlife, his neck was constantly falling. While he was eating, the volunteers had to keep pushing his head up. He was too weak to pull up on a straw. Sharon said squirting liquefied food down his throat with a syringe worked better, but Glenn had so much phlegm and mucus that he was drowning in it. Since he couldn't speak, he was limited to facial

expressions. He worried he wouldn't be seen as intelligent anymore. Sharon said she didn't know how much longer he'd be able to
eat. He could barely take his pills.

One night, Sharon woke in a terrified sweat from a horrible
dream—that Glenn died and there was some legal question about
whether he was dead or not. "I was fighting with the funeral parlor
and everyone, saying, 'No, he's still alive.' He was in the casket. All
embalmed even. And he was trying to get up, to get out, to talk to
me. I said, 'No, he's still alive.' And they said, 'No, he's dead. That's
it.' " Sharon said her dream is the way Glenn now lived day to day.

Finally, Sharon called Dr. Newman for an evaluation. No ALS
specialist had seen Glenn for more than a year because he couldn't
get to their offices—too hard to have an ambulette come to take
him—and they hadn't come for house calls. Although a battalion of
hospice aides and volunteers had come, even the hospice doctors
rarely came anymore.

Dr. Newman suggested to Glenn that he get a feeding tube, a
new, skinny little one that went through the nose to the stomach. It
was too late for him to get one inserted surgically through the
stomach; he couldn't survive the anesthesia. It's normally a simple
procedure, but because Glenn had waited so long he had to be
taken into the hospital. Glenn agreed. Hospice agreed, even though
it flew in the face of their treatment and reimbursement guidelines.
Sharon agreed. Dr. Newman said it would reduce feeding time from
three hours to twenty minutes through the tube.

But on assessing Glenn, Dr. Newman found something more:
He'd begun falling asleep during the day. He had some confusion.
His eyes were glazing over. He had trouble holding complex
thoughts. Sharon had thought he was just stubborn, but Dr.
Newman said that these were the signs of carbon dioxide buildup,
signs in ALS patients that the respiratory system is failing, that the
end is near.

The past three weekends in a row Glenn had had visitors, close
friends and relatives. He'd said good-bye, and he'd asked some of
them to be pallbearers. On Wednesday, September 7, 1994, Dr.
Newman put the tube in place, but then Glenn got an infection and
antibiotics didn't work. On Sunday, September 11, 1994, Dr. Finn
called me to say that Glenn had died.

On the following Tuesday, Sharon called. Saturday night, a

hospice volunteer had come to put him to bed and Sharon had gone in to say good night. The volunteer later told her Glenn had tried to tell him something but he couldn't understand.

Sharon's best friend came over early that morning. "We were sitting having coffee, trying to decide whether we should do the errands we were going to do first, or whether I should wake Glenn up and get him fed and ready," Sharon said. "Then Emelia woke up and I decided to get Glenn ready and then go. So I went inside and I knew as soon as I saw him. His eyes were open, staring at the TV. He was cold, but then he was cold a lot anyway. But I remembered my dream. I didn't want him to think I'd abandoned him if he weren't dead. So I got the stethoscope and listened to see if I could hear his heart. And then I knew he was dead."

Glenn died with his eyes open, during the night, either sleeping or watching TV, maybe *Field of Dreams*. Maybe he just melted with the ballplayers out into that field of corn. In a weird way, whatever it was, Sharon thought the timing of his death was well planned, that he was the one who planned it.

"Glenn was really impressive," Sharon said. "I do think he did a lot of letting go. He knew I was going to have to go out of town [in a few weeks] on business trips, he didn't want to go to that nursing home, he knew that my mom was going to have to have a hysterectomy that week and I was going to have to deal with that," she said. "It was a sunny day; he knew I hated gloomy days. And he knew my friend was going to be here with me. Who knows? Maybe that just seemed like a good time."

Dave Turner was late to the funeral on Friday. Glenn had been right. He had to stand in back because there were so many "babes" there he couldn't find a seat. Glenn was buried wearing his Red Wings T-shirt and his *Field of Dreams* afghan wrapped about the casket. It's the Chinese tradition to send souls off with things they might need in the next life. His family burned incense, to help take his spirit up, gave out candy, because a funeral is considered bad luck and candy sweetens it, and handed out quarters rolled up in paper to buy more candy. His friends threw in some cold beers, a little money, some food, a few baseballs, and some dirt from Detroit's Tigers Stadium.

After Glenn died, the hospice had a debriefing for those who'd taken care of Glenn because they were all so upset. "I think as an organization," Judy Kelterborn said, "we're going to look very hard at ALS patients because their needs are very great and they last a long time, especially young patients. With Glenn it was two and a half years. Death takes a long time."

In Glenn's case, she felt hospice might have set more limits on what they could or couldn't do. "We could've put that feeding tube in six months ago and saved a lot of problems for the staff and for Glenn, but he kept refusing it," she said. "The refusal was the macho man. 'I'll keep eating until I can't and then I'll die,' but by the time he did have it put in, it was too late. Because he couldn't swallow they had to have a big procedure done at Henry Ford Hospital, which cost thousands of dollars."

But the bottom line for many of the hospice workers was the belief that it was hard for Glenn because he "rejected spiritual care," as Judy put it, "and he didn't believe in God." Ironically, on the other hand, they thought Tom Hyde had made some kind of peace with death.

"With Tom, it was sensational," Judy said. "All Dr. Kevorkian's deaths are. But Tom didn't have the problems accepting death that Glenn did. Maybe Glenn just didn't want to die. He was always afraid. I never could crack that. We're all afraid of death in this country. We think it's the worst thing that can happen to us, but how do we know? People who have a spiritual base, whatever that is, can accept that this is the way things go. It doesn't matter how it's done, but what matters is whether they accept death or not."

To Sharon, it had little to do with spirituality. "One often wonders: Why does one person want to go on and not another?" she later mused. "I think it's the person himself and what enjoyment he gets out of life. What help do you have? What was your role before? Were you a breadwinner? The support? Tom Hyde couldn't pick up his daughter or help Heidi. Tom loved taking care of Carmen. Glenn's self-worth diminished when his communication, his ability to speak, began going." It's when the things by which one values oneself are gone, she decided, that life may no longer be worth living.

Heidi Fernandez calls herself and Carmen the youngest "survivors," the term sometimes used by the family and friends of the people whose deaths Dr. Kevorkian made possible. (Dr. Kevorkian gave the early "survivors" gold charms engraved with a number indicating their loved one's place in the chain of those he had helped. Heidi's is number seventeen.)

By the summer of 1997, tallies of acknowledged deaths ranged from forty-nine to fifty-five. For many families, the grieving process after the death was compounded and protracted by the focus of the media, the police, local prosecutors, the courts, and the local medical examiner—who tended to dispute after autopsies the diagnoses of the people who had died.

According to the patients themselves, their families, and most of their own physicians, eighteen of these patients had suffered from cancer, eleven from MS, eight from ALS, two from lung diseases; one each had AIDS, heart disease, chronic fatigue syndrome, Crohn's disease, and quadriplegia. Three had miscellaneous intense pain and two had other neurological or spinal diseases. Many of them also had multiple other problems.

Janet Good, a close associate of Kevorkian who helps to screen his patients, told me that there were many other assisted suicides, deaths that had been more private and remained uncounted. Hundreds more had filed requests with Kevorkian but had not been accepted.

After Tom Hyde died, Dr. Kevorkian was charged with a felony under the new Michigan law banning assisted suicide. Heidi sat in the courtroom, front row center, throughout the trial. Despite Dr. Kevorkian's clear admission that he had helped Tom Hyde die, on May 2 jurors returned a verdict of "not guilty." They were regular people—including a postal worker, a nurse, a clerk, a minister—who understood perfectly the tragedy that had befallen Tom and Carmen and Heidi. Many of them later said that it was Heidi's moving testimony, combined with Tom's video, that led them to this decision.

"Dr. Kevorkian was the only person to help Tom," she told the jury, "the only person who *could* help him. We had seen so many doctors. . . . I had dragged him all over town to see so many people to help stop his suffering and no one could help him. And I couldn't help him." She broke down and sobbed on the stand. After the trial she said it to me again: "No one helped Tom but Jack Kevorkian."

Less than a year later, the Michigan State Commission on Death and Dying recommended that the temporary ban be allowed to sunset when its period was up. Two years after Tom's trial, the law would be ruled unconstitutional by Michigan's Supreme Court because it had been written to stop just one person, Dr. Jack Kevorkian.

In the late winter and spring of 1996, Dr. Kevorkian was tried twice, for a total of four other assisted suicides. In these trials, the charge was murder. And despite Dr. Kevorkian's free admission of his role in these deaths; despite his antics—like coming to court in costumes or in a mock gallows, his courting of the press, his boisterous moral outcries; despite mounting public concern that he may not have adequately evaluated the cases medically or screened them for depression or family abuse, both juries once again found him not guilty.

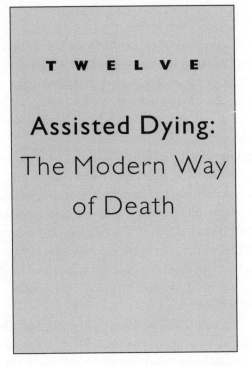

T W E L V E

Assisted Dying: The Modern Way of Death

S hortly after midnight on a freezing January morning, strag-
glers lugging sleeping bags and blankets and thermoses of hot
coffee began to line up beneath the main steps of the U.S.
Supreme Court building in Washington, D.C., like supplicants
waiting to pay homage at the base of a sacred temple.

During the night they kept arriving, in cars, buses, and vans for
the handicapped, from as far as the West Coast and as near as a
block away. By dawn, the line swung down the sidewalk, with
newcomers stomping their feet, or sitting bundled in wheelchairs,
or standing beside their Seeing Eye dogs in the cold, knowing—but
staying anyway in hope—that they were probably too late to get in.
It was said that only fifty seats had been set aside for the general
public.

At 10:00 A.M. on January 8, 1997, the nine justices of the
Supreme Court were to hear two hours of oral arguments from

opposing attorneys, one hour each for the two cases scheduled by the court to be heard in tandem. These cases had been appealed to the nation's highest court after two different regional federal appeals courts, deciding on cases from the states of New York and Washington, had ruled that state laws criminalizing physician-assisted suicide were unconstitutional.

Since appeals courts' rulings apply to all states within their jurisdictions, had these rulings remained unchallenged they would have effectively legalized assisted suicide in twelve states, or nearly a quarter of the nation. Today, attorneys representing Washington and New York—joined in amicus briefs by lawmakers from a number of other states, and by an unusual appeal by the U.S. Solicitor General, the attorney from the Justice Department representing the Clinton administration—were asking the Supreme Court to reverse these rulings.

Amicus briefs opposing legalization were also filed by virtually the entire medical establishment, as well as by organizations connected with the Catholic Church, the National Committee for the Right to Life, and James Bopp and his National Legal Center for the Medically Dependent and Disabled.

Briefs supporting legalization were filed by a large assortment of pro-choice and grassroots groups, including AIDS organizations, the Gray Panthers, the American Civil Liberties Union, the Older Women's League, Unitarian and Jewish groups, affiliates of the National Organization of Women, the Hemlock Society, as well as other lawmakers from various states, and health-care groups breaking rank with their own organizations—including several distinguished medical school professors and hospice professionals. Each side also had its own group of supportive bioethicists, law professors, and family members filing briefs.

While Dr. Kevorkian has probably garnered the most headlines about assisted suicide, neither of these cases involved him. Both the New York and Washington cases were brought by a Seattle-based, grassroots organization called Compassion in Dying, some of whose members are closely affiliated with Derek Humphry and the Hemlock Society.

Humphry, a former *Los Angeles Times* reporter, co-founded the Hemlock Society in 1980. It advocates the right of terminally ill patients to choose the time and manner of their own deaths. Humphry would later write the bestseller *Final Exit,* which gives detailed instructions on how such patients might actually take their lives. Starting in California in 1988, he had also begun to organize a campaign to legalize assisted suicide by putting referendums on the state election ballots.

That year, Humphry's group failed to get enough signatures for a referendum on the California ballot, in part because they were underfunded. But after *Final Exit* became a bestseller, Humphry used the money he made on book sales to help finance more state ballot measures. His supporters began with the state of Washington in 1991. This time they gathered enough signatures to place a "death with dignity" referendum on the ballot.

Polls of voters just prior to the 1991 Washington referendum showed a majority in favor of the ballot measure, but in the last days before the election, opponents poured money into the campaign and helped to defeat it by a slim margin of 54 to 46 percent.

The close tally made it clear that this was not an issue of mere curiosity, but one with deep public support. Some proponents of the measure attributed its loss to negative public reaction to Dr. Kevorkian's double assisted suicide on Bald Mountain on October 23, just a few days before the vote. Others attributed it partly to the measure's wording, which would have legalized both assisted suicide and euthanasia, and partly to its lack of strong protective regulations.

Afterward, some of the referendum's key proponents regrouped. By April 1993, they had launched a counseling organization called Compassion in Dying, under the direction of Unitarian minister Reverend Ralph Mero. On its board and advisory committee were well-respected Seattle-area medical professionals, hospice and long-term care specialists, ethicists, AIDS support group leaders, even the former president of the Washington State Medical Association.

"The organization came from people who had worked very hard to pass a law to legalize physician assisted suicide," says Compassion in Dying's executive director Barbara Coombs Lee.

"They decided to help dying people with these decisions—to prepare them, to help them find doctors and drugs, and to be with them as they died. This went right up to the edge of the law."

Compassion in Dying advocates the right of terminally ill patients to ask doctors for—and for doctors to be able to legally prescribe—medications, such as the barbiturate sleeping pill Seconal, that patients might take in lethal doses if their suffering is so great they no longer want to live.

Organized as a medical service staffed by doctors, hospice nurses, social workers, ministers, and volunteers, working as a team—with patients' own doctors, if they were so inclined—it planned to help terminally ill patients who requested assistance in suicide. It would not help with euthanasia.

Patients who contacted the organization were sent a packet that included strict guidelines on whom it would help. Patients had to meet three key criteria: 1) they had been given a medical prognosis of under six months to live; 2) they were experiencing unbearable suffering that could be relieved no other way; and 3) they were not victims of clinically treatable depression.

To determine eligibility based on these criteria, Compassion in Dying's health-care workers would assess patients' needs and provide referrals or care if pain or symptoms were not well enough addressed or if family support systems needed bolstering. They would confirm that patients were terminally ill, that their suffering was truly untreatable, and that their request for help was really voluntary. Then, if the patient qualified, assistance in dying would be offered.

The organization would not provide prescriptions, but if the patient's own doctor did not provide them, it would make referrals to doctors who would. It also believed that people should not have to be alone when they took the drugs, so it provided volunteers and counseled family members to be with the dying—an act that put them at legal risk.

"When I got back from maternity leave the summer after they began," says Compassion in Dying's feisty attorney, Kathryn Tucker, a thirty-something partner at the prestigious Seattle law firm of Perkins Coie, "I read their material and told them they should be aware of some of the statutes in Washington that make assisted suicide a crime." To protect themselves from prosecution, they decided to take on the law.

Beginning in 1994, Tucker and other Compassion in Dying attorneys filed suit in Washington and in New York, arguing that just as women have the right to make decisions about their bodies in having abortions, terminally ill patients have the right to decide how much pain and suffering they are willing to endure, and to choose when and how they want to die.

They also charged that current end-of-life law created unequal circumstances for patients with different symptoms or illnesses. Patients who need feeding tubes or respirators to survive can legally ask their doctors to shut off their life-support equipment. When doing so, doctors can sedate patients heavily, often to unconsciousness, and withhold food and water, so that patients do not suffer as they die.

Other patients who are in great pain or are suffering from severe breathlessness, nausea, or delirium may also be provided with complete sedation, using barbiturates and anesthesia—and also withholding food and water—until they, too, die.

The legal rationales behind both these end-of-life scenarios are the right of patients to refuse unwanted medical treatment, and the principle of the double effect: So long as the intent is to relieve pain or suffering the intervention is considered legal, even if the unintended side effect is to hasten death.

However, Compassion in Dying attorneys argued, those terminally ill patients who are not in physical pain (nor experiencing severe symptoms such as nausea, breathlessness, or delirium), those who do not want to endure days of terminal sedation as they slowly die, and those who have no life-support equipment to shut off but are suffering nevertheless, cannot legally get assistance in their deaths.

In filing the lawsuits, Compassion in Dying was joined by four physicians in Washington and three in New York, and by three terminally ill patients in each state, all of whom have since died. The patients charged that the state laws prevented their choosing the timing and manner of their own deaths with assisted suicide; the doctors said these laws interfered with good medical practice by preventing proper and humane care for a certain small group of patients whose suffering cannot be relieved in any other way.

One pivotal issue in both suits was the claim that assistance in dying has long been a hidden medical practice—the practice of doctors who give patients with whom they have close relationships legal prescriptions for barbiturates and/or narcotics like morphine, knowing a patient might also use them to end his or her life.

Assisted suicide might have continued on a "don't ask, don't tell" basis, but Compassion in Dying and these doctors and patients wanted to make it more public for four major reasons: Not all patients have close relationships with doctors who are willing to put themselves at legal risk to provide such prescriptions; a secret practice is hard to monitor or regulate, leading to heightened fears of abuse; what is essentially back-alley assisted suicide—like back-alley abortion—could also cause far worse difficulties for patients who botch the job; and, since this is an illegal practice, these patients must either die alone or put their doctors, friends, or family members at risk.

Compassion in Dying's attorneys always had more in mind than just a challenge to Washington's state law. They wanted to change the law of the land. "The classic textbook way to bring a suit to the Supreme Court is to have two different cases decided in different ways," says Carla Kerr, the lead attorney on the New York case and a thirty-something partner in Hughes, Hubbard, and Reed, a prestigious New York law firm headed by Kathryn Tucker's father, Robert Sisk. "Then the high court has to settle the dispute. Mine was the case that was supposed to lose."

Lower courts ruled against both cases, but, much to everyone's surprise, they won in their respective appeals courts. Both courts based their decisions on rights granted by the Fourteenth Amendment to the Constitution, which stipulates that no state may "deprive any person of life, liberty, or property without due process of law, nor deny to any person . . . the equal protection of the laws."

The fundamental challenge had been posed: Do laws against assisted suicide violate our constitutional rights? But the rulings did not agree on *which* rights were involved. On March 6, 1996, the U.S. Court of Appeals for the Ninth Circuit, deciding in the Washington case, held that laws against assisted suicide violated a constitutional *liberty* interest, based on the *due process* clause. In his opinion, Circuit Judge Stephen Reinhardt likened the right to assisted suicide to that of abortion, quoting the Supreme Court's decision in *Planned Parenthood v. Casey.* "The decision about how and when to die," he wrote, "is one of 'the most intimate and personal choices a person may make in a lifetime,' a choice 'central to personal dignity and autonomy.' "

In explaining why laws that interfered with this decision infringed on privacy, he continued, "A competent terminally ill adult, having already lived nearly the full measure of his life, has a strong liberty interest in choosing a dignified and humane death rather than being reduced at the end of his existence to a childlike state of helplessness, diapered, sedated, incontinent. How a person dies not only determines the nature of the final period of his existence, but in many cases, the enduring memories held by those who love him."

On April 2, 1996, the U.S. Court of Appeals for the Second Circuit decided the New York case on different grounds: Laws banning assisted suicide violated the Constitution's *equal protection* guarantee by granting different rights to patients depending on the illness and the symptoms they were suffering.

For this reason, the court held, help in dying is not equally applied, and any law against it is unconstitutional.

Not only were these decisions now being challenged in the Supreme Court, but the court was being asked to resolve these competing opinions. In the face of the dilemmas about life and death created by modern medicine, what guidance could be provided by an antique document composed nearly 150 years before antibiotics, and more than 200 years before artificial life supports, chemotherapy, or organ transplants? Can it be adapted to contemporary realities and still remain true to its original principles?

S upreme Court hearings are not televised on Court TV. The only way to view them—aside from being one of the justices, an attorney granted the privilege to appear before the court, a plaintiff, or a respondent in the case—is to be lucky enough to be granted a hard-to-get privileged seat—or to wait in line. By my rough count that day, some five hundred people qualified—most of them doctors, lawyers, ethicists, or policymakers on end-of-life care, in addition to the first fifty people on the line for the general public.

Starting at 9:50 A.M., some 150 reporters were also led in

small groups by marshals of the court through metal detectors, and jammed single file into a small alcove on the side of the main courtroom. We perched in tight rows on assigned skinny, straight-backed chairs, ensconced behind high marble arches barred by huge metal gates and hung with maroon velvet drapes. We would be able to hear the oral arguments, but we could see almost nothing.

To my left in the back row was a reporter for the *Detroit Free Press,* one of the papers in a city where news of Dr. Kevorkian is almost daily fare. He told me reporters there were tired of covering stories of bodies being wheeled out of cabins or dropped off at hospitals, and welcomed the open debate about legalization.

To my right sat NBC reporter Betty Rollin, author of *Last Wish,* the 1985 book in which she described how she'd helped her dying mother commit suicide. I had never forgotten its first paragraph. "Two hours before my mother killed herself," Rollin began, "I noticed she had put on makeup. This shocked me, but it shouldn't have. Whatever the occasion, my mother liked to look her best. That was her way. Just as it was her way to die as she did—not when death summoned her, but when she summoned death."

Now Rollin, who had also battled her own breast cancer, leaned over to me and whispered that she was amazed to have lived long enough to be here today, to see the legalization of assisted suicide reach the Supreme Court.

As we entered the courtroom, marshals of the court handed us a Supreme Court brochure detailing the court's general procedures, and outlining court etiquette at oral arguments. It also contained numbered photos of the nine justices, the numbers corresponding to a small chart indicating their position on the bench. Since so few of us could see the bench, the court marshals held up the appropriate number of fingers to indicate which justice was speaking at any given time. We became a sea of bobbing heads, looking from our notebooks to the marshals' fingers to the numbered chart.

On this Wednesday morning, as is the case with most oral arguments, precisely an hour is to be given to each of the Compassion in Dying cases—Washington first, New York second. Attorneys for each side are allowed just a half-hour to make their case, including addressing the many questions fired at them by the justices from the bench. Attorneys can share their time with others on the same side, but a white warning light goes off at the lectern in front of them when five minutes remain of the whole half-hour slot. Time's up when the light turns to red. This court believes in precision. Yet it also parleys in affairs of the heart.

I n their dissenting opinion in the 1990 Cruzan case, Justices William Brennan, Thurgood Marshall, and Harry Blackmun, all of whom have now either retired or died, wrote one of the most moving statements in all of constitutional law: "Dying is personal. And it is profound," they said. "For many, the thought of an ignoble end, steeped in decay, is abhorrent. A quiet, proud death, bodily integrity intact, is a matter of extreme consequence."

Over the past decade, new faces have appeared on this bench, representing new and changing times—Ruth Bader Ginsburg, Sandra Day O'Connor (who today spoke quite a lot) and Clarence Thomas (who spoke not at all) among them. As a young woman, Ginsburg had often done her homework beside her dying mother's bed. O'Connor had had a mastectomy in battling breast cancer. Other justices have lost wives or family members to drawn-out, often painful illnesses, or suffered medical emergencies of their own.

At 10:00 A.M. on the dot, a marshal of the court shouts the traditional Supreme Court opening call: "Oyez! Oyez! Oyez!" He orders us to rise as the nine justices enter in a whoosh of long black robes through three separate, velvet-draped doors from behind their long, raised, mahogany legal bench, each taking a high-backed, black leather seat.

Chief Justice William Rehnquist, age seventy, enters from the door in the center with Justices John Paul Stevens and Sandra Day O'Connor—the ones with second and third ranking seniority. Ruth Bader Ginsburg, David Souter, and Antonin Scalia come in through the door on the left, behind where they sit. Anthony Kennedy, Clarence Thomas, and Stephen Breyer come in and sit on the right. In minutes, the arguing attorneys are sworn in as members of the Supreme Court Bar.

10:02 A.M.: William C. Williams, Washington's senior assistant attorney general, taking the place of his boss, attorney general Christine Gregroire (she thought he'd be better in oral arguments), stands at the lectern before them. Williams says he is here to defend his state's legislative policy prohibiting assisted suicide. He says that for centuries medical practice and social policy have been organized around certain lines, with no precedent for assisted suicide.

Almost immediately, Justice Ginsburg interrupts him. In the Cruzan decision, she says, the court recognized a liberty interest in the refusal of treatment, yet it allowed Missouri to impose legislative restrictions to regulate it. She wants to know what the state's interests are here. Should the court decide that dying patients have a constitutional right to assisted suicide, what state interests need protecting?

Williams stammers, then collects himself. These interests, Williams tells Ginsburg—a Clinton appointee who is passionate about the rights of women and children—are to protect life (including the prevention of suicide), to prevent patient abuse, and to regulate the medical profession.

"Precisely because physicians have the capacity to injure or perhaps cause the death of their patients," he says, "the state has an important interest in maintaining a clear line between physicians as healers and curers and physicians as instruments of death of their patients."

Justice Souter, who was close to his aging mother before she died, latches onto this issue of abuse. As he understands it, he says, the risk "is that the practice of assistance is going to sort of gravitate down to those who are not terminally ill—to those, in fact, who have not made a truly voluntary or knowing choice. And ultimately it's going to gravitate out of physician-assisted suicide into euthanasia.

"One of the difficulties that I have," he tells Williams, "is that I'm not sure how I should weight or value that risk or those risks. What the argument raises is plausible. I mean, it's easy to see. But I don't know how realistic it is." He says he wants help.

Williams tells Souter he will hear one good example of such blurring later, in the case from New York, and then goes on to defend the state's right to enact protective laws. Even if this court recognizes a liberty interest in allowing assisted suicide for the dying, he says, state legislatures should be allowed to set guidelines on its use or to prohibit it entirely. Or, he concedes, they might simply decide to authorize it.

Williams steps down. He says he wants to save time for later to rebut his opponent, Kathryn Tucker. For now, he'll also share his time with Walter Dellinger, the U.S. acting Solicitor General from the Justice Department, who takes his place at the lectern.

While Williams claims there is no liberty interest at stake here, Dellinger says there is—but not in assisted suicide. He says those who are terminally ill should have a constitutionally protected right to avoid unwanted pain and suffering. Since the state is charged with the preservation of life, he says, laws against assisted suicide should be upheld, but the dying also have the right to have their pain and suffering aggressively treated. Those who are in pain are not in a position to decide on assisted suicide, he says, and points out that the medical profession is struggling to improve the treatment of pain and depression.

The justices see this as a conundrum, Breyer in particular. Justice Stephen Breyer, a former Harvard Law School professor, is a trustee of the Dana Farber Cancer Institute in Boston, where his wife, Joanna, has been a clinical psychologist for ten years. She specializes in pediatric oncology, working with children who are dying of leukemia. Breyer was one of the speakers at the Sixth Annual Race for the Cure, a marathon run in Washington in June 1995 of pink-capped breast cancer survivors and their supporters.

Breyer tells Dellinger that the briefs submitted by the medical organizations in these cases show that "only between 1 and 2 percent of possibly all people need die in pain, but 25 percent or more do die in pain." Whatever the medical profession's intentions are, he asks, what are these people supposed to do about their suffering?

"The fact that 25 percent unnecessarily die in pain," Dellinger says, "shows the task awaiting the medical profession, but it's not a task that calls for the cheap and easy expedient of lethal medication." Dellinger asserts that legalizing assisted suicide will mitigate against the development of proper pain management and palliative care. Then his time is up.

Now Kathryn Tucker, Compassion in Dying's tiny, thirty-something attorney, stands before the bench like a veritable David in the face of many Goliaths. Tucker is a runner and has the lithe, confident stance assumed by women who work out. She tells the court that terminally ill people definitely do have a liberty interest, and it's in choosing a "humane and dignified death." At stake, she says, are issues of choice in being free of unwanted pain and suffering, individual autonomy, and bodily integrity.

The justices leap on her like lions after an antelope. Choice is not the issue for such patients, one justice tells her; rather, the problem is that these patients want a physician to help them out.

"That is correct, Your Honor," Tucker says, "and the reason why we are focused on that is because these dying patients want a peaceful death, they want a humane death, and they want a dignified death. And, in order to access that kind of death they need the assistance of their physician. The physician is the gatekeeper for the medications that can bring that peaceful end to the suffering that for these patients is intolerable."

And now the gate for questions is also open. "Why is it limited to those on the threshold of death?" says Justice Scalia—known for his aggressive conservatism, high moral tone, and fierce wit. "Why not those in long-term pain?" She tries to speak and he interrupts her. "Why shouldn't I have the right to suicide?" Scalia, a Reagan appointee, believes the Constitution should be interpreted literally and that individual rights must be cautiously bestowed.

"Justice Scalia," she says, "we do draw the line at a patient who is confronting death. That individual has a very different choice than the one you posit. This individual does not have a choice between living and dying. This dying patient whose dying process has begun and is under way, this individual has only the choice of how to die. Will that death be brutal, will that death be peaceful."

"I hate to tell you," he tells her, "but the dying process of all of us has begun and is under way. It's just a matter of time. And it seems to me that the patient who has ten years of agony to look forward to has a more appealing case than the patient who is at the threshold of death."

Justice Ginsburg takes issue with the way terminal illness is defined. How clear is it when a person really is terminal? And, "what about the person who is in such agony that that person is not able to assist in her own suicide so she needs the doctor or the nurse to administer the lethal dose?" she asks. "Isn't that person in a more sympathetic situation than the one you're describing?"

Ginsburg is talking about assisted suicide slipping into euthanasia. Tucker tells her assisted suicide is where she draws the line, and that it has to be voluntary and self-administered.

Ginsburg persists. Could not the state legislatures determine this rather than the court? Why does it have to be a constitutional right? And on what basis can the Constitution differentiate the rights of the patient who can take medication herself and the one who cannot?

Tucker says she wants to balance state interests and individual rights, but Scalia is already interrupting: Why differentiate the person in physical pain from the one whose pain is emotional and feels that life is no longer worth living? Why should the government make a judgment that physical pain is worse than emotional suffering? How can one differentiate emotional illness or instability—where we focus on suicide prevention—from the suffering of those who are dying?

And almost before she can answer him—"mental competency," she says, "is a bright line and the decision as to whether the patient is mentally competent is a clinician's judgment"—Souter and Ginsburg are on her again. Why, if assisted suicide is to be a person's right, should the government or a clinician be involved anyway? Both Rehnquist, a Nixon appointee, and O'Connor, appointed by Reagan, tell her they fear that if the right to assisted suicide is recognized for the terminally ill who are in pain, courts and legislatures will spend years afterward coping with challenges to push that legal line one way or another, just as they have with abortion.

Williams, who still has his time for rebuttal, then tries to tell the justices the results of the one study in America on assisted suicide—the Compassion in Dying study that coupled assistance in suicide with active palliative care measures—but he is cut off. "The one historical thing that I can't get totally out of my mind," says Justice Stevens, "is I'm not aware of any doctor ever being convicted of committing this particular offense. Is that right?" Williams says that it is.

"And it's hard," Stevens continues, "to believe it has never been committed." Williams agrees, but he says it's clear it is still a crime. He argues that even if assisted suicide is already an underground practice, it remains somewhat controlled by its criminal status.

Making it legal, he says, might make the potential for abuse far worse. Plus, the medical community is well on the way to improved palliative care, he says. Legalizing assisted suicide might cut such efforts short. It's 11:04 and time is up.

At 11:05 arguments on the New York case begin. Since the Second Circuit Court of Appeals did not recognize a liberty interest in dying but instead saw the need for equal protection for different categories of dying patients, equality—not liberty—will be the focus of this debate.

"Patients who withdraw from life support are not similarly situated to terminally ill people who are seeking physician-assisted suicide," New York's Attorney General Dennis Vacco starts out by telling the court. Ginsburg cuts directly to the core.

Why, she asks, does he think the "terminally ill person who says 'no more life supports, I want to die,' and the person who wants a pill that will achieve the same end" are in different situations? Are the categories really so neat? "We're told in this wealth of briefs," she says, "there are things in between that go on, like sedation for pain . . . [and] increasing the morphine is not rationally distinguishable from giving a person a pill."

Vacco says his opponents have misstated the facts, that sedation is for the "imminently dying," those in "the last hours of death," and that is "for the purpose of treating four distinct symptoms: nausea, shortness of breath, delirium, and excruciating pain . . ."

Rehnquist stops him sharply. "Is that really a correct use of the word 'sedation'?" he asks. "It seems to me you're talking about analgesics, painkillers, whereas sedation is just to kind of make you feel better, not mind things so much, isn't it?" He wants to know if "it's properly called sedation—or, perhaps, something else."

Ginsburg doesn't mince words. She says it has also been called a barbiturate coma and it is not just in the last hour or hours of life. "You render a person unconscious, you withdraw nutrition and water, and it goes on for days and days and the person finally shrivels up and dies, and that, we're told, is permissible and goes on in hospitals in New York."

Vacco tries to press on. "[T]he suggestion that the death is brought on by virtue of a coma coupled with the termination of nutrition and hydration is simply wrong," he says. "Most medical professionals will agree that the death from the underlying illness or, if the drugs are going to suppress respiration so critically, that death will come from those two reasons long before it comes from starvation as a result of the withdrawal of nutrition and hydration."

Ginsburg disagrees. She says the briefs say this "treatment, or whatever you want to call it, that inevitably will lead to death, will do so in a matter of days, not hours. And how is that rationally distinguishable from a pill that will work . . ."

"Justice Ginsburg," he interrupts, "it's rationally distinguishable because it is consistent medical practice!"

Souter expands on Vacco's point. "I take it you mean that once you accept the right of a patient to withdraw all life support, including hydration and feeding, then the only way to prevent excruciating pain as the person nears death is with these extraordinarily high dosages of painkiller that induce coma. So that your justification for the painkiller and the coma is essentially your justification for preventing excruciating pain," he says, "which is caused by a decision which the individual has a right to make. Is that your argument?" Vacco says that it is.

"So it's not merely that the doctors have been doing this," Souter continues. "The argument is that it's justifiable essentially on the ground that the right to withdraw life support is recognized and the right to ameliorate pain is recognized."

Again, Vacco agrees. "And indeed," he says, "the subsequent administration of the palliative care drugs is consistent with the long-standing notion of the double effect, that the drugs in that instance are not being administered for the purpose of causing the death, they are administered in the context of the post-refusal or post-withdrawal of treatment [in the] palliative care of the patient. And that is distinguishable from the act of purposely and intentionally providing a drug to kill the patient."

"Letting patients die" as opposed to "killing them" is where New York has chosen to draw its legal line, Vacco says. Ginsburg tells him that other states or legislatures or nations might decide— have decided—to draw it elsewhere in an equally rational or irrational way. And why, Justice Stevens wonders, is there any less risk of abuse involved in pulling a plug than there is in physician-assisted suicide?

Ginsburg brings up a different risk: that patients will suffer unnecessarily if the law "makes doctors fearful of putting people out of pain because they don't know whether that's going to constitute physician-assisted suicide or accepted relief of pain." She wants Vacco—and later Dellinger, who shares his time—to address the essential issue of whether this isn't one big sham of "winks and nods" because, she says, "physician-assisted suicide goes on for anybody who is sophisticated enough to want it." And, their time up, they deny that it really does.

Arguing on behalf of Compassion in Dying is Laurence Tribe—a constitutional law expert from Harvard University who regularly appears before this high court—who simply mocks what he describes as a naively irrational, too-neat distinction that does not address how many Americans actually die.

Take Jane Doe, the seventy-six-year-old plaintiff in the New York case. Cancer had wrapped around her esophagus, choking her so that she couldn't eat, couldn't swallow, and could barely breathe. After a long and difficult degenerative process, she needed a surgically implanted feeding tube to survive.

"As she neared death," Tribe says, "she was the recipient of all sorts of medical interventions that she could have said no to. Some of them really weren't lifesaving; they just prevented even greater torment, agony, disintegration." She could have told doctors to remove the feeding tube, even if her sole purpose in doing so was to die, but she was not legally allowed to have her physician give her medication to take her own life.

"Jane Doe didn't want the surgical removal of the tube," Tribe says, "because that would have left her starving and dehydrated—not just in discomfort but . . . in agony for a couple of weeks and she didn't want to be turned into a zombie, she wouldn't have accepted terminal sedation." Yet, she had this right under New York State law. Is this suicide or not? And who monitors this for abuse? And what safeguards are there?

How great, really, is the difference between sedation and assisted suicide, Tribe asks. Is it, in fact, *the technology* that makes the difference in what a dying patient can choose? Why couldn't one just as easily describe a decision to remove life supports as suicide as one could in the decision to take Seconal? Since there are no guidelines for any of it, Tribe maintains, it is all potentially subject to abuse.

"If anyone thinks about what happens in the hospital wards when terminal sedation is given, when the morphine drip is increased, when the person is asleep and it's said that they wanted the respirator disconnected but there are no required witnesses, that's pretty scary," Tribe points out.

"The New York state legislature—which initially outlawed all physician-assisted suicide, not by identifying physicians, but by just saying if A helps B commit suicide, it's a crime—now confronts a rather different regime. It's a regime that says near the end of life, whether or not the intent of somebody is deliberately to die, if certain techniques are used—a combination of morphine and barbiturates, a surgical removal of something implanted—we don't call that suicide. And actually we don't regulate it very much. [But] if the patient is prescribed, at the patient's request, a lethal drug, we make that absolutely forbidden."

"This is a dangerous authority that you would be giving to the medical profession," Justice Ginsburg tells him.

Tribe replies: "They already have it, unfortunately."

Time's up at 12:06 P.M. We all rise, and the justices leave in another whoosh of black robes, out through the marble columns and maroon velvet drapes and the three doors behind them. We are told they will deliberate in two days, but we won't hear their decision until the end of term. It comes down on June 26, 1997.

Today, the modus operandi for medical care at the end of life is to manipulate treatment toward a managed death; what might fairly be called "assisted dying" is, in fact, the way nearly all of us are going to die.

As was noted in Chapter 6, in 1990 the American Hospital Association estimated that 70 percent of the six thousand or so daily deaths in this country are "somehow timed or negotiated, with all concerned parties privately concurring on withdrawal of some death-delaying technology or not even starting it in the first place." A 1997 California study put this number as high as 90 percent.

This means that withholding, withdrawing, or refusing treatment is the way most Americans now die, "letting nature take its course" usually *after* it becomes apparent that further medical interventions would only prolong dying.

Definitions are important here: In *physician-assisted suicide*, a doctor makes available the means of suicide, for example, by providing a prescription for lethal drugs. The patient must take this medication himself; to do so, he must either be able to swallow or have some other means (say, a feeding tube) to ingest it.

In *euthanasia*, on the other hand, a doctor takes some action to intentionally kill a patient, for example, by giving a lethal injection, as might be done in a legal execution, or when a veterinarian puts a pet to sleep.

Relatives or friends of the dying may also offer assistance in suicide or euthanasia. While this, too, is illegal, courts have been notoriously lenient in cases of so-called "mercy killing."

And yet, none of these labels applies—according to the medical profession and the courts—when a life-sustaining treatment is either withheld or withdrawn, or when narcotic or other medication for pain or shortness of breath is increased so much that the unintended side effect is death. Intention is key here so far as medicine and the law is concerned. But intention is often subjective and unspoken.

"It's called passive euthanasia," Norman Fost, director of the Program in Medical Ethics at the University of Wisconsin, told the *New York Times*. "You can ask who's involved and is it really consensual, but there is no question that these are planned deaths. We know who is dying. Patients aren't just found dead in their beds."

As Dr. Joanne Lynn told the *Times* in the same article, "her typical case might be an old man, fragile and with multiple medical problems. She will finally discharge him from the hospital and send him home to his family, knowing that the decision to send him home is a decision to let death come soon. If he develops a fever, there is no reason even to take his temperature, she said. 'The agreement is that he will not come back into the hospital for almost anything.'

"Dr. Lynn added, 'Many of the decisions may be ambiguously

articulated. They may be as much as a nod, something brought up in conversation, 'How do you feel about staying here?' "

However openly or ambiguously it is phrased, the decision to die is made. It might be a decision for an ill, hospitalized, young cancer patient not to have that last round of chemotherapy when her cancer has failed to respond to earlier treatments and has already spread from her breast to her lungs and her bones.

It might be a decision not to use antibiotics to treat pneumonia in a frail elderly woman who has suffered a paralyzing, brain-damaging stroke. Or to reduce heart medications for a man with congestive heart failure who suddenly develops kidney impairment, a bowel obstruction, or other organ failures. Together with a signed "do not resuscitate" order, it is clear to all medical personnel that the patient is being managed toward death.

More obviously, the decision to die might take the form of a choice to remove a respirator or a feeding tube, or even an IV if fluids are causing congestion in the lungs. It might involve giving high doses of narcotics or barbiturates to manage suffering after removal, or to provide terminal sedation for unbearable symptoms.

Perhaps the most extraordinary instance of a modern managed death is in organ transplants, in which death may be engineered to occur on the operating table to allow for speedy harvesting of healthy organs. Transplantation creates a particularly gray area because organs must be maintained within a biologically living body as long as possible to remain viable. This raises uncomfortable new questions: If the organ is "living" when doctors remove it for transplant, is it the physicians themselves that actually cause the death of the person? And, if an organ can be taken within only two minutes after the person's heart has stopped, what are we to make of the fact that, if survival was the motive, CPR might be successful during those two minutes?

Compounding this issue, medications may be given to dying patients designated as organ donors that can hasten death, with the intent to keep the organs healthy. One drug blocks the body's ability to release adrenaline and can harm certain seriously ill patients' ability to rally the body and fight back. Another drug prevents blood clotting and can be harmful to brain-damaged patients with internal bleeding.

In more ordinary situations, the decision to let a patient die is often not made by any one person—even the patient him- or herself. It arises out of a social framework surrounding that patient within a medical-care environment. "Sometimes," Dr. Lynn told me, "it's not even a decision made by anyone but by the force of the clinical situation—it doesn't matter much in terms of survival whether and when we decide to go on treating."

All these medical decisions are considered ethical, legal, even good medical practice. But significantly, it is the doctor—not the patient or the family—who defines the treatment options that lead to these decisions and who is in control of implementing them.

In fact, it seems as if Americans are arguing about two forms of assisted dying—one controlled by doctors (in the best of circumstances, with patient consultation and consent), and the other controlled by patients, asking their doctors for help at a time when they (and not necessarily their doctors) decide it is time.

This fine line has more than a whiff of legal and verbal sophistry about it. The moral line being mapped out by the medical profession is "letting die" as opposed to "making die," but patients and families may see little difference. In hospital beds and corridors, in doctors' offices and in nursing homes, they find themselves forced into careful negotiations with their doctors at the end of a loved one's life. Sometimes these negotiations feel patronizing or humiliating to patients and families. They know that the doctors have the means—as the gatekeepers to drugs—to smooth the passage to death. But those means remain painfully out of reach.

The schisms Americans feel about all of this run deep. Not only is it difficult in many cases even to know what options exist, but it is hard to define the proper role for doctors, what is morally right, where personal choice lies, and how to weigh long-held precepts of family morality.

In the face of this lack of clarity, we are seeing a tidal wave of public opinion wanting to take back control at the end of life from physicians, and of well-meaning physicians both scrambling to do better—and to prevent having to give up control.

Various polls have shown that anywhere from 50 to 75 percent of the American public favor legalization of assisted suicide. Nearly all the major medical organizations in this country oppose it. When polled in private, however, individual physicians' responses are much closer to those of the general public.

In fact, a grassroots movement around assisted suicide has come of age over the past decade. Crowds may not be shouting from the windows—as in the movie *Network*—but the message is the same: "We're made as hell and we're not going to take it anymore!"

It took an Englishman named Derek Humphry to first bring assisted suicide to America's attention. In the early 1970s, Humphry was a successful reporter for the *London Times*, married for nearly two decades to Jean, the mother of their three grown sons. Then they discovered that Jean had breast cancer, and she began chemotherapy.

By 1975 the cancer had spread to her bones. As Humphry describes it, she made him promise that if she needed him to, he would help her die. She asked him to get a doctor to prescribe some lethal drugs and have them ready in case things got too bad. Only after he'd agreed did she consent to another round of chemotherapy.

Soon Jean was completely confined to bed. When she moved, her pain was excruciating. If she leaned forward, her ribs would snap. Humphry got together a strong mix of Seconal and codeine, while Jean lived on pain medication. Then one morning they both knew it was time.

Humphry mixed the drugs in a big mug of coffee with a "lashing of sugar," and put the brew on the bedside to let it cool. After they'd talked awhile, Jean picked up the mug, drank it down, and fell asleep.

Humphry sat with her. About twenty minutes later Jean vomited and Derek panicked. He wasn't sure enough of the drugs had stayed down. He wondered what he'd do if she awoke. He thought if she didn't die she might come back in worse shape than before. He thought about putting a pillow over her head. He willed Jean not to wake up. He sat and watched. About 1:50 in the afternoon, her breathing slowed, and Jean died.

Three years later, Humphry published this story in his 1978 book, *Jean's Way*. By 1980, he'd remarried and moved to Los Angeles to work at the *Los Angeles Times*. That year, he and his second wife, Ann, started the Hemlock Society. A lay organization, now with chapters nationwide, its mission was to give information to terminally ill people who wanted to know how to die.

Humphry and his organization might have remained relatively unknown, but in March 1991, he self-published *Final Exit: The Practicalities of Self-Deliverance and Assisted Suicide for the Dying*. It was a medical how-to, parts of which had been a Hemlock Society handout. Clearly, the country was ready. *Final Exit* blasted onto the *New York Times* best-seller list and stayed there for eighteen weeks.

Final Exit detailed specific drugs, dosages, and exact techniques that would cause death in the quickest, most painless ways. A patient just needed a doctor's prescription; the problem was, it wasn't legal for physicians to give one.

Another problem was the uncertainty of do-it-yourself suicide. Dosages can be inexact, which was the very reason for the book in the first place, and whatever a patient takes, it might not all stay down. Humphry's book underscored the need for a fail-safe. He suggested that in addition to drugs, patients should be ready to put a plastic bag over their heads, and he described just how to tie the bottom. "The fundamental reason why most patients do not choose to do it themselves," Humphry later wrote, "is that they fear a botched attempt."

Although the official suicide rate remained constant, the year after *Final Exit* was published, deaths by asphyxiation with plastic bag in New York City alone rose from eight to thirty-three. Nationally, plastic bag asphyxiations rose from 334 to 437, an increase of 30.8 percent.

For Humphry, *Final Exit* represented only an interim solution. Rather than have deaths like Jean's be surreptitious, illegal, and uncertain affairs, Humphry wanted doctors to be able to help those who were terminally ill die easier, well-planned deaths if they so chose.

Beginning with the failed attempt to put assisted suicide (and euthanasia) on the 1988 California ballot, Humphry became a key player in a series of state ballot drives. After *Final Exit* was published, he used the profits to help finance new initiatives in Washington in 1991, in California in 1992, and in Oregon in 1994.

When the ballot measures in Washington in 1991 and in California in 1992 were both defeated by the identical margin of 54 to 46 percent, proponents went back to the drawing boards, writing new ballot measures that focused on assisted suicide only. They also added specific guidelines as safeguards against possible patient abuse.

In 1994, Oregon voters approved just such a measure—called the Death With Dignity Act—by 51 to 49 percent. The ballot measure legalized assisted suicide for Oregon residents who: 1) were told by their doctor they had an incurable and irreversible disease that would, within reasonable medical judgment, produce death within six months; 2) had this medical prognosis confirmed; 3) seemed to have no evidence of clinical depression or untreated pain or other symptoms; 4) made both an oral and a written request for help in dying. The written request must have been witnessed by at least two other individuals to ensure that the request was voluntary. A fifteen-day waiting period was written in.

In approving this ballot measure, Oregon became the first state to legalize assisted suicide. Before the law could go into effect, however, it was blocked by legal appeals led by James Bopp and others connected with the National Right to Life Committee, Bopp's Indiana-based National Legal Center for the Medically Dependent and Disabled, and the Catholic Church.

The U.S. Ninth Circuit Court of Appeals turned down their appeal to reverse the vote, but when it went back to the Oregon legislature for implementation, state lawmakers refused to put the ballot measure into law. Instead, the legislature sent it back to the voters for a revote in the November 1997 election.

At the time of the 1988 California signature drive, a Hemlock Society poll of doctors in that state found that 57 percent of them had been asked for assistance in dying by their terminally ill patients. Nearly all these doctors made the surprising statement—given the AMA's blanket disapproval—that they thought these requests *rational*, given the patients' conditions. In fact, 76 percent of the California doctors polled thought patients should have the option of physician-assisted suicide, 23 percent said they had helped someone die at least once in their practice (81 percent of these more than once), and 51 percent said they would practice physician-assisted suicide if it were legal.

The year 1988 also saw the publication of a provocative article called "It's Over, Debbie," in the *Journal of the American Medical Association* (*JAMA*). It was purportedly a first-person account by a young gynecology hospital resident of being awakened during the night by a nurse calling to say a patient was having trouble getting some rest. When the sleepy resident arrived, he (or she) found a twenty-year-old, dubbed "Debbie," in the end stage of ovarian cancer, vomiting, in terrible pain, with severe, labored breathing and shortness of breath. She had wasted to 80 pounds, hadn't responded to chemotherapy, and was being given only "supportive care." She hadn't slept or eaten in two days and allegedly said: "Let's get this over with."

Without any discussion with her or with her mother, who was also in her hospital room, the resident filled a syringe with 20 mg of morphine and injected Debbie. Within seconds her breathing slowed to normal while her mother stroked her hair. "I waited for the inevitable next effect of depressing the respiratory drive," the doctor wrote. "With clocklike certainty, within four minutes the breathing rate slowed even more, then became irregular, then ceased. The [mother] stood erect and seemed relieved. It's over, Debbie."

Even though the girl only weighed 80 pounds at the time she died, pain experts later said that 20 mg of morphine wasn't enough to kill a dying cancer patient, especially one on long-term narcotics for pain. These led to questions about the article's authenticity; *JAMA*'s editors backed it, however, claiming it raised issues that needed to be aired.

Indeed, within four months the article had elicited more than 150 letters and set off great controversy. Most of the early letters were from doctors—three-quarters objected to what the young gynecologist had done, and two-thirds lambasted *JAMA* for publishing it. But later letters from the public were very different. They suggested, *JAMA* editor George D. Lundberg, M.D., wrote, "that many of our patients would want active euthanasia if needed, and they would want it performed by doctors."

By 1989, twelve prominent physicians wrote a *New England Journal of Medicine* (*NEJM*) article—the very article that had elated Dr. Kevorkian when he read it in the Royal Oak library—arguing for more aggressive measures to help the dying. "The concept of a good death does not mean simply the withholding of technological treatments that serve only to prolong the act of dying," they wrote. "It also requires the art of deliberately creating a medical environment that allows a peaceful death."

In 1991, the debate escalated to a boiling point over another article in the *NEJM,* this one by Timothy Quill, M.D., a faculty member and primary-care physician at the University of Rochester School of Medicine. Dr. Quill, trained as both an internist and a psychiatrist, is an unassuming man who for eight years was a hospice medical director. In his article, "Death and Dignity: A Case of Individualized Decision Making," Dr. Quill described his part in the death of Patricia Diane Trumbull, a longtime patient of his who was dying of leukemia. He recounted how Diane, as she liked to be called, had decided to refuse a bone marrow transplant—which would have been painful and possibly would have given her a one in four chance of survival—preferring instead to remain at home with her family, with the help of a hospice.

Diane feared a terrible end, and for her own peace of mind, asked Dr. Quill for a prescription for Seconal. These were barbiturate sleeping pills that any doctor might prescribe, but Quill knew—they had discussed it—that she might eventually use them to take her own life. In June 1990, Diane took the pills and died with her family's full knowledge, but to protect them—and Dr. Quill—from prosecution, she ended up dying alone.

Some doctors critical of Dr. Quill said that he hadn't adequately assessed Diane for depression, that he might not have controlled her pain or other symptoms well enough, that he should have been more aggressive about her care. But surprisingly, a good many other doctors, as well as major professional medical organizations, law enforcement bodies, and the general public lent him immediate support.

After the article appeared, state law enforcement authorities and professional licensing bodies investigated Dr. Quill, but they declined to chastise him. A grand jury refused to indict him. The state's Board for Professional Medical Conduct backed him, declaring "it would not be consistent with good medical practice for a physician to refuse to treat terminally ill patients for anxiety, insomnia, or pain because the physician suspects the patient might use the medication to end his or her life." And John R. Ball, M.D., executive vice-president of the American College of Physicians, an organization of the nation's 70,000 internists, wrote to say its ethics committee believed Quill "acted ethically and humanely and in the highest traditions of our profession."

Afterward, Dr. Quill charged that many other doctors secretly do what he had done. "The more fundamental issue is abandonment," he said. "You need to have someone see the process through." His one regret was that because law criminalizes the practice, he'd abandoned Diane by letting her die alone. Not only was Dr. Quill never found guilty of wrongdoing, but no doctor in the history of American law has yet been found guilty for doing what he had done.

It was probably the AIDS epidemic—combined with take-charge baby boomers coming of age—that pushed a good number of physicians over the legal edge.

Among the six patients who were plaintiffs in the assisted suicide cases before the Supreme Court, three had AIDS; two had cancer; and the last had lung disease. Two of the physicians cared primarily for AIDS patients and two more saw AIDS patients as part of their practice. Within the AIDS community, assistance in dying, the sharing of lethal recipes, and the bequeathing after death of leftover drugs had become a near-commonplace practice by the mid-1990s. A February 1997 report in *NEJM* found that more than half of the San Francisco Bay Area physicians treating AIDS patients had helped at least one patient commit suicide.

A 1994 study of physicians in the state of Washington, published in *JAMA* in 1996, found physicians saying they had complied with one-fourth of all patient requests for direct aid in dying. Of 156 patients who asked for assisted suicide, 38 (24 percent) received prescriptions (21 percent of these died as a result). Of the 58 patients who requested euthanasia, 14 (24 percent) received medications from their doctors and died. Patients with AIDS, cancer, and neurological diseases were most likely to ask.

Two different 1996 studies published in *NEJM* found that 60 percent of Oregon physicians believed that physician-assisted suicide should be legal.

By the time they filed their lawsuits, Compassion in Dying

(CID) was able to recruit a roster of distinguished physicians in support of their cases. In addition to Dr. Quill, the New York case included Samuel Klagsbrun, M.D., a psychiatrist who treats both AIDS and cancer patients, the executive medical director of the Four Winds Hospital in Katonah, New York, and an internationally known hospice consultant; and Howard Grossman, M.D., an internist and attending physician at Saint Luke's/Roosevelt Hospital and Saint Vincent's Hospital in New York City, who mainly treats AIDS patients.

The Washington suit was joined by Thomas Preston, M.D., chief of cardiology at Pacific Medical Center and faculty member at the University of Washington; Harold Glucksberg, M.D., an oncologist, also at Pacific Medical Center; Abigail Halperin, M.D., a specialist in family medicine and medical director of the Providence Uptown Medical Care Center in Seattle, where she often sees AIDS patients; and Peter Shalit, M.D., Ph.D., an AIDS specialist.

While opponents of assisted suicide argue that proper pain management and the treatment of depression will eliminate a need for assisted suicide, these physicians maintained that even the best of palliative care might not be good enough for a small group of patients.

"If people think they can guarantee a pain-free death they live on another planet," Dr. Quill told me. "Complicated deaths are not atypical. It's not easy to control pain. It's a trade-off, with various symptoms and side effects. It's all relative, balancing uncomfortable symptoms versus pain."

Dr. Klagsbrun challenges the notion that treatment for depression will eliminate patients' desire for assisted suicide. He distinguishes between clinical—and therefore treatable—depression and what he considers a rational desire to end hopeless and intolerable suffering in the face of life with no other options.

"The best answer for the dying is superb hospice care," he says. "But I moved to the point of wanting to decriminalize assisted suicide when a small number of patients whom I placed in excellent situations still felt, 'I want out.' " He says the mere knowledge that a doctor will help when it is time, he says, can not only lift depression for some patients, but give a sense of control and security that can prolong life.

■   ■   ■

What might legalized assisted suicide look like in practice, given conditions in which there are guidelines and state-of-the-art palliative care?

After Compassion in Dying had been in operation for thirteen months, Dr. Preston and Rev. Mero conducted a study of the three hundred patients who had requested the organization's help. Using guidelines that were nearly identical to those in the Oregon Death With Dignity Act (in fact, the chief architect of the Oregon ballot measure was Barbara Coombs Lee, Compassion's executive director) the organization assessed patients, and made medical referrals for palliative care, and family and patient support. One additional stipulation was added to the guidelines: that inadequate health insurance or other economic concerns did not motivate the suicide request. Compassion charged no fees for its services.

Preston and Mero discovered that as a result of their staff's screening, treatment, social services referral, and counseling efforts, just forty-six of the three hundred people who contacted them actually ended up qualifying for help in dying under the organization's guidelines.

The primary symptoms were shortness of breath—not pain, which generally was well controlled—and nausea, vomiting, loss of excretory function, extreme weakness, and dependency. Of the forty-six offered help, twenty-four people took the drugs prescribed and died—thirteen men and eleven women. They ranged in age from thirty-one to eighty-four. Eleven had cancer, ten had AIDS, two had neurological diseases, and one had lung disease. All were largely confined to a bed or a chair.

"These patients who chose termination of life did so because of what they characterized as unbearable suffering," Preston and Mero wrote. "They expressed their suffering in physical and emotional or spiritual forms. . . . All patients expressed a strong aversion to drifting into a semi-comatose or comatose condition, and many were particularly vehement about not wanting drug-induced coma, which one patient described as 'an indignity worse than death.'

"These patients had between fifteen and forty hours of face-to-face contact with Compassion staff members over an average of five weeks (range two weeks to three months) prior to dying," the study reported. "No suicide attempt was unsuccessful . . . Members of Compassion did not supply drugs, and no physician associated with the organization wrote a prescription for or altered the medical care of any of these patients."

Of the twenty-two who qualified for Compassion in Dying's services but in the end did not use them, "nine were in institutions (hospice, nursing home, hospital) and were unable to obtain medicines necessary to hasten death. Five of these died 'naturally' from their diseases, and four starved to death. We estimate that these nine patients lived from one to six weeks longer than if they had been able to obtain medicines for hastening death."

The remaining thirteen died at home. Eight asked their doctors for medications but the doctors refused, even though in each case these doctors acknowledged that the patient was terminally ill. "Three of these eight subsequently committed suicide," the study read, "two by starvation and one by gunshot. . . . An additional five patients who were able to obtain the necessary medicines died 'naturally' before deciding on suicide." For those, the authors argued, Compassion in Dying's service provided last-resort security.

Opponents of legalization fear patient abuse and say that guidelines to regulate it would never work. Yet this study shows that the guidelines did seem to work. Preston and Mero argue that the availability of prescriptions, paradoxically, can postpone life. Knowing one has a fail-safe at the end can give patients a sense of control, a confidence to endure more, a belief that should things get too bad the means to a quick end are at hand.

Other industrialized countries with advanced medical care are facing similar end-of-life dilemmas, with legalized assisted suicide now hotly debated in the legislatures, courts, and media in Britain, Canada, Israel, Japan, South Africa, Australia, and Colombia, among other countries.

In Germany, assistance in suicide is a legal option, but it is organized as part of a lay movement. There is a huge, voluntary movement for help in dying, but this movement is kept separate from the medical profession. Euthanasia, however, is strictly illegal, primarily because of its negative association with Nazi medical atrocities.

In the Netherlands, assisted suicide and euthanasia are not officially legalized but are publicly condoned and practiced under highly regulated circumstances. The Dutch medical system is state supported, which means health-care and long-term care costs are all covered for families; and local, primary-care family doctors usually know families from birth through death.

Dutch doctors must conform to strict guidelines and report the circumstances of all assisted deaths. Even allowing for some failures to report, this has provided the best data on the practice available anywhere in the world—although the same objective findings are interpreted differently by supporters and opponents.

A national commission, called the Remmelink Commission, examined the 41,587 deaths that occurred between August and December 1990, paying special attention to the 5,197 in which *some* medical decision was made to end life—whether through withdrawal or withholding of treatment, increasing narcotics that might hasten death, or prescribing a prescription or administering a lethal drug (respectively, assisted suicide and euthanasia).

The Dutch require that patients who want assistance in dying make an explicit written request of their doctors, which the doctor must file with the Dutch Medical Society. Based on its study of these reports and of all death certificates, the Commission estimated that over twenty-five thousand patients a year "seek assurance from their doctors that they will assist them if suffering becomes unbearable." About nine thousand people actually make explicit written requests for help in dying. About a third, or less than three thousand, are agreed to by doctors.

As we have seen, debate in the United States on assisted suicide tends to focus on the undertreatment of pain—the argument being that if pain were treated assisted suicide wouldn't be necessary. However, "loss of dignity" was given as the main reason for requesting help in dying by 57 percent of Dutch patients; 46 percent said the reason was intolerable pain. Another 46 percent didn't want to have what they termed an "unworthy dying," 33 percent didn't want to be dependent on others, and 23 percent said they were "tired of life." (These add up to more than 100 percent because people often had several reasons.) In just 10 of 187 cases chosen for special examination of patients' motives was pain cited as the sole reason.

Frits Van Dam, Ph.D., a world-renowned Dutch psychologist and expert in quality-of-life research, contests the notion that treatment of depression is the key to avoiding requests for assisted suicide. "It's an existential decision," he told me. "It's a patronizing response to say 'You're depressed and need medications.' One can also decide to respect human free will and say it's a political and philosophical issue to decide when to die." To him, and to other Dutch physicians, deciding to take one's own life when one is terminally ill has to do with individual choice, free will, dignity, and pride.

Dutch doctors have been publicly attacked by American physicians and ethicists for what some see as free and dangerous practices that could take them down the slippery slope toward involuntary euthanasia. Yet when the Dutch repeated this study several years later, the findings—published in *NEJM* in 1996—showed that the small percentage of deaths that may have involved euthanasia were not expanding in a statistically significant way, but were nearly identical to those in the first study.

More important, on closer examination of statistics comparing the Netherlands and the United States, the figures on how death occurs are surprisingly similar. What Dutch doctors actually do at the end of life resembles what American physicians do in treating their dying patients, with one major difference: In the Netherlands help in dying is provided by family physicians who know their patients and their families over many years, and it is highly public, tightly monitored, and regulated. In the United States, end-of-life care is generally managed by teams of specialists, many of whom are unknown to patients beforehand, and what may be called "assisted dying" is not monitored, regulated, or even openly discussed.

Somewhere between 3 percent and 5 percent of all deaths in the Dutch study reportedly occurred as a result of euthanasia, but the number varies because of uncertainty about whether deaths in which narcotics were increased are accurately termed *euthanasia*. Here we might call those same deaths terminal sedation.

Significantly, the very largest figure given for euthanasia in the Remmelink Commission study—5 percent of deaths—is nearly identical to the most conservative estimate of people requiring aggressive help from doctors in studies here. This figure nearly matches those in the Memorial Sloan-Kettering study, examined in Chapter 4, on requests among cancer patients for direct help in dying, and is the same as the number of patients who either killed themselves or likely received terminal sedation.

Even more interesting, 18 percent of the total Dutch deaths in which *some* medical decision was made to end life were the result of withholding or withdrawing life-sustaining technology. (Comparing this with the 70 to 90 percent estimated in America today, it's hard to know if semantics or more aggressive medical practice is being discussed.) Another 18 percent of the Dutch died when pain medications were increased, a practice that has not yet been studied here, and is no doubt lumped together with nontreatment.

Clearly, from the American figures on withholding treatment and from the Sloan-Kettering study, American physicians are withholding treatment at the end more than the Dutch are and are officially doing less to aggressively help patients end life—at their own request—when it gets unbearable. Nor, as we have seen, are there any legally binding guidelines on withholding or withdrawing medical treatment, or on terminal sedation.

Although pain experts here argue that the Dutch are less sophisticated about palliative care than we are so they have to resort more often to euthanasia, this charge prevents doctors here from recognizing the terrible impact of the modern dying experience for a small but significant number of people whose pain cannot be controlled, and for the large number of those for whom pain, if it exists, is not the primary issue.

B eneath the Supreme Court steps during the oral arguments on January 8 are nearly a hundred activists involved in a group called Not Dead Yet. Some are in wheelchairs, some are missing limbs, some suffering from MS or cerebral palsy, some on respirators and feeding tubes, and some are blind activists led by their guide dogs. They hold makeshift signs and chant loudly: "We're not dead yet! We want to live!" Stephen Lenker, R.N., a former nurse from Indiana who is wheelchair-bound as a result of MS, later tells me, "If this law is made, it will start off with physician-assisted suicide for the terminally ill, but it will spread. If they give us things to lead a productive life we don't want to die, we want to live. But insurance companies don't want to pay for what we need."

"This country is very prejudiced toward those with disabilities," says Diane Coleman, founder of the group. "The medical community isn't trained in disabilities. The health-care system, especially with the growth of managed care, isn't set up to care for those who need expensive long-term care. What 'death with dignity' really means is dying without being disabled." She questions how voluntary a choice to die really will be.

Not all groups representing the disabled agree with them, but it is true that care of the disabled is expensive. In addition to the disabled, many other people worry that in an age of health-care cost containment, it will be more expedient for physicians and families to pressure patients to die than make the effort to care for them.

Already, America is a nation with a two-tier system of health care, one for the rich and the other for the poor. Given the sorry track record of medical care for the poor, and tragic experiments like the Tuskegee syphilis study, it is not surprising that many— particularly those who are poor or minorities—fear abuse at the hands of the physicians.

These fears show up in polls on assisted suicide. One telephone poll, conducted in 1996 by the *Washington Post*, found that 51 percent of the total number of people polled thought assisted suicide should be legalized. However, 55 percent of those who were white thought so, as opposed to 20 percent of those who were black. And while 58 percent of those with incomes over $75,000 said it should be legal, only 37 percent of those with incomes under $15,000 did.

Men and women also responded differently: 54 percent of the men felt it should be legalized, but only 47 percent of the women did. There were similar breakdowns by age: 52 percent of those between 18 and 29 years of age thought assisted suicide should be legalized, as opposed to 35 percent of those who were over 70.

In short, those who feel relatively powerful within our society are far more comfortable with the notion of assisted suicide than more vulnerable groups.

Doctors, too, worry that in a managed-care environment they

might be required to help patients die. "The ban on physician assisted suicide," the AMA's amicus brief states, "helps ensure that patients will never lose the trust that must exist for the relationships between health care professionals and patients to flourish."

"All doctors help patients die," says Dr. Joanne Lynn, who joined in a brief filed by the American Geriatric Society opposing legalization of assisted suicide. "The question is do they do it in a way that breaks the law?" While she admits seeing the need for aggressive help for a few patients whose level of suffering cannot be relieved by any other means, she says that the benefit of legalization for the few are outweighed by a greater risk of abuse for the many.

Dr. Lynn says the idea of autonomous decision making by a patient at the end of life implies that the person can think clearly, which for someone who is dying and frail is no more possible than for a woman in the midst of a long and tough labor. The overwhelming emotional and physical experience raises for her the question of what *voluntary* means in such a situation.

"Fragile, old, and dying people want to please their families and doctors, not to be a burden," she says, "and they don't know what to do at the end, especially amid the choices of modern medicine. They can easily be swayed by children who might say, 'How?' when these old people say they want to die, rather than, 'How can I help you, Mom? I love you, and I want you to live.' "

Dr. Lynn also raises the question of what would happen if physician-assisted suicide didn't work. She imagines a hospital or a nursing home, with a frail elderly person, usually a woman. A barbiturate like Seconal is not the best medication to take life, she says. The lethal dosage varies with the individual; the patient may vomit—or be unable to swallow at all. Lethal injections are in fact swifter, surer, and more humane, but of course these would be classified as euthanasia under current definitions of assisted suicide.

So what happens, Dr. Lynn asks, if the pills she is supposed to give the patient don't work? Will she be forced to break the law by giving a lethal injection anyway? Will she have to resort to placing pillows over the patients' heads? Will she then be open to charges of malpractice if her patient doesn't die, or worse, if the failed attempt causes brain damage? Furthermore, she says, why should she have to do this just because she is a physician? Why not someone else?

On June 26, 1997, the Supreme Court announced its unanimous decision that assisted suicide was not a Constitutional right, that the laws that criminalized it in Washington and New York violated neither Americans' liberty interests nor the equal protection clause.

The main opinion in the Washington case, written by Chief Justice Rehnquist, cited Western civilization's long-standing opposition to both suicide and assisting in suicides. The opinion also cited the fear of patient abuse and the possibility that assisted suicide would blur into euthanasia.

In the New York case, the court upheld the distinctions between "letting a patient die" and "making that patient die"—the legal line the state had drawn between withdrawal of treatment and assisted suicide.

These decisions, however, in no way shut the door to legalization. Both specifically returned the issue to the states for further action. They also left open the possibility that the Supreme Court would be willing to hear future cases involving assisted suicide.

"Throughout the Nation," Rehnquist wrote in the Washington case, "Americans are engaged in an earnest and profound debate about the morality, legality, and practicality of physician assisted suicide. Our holding permits this debate to continue, as it should in a democratic society."

Five of the other justices—Ginsburg, Stevens, Souter, Breyer, and O'Connor—wrote opinions of their own, exploring particular aspects of the cases. These concurring opinions may also be cited as precedents. Justice O'Connor took care to note that while there may not be a generalized right to assisted suicide, individual dying patients do have the right to have their pain and terrible symptoms well controlled.

Breyer rejected the way Rehnquist had formulated the liberty interest the court considered. Rather than see it as a "right to commit suicide with another's assistance," he found that there may be a right to a humane and dignified death, a "right to die with dignity. But irrespective of the exact words used, at its core would lie personal control over the manner of death, professional medical assistance, and the avoidance of unnecessary and severe physical suffering—combined." State laws that impede proper pain management, he said, may have to be changed.

Stevens suggested that a blanket statement against assisted suicide as a Constitutional right did not mean it might not be right "as an aspect of individual freedom." He suggested that a valid case for help in dying might be made by an individual patient, and pointedly challenged the medical profession to do better.

"Encouraging the development and ensuring the availability of adequate pain treatment is of utmost importance; palliative care, however, cannot alleviate all pain and suffering," he held. "An individual adequately informed of the care alternatives thus might make a rational choice for assisted suicide. For such an individual, the State's interest in preventing potential abuse and mistake is only minimally impacted."

He also pointed out that even without assisted suicide, doctors are increasingly complicit with death. "[B]ecause physicians are already involved in making decisions that hasten the death of terminally ill patients—through termination of life support, withholding of medical treatment, and terminal sedation—" he wrote, "there is in fact significant tension between the traditional view of the physician's role and the actual practice in a growing number of cases."

Thus, the Supreme Court's decision did not end the dispute, but rather issued a starting shot in what is sure to become a long state-by-state battle in legislatures and in the courts. Even as the decision was announced, organizers were gearing up for the November 1997 revote on Oregon's Death with Dignity Act, and a signature drive was under way in Michigan to put a referendum on legalized assisted suicide on the ballot.

Perhaps even more important is the intense public scrutiny stimulated by the Supreme Court cases, the open acknowledgment on all sides that modern medicine has created a crisis in end-of-life care in this country. To address it requires major changes in our medical system, in our health-care financing, and in our personal priorities. Some of these changes are already under way.

Conclusion: Toward a New Kind of Hope

Doctors have long feared telling patients the truth and believed that giving someone *bad news* takes away hope. But in this age of seemingly ever-possible cures and chronic decline, when life may be prolonged nearly indefinitely, *hope* needs to be redefined. Today, hope for the dying is the hope for a good death, however the person who is dying might define it.

The good deaths I have seen or learned about often have these things in common:

1. *Open, ongoing communication.* Honest and coordinated discussion among doctors, the patient, and the family begins well in advance of the terminal stage of illness and addresses the chances of recovery, as well as the benefits and burdens of treatment, for both patient and family. Advance directives are reviewed and, if necessary, revised as the situation changes.

2. *Preservation of the patient's decision-making power.* The patient is granted as much decision making as she wants at every stage of her illness, and can be confident that her wishes will be carried out even when she can no longer express them.

3. *Sophisticated symptom control.* Pain and other troubling or humiliating symptoms are managed aggressively and well. Narcotics are used without fear of addiction, and calibrated to balance what the patient determines to be good pain control with an acceptable level of sedation.

4. *Limits are set on excessive treatment.* Excessive treatment— defined as medical interventions that extend the process of dying longer than *the person who is dying* wants it extended—is not given.

5. *A focus on preserving patient quality of life.* Communication about treatment takes into account the patient's autonomy and how he defines Self, and weighs both the physical and existential questions of life: What does he most value? When are pain and loss of function so great that they become intolerable? What constitutes a meaningful life? What constitutes loss of Self for the person who is dying?

6. *Emotional support.* Psychological issues are addressed, especially those having to do with depression, sadness, and loss. Attention is also paid to finishing old business and family reconciliation.

7. *Financial support.* Decisions about palliative care, acute medical care, home care, or long-term care are not dictated primarily by financial considerations. Costs are adequately covered, whether by public or private health insurers.

8. *Family support.* Decision making occurs within the context of a functioning family, with attention paid to the needs of the family and primary caregivers as well as to the patient. Support is given so that the family is not torn apart, and it is provided according to that family's system of values. There is a recognition of the need for family strength, an understanding that the good or bad legacy this death creates will endure in family lore.

9. *Spiritual support.* Spiritual issues are considered regarding what it means to *this person* to have a meaningful, dignified, and peaceful closure. Physicians, medical and care personnel, and rela-

tives and friends are open to the spiritual needs of the individual patient, however that patient might define them.

10. *The patient is not abandoned by medical staff even when curative treatment is no longer required.* The dying person does not feel isolated, nor does she have to die alone. Doctors and other medical personnel are supportive even when a cure is no longer possible, helping to manage dying well, through to the end.

S ince almost all end-of-life care today involves decisions about medical interventions, a good death must be orchestrated and planned, with doctors, patients, and families acting as a team. This includes whether and how to withhold treatment of the underlying condition, how aggressively to treat pain and other symptoms, when to withdraw treatment that might prolong life, whether to use treatment that may hasten death.

For the majority of Americans such planning is still more the exception than the rule. In order to ensure a good death—one with all these elements—a number of medical, institutional, and cultural attitude and policy changes must be made. Some are already on the way.

· In 1995, George Soros's Open Society Institute launched the Project on Death in America, a multimillion-dollar grant-funding organization aimed at stimulating research, education, and care for the seriously ill and dying.

· In 1996, the Center to Improve Care of the Dying, at George Washington University in Washington, D.C., was founded to develop educational programs and public policy to improve the health-care system at the end of life.

· In 1997, the Robert Wood Johnson Foundation, which funded the SUPPORT study, launched a $1.7 million Last Acts initiative campaign to seek reforms that alter the behavior of doctors, medical-care providers, insurers, hospitals and nursing homes, and consumers themselves in order to improve the care of the dying. The campaign, led by former First Lady Rosalynn Carter, is a coalition of seventy-two organizations, including the American Association of Retired Persons, the American Medical Association, the American Hospital Association, Cancer Care, and the National Hospice Organization.

· In 1997, the American Medical Association established an Institute for Ethics to rate hospitals and insurers, improve the care of dying patients, and "help reinstitute ethics to its time-honored and much-needed place as an integral part of the practice of medicine."

· In 1997, the American Geriatric Society issued a ten-point program urging excellence in treatment at the end of life. This included a call for improved symptom management, including emotional care as well as treatment of pain, shortness of breath, fatigue, nausea, and skin breakdown; more concern for adhering to advance directives; programs to preserve family strength; and services for family bereavement.

· In 1997, the Institute of Medicine, an affiliate of the National Academy of Sciences, issued a major report called *Approaching Death: Improving Care at the End of Life.* The report proposed, among other things, the creation of interim medical facilities between hospital and home, better pain and symptom management, better preparation of families and patients for death, and better training of physicians.

Additional and aggressive efforts are also required in the following areas:

1. *The definition of terminal illness must change.* Today's definition of terminal illness—based on congressional regulations for Medicare coverage of hospice care—is a prognosis of six months to live. But in the present medical system, in which life can be prolonged nearly indefinitely, it is hard to know exactly when an illness is likely to be fatal, especially for illnesses other than cancer. Studies show that doctors sometimes offer mistaken prognoses even within twenty-four hours of death.

Dr. Joanne Lynn, director of the Center to Improve Care of the Dying, now suggests that we speak not of terminal illness but of living with a *life-defining, eventually fatal condition.* This would allow people to plan along dual tracks: one, that they recover; the other, that they do not.

Instead of talking about the odds of survival, we should talk instead of quality of life, but only *as that is determined by the person who is dying*. Doctors must be able to discuss the ambiguities of prognoses, addressing quality-of-life issues as patients decline. They need to talk about what symptoms to expect, how these might impair patients' daily function, what impact they have on families, and how both patients and families can anticipate and adjust to them. Physicians, patients, and families also need to be able to talk about how to know when enough's enough, and what happens then.

Conversations like these cannot wait for the last stages of an illness; they must be part of an ongoing discussion that is intrinsic to medical planning, not one that takes place only when a living will is signed or just at the very end of life. Studies show that as patients come closer to death what they can cope with may change; some people find they can cope with more than they'd thought, some with far less. Open discussion allows preparation in advance of medical turning points, and prevents poorly considered decisions being made during a medical crisis.

2. *Medical training must change*. Doctors today are trained in acute, rather than in chronic, long-term care. Rather than view death as the failure to find a cure, the medical community must learn to view as an alternate kind of success the goal of ensuring a good death. To do so requires knowing how to help patients and families navigate a bearable course through what is often a lengthy, messy journey.

Doctors need help knowing when and how to decide *not* to treat, when and how to withhold or withdraw life-extending treatment, when and how to provide it if the family so wishes, and how to pay attention to patient preferences as stated verbally or in advance directives.

If patients decide against further treatment, doctors need to learn how not to abandon them—whether to burdensome pain and other physiological symptoms or to emotional or physical isolation.

A new board certification should be established in palliative care. In addition, all doctors, whatever the nature of their practice, should be taught the pain treatment principles outlined by the U.S. Department of Health and the World Health Organization. They should also be tested on their expertise in pain and symptom management on all licensing exams.

Hospitals and nursing homes should require that such assessment be included in patient charts, and standards should be set for institutions—and included in criteria for accreditation—on the quality of pain and symptom control.

Many medical organizations—such as the American Medical Association, the Joint Commission on Accreditation of Hospitals and Health Care Systems, the American Nurses Association, the Health Care Financing Administration, and the National Hospice Organization—have already begun designing programs to work toward these goals. These programs should be supported.

3. *The goals of medical treatment must be expanded.* While cure is always the first goal of treatment, the preservation of dignity, function, and autonomy cannot be far behind. Symptom control is key. Today there is no excuse for medical neglect or mismanagement of symptoms such as pain, breathlessness, nausea, constipation, or the inability to sleep.

Symptoms that are more difficult to control—the inability to walk, to move, to have a sexual relationship, to think clearly, to see, or to eat well; to be free of tremors, muscle spasms, incontinence, fatigue, weakness—should not be minimized. They may not be medically significant to doctors, but they can end up being of great emotional consequence to patients and should therefore be aggressively considered and responsibly managed.

It is crucial in diseases of degenerative decline that an assessment is made of the burden of particular symptoms, not according to some broad theoretical or medical view, but only *for the individual who is dying.* The point is to allow those living with potentially fatal illnesses to function as well as they can in everyday life, even as they move toward death.

4. *Emotional, spiritual, and psychological support must be provided.* These supports are particularly significant in chronic, ultimately fatal decline. Good palliative care means helping patients sort through the progression of psychological symptoms. Medical and other support personnel need more skill in evaluating and treating clinical depression, while continuing to honor the profound sadness inherent in normal dying.

Recognizing the value of "midwives to the dying," training that addresses suffering in its broadest sense might be given to a new group of dying specialists. It might also be given to psychologists, psycho-oncologists, social workers, spiritual counselors, and physicians themselves. Such training should be disease specific, recognizing different disease trajectories from illness to death. Care should also be individualized for each person dying, taking into account who that person is in the deepest sense, and their personal needs for meaning and closure.

5. *National health-care financing structures must change.* The financial costs of death today create a terrifying burden for patients and families alike.

American medical institutions and medical reimbursement systems are built on acute care, while long-term medical and physical care, including sophisticated palliative care, are drastically underfunded. Proposed cuts in Medicare, Medicaid, and private managed care programs, however, are most often proposed for exactly this kind of care. The peril of cuts in coverage for home care, cutbacks in nursing home inspections, in the lack of growth of long-term care facilities all threaten the shaky structure on which modern dying now rests.

In addition, health-care rationing and health-maintenance organizations that limit patient care and decision making threaten to take away control over our own dying, control that has come after nearly thirty years of advocacy, court cases, and changes in the law. We need a national overhaul of our medical funding and long-term care systems so that the chronically ill and the dying—including their beleaguered families—receive the money and attention they deserve.

6. *More support needs to be available to patients and their families.* Few families are able by themselves to meet the tremendous legal, financial, and physical needs of ill relatives at the end of life, which today—as we have seen—can often be lengthy and problematic. They need more supportive care at home and expanded short- and long-term care options. Hospice care, nursing homes, respite and day care, and new institutions such as graduated-care facilities all need to be supported and improved.

Employers need to encourage and support employees to make use of the federal Family and Medical Leave Act so that (as with maternity leave) these employees might be able to stay home to care for a close relative or friend who is seriously ill or dying.

This need for help at home will continue to increase. The

portion of the population that is over eighty-five is projected to grow exponentially into the twenty-first century, and with it the frequency of Alzheimer's or some other form of dementia, and other chronic and disabling illnesses.

This intense kind of long-term care is especially crucial in an era when women, the traditional caretakers, are now likely to be at work, and when social and emotional support for caretakers is often lacking.

7.   *Laws and regulations governing the use of drugs in palliative care should be revised.* Today, restrictive drug laws block patient access to medications that might improve daily life for the terminally and chronically ill, not only in a patient's last weeks or months, but also during the whole course of illness and decline.

This includes narcotics like morphine, as well as substances now designated as Schedule I drugs, including marijuana, heroin, and LSD, if they are medically indicated. Professional licensing bodies and governmental agencies that put a damper on effective prescribing must be better educated about the need for these changes.

8.   *There should be watchdog committees or regulatory procedures governing managed care to ensure patient and family decision making.*

In an age of HMOs and managed care, when insurers can supersede even doctors' medical decisions in the name of cost cutting, the principles of informed consent and patient autonomy may have little practical meaning. Solutions are fast needed to ensure that these basic principles of care are not threatened by a rush to increase profits, by our concern to curb our rising national health-care costs, or by the pressure for medical research.

9.   *There should be stricter regulatory procedures and legal guidelines governing organ transplant procedures, experimental medical research, withholding of treatment, and terminal sedation—in addition to the procedures already in place for the withdrawal of treatment.*

Americans today feel a loss of control at the end of life. They fear a loss of the ability to pay for care or to provide that care for themselves or their families. They worry about being guinea pigs— knowing and unknowing—in the march for medical progress, even fear whether their organs will be taken prematurely for transplant.

They both fear and desire the withdrawal, withholding, and granting of pain and symptom-management treatments when they are dying.

Against such a backdrop, it is understandable that Americans now both *desire* the legalization of assisted suicide and also fear that it might open them to risks of abuse. It is this loss of control at the end of life that needs to be addressed. The fear of abuse now requires adequate governmental regulation of all these ethically difficult situations of medical care at the end of life.

10. *Assisted suicide should be legalized for the dying, while ensuring that there are adequate fail-safes against substandard palliative care and against abuse.*

Even if all the reforms suggested above are put into effect, there will remain a small percentage of patients whose personal definitions of unbearable suffering cannot be adequately addressed by any means other than by hastening their own death.

After six years of investigating death in America I have come to the conclusion that assisted suicide must be made legally available for this group of people, should they request it. Not only does it validate some people's sense of choice and informed consent, but for others it provides the security they need to keep on living—knowing they can get ultimate relief from their suffering if that suffering truly becomes too much for them, and that they can have the kind of support they require from their physicians and families.

Like *all* other end-of-life care that might lead to death—including withholding and withdrawing medical treatment, sedation to unconsciousness (including withholding artificial nutrition and hydration), organ transplantation policy, medical experimentation—assisted suicide must be strictly regulated in order to prevent abuse.

Hospice helped us put dying back into the realm of the human. We may now need to take the hospice vision a step further, incorporating the hospice philosophy into mainstream end-of-life medical care—whether we die in our own bedrooms or living rooms, in nursing homes, or in hospitals.

The end result might be an environment that resembles modern childbirth. Good deaths, like good births, can occur in a variety of well-managed settings. The kind and quality of medical care and patient-family support are what matter, and that care can be offered at home (as in home births), in hospice inpatient units or nursing homes (as at hospital-based birthing centers), or in high-tech hospitals (as are most births in America today). Where death occurs should be determined more by the medical complications involved in managing it well than on the locale. When a cure is unlikely, the way in which we die should be the way of most comfort and peace.

Epilogue: The Good Death of Jack Sheedy

Modern medicine may have made dying harder, but it has also given us the gift of time—the time to prepare, the time to heal family wounds, the time to bring psychological and spiritual closure. If we can take advantage of it, it has given us something unique in history: the time to tie up loose ends and orchestrate a death that is good.

After I had been at work on this book for nearly three years, my family and I had the sad opportunity to test what I had learned about planning a good death. My father-in-law, Jack Sheedy—Gramps, as nearly everyone called him—was terminally ill with cancer. As with all good deaths, the person Jack Sheedy was in life had everything to do with how he died.

Gramps was eighty-nine when I met him, my neighbor at a summer house I'd rented on rural Fire Island. The house belonged to his son, John, my future husband, though I didn't know that at the time. Outside the front door was a little patch of dirt I thought would make a good garden. I wanted to put in a few tomatoes, a little spinach, some herbs. But as I began to dig, Gramps came out and said: "Don't plant a garden there!" Being merely a weekend gardener, I'd failed to notice that the spot was full of poison ivy.

I never met anyone as old as Jack and still that spry. Each morning he'd walk a mile on the beach, often with Honey Bear, John's dog. He'd eat eggs only on Tuesdays and Saturdays; he had meat only on Thursdays. Jack was tanned and ruddy. Usually he wore a white Irish fisherman's sweater, shorts, and a baseball cap.

His younger brother was eighty-eight-year-old Father Tom, the priest whom we met in Chapter 9 who'd died in a Gulfport, Mississippi, hospital from injuries suffered in a car accident. His older sister was Peggy, whom Father Tom had worried about because she was comatose on a feeding tube in a nursing home and died at ninety-five. This was a family that was long-lived.

Gramps was a legend on Fire Island, where just a few diehards stay year round. The island is a small strip of sand, technically a barrier reef, off the coast of Long Island. Only a few cars are allowed off-season, and none at all except utility trucks and emergency vehicles from Memorial Day through Labor Day. The only way to get around is on foot, dragging things through the sand in one of the island's trademark little red wagons. Where Gramps lived for six months a year was a mile from the closest ferry dock, straight west over deep sand.

Each year, as he had for twenty-seven years, Gramps came out in April, when it was still cold. Few stores were open yet so he had to lug his own food in canvas L. L. Bean bags piled into his wagon. He stayed at the house until mid-November. The house was unheated but he was used to staying warm near the fireplace. He had some tiny space heaters, but he didn't like to spend money on electricity. (Gramps was a notorious penny-pincher.) He also kept a woodpile out back, pieces of wood or old junk piled high. You never knew, he said, when an old screen door would come in handy, or a board to fix a table that broke. He retrieved old sheets from the garbage, just in case someone broke a leg, he said, and needed to tear them in pieces for a splint.

Since the walk to the grocery store was long, Gramps tucked tiny pieces of cheese or leftovers throughout his refrigerator, wrapped in foil that he pressed down and reused, over and over. He also fished a lot. He fished from the shore when the bluefish were running. Sometimes a fisherman heading out to the bay would take him along on a boat to fish for sea bass and blues. He walked barefoot in the Great South Bay, wiggling his heel in hopes of finding clams, and he always found them. He spoke little, noticed all.

Most of all, Gramps had a magnificent garden. People came from all over Fire Island to see it. Each fall he'd cover the spot with seaweed. He'd compost all year and transform a fifteen- by twenty-five-foot spot of sandy desert into a lush plot of land that grew the largest tomatoes, lettuce, peppers, rhubarb, and zucchini, and the healthiest herbs on the island. Stuffed among his rain forest of greens grew secret medicinal plants. When Gramps was ill, he'd make his way out there and chew a little comfrey or whatever else he needed to fix what ailed him.

Gramps's philosophy was use it or lose it. He did the *New York Times* crossword puzzle daily and always finished. No one ever beat him at pinochle. He said you had to do that to keep your mind active, and no doubt about it, his mind was alert until the very end. He said the hardest part of getting old was remembering all those birthdays—the children, the grandchildren, the great-grand-children, the one great-great grandson. It was also expensive, since he had to buy thirty-six birthday cards, and he put a $5 check in each one.

By the time I met Gramps he had been married nearly seventy-five years. No one knew what had gone wrong but it was clear that their relationship was difficult and full of tension. Gramps and Marie had a schedule. Each month he'd walk to town, take the ferry and then the train back from Fire Island to Bronxville to give her cash to pay the rent. He would always pay in cash, a habit left over from the Depression.

In November, long after John or his kids had stopped coming, John would go to Fire Island to take Gramps home. He and Marie would live together in their apartment for a few weeks, but by the end of the month, Marie would go to their daughter's in Westport to help her set up for Thanksgiving. Christmas was important to this family and it would always be back at their house. Then Gramps came to visit John for a week in January. Easter would be back in Westport. And then he'd go back to Fire Island.

But Christmas was also important to Gramps for another reason. Early December is when the seed catalogs came. He would go
over them with John and place their orders. The seed packets would
start arriving at John's house in the mail while Gramps stayed with
him in the city in January. When they came, Gramps would finger
the little envelopes, put them in rows in a box. In April, he was like
a little kid discovering spring anew, when he'd get John to trudge
through the sand to Fire Island to open the house again, taking his
seeds and his lists and his thirty-six birthday cards with him. They'd
spend that first weekend digging the garden, playing pinochle, and
planting the first seeds of the year.

A year after John and I married, Easter was at our house. That
year, just after Christmas, Honey Bear died after being sick for
many months. Gramps was now ninety-six, and when he arrived he
looked pale; he said he had a pain in his side and hadn't been able to
keep anything down for three days. He hadn't called anyone or
gone to a doctor. John took him to Marie's doctor in Bronxville.
From there he was sent to get an X ray. They said he had a
"blockage" and admitted him to Lawrence Hospital in Bronxville.
They found that Gramps had advanced prostate cancer.

They said his enlarged prostate was blocking his urinary tract
and they wanted to do exploratory surgery to see whether there
were any kidney stones or other blockages. Gramps was given light
anesthesia. When he came back to his room he told us he knew it
was bad. Staff gave him Demerol for his pain. I was concerned that
Demerol can be toxic for elderly patients, particularly those with
kidney problems, but the hospital gave it to him anyway because
they said it was hospital policy. Gramps promptly had seizure after
seizure—as we said he might—and hallucinated for the next thirty-
six hours. He thought there were rats in the room; he thought he
was eating and used a pretend spoon to feed himself, over and over;
he talked about his relationship with his mother; he said he was
getting his ticket out of his drawer to take a boat trip.

We stayed with him, talked to him, and held his hand, partly to
calm him and partly because I'd learned from Sister Loretta to pay
attention to the content of hallucinations. It was a bad sign, we
thought, when he began talking about getting ready for a journey
and the long-dead relatives who were coming to see him.

But Gramps also began talking about old memories, about

things he'd done as a child, about old girlfriends from the time he was in his teens, about things he remembered doing and people he'd met on Fire Island. (It was a good sign that not *all* of these people were dead.) In fact, Gramps talked more than he'd talked in his whole life. When we asked him how likely he was to take his journey, he said the chances were fifty-fifty. We knew he was talking about whether he would live or die, and that even he wasn't really sure.

This was a man who was nearly a hundred, who was born in the last century, who had only been in a hospital once—in 1941, when he had had his appendix removed, before his present doctor was born. Even if he had not been mentally confused, he would not have understood well enough any of his modern medical choices.

Yet, knowing Gramps, and having talked at length with him about both Peggy and Father Tom, we did make some basic decisions we never went back on. In the exploratory surgery doctors found cancer not only in the prostate but also in his kidney. Other tests showed he'd had kidney failure and that the cancer had probably already spread to his bones.

We realized that at ninety-six, with cancer that had already metastasized, Gramps was likely to die. There wasn't much we could do to avoid it. We decided that our goal was for Gramps to have a good and peaceful death rather than to prolong his life with aggressive treatment such as chemotherapy or surgery. With this decision, we were trading weeks, maybe months, but months spent with the pain and discomfort of treatment as opposed to months spent in peace and, if he had any, well-controlled pain. We also decided Gramps would be better off dying earlier of kidney or heart failure than of bone cancer, since those were deaths that were likely to be gentle and pain free, and bone cancer definitely was not.

Since the cancer was so advanced and he was frail, the first good decision we made was to decline aggressive treatment. We all decided as a family not to have chemotherapy; the chances seemed low of arresting prostate cancer that had already spread to the bones, and the difficult side effects of chemotherapy were not ones Gramps could either tolerate or want to cope with in the final phase of his life. His doctors agreed.

But they did not agree when we declined surgery—after talking it over with Gramps as much as he was able—to remove his

testicles. After consulting with specialists ourselves, and after doing a search of the Internet's computerized medical libraries, we
discovered two drugs said to have the same effect as the surgery:
They would stop growth of the offending male hormone, a hormone that would have continued to spread this cancer. When we
asked his doctor about them he told us that in older patients
compliance with taking the drugs is a problem. Dumbfounded, we
told him we would give the pills to Gramps ourselves and take
him to get his shots.

In the end, the prostate never did shrink sufficiently. He had to
keep in a catheter, which carried a risk of infection, but there's no
way to know whether surgery would have shrunk the cancer either,
nor whether Gramps would have survived or tolerated it. We
tended to doubt it.

The second good decision we made was to get hospice care.
After all those years with time apart, Marie wanted Gramps home.
She wanted to take care of him and he wanted to be with her. On his
primary-care doctor's suggestion, we enrolled Gramps in a local
hospice program. From then on, a hospice aide came to help Marie
at home for four hours a day; a nurse came three times a week.
John's eldest sister came up from North Carolina and stayed for a
few months, helping Marie take care of him. John and his other two
sisters ran errands. We took turns so that someone was there every
day. And it worked—as long as Gramps could still get around with
the help of a walker.

That's how it was for another five months, with Marie making
his favorite foods, talking with him and holding his hand at home.
During this time Marie and Jack fell in love again. They listened to
old songs, they talked about old times. "My mother is incredibly
caring," John found himself telling me. "This togetherness they
have is important not only for them but for all of us witnessing it."

But Jack still lost his temper sometimes, just as he must have
when he and Marie moved apart. He yelled at her, furious at his
disease. She was hurt, they stopped speaking. But the children
came and helped them talk out their troubles. In the end, they
resolved many of them. Jack stopped being mean; Marie overlooked it if he was.

That summer, John planted the garden, and each day he visited,
Gramps would ask what the plants each looked like, what color

and shape they were, how high, how close to the others. Finally, he started to share his gardening secrets, making John write them down in a book. John followed his instructions, pinching back plants when he said, watering just when he said, giving extra mulch or fertilizer. Gramps made John take pictures so he could better tell him what to do. The garden grew lush and huge. We brought Gramps a basil and a tomato plant, each in a pot, and he took care of those himself on the windowsill in his apartment. And as he talked, he made peace with them all, with John, with his daughters, with Marie.

At the end of September, Gramps stopped eating. Marie thought it was her cooking, but it wasn't. One daughter refused to believe he was dying and kept trying to feed him, telling him he needed to eat so he could get well. The daughters fought. Gramps just slept in his chair all day, because he was weak and because when he tried to move, he fell down. Marie, who was ninety-four, couldn't pick him up. She couldn't sleep at night for fear he'd fall on the way to the bathroom.

We decided that though hospice was wonderful, Marie was drained. For her to go on caring for Gramps at home would have meant two deaths instead of one. The third good decision we all made was for Gramps to go to Calvary Hospital, in a nearby town.

It turned out that Calvary is the one hospital in the entire country that specializes only in the acute, palliative care of cancer patients. Though such hospitals do exist in Canada and Great Britain, they don't exist here, partly because of our peculiar health-care financing system, which gives preferential benefit to acute, curative care, and partly because of the ethos of aggressive, end-stage treatment. Calvary gives no curative treatment, but instead aggressively manages the symptoms of dying.

Gramps was glum. He knew Marie wasn't able to take care of him anymore and that hospice home-care aides weren't enough for what he now needed. Yet he didn't want to leave home. He would mouth the words that it was best for him to go, but he was mad. He'd stopped eating before he left and we all thought he was determined to die.

But at Calvary he had his own room. It was light, cheery, airy. While Marie couldn't even turn him, here were nurses who could make him comfortable, who would turn him every two hours to avoid bedsores. He also liked that it was a Catholic hospital. He'd long ago stopped practicing religion but here he felt at home. There were Irish nurses, a cross over the bed, a priest if he wanted to talk. He even got the anointment for the sick.

In fact, Gramps could have whatever he wanted—his regular vodka and tonic at dinner, a massage, a chocolate milk shake any time of day. There was a great, chatty Irish nurse named Ania to talk to. We put a large photo of Gramps and his best friend, Charlie, on the wall at the foot of his bed, next to one of him fishing for bluefish off the beach at Fire Island, and nearby a picture of young Gramps and Marie courting.

Gramps began eating again, happy to be in a place that was sophisticated enough to take such good care of him. Marie was fine, and Gramps perked up. He had a speaker phone by his bed and all the children and grandchildren and great-grandchildren could call. He had his button for the TV and a free *New York Times* came each day so he could follow the news and sports and do the crossword puzzle.

Not only did Gramps not die, he got better—so much so that Calvary finally told us he might need to get out. A Medicare administrator had told Calvary, they said, that Gramps no longer qualified for their treatment benefits. He wasn't in pain; he didn't have a fever; he wasn't getting worse. Gramps no longer needed *skilled medical care,* they said, so Medicare wouldn't cover his costs there.

We were told to look at nursing homes with *custodial care.* All of them were awful. It was appalling, John told the doctor at Calvary, that they were going to move this man to such places at the end of his life. None was as lovely as Calvary.

In the beginning of November, Gramps's sister, Peggy, died after being on the feeding tube for six years. Her heart just gave out. When John told Gramps it was as if he already knew. He looked at John and said, "Good." For years both he and John had asked doctors to remove her tube but they'd refused; no one had the energy to go to court, which is the only thing the nursing home said they could do. Peggy had long since curled into a fetal position, in an irreversible coma from which there was no hope of her ever coming out. The feeding tube had been put in without anyone's permission.

Medicare paid for her every day, comatose or not. But ironically, if Gramps improved too much, even though he would shortly die, spry as he was, it wouldn't pay for Calvary. The doctor whispered that we should stall, and we did. When Peggy died, everyone was sadly relieved. It seemed as if she'd actually died years ago and now we were just going through the rituals of saying good-bye. When we told Gramps he just wanted to know how her funeral was going to be paid. We knew he was also thinking of his own.

John or one of the sisters visited every day. Marie was at the hospital, holding Gramps's hand. Relatives from everywhere sent cards. Gramps started asking about Thanksgiving and who was coming up to visit from the North Carolina daughter's family. We knew he was thinking of beginning to say good-bye. Everyone who could decided to come. Then Gramps took what's euphemistically called *a turn for the worse* and Calvary stopped suggesting he leave. He was put on the critical list. He got an infection, which we fought over, but they decided to treat. They gave him antibiotics, but the fact is, Gramps didn't say no. He was waiting; he wasn't quite ready to die. We brought him a plant that actually bloomed in his room, and a tiny Christmas tree, which we decorated. During Thanksgiving week, a parade of children and grandchildren put ornaments on the tree and kissed him good-bye.

A week later, he got worse. Even though his infection had cleared up, he stopped eating altogether, barely had anything to drink—he couldn't hold it down—and started having trouble breathing. His lungs filled with fluids, as if he were drowning. We saw he was still getting IV fluids and doctors were still taking blood for tests. They told us he couldn't swallow so he couldn't take his heart medications or pills for his gout. The tests were to ascertain his potassium levels to try to stabilize his heart. We asked them to stop, to leave him alone. With the fluids going in, and his body less and less able to excrete or manage it, the fluids were collecting in his chest. Medical personnel were suctioning him, which causes discomfort. His nurse Ania told us it would be better to stop; we also checked with physicians and found she was right.

Without food or water the body slowly shuts itself down, as if producing its own anesthetic, and the patient slowly gets sleepy and dozes off. When fluids are administered, they can build to an uncomfortable level. There are two schools of thought—give fluids and suction them out, or do nothing. We found that at Calvary one reason for the fluids was that the hospital's funding is based on acute medical care. They had to go this route unless asked to do otherwise. We asked. His fluids were cut back, though not entirely, and the buildup in his chest diminished.

Gramps could hear us throughout, but he was too weak to move, and it was a big effort to respond. We asked if he wanted to be suctioned, and time and again he shook his head no. A priest even came into the room to confirm this, and when he asked Gramps himself if he wanted to be suctioned—explaining to him the reasons why—Gramps again shook his head no.

It was time to make another decision. We requested that Calvary begin treatment with narcotics; Gramps wasn't in pain but he was experiencing breathlessness. With shortness of breath, as with pain, narcotics such as morphine and other opioids can reduce the feelings of suffocation or discomfort. In his case, his doctor chose Levorphanol, a drug like morphine, but longer acting and with less potential for side effects for Gramps, who had had a reaction to Demerol.

This was a doctor who knew how to use narcotics well. But he gave it to him by injection, since "Levo," as it's called, can build up in the system over time and is better given as needed, he'd said, rather than in a regular IV drip. Whenever Gramps had trouble breathing we asked for a shot and it helped. Someone was with him the entire time—Marie, John and I, one of John's sisters, a brother-in-law, one of his many grandchildren, and Ania, who knew when to give the shots and how to calm his fears.

By then, Gramps's main communication was intense eye contact. He'd stare at you, through you, inside you, intimately, as one stares at a lover in sex. We'd hold his hand, stroke his arm, his brow. And we'd play music. John's son-in-law—Irish like Gramps—had made a tape of old Irish tunes. We began to play them for him on a cassette recorder.

The first time we played the tape, Marie was sitting beside him. In the beginning, he barely acknowledged the music. Then an old song came on called "After the Ball." Gramps turned and stared at Marie. He took her hand in his and they both smiled. When they were in their twenties and courting, at the time the photo in his room was taken, it turned out, this was their song. They'd danced to it, made out to it, and later made love to it. And now as he lay dying, they looked at each other, held hands, stared, and smiled. We played these songs most of the next few days, as Gramps's children came to say a final good-bye.

In the last two days, Gramps began to stare at a spot on the ceiling. He barely talked but he heard everything. John and I sat quietly, stroking his arms, John on one side of the bed, Marie and I on the other. We thought maybe he was comatose. John was doing the *Times* crossword puzzle now, and at one point he said to me, "What's a seven-letter word for a cousin of a carrot?" Before I could answer, a hoarse whisper came from the bed. Gramps answered, "Parsnip."

Now everyone had said good-bye but his daughter from North Carolina wanted to be there at the end. We called her. Friday we told Gramps she'd come Sunday, and we told him the time of her plane. Later, we realized he pretty much planned exactly when he would go.

Those last days, the room was enormously peaceful. Gramps was still wheezing, with one side better for him than the other. Nurses turned him every two hours, trying to prevent bedsores. But Gramps didn't seem to mind. He never ate or drank, but we put chips of ice on his tongue and Vaseline swabs on his lips. He couldn't swallow. They gave him no medication but the Levo. John said some private good-byes. He said Gramps understood completely, held his hand tightly, and stared at him with those totally open eyes. He had no pain. But soon he began staring more at the ceiling.

Saturday night was wet and foggy. John came back to stay with him. John is a businessman, not the type to talk like this, but he said the room seemed to be full of a powerful energy and also incredibly peaceful. Gramps's breathing became more shallow. John held his hand and played the Irish songs. After a while, Gramps began scanning the spot he'd been staring at, as if it had become wider. Suddenly he held out an arm as if he were pointing at that spot. John thought he was upset, so he told Gramps it was okay. Soon Gramps pointed again, as if he were reaching for someone. Then a third time he reached and seemed surprised.

I was asleep at home but for some reason, I suddenly found myself wide-awake, and as I woke up I found myself saying these words out loud: "Don't stay here, Jack. Go with your brother, Father Tom. Follow the light." John came home an hour later, so energized he couldn't sleep. I told him what had happened to me. Eerily, we both felt sure that Gramps's brother, Father Tom, had come for him, probably with Peggy as well.

That morning, John had already gone to get his sister at the airport when Gramps's doctor called to say that he had died. When the three of us walked into Gramps's room he'd been dead just an hour. He'd died as John's sister's plane was landing. Could be that Gramps planned it so she could spend her time focusing on Marie.

We expected that energy still to be in the room, but it wasn't when we arrived. A priest was there. When John told him what had happened the night before he said that was not at all an uncommon experience in the hospital. His explanation was that God had come for him. Other relatives had more mundane explanations, that it was probably his mother or Peggy or Father Tom. Gramps left quickly, just the way he always had when he got to Fire Island, stepped off the ferry, and ran toward the house. But his eyes were still wide open, staring at that spot. And on his face was the biggest smile.

We lined the inside of the coffin with photos, John and I kissing Gramps at our wedding, pictures of him petting Honey Bear, Gramps with each of his four children and with Marie. The eighteen grandchildren, bearing notes and pictures from the seventeen great-grandchildren and the great-great grandson, each tucked small treasures inside with him. We also put in photos of Gramps's garden, some taken this year showing the results of the secrets he'd shared with John. The tomatoes and lettuce plants were bigger than ever, the vines with the peas and the beans blanketing the garden fence.

We held the funeral Mass in the chapel at the Monastery of the Sacred Heart in Yonkers. The chapel was nearly full. Gramps had friends of all ages. All his children were there, as were sixteen of his grandchildren and great-grandchildren and his great-great grandson. John read the eulogy he'd stayed up the night before writing.

"His death was remarkable, just like his life," he began. "He never complained. He died with great strength and with enormous dignity. There was so much love in that hospital room of his. You could just feel it. In dying, he accomplished a number of things that probably couldn't have happened if we had tried to talk about them. He united his family. We met. We talked. We didn't always agree but we became a family again.

"So, these are the lessons my father has taught us in dying: Uniting. Caring. Loving those who are important to you in life. Albert Camus once said: 'There is but one freedom, to put oneself right with death, after that, all is possible.' My father was fortunate. He put himself right with death."

Notes

The following list contains abbreviations of publications frequently used in this section:

American Family Physician	*AFP*
Annals of Internal Medicine	*AIM*
Archives of Internal Medicine	*Arch*
Clinical Practice Guidelines: Acute Pain Management: Operative or Medical Procedures and Trauma (February 1992)	*Acute Pain Management*
Clinical Practice Guidelines No. 9: Management of Cancer Pain (March 1994)	*Management of Cancer Pain*
Journal of Near Death Studies	*JNDS*
Journal of Pain and Symptom Management	*JPSM*
Journal of the American Medical Association	*JAMA*
New England Journal of Medicine	*NEJM*
U.S. Department of Health and Human Services, Agency for Health Care Policy and Research	USDHHS, AHCPR

A Personal Introduction

Page

xxiv ... *I wrote an article for* New York: This article appeared as "The Art of Dying," 23 November 1992.

O N E   Dying Well: The Death of Judith Obodov Hardin

Page

1   All personal information about Judith Hardin's death is based on extensive
     interviews between July 1994 and April 1996—after her August 1990
     death—with her husband, Moh Hardin, her mother, Adele Obodov (16 and
     18 October 1994), her son, Justin Hardin (19 July 1994), her daughter,
     Cecily Hardin (23 February 1996), and her friend Connie Berman (16–18
     March 1995). Additional information came from a letter Moh wrote to his
     close friends shortly after Judith died that he later shared with me in private
     correspondence.

9   *Reliable researchers estimate:* B. Cassileth et al., "Contemporary Unor-
     thodox Treatments in Cancer Medicine," *AIM* 101 (1984): 105–12; Jimmie
     Holland, M.D. et al., "Alternative Cancer Therapies," in *Handbook of
     Psycho-oncology,* ed. Jimmie C. Holland, M.D. and Julie H. Rowland, Ph.D.
     (New York: Oxford University Press, 1989): 508–15; Bernie S. Siegel, M.D.,
     Love, Medicine and Miracles; (New York: Harper & Row, 1986).

10   *"We found a book . . .":* The early book on visualizations for cancer patients
     that Moh and Judith Hardin used was O. Carl Simonton, Stephanie Simon-
     ton, and James Creighton, *Getting Well Again: A Step-by-Step Self-Help
     Guide to Overcoming Cancer for Patients and Their Families* (New York:
     Jeremy P. Tarcher, Inc., 1978).

     . . . in her study of Buddhism: Judith's Buddhist teacher was the late Eleventh
     Venerable Chögyam Trungpa, Rinpoche, of the Kagyu and Nyingma schools
     of Tibetan Buddhism.

15   *. . . Joe Vest, a filmmaker:* Judith Hardin's friend Joe Vest wanted to compose
     a piece of music before he died that would celebrate the joy and beauty of
     life. And he did. The world premiere of his exquisite *Requiem,* set to Walt
     Whitman's *Leaves of Grass,* was performed in Boulder at the First United
     Methodist Church on 8 July 1990, with an orchestra of members of the
     Denver Philharmonic Orchestra led by David Lockington, and a chorus, led
     by Erick Brunner, made up of choir members from the Denver/Boulder area.
     It was subsequently performed several times again, and video and audio
     tapes were made by Chariot Productions, in Boulder, and are available for
     sale. Joe died on 20 April 1994.

17   *Dr. Sierpina recommended hospice:* Medical information about Judith's
     death, given at the request of her husband, was based on interviews with Dr.
     Paul McIntyre and Dr. Victor Sierpina. Dr. McIntyre was interviewed 2 April
     1996. Dr. Sierpina was interviewed 30 March 1996.

23   *"Very little was said. . . .":* The following description of Judith's death is
     quoted from a personal letter Moh wrote to friends in fall 1990. Used with
     his permission.

26   *"I had no idea . . .":* Connie was less willing to embrace this crooked-picture
     scenario than Moh was and, in her interviews, always wanted this noted.
     "The picture thing was kind of a joke," she said, "not a serious conversation,
     but 'wouldn't it be great if you could send a signal by tilting the pictures.'
     There were two dinky little pictures over the bed. It was a rental house. So we
     said, 'Oh, turn the pictures.' But we were practicing, and Moh, I thought,
     said, 'Look at the pictures.' I remember thinking the mirror I first saw them
     in was wavy, but then we looked, and they were slightly off. Not forty-five

degrees. But we were thinking, 'Were they crooked before? Did we not notice?' It was interesting, weird, but definitely not clearly supernatural. Just ironic."

T w o The Sorcerer's Apprentice: Beyond the Age of Medical Miracles

Page

29 *"She went into respiratory failure"*: At Moh Hardin's request, medical information on Judith was provided by Dr. Victor Sierpina, in an interview 30 March 1996, and by Dr. Paul McIntyre, 2 April 1996.

31 *. . . more people were going to hospitals,*: Data on where we die in America was based on numerous studies and reports, including: Dwight Brock, Ph.D., and Daniel J. Foley, M.S., "Demography and Epidemiology of Dying in the United States, with Emphasis on Deaths of Older Persons"; paper prepared for a symposium of The Center to Improve Care of the Dying, "A Good Dying: Shaping Health Care for the Last Months of Life," Washington, D.C., 30 April 1996; Vincent Mor, Ph.D., "Available Data for Studying Dying in America"; Kathleen M. Foley, M.D., "Epidemiology of Death: The How, Why, Where and Symptoms of Dying"; and *Summary of Committee Views and Workshop Examining the Feasibility of an Institute of Medicine Study of Dying, Decisionmaking and Appropriate Care,* ed. Marilyn J. Fields, Ph.D., Division of Health Care Sciences, Institute of Medicine, Washington, D.C., February 1994. (Copies available from Institute of Medicine, 2101 Constitution Avenue N.W., Washington, DC 20418.) Also D. Merrill and V. Mor, "Pathways to Hospital Death Among the Oldest Old," *Journal of Aging and Health* 5 (November 1993): 516–35; D. Merrill and V. Mor, "Where People Die: Health and Social Determinants," paper presented at the Gerontological Society of America, San Francisco, 1991; V. Mor et al., "The Effect of Hospice Care on Where Patients Die," in *The Hospice Experiment,* eds. V. Mor et al. (Baltimore: Johns Hopkins University Press, 1988); A. McMillian et al., "Trends and Patterns in Place of Death for Medicare Enrollees," *Health Care Finance and Review* 12 (1990): 1–7; and M. Sager et al., "Changes in the Location of Death after Passage of Medicare's Prospective Payment System," *NEJM* 320 (1989): 433–39.

32 *Only a hundred years ago:* Research on the history of medicine was based on historical sections in *Deciding to Forego Life-Sustaining Treatment,* a document of the President's Commission for the Study of Ethical Problems in Medicine and Biomedical and Behavioral Research, 1983; interviews with Joanne Lynn, M.D. 24–25 May, 1994; Albert S. Lyons, M.D. and R. Joseph Petrucelli II, M.D., *Medicine: An Illustrated History* (New York: Abradale Press, Harry N. Abrams, 1987); and various texts in the rare book room of the library of the New York Academy of Medicine. Also important is Paul Starr, *The Social Transformation of American Medicine* (New York: Basic Books, 1984).

The cessation of heart: The President's Commission's first document was the seminal work, *Defining Death* (July 1981), used by the American Bar Association, the American Medical Association, and the National Conference of Commissioners on Uniform State Laws to create a proposed new statute, the

Uniform Determination of Death Act, now adopted by all states as the legal definition of death. Much of the initial thinking on brain death definitions was outlined by the ad hoc Committee of the Harvard Medical School to Examine the Definition of Brain Death, in "A Definition of Irreversible Coma," *JAMA* 205 (1968): 337.

33 *... diseases that once killed:* Data on the changing patterns of illness is based on various interviews, speeches, and workshops, from October 1993 through October 1994, with Daniel Callahan, Ph.D., former president of the Hastings Center, and his book *The Troubled Dream of Life: Living with Mortality* (New York: Simon & Schuster, 1993); and with Dr. Joanne Lynn, in many interviews, May 1994–January 1997. See also Field and Cassel, eds., *Approaching Death* (Washington, D.C.: National Academy Press, 1997): 2–5 to 2–6.

... an "epidemiologic transition,": Dr. Abdel R. Omran in "The Epidemiologic Transition: A Theory of the Epidemiology of Population Change," *Milbank Memorial Fund Quarterly* 49 (winter 1971): 509–38; interviews with Dr. S. Jay Olshansky, and Olshansky and Ault, "The Fourth Stage of the Epidemiologic Transition: The Age of Delayed Degenerative Diseases," *Milbank Quarterly* (fall 1986): 64; and Olshansky et al., "Trading Off Longer Life for Worsening Health: The Expansion of Morbidity Hypothesis," *Journal of Aging and Health* 3 (May 1991): 194–216.

... new infectious diseases: Data on emerging infectious diseases were based on an interview with Dr. Robert W. Pinner of the National Center for Infectious Diseases, January 1996, and his research as the lead author of "Trends in Infectious Diseases Mortality in the United States," *JAMA* 273 (January 1996). "It is principally a matter of perspective," Dr. Pinner says, on the recent reemergence of infectious diseases. "As societies develop, causes of death shift from being infectious to chronic. . . . Infectious diseases *are* going up, especially because of AIDS. [But that] doesn't mean there aren't huge differences since the turn of the century."

34 *But by the 1990s:* Cancer survival data was provided by the Cancer Statistics Branch of the National Cancer Institute.

... death from heart disease: Heart survival data is taken from R. A. O'Rourke, "Overview of Trends in Heart Disease: Changing Prognosis after Myocardial Infarction," *The Annals of Epidemiology* 3 (September 1993): 541–46; and from an interview on 8 April 1996 with Daniel Levy, M.D., director of the Framingham Heart Study.

35 *Daily teaching rounds:* I did follow-up interviews for the section on rounds at Mount Sinai Hospital with Arthur Kennish, M.D. (on many occasions from August 1993–April 1996), Salmin Sharma, M.D. (11 April 1996), Diane Meier, M.D. (14 January 1994), all physicians at Mount Sinai School of Medicine—and with spokesmen from the National Office of Organ Transplantation (April 1996).

37 *The past two decades:* Data provided by the American Medical Association, in *Physician Characteristics and Distribution in the United States,* based on 1993 figures.

38 *I've identified him:* I agreed with Dr. Kennish, who took me on rounds, not to use the real names of any Mount Sinai patients.

40 *Study one, in the* Lancet: RITA Trial Participants. "Coronary Angioplasty

Versus Coronary Artery Bypass Surgery: The Randomized Intervention Treatment of Angina (RITA) trial," *Lancet* 341 (8845) (6 March 1993): 573–80.

Study two, ... AIM: Daniel B. Mark, M.D. et al., "Effects of Coronary Angioplasty, Coronary Bypass Surgery, and Medical Therapy on Employment in Patients with Coronary Artery Disease," *AIM* 120 (January 15, 1994): 111–17.

Study three, in JAMA: Harold S. Luft, Ph.D. and Patrick S. Romano, M.D., "Chance, Continuity, and Change in Hospital Mortality Rates," *JAMA* 270 (21 July 1993): 331–37.

Study four discusses: D. C. McCory et al., "Predicting Complications of Carotid Endarterectomy," *Stroke* 24 (1993): 1285–91.

42   *"At teaching hospitals":* Interview with Dr. Diane Meier on 14 January 1994.

45   *"The antirejection drugs cause cancer":* There are warnings in the pharmacology guides, but studies also confirm the possibility. These studies include: M. G. and Delfino Perlroth, "Cyclosporine in Heart Transplantations: The Authors' Personal Experience," *Recenti Progressi in Medicina* 85 (October 1994): 471–74; and S. H. Chu et al., "Prognosis of Posttransplant Lymphomas in Patients Treated with Cyclosporine, Azathioprine, and Prednisolone," *Transplantation Proceedings* 26 (August 1994): 1981–82. On the other hand, some studies dispute this, including S. B. Gaya et al., "Malignant Disease in Patients with Long-Term Renal Transplants," *Transplantation* 59 (27 June 1995): 1705–09.

46   *Osler used these:* Sir William Osler, *Principles and Practice of Medicine* (New York: Appleton and Co., originally published in 1892).

Cecil Textbook of Medicine ...: Wyngarden et al., eds., *Cecil Textbook of Medicine,* 19th ed. (Philadelphia: Saunders, 1992). In 1996, the twentieth edition of *Cecil Textbook of Medicine* was published too late for thorough review in this text.

... *Christine K. Cassel, M.D.* ... *one of the major voices:* Chair of the National Academy of Science's Institute of Medicine's Committee on Care at the End of Life, and coeditor, *Approaching Death: Improving Care at the End of Life* (Washington, D.C.: National Academy Press, 1997), vols. 1 and 2.

Another major text: Kurt J. Isselbacher et al., ed. *Harrison's Principles of Internal Medicine* (New York: McGraw-Hill, 1994).

47   *In 1996, researchers:* Reported on 15 March 1996, to the editors of the textbooks, and shared with me by the Center to Improve Care of the Dying in private communication.

This study's essential findings: Report of the AMA's Council on Scientific Affairs, "The Good Care of the Dying Patient," *JAMA* 275 (14 February 1996): 474.

48   *It wasn't until the spring of 1993:* Derek Doyle et al., eds. *The Oxford Textbook of Palliative Medicine* (New York: Oxford University Press, 1993). *The World: Cancer Pain Relief,* guidelines for treatment, were published in 1986 and essentially adopted in 1991 by the American Pain Society.

... *the American Society:* Board of Directors of the American Society of Clinical Oncology, *Cancer Pain Assessment and Treatment Curriculum*

Guidelines Teaching Syllabus and Slide Sets (Conference on Cancer Pain, Pittsburgh, 18–19 September 1993).

. . . *the U.S. Department:* Ada Jacox et al., USDHHS, AHCPR, *Management of Cancer Pain* (Washington, D.C.: U.S. Department of Health and Human Services, March 1994).

The Study to Understand: The main thesis was published in William A. Knaus, M.D., Joanne Lynn, M.D. et al., "A Controlled Trial to Improve Care for Seriously Ill Hospitalized Patients," *JAMA* 274 (22/29 November 1995): 1591–98, but additional parts of this study have appeared in many other medical journals, including Lynn et al., "Perceptions by Family Members of the Dying Experience of Older and Seriously Ill Patients," *Annals of Internal Medicine (AIM),* 126 (15 January 1997): 97–106; various other issues of *AIM* in February, March, and April 1995; and the *Journal of General Internal Medicine* (October 1994) (April 1995). This study has also been widely reported and commented on within the medical and medical ethics communities and in the popular press. Special reports on the study were published by a broad range of media, from the *Hastings Center Report* (November–December 1995) to *People* magazine (19 February 1996) and *U.S. News and World Report* (4 December 1995).

49   *The $28 million SUPPORT project:* The SUPPORT project was funded largely by the Robert Wood Johnson Foundation.

All of these were seriously ill: The hospitals in the SUPPORT study were Beth Israel Hospital in Boston; the University of California at Los Angeles Medical Center; Duke University Medical Center, in Durham; MetroHealth Medical Center, in Cleveland; and Marshfield Medical Research Foundation/ Saint Joseph's Hospital, in Marshfield, Wisconsin.

51   *"It used to be that death":* Jennifer Mendelsohn, "Last Passage: Can Doctors Learn to Allow Patients to Choose Death with Dignity?" *People* (19 February 1996): 83.

52   *"Twenty years from now":* Personal interview with Dr. Lynn, 24 May 1994.

53   *"The dilemma we face":* S. Jay Olshansky, Ph.D., Bruce A. Carnes, Ph.D., and Christine K. Cassel, M.D., "The Aging of the Human Species," *Scientific American* (April 1993): 46–52.

T H R E E   Dying Hard: The Death of Peter Ciccone

Page

54   . . . *Peter Ciccone made a tape recording:* Peter Ciccone's story is based on extensive in-person and telephone interviews with him and Ron Burris, April 1992–September 1993—when Peter died—and afterward, with Ron Burris, until March 1997. Also interviewed were Peter's sister Fran Mack and his brother Dominick ("Donny") Ciccone. In addition, extensive interviews took place, April 1992–February 1997, with Sister Loretta Palamara, spiritual counselor at Cabrini Hospice; with Mary Cooke, the hospice director; and with Dr. Daniel Kao, the hospice medical director. Also interviewed was Peter's home-care nurse, Mary Iades, 15 April 1996. The weather in the summer of 1993, when Peter died, was confirmed with data provided by the National Climatic Data Center, in Asheville, North Carolina.

56   *Laboratories all over the world:* Data on increased AIDS survival time

includes: E. G. Apolonio et al., "Prognostic Factors in Human Immunodeficiency Virus-Positive Patients with a CD4+ Lymphocyte Count < 50/microL," *Journal of Infectious Diseases* 171 (April 1995): 829–36; L. P. Jacobson et al., "Changes in Survival after Acquired Immunodeficiency Syndrome (AIDS): 1984–91, *American Journal of Epidemiology (AJE)* 138 (1 December 1993): 952–64; S. Blum et al., "Trends in Survival Among Persons with Acquired Immunodeficiency Syndrome in New York City," *AJE* 139 (15 February 1994): 351–56; L. P. Jacobson, "AIDS Survival Time Has Nearly Doubled Since 1984," *AFP* 48 (August 1993): 319; and D. Osmond et al., "Changes in AIDS Survival Time in Two San Francisco Cohorts of Homosexual Men, 1983 to 1993," *JAMA* 271 (13 April 1994): 1083–87. The difficulty in pinpointing survival time has been compounded by lack of clarity about when HIV was contracted (since testing might occur at any time) and also by changes in medical definitions. See R. E. Chaisson et al., "Impact of the 1993 Revision of the AIDS Case Definition on the Prevalence of AIDS in a Clinical Setting," *AIDS* 7 (June 1993): 857–62; and the WHO International Collaborating Group for the Study of the WHO Staging System, "Proposed 'World Health Organization Staging System for HIV Infection and Disease': Preliminary Testing by an International Collaborative Cross-sectional Study," *AIDS* 7 (May 1993): 711. See an AIDS update by John Leland, "The End of AIDS?" and companion articles by other reporters, in *Newsweek* (2 December 1996): 65–73.

57 "*. . . especially with the advent of protease inhibitors:* David Brown, "Triple-Drug Therapies Are Changing Patterns, Costs of AIDS Treatment," *Washington Post,* 27 January 1997.

However, researchers lament: Data on the increased need for palliative care come, among many studies, from C. Kemp and L. Stepp, "Palliative Care for Patients with Acquired Immunodeficiency Syndrome," *The American Journal of Hospice Palliative Care* 12 (November–December 1995): 14, 17–27; R. J. Miller, "Some Notes on the Impact of Treating AIDS Patients in Hospices," *Hospice Journal* 7 (1991): 1–12; and most especially from the AIDS Educational Summit, a task force of the National Hospice Organization that met in San Francisco on 14 February 1994, and from the work of Tom Grothe, R.N. (interviews 10 and 21 February 1994) of the Visiting Nurses and Hospices of San Francisco and director of Coming Home Hospice in the Castro district, where many in the Bay Area's gay community live. *Studies also show:* This statement is based on the research with AIDS and cancer patients of Russell K. Portenoy, M.D., cochief of the pain and palliative-care service, and the work of William S. Breitbart, M.D., and Steven Passik, Ph.D., of the psychiatry service at Memorial Sloan-Kettering Cancer Center. Dying patients have multiple symptoms; it is the prevalence of these symptoms, their frequency and their intensity, that can lead to what these researchers refer to as "global distress." This is what turns out to be the most crucial marker in measuring patients' perceptions of their quality of life, their will to keep on going versus their sense of hopelessness, and their tendency to have what these physicians call "suicidal ideation," or the desire to end their lives. This work has been published in many medical texts and journals; it was thoroughly described at a conference, Psycho-Oncology V: Psychosocial Factors in Cancer Risk and Survival, at Memorial

Sloan-Kettering in New York City, 2–4 October 1993, and to me in many interviews with these physicians and their colleagues at numerous times, November 1992–April 1996.

. . . further disabling the body's immune system: See studies on psychoimmunology, notably the work of Steven E. Locke, M.D., professor of psychiatry, Harvard Medical School; Janice Kiecolt-Glaser, Ph.D., a psychologist; and Ronald Glaser, M.D., an immunologist, at Ohio State University. This work was reported by Dr. Locke at an international conference, held in Montreal 20–23 June 1993. See Steven E. Locke, M.D., "Immunity," in *Healing: Beyond Suffering or Death* (Le Processus de Guérison: Par-Delà la Souffrance ou la Mort), ed. Luc Bessette, M.D. (Montreal: MNH, 1993): 73–75.

. . . the means to relieve some of them: See, in particular, the research of Dr. Russell Portenoy; Kathleen Foley, M.D., especially in C. Richard Chapman and Foley, *Current and Emerging Issues in Cancer Pain* (New York: Raven Press, 1993); C. Stratton Hill Jr., M.D., *Advances in Pain Research and Therapy: Drug Treatment of Cancer Pain in a Drug-Oriented Society* (New York: Raven Press, 1989); and William Breitbart, M.D., "Pharmacotherapy of Pain in AIDS"; ed. Gary P. Wormser, *A Clinical Guide to AIDS and HIV* (Philadelphia: Lippincott-Raven, 1996): 359–78. I was not given access to Peter Ciccone's actual medical records, but the drugs and dosage reports I used were provided by Ron Burris and by Cabrini Hospice's director, Mary Cooke. What they each gave me matched fairly well. Although Dr. Kao tried some of these additional drugs, when comparing these reports with the recommendations of internationally known pain experts, it seemed he did not try them all, and possibly not in doses high enough to help Peter.

58 *" '. . . get a gun and shoot me.' ":* In an interview with Donny Ciccone, Peter's brother, in January 1996, he said that he and his sister, Fran Mack, doubted that his mother would have said, "Please get a gun and shoot me." He said she was so religious they "didn't think she would say such a thing." Yet, these are the words Peter used when he told this story to me.

59 *. . . in 1986, AIDS was still barely known:* This brief history of AIDS was based on the work of the late journalist Randy Shilts, *And the Band Played On* (New York: St. Martin's Press, 1987).

60 *In March 1987:* Gina Kolata, "FDA Approves AZT," *Science* 235 (March 27, 1987): 1570.

62 *. . . most of the medical community:* See Shilts's heartbreakingly compelling account, which first broke the news of the enormity of the AIDS epidemic and how it was being ignored. Shilts, *And the Band*.

. . . psychiatrist, however, was able to come: Although Ron gave me the names of the dermatologist and the psychiatrist, and gave them his permission for them to share Peter's medical history with me, neither returned my calls. This is therefore solely from Peter's and Ron's own accounts.

. . . between 40 and 80 percent: Based on interviews and the research of Dr. William Breitbart, Dr. Steven Passik, and Dr. Russell Portenoy; of Mathew Lefkowitz, M.D., director of the pain management service at SUNY Health Science Center, Brooklyn, N.Y.; Richard Patt, M.D., Gayle Newshan, R.N., and Mary Jo Hoyt, R.N., of the AIDS center program at Saint Vincent's Medical Center. Also see section on AIDS pain, USDHHS, AHCPR, *Management of Cancer Pain* (Washington, D.C.: U.S. Department of Health and

Human Services, 1994): 139; Joan Stephenson, Ph.D., "Experts Say AIDS Pain 'Dramatically Undertreated,'" *JAMA,* 6 November 1996; William Breitbart et al., "The Undertreatment of Pain in Ambulatory AIDS Patients," *Pain* 65, 1996: 243–49.

63 *Hospices hark back:* This history and current status of hospice is based on accounts from Sandol Stoddard, *The Hospice Movement* (New York: Vintage Books, 1992); from interviews with Jay Mahoney, director of the National Hospice Organization (NHO), on 18 January 1994, 21 February 1994, and 5 March 1996; and from an interview with Florence Wald, R.N., founder of Connecticut Hospice, America's first hospice, in September 1995. Data provided by NHO.

64 *"If someone wants":* I had many interviews, both in person and on the phone, with Mary Cooke, April 1992 through 24 April 1996, when this one took place.
In fact, by 1996: Robert A. Rosenblatt, "U.S. Targets Hospices If Patients Live Too Long," *Los Angeles Times,* 15 March 1997.

65 *It is hard:* Joanne Lynn, M.D. et al., "Defining the 'Terminally Ill': Insights from SUPPORT," *Duquesne Law Review* 35 (1996): 311.
. . . AIDS patients who make peace: G. M. Reed et al., "Realistic Acceptance as a Predictor of Decreased Survival Time in Gay Men with AIDS," *Health Psychology* 13 (July 1994): 299–307.
Since Peter died, protease: Robin Estrin, "Fewer AIDS Patients Enter Hospices," Associated Press, 22 January 1997.

68 *. . . neuropathy—the kind of nerve pain:* Information about pain and neuropathies is based on extensive interviews with numerous world-renowned pain experts and on extensive reading and study of the research, including that of the following physicians: Kathleen Foley, Russell Portenoy, William Breitbart, Steven Passik, C. Stratton Hill Jr., Richard Patt, Mathew Lefkowitz, Robert Brody, and Michael Levy. These experts all say that neuropathic pain is among the toughest to treat, requiring very careful assessment since many different kinds of pain syndromes may be operating at once, each possibly needing a different approach—surgical, medical, different ways of delivering medication, and high doses. In general, though, neuropathic pain requires higher doses of narcotics than is normally seen by physicians (and patients and families), often in combination with high doses of tricyclic antidepressants, anticonvulsants (often at seizure-level doses), antiarrhythmics, and local anesthetics in internal preparations. For specific treatment methods see William Breitbart, M.D., "Pharmacotherapy of Pain in AIDS," in *A Clinical Guide to AIDS and HIV,* ed. Gary P. Wormser (Philadelphia: Lippincott-Raven Publishers, 1996): 359–78.
Neuropathic pain: See AHCPR cancer pain guidelines, p. 140; and "Psychological and Psychiatric Interventions in Pain Control," *Oxford Textbook of Palliative Medicine* (New York: Oxford University Press, 1993): 244. Also see Breitbart et al., "The Undertreatment of Pain in Ambulatory AIDS Patients," *Pain* 65 (1996): 243–49; and Breitbart, "Pain in AIDS: Bridging the Gap Between Pain Experts and AIDS Specialists," *American Pain Society Bulletin* 5 (July/August 1995): 1.
Yet, its severity: Breitbart and McDonald report that in their studies only 6 percent of AIDS patients reporting severe pain were being given a strong

opioid. "This degree of undermedication of pain in AIDS (85 percent)," they reported, about a second study, "far exceeds published reports of 40 percent undertreatment of pain in cancer populations." See "Pharmacologic Pain Management in HIV/AIDS," *Journal of the International Association of Physicians in AIDS Care* 2 (July 1996): 17–26.

Dr. Kao considered him: Interviews with Dr. Daniel Kao in person and on the phone occurred periodically, October 1992–February 1994. This interview followed a lecture on pain management that Dr. Kao gave to prospective hospice volunteers at Cabrini, 11 October 1993. Available pain assessment methods and scales are described in the USDHHS, AHCPR's *Management of Cancer Pain.*

69   *"I fought over and over again":* Interview with Donny Ciccone on 18 January 1996.

"In 1978, when I came": The pages that follow are based on an interview with Dr. Kao, 19 January 1994.

By 1994, there were still: Data on hospice doctors provided by the National Academy of Hospice Physicians, now renamed the American Academy of Hospice and Palliative Medicine.

71   *In all, I asked more than:* These pain experts include the list of physicians mentioned earlier as neuropathic pain specialists, as well as Nessa Coyle, R.N., Gayle Newshan, Ph.D., and Mary Jo Hoyt, R.N. and the late John Bonica, M.D. I talked in more general terms about AIDS, neuropathic pain, and/or problems of using narcotics in prior drug-dependent or current substance-abuse populations, and/or problems of costs with all of the above, with Betty Ferrell, Ph.D., City of Hope Medical Center, Duarte, California; Dr. Joanne Lynn; Paul Brenner, director of the Jacob Perlow Hospice at Beth Israel Medical Center in New York; and NHO director Jay Mahoney.

In addition, I attended lectures of leading pain and symptom specialists, among them: Howard Fields, M.D., Ph.D., of the University of California in San Francisco; Charles E. Inturrisi, Ph.D., professor of pharmacology at Cornell University Medical Center, New York City; Eduardo D. Breura, M.D., director of palliative care, Edmonton General Hospital, University of Alberta; Ehud Arbit, M.D., then the chief of the neurosurgical service and Subhash Jain, M.D., director of anesthesiology pain management, both at Memorial Sloan-Kettering; Neil Ellison, M.D., Geisinger Medical Center, Danville, Pennsylvania; Stuart L. Du Pen, M.D., director of pain consultation, Swedish Hospital, Seattle; Mark Lema, M.D., chairman of the cancer pain service at Roswell Park Cancer Institute, in Buffalo; and Margo McCaffery, R.N., a nationally known consultant, based in Los Angeles, who specializes in assessment and holistic approaches to the nursing care of patients with pain.

I talked in general about the psychology of pain with Dr. Jimmie Holland, coeditor with Julia H. Rowland, Ph.D., of the *Handbook of Psychooncology* (New York: Oxford University Press, 1990) and chief of psychiatry at Memorial Sloan-Kettering.

72   *Dr. Portenoy has written:* Portenoy et al., "The Nature of Opioid Responsiveness and Its Implications for Neuropathic Pain: New Hypotheses Derived from Studies of Opioid Infusions," *Pain* (December 1990): 273–86.

73   *. . . a much-quoted 1990 study:* Nessa Coyle, R.N., Jean Adelhardt, R.N., Kathleen Foley, M.D., and Russell Portenoy, M.D., "Character of Terminal

Illness in the Advanced Cancer Patient: Pain and Other Symptoms During the Last Four Weeks of Life," *JPSM* 5 (April 1990): 83–93.

"*The pain in AIDS*": Interviews with Dr. Richard Patt, 1 February 1994, at the time of publication of his book—Richard B. Patt, M.D. with Susan S. Lang, *You Don't Have to Suffer: A Complete Guide to Relieving Cancer Pain for Patients and their Families* (New York: Oxford University Press, 1994); at the First National Conference on Clinical Hospice Care/Palliative Medicine, sponsored by the NHO and the National Academy of Hospice Physicians, San Francisco, 20–23 February 1994; and in private correspondence in February 1997.

74   "*Fifty milligrams an hour*": Interview with Dr. Robert Brody, February 1994.

75   . . . *Peter's pain was* spiritual, *not physical*: Interview with Mary Cooke, 24 April 1996.

       "*Peter had the trouble of being Catholic*": Interview with Sister Loretta, 15 April 1996.

76   "*We tried to*": Interview with Peter's home-care nurse, Mary Iades, 15 April 1996.

       A 1994 study: Study of homophobia in the medical profession reported by the AMA's Council on Scientific Affairs report, "Health Care Needs of Gay Men and Lesbians in the United States," *JAMA* 275 (1 May 1996): 1354–59. (Study is described on page 1356.)

       "*There were no provisions*": Diagnosis-related groups (DRGs) is how Medicare and other health-care reimbursement programs classify payment amount allotted for each category of hospitalized care, for example, pneumonia, bypass surgery, appendectomy, or gallbladder surgery.

77   *In 1996, the U.S. Health Care*: Christine K. Cassel, M.D. and Bruce C. Vladeck, Ph.D., "Sounding Board: ICD-9 Code for Palliative or Terminal Care," *NEJM* (17 October 1996): 1232–33. Notes on its current use and availability are from Dr. Russell K. Portenoy, in private correspondence, 20 January 1997, and Dr. Joanne Lynn, in an interview 2 February 1996.

       "*What we usually do*": Dr. Joanne Lynn.

F O U R When Death Becomes a Blessing: The Problem
             of Pain

Page
81   *On Saturday, September 18, 1993*: American Society of Clinical Oncology Conference on Cancer Pain, Pittsburgh, 18 and 19 September 1993. Dr. Kathleen Foley's address was on Saturday morning, September 18, and is the basis for this section of the chapter. However, from this lecture onward, through April 1996, I also interviewed Dr. Foley numerous times on the phone and in person, attended many of her other lectures, including those at Memorial Sloan-Kettering, Beth Israel Hospital, and as part of The Project on Death in America, of which she became chairman in 1995, and read most of her textbooks on pain and her medical research papers.

85   . . . *the group eventually helped draft*: Comprehensive Pain Management Group (CPMG), *Method of Relief of Cancer Pain* (later known as *Annex 1*) (Geneva, Switzerland: World Health Organization, 1983).

86   ... *American College of Physicians: AIM* 99 (1983): 870–73.

In 1984, in JAMA: W. T. McGivney and G. M. Crooks, "The Care of Patients with Severe Chronic Pain and Terminal Illness," *JAMA* 251 (1984): 1182–88.

By 1986, the organization: CPMG, *Cancer Pain Relief* (Geneva, Switzerland: World Health Organization, 1986). (WHO Publications Center, USA, 49 Sheridan Avenue, Albany, NY 12210).

... *the American Pain Society:* American Pain Society (APS), *Guidelines for the Use of Narcotic Analgesics in Acute and Chronic Pain* (1986). Also updated: APS, "Principle of Analgesic Use in the Treatment of Acute and Chronic Cancer Pain: A Concise Guide to Medical Practice," 2nd ed. (1989), and 3rd ed. (1992). (To get a copy call: 708-966-0050.)

... *for acute, postsurgical pain management:* USDHHS, AHCPR, *Acute Pain Management* (Washington, D.C.: U.S. Department of Health and Human Services, February 1992). (To order guidelines, request Publication No. 92-0032, from USDHHS, AHCPR, Rockville, MD 20852, or call 800-358-9295 for a copy.)

... *the agency published a second:* USDHHS, AHCRP, *Management of Cancer Pain* (Washington, D.C.: U.S. Department of Health and Human Services, March 1994). (To order, request Publication No. 94-0592, from USDHHS, AHCPR, Rockville, MD 20852, or call 800-358-9295).

87   ... *Dr. Foley published seminal papers:* Kathleen M. Foley, M.D. with Charles E. Inturrisi, M.D., *Opioid Analgesics in the Management of Clinical Pain: Advances in Pain Research and Therapy* 8 (New York: Raven Press, 1986); and "The Treatment of Cancer Pain," *NEJM* 313 (1985): 84–95.

In 1991, Dr. Cleeland's: A. K. Hatfield et al., *An ECOG Pilot Study: Results of an Outpatient Pain Survey in Outpatient Cancer Centers,* presented at a meeting of the American Society of Clinical Oncology, Houston, 19–21 May 1991.

88   ... *researchers conducted a nationwide survey:* David E. Joranson, M.S.S.W. et al., "Opioids for Chronic Cancer and Non-Cancer Pain: A Survey of State Medical Board Members," *Federation Bulletin: The Journal of Medical Licensure and Discipline* 79 (1992): 15–49.

89   *In 1993, Dr. Cleeland reported:* Janie H. Von Roenn, M.D. et al., "Physician Attitudes and Practice in Cancer Pain Management: A Survey from the Eastern Cooperative Oncology Group," *AIM* 119 (15 July 1993): 121–26.

90   *In March 1994, the Wisconsin researchers:* Cleeland et al., "Pain and its Treatment in Outpatients with Metastatic Cancer," *NEJM* 330 (March 1994): 592–96.

"The guidelines very clearly state": Dr. Kathleen Foley, speaking on a video uplink of a national Cancer Pain Video Conference, sponsored by the American Pain Society, 21 April 1994.

... *about half of all Americans:* See the findings of the SUPPORT study, *JAMA* 274 (22/29 November 1995): 1591–98, for patients with other illnesses besides cancer, including heart, liver, or respiratory diseases, or organ system failures. Also see David E. Joranson, of the WHO Collaborating Center for Symptom Evaluation in Cancer Care at the University of Wisconsin, in an interview in *The New York Times,* 21 October 1994, plus the research of his team, the pain teams at Memorial Sloan-Kettering, at M. D. Anderson, and at many other cancer and pain research centers.

91 *Federal AHCPR cancer pain guidelines:* AHCPR, *Management of Cancer Pain,* p. 8.

... *in America today, undertreated pain:* Ibid., as well as a host of other references.

... *because cancer pain:* A third of all cancer patients have moderate to severe pain during the treatment phase of their illness, as do about 60 to 90 percent of those with advanced cancer. This is reported in Foley, "Supportive Care and the Quality of Life of the Cancer Patient," *Principles and Practice of Oncology,* 4th ed., ed. V. T. DeVita Jr. et al. (Philadelphia: Lippincott, 1993), 2417–48, as well as in many other books and research papers. (An earlier version of this piece was written with E. Arbit, M.D.)

... *half of all patients with a variety:* See Joanne Lynn, M.D. et al., "Perceptions by Family Members of the Dying Experience of Older and Seriously Ill Patients," *AIM* 126 (15 January 1997): 97–106. (This article is taken from a portion of the SUPPORT study.)

They believe, wrongly: This information is taken from the work of—and interviews with—numerous pain experts, including Dr. Foley and other authors of the many pain management guidelines already mentioned, but it is also outlined at length in all the highly influential pain management guides, including that published by AHCPR.

Consider what happened to Ronald Blum: Based on interviews with Dr. Blum on 6 December 1993, and with John Eadie, Director of the Division of Public Health Protection of the New York State Department of Health, 24 January 1994. For background material, see Martha McKinney, Ph.D. and Lou Fintor, "News: How Physicians Handle Drug Investigations," *Journal of the National Cancer Institute* 83 (18 September 1991): 1282–84.

93 *If the charges had stuck:* As of this writing in 1997, in 1987 when Dr. Blum faced these possible charges, New York State law requires that doctors list as an *addict* or *habitual user* anyone—including terminally ill patients—who uses narcotics for more than three months. In addition, that patient's name, age, and the drug being prescribed must be listed. When the forms aren't filled in properly, the state's computer automatically writes "21" in the age blank.

"When you have a lot of twenty-one-year-old people, it's one of two things, both of which are wrong," Thomas Coffey, the director of the Bureau of Controlled Substances in New York's State Department of Health, explained to a reporter for the *Journal of the National Cancer Institute* in 1987. "One is a technical matter, one is a substantial matter. But the only way to determine that really is to try and find out from the doctor's office how old these patients are."

Federal drug control: This discussion of the early history of drug laws is based on a keynote address by C. Stratton Hill Jr., "A World View of Pain Management," at A Total Quality Approach to Cancer Pain Management, a conference sponsored by Beth Israel Medical Center, New York, 17 November 1993.

... *until 1953, when Dr. Bonica:* John Bonica, M.D., *The Management of Pain* (Philadelphia: Lea and Febiger, 1953). See *Current and Emerging Issues in Cancer Pain: Research and Practice,* ed. C. R. Chapman, M.D. and K. M. Foley, M.D. (New York: Raven Press, 1993), p. vii, for a discussion of the critical role of Dr. Bonica's book.

The federal Controlled Substances Act: The history of drug laws after 1970 is based on the work of David E. Joranson, "Federal and State Regulation of Opioids," *JPSM* 5 (February 1990): 12–23.

94   *. . . drugs were ranked in terms of five schedules:* Taken from regulations of the Controlled Substances Act of 1970.

95   *. . . international law:* David E. Joranson, "Guiding Principles of International, Federal and State Laws Pertaining to Medical Use and Diversion of Controlled Substances," paper in press, Pain Research Group, University of Wisconsin, Madison, WI, 1993.

96   *. . . the states jumped the gun:* Joranson, "Federal and State Regulation": 15–16.

The New York State law: Based on personal interviews and the work of Robert T. Angarola, 20 January 1994 (work includes "Single-Copy Serialized Prescriptions: Old Regulation in New Clothing," *American Pain Society Bulletin* (November 1992), and a series of other articles in that journal on other dates; and "Regulatory Affairs and Government Regulations for Pain Management," paper presented at a Memorial Sloan-Kettering conference, Current Concepts in Acute, Chronic and Cancer Pain Management (8 December 1993); interview with David Joranson, 25 January 1994; and interviews with John Eadie, 24 January 1994, and June Dahl, Ph.D., 25 January 1994.

97   *"To keep their licenses":* Personal interview with Dr. Arthur Kennish, January 1994.

. . . Wisconsin State Cancer Pain: The Wisconsin State Cancer Pain Initiative (an educational and lobbying group that aims to improve the pain management of cancer patients) has since been copied by lobbying groups in other states, some of which—like New York—also include efforts to improve not only cancer but AIDS pain treatment. For information, write the Wisconsin Pain Initiative, 1300 University Avenue, Room 3675, Madison, WI 53706.

After officials in Texas: From a personal interview and lecture in New York, 17 November 1993; and in C. Stratton Hill Jr., M.D., "The Intractable Treatment Act of Texas," *Texas Medicine* 88 (February 1992); "Influence of Regulatory Agencies on the Treatment of Pain and Standards of Medical Practice for the Use of Narcotics," *Pain Digest* 1 (1991): 7–12; "Relationship Among Cultural, Educational, and Regulatory Agency Influences on Optimum Cancer Pain Treatment," *JPSM* 5 (February 1990): 37–45.

98   *A 1988 study of ninety-four:* Ronald M. Kanner, M.D. and Russell K. Portenoy, M.D., "Unavailability of Narcotic Analgesics for Ambulatory Cancer Patients in New York City," *JPSM* 1 (Spring 1986): 87–89.

National studies show similar numbers: Personal interview with Dr. Ronald Kanner, chairman of the neurology department, Long Island Jewish Hospital, New Hyde Park, New York, February 1994.

"Stocking opioid drugs: Interview with Ivan Jourdain, February 1994.

99   *. . . the mounting psychological stress:* In personal interviews with Dr. Foley, as well as in her article, "The Relationship of Pain and Symptom Management to Patient Requests for Physician-Assisted Suicide," *JPSM* 6 (July 1991); and her paper, "Physician-Assisted Suicide," presented at a conference at Memorial Sloan-Kettering on Current Concepts in Acute, Chronic and Cancer Pain Management, 10 December 1993.

100   ... *these six rules:* These pain principles are outlined by Dr. Foley in lectures and books and are the core of the international WHO and federal AHCPR pain treatment guidelines. They were reviewed by Dr. Russell K. Portenoy, Dr. Richard Patt, and Dr. Joanne Lynn.

103   *In 1990, a North Carolina jury:* A summary of the case of the family of Henry James was provided by his attorney, Ron Manasco, of the law firm Henson and Fuerst, of Rocky Mount, N.C. Additional information came from an interview with Manasco on 25 January 1994.

   "Patients have to understand": Interview with Dr. Foley, 8 December 1993.

   In December 1993, about a year: The following discussion is based on an interview with Dr. John Bonica, 10 December 1993, and subsequent biographical material he provided me.

105   *The patient is Laura:* I agreed with Memorial Sloan-Kettering not to use the real names of any patient at the hospital.

110   *Dr. Van Dam scoffs:* Interview on Tuesday, 14 December 1993.

111   *William Breitbart is a physician:* This section is based on many interviews with Dr. William Breitbart, October 1993–June 1996, as well as lectures he gave at psychology conferences and in pain management rounds at Memorial Sloan-Kettering, December 1993–January 1994; at Psycho-Oncology V: Psychosocial Factors in Cancer Risk and Survival, 2–4 October 1993, Concepts in Acute, Chronic and Cancer Pain Management, 8–10 December 1993, both conferences at Memorial Sloan-Kettering; at the First National Conference on Clinical Hospice Care/Palliative Medicine, sponsored by the National Hospice Organization and the National Academy of Hospice Physicians, San Francisco, 20–23 February 1994; at a seminar of The Project on Death in America, 12–13 January 1995; and based on his work in numerous publications, including *The Handbook of Psycho-Oncology,* ed. Holland and Rowland (1990), *The Oxford Textbook of Palliative Medicine,* ed. Doyle, Hanks, and Macdonald (1993), and many journal articles.

112   *... a research specialist on the reasons patients:* See, among other work, Breitbart, Barry D. Rosenfeld, Ph.D., and Steven Passik, Ph.D., "Interest in Physician-Assisted Suicide Among Ambulatory HIV-Infected Patients," *American Journal of Psychiatry* 153 (February 1996): 238–42.

   Recent research in mind/body medicine: This view is promulgated by researchers in psychoimmunology like Dr. Steven Locke, professor of psychiatry at Harvard Medical School (see "Immunity," a paper he gave at Healing: Beyond Suffering or Death, a conference in Montreal 21 June 1993). On the other hand, Dr. Jimmie Holland of Memorial Sloan-Kettering takes issue with this theory (see "Living with Cancer," *Scientific American* 275 (September 1996): 158–61.

115   *... Dr. Breitbart often:* This section is taken from Breitbart and Steven Passik, Ph.D., "Psychiatric Aspects of Palliative Care," *Oxford Textbook,* 617.

   Still, to some who disagree: See in particular "Physician-Assisted Suicide," a paper presented at Concepts in Acute, Chronic and Cancer Pain Management.

   Others—like Dr. Van Dam: Interview with Dr. Frits S.A.M. Van Dam, 14 December 1993.

   To still others—including psycho-oncologist: Rachel Naomi Remen, M.D., interview 22 April 1995.

116 *An even higher percentage of AIDS:* See Breitbart et al., "A Double-Blind Trial of Haloperidol, Chlorpromazine, and Lorazepam in the Treatment of Delirium in Hospitalized AIDS Patients," *American Journal of Psychiatry* 153 (February 1996): 231–37.
"There are different kinds of hallucinations": Interview with Dr. Breitbart in April 1995.

117 *"We know from one study:* Interview with Jon Levenson, M.D., 22 April 1992.

118 *In 1990, he shocked pain specialists:* See Vittorio Ventafriddal et al., "Symptom Prevalence and Control During Cancer Patients' Last Days of Life," *Journal of Palliative Care* 6:3 (1990): 7–11.

119 *... like Memorial Sloan-Kettering:* Based on interviews with Dr. Foley, Dr. Portenoy, and Nessa Coyle, and others at Memorial Sloan-Kettering; and with Dr. Michael Levy at Fox Chase Cancer Center.
Some doctors consider terminal sedation: This difference in treatment, and therefore in equal protection under the law, is what prompted the federal United States Court of Appeals for the Second Circuit to decide on 2 April 1996, that all laws against assisted suicide are unconstitutional, ultimately sending the question of legalizing assisted suicide to the U.S. Supreme Court.

120 *Others add severe nausea:* Interview with Dr. Portenoy in November 1992; Paul Rousseau, "Terminal Sedation in the Care of Dying Patients," *Archives of Internal Medicine* 9 (September 1996): 1785ff.; N. Cherney and R. Portenoy, "Sedation in the Management of Refractory Symptoms—Guidelines for Evaluation and Treatment," *Journal of Palliative Care* 10 (1994): 31–38; Troug et al., "Barbiturates in the Care of the Terminally Ill," *NEJM* 327 (1992): 1678–82.
... by an important 1990 study: See Coyle et al., "Character of Terminal Illness in the Advanced Cancer Patient: Pain and Other Symptoms During the Last Four Weeks of Life," *JPSM* 5 (April 1990): 83–93.

123 *However, there are some 6,000 deaths:* See reference to figures provided by a 1990 study of the American Hospital Association, in Alan Meisel, "The Legal Consensus about Foregoing Life-Sustaining Treatment: Its Status and Its Prospects," *Kennedy Institute of Ethics Journal* 2 (1993): 309–45. See especially n. 8, p. 335.
Still, even cancer specialists say: Interview with Dr. Joanne Lynn, April 1996. See also Gina Kolata, "Living Wills Aside, Dying Cling to Hope," *The New York Times,* 15 January 1997.

124 *... most Americans die:* See Meisel, "The Legal Consensus," p. 335, n. 6 especially.
... the issue the U.S. Supreme Court considered: In *Vacco v. Quill* and *Washington v. Glucksberg,* argued 8 January 1997.

F I V E   **Tough Love:** The Legacy of Karen Ann Quinlan

Page

126 *About a week before she lost:* Information about Karen Ann Quinlan's personal story was based on a number of sources. These include personal interviews with her parents, Julia and Joe Quinlan, in February 1995, and two conferences—Managing Mortality: Ethics, Euthanasia, and the Termi-

nation of Medical Treatment (3–5 December 1992), Minneapolis, Minn.; Quinlan: A Twenty Year Retrospective (12–13 April 1996), in Princeton, N.J., at which the Quinlans and others spoke. (Tapes are available of these respective conferences through TagTeam Film and Video, Inc., 612-338-3360, or Continuing Medical Education, at the University of Minnesota, 612-626-7600; and Martin's Video, in Mays Landing, N.J., 609-625-6633.) This report also draws on accounts in *The Philadelphia Inquirer* and *The New York Times*; Joan Kron, "The Girl in the Coma," *New York*, 6 October 1975: 32–5; Joan Kron, "Did the Girl in the Coma Want Death with Dignity," *New York,* 27 October 1975: 60–62; Joseph and Julia Quinlan with Phyllis Batelle, *Karen Ann* (New York: Doubleday, 1977) and Paul Armstrong, interviewed by the author, 14 February 1995.

131 *Though Valium was found . . .:* Interview with Dr. Julius Korein, 3 March 1995.

132 *". . . big warnings not to drink with Darvon":* Warnings about mixing Darvon, whose generic name is propoxyphene hydrochloride, and alcohol, appear in modern lay and physician desk references, as for example, *The Pill Book, 7th Revised Edition,* Harold M. Silverman, Pharm. D., ed. (New York: Bantam Books, 1996), 956–57.

A clot could have formed: This is based on communications and/or conversations with several doctors, including Russell K. Portenoy, M.D., neurology pain service, Memorial Sloan-Kettering Cancer Center, 20 May 1997, and Joanne Lynn, M.D., former staff director for medicine of the President's Commission for the Study of Ethical Problems in Medicine and Biomedical and Behavioral Research, 14 May 1997.

133 *. . . even after reviewing autopsy data:* H. C. Kinney et al., "Neuropathological Findings in the Brain of Karen Ann Quinlan," *NEJM* 330 (26 May 1994): 1469–75.

134 *This supposition is based on:* Astonishingly, one 1977 study found that "more than half the children undergoing major surgery in the study group—including limb amputations, excisions of cancerous neck masses and heart surgery—were not given *any* analgesics, and the rest received inadequate doses." Even studies as late as 1986 found that children received half to a third of the amount of analgesics that adults did (prorated to their weight) when their surgeries and ailments were matched. "Recent studies, using the assessment tools available to us," Ronald Melzack, M.D., president of the International Association for the Study of Pain, wrote in 1988, "indicate that children experience the same qualities and intensities of pain felt by adults. But they are horribly undermedicated."

See J. M. Erland and J. E. Anderson, "The Experience of Pain in Children," as reported in Ronald Melzack, M.D., "The Tragedy of Needless Pain: A Call for Social Action," *Proceeding of the 5th World Congress on Pain,* ed. R. Cubner, G. F. Gebhart, and M. R. Bond (New York: Elsevier Science Publishers, 1988); N. L. Schecter, D. A. Allen, and K. J. Hanson, "The Status of Pediatric Pain Control: A Comparison of Hospital Analgesic Usage in Children and Adults," *Pediatrics* 77 (1986): 11–15.

Yet, other physicians: Commentary in personal correspondence with Dr. Joanne Lynn, former staff director for medicine of the President's

Commission for the Study of Ethical Problems in Medicine and Biomedical
and Behavioral Research (President's Commission), May 1997.

135 *In 1992, Raj Narayan, M.D.:* In Gina Kolata, "Ethicists Debate New Definition of Death," *The New York Times,* 29 April 1992.
Ronald Cranford, M.D., a neurologist: Ibid.
"Karen Quinlan would have been handled": Dr. Ronald Cranford, interview
by author, 26 July 1996.

136 *. . . Gary Dockery:* See Ronald Smothers, "Injured in '88, Officer Awakes in
'96," *The New York Times,* 16 January 1996. Update in "The Miracle That
Faded Away," *People* magazine, 30 December 1996–6 January 1997 double
issue, p. 167. Dockery died 15 April 1997, as reported in *People,* 28 April
1997.
. . . neurologist Dr. Julius Korein said: Korein interview by author, 3 March
1995.
The Catholic Church has a long history: Information on the Church's theological position is from an interview with Richard Doerflinger on 21 February 1996, and from Monsignor (formerly Father) Thomas Trapasso, at the
conference, Quinlan: A Twenty Year Retrospective. Also see Reverend Kevin
O'Rourke, "Pain Relief: The Perspective of Catholic Tradition," *Journal of
Pain and Symptom Management* (November 1992): 485–91; Sacred Con-
gregation for the Doctrine of the Faith, *Declaration on Euthanasia* (Boston:
Saint Paul Books and Media, 5 May 1980); Committee for Pro-Life Activities of the National Conference of Catholic Bishops, *Nutrition and Hydration: Moral and Pastoral Reflections* (Washington, D.C.: United States
Catholic Conference, 4 April 1992).

137 *"Often a terminally ill patient":* Karen Ann, p. 92.

138 *On Wednesday, July 30, 1975:* Recollections of these conversations and the
meeting between the Quinlans and Dr. Morse, in Quinlan et al., *Karen Ann,*
116 ff. The Quinlans say it was Wednesday, 31 July 1975, but that year July
31 fell on a Thursday, not a Wednesday, so it isn't clear whether the meeting
took place on Wednesday or Thursday. I have therefore adjusted all dates by
the day of the week rather than the calendar date since it is doubtful that a
meeting with hospital administrators held later that week would have occurred on a Sunday.

142 *Meanwhile, the theological controversy:* Quinlan et al., *Karen Ann,* p. 225.
The New Jersey Supreme Court: Legal information on the Quinlan case comes
from their attorney Paul Armstrong, and from the legal opinion handed down
In the Matter of Karen Quinlan, An Alleged Incompetent, by New Jersey State
Supreme Court Justice Robert Hughes, on 31 March 1976.

143 *The New Jersey Catholic:* Bishop Casey's amicus brief is also contained in
that opinion.

144 *"That night I thought my mother":* Quinlan et al., *Karen Ann,* p. 285. *A
federal commission:* The President's Commission, *Deciding to Forego Life-
Sustaining Treatment* (Washington, D.C. 1983): footnote on p. 183, quoting
testimony in Quinlan and Quinlan, *supra* note 1, at 287.

145 *". . . Dr. Morse replied, 'For as long as it takes. . . .' ":* I tried to contact Dr.
Morse to ask his side of this story and learned that he had died 1 April 1987.
An amateur pilot, his small Cessna airplane crashed in the woods near
Seneca Lake, in Morris County, New Jersey, killing him, at forty-seven,

along with his fourteen-year-old son and two friends of his son, ages fourteen and seventeen.

. . . Sister Mary Urban, the president: Joe Quinlan wrote this in *Karen Ann,* p. 291. On 29 April 1996, I called Sister Mary Urban, who was still at Saint Clare's, to arrange an interview. Over the phone she told me she had long been "misinterpreted," and she scheduled a time in which we could meet; she wanted to explain. But the next day, before the interview could take place, Larry Stern, the same public relations officer who represented her and Saint Clare's in 1975, called to cancel it.

"She called me in a panic," he said. "She doesn't want to dredge it up again. She's in her eighties now and it's too painful. She has never talked to the press and she doesn't want to make any public statements." When asked if she would disagree if quoted, as the Quinlans reported, that she said, "In this hospital we don't kill people," he said: "No. You have to do what you have to do."

Dr. Arshad Javed was still a pulmonary specialist in New Jersey. When called for an interview, he had his assistant send back a fax asking, among other things, whether he would be compensated for his time and expertise. I have not compensated anyone for interviews in this book, so I did not go ahead with this one.

147 *"Nutrition and Hydration":* Op. cit.
When I interviewed him: Richard Doerflinger, 21 February 1996.

148 *. . . ad hoc committee at Harvard:* See a thorough discussion in The President's Commission for the Study of Ethical Problems in Medicine and Biomedical and Behavioral Research, *Defining Death: Medical, Legal and Ethical Issues in the Determination of Death* (Washington, D.C., 1981): 24 ff.

150 *"The commission decided,":* In private communication with Dr. Joanne Lynn, spring 1996.
"Weaning a permanently unconscious patient": The President's Commission for the Study of Ethical Problems, *Deciding to Forego,* in footnotes, p. 191, referring also to editorial by A. Grenvik, "Terminal Weaning: Discontinuance of Life-Supporting Therapy in the Terminally Ill Patient," *Critical Care Medicine* (May 1983).

152 *"They believed in the right of people":* Joseph Quinlan's obituary: Robert Hanley, "Joseph Quinlan, 71, Sought Daughter's Right to Die," *The New York Times,* 11 December 1996.

S I X   **Who Decides?** Law and Politics at the Edges of Life

Page
154 *On Monday, December 17, 1990:* Accounts of the protest were based on the following newspaper articles: Paul Hendrickson, "The Mourning After: In a Small Missouri Town, the Nancy Cruzan Vigil Ends. The Debate Doesn't," *Washington Post,* 28 December 1990; Pamela Warrick, "Protesters Plotted 'Rescue'—and Then It Was Too Late," *Los Angeles Times,* 10 January 1991.

155 *. . . decided by the U.S. Supreme Court:* Case law analysis and descriptions taken from Alan Meisel, J. D., *The Right to Die* 2nd edition, Vol. 1 and Vol.

2 (New York: John Wiley & Sons, 1995); Managing Mortality: Ethics, Euthanasia, and the Termination of Medical Treatment conference sponsored by The Center for Biomedical Ethics, University of Minnesota, Minneapolis, Minn., 3–5 December 1992). Case histories in conference brochure were prepared by The Society for the Right to Die (now Choice in Dying), 200 Varick St., New York, NY 10014; 212-366-5540.

In the early hours: Synopsis of what happened to Nancy Cruzan is taken from *Nancy Beth Cruzan, by Her Parents and Co-guardians, v. Director, Missouri Department of Health,* Sup. Ct. Case No. 88–1503 (25 June 1990). The same story was told by the Cruzan family at the Managing Mortality conference, 3 December 1992. (See *Managing Mortality,* the conference report. Tapes are available through TagTeam Film & Video, Inc., 2525 Franklin Avenue E, Suite 203, Minneapolis, MN 55406.) Malcolm Gladwell, "Woman in Right-to-Die Case Succumbs; Cruzan Was in Coma for 8 Years; Court Ruling Allowed Tube Removal," *Washington Post,* 27 December 1990.

156   *The formula needed to be:* U.S. Supreme Court, *Cruzan v. Director.* See the opinion of Justices Brennan, Marshall, and Blackmun.

"It took us three and a half years": Interview with Chris Cruzan White, 5 October 1996.

157   *According to Donald Lamkins:* Interview with Donald Lamkins, 17 January 1997.

. . . Nancy had told many relatives: U.S. Supreme Court, *Cruzan v. Director;* see footnotes 19 and 20 in the opinion of Justice Brennan, joined by Justices Marshall and Blackmun, describing conversations that Nancy had had with Athena Comer, her long-time friend, coworker, and a housemate for several months, after Comer's sister suddenly became ill and died during the night. "The Comer family had been told that if she had lived through the night, she would have been in a vegetative state. Nancy had lost a grandmother a few months before. Ms. Comer testified: 'Nancy said she would never want to live [in a vegetative state] because if she couldn't be normal or even, you know, like halfway, and do things for [her]self, because Nancy always did, that she didn't want to live . . . and we talked about it a lot.' "

That half-hour "serious" conversation took place about a year before Nancy's accident, and about six months after a similar conversation she'd had with Chris, after their niece was stillborn. Had she lived, doctors said she would have been badly damaged. Nancy told Chris, "Maybe it was part of a 'greater plan' that the baby had been stillborn and did not have to face 'the possible life of mere existence.' "

159   *"There's a link between the two,":* Laura Echevarria, interview 9 January 1997. This interview provides much of the background for the short history and political mission statement of the National Right to Life Committee, Inc., Suite 500, 419 Seventh Street N.W., Washington, DC 20004-2293, 202-625-8800. Although repeated requests were made, no press or background material was provided by the National Right to Life press office, no calls were returned, and no requested interviews arranged.

Bill Webster, the Republican: The story of Attorney General William Webster is based on Christopher Clark and Chris Bentley, "Once a Dynasty," *Springfield News-Leader,* 2 June 1993.

160   ... *attorney James Bopp Jr.:* The information on the National Legal Center for the Medically Dependent and Disabled, Inc. is from the organization's mission statement. The views and history of legal cases taken by the center are also based on an interview with Daniel Avila, its chief staff counsel, 20 November 1996. James Bopp did not return my calls, nor, again, did officials of the National Right to Life Committee (other than to send some literature and to finally have the press secretary, Laura Echevarria, talk with me), although interviews were requested, among them with Wanda Franz, the president, and Burke J. Balch, director of the Committee's medical ethics department.

While other groups representing the disabled: Summary Report, Managing Mortality, a conference sponsored by The Center for Biomedical Ethics, University of Minnesota, 3–5 December 1992, p. 9, comment by Jan Lawrence, the sister of Sue Ann Lawrence, noted: "The Indiana chapter of the Association for Retarded Citizens had passed a resolution recognizing a clear distinction between a retarded citizen and a person in a PVS."

Many of the disabled: Based on my own interviews with many disabled protesters representing a group called Not Dead Yet at the U.S. Supreme Court hearing on arguments to legalize assisted suicide, 8 January 1997, and on conversations during that same period on ERGO, the Hemlock Society's E-mail list in which Not Dead Yet members participated, and on an interview with Diane Coleman, the group's founder, 28 March 1997.

... *her care cost taxpayers $130,000:* Henry R. Glick, *The Right to Die* (New York: Columbia University Press, 1992): p. 2.

Nancy's condition was not strictly terminal: Nancy would have died without her feeding tube and the round-the-clock, high intensity care she was getting, but perhaps not if she received that care. Her attorney William Colby says, however: "Her condition was terminal in my opinion. I once asked for a show of hands from about three hundred doctors and nurses at a National Hospice Organization meeting on that question. It split about fifty-fifty."

... *in nearly all of the major antiabortion cases:* The cases are listed in James Bopp's résumé, as provided by his law firm, Bopp, Coleson & Bostrom, of Terre Haute, Indiana. Also see the following references to these legal cases in: Aaron Epstein, "Justices to Review Abortion Limits, Basic Right Question Won't Be Addressed," *Detroit Free Press,* 22 January 1992; Christopher Scanlan, "Hopes for Fetal Tissue Wait, Abortion Foes Oppose Research on Its Healing Value," *Detroit Free Press,* 7 October 1991; Sara Engram, "Abortion Foes Battle Right to Die," *Detroit Free Press,* 12 August 1991; Aaron Epstein and Jacquelynn Boyle, "High Court Ruling Lets Teen Obtain an Abortion," *Detroit Free Press,* 19 May 1989; Dolores Kong, "Ethics Arguments Disrupt Fetal Research," *Detroit Free Press,* 4 April 1989; Aaron Epstein, "High Court Snubs 'Father's Rights,' Justices Refuse to Hear Appeal on Abortion," *Detroit Free Press,* 15 November 1988.

161   *On July 3, 1989, the same day:* William H. Colby, "The Lessons of the Cruzan Case," *The University of Kansas Law Review* (spring 1991): p. 524. *In all, more than fifty briefs:* Information provided by the press office of the U.S. Supreme Court, and in correspondence with Colby, February 1997.

"I feel like a spectator": *Frontline* did three documentaries on the Cruzans

that aired in July 1987, in March 1988, and in March 1991, all produced by Elizabeth Arledge.

163 *About a dozen right-to-life protesters:* This section, including the quotes from Randall Terry, is based on an unsigned UPI story, dateline Mount Vernon, 21 December 1990, UPI News Service, available on-line through Dialog/Knowledge Index.

In fact, the fortunes of Bill Webster: U.S. Department of Justice, Western District of Missouri, Office of U.S. Attorney Marietta Parker, press release, 21 September 1993; also from numerous articles in the *Springfield News-Leader.*

164 *"We have a way of knowing":* Interview with Wanda Frye, 10 January 1997.

167 *Sheriff Doug Seneker headed up:* Interview with Sheriff Seneker, 10 January 1997. *"Her death was as peaceful": Managing Mortality.*

168 *Consent has a long basis:* Meisel, *Right,* Vol. 1, p. 57.

. . . *established four additional legal precedents:* The legal precedents are compiled from Meisel, *Right to Die;* talks presented at Managing Mortality conference and *Case Histories,* prepared by Choice in Dying P.N.J. 1. *In the Matter of Karen Quinlan,* Case 70 N.J. 10, 355 A 2nd 647 before the New Jersey Supreme Court decided 31 March 1976; *Quinlan: A Twenty Year Retrospective* talks presented at conference in Princeton, N.J., 12–13 April 1996; Paul Armstrong, interview by author, February 1995.

169 *"Patient's right to privacy": In the Matter of Karen Quinlan,* N.J. Sup. Ct. (argued 26 January 1976, decided 31 March 1976).

170 *Justice Hughes had ruled that hospital:* Meisel, *Right,* Vol. 1, pp. 291–92. *The first model living will:* This section on advance directives is based on information provided by Choice in Dying, particularly its publication, *Concern for Dying/Society for the Right to Die, 1990–1991 Annual Reports,* p. 3. Henry R. Glick, *The Right to Die* (New York: Columbia University Press, 1992). See also the history and literature provided by the Death With Dignity Education Center, San Mateo, Calif.

171 *Keene had befriended a neighbor:* See Glick, *Right to Die,* pp. 92–104, for a discussion of the California Natural Death Act.

. . . *laws creating a brain-based definition of death:* See a thorough discussion in the report by the President's Commission for the Study of Ethical Problems in Medicine and Biomedical and Behavioral Research, *Defining Death: Medical, Legal and Ethical Issues in the Determination of Death,* (Washington, D.C.: GPO, 1981), 24ff.

172 . . . *National Conference of Catholic Bishops:* Glick, *Right to Die,* pp. 171 ff.

174 *Despite this effort:* Information provided by Choice in Dying, and by Alan Meisel in private correspondence, spring 1997.

175 *"[It's] an unreal standard,":* Interview with Julie Chase Delio, November 1993. See also her discussion at the Managing Mortality conference. Case summary for this conference was prepared by Choice in Dying.

Between 1976 and 1993, lower trial courts: Alan Meisel, "The Legal Consensus about Forgoing Life-Sustaining Treatment: Its Status and Prospects," *Kennedy Institute of Ethics Journal* 2: 4 (1993): 313; and in personal correspondence with Alan Meisel.

176 *The 1995 Study to Understand: JAMA* 274 (22 and 29 November 1995): 1591–98. Interviews with Dr. Joanne Lynn, May 1994–May 1997.

Why would a doctor ignore: See a thorough discussion of SUPPORT in *Dying Well in the Hospital: The Lessons of SUPPORT, Hastings Center Report* (November–December 1995); Gina Kolata, "Living Wills Aside, Dying Cling to Hope," *The New York Times,* 15 January 1997. The studies cited here were also discussed in an interview with Diane Meier, M.D., December 1993.

177   *. . . Dr. Lynn . . . has made it a point:* Joanne Lynn, M.D., "Why I Don't Have a Living Will," *Law, Medicine and Health Care* 19: 1–2 (spring/summer 1991): 101–4.

178   *. . . the Indiana family of a . . . comatose woman:* The Lawrence family had requested a court order to remove Sue Ann Lawrence's feeding tube in March 1991; she had been brain damaged since an accident at the age of nine, and in a PVS for the prior three and a half years. "We were afraid the judge was going to award Sue's guardianship to a former bouncer at a massage parlor," Jan Lawrence says, at the Managing Mortality conference, "instead of a family who had nurtured a brain-damaged sibling and daughter for thirty-three years since a childhood injury—including her final three and a half years in a persistent vegetative state after a stroke."

Tapes of this conference are available through TagTeam Film and Video, Inc., 2525 Franklin Avenue E, Suite 203, Minneapolis, MN 55406, 612-338-3360.

179   *"Before this, there was":* Robert Burt, interview by author, January 1996.

180   *. . . Helga Wanglie tripped:* Described by Ruth Wanglie at the Managing Mortality conference. Case summary prepared for this conference by Choice in Dying. Tapes available, TagTeam Film and Video.

182   *. . . "uncomfortable taking care of her":* Dr. Ronald Cranford, interview by author, 26 July 1996.

183   *"Our society is basically putting":* Arthur Caplan, Ph.D., Managing Mortality conference, and further explained in a personal interview on 3 March 1996.
In 1976, when Justice Hughes: Meisel, *Right,* Vol. 1, p. 291ff.
In 1992, the Joint Commission: Judith Wilson Ross et al., *Health Care Ethics Committees: The Next Generation* (Chicago: American Hospital Association, 1993): p. ix.

184   *"It quickly became apparent":* Albert R. Jonson, ed., "Special Supplement: The Birth of Bioethics," *Hastings Center Report* 23: 6 (November–December 1993).
The dubious precedent was set: This section is based on David J. Rothman, *Strangers at the Bedside* (New York: Basic Books, 1991).

186   *He published an article in the prestigious:* Henry K. Beecher, "Ethics and Clinical Research," *NEJM* 274 (1966): 1354–60.
Yet, it was a 1972 news report: "Syphilis Victims Got No Therapy," *The New York Times,* 26 July 1972, as reported in Arthur L. Caplan, "Twenty Years After: The Legacy of the Tuskegee Syphilis Study/When Evil Intrudes," *Hastings Center Report* (November–December 1992): 29–32.

187   *"Medical practice":* Jay Katz, "Do We Need Another Advisory Commission on Human Experimentation?" *Hastings Center Report* (January–February 1995): 29–31. See also Jay Katz, "Ethics and Clinical Research Revisited: A Tribute to Henry K. Beecher," *Hastings Center Report* (September–October 1993): 31–39.

Today, newer issues and revelations: "The Advisory Committee on Human Radiation Experiments (ACHRE) was established by President Clinton in April 1995 in response to allegations of abuses of human subjects in government-sponsored research conducted during the Cold War. The suspect research included experiments in which hospital patients were injected with plutonium and uranium, institutionalized children were administered radioactive tracers, and prisoners were exposed to testicular irradiation. In addition to investigating the facts of these and other cases, ACHRE was charged with identifying appropriate standards by which to evaluate the ethics of these experiments." *JAMA News Release Packet* (Chicago: AMA, 20 November 1996).

In another of the Nuremberg-related articles in that issue, "ACHRE Reports the Findings on the Nuremberg Code's Influence on the Norms and Practices of U.S. Medical Researchers," according to a 20 November 1996 AMA press release.

. . . in November 1996, on the fiftieth anniversary: Gina Kolata, "Ban on Medical Experiments Without Consent Is Relaxed," *The New York Times,* 5 November 1996. Also see "Trusting Science," *Hastings Center Report,* a special issue on Nuremberg and human radiation experiments, September–October 1996; and "Special Communications," *JAMA,* special section, 27 November 1997.

188 *"The patients must have a life-threatening condition":* Ibid.
The lifting of this ban: See "Trusting Science," *Hastings Center Report,* and "Special Communications," *JAMA.* In addition, James Lindemann Nelson, Ph.D., a bioethicist at the department of philosophy at the University of Tennessee and coauthor (with Hilde Lindemann Nelson) of *The Patient in the Family* (New York: Routledge, 1995), notes in personal correspondence that under this new FDA ruling, "subjects can get randomly assigned to an experimental treatment or [get] nothing at all when the field is in a state known as equipose—that is, [when] we don't know whether the experimental treatment is better than nothing (that's why the experiment is going on). I think it would be good for people to realize this more generally than they do. It removes at least a little bit of the cold-hearted image of people being denied care. (The randomization is not always between the experiment and nothing, of course; sometimes there is a standard treatment that the field is trying to improve, and the assignment is between experiment and standard.)"

189 *. . . the American Hospital Association estimates:* Meisel, "The Legal Consensus," *Kennedy Journal,* 334–35, footnote 6.

190 *. . . press reports speculated:* Colby takes issue with the word *speculated,* saying, "It was reported as fact, incorrectly, by a young *New York Times* reporter. Then it becomes citable." Joe Cruzan never felt, he says, that what he'd done for Nancy was wrong, only that that is what she would have wanted.
"One of the things people don't realize": Chris Cruzan White, phone interview by author, 5 October 1996.

191 *"The psychiatry books are filled":* William H. Colby's eulogy at Joe Cruzan's funeral, printed in the *Webb City Sentinel* (Kansas City), 23 August 1996. Interview with William Colby, 6 January 1997.

S E V E N   Bearing the Burden: Families in Distress

Page

192 *Twentieth-century medicine has reshaped our lives:* Peter Uhlenberg, "Death and the Family," Arlene S. Skolnick and Jerome H. Skolnick, eds., *Families in Transition*, 6th ed. (Glenview, Ill.: Scott, Foresman, 1989). Andrew Cherlin, "The Trends: Marriage, Divorce, Remarriage," *ibid.* Tamara K. Hareven, "American Families in Transition: Historical Perspective on Change," *ibid.* Uhlenberg, "Population Aging and Social Policy," *Annual Review of Sociology* 18 (1992): 449–74.

... *life expectancy has soared:* Kenneth D. Kochanek, M.A. and Bettie L. Hudson, "Advance Report of Final Mortality Statistics, 1992," *Monthly Vital Statistics Report* (Washington, D.C.: U.S. Department of Health and Human Services, Division of Vital Statistics, National Center for Health Statistics, 22 March 1995).

193 *In 1900, only one household:* Daniel Scott Smith, "Life Course, Norms and the Family System of Older Americans in 1900," *Journal of Family History* 4, no. 3 (Fall 1979): 2285–98.

Today, the figure is one household: U.S. Bureau of the Census, interview with statisticians in the Marriage and Family Statistics Department of the Population Division.

More than half of all midlife adults: Gina Kolata, "Family Aid to Elderly Is Very Strong, Study Shows," *The New York Times*, 3 May 1993. Data mentioned in article taken from National Institute of Child Health and Human Development, *National Survey of Families and Households*.

Nineteenth-century families: Jack Larkin, *The Reshaping of Everyday Life: 1790–1840* (New York: HarperCollins, 1988), 9–14.

194 *A study by the National Institute on Aging:* Kolata, "Family Aid," op. cit., reporting on Thomas F. Juster, "Survey Sketches New Portrait of Aging America: The Health and Retirement Survey," National Institute on Aging, National Institutes of Health (Gaithersburg, Md.: 1993).

The second study: Kolata, "Family Aid," op. cit. The AARP study, which took place in 1993, was directed by Robert Harootyan; the National Center for Health Statistics performed a similar study that also confirmed these findings. Both studies are mentioned in the Kolata article.

... *Alzheimer's is the fourth leading cause:* Associated Press, "Third Gene Tied to Early Onset Alzheimer's," *The New York Times*, 18 August 1995. Dr. Joanne Lynn estimates that the number of people who die each year having Alzheimer's may be as high as 1 million, since it does not always show up on death certificates as the specific cause of death. Lynn, private correspondence with author, February 1997.

In 1990, a man whom I will call: This story is based on extensive interviews by author with several members of the family, April 1992–October 1996. The names, identifying characteristics, and many details of the story have been changed to protect the privacy of the Cobb family, at its request.

206 ... *Jean Elbaum, who was comatose:* Alan Meisel, *The Right to Die: 1994 Cumulative Supplement No. 2* (New York: John Wiley & Sons, 1994), vii ff.

207 ... *attend support groups for cancer, AIDS:* Many of these groups are

organizations with self-help components, such as Cancer Care (800-813-HOPE); the Gay Men's Health Crisis, New York City; the National Multiple Sclerosis Society (800-LEARN-MS); the Well Spouse Foundation (212-644-1241); the Alzheimer's Association (in many cities; the New York chapter is 212-983-0700) or the ALS Association (212-679-4016 in New York, or 818-990-2151 in Sherman Oaks, Calif.).

"We know from experience": Diane Blum, letter September 1996. See also Blum et al., *A Helping Hand: The Resource Guide for People with Cancer* (New York: Cancer Care, 1996). For information, call 212-221-3300.

Recall the SUPPORT study: Knaus, Lynn et al., "A Controlled Trial to Improve Care for Seriously Ill Hospitalized Patients: Study to Understand Prognoses and Preferences for Outcomes and Risks of Treatment," *JAMA* 274, no. 20 (22/29 November 1995): 1591–98.

Among the study's major findings: Kenneth E. Covinsky, M.D. et al., "The Impact of Serious Illness on Patients' Families," *JAMA* 272, no. 23 (21 December 1994): 1839–44.

208 *One study of four hundred cancer patients*: K. Siegel et al., "Caregiver Burden and Unmet Patient Needs," *Cancer* 68 (1991): 1131–40.

A second study, of heart bypass patients: M. Stanley and R. Frantz, "Adjustment Problems of Spouses of Patients Undergoing Coronary Bypass Graft Surgery During Early Convalescence," *Heart Lung* 17 (1988): 677–82.

A third found that spouses of patients: R. A. Pruncho and S. L. Potashnik, "Caregiving Spouses: Physical and Mental Health in Perspective," *Journal of American Geriatric Society* 37 (1989): 697–705.

209 *In fact, when researchers*: Covinsky et al., "Is Economic Hardship on the Families of the Seriously Ill Associated with Patient and Surrogate Care Preferences?" *Archives of Internal Medicine*, 12/26 August 1996, pp. 1737–41.

Interestingly, while some other researchers: E. J. Emanuel and L. L. Emanuel, "Proxy Decision Making for Incompetent Patients: An Ethical and Empirical Analysis, *JAMA*, 15 April 1992, pp. 2067–71; and A. E. Buchanan and D. W. Brock, *Deciding for Others* (New York: Cambridge University Press, 1989).

. . . *the SUPPORT study found*: Covinsky et al., "Is Economic Hardship . . .?" op. cit.

"Families are those who grieve": Joanne Lynn, M.D., "Why I Don't Have a Living Will," *Law, Medicine and Health Care* 19, no. 1–2 (Spring–Summer 1991): 103.

210 *Among the more astounding findings*: David Reiss, M.D., Sandra Gonzales, Ph.D., and Norman Kramer, M.D., "Family Process, Chronic Illness, and Death: On the Weakness of Strong Bonds," *Archives of General Psychiatry* 43 (August 1986): 795–804. Gonzales, Peter Steinglass, M.D., and Reiss, "Putting the Illness in Its Place: Discussion Groups for Families with Chronic Medical Illnesses," *Family Process* 28 (March 1989): 69–87.

211 . . . *there seem to be three different trajectories*: Froma Walsh, Ph.D., and Monica McGoldrick, eds., *Living Beyond Loss: Death in the Family* (New York: W. W. Norton, 1991). The information contained here came from Dr.

Walsh's book as well as a seminar she gave, "Helping Families with Loss," at the National Hospice Organization and the NHO Council of Hospice Professionals 15th Annual Symposium and Exhibition, Salt Lake City, 13–16 October 1993. Tape available from Teach 'em, 160 East Illinois Street, Chicago, IL 60611; 1-800-225-3775.

214 *... Dr. Koenig told a* New York Times *reporter in 1995:* Seth Mydans, "Should Dying Patients Be Told? Ethnic Pitfall Is Found," *The New York Times,* 13 September 1995.

American families in fact have widely differing: Monica McGoldrick et al., "Mourning Rituals," *Family Therapy Networker* 10, no. 6 (November–December 1986): 28–36. McGoldrick's article compares attitudes toward terminal illness and death among Irish, African-American, Puerto Rican, and Chinese families. See also, Jennie Chin Hanson, R.N., "Cultural Aspects of Aging," a paper presented at the National Hospice Organization's 15th Annual Symposium, Salt Lake City, 13–16 October 1993. Hanson's seminar includes a discussion about ethnic differences in long-term care. Tape available from Teach 'em.

215 *One study of eight hundred elderly patients:* Mydans, "Should Dying Patients."

Medical social workers have found: David Brennan, M.S.W., "Families Under Stress: Hospice Care from a Family Systems Perspective," a workshop presented at the National Hospice Organization's First National Conference on Clinical Hospice Care/Palliative Medicine, San Francisco, February 1994. Tape available through Teach 'em.

And many Asian cultures: An informal talk given by Pat Bregant, the volunteer coordinator at Coming Home Hospice, San Francisco, 20 February 1994.

As of 1996, the Decisions staff: Mildred Solomon, Ed.D., interview by author, 22 May 1996. Solomon et al., "Moving Beyond the PSDA: Helping Hospitals and Nursing Homes Handle Tough Cases," *The Quality Letter/ Perspective* (October 1992): 9–13.

216 *Dr. Solomon cites as an example:* Solomon, "Autonomy: Refusing, Accepting, and Demanding Treatment," part of a panel presentation at Quinlan: A Twenty-Year Retrospective conference, Princeton, N.J., 12–13 April 1996.

In another program, in the Southwest: Pilar Baca-Assay, R.N., letter to author, February 1990.

"It's important in the dying process": Brennan, "Families Under Stress," op. cit.

Grothe says each person he sees: Tom Grothe, R.N., interview, 22 February 1994. It is Grothe who first alerted me to—and fully explained the grave significance of—the presence of multiple loss and its consequent effect on grief and the grieving and dying process in the AIDS community.

E I G H T   Hospice: The Birth of the Modern Art of Dying

Page
218 *"Joseph was actively dying,":* Sister Loretta Palamara, interviews by the

author, April 1992. Additional interviews with Sister Loretta took place both in person and by phone over the period from 1982 to 1997, during which time she was interviewed by the author on numerous subjects related to dying.

220 *She is now:* Sister Loretta died of a brain hemorrhage on 25 February 1997.

... *Audrey Hill is "actively dying.":* Audrey and Jonathan Hill, talks and interviews by the author on many occasions, April–June 1992, until Audrey's death, and with Jonathan Hill again in October 1996.

224 *In America, hospice has pioneered:* Information in this section comes from National Hospice Organization's (NHO) First Conference on Clinical Hospice Care/Palliative Medicine, San Francisco, 20–23 February 1994; NHO's 16th Annual Symposium and Exhibition, Washington, D.C., 18–22 October 1994; NHO's 15th Annual Symposium and Exhibition, Salt Lake City, 13–16 October 1993; NHO's *Standards of a Hospice Program of Care* (Arlington, Va.: NHO, 1993); Sandol Stoddard, *The Hospice Movement* (New York: Vintage Books, 1992); and interviews with Jay Mahoney, NHO president, interviews by author, February 1994; October 1995; and in personal correspondence February 1997.

Also Dame Cicely Saunders, "Managing Terminal Illness: An Update," a paper presented at the Ninth Annual Conference of the International Hospice Institute, London, 15 July 1993. (A tape of the conference is available through Rollin' Recordings, 208 River Ranch Road, Boerne, TX 78006, 210-736-5483.)

And Saunders and Mary Baines, *Living With Dying: The Management of Terminal Disease* (Oxford, Eng.: Oxford University Press, 1989); Saunders, "Foreword," *Oxford Textbook of Palliative Medicine* (New York: Oxford Medical Publications, 1993), pp. v–viii.

225 *During these same years, Elisabeth Kübler-Ross:* Kübler-Ross, interview by author in Head Water, Virginia, May 1993; lecture in Head Water, May 1993; lecture in New York City, October 1993.

See also Kübler-Ross's seminal books, most notably *On Death and Dying* (New York: Macmillan, 1969); *Questions and Answers on Death and Dying* (New York: Macmillan, 1974); *Death: The Final Stage of Growth* (New York: Simon & Schuster, 1975); *Living with Death and Dying* (New York: Macmillan, 1981); *On Children and Death* (New York: Macmillan, 1983); *AIDS: The Ultimate Challenge* (New York: Macmillan, 1987); *On Life After Death* (Berkeley, Calif.: Celestial Arts, 1991), a collection of lectures given throughout the 1970s and 1980s; and her biography: Derek Gill, *Quest: The Life of Elisabeth Kübler-Ross* (New York: Ballantine, 1982); and her autobiography, *The Wheel of Life* (New York: Scribner, 1997).

226 *The first hospice in America:* Florence Wald, interview, September 1995; Wald, "Finding a Way to Give Hospice Care," Inge B. Corless, R.N., Ph.D. et al., eds., *Death, Dying and Bereavement: Theoretical Perspectives and Other Ways of Knowing* (Sudbury, Mass.: Jones and Bartlett Publishers, 1994), pp. 31–47.

228 *"Sometimes I'm flabbergasted to discover":* Interviews with Sister Loretta Palamara, April and May 1992.

229 *"A child," she says, "needs to have":* Penelope Buschman, interview by author, April 1992.

230 *Because parents often have so difficult:* Genevieve Foley, Stephanie Vitalano, interviews by author, April 1992.

231 *"Children have the potential of moving":* Diane Haug, interview by author, February 1995.

233 *... giants in the emerging field of humanistic psychology:* Some examples of the writings of these theorists can be found in the following books: Carl G. Jung, *Modern Man in Search of a Soul* (New York: Harcourt, 1933); *ibid., Psychological Reflections* (New York: Pantheon Books, 1953); *ibid., The Undiscovered Self* (London: Kegan Paul, 1958); *ibid., Memories, Dreams and Reflections* (New York: Pantheon Books, 1963). Gordon W. Allport, *Pattern and Growth in Personality* (New York: Holt, Rinehart and Winston, 1961); *ibid., Becoming: Basic Considerations for a Psychology of Personality* (New Haven: Yale University Press, 1955). Carl Rogers, *On Becoming a Person* (Boston: Houghton Mifflin, 1961). Rollo May, *Existence* (New York: Basic Books, 1958); *ibid., Existential Psychology* (New York: Random House, 1961). Erik Erikson, *Childhood and Society* (New York: W. W. Norton, 1950); *ibid.,* "Identity and the Life Cycle," *Psychological Issues* 1, monograph 1 (1959). Abraham Maslow, *Toward a Psychology of Being* (New York: Van Nostrand Reinhold, 1968).

234 *In 1963, Robert Butler, M.D.:* Robert N. Butler, "The Life Review: An Interpretation of Reminiscence in the Aged," *Psychiatry* 26 (1963): 65–76; "Twenty-five Years of the Life Review: Theoretical and Practical Consideration," Robert Disch, ed., *Journal of Gerontological Social Work* 12, no. 3/4, 1988; *Why Survive? Being Old in America* (New York: Harper & Row, 1975); with Myrna Lewis and Trey Sunderland, *Aging and Mental Health*, 4th ed. (New York: Maxwell Macmillan, 1991).

In 1996, in a chapter: Robert N. Butler, "Life Review," *Encyclopedia of Gerontology*, vol. 1; also a paper presented at the Conference on Dying and the Inner Life, sponsored by The Fetzer Institute, The Nathan Cummings Foundation, and The Project on Death in America, 31 May–2 June 1996.

235 *And, in fact, that is:* Ira Byock, *Dying Well* (New York: Putnam, 1997). Byock, interviews by author, February 1994, January 1995, October 1995. "Beyond Symptom Management: Growth at the End of Life," paper presented at the National Hospice Organization's First Conference on Clinical Hospice Care, February 1994; and at the International Hospice Institute, London, July 1993; "Medical, Palliative Care and Hospice Issues," from symposium of The Project on Death in America, January 1995; "The Hospice Clinician's Response to Euthanasia/Assisted Suicide," an address at the meeting of the Academy of Hospice Physicians, February 1994. (Tapes of some of these speeches are available through Teach 'em, 160 East Illinois Street, Chicago, IL 60611, 800-225-3775; and Rollin' Recordings, 208 River Ranch Road, Boerne, TX 78006, 210-736-5483.)

... Tibetan Buddhist teacher Chögyam Trungpa, Rinpoche: The late Eleventh Venerable Chögyam Trungpa, Rinpoche, was a lineage holder of the Kagyu and Nyingma traditions of Tibetan Buddhism, and Supreme Abbot of the Surmang Monasteries in Eastern Tibet until the Chinese takeover in 1959. See Chapter 9.

Beginning in 1970, he established Vajradhatu International and Shambhala International, Buddhist organizations that include Naropa Institute, Boulder, retreat centers in Colorado and Vermont, and meditation centers in cities throughout North America and Europe. He was the author of *Meditation in Action* (Berkeley, Calif.: Shambhala Publications, 1969) and *Cutting Through Spiritual Materialism* (Berkeley, Calif.: Shambhala Publications, 1973), and he wrote the commentary for *The Tibetan Book of the Dead* (Berkeley, Calif.: Shambhala Publications, 1975) and *Shambhala: The Sacred Path of the Warrior* (Boulder, Colo.: Shambhala Publications, 1984). (Tapes are available through Kalapa Recordings, 1084 Tower Road, Halifax, NS, Canada B3H 2Y5, 902-421-3214.)

. . . at which many teachers from Christian: Those at Naropa Institute include Ram Dass (Richard Alpert, Ph.D.), Stephen and Ondrea Levine, Rabbi Zalman Schachter-Shalomi, Brother David Stendl-Rast, Tibetan Buddhist teachers from the Kagyu, Nyingma, Sakya, and Galupa schools, and teachers from Vietnamese and Japanese traditions.

"Suffering occurs not merely in the presence": Eric Cassell, M.D., *The Nature of Suffering* (New York: Oxford University Press, 1991).

236 *Among the major findings:* Joanne Lynn, M.D. et al., "Defining the 'Terminally Ill': Insights from SUPPORT," *Duquesne Law Review*, Vol. 35:311, 1996, pp. 311–36; Joanne Lynn, M.D. et al., "Prognoses of Seriously Ill Hospitalized Patients on the Days Before Death: Implications for Patient Care and Public Policy," *New Horizons,* Vol. 5:1, 1997, pp. 56–61.

Like AIDS patients: "Death is death, no matter what the disease," Barbara Karnes, R.N., says. "It depends on how much medication you're pumping them with. The description I give is how death looks. But AIDS does look different. It has a roller-coaster effect in which patients go through a crisis and come back, but with a little less strength each time. One time they just die, but to the relatives it seems unexpected. It is harder on the grieving process, but it is just different." Interview, 15 May 1997.

238 *"[In the days] when Grandma died at home,":* Barbara Karnes, "The Dynamics of Dying: What Is It Like to Die?," a workshop at the National Hospice Organization's 15th Annual Symposium, Salt Lake City, 13–16 October 1993. (Tape is available through Teach 'em, 160 East Illinois Street, Chicago, IL 60611, 800-225-3775.) See also *ibid., Gone from Sight: The Dying Experience* (pamphlet; P.O. Box 335, Stilwell, KS 66085). Other booklets with similar information are available through NHO and individual hospices, for example: *Preparing for the Death of a Loved One: A Guide for Families*, and *Lasting Is the Song,* (New York: Cabrini Hospice), Pamphlets also available from Cabrini Hospice, 227 East Nineteenth Street, New York, NY 10003. Karnes, interview by author, 23 January 1997.

243 *Their studies of dying patients:* Karlis Osis, Ph.D., and Erlendur Haraldsson, Ph.D., *At the Hour of Death* (Mamaroneck, N.Y.: Hastings House Publishers, 1977). Introduction by Kübler-Ross.

244 *"If you believe in an afterlife":* Osis, interview by author, 26 February 1995.

245 *Moody's book:* Raymond A. Moody Jr., M.D., *Life After Life* (New York: Bantam Books, 1975). See also *Reflections on Life After Life* (New York: Bantam Books, 1978); *The Light Beyond* (New York: Bantam Books, 1988). Interview by author, 18 November 1993.

. . . also by cardiologists and paramedics: See, for example, Michael Sabom, M.D., *Recollections of Death: A Medical Investigation of the Near-Death Experience* (New York: Harper & Row, 1981).

"The light immediately communicated with me": Tom Sawyer, interview by author, December 1994. See also, Sidney Saylor Farr, *What Tom Sawyer Learned from Dying* (Charlottesville, Va.: Hampton Roads Publishing Co., 1993).

246 *Even children—untutored in the popular accounts:* Reports of children's experiences are also described in Melvin Morse, M.D., with Paul Perry, *Closer to the Light: Learning from the Near-Death Experiences of Children* (New York: Ivy Books, 1990); Diane M. Komp, M.D., *A Window to Heaven: When Children See Life in Death* (Grand Rapids, Mich.: Zondervan Publishing House, 1992). Komp, interview by author, May 1992.

... *the accounts were remarkably the same:* Kenneth Ring, Ph.D., *Life at Death: A Scientific Investigation of the Near-Death Experience* (New York: William Morrow, 1980); *Heading Toward Omega: In Search of the Meaning of the Near-Death Experience* (New York: Morrow, 1984); *The Omega Project* (New York: Morrow, 1992); P. M. H. Atwater, *Coming Back to Life* (New York: Ballantine Books, 1988); Barbara Harris and Lionel C. Bascom, *Full Circle* (New York: Pocket Books, 1990); Morse with Perry, *Transformed by the Light* (New York: Ivy Books, 1992).

Still, George Gallup Jr., ... estimated: George Gallup Jr., *Adventures in Immortality* (New York: McGraw-Hill, 1982).

By 1993, the Gallup organization: Robert Bezilla, ed., *Religion in America* (Princeton, N.J.: The Princeton Religion Research Center, 1993).

International Association of Near Death Studies: The association's address is P.O. Box 502, East Windsor Hill, CT 06028; *Journal of Near-Death Studies* can be obtained from Human Sciences Press, 233 Spring Street, New York, NY 10013.

... *stories were regularly appearing on best-seller lists:* Some examples of such books include the following: Morse with Perry, *Closer to the Light;* Betty J. Eadie, with Curtis Taylor, *Embraced by the Light,* Foreword by Dr. Melvin Morse (Placerville, Calif.: Gold Leaf Press, 1992); Dannion Brinkley with Perry, *Saved by the Light,* Introduction by Dr. Raymond A. Moody (New York: Villard Books, 1994).

"The most common words used to describe": Interview with Dr. Kenneth Ring, 23 April 1993; by phone at other times, 1993–1995; at lectures 2 March 1993 and 2 April 1995. Eadie, interview by author, June 1993, October 1993, and April 1995. These words were also used to describe NDEs by participants at "The Near-Death Experience: Gateway to Learning," The International Association for Near-Death Studies North American (IANDS) Conference, in Saint Louis, Missouri, June 1993, and in an NDE support group at the University of Connecticut, May 1993.

247 *These peak experiences ... can be elicited:* Dr. Ring, interview by author, 23 April 1993.

Medical and psychiatric researchers offer: This issue has been debated at length in many articles in the *Journal of Near-Death Studies,* including a special issue on the neurobiological model, with articles by the following: Juan C. Saavedra-Aguilar, M.D., and Juan S. Bomez-Jeria, M.D., "A Neurobiological Model for Near-Death Experiences," *JNDS* 7, no. 4 (1989): 205–22; and "Responses to Commentaries on 'A Neurobiological Model,' " 265–72; Russell Noyes, M.D., "Comments on 'A Neurobiological Model for

Near-Death Experiences,'" *ibid.*: 249–50; Daniel B. Carr, M.D., "Comments on . . . ," *ibid.*, 251–54. Also, Glen O. Gabbard, M.D., and Stuart W. Twemlow, M.D., "Do 'Near-Death Experiences' Occur Only Near Death?— Revisited," *JNDS* 10, no. 1 (1991): 41–47; and "Explanatory Hypotheses for Near-Death Experiences," *Revision* 4, no. 2 (1981): 68–71.

Articles in other journals include: Noyes, "Attitude Change Following Near-Death Experiences," *Psychiatry* 43, no. 3 (1980): 234–41; Bruce Greyson, M.D., "Varieties of Near-Death Experience," *Psychiatry: Interpersonal & Biological Processes* 56, no. 4 (1993): 390–99; and Ian Stevenson, M.D. et al., "Are Persons Reporting 'Near-Death Experiences' Really Near Death? A Study of Medical Records," *Omega: Journal of Death & Dying* 20, no. 1 (1989–1990): 45–54.

248 *Daniel Dennett . . . says these experiences:* Daniel Dennett, Ph.D., *Consciousness Explained* (Boston: Little, Brown, 1991); *Content and Consciousness* (New York: Routledge, 1986); "Time and the Observer: The Where and When of Consciousness in the Brain," *Behavioral & Brain Sciences* 15, no. 2 (1992): 183–247; "The Art of Dying," *New York*, 23 November 1992, p. 50.

. . . the brain's biochemical way of dealing: See Susan Blackmore, *Dying to Live* (Amherst, N.Y.: Prometheus Books, 1993). Blackmore, a senior lecturer in psychology at the University of the West of England, takes a very close look at all of these scientific explanations. One would expect her to find merit in at least one of them, since she is also a fellow of the Committee for the Scientific Investigation of Claims of the Paranormal and one of the world's leading experts on near-death experiences, yet she finds holes in all of them.

. . . NDEs and deathbed visions: See Mary D. McEvoy, "The Near-Death Experience: Implications for Nursing Education," *Loss, Grief & Care* 4, no. 1–2 (1990): 51–55. McEvoy, of the University of Pennsylvania School of Nursing, Philadelphia, suggests that nurses talk with dying patients about NDEs. Linda Barnett, "Hospice Nurses' Knowledge and Attitudes Toward the Near-Death Experience," *JNDS* 9, no. 4 (1991): 225–32. Barnett reports that of sixty hospice nurses surveyed, 63 percent said they'd worked with an NDE patient, 52 percent were adequately knowledgeable about the NDE, and all the nurses had a positive attitude toward near-death phenomena and toward caring for NDE patients. This researcher recommended including NDEs as part of nursing education.

Pamela Kircher . . . took an informal survey: Kircher, "Near-Death Experience and Hospice Work," paper presented at the annual IANDS Conference, in Saint Louis, Missouri, 27 June 1993.

249 *From this material came their book:* Maggie Callanan and Patricia Kelley, *Final Gifts* (New York: Poseidon Press, 1992). Information in this section is based on Callanan, "Final Gifts," the keynote address at the IANDS Conference, Saint Louis, Missouri, 25 June 1993, and on an interview by author, June 1992.

N I N E   New American Sacred: The Return of Prepared Dying

Page

250 *It's the morning of May 26, 1987:* The account of the cremation of Venerable Chögyam Trungpa, Rinpoche, is from my own observations and interviews.

See also, Gregory Jaynes, "In Vermont: A Spiritual Leader's Farewell," *Time*, 22 June 1987, p. 10; Rick Fields, "The Vidyadhara Trungpa Rinpoche Dies in Nova Scotia; Cremation Rites Held at Karme Choling," *Vajradhatu Sun*, Special Issue, June/July 1987; Ari Goldman, various articles in *The New York Times*; local Vermont papers.

251 *Officially, he was the Eleventh Trungpa Rinpoche:* Chögyam Trungpa, Rinpoche, *Born in Tibet* (Boston: Shambhala Publications, 1986).

"I received this transmission at the age of eight": Francesca Fremantle and Chögyam Trungpa, trans., *The Tibetan Book of the Dead: The Great Liberation through Hearing in the Bardo* (Berkeley, Calif.: Shambhala Publications, 1975), p. xii.

In 1959, when the Chinese invaded: Chögyam Trungpa, *Tibetan*, pp. 143ff. Rick Fields, *How the Swans Came to the Lake: A Narrative History of Buddhism in America* (Boulder: Shambhala Publications, 1981). Fields describes the progress of Buddhism in the West.

252 *In the West, Chögyam Trungpa, Rinpoche, was controversial:* See the following: Georg Feuerstein, *The Shock Tactics and Radical Teachings of Crazy-Wise Adepts, Holy Fools and Rascal Gurus* (New York: Paragon House, 1991); Jaynes, "In Vermont."

He died ... of liver disease: Mitchel Levy, M.D., interview by author, February 1995; Michael Baime, M.D., interview by author, July 1996. Dr. Levy specializes in critical care medicine at Brown University Hospital. Dr. Baime is chief, division of general internal medicine, University of Pennsylvania Graduate Hospital. Both doctors were Rinpoche's personal physicians.

254 *All of the world's cultures:* The following discussion is drawn from these resources: Stanislav Grof, M.D., and Joan Halifax, Ph.D., *The Human Encounter with Death* (New York: E. P. Dutton, 1977); Philip Aries, *Western Attitudes Toward Death* (Baltimore: Johns Hopkins University Press, 1974); *ibid., At the Hour of Our Death* (New York: Oxford University Press, 1981); Carol Zaleski, Ph.D., *Otherworld Journeys* (New York: Oxford University Press, 1987). See also, Vicki Goldberg, "Looking Straight into the Eyes of the Dying," *The New York Times*, 31 March 1996.

255 *Philosopher William James:* William James, *The Varieties of Religious Experience* (New York: Macmillan, 1961); see particularly the chapter "Mysticism," pp. 299–336. See also, John White, ed., *The Highest State of Consciousness* (New York: Anchor/Doubleday, 1972).

256 *When the Grand Rebbe Menachem Mendel Schneerson:* Joshua Johnson, "After Procedure, Faithful Foresee Rebbe's Recovery," *Newsday*, 12 June 1994; Paul Moses and Juan Forero, "End of the Lineage: Lubavitchers Keep Waiting for 'Moshiach,' " *Newsday*, 13 June 1994; Russ Buettner et al., "Menachem Mendel Schneerson, 1902–1994: Lubavitch Rebbe Dies; Revered Hasidic Leader Spread Faith Around the Globe," *Newsday*, 13 June 1994.

When Cardinal Joseph Bernardin: Cardinal Joseph Bernardin, *The Gift of Peace* (Chicago: Loyola Press, 1997); excerpts in *Newsweek*, 25 November 1996.

... this secular generation is looking: Also according to the Gallup surveys, Americans' conception of heaven has changed over the years. For a more thorough discussion, see Robert Bezilla, ed., *Religion in America: 1992 to 1993, 25th Anniversary Edition* (Princeton, N.J.: The Princeton Religion

Research Center, 1993); George Gallup Jr. and Sarah Jones, *100 Questions and Answers: Religion in America* (Princeton, N.J.: Princeton Religion Research Center, 1989).

. . . powerful help in getting ready to die: On Friday, April 4, 1997, on the morning of the tenth anniversary of his teacher Trungpa Rinpoche's death, poet Allen Ginsberg, who was suffering from liver cancer, had a stroke and slipped into a coma. He died two hours after midnight.

During the weeks before he died, Ginsberg practiced the meditation he'd been taught by Geluk Rinpoche, the Tibetan Buddhist who had become his teacher after Trungpa died. American Buddhists meditated at his side, taking shifts round the clock; Geluk Rinpoche and other Buddhists were there when he died. His funeral, which I attended, was held Monday, April 7, in the shrine room of the Shambhala Center in New York, which was founded by Trungpa Rinpoche.

Among the numerous teachers: See pages 449–50 (note for page 235) for list of Chögyam Trungpa, Rinpoche's books; Dilgo Khyentse, Rinpoche, *The Heart Treasures of the Enlightened Ones* (Boston: Shambhala Publications, 1992); Chagdud Tulku, Rinpoche, *Lord of the Dance: The Autobiography of a Tibetan Lama* (Junction City, Calif.: Padma Publishing, 1992); *ibid., Life in Relation to Death* (Junction City, Calif.: Padma Publishing, 1987); Sogyal Rinpoche, *The Tibetan Book of Living and Dying* (San Francisco: Harper-SanFrancisco, 1992); Dalai Lama, *A Flash of Lightning in the Dark of Night* (Boston: Shambhala Publications, 1994); *ibid., Essential Teachings* (Berkeley: North Atlantic Books, 1995); *ibid., Way to Freedom* (San Francisco: Harper-SanFrancisco, 1994); Robert A. F. Thurman, "Introduction," *The Tibetan Book of the Dead* (New York: Bantam Books, 1994). Much of their teaching is also available on tapes from Sounds True Recordings, 735 Walnut Street, Boulder, CO 80302, 303-449-6229, or from The New York Open Center and Tibet House, Art of Dying Conferences, 1995 and 1997, in New York.

257   *. . . The Tibetan Book of Living and Dying:* Information on book sales provided by HarperSanFrancisco.

258   *Chögyam Trungpa's heir . . . Tendzin was a controversial teacher:* Associated Press, "Vajra Regent Osel Tendzin, 47; Former Leader of Buddhist Sect," *Boston Globe,* 28 August 1990; "Osel Tendzin; 1st Westerner to Head Tibet Buddhist Sect," *Los Angeles Times,* 27 August 1990.

"You and I and all of us have traveled": Osel Tendzin, private letter to Judith Hardin, 23 December 1989. Shared with author by Moh Hardin.

259   *Osel Tendzin once described the effects:* Material drawn from a teaching session in Ojai, Calif., August 1990.

"Consider [this mind of the Buddha]": Ibid.

260   *It is April Fool's Day, 1995.:* The following discussion is based on Rachel Naomi Remen, M.D., "Living Well and Dying Well," lectures presented at Art of Dying Conferences, New York City, 1 April 1995 and 21 March 1997; interviews by author, 22 April 1995 and 31 March 1997; *On Healing* (Bolinas, Calif.: Institute for the Study of Health and Illness, 1993), a collection of her lectures and papers (provided by her offices at Commonweal and the Institute for the Study of Health and Illness). *Kitchen Table Wisdom* (New York: Riverhead Books, 1996).

265   *"Between April 14 and April 21":* Edward Rothstein, "On the Web, Tuning

in to Timothy Leary's Last Trip, Live from His Deathbed," *The New York Times,* 29 April 1996. Laura Mansnerus, "At Death's Door, the Message Is Tune In, Turn On, Drop In," *ibid.,* 26 November 1995, and "Timothy Leary, Pied Piper of Psychedelic 60's, Dies at 75," *ibid.,* 1 June 1996.

266 *He died . . . The night before:* Ibid.

Leary's method . . . In the early 1960s: Ram Dass, "Work with the Dying," paper presented at Conference on Dying and the Inner Life, at the Fetzer Institute, Kalamazoo, Mich., 31 May–2 June 1996. (Paper adapted from forthcoming book on consciousness and aging. Ram Dass says Aldous Huxley was "one of our group" at Harvard. Huxley is known for having explored psychotropic plants and psychedelic drugs for their mind-altering capacities. See Huxley, *The Doors of Perception* (New York: Harper & Row, 1954), and *Island* (New York: Harper & Row, 1962).

267 *Huxley was . . . the work of Albert Hofmann:* Bernard Gavzer, "Warning: Don't Be Casual about LSD," *Parade,* 21 August 1994.

Additional background material for this discussion is from Rick Strassman, M.D. (psychiatry faculty, University of New Mexico Medical School, Albuquerque), private correspondence and grant proposals; Charles S. Grob, M.D. (psychiatry faculty, UCLA Medical School and Harbor-UCLA Medical Center); Rick Doblin (president of the Multidisciplinary Association for Psychedelic Studies, Charlotte, N.C.); Ethan A. Nadelmann (director of the Lindesmith Center), Drug Policy Seminars, sponsored by the Open Society Institute, Spring 1995.

Among the most interesting work: Grof and Halifax, *Human Encounter;* lecture at Naropa Institute, August 1974. (Tape of lecture is available through Kalapa Recordings, see page 450; information about Naropa is available from Naropa Institute, 2130 Arapahoe Avenue, Boulder, CO 80203, 303-444-0202.)

268 *Since then . . . some researchers are attempting:* Strassman, Grob, and Doblin, interviews by author, The Lindesmith Center's Drug Policy Seminars; Charles Tart, Ph.D. (formerly on faculty of University of California, Irvine), interview June 1993.

269 *One of Dr. Grof's and Dr. Halifax's patients:* Grof and Halifax, talk at Naropa Institute, summer 1974. (Tape is available from Kalapa Recordings.)

Dr. Grof has since created: Grof, interview by author, February 1995; also, lectures and workshops in New York and Montreal, 1993. See also, *ibid., The Holotropic Mind* (San Francisco: HarperSanFrancisco, 1990).

270 *Dr. Halifax uses various forms:* Halifax, interview by author, January 1995; also a presentation on the panel "Spiritual Issues," at a conference sponsored by the Project on Death in America, 13 January 1995. Also of interest are Dr. Halifax's lectures at these conferences: Buddhism in America, Boston, 17–19 January 1997; Art of Dying Conference 2, New York City, 21–23 March 1997.

271 *After he was fired . . .:* Ram Dass, "Work with the Dying."

. . . he went to the East, looking for a teacher: Ram Dass, *The Only Dance There Is* (New York: Anchor/Doubleday, 1970); with Stephen Levine, *Grist for the Mill* (Santa Cruz, Calif.: Unity Press, 1977).

. . . that he and Leary . . . wrote a book: Ram Dass, Timothy Leary et al., *The Psychedelic Experience* (New York: Citadel Press, 1976).

He also wrote Be Here Now: Ram Dass, *Be Here Now* (New York: Crown, 1971); *The Only Dance;* and *Grist* (*Grist* contains "Dying: An Opportunity for Awakening."); "Work with the Dying," paper presented at Dying and the Inner Life conference; "Facing Death," a paper presented at Conscious Dying/Conscious Aging, conference sponsored by Omega Institute, 1 May 1992 (available through Sounds True Conference Recordings, 735 Walnut Street, Boulder, CO 80302; 303-449-6229).

272 *On this spring day in 1992: Ibid.*

274 *Stephen and Ondrea Levine have written:* Levine and Levine, *A Gradual Awakening* (New York: Anchor/Doubleday, 1979); *Who Dies?: An Investigation of Conscious Living and Conscious Dying* (*ibid.,* 1982); *Meetings at the Edge* (*ibid.,* 1984); *Healing into Life and Death* (*ibid.,* 1987); *Guided Meditations, Explorations and Healings* (*ibid.,* 1991); and *ibid., A Year to Live* (New York: Bell Tower, 1997). (Guided meditation and workshop tapes are available through Warm Rock Tapes, P.O. Box 108, Chamisal, NM 87521, 415-883-6111.) Discussion in this section based on Stephen Levine, interview by author, May 1992, 22 March and 11 April 1997; and Ondrea Levine, interview by author, 15 and 24 October 1993 and 22 March 1997; and attendance at Conscious Living/Conscious Dying Workshop, 21–23 October 1993.

279 *On Sunday evening, October 3, 1993:* The story of Father Tom Sheedy's death is based on Father Vincent Keenan and Sister Martina Fox, interviews by author, October 1993; Father Tommy Conway, interview by author, October 1993 and December 1994; Larry Killebrew, M.D., interview by author, 1 December 1993. Further material drawn from personal observation, interviews with family members and many of Father Tom's parishioners, and on his official church biography.

T E N   **Wisdom's Portraits:** Midwives at Death's Door

Page

286 *Dr. Elisabeth Kübler-Ross is sitting:* Life, Death and Transition Workshop, at the Elisabeth Kübler-Ross Center, Head Waters, Va., 24–28 May 1993; Kübler-Ross interviewed by author while attending workshop. See also, Derek Gill, *Quest: The Life of Elisabeth Kübler-Ross* (New York: Ballantine Books, 1980).

300 *Around noon, on Thursday, October 6, 1994:* See Carlos Santos, "Highland Fire Leaves Author Saddened and Angry; Kübler-Ross Lost House, Art and Manuscripts," *Richmond Times-Dispatch,* 13 October 1994; *ibid.,* "Fire and Theft at Farm Probed," *Richmond Times-Dispatch,* 11 October 1994; Associated Press, "Arson Suspected in Fire at Home of 'Death and Dying' Author," *Richmond Times-Dispatch,* 8 October 1994.

301 *In 1995, after her home was destroyed:* According to one of her "trainers," David Mullins, the Elisabeth Kübler-Ross Center was closed, the organization "dead," and Elisabeth had officially retired.

By spring 1997, Kübler-Ross was living alone with a housekeeper in Scottsdale and had published two more books, *Cocoon and the Butterfly* (Barrytown, N.Y.: Barrytown, Ltd., 1997) and her autobiography, *The Wheel of Life* (New York: Scribner, 1997). See also Leslie Bennetts, "Elisabeth Kübler-Ross's Final Passage," *Vanity Fair,* June, 1997.

The American past provides models: Sheila Rothman, Ph.D., "The New England Way of Death: What the Past Can Teach the Present," lecture and paper presented at symposium of the Project on Death in America, 12 January 1995. See also *ibid., Living in the Shadow of Death: Tuberculosis and the Social Experience of Illness in American History* (Baltimore: Johns Hopkins University Press, 1995).

303 *You hear her shriek in Brooklynese:* Author visited Ma and Kashi Ranch in March 1995, and interviewed her then and by phone in January 1996. Background information also comes from her forthcoming autobiography, which she shared with author in manuscript form.

. . . *as novelist Paul Monette:* Paul Monette, *Borrowed Time* (New York: Avon Books, 1990); *Afterlife* (New York: Crown, 1990), *Halfway Home* (New York: Avon, 1992), and *Becoming a Man* (San Diego: Harcourt Brace, 1992). On Monette's relationship with Ma, see "My Priests," *Last Watch of the Night* (San Diego: Harcourt Brace, 1994), and the eulogy Ma gave at his memorial service in February 1995, shared with author in private correspondence.

. . . *as Kimberly Bergalis did:* Anna and Harry Bergalis, interview by author, March 1995. The Bergalises, Kimberly's parents, also furnished author with a copy of sections of her diary.

304 . . . *a tempest has gathered around her:* See Ram Dass, "The Mellow Drama," *Grist for the Mill* (Santa Cruz, Calif.: Unity Press, 1977), pp. 58–72; Jenny Vogt, "Guru Ma: Saintly or Sinister?," *Palm Beach Post,* 21 March 1992. Interviews by author with several former students who want to maintain their anonymity also were used in this discussion.

311 *Therese Schroeder-Sheker, founder of:* This section is based on interviews with Schroeder-Sheker, professor of music thanatology and academic dean of the Chalice of Repose, May 1994 and April 1995, on presentations at Art of Dying Conferences, 3 April 1995 and 23 March 1997; and from material furnished by Schroeder-Sheker and the Chalice of Repose staff.

315 *On Father's Day in Montreal:* This scene was viewed by author on visit to the Palliative Care Unit, Royal Victoria Hospital, Montreal, June 1993; Dr. Balfour Mount and Yvonne Corbeil, his assistant director of palliative care medicine, interviews by author, 18 June 1993; also many tapes, written material, and transcripts of lectures provided by them of nine years of international congresses on the care of the terminally ill.

See also Mount, *Sightings: Reflection on Dying* (Downers Grove, Ill.: InterVarsity Press, 1983); "Death and Dying: Attitudes in a Teaching Hospital," *Urology* IV, no. 6 (December 1974): 27–33; Mount and Ina Ajemian, eds., *The R.V.H. Manual on Palliative/Hospice Care* (Salem, New Hampshire: The Ayer Co., 1982).

E L E V E N Dr. Kevorkian's Challenge: Two Deaths in Michigan

Page

321 *When they met in 1988:* The story of Tom Hyde's death is based on numerous interviews with Heidi Fernandez, on the phone and in person, beginning in November 1993 through September 1994; on her testimony

and that of Sean Hyde and others during Dr. Kevorkian's trial in April and May 1994; on an interview with Sylvia Shadrick, Tom's mother, in June 1994; and on the video made on 1 July 1993, in which Tom asks Dr. Kevorkian for help in dying. An early version of this story first appeared in *Glamour* magazine, September 1994.

324   *I also subsequently talked in depth with the families:* Cheryl Gale (about her husband, Hugh Gale) November 1994; Sharon Welsh (about her best friend, Sherry Miller), November 1994; Ron Adkins (about his wife, Janet Adkins) 23, 24, and 25 August 1996; Carol Loving (about her son Nicholas) 22, 23, 24, 25 August 1996; Carol Poenisch, 23, 24, 25 August 1996 and 8 January 1997, and Connie Frederick 25 August 1996 (about their mother, Merian Frederick); and Dave Ball, 23, 24, 25 August 1996, and Judy Brown, September 1996 (about their father, Stanley Ball). In addition I talked with Dawn Haselhuhn, founder of a support group called Friends of Dr. Kevorkian, 6 November 1993.

In addition, I visited hospitals and hospices: Interviews with the following people occurred on the dates given: Sherry Roggow, staff member, Michigan State Commission on Death and Dying, 1 November 1993; Alvin Bowles, M.D., chairman of the ethics committee, Detroit Medical Center, and J. Edson Pontes, M.D., professor and chairman of the urology department, Wayne State University School of Medicine and at the Detroit Medical Center, 1 November 1993; John Finn, M.D., in interdisciplinary hospice rounds at the Detroit Medical Center, 1 and 2 November 1993, and in interviews 18 and 30 November 1993, and 22 February 1997; Lawrence Crane, M.D., clinical director of the AIDS program, Detroit Medical Center, 3 November 1993; John D. O'Hair, Wayne County prosecutor and chair of the Michigan State Commission, and Eric Cholack, assistant prosecuting attorney, Wayne County, and staff members for the commission, 8 November 1993; and Father James L. Meyer, director, department of pastoral care, Hutzel Hospital, Detroit Medical Center, 3 November 1993.

325   *Jack Kevorkian catapulted . . .:* The information on Jack Kevorkian, M.D., is based on extensive interviews with Janet Good, founder of the Michigan Hemlock Society and long-time assistant to Dr. Kevorkian, 6 November 1993 and 22–25 August 1996; Michael Betzold, *Appointment with Doctor Death* (Troy, Michigan: Momentum Books, 1993); more than one hundred articles from the *Detroit Free Press, The New York Times, Newsweek, Time,* and *People* from September 1989 to May 1997; Jack Kevorkian, M.D., *Prescription: Medicine* (Buffalo: Prometheus Books, 1991); articles written by Dr. Kevorkian for European medical journals; on an interview with Dr. Kevorkian, 5 November 1993; on press conferences attended by author in Detroit, November 1993; on televised press conferences and interviews, November 1993 through February 1997. I also visited Royal Oak, where he then lived, in November 1993, to describe the community and interview shopkeepers about his lifestyle.

326   *"The patient was a helplessly immobile woman":* Kevorkian, *Prescription,* p. 188.

327   *. . . Humphry declined this offer:* Interview with Derek Humphry, February 1997.

328   *. . . (a CD of him performing his own music . . .):* A Very Still Life, on the

Lucid Label from Resist Records, available at Tower Records, Virgin, and Blockbuster chains; $18.95.

That month he came across an article: Sidney H. Wanzer, M.D. et al., "The Physician's Responsibility Toward Hopelessly Ill Patients: A Second Look," *NEJM* 320, no. 13 (30 March 1989): 844–849.

That summer, a thirty-eight-year-old man named David Rivlin: Dr. John Finn, interview by author, February 1994.

329 *Art Humphrey, a Detroit television reporter:* Art Humphrey: "A Time to Care," TV special on WDIV, Detroit, October 1989.

330 *Ron Adkins ran his own investment firm:* Ron Adkins, interview by author, 23, 24, and 25 August 1996. *Ibid.,* informal talk, Managing Mortality Conference in Minneapolis, 3–5 December 1992. Also numerous articles in *The New York Times, Detroit Free Press,* and *People* magazine, June 1990 to March 1997.

332 *"Thank you, thank you":* Kevorkian, *Prescription,* p. 230.

333 *To stop Dr. Kevorkian:* Associated Press, "Doctor Assists 2 More Suicides in Michigan," *The New York Times,* 16 December 1992; also see, among other articles in the *The New York Times* and *Detroit Free Press,* David Zeman, "Kevorkian Jurors Face Intense Grilling Trial, Weeding Out Process Begins Today," *Detroit Free Press,* 19 April 1994, which contains a chronology of charges against Kevorkian.

336 *He was released . . . a doctor took them aside:* The name of this doctor was not provided, nor did Heidi recall his name. When asked later about this incident by a researcher at *Glamour,* Dr. Daniel Newman said it was not he who had said this to Heidi and Tom, but another physician at his clinic. He had been out of town at the time it occurred, he said, and did not know they had been given this information.

342 *"I have to practice with Dr. Kevorkian":* Dr. John Finn, testimony at Michigan Commission on Death and Dying, public hearings, 8 November 1993; interviews by author, November 1993 and 22 February 1994.

His skill is motivated: Ibid., 22 February 1994.

343 *Other Michigan doctors:* Dr. Howard Brody, interview, 20 October 1993. In this interview, Dr. Brody provided a history of the issue of assisted dying as it was addressed by the Society from December 1990 onward. See also Diane Gianelli, "Michigan 'Neutral' on Suicide," *American Medical News* 36, no. 20 (24 May 1993): 2; and Howard Brody, M.D., "Assisted Death: A Compassionate Response to a Medical Failure," *NEJM,* 327, no. 19 (5 November 1992): 1384–88.

. . . assisted suicide should be made legal: Michigan Commission on Death and Dying, public hearings, 8 November 1993; final report, Lansing, Michigan, Legislative Service Bureau, Commission on Death and Dying, 12 April 1994.

Joan Hull, Ph.D., the staff psychologist: Dr. Joan Hull, interviews by author 30 October, 1–3 and 17 November 1993. Author accompanied Dr. Hull on her daily rounds; protocols are under the hospice's letterhead.

344 *"When you're confronted with death":* Carolyn Fitzpatrick-Cassin, interview, October 1994.

345 *. . . regulatory fraud enforcement programs:* Beverly Beyette, " 'What If I Don't Die in 6 Months?,' " *Los Angeles Times,* 4 April 1997; Robert

Rosenblatt, "U.S. to Bolster Health Care Fraud Attack," *Los Angeles Times,* 26 March 1997; Robert Rosenblatt, "U.S. Targets Hospices If Patients Live Too Long," *Los Angeles Times,* 15 March 1997.

346 *Glenn Leung was half Irish:* The story of Glenn Leung is based on extensive interviews, both in person and by phone, with him, his sister, Sharon Siens Tse, and with Dave Turner, volunteer coordinator for the Hospice of Southeastern Michigan (HSEM); Dr. John Finn (see dates on page 459), the hospice's medical director; Judy Kelterborn, M.S.W., Glenn's hospice social worker; Joan Hull, Ph.D., his psychologist and director, behavioral medicine, HSEM, on 30 October and 1–3 and 17 November 1993; and Carolyn Fitzpatrick-Cassin, the hospice's president and CEO, 24 and 26 November 1993. These interviews and visits began in November 1993 and lasted through January 1995.

349 *"I want to sign it today":* Associated Press, "Doctor Assists 2 More Suicides in Michigan," *The New York Times,* 16 December 1992.

353 *Judy Kelterborn, the hospice social worker:* Interview by author, January 1995.

359 *According to the patients themselves:* See "The Kevorkian File," at http://www.FinalExit.org/Kevorkian.html or http://www.efn.org/ergo/ Kevorkian.html for a complete list of patients and their illnesses as of May 1997 (compiled by DeathNet, run by John Hofsess, and by ERGO, run by Derek Humphry). Also see "The Suicide Machine," *Free Press,* for a listing through March 1997, and more extensive biographies.

360 *In the late winter:* Dr. Kevorkian's jury trials in addition to the one for the death of Tom Hyde includes those for Sherry Miller and Marjorie Wantz, and Dr. Ali Khalili and Merian Frederick, both in the spring of 1996.

T W E L V E Assisted Dying: The Modern Way of Death

Page

361 *Shortly after midnight:* All descriptions pertaining to the U.S. Supreme Court's oral arguments on assisted suicide, 8 January 1997, are from personal observations and interviews by the author, except where otherwise noted.

At 10:00 A.M. . . . two cases: Washington et al., Petitioners v. Harold Glucksberg et al., No. 96-110, and *Dennis C. Vacco, Attorney General of New York et al., v. Timothy E. Quill et al.,* No. 95-1858. Transcripts of the proceedings may be obtained through Alderson Reporting Company, 1111 Fourteenth Street N.W., Washington, DC 20005-5650, 202-289-2260.

362 *. . . two different regional federal appeals courts:* United States Court of Appeals for the Ninth Circuit, deciding on *Compassion in Dying, a Washington nonprofit corporation; Jane Roe; John Doe; James Poe; Harold Glucksberg, M.D., Plaintiffs-Appellees, v. State of Washington; Christine Gregoire, Attorney General of Washington, Defendants-Appellant,* No. 94-35534; and United States Court of Appeals for the Second Circuit, deciding on *Timothy E. Quill, M.D.; Samuel C. Klagsbrun, M.D.; and Howard A. Grossman, M.D., Plaintiffs-Appellants, v. Dennis C. Vacco, Attorney General of the State of New York; George E. Pataki, Governor of the State of New York; Robert M. Morgenthau, District Attorney of New York County, Defendants-Appellees,* No. 95-7028.

. . . an unusual appeal by . . . the Clinton administration: Walter Dellinger, acting Solicitor General et al., No. 96-110, In the Supreme Court of the United States, October Term, 1996, *Washington et al., Petitioners v. Harold Glucksberg et al., Respondents, On Writ of Certiorari to the United States Court of Appeals for the Ninth Circuit, Brief for the United States as Amicus Curiae Supporting Petitioners;* ibid., No. 95-1858, In the Supreme Court of the United States, October Term, 1996, *Vacco et al., Petitioners v. Quill et al., Respondents, On Writ of Certiorari to the United States Court of Appeals for the Second Circuit, Brief for the United States as Amicus Curiae Supporting Petitioners.* Also see Linda Greenhouse, "Administration Asks Justices to Rule Against Assisted Suicide," *The New York Times,* 13 November 1996. *Amicus briefs opposing legalization:* A partial list opposing legalization of assisted suicide includes briefs filed by the American Medical Association together with the American Nurses Association, the American Psychiatric Association et al.; the American Geriatrics Society; the American Hospital Association; the United States Catholic Conference with the Catholic Conferences of New York, Washington, Oregon, Michigan, and California and the Christian Life Commission of the Southern Baptist Convention, the National Association of Evangelicals, the Lutheran Church–Missouri Synod, Wisconsin Evangelical Lutheran Synod–Lutherans for Life, the Evangelical Covenant Church, and the American Muslim Council; Not Dead Yet and American Disabled for Attendant Programs Today; the National Legal Center for the Medically Dependent and Disabled, Inc. et al.; Christian Legal Society, Christian Medical and Dental Society, Christian Pharmacists Fellowship International, Nurses Christian Fellowship, and Fellowship of Christian Physicians; National Association of Prolife Nurses, National Association of Directors of Nursing Administration in Long Term Care et al.; American Suicide Foundation; the National Spinal Cord Injury Association; the Union of Orthodox Jewish Congregations of America and the Rabbinical Council of America; the American Association of Homes and Services for the Aging; the National Hospice Organization; the Project on Death in America; and the National Committee for the Right to Life. *Briefs supporting legalization:* A partial list of those in support include the American Civil Liberties Union, the American Civil Liberties Union of Washington, the National Gray Panthers Project Fund, the Japanese American Citizen League, Humanists of Washington, the Hemlock Society, the Euthanasia Research and Guidance Organization, AIDS Action Council, Northwest AIDS Foundation, Seattle AIDS Support Groups, Local 6 of the Service Employees International Union, Temple De Hirsch Sinai, the Older Women's League; the American Medical Student Association and a Coalition of Distinguished Medical Professionals; a Group of Law Professors; Americans for Death with Dignity and the Death With Dignity Education Center; the American College of Legal Medicine; Bioethicists; Center for Reproductive Law and Policy; Coalition of Hospice Professionals; the Gay Men's Health Crisis and Lambda Defense and Education Fund et al.; National Women's Health Network and Northwest Women's Law Center; Washington State Psychological Association, the American Counseling Association, the Association for Gay, Lesbian, and Bisexual Issues in Counseling, and a Coalition of Mental Health Professionals; and State Legislators in Support.

Each side also had its own group: A hundred pro and con amicus briefs were filed in all—forty-eight for *Vacco v. Quill* and fifty-two for *Washington v. Glucksberg*—which would have been the Supreme Court's all-time record had these not been two separate cases. As it was, that record was set by the 1989 antiabortion case from Missouri in *Webster v. Reproductive Health Services,* in which seventy-seven briefs were filed.

. . . some of whose members are closely affiliated: Much of the material that follows is based on interviews with the principal players in the Compassion cases, including Barbara Coombs Lee, executive director (7 January, 27 March, and 1 April 1997); Faye Girsh, executive director of the Hemlock Society (7 January 1997); Compassion's attorney Kathryn Tucker (8 January and 28 March 1997); Charlotte Ross, executive director of the Death with Dignity Education Center (7 and 8 January 1997); and Derek Humphry (several interviews and/or personal communications, 31 July 1996 to April 1997).

363   *Polls of voters just prior to the 1991:* Derek Humphry, *Dying with Dignity* (New York: Carol Publishing Group, 1992): 39–45.

364   *Compassion in Dying advocates:* Information from a press packet of background information was provided by Compassion in Dying. It included Robert A. Free et al., "Terminal Patients Turn to Family When Living Becomes Unbearable," *The Seattle Times,* 12 January 1997; William Carlsen, "Seattle Group Gives Assisted Suicide Momentum in Courts," *San Francisco Chronicle,* 3 June 1996; and David Friedman, "One Last Choice," *Vogue,* February 1997. Interviews by author with Barbara Coombs Lee, its executive director, were also held on 7 January, 27 March, and 1 April 1997. Also see "New Group Offers to Help the Ill Commit Suicide," *The New York Times,* 13 June 1993.

Organized as a medical service: The material that follows is from the Compassion press packet and interviews with Coombs Lee (1 April 1997) and Kathryn Tucker (28 March 1997).

365   *Beginning in 1994, Tucker and other Compassion in Dying attorneys:* Compassion in Dying, a Washington nonprofit corporation; Jane Roe, John Doe, James Poe, Harold Glucksberg, M.D., Abigail Halperin, M.D., Thomas Preston, M.D., and Peter Shalit, M.D., Ph.D., v. The State of Washington and Christine Gregoire, Attorney General of Washington, No. C94-119, filed in United States District Court, Western District of Washington at Seattle, 24 January 1994; Timothy E. Quill, M.D., Samuel C. Klagsbrun, M.D., Howard A. Grossman, M.D., Jane Doe, George A. Kingsley, and William A. Barth v. G. Oliver Koppell, Attorney General of the State of New York, No. 94 Civ. 5321, filed in Southern District of New York United States District Court, 20 July 1994.

366   *One pivotal issue:* Among the more recent and significant such studies are Anthony L. Back, M.D. et al., "Physician-Assisted Suicide and Euthanasia in Washington State," *JAMA* 275 (27 March 1996): 919–25; L. R. Slome et al., "Physician-Assisted Suicide and Patients with Human Immunodeficiency Virus Disease," *NEJM* 336 (6 February 1997): 417–21.

This latter, a study of San Francisco Bay Area physicians who treat AIDS patients, found that more than half (53 percent) have assisted a terminally ill patient to end his or her life. The figure marks the highest prevalence of physician-assisted suicide in a published report to date. Another important finding of the study was the response to a hypothetical case vignette in which approximately half of the physicians (48 percent) said they are now willing to assist a terminally ill patient in ending his or her life, in contrast to a 1990 study which found that 28 percent would be likely to lend assistance.

Physician-assisted suicide, in both the 1990 and the current study, was defined as a physician providing a sufficient dose of narcotics to enable a patient to kill himself or herself. Respondents were to assume that the patient was a mentally competent, severely ill individual facing imminent death. Such a situation is in contrast to active euthanasia (administering a lethal injection) or passive euthanasia (withdrawing life support in response to a patient's advance directive), which were not investigated in these studies.

By 1997, a network of medical ethics committees in the San Francisco area had "issued a formal protocol for the practice of 'hastened death.' It is to be published in the June 1997 issue of *The Western Journal of Medicine,* and while it is not the first set of guidelines to be published, it marks the first time any community has reached a consensus." (Sheryl Gay Stolberg, "Considering the Unthinkable: Protocol for Assisted Suicide," *The New York Times,* 11 June 1997.)

See also Margaret A. Drickamer, M.D. et al., "Practical Issues in Physician-Assisted Suicide," *AIM* 126 (15 January 1997): 146–51; Sheryl Stolberg, "Ending Life on Their Own Terms," *Los Angeles Times,* 1 October 1996; Daniel Golden, "A Time to Die: Increasingly the Terminally Ill Are Turning to Suicide Out of Horror," *Boston Globe,* 7 October 1990; Dick Lehr, "Death and the Doctor's Hand," *Boston Globe,* 25–27 April 1993. *"The classic textbook way"*: Interview with Carla Kerr, 24 March 1997. *"The decision about how"*: Decision of the U.S. Ninth Circuit Court of Appeals, see "Section IV. Is There a Liberty Interest?" Part F. "Liberty Interest Under Casey," paragraph 4.

367   *"A competent terminally ill adult"*: Ibid., paragraph 4.

    ... the Constitution's equal protection *guarantee:* See "Discussion" section, part III, on "Equal Protection."

368   *To my left...:* Aaron Epstein wrote "A Setback for Assisted Suicides? Justices Hammer Backers with Tough Questions," *Detroit Free Press,* 9 January 1997.

    "Two hours before my mother": Betty Rollin, *Last Wish* (New York: Simon & Schuster, 1985), p. 5.

    ... who had also battled: See Rollin, *First, You Cry* (New York: Lippincott, 1976).

    ... a Supreme Court brochure: Supreme Court of the United States, *Visitor's Guide to Oral Arguments.*

    "Dying is personal": Supreme Court of the United States, *Nancy Beth Cruzan, by her parents and co-guardians, Lester L. Cruzan et ux., Petitioners v. Director, Missouri Department of Health et al.,* No. 88-1503, Section II A., paragraph 3 of the dissenting opinions of Justices William Brennan, Thurgood Marshall, and Harry Blackmun.

369   *O'Connor had had a mastectomy:* Personal information about the Supreme Court Justices provided upon request by the press office of the U.S. Supreme Court.

... *the traditional Supreme Court opening call:* The Supreme Court Historical Society, *The Supreme Court of the United States,* p. 14.

10:02 A.M.: The following is from my own reporting and from *Official Transcript, Proceedings Before the Supreme Court of the United States, Vacco v. Quill, 8 January 1997,* Alderson Reporting Company, 1111 Fourteenth Street N.W., Washington, DC 20005-5650, 202-289-2260.

371 *Justice Stephen Breyer ... a trustee of the Dana Farber Cancer Institute:* Lloyd Grove, "The Courtship of Joanna Breyer," *Washington Post,* 11 July 1994; John Manaso, "26,000 Join to Run for Our Lives," *Washington Post,* 18 June 1995; Malcolm Gladwell, "Judge Breyer's Life Fashioned Like His Courthouse," *Washington Post,* 26 June 1994.

372 *... Justice Scalia—known for his:* Joan Biskupic, "Nothing Subtle About Scalia," *Washington Post,* 18 February 1997; ibid., "Scalia Makes the Case for Christianity," *Washington Post,* 10 April 1996.

374 *At 11:05 arguments on the New York case:* Based on my own reporting and from *Official Transcript, Proceedings Before the Supreme Court of the United States, Vacco et al., v. Quill et al.,* Alderson Reporting Company.

377 *... the modus operandi for medical care:* The note that the American Hospital Association estimates that 70 percent of the 6,000 or so daily deaths in America occur as a result of withholding or withdrawing treatment is included in the amicus brief of the American Hospital Association filed in the case of Nancy Cruzan, 1 September 1989.

A 1997 California study: T. J. Prendergast and J. M. Luce, "Increasing Incidence of Withholding and Withdrawal of Life Support from the Critically Ill," *American Journal of Respiratory and Critical Care Medicine* 155 (January 1997): 15–20.

378 *... withholding, withdrawing, or refusing treatment is the way ...:* Alan Meisel, "The Legal Consensus about Forgoing Life-Sustaining Treatment: Its Status and Its Prospects," *Kennedy Institute of Ethics Journal* 2, no. 4 (1993): 309–45. See reference to figures provided by a 1990 study of the American Hospital Association, in footnote 8, p. 335.

"It's called passive euthanasia,": Gina Kolata, " 'Passive Euthanasia' in Hospitals Is the Norm, Doctors Say," *The New York Times,* June, 1997.

Perhaps the most extraordinary instance ...: The following discussion is based on: Linda L. Emanuel, "Reexamining Death: The Asymptotic Model and a Bounded Zone Definition," *Hastings Center Report,* July–August 1995, 27–35; Robert D. Troug, "Is It Time to Abandon Brain Death?" *Hastings Center Report,* January–February 1997, 27–37; Robert Cooke, "Organ-Donor Injections Disputed," *Medical News,* 12 April 1997; Reuters, "Transplant Organs Said Removed Before Donors Die," 10 April 1997; CBS, *60 Minutes,* 13 April 1997; press release, "Response to CBS *60 Minutes* Story on Non-Heartbeating Donor Protocols," United Network for Organ Sharing news release, 9 April 1997; Charles Siebert, "Miracle in a Picnic Cooler," *The New York Times Magazine,* 13 April 1997.

380 *All these medical decisions:* The American Medical Association's Council on Ethical and Judicial Affairs, "Decisions Near the End of Life," *JAMA* 267 (22–29 April 1992): 2229–33.

Various polls have shown ...: An April 9–10, 1996 Gallup poll showed 75 percent of Americans favored "a law which would allow doctors to end a patient's life by some painless means if the patient and his family request it." A Gallup poll asking the same question on April 25–28, 1996, showed 68 percent in favor. This had increased from 65 percent in favor in 1990 and 53 percent in favor in 1973. (Information provided by the Gallup Organization.)

Judy Foreman, "Choosing a Good Death," *Boston Globe,* 23 June 1996 ("an April [1996] CNN/*USA Today*/Gallup poll found that 75 percent of Americans—up from 65 percent in 1990 and 53 percent in 1973—feel that if a person has an incurable disease, doctors should be legally allowed to end the patient's life painlessly if the patient and family request it."); Richard A. Knox, "Poll: Americans Favor Mercy Killing," *Boston Globe,* 3 November 1991 (a *Boston Globe*/Harvard poll found that 64 percent of a national sample of 1,311 adults approved assisted suicide and euthanasia for terminally ill patients who requested it); a Gallup poll 25–28 April 1996 put public support for doctor-assisted suicide at 68 percent.

Robert J. Blendon et al., "Should Physicians Aid Their Patients in Dying? The Public Perspective," *JAMA* 267 (20 May 1992): 2658–62, found that polls show that in a breakdown of respondents by religion, Catholics are most supportive of euthanasia. One poll "shows that 72% of Catholics polled] agree that physicians should be allowed by law to end patients' lives if patients and their families request it. In comparison, 68% of Jews and 59% of Protestants (including 66% of fundamentalists and 54% of born-again Christians) support legalizing euthanasia.

"Furthermore, the depth of an individual's religious beliefs, or religiosity, appears to affect support for euthanasia among Protestants but not among Catholics. Only 57% of very and somewhat religious Protestants support allowing euthanasia, while 84% of 'not very' and 'not at all' religious Protestants favor such legislation. Among Catholics, however, support for allowing euthanasia remained relatively constant at 71% to 72% across the religiosity spectrum."

Nearly all the major medical organizations . . .: Major medical organizations filing amicus briefs in the cases before the Supreme Court opposing legalization of physician-assisted suicide included the American Medical Association, the American Hospital Association, the American Psychiatric Association, the American Nurses Association, the American Academy of Pain Management, the American Academy of Pain Medicine, the American Academy of Physical Medicine and Rehabilitation, the American Academy of Hospice and Palliative Medicine, the National Hospice Organization, and at least twenty-three state-affiliated medical associations or societies. . . . *When polled in private, however, individual physicians' responses* . . .: Susan Okie, "Country's Doctors Remain Divided over Physician-Assisted Suicide," *Washington Post,* 8 January 1997, put physician support at 60 percent. Back et al., "Physician-Assisted Suicide . . ." *JAMA* 275 (27 March 1996): 919–25; Slome et al., "Physician-Assisted Suicide and Patients . . ." *NEJM* 336 (6 February 1997): 417–21.

381 *It took an Englishman named Derek Humphry:* This section is based on periodic personal interviews with Humphry 31 July 1996 to April 1997; on "Playboy Interview: Derek Humphry," *Playboy,* August 1992; Derek Humphry, *Lawful Exit* (Junction City, Oregon: Norris Lane Press, 1993); ibid., *Death*

With Dignity (New York: Carol Publishing, 1992); ibid., *Final Exit* (Eugene, Oregon: The Hemlock Society, 1991); and Derek Humphry with Ann Wickett, *The Right To Die* (Eugene, Oregon: The Hemlock Society, 1990).

. . . Jean's Way: Derek Humphry and Ann Wickett, *Jean's Way* (New York: Quartet Books, 1978.)

382   *A lay organization:* The Hemlock Society USA has chapters in most states. Its national headquarters: P.O. Box 101810, Denver, CO 80250-1810, 1-800-247-7421.

. . . *he self-published* Final Exit: See for commentary "Final Exit," *Time,* 19 August 1991. A collection of some of the material in *Final Exit* was contained in *Let Me Die Before I Wake: Hemlock's Book of Self-Deliverance for the Dying,* published by the Hemlock Society and distributed by Grove Press; republished by Dell in 1992. *Final Exit: The Practicalities of Self-Deliverance and Assisted Suicide for the Dying* was first published by the Hemlock Society in March 1991 and became number one on the *New York Times* best-seller list shortly afterward. It was bought by Dell and republished in September 1992. It has been translated into twelve languages and is on sale worldwide. Dell published an updated edition in 1997.

. . . *deaths by asphyxiation with plastic bag:* Elisabeth Rosenthal, "Study Finds Suicides Follow a Book," *The New York Times,* 6 November 1993.

. . . *after* Final Exit . . . *to help finance:* Humphry says: "I started up all the groups in [California, Washington, and Oregon], which within a couple of years began initiative drives—California [in] 1988 and 1992, Washington [in] 1991, and Oregon [in] 1994. Of course I didn't run the political campaigns but either through Hemlock or my own individual efforts at fundraising, I got them supplied with the bulk of their money. I recently got from Hemlock's treasurers these figures for political expenditures by the organization since 1988:

"California, 1988, $210,000; Washington, 1991, $300,000; California, 1992, $100,000; Oregon, 1994, $205,000; total $815,000. I can assure you this was all done within the tax-code laws because the IRS audited Hemlock thoroughly from 1980 to 1992. Note, these figures are money given by Hemlock Society directly to its political arm." Personal correspondence, 29 December 1996. Also see Humphry, *Death with Dignity,* for a full description of these ballot initiatives.

383   *When the ballot measures in Washington in 1991:* "On November 5, 1991," read an article in *JAMA,* "voters in Washington State defeated an initiative to legalize physician aid-in-dying by a relatively narrow margin of 54% to 46%. The question failed by fewer than 100,000 votes out of 1.3 million votes cast and would have been the first law of its kind in the United States if it had passed. At present, similar initiatives can be found in at least 20 states across the country." Blendon et al., "Should Physicians Aid Their Patients in Dying?" *JAMA* 267 (20 May 1992): 2658–62.

. . . *and in California:* Derek Humphry, *Lawful Exit,* for his analysis of the two California and the Washington campaigns, pp. 93–109.

In 1994, Oregonian voters: Early returns set the vote at 52 to 48 percent: Associated Press, "Voters in Oregon Allow Doctors to Help the Terminally Ill Die, *The New York Times,* 11 November 1994; Associated Press, "Here are the latest, unofficial returns for the ballot measure in Oregon that would bar prosecution of doctors who help dying patients commit suicide," 9 November 1994 (99 percent of the vote, or 2,283 to 2,300 precincts, were in, with 492,085 votes approving the bill, and 453,054 voting against it); Mark O'Keefe, "Euthanasia Debate Not Just in Oregon," *The Oregonian,* 4 August 1995; ibid., "Assisted-Suicide Measure Survives Heavy Opposition," *Oregonian,* 10 November 1994 (a summary of the Washington, California, and Oregon votes can be found in this article.)

A poll in March 1997 found 61 percent of the voters were now in support ("Surveys: More Favor Assisted-Suicide Law," *The Oregonian,* 11 March 1997), but lawmakers were about to send it back for a November revote ("Foes of Assisted Suicide Lobby Senators," *The Eugene Register-Guard,* 29 May 1997). Later figures, counting absentee ballots and untallied precincts, set the vote at 51 to 49 percent, "Foes," *The Eugene Register-Guard;* personal communication from Derek Humphry on 3 June 1997.
. . . *a Hemlock Society poll:* Diane Meier, M.D., "Doctors' Attitudes and Experiences with Physician-Assisted Suicide," shared with me in galley form, refers to *A 1987 Survey of California Physicians Regarding Voluntary Active Euthanasia for the Terminally Ill,* The National Hemlock Society, 17 February 1988. For a copy of this paper, contact Dr. Meier, Department of Geriatrics and Adult Development, Mount Sinai Medical Center, Fifth Avenue and 101st Street, New York, NY.

384　*The year 1988 . . . "It's Over, Debbie":* Name withheld by request, "It's Over, Debbie," *JAMA* 259 (8 January 1988): 272.
. . . *pain exerts later said that 20 mg:* See the letter of Kenneth L. Vaux, Ph.D., in *JAMA* 259 (8 January 1988): 2141; Kathleen M. Foley, M.D., "Physician-Assisted Suicide," a paper presented at Current Concepts in Acute, Chronic and Cancer Pain Management, a conference at Memorial Sloan-Kettering, 10 December 1993, in the conference papers, p. 644.
. . . *elicited more than 150 letters . . . :* "Letters," 2094–98 and "Commentaries," *JAMA* 259 (8 January 1988): 2139–45. Public responses also printed in *JAMA,* 12 August 1988.
. . . *JAMA editor George D. Lundberg, M.D., wrote . . . : JAMA* 259 (8 April 1988): 2142–43.
By 1989, twelve prominent physicians: Sidney H. Wanzer, M.D. et al., "The Physician's Responsibility toward Hopelessly Ill Patients: A Second Look," *NEJM* 320 (30 March 1989): 844–49.

385　*In 1991 . . . Timothy Quill, M.D.:* Timothy Quill, M.D., "Sounding Board: Death and Dignity; A Case of Individualized Decision Making," *NEJM* 324 (7 March 1991): 691–94. Also see Quill, *Death and Dignity* (New York: Norton & Co., 1993); and *A Midwife through the Dying Process* (Baltimore: The Johns Hopkins University Press, 1996). Many interviews and personal communications took place between Dr. Quill and this author, from 24 January 1994 through May 1997.
Some doctors critical of Dr. Quill: Dr. Kathleen Foley, book review given to me in draft by Dr. Foley, and ibid., "Physician-Assisted Suicide," a paper presented at Current Concepts, 10 December 1993, p. 644.
But surprisingly, a good many other doctors: Timothy E. Quill, M.D., Christine K. Cassel, M.D., and Diane E. Meier, M.D., "Care of the Hopelessly Ill: Proposed Clinical Criteria for Physician-Assisted Suicide," by

NEJM 327 (5 November 1992): 1380–84. Dr. Cassel and Dr. Meier are greatly respected in the medical profession and the piece these three doctors published in *NEJM* had a large impact in that it was much referred to at medical meetings and widely quoted.

A grand jury refused to indict: Associated Press, "No Case in Tranquilizer Suicide," *The New York Times,* 13 April 1991; Lawrence Altman, "Jury Declines to Indict a Doctor Who Said He Aided in a Suicide," *The New York Times,* 27 July 1991.

The state's Board for Professional Medical Conduct: The organization wrote a statement of findings, dated 16 August 1991, on "the matter of Dr. Timothy Quill."

386 *... American College of Physicians:* John R. Ball, M.D., executive director of the American College of Physicians, sent a letter to this effect to the Monroe County Grand Jury, dated 11 July 1991.

Afterward, Dr. Quill charged that many other doctors: Quill et al., "Care of the Hopelessly Ill," *NEJM* 327 (5 November 1992): 1380–84; Quill, "The Care of Last Resort," *The New York Times,* July 1994.

"The more fundamental issue": Personal interview, 24 January 1994.

... no doctor in the history of American law: Oral arguments before the Supreme Court, 8 January 1997. A Sebring, Florida, physician, however, was scheduled to be tried for murder in June 1997 in the death of a terminally ill lung cancer patient (United Press International, "Florida: Jury Set for M.D. Murder Trial," 28 May 1997).

Among the six patients ... three had AIDS: In the New York case, George Kingsley and William Barth; in the Washington case, John Doe.

Two of the physicians cared primarily for AIDS: In the New York case, Dr. Howard Grossman (Dr. Samuel Klagsbrun also sees AIDS patients as part of his practice); in the Washington case, Dr. Peter Shalit (Dr. Abigail Halperin sees AIDS patients as part of her practice).

Within the AIDS community, assistance in dying: Dick Lehr, "Death and the Doctor's Hand," *Boston Globe,* 25–27 April 1993.

A February 1997 ... Bay Area physicians: Slome et al., "Physician-Assisted Suicide ..." *NEJM* 336 (6 February 1997): 417–21.

... A 1994 study of physicians: Back et al., "Physician-Assisted Suicide and Euthanasia in Washington State," *JAMA* 275 (27 March 1996): 919–25. "The patient concerns most often perceived by physicians," the study read, "were worries about loss of control, being a burden, being dependent on others for personal care, and loss of dignity. Physicians provided assistance more often to patients with physical symptoms. Physicians infrequently sought advice from colleagues."

Researchers concluded: "Patients' requests for physician-assisted suicide and euthanasia are not rare. As perceived by physicians, the most common patient concerns at the time these requests are made are nonphysical. Physicians occasionally provide these practices, even though they are currently illegal in Washington State. Physicians do not consult colleagues often about these requests. These findings raise the question of how to ensure quality in the evaluation of patient requests for physician-assisted death."

A partial history of how doctors came to be the gatekeepers for drugs is in David E. Joranson, *Guiding Principles of International, Federal and State*

Laws Pertaining to Medical Use and Diversion of Controlled Substances, in press, available through Joranson, Associate Director for Policy Studies, Pain Research Group, University of Wisconsin–Madison Medical School, 610 Walnut Street, Madison, WI 53705.

Two different 1996 studies: See, for example, M. A. Lee et al., "Legalizing Assisted Suicide—Views of Physicians in Oregon," *NEJM* 334 (1 February 1996): 310–15.

387 *"If people think they can guarantee":* Interview with Dr. Quill, 25 January 1994.

. . . *Dr. Klagsbrun challenges:* Interview with Dr. Klagsbrun, 28 March 1997. It is also important to note again that clinical depression is undertreated in the dying. Studies at Memorial Sloan-Kettering by William Breitbart, M.D., and others, particularly with AIDS patients, show that the strongest predictor of interest in assisted suicide is depression. Breitbart et al., "Interest in Physician-Assisted Suicide among Ambulatory HIV-Infected Patients," *American Journal of Psychiatry* 153 (February 1996): 238–42; Jane Brody, "Depression May Lead Dying Pahtients to Seek Suicide," *The New York Times,* 18 June 1997.

388 *After Compassion in Dying had been in operation:* Thomas A. Preston and Ralph Mero, "Observations Concerning Terminally Ill Patients Who Choose Suicide," *Journal of Pharmaceutical Care in Pain and Symptom Control,* 4, no. 1–2 (1996): 183–92.

389 *Other industrialized countries:* Susan Hattis Rolef, "Ending the Pain," *Jerusalem Post,* 9 December 1996; "Public Supports Euthanasia for Most Desperate Cases," *British Medical Journal* 313 (7 December 1996): 1423; Clyde H. Farnsworth, "Woman Who Lost a Right-to-Die Case in Canada Commits Suicide," *The New York Times,* 15 February 1994; "Estimated 10,000 Submissions to Euthanasia Inquiry," Australian Broadcasting Corporation story on 16 December 1996, in preparation for a Senate Committee inquiry into the Northern Territory's passage of a law legalizing voluntary euthanasia. (The Australian federal government later overruled the Northern Territory's law, but a national battle is still raging.)

In Germany: Margaret P. Battin, Ph.D., "Euthanasia: The Way We Do It, The Way They Do It," *JPSM* 6 (July 1991): 298–305; ibid., "Assisted Suicide: Can We Learn from Germany?" *Hastings Center Report,* March–April 1992.

390 *In the Netherlands:* Marcia Angell, M.D., "Euthanasia in the Netherlands: Good News or Bad?" *NEJM* 335 (28 November 1996): 1676–78; Marlise Simons, "Dutch Move to Enact Law Making Euthanasia Easier," *The New York Times,* 9 February 1993; ibid., "Dutch Doctors to Tighten Rules on Mercy Killings," *The New York Times,* 11 September 1995; Herbert Hendin, M.D., "Seduced by Death: Doctors, Patients and the Dutch Cure," *Issues in Law and Medicine* 10 (2 November 1994): 123ff.

. . . *A national commission:* Paul J. Van Der Mass et al., "Euthanasia and Other Medical Decisions Concerning the End of Life," *Lancet* 338 (14 September 1991): 669–74; report of the first Remmelink Commission study. *As we have seen, debate in the United States . . . undertreatment of pain:* Kathleen M. Foley, M.D., "The Relationship of Pain and Symptom Management to Patient Requests for Physician-Assisted Suicide," *JPSM* 6 (July 1991): 289–97; ibid., "Competent Care for the Dying instead of Physician-

Assisted Suicide," *NEJM* 336 (2 January 1997): 54–58. Undertreated pain can spiral out of control, leading to increased depression, and possibly to a desire for physician-assisted suicide.

391 *"It's an existential decision":* Frits S.A.M. Van Dam, Ph.D., interview 14 December 1993.

Yet when the Dutch repeated: P. J. Van Der Mass et al., "Euthanasia, Physician-Assisted Suicide, and Other Medical Practices Involving the End of Life in the Netherlands, 1990–1995," *NEJM* 335 (28 November 1996): 1699–1705; G. Van Der Wal et al., "Evaluation of the Notification Procedure for Physician-Assisted Death in the Netherlands," *NEJM* 335 (28 November 1996): 1706–11.

The Van Der Mass study found that while "euthanasia seems to have increased in incidence since 1990, and the ending of life without a patient's explicit request seems to have decreased slightly," the findings suggested that "most of the cases in which life was ended without the patient's explicit request were more similar to cases involving the use of large doses of opioids than to cases of euthanasia. As compared with 1990, there was a small decrease in the proportion of these cases." The overall conclusions were that doctors are not heading down a "slippery slope" toward involuntary killings, but that assistance in dying is a carefully considered option for a small number of people at the end of life.

This study is hotly debated, however, with a highly critical report of the Dutch study, and a reinterpretation of the same figures in *JAMA* by, among others, Herbert Hendin, director of the American Suicide Foundation, an anti–assisted suicide group, and Zbignew Zylicz, a Dutch hospice doctor. Hendin et al., "Commentary: Assisted Suicide and Euthanasia in the Netherlands," *JAMA* (4 June 1997), charge that doctor-assisted deaths have increased 27 percent in the Netherlands in the past five years, and that in a number of those cases physicians administered lethal medications to "fully competent" patients without first getting their approval.

The authors of the initial study published in *NEJM* countercharge that this new report is a distortion of the figures, and does not take into account the rising numbers of the elderly and of cancer patients in the population, that the rise overall was not statistically significant, and that many patients had expressed requests for lethal medications to their physicians way in advance of their deaths as part of advance planning. Hendin et al. also did not seem to differentiate terminal sedation from assisted suicide.

Somewhere between 3 percent and 5 percent: Taking what the study called a "best estimate" figure of 3 percent of the deaths as euthanasia—in 1.8 percent of them, a doctor injected a patient with a lethal drug; 0.3 percent were strictly assisted suicides. All these were the result of voluntary, written requests on the part of patients. But an additional 0.8 percent were cases in which "life-terminating" acts were done *without* explicit written requests. It is this figure that has caused the major furor here over fears of abuse.

It should be noted, however, that in those rocky 0.8 percent of the cases in which doctors euthanized a patient without an explicit written request (required in Holland if the doctor is to avoid legal censure), the Commission found that the patient seemed to have been unconscious. Remember, these deaths took place in family practices, in the context of long-term patient-physician relationships in which dying had been discussed over a long period of time. It was not like our medical system in which a team of specialists—and strangers—is often summoned to the bedside at death and does not know this patient or his deepest beliefs.

392 *This figure nearly matches ... the Memorial Sloan-Kettering:* Coyle et al., "Character of Terminal Illness in the Advanced Cancer Patient: Pain and Other Symptoms During the Last Four Weeks of Life," *JPSM* 5, no. 2 (April 1990): pp. 83–93.

Stephen Lenker: Interview with Stephen Lenker, 8 January 1997.

393 *"This country is very prejudiced:* Interview with Diane Coleman, 28 March 1997.

Not all groups representing the disabled: Interview with Andrew Batavia, 8 January 1997, a Miami attorney representing other disabled people who filed a Supreme Court brief in favor of legalized doctor-assisted suicide.

These fears also show up in polls: David Rosenbaum, "Americans Want a Right to Die. Or So They Think," *The New York Times,* 8 June 1997.

394 *... "The ban on physician assisted suicide: American Medical Association et al., State of Washington et al. v. Glucksberg et al.,* amicus brief submitted to the Supreme Court, 12 November 1996, p. 30.

"All doctors help patients die": Interview with Dr. Joanne Lynn, 8 April 1997.

Will she be forced to break the law: This is a point of contention over the return of the Oregon state referendum to voters for a revote. As reported in "Foes of Assisted Suicide," *The Eugene Register-Guard,* 28 May 1997, opponents of the law are gathering steam based on what they claim is a major flaw in that law. They cite a new "study in the Netherlands that shows 25 percent of patients who take the prescribed dose of pills don't die immediately. In those cases, the doctors then give patients a lethal injection, an option that isn't allowed under Measure 16 [the Oregon assisted-suicide ballot measure].

"Advocates of the law said voters made an informed choice to let terminally ill people end their painful lives by seeking deadly medication prescribed by a doctor. 'There's no doubt what the voters want today,' said Barbara Coombs Lee, the chief petitioner of Measure 16, the Oregon Death With Dignity Act. 'The momentum against repeal is building.' "

396 *... organizers were gearing up for the November 1998 revote:* Steve Suo, "Big Purse Expected for Round Two," *Portland Oregonian,* 8 June 1997, predicts "the repeal campaign will draw even more money than in 1994." That year opponents spent $1.5 million as opposed to the $600,000 spent by supporters of assisted suicide. For the 1997 campaign they had already hired Brooke Bodney, a fund-raiser for the Dole-Kemp presidential campaign, and Chuck Cavalier, a political consultant "who specializes in fighting assisted-suicide measures."

Cavalier had helped defeat the referendums in California in 1992 (polls there showed support at 74 percent before Cavalier's TV campaigns, but the measure failed by 54 to 46 percent of the vote afterward) and in Washington in 1991, and persuaded Australian lawmakers to repeal a suicide measure in the Northern Territory in 1996.

Bodney told the *Oregonian* he "expects the campaign to be among the most expensive ballot measure efforts in Oregon history. That would put it in the league with the $4.9 million spent in 1992 by Portland General Electric against measures to close the Trojan Nuclear Plant and the $4.8 million in tobacco interests spent last year to kill a cigarette tax increase." Financial support for defeating the ballot measure is expected to come, as it did in 1994, "from Catholic dioceses and Catholic hospitals in Oregon and elsewhere [and] from various Knights of Columbus chapters."

. . . *a signature drive was under way in Michigan:* This drive, called Merian's Friends, was being organized by Carol Poenisch, daughter of ALS patient Merian Frederick, who was Dr. Jack Kevorkian's nineteenth patient, and one of the deaths for which he was found not guilty. Interviews with Carol Poenisch, 22–26 August 1996 and 8 January 1997.

Index